JAMES HALLIDAY'S
POCKET COMPANION

TO

AUSTRALIAN
AND
NEW ZEALAND
WINES

Angus&Robertson
An imprint of HarperCollins*Publishers*

Angus&Robertson
An imprint of HarperCollins*Publishers*, Australia

First published in Australia in 1995

Copyright © James Halliday 1995

HarperCollins*Publishers*
25 Ryde Road, Pymble, Sydney NSW 2073, Australia
31 View Road, Glenfield, Auckland 10, New Zealand
77–85 Fulham Palace Road, London W6 8JB, United Kingdom
Hazelton Lanes, 55 Avenue Road, Suite 2900, Toronto, Ontario M5R 3L2
and 1995 Markham Road, Scarborough, Ontario, M1B 5M8, Canada
10 East 53rd Street, New York NY 10022, USA

National Library of Australia Cataloguing-in-Publication data:
Halliday, James, 1938 –
James Halliday's pocket companion to Australian and New Zealand wines.

  ISBN 0 207 18860 2.
  1. Wine and wine making – Australia. 2. Wine and wine making – New
  Zealand. 3. Wineries – Australia – Directories. 4. Wineries – New Zealand
  – Directories.
  I. Title. II. Title: Pocket companion to Australian and New Zealand wines.
  663.20099

Printed in Australia by Griffin Paperbacks

9 8 7 6 5 4 3 2 1
98 97 96 95

CONTENTS

HOW TO USE THIS BOOK

Hopefully, the *Pocket Companion* will be self-explanatory, but I will briefly take you through the information for each entry.

WINERY ENTRIES

CASSEGRAIN VINEYARDS

★★★☆ 8.95–29 R AUS182 UK39 US9

Hastings Valley **Est.** 1980

Hastings Valley Winery, Pacific Highway, Port Macquarie, NSW 2444

Ph (065) 83 7777 **Fax** (065) 84 0354

Open 7 days 9–5 **Production** 42 000

Winemaker(s) John Cassegrain, Drew Noon

A very substantial operation based in the Hastings Valley, drawing some of its more interesting grapes from estate-owned and associated vineyards there, but also from the Hunter Valley and elsewhere. The quality of the wines varies significantly from year to year and from one variety to the next, making it a little difficult to follow.

Principal Wines Chardonnay, Semillon, Verdelho, Shiraz, Pinot Noir, Merlot, Chambourcin; Fromenteau Chardonnay; First Ridge Semillon; Morillon Pinot Noir; Five Mile Hollow Red and White.

WINERY NAME: CASSEGRAIN VINEYARDS

Although it might seem that stating the winery name is straightforward, this is not necessarily so. To avoid confusion, wherever possible I use the name which appears most prominently on the wine label and do not refer to any associated trading name. Wineries that are new entries are followed by an asterisk *.

RATINGS: ★★★☆

The winery star system may be interpreted as follows:

★★★★★ Outstanding winery regularly producing exemplary wines.
★★★★☆ Extremely good; virtually on a par with a five-star winery.
★★★★ Consistently produces high-quality wines.
★★★☆ A solid, reliable producer of good wine.
★★★ Typically good, but may have a few lesser wines.
★★☆ Adequate.

If the ratings seem generous, so be it. The fact is that Australia is blessed with a marvellous climate for growing grapes, a high degree of technological skill, and a remarkable degree of enthusiasm and dedication on the part of its winemakers. Across the price spectrum, Australian wines stand tall in the markets of the world. I see no reason, therefore, to shrink from recognising excellence. NR = not rated.

PRICE RANGE: 8.95–29 R

The price range given covers the least expensive through to the most expensive wines usually made by the winery in question. Hence there will be a significant spread. That spread, however, may not fully cover fluctuations which occur in retail pricing, particularly with the larger companies. Erratic and often savage discounting remains a feature of the wine industry, and prices must therefore be seen as approximate. NA = information was not available.

The Australian winery prices are for purchase in Australia, in Australian dollars; those for New Zealand are for purchase in New Zealand, in New Zealand dollars.

In each instance I have indicated whether the price is cellar door (CD), mailing list (ML) or retail (R); by and large the choice has been determined by which of the three methods of sale is most important to the winery.

The price of Australian and New Zealand wines in other countries is affected by a number of factors, including excise and customs duty, distribution mark-up and currency fluctuations. Contact your wine distributor for details.

METHODS OF DISTRIBUTION: AUS182 UK39 US9

On pages 584–604 you will find distributor lists for Australia, New Zealand, the United Kingdom and the Unites States. For example, Cassegrain Vineyards wines are distributed by the Western Wine Agency (see Australian distributor number 182, page 595). Alternatively, you will find the code AUSSD or NZSD, which means that the winery sells all of its wine direct, even if to resellers such as restaurants and retailers.

A list of Canadian distributors of Australian wines appears on page 605. This is a general contact list only; no corresponding codes are given throughout the book.

REGION: Hastings Valley

Changes to the nationwide regional winery boundaries are under way; in due course these will become enshrined in law. Because there will be last-minute challenges and changes of heart, before and while this book is being published, I have basically used the regional names which have appeared in prior editions of my wine guides.

YEAR OF ESTABLISHMENT: Est. 1980

A more or less self-explanatory item, but keep in mind that some makers consider the year in which they purchased the land to be the year of establishment, others the year in which they first planted grapes, others the year they first made wine, others the year they first offered wine for sale ... and so on. There may also be minor complications where there has been a change of ownership or a break in production.

ADDRESS, TELEPHONE AND FACSIMILE DETAILS:
Hastings Valley Winery, Pacific Highway,
Port Macquarie, NSW 2444
Ph (065) 83 7777 **Fax** (065) 84 0354

The details are usually those of the winery and cellar door but, in a
few instances, may simply be of the vineyard — this occurs when
the wine is made at another winery under contract and is sold only
through retail.

CELLAR DOOR SALES HOURS: **Open** 7 days 9–5

Although a winery might be listed as not open or only open on
weekends, some may in fact be prepared to open by appointment.
Many will, some won't; a telephone call will establish whether it is
possible or not. Also, virtually every winery that is shown as being
open only for weekends is in fact open for public holidays as well.
Once again, a telephone call will confirm this.

PRODUCTION: 42 000

The figure (representing the number of cases produced each year)
given is merely an indication of the size of the operation. Some
wineries (principally but not exclusively the large companies)
regard this information as confidential; in that event NFP (not
for publication) will appear.

WINEMAKER(S): John Cassegrain, Drew Noon

In the large companies, the winemaker is simply the head of a team;
there may be many executive winemakers actually responsible for
specific wines.

SUMMARY: A very substantial operation based in the Hastings
Valley, drawing some of its more interesting grapes from estate-
owned and associated vineyards there, but also from the Hunter
Valley and elsewhere. The quality of the wines varies significantly
from year to year and from one variety to the next, making it a little
difficult to follow.

My summary of the winery; little needs to be said, except that I
have tried to vary the subjects I discuss in this part of the winery
entry.

PRINCIPAL WINES: Chardonnay, Semillon, Verdelho, Shiraz,
Pinot Noir, Merlot, Chambourcin; Fromenteau Chardonnay;
First Ridge Semillon; Morillon Pinot Noir; Five Mile Hollow Red
and White.

Particularly with the larger companies, it is not possible to give a
complete list of the wines; the saving grace is that these days most of
the wines are simply identified on their label by their varietal
composition.

WINE ENTRIES AND TASTING NOTES

CASSEGRAIN FROMENTEAU CHARDONNAY
●●●●) $29
Compelling proof that the Hastings Valley, on the north
coast of New South Wales, can produce Chardonnay of
exceptional quality. From the 2.5-hectare estate-owned
Fromenteau Vineyard, planted in 1981, it has always
produced very striking wine, hitting a probably never-to-be-
repeated peak in the warm dry vintage of 1991. Only
950 cases produced.
Cellaring Quick developing style.
Best Vintages '89, '91 **Current Vintage** '91
Matching Food Rich chicken or veal.
Tasting Note 1991 Glowing yellow-green; extremely
complex, nutty honeyed fruit with strong barrel ferment
influence. A compellingly complex, plush, layered palate
with a huge volume of fruit, high-class French oak and
almost overwhelming impact.

WINE NAME: CASSEGRAIN FROMENTEAU CHARDONNAY

The wine's name will in most cases be prefaced by the name of
the winery.

RATING: ●●●●)

A rating is given for each wine as follows.

●●●●● Outstanding; as near to perfect as one can get in an
imperfect world

●●●●) Excellent wine, full of character, and usually well priced.

●●●● High-quality wine, with clear varietal definition.

●●●) Good, fault-free wine.

●●●● A sound commercial wine with adequate flavour.

●●) Somewhat idiosyncratic or perhaps a little weak.

Another perspective is to regard 4.5 to 5 ● wines of gold medal
standard; 3.5 to 4 ● as silver medal quality; and 3 ● as bronze
medal standard.

You will see that almost all of the wines reviewed in this book
rate 3.5 ● or better. This is not wanton generosity on my part — it
simply reflects the fact that the 1000 or so wines selected for specific
review are the tip of over 5000 tasting notes accumulated over
the last year. In other words, the wines described are among
Australia's top 20%.

PRICE: $29

This is a recommended retail price only.

BACKGROUND: Compelling proof that the Hastings Valley, on the north coast of New South Wales, can produce Chardonnay of exceptional quality. From the 2.5-hectare estate-owned Fromenteau Vineyard, planted in 1981, it has always produced very striking wine, hitting a probably never-to-be-repeated peak in the warm dry vintage of 1991. Only 950 cases produced.

Like the summary information given in the winery entries, I have tried to vary the approch of my discussions.

CELLARING: Quick developing style.

I will usually give a range of years (e.g. 1–3 years), or a more specific comment, as above, but whatever my cellaring recommendation, always consider it with extreme caution, and as an approximate guide at best. When to drink a given wine is an intensely personal decision which only you can make.

BEST VINTAGES: '89, '91

Self-explanatory information, but a note of caution: wines do change in bottle, and it may be that were I to taste all of the best vintages listed, I would demote some, and elevate some not mentioned.

CURRENT VINTAGE: '91

Self-explanatory; usually the vintage of the tasting note.

MATCHING FOOD: Rich chicken or veal.

Again, merely a suggestion — a subliminal guide to the style of wine.

TASTING NOTE: 1991 Glowing yellow-green; extremely complex, nutty honeyed fruit with strong barrel ferment influence. A compellingly complex, plush, layered palate with a huge volume of fruit, high-class French oak and almost overwhelming impact.

The tasting note opens with the vintage of the wine tasted. With the exception of a very occasional classic wine, this tasting note will have been made within the twelve months prior to publication. Even that is a long time, and during the life of this book the wine will almost certainly change. More than this, remember that tasting is a highly subjective and imperfect art.

AUSTRALIAN
WINERIES
AND
WINES

ABBEY VALE VINEYARD

★★☆ 12–18 CD AUS67
Margaret River **Est.** 1988
Wildwood Road, Margaret River, WA 6282
Ph (097) 55 2277 **Fax** (097) 55 2286
Open 7 days 10.30–5 **Production** 3500
Winemaker(s) Dorham Mann
The former Kidepo Valley sells the major portion of the grapes from its substantial 25 hectare vineyard to Houghton, which used to make its wines. Since 1994 that arrangement has terminated, and with the exception of the crisp, grassy 1994 Festival White, showed a range of ambient temperature, fermentation-related problems.
Principal Wines Festival White, Semillon, Verdelho, Sauvignon Blanc, Sunburst Verdelho, Cabernet Sauvignon; Moonshine Ale.

ABBEY VALE SEMILLON

●●●● $18
The '89 vintage, made by Houghton, was still on sale at cellar door in late 1994, and had matured into a most interesting wine, which won a silver medal at the 1994 Mount Barker Wine Show.
Cellaring Drink now. **Best Vintages** NA **Current Vintage** '89
Matching Food Marron.
Tasting Note 1989 Glowing yellow-green; a very complex bouquet with an amalgam of honey and herbal aromas. The herbaceous varietal character of the semillon, in typical Margaret River style, has not altered with age on the palate, giving an intense, tangy core surrounded by softer, buttery bottle-developed characters.

AFFLECK

★★★ 9–15 CD AUSSD
Canberra **Est.** 1976
RMB 244 Millynn Road off Gundaroo Road, Bungendore,
NSW 2621
Ph (06) 236 9276
Open By appt **Production** 120
Winemaker(s) Ian Hendry

The 1994 cellar door and mail order price list says that the wines
are 'grown, produced and bottled on the estate by Ian and Susie
Hendry with much dedicated help from family and friends'. The
2.5-hectare vineyard, situated on the shale of the Lake George
escarpment, is very much a weekend and holiday occupation for
the Hendrys, who lead busy weekday professional lives.

Principal Wines Chardonnay, Pinot Noir, Late Harvest Sauvignon
Blanc, Cabernet Shiraz, Muscat.

ALKOOMI

★★★★☆ 11–22 R AUS17, 28, 70, 75, 143,
156, 164, 173 UK1
Great Southern **Est.** 1971
Wingeballup Road, Frankland, WA 6396
Ph (098) 55 2229 **Fax** (098) 55 2284
Open 7 days 10.30–5 **Production** 25 000
Winemaker(s) Grant Mitchell

For those who see the wineries of Western Australia as suffering
from the tyranny of distance, this most remote of all wineries shows
there is not tyranny after all. It is a story of unqualified success due to
sheer hard work and no doubt to Merv and Judy Lange's aversion to
borrowing a single dollar from the bank.

Principal Wines Classic White, Rhine Riesling, Chardonnay,
Sauvignon Blanc, Late Harvest Riesling, Classic Red, Malbec,
Cabernet Sauvignon, Sparkling Alkoomi, Tawny Port.

ALKOOMI CABERNET SAUVIGNON

●●●●● $22

The standard Cabernet Sauvignon retails for $16; in exceptional
years, small quantities of Cabernet Sauvignon are released under
a Reserve label, and given 100% new wood maturation, with the
inclusion of a percentage of merlot. The tasting note given is for a
wine entered at the Mount Barker Wine Show, and not yet released.
I can only assume it will be a Reserve release. Top gold medal in its
class.

Cellaring 10 years. **Best Vintages** '83, '84, '86, '90, '93, '94
Current Vintage '93
Matching Food Rare rump steak.
Tasting Note 1993 Medium to full red-purple; sweet, rich, dark
berry/cassis fruit with stylish, subtle oak. A lovely wine on the palate
with fresh, sweet harmonious fruit and oak, finishing with fine-
grained tannins.

ALKOOMI CHARDONNAY
●●●● $15
Produced from 5 hectares of estate plantings, and barrel fermented
and matured in a mixture of oak, predominantly French Nevers and
Vosges from Seguin Moreau. Both the 1993 and 1994 are good
wines; the Langes believe the '94 is the best yet made at Alkoomi.
Cellaring 2–3 years. **Best Vintages** '85, '88, '90, '92, '94
Current Vintage '94
Matching Food Stir-fried chicken with cashew nuts.
Tasting Note 1994 Light to medium yellow-green; clean fruit with
sweet tropical/peach aromas and a nice touch of spicy oak. The
palate has similar melon and peach flavours, spicy/nutmeg oak,
and a long finish.

ALKOOMI CLASSIC RED
●●●● ▶ $12
Predominantly made from estate-grown shiraz, with a significant
percentage of cabernet sauvignon, and small amounts of merlot,
malbec and cabernet franc. It is the shiraz which drives the wine;
it is not surprising that each release of this wine sells out long before
the next becomes available. The '93 is an outstanding wine at the
price.
Cellaring 2–3 years. **Best Vintages** '83, '84, '86, '90, '93, '94
Current Vintage '93
Matching Food Steak Diane.
Tasting Note 1993 Deep, bright red-purple; a vibrant bouquet
filled with spicy cherry/berry fruit. The palate is rich and potent with
spicy shiraz flavours and abundant soft tannins providing structure
throughout. The oak influence is negligible.

ALKOOMI CLASSIC WHITE
●●● ▶ $12
A blend of 60% semillon, 25% chardonnay and 15% sauvignon
blanc, following more or less in the footsteps of the classic white
Margaret River blends. It is deliberately aimed at the mid market,
made without oak but with appreciable residual sugar.
Cellaring Drink now. **Best Vintages** NA **Current Vintage** '94
Matching Food Pasta carbonara.
Tasting Note 1994 Light green-yellow; a crisp and clean bouquet
with citrus, herb and pineapple aromas. The palate is rich and
weighty, with a similar range of flavours, finishing moderately sweet.

ALL SAINTS ESTATE
★★★★☆ 9–37 CD AUS14, 15, 103
North East Victoria **Est.** 1864
All Saints Road, Wahgunyah, Vic 3687
Ph (060) 33 1922 **Fax** (060) 33 3515
Open 7 days 9–5 **Production** 30 000
Winemaker(s) Neil Jericho
Brown Brothers have spent both time and money on restoring All
Saints since acquiring it in 1991. While there is a creditable range

of table wines, the focus is on the fortifieds, with a complicated but interesting Futures Release scheme for the latter wines, which are also sold by conventional methods.

Principal Wines Chardonnay, Marsanne, Shiraz, Cabernet Sauvignon, Late Harvest Semillon, Late Picked Muscadelle. The real focus is on Classic Release Liqueur Muscat and Liqueur Tokay and on Show Reserve Liqueur Muscat and Liqueur Tokay.

ALL SAINTS CLASSIC RELEASE LIQUEUR MUSCAT
●●●● $16.50

The blend has an average age of 10 years, and, even if not showing the same outstanding varietal character as its sister wine, the Liqueur Tokay, is an impressive wine, attesting to the depth of the fortified stocks still held at All Saints.

Cellaring Not required. **Best Vintages** NA
Current Vintage NV
Matching Food Coffee and chocolates.
Tasting Note NV Medium tawny with just a hint of brown on the rim; soft, raisiny varietal muscat with fractionally earthy spirit. The palate is quite luscious, with good raisined fruit, starting sweet and finishing with cleansing acidity.

ALL SAINTS CLASSIC RELEASE LIQUEUR TOKAY
●●●● ▸ $16.50

An exceptionally good wine at the price, with an average blend age of eight years. The varietal definition is excellent, the blend a delightful amalgam of old and young material.

Cellaring Not required. **Best Vintages** NA
Current Vintage NV
Matching Food Try it as an aperitif.
Tasting Note NV Light golden brown; rich and sweet malt and tea-leaf aromas with barely perceptible fortifying spirit. The palate is of medium to full weight, with malty/toffee/caramel/tea-leaf flavours, finishing with well balanced acidity.

ALL SAINTS LATE HARVEST SEMILLON (375 ML)
●●●● ▸ $14

A new product, first made in the 1994 vintage and which immediately had show success, promptly winning two gold and two silver medals. Winemaker Neil Jericho has had long experience in making such styles, but it does appear to be very fast developing.

Cellaring Drink now. **Best Vintages** NA **Current Vintage** '94
Matching Food Sweet, fruit-based tarts.
Tasting Note 1994 Full yellow-green; there are intense, almost essency, dried apricot and peach aromas on the bouquet, indicating a high level of botrytis infection. The palate is rich and powerful, again with flavours of dried apricots, and subtle oak.

ALL SAINTS SHIRAZ
●●●● $14

A typical concentrated Rutherglen Shiraz in terms of fruit, but not so typical in terms of the addition of a considerable degree of new

American oak. The marriage works well.
Cellaring 5–7 years. **Best Vintages** NA
Current Vintage '92
Matching Food Venison.
Tasting Note 1992 Full red-purple; concentrated and deep
blackberry fruit aromas, balanced by potent vanillin American oak.
The palate is chewy and dense, with spicy blackberry fruit,
considerable tannins and lashings of vanillin oak.

ALL SAINTS SHOW RESERVE LIQUEUR TOKAY
●●●●● $37
While some of the best stocks of All Saints were sold to other
purchasers before Brown Brothers completed the acquisition of the
entire property, certain of the very best material remained. This has
in turn formed the base of this show blend, which has an average
age of 20 years, and which has already accumulated a large
number of trophies and gold medals.
Cellaring Not required. **Best Vintages** NA
Current Vintage NV
Matching Food A meal in itself.
Tasting Note NV Deep golden brown; wonderfully concentrated
and rich caramel, toffee and molasses aromas lead on to a
sensuously luscious and complex toffee, tea-leaf and butterscotch-
flavoured palate.

ALLANDALE
★★★★ 13.95–15.50 R AUS35, 58, 178
Hunter Valley **Est.** 1978
Lovedale Road, Pokolbin via Maitland, NSW 2321
Ph (049) 90 4526 **Fax** (049) 90 1714
Open Mon–Sat 9–5, Sun 10–5 **Production** 15 000
Winemaker(s) Bill Sneddon
Unostentatious, medium-sized winery which has been under the
control of winemaker Bill Sneddon for well over a decade. Has
developed something of a reputation as a Chardonnay specialist
over the past few years.
Principal Wines Semillon Sauvignon Blanc, Chardonnay,
Matthew Shiraz, Cabernet Sauvignon, Methode Champenoise.

ALLANDALE CHARDONNAY
●●●● ▶ $15.50
Draws upon 3 hectares of estate plantings. The occasional special
release (as in 1991) and wines such as the current vintage have kept
the winery in the public eye. The wine shows excellent use of a mix
of French and American oak.
Cellaring 2–3 years. **Best Vintages** '91, '94
Current Vintage '94
Matching Food Smoked salmon.
Tasting Note 1994 Medium to full yellow-green; a rich and
complex bouquet with tangy melon and citrus fruit perfectly
interwoven with oak. The palate is tangy and lively, of medium

to full weight with grapefruit, fig and melon flavours, and perfectly balanced oak.

ALLANDALE MATTHEW SHIRAZ
●●● ▶ $16.95
Always made in a relatively soft style, with a noticeable but not overblown American oak contribution; recent vintages have seen even better oak balance and integration resulting from partial barrel fermentation in American oak.
Cellaring 2–5 years. **Best Vintages** '86, '87, '89, '91, '93
Current Vintage '93
Matching Food Veal chops.
Tasting Note 1993 Medium purple-red; the bouquet is of light to medium intensity with obvious but well integrated American oak and earthy shiraz in the background. In the mouth, elegantly weighted and structured, though the flavours are undeniably, albeit gently, driven by vanillin and cedar oak.

ALLANDALE SEMILLON SAUVIGNON BLANC
●●●● $14.95
A blend of 80% semillon and 20% sauvignon blanc, a combination which is surprisingly rare in the Hunter Valley (and far more commonly encountered in regions such as McLaren Vale and the Margaret River). The blend works well, and the wine shows once again what an excellent vintage 1994 was for white wines in the Hunter.
Cellaring Now–3 years. **Best Vintages** NA
Current Vintage '94
Matching Food Seafood risotto.
Tasting Note 1994 glowing yellow-green; the bouquet is of above-average intensity and concentration, with fruit the driving force. There is plenty of varietal character and bite on the palate, with herbaceous though not green flavours. An unwooded wine with excellent structure and which will age well.

ALLANMERE WINES
★★★★ 12.50–18 CD AUS10
Hunter Valley **Est.** 1984
Allandale Road, Allandale via Pokolbin, NSW 2321
Ph (049) 30 7387 **Fax** (049) 30 7387
Open Mon–Tues, Thur–Fri 11–4, W'ends 9.30–5
Production 4000
Winemaker(s) Geoff Broadfield, Newton Potter
For the time being at least, Newton Potter, assisted by long-term part-time winemaker Geoff Broadfield (who also officiates at Wandin Valley Estate), continues to own and run Allanmere, producing beautifully crafted white and red wines.
Principal Wines Gold Label Chardonnay, Semillon, Trinity White (Chardonnay, Semillon, Sauvignon Blanc), Cabernet Sauvignon, Trinity Red (Cabernet blend), Cabernet Shiraz. Durham Chardonnay is top-of-the-range Chardonnay.

ALLANMERE DURHAM CHARDONNAY
●●●● $18

Allanmere has no vineyards of its own, but has long-term grower contracts in the Hunter Valley, and has always been able to source chardonnay (and other grapes) of high quality. Geoff Broadfield's skills, together with the opulent use of oak, produces a wine of great opulence.

Cellaring Short term — quick developing. **Best Vintages** '86, '87, '91, '93 **Current Vintage** '93

Matching Food Smoked chicken.

Tasting Note 1993 Medium to full yellow-green; peachy fruit is enveloped in masses of smoky bacon oak on the bouquet. The palate, too, shows opulent Francois Freres style oak in abundance, along with rich peachy/buttery fruit.

AMBERLEY ESTATE

★★★★ 11–16 CD AUS56
Margaret River **Est.** 1986
Thornton Road, Yallingup, WA 6282
Ph (097) 55 2288 **Fax** (097) 55 2171
Open 7 days 10–4.30 **Production** 24 000
Winemaker(s) Eddie Price

Has grown rapidly on the basis of its ultra-commercial, fairly sweet and bland Chenin Blanc. In fact, almost all of the other wines in the portfolio are significantly better, even if more expensive. The winery also offers a high quality restaurant (bookings recommended).

Principal Wines Semillon Sauvignon Blanc, Margaret River White Burgundy, Classic Margaret River White (Semillon, Chardonnay, Sauvignon Blanc), Sauvignon Blanc, Semillon, Chardonnay, Chenin Blanc, Nouveau, Cabernet Merlot.

AMBERLEY ESTATE CABERNET MERLOT
●●●● $15

A blend of cabernet sauvignon, merlot and cabernet franc. Both the '91 and '92 vintages show great concentration and backbone — in stark contrast to the style of most of the white wines.AUS56

Cellaring 5–7 years. **Best Vintages** '91, '92

Current Vintage '92

Matching Food Rack of lamb.

Tasting Note 1992 Medium red, with just a touch of purple; clean, firm, briary fruit in typical, slightly gravelly, Margaret River style. The palate is powerful, potent and concentrated with dark berry/briary fruit and marked tannins. The oak influence is subtle throughout.

AMBERLEY ESTATE SAUVIGNON BLANC
●●● ▶ $15

Made without oak, which is understandable, and bolstered by a touch of residual sugar, likewise understandable but less desirable, perhaps. For all that, a pleasant wine.

Cellaring Drink now. **Best Vintages** NA **Current Vintage** '94

Matching Food Stuffed mussels.

Tasting Note 1994 Light to medium yellow-green; a fragrant bouquet with tropical passionfruit/gooseberry aromas of light to medium intensity. The palate is of similar weight, and perhaps for that reason, has been fleshed out with a touch of sugar.

AMBERLEY ESTATE SEMILLON
●●●● $16

Made in a quite different mould from most Margaret River Semillons, with lots of rich barrel ferment oak producing a wine which, in many ways, has more in common with a ripe year Hunter Valley Semillon than that which one usually finds in the Margaret River.
Cellaring Drink now. **Best Vintages** NA **Current Vintage** '93
Matching Food Roast chicken.
Tasting Note 1993 Glowing yellow-green; an intense and complex bouquet with abundant spicy vanillin oak with toasty/nutty fruit just holding its own. The palate is similarly rich, high-flavoured and concentrated with some tangy/herbal fruit and expansive, toasty barrel ferment oak.

AMBERLEY ESTATE SEMILLON SAUVIGNON BLANC
●●● ▶ $14

A traditional Margaret River blend, made in a more traditional fashion than the Semillon. There is a light touch of oak, possibly introduced during tank fermentation, and highly aromatic fruit.
Cellaring Drink now. **Best Vintages** NA **Current Vintage** '94
Matching Food Richer Asian seafood dishes.
Tasting Note 1994 Medium yellow-green; interesting fragrant and aromatic aromas ranging from herbal/vegetal through gooseberry to more floral/minty characters. The palate, too, has a range of con-centrated flavours, before finishing with appreciable residual sugar.

ANDERSON WINERY

NR 9–17.50 CD AUSSD
North East Victoria **Est.** 1993
Lot 12 Chiltern Road, Rutherglen, Vic 3685
Ph (060) 32 8111 **Fax** (060) 32 9028
Open Mon–Sat 9–5, Sun 10–5 **Production** 1500
Winemaker(s) Howard Anderson
With a winemaking career spanning 30 years, including a stint at Seppelt Great Western, Howard Anderson and family have started their own winery, ultimately intending to specialise in sparkling wine made entirely on site. Most recently, Howard Anderson was a partner in Cofield Wines, but each has gone its own way.
Principal Wines Classic White, Chardonnay, Doux Blanc, Pinot Noir, Shiraz, Soft Cabernet, Late Harvest Tokay, Sparkling, Fortifieds.

ANDREAS PARK ESTATE *

NR NA AUSSD
Mudgee **Est.** 1960
Cassilis Road, Mudgee, NSW 2850

Ph (02) 415 1649 **Fax** (02) 413 1112
Open Not **Production** 300
Winemaker(s) Ian MacRae (Contract)
I know little of Andreas Park Estate except that Ian MacRae (of
Miramar) is the contract winemaker, and that most of the grapes
from the substantial and now very old vineyards are sold to others.
The 1994 Shiraz made by Ian MacRae won the top gold medal at
the Mudgee Wine Show of that year.
Principal Wines Shiraz.

ANDREW GARRETT WINES

★★★★ 8.95–19.90 R AUS13, 36, 48, 107, 109,
149, 163 UK8
Southern Vales **Est.** 1983
Kangarilla Road, McLaren Vale, SA 5171
Ph (08) 323 8853 **Fax** (08) 323 8550
Open 7 days 10–5 **Production** 95 000
Winemaker(s) Warren Randall
Now controlled by Suntory of Japan, this high-flying winery was a
major topic of conversation in the second half of the 1980s as its
production soared and its aggressive purchasing helped push grape
prices to unsustainable heights, but has since adopted a much lower
profile. Well-crafted wines are sourced from all the major South
Australian regions, with a recent much-publicised push into the
Mornington Peninsula.
Principal Wines Chardonnay, Riesling, Fumé Blanc, Semillon,
Pinot Noir, Cabernet Merlot, Bold Style Shiraz, Mornington
Peninsula Cabernet Sauvignon, Sparkling; Randall is premium
sparkling label.

ANDREW GARRETT BOLD STYLE SHIRAZ
●●● ▶ $12.10
As the name implies, made so as to focus all of the attention onto the
fruit flavours. Made from McLaren Vale shiraz, it is released young,
yet is in no sense a light red. There is a hint of spicy/charry
American oak probably introduced during fermentation, and the
style works well.
Cellaring Short term. **Best Vintages** '92, '93
Current Vintage '93
Matching Food Italian cuisine, soft cheeses.
Tasting Note 1993 Vibrant red-purple; the aromas are bright,
fresh and very juicy, with similar masses of juicy fruit and just a flick
of spicy oak; the wine has been kept very fresh before going to
bottle. Soft tannins.

ANDREW GARRETT CHARDONNAY
●●●● $13.95
Made in consistent style over recent vintages, showing the
sophisticated use of oak and grapes grown in a range of mild to
cool South Australian climates, giving a fresh, crisp, well balanced
wine.

Cellaring Best enjoyed while fresh. **Best Vintages** '92, '93, '94
Current Vintage '94
Matching Food Seafood, Coquilles St Jacques.
Tasting Note 1994 Light to medium yellow-green; a lively bouquet
with tangy melon and citrus fruit and subtle oak. The palate is
elegant and crisp in an unforced style; perhaps needs a touch
more weight for gold medal points.

ANDREW GARRETT MORNINGTON PENINSULA CABERNET SAUVIGNON
●●●● $16.50
Warren Randall was always the man to step into Andrew Garrett's
shoes, once the latter had left Andrew Garrett Wines, for both are
nothing if not full of self-confidence. Thus Randall introduced this
wine with a fanfare of trumpets, announcing, 'at last a Mornington
Peninsula Cabernet with real flavour'. He might be more than half
right. From Sir Peter Derham's Red Hill Estate and from Willow
Creek Vineyard.
Cellaring 3–4 years. **Best Vintages** NA **Current Vintage** '93
Matching Food Peking duck.
Tasting Note 1993 Medium to full purple-red; a smooth, clean
and ripe aroma with luscious berry fruit and minimal oak. The palate
has lots of dark berry and cassis fruit flavours with good tannin
structure. In all respects a most interesting wine.

ANDREW GARRETT SAUVAGE PINOT CHARDONNAY
●●●● $25
Winemaker Warren Randall's stint at Seppelt Great Western has
reflected itself in the sparkling wines from Andrew Garrett. This
blend of pinot noir and chardonnay from various South Australian
regions is unusual in having no dosage (or sugar) added at
disgorgement, hence the Sauvage name. Winner of Thorpe Trophy
for Best Sparkling Wine 1994 Sydney Wine Show.
Cellaring None required, but will hold for several years.
Best Vintages '91 **Current Vintage** '91
Matching Food Aperitif style.
Tasting Note 1991 Light straw-green; complex
nutty/biscuity/bready autolysis and pinot noir aromas. The palate is
firm, with delicate dusty fruit and a long, bone-dry finish.

ANGOVE'S

★★★☆ 4–19 R AUS4–9 UK30
Riverlands **Est.** 1886
Bookmark Avenue, Renmark, SA 5341
Ph (085) 85 1311 **Fax** (085) 85 1583
Open Mon–Fri 9–5, Sat 9–1 **Production** 750 000
Winemaker(s) Frank J Newman
Exemplifies the economies of scale achievable in the Australian
Riverlands without compromising potential quality. Very good
technology provides wines which are never poor and which can
sometimes exceed their theoretical station in life. The white varietals

are best. Recently spreading its wings with varietals from premium
regions outside the Riverlands.
Principal Wines Classic Reserve Colombard, Sauvignon Blanc,
Chardonnay, Cabernet Sauvignon; Padthaway Chardonnay,
Cabernet Sauvignon; Floreate; Cheaper Butterfly Ridge varietals and
Misty Vineyards generics; also specialist Brandy producer; Fortifieds.

ANGOVE'S CLASSIC RESERVE COLOMBARD
●●● $7.95
One of the range of varietal wines produced from Angove's, vast
Nanya Vineyard, the others being Riesling, Chardonnay, Sauvignon
Blanc, Pinot Noir, Shiraz and Cabernet Sauvignon. Cold-fermented
in stainless steel, and early-bottled without oak maturation.
Cellaring Drink now. **Best Vintages** '88, '93, '94
Current Vintage '94
Matching Food Grilled fish.
Tasting Note 1994 Light green-yellow; a clean and fresh bouquet
with faint citrus aromas leads on to a clean, fresh and lively palate
with some citrus and melon flavours. Outpointed the Chardonnay
and Sauvignon Blanc of the same year, both of which are very
developed.

ANGOVE'S FLOREATE
●●●● $9.95
A very unusual and rare late harvest Sauvignon Blanc from
Angove's, Nanya Vineyard which is not, however, botrytised.
Although Angove's is not specific, it is likely to have been cane cut,
for it has 12% alcohol and 6.3¡ baume of residual sugar.
Cellaring Drink now. **Best Vintages** '92 **Current Vintage** '92
Matching Food Baked apple, créme brûleé.
Tasting Note 1992 Deep golden yellow; a complex bouquet with
obvious oak influence leads on to a palate with cumquat and toffee
flavours, finishing with nicely balanced acidity.

ANGOVE'S PADTHAWAY CABERNET SAUVIGNON
●●●● $17
A new venture for Angove's which has hitherto produced almost all
of its wines from its Nanya Vineyard in the Riverlands, making
occasional Limited Release/Winemaker Selection with grapes
purchased from various premium areas. 1993 is the inaugural
vintage.
Cellaring 3–5 years. **Best Vintages** '93 **Current Vintage** '93
Matching Food Lamb casserole.
Tasting Note 1993 Medium to full red; rich, ripe chocolate and
dark berry fruit aromas with subtle oak. The palate is generous, rich
and ripe; a fruit-driven style with soft tannins and subtle oak.

ANGOVE'S PADTHAWAY CHARDONNAY
●●● ▶ $17
A new venture for Angove's which has hitherto produced almost all
of its wines from its Nanya Vineyard in the Riverlands, making
occasional Limited Release/Winemaker Selection wines with grapes

purchased from various premium areas. 1993 is the inaugural vintage.

Cellaring 1–2 years. **Best Vintages** NA **Current Vintage** '93
Matching Food Richer seafood, salmon.
Tasting Note 1993 Advanced but brilliant yellow-green; smooth with regional citrus/vegetal aromas which are attractive; the palate has ample tangy melon and citrus fruit with a distinct cut to the finish. Subtle oak.

ANTCLIFFE'S CHASE

NR 10.50–17 CD AUS16
Goulburn Valley **Est.** 1982
RMB 4510, Caveat via Seymour, Vic 3660
Ph (057) 90 4333 **Fax** (057) 90 4333
Open W'ends 10–5 **Production** 500
Winemaker(s) Chris Bennett, Ian Leamon
A small family enterprise which commenced planting the vineyards at an elevation of 600 metres in the Strathbogie Ranges in 1982, but which has only recently commenced wine production from the 4-hectare vineyard. As the scarecrow label indicates, birds are a major problem for remote vineyards such as this.
Principal Wines Riesling, Chardonnay, Pinot Noir, Cabernet Franc.

AQUILA ESTATE *

★★★ 11–15 R AUS101
South-west Coastal Plain **Est.** 1993
85 Carabooda Road, Carabooda, WA 6033
Ph (09) 407 5100 **Fax** (09) 407 5070
Open Not **Production** 10 000
Winemaker(s) Elaine Washer, Mike Davies
Aquila Estate has appeared out of nowhere, as it were. It is situated on the Washer family's 15-hectare avocado plantation at Carabooda, north of Perth, which has 4 hectares of estate vines coming into production. Most of the grapes will, however, come from the Margaret River and Boyup Brook regions under long-term contracts. Winemaker and chief executive Elaine Washer is a 23-year-old science graduate with an Honours Degree in genetic engineering. Her brother Stewart is a specialist in DNA research.
Principal Wines Semillon, Sauvignon Blanc, Chardonnay, Reflections (white blend), Cabernet Sauvignon, Flame (red blend).

AQUILA ESTATE CABERNET SAUVIGNON
●●● ▶ $15
Made from Margaret River cabernet sauvignon, and a silver medal winner at the 1994 Mount Barker Show. An unusual wine, with strong oak impact.
Cellaring 2–4 years. **Best Vintages** NA **Current Vintage** '93
Matching Food Spiced beef.
Tasting Note 1993 Medium red; there are bright, juicy, black and

redcurrant aromas with cinnamon and nutmeg oak. The palate is
high-flavoured with tangy cinnamon and lemon rind characters
along with more conventional black fruit flavours; soft, lingering
tannins on the finish.

AQUILA ESTATE CHARDONNAY
●●● $15
The first release from Aquila Estate, produced in very limited
quantities, and launched in October 1993. Barrel fermented in
French oak, and certainly shows the handling.
Cellaring 1–2 years. **Best Vintages** NA **Current Vintage** '93
Matching Food Scampi.
Tasting Note 1993 Medium yellow-green; the bouquet is complex
with attractive melon fruit and strong barrel ferment oak aromas. The
barrel ferment and malolactic ferment characters do tend to sit on
top of the fruit somewhat on the palate, but the wine has good
texture.

ARLEWOOD ESTATE
NR 10–15 CD AUS182
Margaret River **Est.** 1988
Harmans Road South, Willyabrup, WA 6280
Ph (097) 55 6267 **Fax** (097) 55 6267
Open By appt **Production** 1000
Winemaker(s) Mike Davies, Jan Davies
Liz and John Wojturski have established their 2.5-hectare vineyard
between Ashbrook and Vasse Felix, with contract winemaking by
Mike and Jan Davies. Production is projected to peak at 2000 cases
in the medium term.
Principal Wines Semillon, Sauvignon Blanc Semillon, Estate White
(Semillon Sauvignon Blanc Verdelho), Liaison (Fully Sweet), Cabernet
Sauvignon, Port.

ARROWFIELD
★★★☆ 9.50–20.95 R AUS12 US1
Upper Hunter Valley **Est.** 1968
Denman Road, Jerry's Plains, NSW 2330
Ph (065) 76 4041 **Fax** (065) 76 4144
Open 7 days 10–5 **Production** 110 000
Winemaker(s) Simon Gilbert, Liz Radcliffe
After largely dropping the Arrowfield name in favour of Mountarrow
and a plethora of other brands, this Japanese-owned company has
come full circle once again marketing the wines solely under the
Arrowfield label. Its principal grape sources are Cowra and the
Upper Hunter, but it does venture further afield from time to time.
Principal Wines Top-of-the-range Show Reserve Chardonnay,
Late Harvest Rhine Riesling, Shiraz, Cabernet Sauvignon; Cowra
Chardonnay, Sauvignon Blanc, Pinot Noir; Arrowfield varietals
Chardonnay, Semillon Chardonnay, Semillon Sauvignon Blanc,
Traminer, Shiraz Cabernet, Cabernet Merlot; Sparkling and

Fortifieds; also Simon Whitlam range of Semillon, Semillon
Chardonnay, Shiraz, Cabernet Sauvignon.

ARROWFIELD SHOW RESERVE CABERNET SAUVIGNON
●●● ▶ $17.95
A blend of Central Victorian, Cowra and McLaren Vale grapes. Like
the Show Reserve Chardonnay, made in very limited quantities: only
2115 cases were produced of the '91 vintage, which was held back
until its release in 1995.
Cellaring 2–5 years. **Best Vintages** NA **Current Vintage** '91
Matching Food Fillet steak.
Tasting Note 1991 Medium to full red; the bouquet is presently
fractionally closed, with oak tending to dominate. The wine opens up
on an elegant palate with cedary notes, finishing with fine tannins.

ARROWFIELD SHOW RESERVE CHARDONNAY
●●●● ▶ $17.95
A blend of the best Hunter Valley and Cowra grapes available
to Arrowfield out of the 1994 vintage. 2700 cases were made,
producing one of the best wines for many years to come from
Arrowfield. Often the oak handling seems overblown; in this wine
it has been judged to perfection in both 1993 and 1994.
Cellaring 1–2 years. **Best Vintages** '93, '94
Current Vintage '94
Matching Food Moreton Bay bugs.
Tasting Note 1994 Glowing yellow-green; a complex bouquet
of medium to full intensity with excellent fruit and oak balance and
integration. The palate is quite tightly structured with crisp, slightly
stony melon fruit backed by plenty of toasty barrel ferment oak.

ARROWFIELD SHOW RESERVE LATE HARVEST RIESLING (375 ML)
●●●●● $17.95
A superb botrytised Riesling which deservedly won a gold medal at
the 1994 Australian National Wine Show in Canberra.
Cellaring 1–3 years. **Best Vintages** NA **Current Vintage** '93
Matching Food Richer sorbets.
Tasting Note 1993 Light green-yellow; bright, fresh and intense
lime and mandarin aromas. The palate is lively, fresh and crisp, with
near perfect botrytis riesling flavours, finishing with just the right
amount of acid.

ARTHURS CREEK ESTATE *
★★★★☆ 16.95–19.95 R AUS148
Macedon **Est.** 1976
Strathewen Road, Arthurs Creek, Vic 3099
Ph (03) 9827 6629 **Fax** (03) 9824 0252
Open Not **Production** 585
Winemaker(s) Mitchelton (Contract), Gary
Baldwin (Consultant)
A latter-day folly of leading Melbourne QC, S E K Hulme, who
planted one and a half hectares each of semillon, chardonnay, and

cabernet sauvignon at Arthurs Creek in the mid 1970s, and
commenced to have wine made by various people, including Tom
Lazar, John Flynn, Lou Knight, Ian Leamon, David Creed and Don
Lewis for 15 years before deciding to sell any of it. A ruthless
weeding out process followed, with only the best of the older
vintages offered. The young vintages are full of promise.
Principal Wines Chardonnay, Cabernet Sauvignon.

ARTHURS CREEK ESTATE CABERNET SAUVIGNON
●●●●) $19.95
Since 1992 the winemaking has been carried out by Mitchelton; at
the 1994 Victorian Wine Show the '92 Cabernet Sauvignon won
the top gold medal in Class 22 (1992 and older Cabernets), the
1992 won a silver medal in Class 18, while the 1994 Cabernet
Sauvignon was awarded the trophy for Best Cabernet Sauvignon
of Show.
Cellaring Up to 10 years or more. **Best Vintages** '82, '87, '89,
'91, '92, '93, '94 **Current Vintage** '89
Matching Food Lamb fillets.
Tasting Note 1982 Light to medium red; clean, fine and fragrant,
with strong overtones of Bordeaux. A genuinely elegant wine on the
palate with spotlessly clean, slightly minty cool-grown fruit. (Tasted
early 1994.)

ARTHURS CREEK ESTATE CHARDONNAY
●●●●) $16.95
Produced from 1.5 hectares of estate plantings. The two initial
releases were 1988 and 1990, which came onto the market in late
1993. The 1988 was made by Lou Knight at Knight's Granite Hills;
the 1990 by David Creed at Lovegrove at Cottles Bridge.
Cellaring 3–5 years. **Best Vintages** '88, '90, '92, '93, '94
Current Vintage '91
Matching Food Veal fricassee.
Tasting Note 1990 Light to medium yellow-green; classic melon
and fig cool-climate aromas with subtle oak. The palate is in the
same classically reserved mould, very harmonious and has
developed quite beautifully in bottle.

ASHBROOK ESTATE
★★★★☆ 13.95–21 R AUS2, 96, 161, 168, 170 UK62
Margaret River **Est.** 1975
Harmans South Road, Willyabrup, WA 6280
Ph (097) 55 6262 **Fax** (097) 55 6290
Open W'ends 11–5 **Production** 8000
Winemaker(s) Tony Devitt, Brian Devitt
A fastidious maker of outstanding table wines but which shuns
publicity and the wine show system alike, and is less well known
than it deserves to be. No recent tastings, but I have yet to sample
a bad wine from Ashbrook Estate.
Principal Wines Semillon, Sauvignon Blanc, Riesling,
Chardonnay, Verdelho, Cabernet Sauvignon.

ASHER VINEYARD *

NR 10 CD AUSSD
Geelong **Est.** 1975
360 Goldsworthy Road, Lovely Banks, Vic 3221
Ph (052) 76 1365
Open Sat, Public hols 10–5, Sun 12–5 **Production** Minuscule
Winemaker(s) Brian Moten
A tiny, semi-home-winemaking operation situated at the picturesquely
named Lovely Banks on the outskirts of Geelong.
Principal Wines Sauvignon Blanc, Cabernet Sauvignon, Malbec.

ASHTON HILLS

★★★★ 14.95–22 R AUS56, 166 UK11
Adelaide Hills **Est.** 1982
Tregarthen Road, Ashton, SA 5137
Ph (08) 390 1243 **Fax** (08) 390 1243
Open Fri–Sun 10–5 **Production** 900
Winemaker(s) Stephen George
Stephen George wears three winemaker hats: one for Ashton Hills,
drawing upon a 3.5-hectare vineyard high in the Adelaide Hills;
one for Galah Wines (see separate entry) and one for Wendouree
(likewise). It would be hard to imagine three wineries producing
more diverse styles, with the elegance and finesse of Ashton Hills at
one end of the spectrum, the awesome power of Wendouree at the
other.
Principal Wines Chardonnay, Riesling, Pinot Noir, Obliqua,
Merlot Cabernet.

ASHTON HILLS PINOT NOIR
●●● ▶ $21.95
As with all the Ashton Hills wines, these are Pinots relying on finesse
and elegance, rather than on power or obvious fruit flavours.
Winemaker Stephen George employs the full gamut of winemaking
techniques, and has an extraordinary 19 different clones of pinot
planted, necessarily providing yet further complexity.
Cellaring 2–3 years. **Best Vintages** '88, '92, '92, '93
Current Vintage '93
Matching Food Quail, guinea fowl.
Tasting Note 1993 Medium red-purple; faintly plummy, sweet fruit
of medium intensity; similar plummy fruit flavours on the palate,
which has good structure and mouthfeel. The richest yet of the
Ashton Hills Pinots.

ASHTON HILLS RIESLING
●●● ▶ $15
A wine of unusually consistent style, and which invariably ages
slowly. The natural acidity is high, and the fruit always tight and
often inexpressive when the wine is young, slowly opening up as it
evolves in bottle. These are elegant wines which are ideally suited to
food. In mid 1994 vintages back to 1989 were available from the
mailing list.

Cellaring 5 years or more. **Best Vintages** '89, '90, '91, '93
Current Vintage '94
Matching Food Fresh asparagus.
Tasting Note 1994 Light to medium green-yellow; the bouquet is typically tight, neither particularly aromatic nor fruity, but fine and clean. The palate is similarly firm and tight, with hints of citrus and spice.

AUGUSTINE

★★★★ 12.95 R AUS176
Mudgee **Est.** 1918
George Campbell Drive, Mudgee, NSW 2850
Ph (063) 72 3880 **Fax** (063) 72 2977
Open 7 days 10–4 **Production** 7000
Winemaker(s) Rothbury Estate
The historic Augustine Vineyard, established by the Roth family but purchased by Dr Thomas Fiaschi in 1917, passed into the control of Rothbury Estate in 1993. The new Augustine wines are made at Rothbury and are a handsome demonstration of the quality of Mudgee fruit.
Principal Wines Chardonnay, Cabernet Merlot.

AUGUSTINE CABERNET MERLOT
●●●●) $12.95
A singularly auspicious debut for this wine, coming from the cabernet sauvignon and merlot established among the 45 hectares of estate plantings acquired (under lease) by Rothbury in 1993.
Cellaring 3–5 years. **Best Vintages** NA
Current Vintage '93
Matching Food Braised oxtail.
Tasting Note 1993 Medium to full red-purple; smooth, sweet cassis berry fruit aromas of medium to full intensity with just a hint of oak. The palate shows similarly attractive, clean, sweet blackcurrant fruit with a hint of chocolate, finishing with soft, fine tannins and well integrated oak.

AUGUSTINE CHARDONNAY
●●●) $12.95
Mudgee can fairly claim to be one of the birthplaces of Australian chardonnay, providing the source material (from a high quality pre-phylloxera clone) for much of the explosion of plantings in the 1970s. This wine was part tank fermented and part barrel fermented in new Missouri oak.
Cellaring 2–3 years. **Best Vintages** NA
Current Vintage '94
Matching Food Grilled trout.
Tasting Note 1994 Light to medium yellow-green; clean peach and melon fruit with a touch of vanillin oak. The palate is not particularly rich, but is crisp and lively with lemony/melon fruit and restrained oak.

AULDSTONE

NR 8–16 CD AUSSD
North East Victoria **Est.** 1989
Booths Road, Taminick via Glenrowan, Vic 3675
Ph (057) 66 2237
Open Thurs–Sun 9–5 **Production** 1600
Winemaker(s) Contract
Michael and Nancy Reid have restored a century-old stone winery
and are replanting the largely abandoned vineyard around it.
Gourmet lunches are available on weekends.
Principal Wines Chardonnay, Semillon, Traminer Riesling,
Pinot Noir, Cabernet Sauvignon, Aleatico, Sparkling Burgundy.

AUSTIN'S BARRABOOL WINES

NR 10.95–17.95 R AUS55
Geelong **Est.** 1982
50 Lemins Road, Waurn Ponds, Vic 3221
Ph (052) 41 8114
Open By appt **Production** 600
Winemaker(s) John Ellis (Contract)
A tiny winery which has made its mark with a gold medal-winning,
full-flavoured, intense 1990 Rhine Riesling and a trophy-winning
Chardonnay, a quite superb wine with tangy, barrel ferment fruit.
However, the pace of intended development seems to have slowed
significantly.
Principal Wines Riesling, Chardonnay, Cabernet Sauvignon.

AVALON VINEYARD

★★☆ 9.50–16.40 CD AUSSD
North East Victoria **Est.** 1981
RMB 9556 Whitfield Road, Wangaratta, Vic 3678
Ph (057) 29 3629
Open 7 days 10–5 **Production** 360
Winemaker(s) Doug Groom
Avalon Vineyard is situated in the King Valley, 4 kilometres north
of Whitfield. Much of the production is sold to other makers, with
limited quantities made by Doug Groom, a graduate of Roseworthy,
and one of the owners of the property. No recent tastings, but earlier
tastings showed variable quality, perhaps due to limited winery
facilities.
Principal Wines Chardonnay, Riesling, Semillon, Cabernet
Sauvignon, Pinot Noir, Sparkling.

AVALON WINES

★★★☆ 10–14 CD AUSSD
Darling Range **Est.** 1986
1605 Bailey Road, Glen Forrest, WA 6071
Ph (09) 298 8049

Open By appt **Production** 150
Winemaker(s) Lyndon Crockett
One of the newest wineries in the Perth Hills, drawing upon one
hectare each of chardonnay, semillon, and cabernet sauvignon. The
'93 Cabernet is a little raw and unfinished, but the Chardonnay is
quite impressive.
Principal Wines Chardonnay, Semillon, Cabernet Sauvignon.

AVALON WINES CHARDONNAY
●●● ▶ $14
Produced in minuscule quantities from one hectare of estate
vineyards in the picturesque Perth Hills. An impressive wine given
the tiny production.
Cellaring Up to 3 years. **Best Vintages** NA
Current Vintage '93
Matching Food Chicken or veal.
Tasting Note 1993 Medium to full yellow; a concentrated
bouquet, with nutty fruit and well handled oak. The palate is
complex and structured, with the flavours into secondary characters,
probably due to ambient temperature barrel fermentation techniques,
but which work well enough.

BAILEYS

★★★★★ 8.95–50 CD AUS176 UK94
North East Victoria **Est.** 1870
Cnr Taminick Gap Road & Upper Taminick Road, Glenrowan,
Vic 3675
Ph (057) 66 2392 **Fax** (057) 66 2596
Open Mon–Fri 9–5, W'ends 10–5 **Production** 60 000
Winemaker(s) Steve Goodwin, Colin Slater
Part of the rapidly expanding Rothbury group of companies, and
moving with the times, seeking to upgrade the quality of its white
wines and, more particularly, cashing in on the interest in full-bodied
Shiraz. For all that, its greatest strength lies in its fortified wines.
Principal Wines Classic Chardonnay, Riesling, Hermitage;
1920's Block Shiraz; Warby Range; Founder and Winemaker's
Selection Tokay and Muscat.

BAILEYS 1920'S BLOCK SHIRAZ
●●●●● $22.50
Baileys was founded in 1870 by Varley Bailey, and in 1920 — to
celebrate the 50th anniversary — a special block of shiraz was
planted. It is from these vines that the wine is made, first produced in
1991 and immediately proclaiming its class. Only 900 cases of the
wine are produced each year.
Cellaring Up to 20 years. **Best Vintages** '91, '92, '93
Current Vintage '93
Matching Food Rare rump steak, venison.
Tasting Note 1993 Typical medium to full red-purple; a rich
bouquet showing strong varietal character with dark cherry fruit,
some spicy notes and subtle oak. In the mouth, extremely powerful

and concentrated, with liquorice and cherry flavours, finishing with pronounced tannins. Fruit- rather than oak-driven.

BAILEYS CLASSIC STYLE HERMITAGE
●●●● ▶ $11.95

Possessed of what is arguably the most distinctive label in Australia, as visually powerful (with its diagonal 'Hermitage' in such large typeface) as the wine in the glass is potent. The wine is deliberately made in the traditional North East Victorian style to emphasise the richness and power of the fruit. There is some vintage variation, but the current release is an outstanding wine.
Cellaring 10–15 years. **Best Vintages** '85, '86, '88, '92, '94
Current Vintage '92
Matching Food Powerful red meat or cheese.
Tasting Note 1992 Dense red-purple; concentrated dark berry and liquorice fruit aromas with just the faintest hint of American oak. In the mouth, a massive wine with heaps of juicy black fruit flavours finishing with soft but persistent tannins. Gold medal 1994 Sydney International Top 100.

BAILEYS FOUNDER LIQUEUR MUSCAT
●●●● ▶ $13.95

Made from brown frontignac, otherwise known as brown muscat, and the best known of the fortified wines of North East Victoria. As one would expect, in the rich Baileys mould. One of four Muscats produced, starting at the bottom with Warby Range, then Founder Liqueur, then Gold Label and ultimately Winemaker's Selection.
Cellaring Indefinite. **Best Vintages** NA **Current Vintage** NV
Matching Food After coffee; alternative to Cognac.
Tasting Note NV Medium red-brown; an arresting bouquet with hints of spice to the sweet, ripe, complex fruit. The same unusual spicy/cinnamon aspects are apparent on the rich and complex palate.

BAILEYS FOUNDER LIQUEUR TOKAY
●●●● ▶ $13.95

The midpoint of the Tokays produced by Baileys, coming between Warby Range at the bottom end and Winemaker's Selection at the top end. In the totally distinctive, rich and sweet Baileys style, with more accent on complexity and less on primary fruit than that of Morris; one of the great classics.
Cellaring Indefinite. **Best Vintages** NA **Current Vintage** NV
Matching Food Winter aperitif; summer after dinner.
Tasting Note NV Medium golden brown; full, complex sweeter style of Tokay with clean spirit. The palate is rich, full and textured with flavours of butterscotch and sweet biscuit, and a chewy texture, but finishing long and clean.

BAILEYS WINEMAKER'S SELECTION OLD LIQUEUR MUSCAT
●●●●● $50

For many, Muscat is the greatest expression of North East Victorian fortified wines. This particular wine shows the essential blending skills, with a balance of very old and younger material, simultaneously providing complexity and freshness.

Cellaring Indefinite. **Best Vintages** NA **Current Vintage** NV
Matching Food After coffee; alternative to Cognac.
Tasting Note NV Dark brown tending to olive on the rim; complex, faintly earthy spirity aromas, with an almost nutty edge to the raisined muscat fruit. A tremendously powerful and concentrated wine in the mouth with excellent balance and a wonderful finish. Iron fist in a velvet glove.

BAILEYS WINEMAKER'S SELECTION OLD LIQUEUR TOKAY
●●●●● $50

Made in very limited quantities, and these days released on strict allocation as the popularity of these very old wines has deservedly grown. Made from muscadelle (as are all North East Victorian Tokays) and is preferred by many winemakers to Muscat because of its greater elegance.

Cellaring Indefinite. **Best Vintages** NA **Current Vintage** NV
Matching Food After coffee; alternative to Cognac.
Tasting Note NV Deep brown; the bouquet shows obvious barrel aged rancio characters, very complex but still retaining good varietal character. The wine has outstanding structure in the mouth, with complexity apparent immediately the wine is tasted. The flavours run in the cold tea/butterscotch/brandysnap spectrum, finishing with cleansing acidity.

BALD MOUNTAIN
★★★☆ 8.90–11.50 CD AUSSD
Granite Belt **Est.** 1985
Old Wallangarra Road, Wallangarra, Qld 4383
Ph (076) 84 3186 **Fax** (076) 84 3433
Open 7 days 10–5 **Production** 3000
Winemaker(s) Simon Gilbert (Contract)
Denis Parsons is a self-taught but exceptionally competent vigneron who, in a few short years, has turned Bald Mountain into the viticultural showpiece of the Granite Belt. In various regional and national shows in 1994 Bald Mountain wines received 10 bronze and 2 silver medals, placing it at the forefront of the Granite Belt wineries.
Principal Wines Sauvignon Blanc, Chardonnay, Shiraz, Shiraz Cabernet.

BALD MOUNTAIN CHARDONNAY
●●● ▶ $11.50

Produced from 1.5 hectares of immaculately maintained estate plantings. The wine has a very particular and distinctive bouquet which is strongly reminiscent of many Hunter Valley Chardonnays, notably when fermented with a particular type of yeast. It is interesting to see the character also appear in the Granite Belt.

Cellaring 1–2 years. **Best Vintages** '92, '93
Current Vintage '93
Matching Food Seafood pasta.
Tasting Note 1993 Medium yellow-green; strong smoky, slightly burnt overlay to fruit of medium intensity, with peachy notes underneath. The palate has good structure and weight, with honeyed/peachy fruit, and light but slightly resinous oak.

BALD SPUR ESTATE

★★ NA AUSSD
Yarra Valley **Est.** 1983
c/o 40 Grand Bud, Montmorency, Vic 3094
Ph (03) 9439 8241
Open Not **Production** 1500
Winemaker(s) Lindsay Belbin
A new venture situated in the Eltham Shire which is part of the Yarra Valley viticultural region; owner Lindsay Belbin commenced making Meads in 1985, and the first Cabernet Sauvignon in 1988.
Principal Wines Cabernet Sauvignon; also Meads under the Miruvore label.

BALDIVIS ESTATE

★★★ 8.95–14.95 R AUS58 109 UK46
South-west Coastal Plain **Est.** 1982
Lot 165 River Road, Baldivis, WA 6171
Ph (09) 525 2066 **Fax** (09) 525 2411
Open Mon–Fri 10–4, W'ends, Hols 11–5 **Production** 6000
Winemaker(s) Jane Gilham
Part of very large mixed horticultural enterprise on the Tuart Sands of the coastal plain. There is ample viticultural and winemaking expertise; although the wines are pleasant, soft and light bodied, they tend to lack concentration.
Principal Wines Wooded and Unwooded Chardonnay, Cabernet Merlot, Classic Semillon, Sauvignon Blanc, Late Picked Semillon.

BALDIVIS ESTATE UNWOODED CHARDONNAY
●●● ▶ $14.95
Baldivis releases both a wooded (in fact lightly oaked) and unwooded Chardonnay. Both won bronze medals at the 1994 Mount Barker Wine Show, both in turn showing light and basically overcropped fruit characters. There is no problem with the winemaking, and in fact the unwooded style works best.
Cellaring Drink now. **Best Vintages** NA
Current Vintage '94
Matching Food Fish consommé.
Tasting Note 1994 Light to medium green-yellow; a clean bouquet of light to medium intensity with some citrus/herbal/floral notes. The palate is fresh and crisp, somewhat akin to a cross between sauvignon blanc and chardonnay, lacking intensity but nicely balanced.

BALGOWNIE ESTATE

★★☆ 9.95–18.95 R AUS104
Bendigo **Est.** 1969
Hermitage Road, Maiden Gully, Vic 3551
Ph (054) 49 6222 **Fax** (054) 49 6506
Open Mon–Sat 9–5 **Production** 13 000
Winemaker(s) Lindsay Ross
When in the hands of founder Stuart Anderson, famous for its
estate-produced Hermitage and Cabernet Sauvignon, but has not
flourished under the Mildara Blass ownership. Recent vintages
(including '92) of the Cabernet Sauvignon have been very tannic
and harsh, needing infinite patience, with no certainty of reward.
Principal Wines Estate-produced Hermitage and Cabernet
Sauvignon; Premier Cuvée (second non estate label), Chardonnay
and Cabernet Hermitage.

BALLANDEAN ESTATE

★★★ 6–15 CD AUS169
Granite Belt **Est.** 1970
Sundown Road, Ballandean, Qld 4382
Ph (076) 84 1226 **Fax** (076) 84 1288
Open 7 days 9–5 pm **Production** 9000
Winemaker(s) Angelo Puglisi, Adam Chapman
The senior winery of the Granite Belt, and by far the largest. The
white wines are of diverse but interesting styles, the red wines
smooth and usually well made. The currently available Auslese
Sylvaner is a particularly interesting wine of good flavour.
Principal Wines Chardonnay, Semillon, Sauvignon Blanc,
Auslese Sylvaner, Shiraz, Cabernet Sauvignon.

BALNARRING VINEYARD

★★★☆ 11–15 ML AUSSD
Mornington Peninsula **Est.** 1982
Bittern-Dromana Road, Balnarring, Vic 3926
Ph (059) 83 5258
Open 7 days 10–4 **Production** 1200
Winemaker(s) Bruce Paul, Stan Paul
Over the years, the wines of Balnarring have been made at various
wineries under contract, but have shown a consistent vineyard style,
with the red wines in particular possessing exceptional colour and
depth of flavour. Winemaking is now carried out by owners Bruce
and Stan Paul.
Principal Wines Chardonnay, Riesling, Gewurztraminer, Pinot
Noir, Merlot, Cabernet Merlot, Cabernet Sauvignon.

BALNAVES OF COONAWARRA

★★★☆ 14.60–15.80 R AUSSD
Coonawarra **Est.** 1975
Main Road, Coonawarra, SA 5263

Ph (087) 37 2946 **Fax** (087) 37 2945
Open Mon–Fri 9–5, W'ends 10–5 **Production** 2800
Winemaker(s) Ralph Fowler (Contract)
Former Hungerford Hill vineyard manager and now viticultural
consultant-cum-grape grower Doug Balnaves established his vineyard
in 1975, but did not launch into winemaking until 1990, with
colleague Ralph Fowler as contract maker. Only a small part of the
production from the 25-hectare vineyard is vinified under the
Balnaves label.
Principal Wines Chardonnay, Sparkling Burgundy, Shiraz, Merlot
Cabernet Franc, Cabernet Merlot, Cabernet Sauvignon.

BALNAVES OF COONAWARRA CABERNET MERLOT
●●● ▶ $15.80
A blend of 50% merlot and 50% cabernet sauvignon, matured in
used French and American hogsheads for 12 months. The 1993
vintage does not have the richness of the 1990 or 1991 vintages,
no doubt due to the very cool growing season.
Cellaring 2–3 years. **Best Vintages** '90, '91, '92
Current Vintage '93
Matching Food Calf's liver Italian style.
Tasting Note 1993 Medium red; fragrant fruit aromas with
distinctly leafy/minty notes. The palate is powerful in terms of fruit,
with a range of herb, asparagus, capsicum and mint flavours
backed by subtle oak.

BALNAVES OF COONAWARRA CABERNET SAUVIGNON
●●● ▶ $15.80
Drawn from a little over 16 hectares of estate plantings, the majority
of the grapes are sold to other leading Coonawarra winemakers. As
with the Cabernet Merlot, the '93 vintage is very much lighter than
the '90 (a marvellous wine) or the '91 (very good).
Cellaring 2–3 years. **Best Vintages** '90, '91
Current Vintage '93
Matching Food Veal chops.
Tasting Note 1993 Light to medium red-purple, with a fair amount
of gas evident. The bouquet is light, with hints of cherry and berry
underlying more leafy characters. The palate shows a range of
flavours from sweet berry through to tobacco leaf, of light to medium
intensity. Does not really show its 12.8% alcohol.

BALNAVES OF COONAWARRA CHARDONNAY
●●● ▶ $14.60
Produced from 1.6 hectares of estate plantings, which comprise but
a small fraction of the total vineyard. Fermented in used French
hogsheads and matured on lees for five months before bottling to
produce a pleasant but fairly light-bodied wine.
Cellaring 2–3 years. **Best Vintages** '92, '93
Current Vintage '94
Matching Food Robe crayfish.
Tasting Note 1994 Light yellow-green; a fresh, clean and light
bouquet with melon fruit and imperceptible oak. The palate is still

very light with melon fruit and just a hint of oak in the background.
May develop more richness over the next one to two years.

BANNOCKBURN VINEYARDS

★★★★★ 19–29 R AUS170 UK38
Geelong **Est.** 1974
Midland Highway, Bannockburn, Vic 3331
Ph (052) 81 1363 **Fax** (052) 81 1349
Open By appt **Production** 6000
Winemaker(s) Gary Farr
With the qualified exception of the Cabernet Merlot, which can be a
little leafy and gamey, produces outstanding wines across the range,
all with individuality, style, great complexity and depth of flavour.
The low-yielding estate vineyards play their role, but so does the
French-influenced winemaking of Gary Farr.
Principal Wines Sauvignon Blanc, Chardonnay, Cabernet Merlot,
Pinot Noir, Saignee (Rosé), Shiraz.

BANNOCKBURN CHARDONNAY
●●●●● $30
As with all the Bannockburn wines, 100% estate-grown from
plantings made in 1974, 1981 and 1987 which are typically low-
yielding and produce fully ripe grapes with very concentrated
flavour. What are described as traditional French techniques, with
roughly settled juice, barrel fermented, natural yeast and natural
malolactic fermentation, result in wines of great complexity.
Cellaring 5–10 years. **Best Vintages** '88, '90, '91, '92, '94
Current Vintage '93
Matching Food Pan-fried veal.
Tasting Note 1993 Medium yellow-green; the aromas are very
complex, with malty/nutty overtones from barrel fermentation and
malolactic fermentation. The palate, too, is very generous, with nutty
cashew flavours to the mid palate and finish; strongly structured
throughout.

BANNOCKBURN PINOT NOIR
●●●●● $31
Widely acknowledged as one of Australia's best Pinot Noirs, made
in a very distinctive style with strong French influences from low
yielding vineyards at Geelong, near Melbourne. Winemaker Gary
Farr begins making the Pinot Noir in the vineyard, but does not finish
his work until the wine is bottled. Even then, a certain degree of
patience is required to allow the wine to show its best.
Cellaring 4–7 years. **Best Vintages** '84, '86, '88, '89, '90, '91,
'92, '93 **Current Vintage** '93
Matching Food Rare roast squab.
Tasting Note 1993 Medium red; as with all the Bannockburn
wines, a complex bouquet, with many aromas ranging from forest
floor through to strawberry and spice. The palate flows logically on,
with potent stemmy/briary/berry flavours, finishing with soft but
lingering tannins.

BANNOCKBURN SHIRAZ
●●●●● $21
Gary Farr has made wine in France every year since 1983. While based at Domaine Dujac in Burgundy, he has closely watched the methods of Rhone winemakers, including Alain Graillot of Crozes Hermitage (who himself worked at Dujac), and this wine is strongly, and very deliberately, Rhone-influenced in style.
Cellaring 5–7 years. **Best Vintages** '88, '91, '92, '93
Current Vintage '93
Matching Food Rich game, strong cheese.
Tasting Note 1993 Medium red-purple; a vivid bouquet with gamey/earthy/barnyard characters strongly reminiscent of the northern Rhone Valley. The palate is similarly complex with game, spicy, cherry and liquorice flavours all intermingling with fine tannins.

BARONGVALE

NR 6–12 CD AUSSD
Geelong **Est.** 1988
East West Road, Barongarook, Vic 3249
Ph (052) 33 8324
Open W'ends, Public hols 10–5 **Production** NFP
Winemaker(s) Stuart Walker
One of the most remote wineries in the West Geelong region, making a surprisingly wide range of wines of (to me) unknown quality, but directed at tourists headed to the Otways. It draws upon 4 hectares of estate vineyards.
Principal Wines Chardonnay, Colombard, Riesling/Traminer, Cabernet Sauvignon, Shiraz Pinot Cabernet, Sherry, Port-style Blackberry Wine.

BAROSSA SETTLERS

★★★ 7.50–19.50 CD AUSSD
Barossa Valley **Est.** 1983
Trial Hill Road, Lyndoch, SA 5351
Ph (085) 24 4017
Open Mon–Sat 10–4, Sun 1–4 **Production** 700
Winemaker(s) Howard Haese
A superbly located cellar door is the only outlet (other than mail order) for the wines from this excellent vineyard owned by the Haese family. Production has slowed in recent years, with the grapes from the 31-hectare vineyard being sold to others.
Principal Wines Champagne, Chardonnay, Riesling, Auslese Riesling, Shiraz, Cabernet Sauvignon, Port.

BAROSSA VALLEY ESTATE

★★★ 7.95–25 R AUS22 UK18
Adelaide Plains **Est.** 1984
Heaslip Road, Angle Vale, SA 5117

Ph (08) 284 7000 **Fax** (08) 284 7219
Open Mon–Fri 9–5, Sat 11–5, Sun 1–5 **Production** 100 000
Winemaker(s) Colin Glaetzer
The brand of Valley Grower's Co-Operative, is one of the last and
largest cooperative-owned wineries in Australia. Across the board,
the wines are full flavoured and honest, although poor-quality corks
did not help the cause of the wines.
Principal Wines Chardonnay, Semillon Sauvignon Blanc,
Traminer, Late Picked Frontignac, Shiraz, Cabernet Sauvignon,
Pinot Noir, Alicante Bouchet; Ebenezer Chardonnay, Malbec Merlot
Cabernet Sauvignon, Shiraz, Sparkling Pinot Noir; E & E Black
Pepper Shiraz, Sparkling Shiraz.

BAROSSA VALLEY ESTATE BLACK PEPPER SHIRAZ
●●● $25
The wine comes from two vineyard estates, both of which are
regarded as outstanding, one with very old vines, the other with
newer plantings. This wine, recently joined by E & E Black Pepper
Sparkling Shiraz, is the flagship of Barossa Valley Estate, and is
in keen demand notwithstanding its price. I personally have
reservations about the style, which others clearly appreciate
more than I.
Cellaring 5 years or more. **Best Vintages** '90, '91, '92
Current Vintage '91
Matching Food Lamb, rabbit or hare.
Tasting Note 1991 Medium to full red; notwithstanding the name,
there is no spice or black pepper on either the bouquet or palate,
but a great deal of vanillin American oak, and solid, traditional ripe
Barossa fruit hiding underneath that oak.

BARRETTS WINES

NR 9–14 CD AUSSD
South West Victoria **Est.** 1983
335 Portland-Nelson Highway, Portland, Vic 3305
Ph (055) 26 5257
Open 7 days 10–6 **Production** 600
Winemaker(s) Rod Barrett, Simon Clayfield (Contract)
The second (and newer) winery in the Portland region. The initial
releases were made at Best's, but since 1992 all wines have been
made on the property by Rod Barrett with consultant advice from
Best's winemaker Simon Clayfield.
Principal Wines Riesling, Traminer, Botrytis Riesling, Cabernet
Pinot Noir.

BASEDOW WINES

★★★ 8.95–27.95 R AUS36, 76, 107, 109 UK16
Barossa Valley **Est.** 1896
161–165 Murray Street, Tanunda, SA 5352
Ph (085) 63 3666 **Fax** (085) 63 3597
Open Mon–Fri 9–5, W'ends 11–5 **Production** 40 000
Winemaker(s) Grant Burge

Purchased by Grant Burge Wines in late 1993 after a long period of financially troubled ownership by MS McLeod. The wines have always been honest and full flavoured, the White Burgundy once one of the great bargains, although the most recent vintages are slightly less convincing.
Principal Wines White Burgundy, Chardonnay, Cabernet Sauvignon, Shiraz, Port.

BASEDOW CHARDONNAY
●●● ▶ $12.95
Made in mainstream Barossa style, with plenty of ripe fruit flavours and a reasonable dollop of oak; generous, hearty and quick-developing.
Cellaring Neither necessary nor recommended.
Best Vintages '90, '92, '94 **Current Vintage** '94
Matching Food Avocado, pasta.
Tasting Note 1994 Medium yellow-green; full, rich peachy fruit aromas with honey/buttery characters. Some peach, lemon and peppermint fruit, finishing with slightly raw oak.

BASEDOW WHITE BURGUNDY
●●● $9.95
For more than a decade, a wine which offered extraordinary value for money, and not infrequently, surprising style. Made from once-unfashionable Barossa Valley semillon, with significant oak influence. Former winemaker Doug Lehmann insisted no chips were used, but the current vintages certainly seem to involve the use of either chips or Innerstave oak.
Cellaring Better vintages — up to 5 years. **Best Vintages** '86, '88, '90, '92 **Current Vintage** '94
Matching Food Full-flavoured white meat dishes; Italian, Chinese.
Tasting Note 1994 Medium to full yellow-green; big, broad highly aromatic bouquet with pungent oak. The palate is likewise rich but very oaky in an assertive, and to me, not terribly attractive style.

BASKET RANGE WINES

NR 12 ML AUSSD
Adelaide Hills **Est.** 1980
Blockers Road, Basket Range, SA 5138 ; c/o PO Basket Range, SA 5138
Ph NA **Fax** NA
Open Not (Vineyard only) **Production** 300
Winemaker(s) Phillip Broderick
A tiny operation known to very few; the '89 Basket Range is the most recently tasted, with pleasant red berry plum and spice fruit.
Principal Wines A single Bordeaux-blend of Cabernet Sauvignon, Cabernet Franc, Merlot, Malbec.

BASS PHILLIP

★★★★★ 14.50–36 ML AUSSD US2
South Gippsland **Est.** 1979

Tosch's Road, Leongatha South, Vic 3953
Ph (056) 64 3341 **Fax** (056) 64 3209
Open 7 days 11–6 Summer & Autumn **Production** 700
Winemaker(s) Phillip Jones
Phillip Jones has retired from the Melbourne rat-race to hand-craft tiny quantities of superlative Pinot Noir which, at its best, has no equal in Australia.
Principal Wines Tiny quantities of Pinot Noir in three (sometimes four) categories: Pinot Blend, Pinot Noir and an occasional barrel of Reserve. A hatful of Chardonnay also made.

BASS PHILLIP PINOT NOIR
●●●●● $30
The wine is in fact released in three, and sometimes four grades each year. The Pinot Blend is from younger vines with the incorporation of 10% of gamay; the Bass Phillip Pinot Noir is the standard wine (if it can be called that) and is made in by far the greatest volume; there is then the scarce Premium, anchored upon the initial one acre of vines planted on the best soil; and occasionally a single barrel Reserve selection from the Premium. With the exception of the Reserve, the hierarchy is basically determined in the vineyard.
Cellaring 4–10 years. **Best Vintages** '84, '85, '89, '91, '92, '93, '94 **Current Vintage** '93
Matching Food Saddle of hare.
Tasting Note 1993 Premium. Medium red-purple; a fragrant, earthy bouquet, vaguely reminiscent of the '85, with well balanced and integrated oak. Round, sweet and delicious in the mouth, with fine tannins and good acid. Excellent balance and structure, but early maturing.

BELBOURIE VINEYARDS
★★☆ 15–16 CD AUSSD
Hunter Valley **Est.** 1963
Branxton Road, Rothbury, NSW 2330
Ph (049) 38 1556
Open W'ends, Hols 10–Sunset **Production** 2000
Winemaker(s) Bob Davies
A winery with a rich, and at times fascinating, history of wine and winemaking, but these days tending more to the conventional. It has always sought to encourage cellar door and mailing list sales, focusing on monthly wine and food events, and has a loyal clientele.
Principal Wines Barramundi Chardonnay, Belah Semillon Chardonnay, Hermitage.

BELLINGHAM VINEYARDS
★★★ 5.50–8 ML AUS156
Pipers Brook **Est.** 1984
Pipers Brook, Tas 7254
Ph (003) 82 7149

Open By appt **Production** 560
Winemaker(s) Greg O'Keefe (Contract)
Dallas Targett sells most of the grapes from his 13-hectare vineyard
to Greg O'Keefe; a small part has been made for the Bellingham
label. 1991 Pinot Noir is a delicious wine with fragrant,
sappy/spicy aroma and bouquet. The prices are most unTasmanian.
Principal Wines Rhine Riesling, Chardonnay, Pinot Noir,
Cabernet Sauvignon.

BELUBULA VALLEY VINEYARDS

NR NA AUSSD
Central Highlands **Est.** 1986
Golden Gully, Mandurama, NSW 2798
Ph (063) 67 5236 **Fax** (02) 362 4726
Open Not **Production** 1000
Winemaker(s) David Somervaille
Belubula Valley is a foundation member of the Central Highlands
Grapegrowers Association, centred on Orange; the vineyard is
located on the Belubula River, near Carcoar, and the small amounts
of wine made to date have not yet been commercially released.
David Somervaille, incidentally, is Chairman of partners of the
national law firm Blake Dawson Waldron.
Principal Wines Cabernet Sauvignon.

BENFIELD ESTATE

★★☆ 7–13 CD AUSSD
Canberra **Est.** 1985
Fairy Hole Road, Yass, NSW 2582
Ph (06) 226 2427
Open W'ends, Public hols 10–5 **Production** 850
Winemaker(s) David Fetherston
David Fetherston has had a hard time of it recently. The 1993
vintage was destroyed by frost, while gales in November 1994
rendered the house uninhabitable. Wine quality, too, has suffered
somewhat, with the currently available wines suffering from rather
aggressive, green oak.
Principal Wines Riesling, Semillon, Chardonnay, Merlot,
Cabernets.

BERESFORD WINES

★★☆ 14 R AUS163 UK26
Southern Vales **Est.** 1985
49 Fraser Avenue, Happy Valley, SA 5159
Ph (08) 322 3611 **Fax** (08) 322 3610
Open Mon–Fri 9–5, W'ends 11–5 **Production** NFP
Winemaker(s) Robert Dundon
Notwithstanding the vast industry experience of Rob Dundon (for
many years winemaker at Thomas Hardy) the Beresford wines fail to
excite; recent tastings include the '94 Chardonnay. The brand is part

of the large, export-oriented Crestview operation (see separate entry).

Principal Wines Chardonnay, Semillon Sauvignon Blanc, Riesling, Cabernet Merlot.

BERRI ESTATES

★★ 3–17.95 R AUS22 UK42
Riverlands **Est.** 1916
Sturt Highway, Glossop, SA 5344
Ph (085) 82 0300 **Fax** (085) 83 2224
Open Mon–Sat 9–5 **Production** NFP
Winemaker(s) Reg Wilkinson
Strictly a producer of bulk wine with no pretensions to grandeur, and with a substantial part of the production exported in bulk. Part of the BRL Hardy Group.

Principal Wines Light Fruity Lexia, Fruity Gordo Moselle, Chablis, Claret, Rosé, White Lambrusco, all in cask form.

BEST'S WINES

★★★★☆ 4.60–35 CD AUS35, 48, 72, 96, 131 UK24, 102
Great Western **Est.** 1866
2kms off Western Highway, Great Western, Vic 3377
Ph (053) 56 2250 **Fax** (053) 56 2430
Open Mon–Fri 9–5, Sat 9–4, Sun of long w'ends and hols 12–4
Production 25 000
Winemaker(s) Viv Thomson, Simon Clayfield
An historic winery, owning some priceless vineyards planted as long ago as 1867 (other plantings are, of course, much more recent) which has consistently produced elegant, supple wines which deserve far greater recognition than they in fact receive. The Shiraz is a classic; the Centenary Shiraz magnificent.

Principal Wines Chardonnay, Rhine Riesling, Chenin Blanc, Ondenc, Golden Chasselas, Pinot Noir, Dolcetto, Shiraz, Cabernet Sauvignon, Centenary Shiraz, together with a large range of fortified wines sourced from St Andrews at Lake Boga. Some of these wines are available only at cellar door.

BEST'S WINES CENTENARY SHIRAZ
●●●●● $35
A magnificent wine released in late 1994 to commemorate the Centenary of Best's Great Western Vineyards. It is made entirely from vines planted by Henry Best in late 1860s, and was matured in small French oak. Also available in magnums ($74 cellar door).
Cellaring 20+ years. **Best Vintages** NA **Current Vintage** '92
Matching Food Stir-fried beef.
Tasting Note 1992 Strong purple-red; spotlessly clean bouquet redolent of plum, cherry and berry fruit, and just a hint of French oak. The palate is powerful and concentrated, but very much the iron fist in a velvet glove style. Spotlessly clean, and the dark cherry fruit has all but swallowed up the new French oak. Will mature magnificently.

BEST'S WINES SHIRAZ
●●●●● $15
One of the more understated classic wines, produced entirely from
estate-grown grapes, made with a minimum of artifice and with high
quality fruit, rather then oak, doing the work.
Cellaring Up to 30 years. **Best Vintages** '62, '70, '77, '78, '85,
'88, '90, '91, '92 **Current Vintage** '91
Matching Food Roast veal, mature cheddar.
Tasting Note 1991 A deeply-coloured, concentrated and ripe
wine with fragrant spice, mint and cherry fruit, finishing with nicely
balanced tannins.

BETHANY WINES

★★★★ 12–19 CD AUS2, 34, 114, 143, 178, 183
Barossa Valley **Est.** 1977
Bethany Road, Bethany via Tanunda, SA 5352
Ph (085) 63 2086 **Fax** (085) 63 0046
Open Mon–Sat 10–5, Sun 1–5 **Production** 15 000
Winemaker(s) Geoff Schrapel, Robert Schrapel
The Schrapel family has been growing grapes in the Barossa Valley
for over 140 years, but the winery has only been in operation since
1977. Nestling high on a hillside in the site of an old quarry, it is
run by Geoff and Rob Schrapel, who produce a range of
consistently well made and attractively packaged wines. Their
moment of glory came at the 1994 National Wine Show with the
Shiraz Trophy for the '92 Shiraz.
Principal Wines Riesling (Dry, Late Harvest), Chardonnay,
Semillon, Cabernet Merlot, Shiraz, Grenache, Sparkling, Port.

BETHANY CABERNET MERLOT
●●●● $16.85
The cabernet sauvignon component of the wine comes from 30-year-
old vines planted on the 'Old Mulberry' Vineyard with a mulberry
tree planted by Gottlob Schrapel in 1845 still flourishing on the dark
soils. The wine is typically ripe, but has a real touch of class.
Cellaring 3–5 years. **Best Vintages** '88, '90, '91, '92, '94
Current Vintage '92
Matching Food Fillet of lamb.
Tasting Note 1992 Medium red-purple; a solid bouquet with berry
and earth flavours married with subtle oak. The palate shows typical,
pleasantly ripe currant/berry flavours interwoven with subtle oak,
finishing with soft tannins. As ever, harmonious.

BETHANY PRESSINGS GRENACHE
●●● ❯ $14.35
Yet another demonstration of the recovery in the fortunes of
grenache. For good measure, this is a pressings version,
incorporating the last drop of juice squeezed from the berries during
the pressing cycle after fermentation.
Cellaring 5–7 years. **Best Vintages** NA **Current Vintage** '94
Matching Food Game casserole.

Tasting Note 1994 Deep red; the bouquet is lusciously sweet, redolent with juicy/jammy red berry fruit. The same flavours are apparent on a striking palate, with vivid juicy flavours, like the bouquet bordering on jammy. A very authentic rendition of super-ripe grenache.

BETHANY SHIRAZ
●●●●● $19.95
The 1988 Bethany Shiraz won the top gold medal in its class at the 1990 Melbourne Wine Show and was selected in the Top 100 in the 1991 Sydney International Wine Competition. However, the 1992 vintage has had even greater success, following its gold medal at the 1994 Barossa Valley Wine Show with the prestigious Australian National Wine Show Trophy for Best Shiraz in November 1994. Estate-grown, hand-pruned and hand-picked, and matured for two years in American oak.
Cellaring 3–6 years. **Best Vintages** '88, '90, '91, '92
Current Vintage '92
Matching Food Mild curry.
Tasting Note 1992 Medium to full purple-red; abundant, fresh cherry and plum fruit aromas which are generously ripe, but not overripe. The palate is plush, with lots of sweet cherry fruit and nicely balanced American vanillin oak, finishing with soft tannins.

BETHANY SPECIAL SELECT LATE HARVEST RIESLING
●●● ▶ $11.50
Made using the Cordon Cut technique, which involves cutting the cane on which the grapes hang, but leaving it on the vine for over a month (until May) during which time the grapes lose much of their moisture and may occasionally be infected by botrytis.
Cellaring Short term only. **Best Vintages** '89, '90, '92, '93
Current Vintage '92
Matching Food Fresh fruit.
Tasting Note 1992 Medium yellow-green; intense apricot and peach aromas; good flavour and balance with white peach and apricot fruit and well balanced but relatively soft acidity.

BIANCHET WINERY

★★★ 8–17 CD AUSSD
Yarra Valley **Est.** 1976
Lot 3 Victoria Road, Lilydale, Vic 3140
Ph (03) 9739 1779 **Fax** (03) 9739 1277
Open W'ends 10–6 **Production** 2000
Winemaker(s) Tony Inglese
Produces very full-flavoured wines sold with considerable bottle age; in late 1994 the current vintages were '90 and '92. The style is somewhat rustic, but wine such as that made from the rare Italian grape verduzzo make the cellar door well worth a visit. In late 1994 it seemed likely that the winery would be sold in the sad aftermath of family deaths and illness.
Principal Wines Traminer, Semillon, Chardonnay, Verduzzo, Pinot Noir, Shiraz, Cabernet Sauvignon, Merlot.

BIN BILLA *

NR NA AUSSD
Bendigo **Est.** 1974
Hogans Road, Daylesford, Vic 3460
Ph (053) 48 6539 **Fax** (053) 48 6556
Open 7 days 10–5 **Production** 1500
Winemaker(s) John Hayes
The former Fern Hyll Estate, which draws upon 8 hectares of estate
vineyards, and has a barbecue area and restaurant with historic
tasting rooms.
Principal Wines Riesling, Chardonnay, Pinot Noir, Shiraz,
Malbec, Cabernet Sauvignon.

BINDI *

NR NA AUSSD
Macedon **Est.** 1988
145 Melton Road, Gisborne, Vic 3437
Ph (054) 28 2564
Open Not **Production** 500
Winemaker(s) John Ellis (Contract), Michael Dhillon
A new arrival in the Macedon region, owned and run by the Dhillon
family, with contract winemaking at Hanging Rock. The wines are
dedicated to Kostas Rind (1909–1983), a Lithuanian sage.
Principal Wines Table and sparkling wines under the Bindi and
Kostas Rind labels.

BIRDWOOD ESTATE

★★☆ 14–15 ML AUSSD
Adelaide Hills **Est.** 1990
Narcoonah Road, Birdwood SA 5234
Ph (08) 263 0986
Open Not **Production** 500
Winemaker(s) Oli Cucchiarelli
Birdwood Estate is still feeling its way, the vineyard having been
slowly enlarged from a few vines to five hectares, not all in
production.
Principal Wines Chardonnay, Riesling, Cabernet Sauvignon.

BIRDWOOD ESTATE CHARDONNAY

●●● $19.95
Produced in tiny quantities from a 5-hectare vineyard planted at an
altitude of 450 metres to rhine riesling, chardonnay, cabernet
sauvignon, merlot and cabernet franc. This release represents a
quantum leap in quality over earlier vintages, and shows the delicate
Adelaide Hills style to good advantage.
Cellaring 1–4 years. **Best Vintages** '90, '91, '93, '94
Current Vintage '94
Matching Food Blue swimmer crab.
Tasting Note 1994 Medium yellow-green; a delicate, discrete

cool climate bouquet with citrussy aromas and subtle oak. Lurking in
the bouquet and palate is a hint of matchstick-like bitterness, which
did appear to dissipate with aeration. The palate may well develop
attractive flavours with bottle age.

BLACKWOOD CREST

★★☆ 10–14 CD AUSSD
Warren Valley **Est.** 1976
RMB 404A Boyup Brook, WA 6244
Ph (097) 67 3029 **Fax** (097) 62 3029
Open 7 days 10–6 **Production** 1000
Winemaker(s) Max Fairbrass
A remote and small winery which has produced one or two striking
red wines full of flavour and character; worth watching.
Principal Wines Riesling, Classic White, Sweet White, Shiraz,
Cabernet Sauvignon.

BLANCHE BARKLY WINES

NR 10–16.50 CD AUSSD
Bendigo **Est.** 1972
Rheola Road, Kingower, Vic 3517
Ph (054) 43 3664
Open W'ends, Public hols 10–5 **Production** NFP
Winemaker(s) David Reimers
Sporadic but small production and variable quality seem to be the
order of the day; the potential has always been there. No recent
tastings.
Principal Wines Shiraz, Cabernet Sauvignon.

BLEASDALE VINEYARDS

★★★☆ 6.75–27 R AUS29–33
Langhorne Creek **Est.** 1850
Wellington Road, Langhorne Creek, SA 5255
Ph (085) 37 3001 **Fax** (085) 37 3224
Open Mon–Sat 9–5, Sun 11–5 **Production** 60 000
Winemaker(s) Michael Potts
One of the most historic wineries in Australia drawing upon
vineyards which are flooded every winter by diversion of the
Bremer River, and which provides moisture throughout the dry,
cool, growing season. The wines offer excellent value for money.
Principal Wines Late Picked Riesling, Chardonnay, Verdelho,
Malbec, Cabernet Sauvignon, Shiraz Cabernet Sauvignon,
Cabernet Malbec Merlot, Sparkling, Fortified.

BLEASDALE CABERNET MALBEC MERLOT
●●●● $11
Another recent introduction to the Bleasdale range, although both
cabernet and malbec have long been grown in the Langhorne Creek
area. A no-frills style in which the vineyard is doing most of the
work.

Cellaring 3–5 years. **Best Vintages** NA **Current Vintage** '92 **Matching Food** Medium-weight red meat dishes.
Tasting Note 1992 Medium to full red-purple; spotlessly clean cassis/berry fruit aromas of medium to full intensity. The same sweet cassis fruit flavours lead the palate, which is of medium weight, finishing with soft tannins.

BLEASDALE VERDELHO
●●● ▶ $9.75
Verdelho has been grown at Potts Bleasdale for a very long time, originally dedicated entirely to make a very distinctive fortified wine (which is still available from cellar door at $27 per bottle with an average age of 16 years). Part now goes to make an attractive, fresh, lightly wooded dry table wine.
Cellaring 2–3 years. **Best Vintages** NA **Current Vintage** '92 **Matching Food** Avocado.
Tasting Note 1992 Medium yellow-green; clean fruit with a nicely judged touch of spicy oak. The palate is well balanced with gently honeyed fruit and again a touch of spicy/charry American oak, probably introduced in tank.

BLEWITT SPRINGS WINERY

★★★☆ 10.60–13.70 R AUS43
Southern Vales **Est.** 1987
Fraser Avenue, Happy Valley, SA 5159
Ph (08) 322 3611 **Fax** (08) 322 3610
Open Not **Production** 4000
Winemaker(s) Brett Howard
A newcomer to the scene which has attracted much attention and praise for its voluptuous Chardonnays, crammed full of peachy, buttery fruit and vanillin American oak. Oak also plays a major role in the Semillon and the red wines; a lighter touch might please some critics.
Principal Wines Rhine Riesling, Chardonnay, Semillon, Shiraz, Cabernet Sauvignon.

BLOODWOOD ESTATE

★★★ 9–18 ML AUSSD
Central Tablelands **Est.** 1983
4 Griffith Road, Orange, NSW 2800
Ph (063) 62 5631
Open By appt **Production** 2500
Winemaker(s) Stephen Doyle, Jon Reynolds
The Orange district of New South Wales may well prove to be an important viticultural area if the wines of Bloodwood Estate are any indication. Delicious Rosé of Malbec and stylish Chardonnay have impressed, although it would seem that 1994 was a difficult vintage for the estate (the wines of which are made by Jon Reynolds at Reynolds Yarraman).
Principal Wines Rosé of Malbec, Chardonnay, Noble Riesling, Cabernet Merlot.

BONEO PLAINS *

NR NA AUSSD
Mornington Peninsula **Est.** 1988
RMB 1400 Browns Road, South Rosebud, Vic 3939
Ph (059) 88 6208 **Fax** (059) 88 6208
Open By appt **Production** NFP
Winemaker(s) Larry Keech
A 9-hectare vineyard and winery established by the Tallarida family,
well known as manufacturers and suppliers of winemaking
equipment to the industry. I have not seen or tasted any of the wines
so far produced; the operation is in its infancy.
Principal Wines Chardonnay, Merlot, Cabernet Sauvignon.

BONNEYVIEW

NR 6–10 CD AUSSD
Riverlands **Est.** 1975
Sturt Highway, Barmera, SA 5345
Ph (085) 88 2279
Open 7 days 9–5.30 **Production** 2000
Winemaker(s) Robert Minns
The smallest Riverlands winery selling exclusively cellar door,
with an ex-Kent cricketer and Oxford University graduate as its
owner/winemaker.
Principal Wines Chardonnay, Sauvignon Blanc, Shiraz, Cabernet
Merlot, Fortifieds.

BOOTH'S TAMINICK CELLARS

NR 5–11 CD AUSSD
North East Victoria **Est.** 1900
Taminick via Glenrowan, Vic 3675
Ph (057) 66 2282
Open Mon–Sat 9–5, Sun 10–5 **Production** NFP
Winemaker(s) Cliff Booth
Ultra conservative producer of massively flavoured and concentrated
red wines, usually with more than a few rough edges which time
may or may not smooth over.
Principal Wines Trebbiano, Chardonnay, Late Harvest Trebbiano,
Shiraz, Cabernet Merlot, Cabernet Sauvignon, Ports, Muscat.

BOROKA VINEYARD

★★ 7.50–12 CD AUSSD
Great Western **Est.** 1974
Pomonal Road, Halls Gap, 3381
Ph (053) 56 4252
Open Mon–Sat 9–5, Sun, Public hols 10–5 **Production** 1500
Winemaker(s) Bernard Breen
Out of the mainstream in terms of both wine quality and location,
but does offer light lunches or picnic takeaways, and the views are
spectacular.

Principal Wines Chablis and Riesling blends, Dry Rosé, Shiraz, Cabernet Sauvignon, Reserve Port.

BOSTON BAY WINES

★★★ 8–32 CD AUS16
Port Lincoln **Est.** 1984
Lincoln Highway, Port Lincoln, SA 5606
Ph (086) 84 3600 **Fax** (086) 84 3600
Open W'ends, School/Public hols 11–30–4.30 **Production** 2500
Winemaker(s) Stephen John (Contract)
A strongly tourist-oriented operation which has extended the viticultural map in South Australia. The wines are contract made; rich, lime-accented Rhine Riesling akin to McLaren Vale in style and soft, leafy Baudin's Blend Cabernet Merlot are best.
Principal Wines Riesling, Spatlese Riesling, Chardonnay, Cabernet Sauvignon, Cabernet Merlot, Baudin's Blend (Magnum).

BOTOBOLAR

★★★ 7–10.50 CD AUS63, 161 UK95
Mudgee **Est.** 1971
Botobolar Lane, Mudgee, NSW 2850
Ph (063) 73 3840 **Fax** (063) 73 3789
Open Mon–Sat 10–5, Sun 10–3 **Production** 5500
Winemaker(s) Kevin Karstrom
One of the first organic vineyards in Australia with new owner Kevin Karstrom continuing the practices established by founder Gil Wahlquist. 1994 preservative Free Dry White and Dry Red extend the organic practice of the vineyard to the winery.
Principal Wines Chardonnay, Marsanne, Shiraz, Cabernet Sauvignon; St Gilbert Dry Red and White; Preservative Free White and Red.

BOWEN ESTATE

★★★★ 9–15 CD AUS27, 48, 49, 167, 169, 170 UK11
Coonawarra **Est.** 1972
Penola-Naracoorte Road, Penola, SA 5277
Ph (087) 37 2229 **Fax** (087) 37 2173
Open Mon–Sat 9–5 **Production** 8000
Winemaker(s) Doug Bowen
One of the best known names among the smaller Coonawarra wineries with a great track record of red winemaking; Chardonnay has joined the band, and the Riesling ended with the '93 vintage.
Principal Wines Chardonnay, Shiraz, Cabernet Sauvignon Merlot Cabernet Franc, Cabernet Sauvignon, Sanderson Sparkling.

BOWEN ESTATE CABERNET SAUVIGNON

●●● ▶ $14
As with the Shiraz, Doug Bowen believes in ripeness, the '92 weighing in with 15% alcohol. Whereas it can work with a Shiraz, I

think it sits less happily with Cabernet Sauvignon, and prefer the years of lower alcohol.

Cellaring 5–8 years. **Best Vintages** '84, '86, '90, '91
Current Vintage '92
Matching Food Richly-sauced beef casserole.
Tasting Note 1992 Medium to full red, showing some development; plummy/briary/berry fruit on the bouquet, and massive, ripe chocolate, berry and earth fruit flavours on the palate. A most unusual style for Coonawarra, or anywhere else for that matter.

BOWEN ESTATE SHIRAZ
●●●● $13

A wine which has given tremendous pleasure over the years, always crammed full of personality and flavour. Doug Bowen certainly prefers to allow the grapes to ripen fully, sometimes to frightening levels. I personally prefer the less-ripe years where a little more varietal spice and pepper comes through.

Cellaring 10 years or more in good vintages. **Best Vintages** '84, '86, '90, '91, '92
Current Vintage '92
Matching Food Kangaroo fillet.
Tasting Note 1992 Dark red; big briary, slightly jammy fruit aromas with considerable concentration, and just a hint of spicy oak. The palate shows similar ripe briary/berry fruit with fruit and alcohol sweetness combining; a luscious, overwhelming style. The American oak is a fraction distracting.

BOYNTON'S OF BRIGHT

★★★★ 10–16 CD AUSSD
North East Victoria **Est.** 1987
Ovens Valley Highway, Bright, Vic 3747
Ph (057) 56 2356 **Fax** (057) 56 2610
Open 7 days 10–5 **Production** 4800
Winemaker(s) Kel Boynton
The 12.5-hectare vineyard is situated in the Ovens Valley, north of the township of Bright, under the lee of Mt Buffalo. Over 120 tonnes of grapes are produced each year, half being sold, and half being vinified at the estate winery.
Principal Wines Riesling, Sauvignon Blanc, Sauvignon Blanc Semillon, Chardonnay, Spatlese Lexia, Mataro, Shiraz, Cabernet Sauvignon, Port, Sparkling.

BOYNTON'S SAUVIGNON BLANC SEMILLON
●●●● $12

A new arrival, earlier vintages being made only from sauvignon blanc. Made without oak input, the semillon adding both flesh and flavour.

Cellaring 1–2 years. **Best Vintages** '90, '91, '93, '94
Current Vintage '93
Matching Food Sugar-cured salmon.

Tasting Note 1993 Light green-yellow; fine, tight citrussy lemony fruit aromas lead on to a high-toned, lively palate with honeysuckle flavours and a tangy finish.

BOYNTON'S SHIRAZ
●●●● ▶ $14
Along with Cabernet Sauvignon, the wine which really established the reputation of Boynton's. The early vintages won numerous gold medals and trophies, all exhibiting very strong American oak influence. The current release is much less oaky, and I prefer it greatly, for it allows the very good varietal fruit flavour to come through.
Cellaring 4–6 years. **Best Vintages** '89, '90, '91, '93
Current Vintage '93
Matching Food Pasta with a tomato or meat sauce.
Tasting Note 1993 Medium red-purple; spotlessly clean aromas with spicy varietal fruit and subtle oak. The palate is fresh and lively with spicy cherry fruit and soft, fine tannins. An attractive early-drinking style.

BRAHAMS CREEK WINERY
NR 10.95 CD AUSSD
Yarra Valley **Est.** 1985
Woods Point Road, East Warburton, Vic 3799
Ph (03) 9560 0016 **Fax** (03) 9560 0016
Open W'ends 10–6 **Production** 900
Winemaker(s) Geoffrey Richardson
Owner Geoffrey Richardson did not start marketing his wines until 1994, and was then offering a range of wines from the 1990 and 1991 vintages, the youngest being a '92 Sauvignon Blanc. I have not tasted the wines.
Principal Wines Chardonnay, Sauvignon Blanc, Pinot Noir, Cabernet Sauvignon, Merlot.

BRANDS LAIRA
★★★★ 12–20 R AUS100 UK98
Coonawarra **Est.** 1965
Penola-Naracoorte Road, Coonawarra, SA 5263
Ph (087) 36 3260 **Fax** (087) 36 3208
Open 7 days 9–5 **Production** NFP
Winemaker(s) Jim Brand
Having first acquired 50% of the business, McWilliam's now owns 100%, although the Brand family remains very much involved, with Jim Brand now group viticulturist. Hopefully, the ownership of McWilliam's will see less use of cheaper American oak, and greater use of more expensive (and better) French oak. The vineyard deserves it.
Principal Wines Riesling, Chardonnay, Cabernet Merlot, Shiraz, Cabernet Sauvignon.

BRANDS LAIRA CABERNET SAUVIGNON
●●●● $15.95

First made in 1971, and over the intervening years has produced
some wonderful wines; the earlier vintages, in particular, were pacesetters. Since then the field has caught up and indeed passed
Brands, but the viticultural resources are there, and there is no
doubting the honesty of the wine.

Cellaring 10+ years. **Best Vintages** '86, '90, '91, '92, '94
Current Vintage '93
Matching Food Barbecued red meat.
Tasting Note 1993 Medium red-purple; the bouquet shows gently
ripe dark berry fruits with some earth and chocolate notes. The
palate has an altogether warm feel to it, with chewy
earthy/chocolatey flavours, and abundant mouthfeel and richness.

BRANDS LAIRA CHARDONNAY
●●● ▶ $15.95

A relatively recent arrival on the scene for Brands, the style of which
has improved greatly since McWilliam's became involved. The
advent of substantial oak input with the '93 vintage is further
evidence of the McWilliam's involvement, but I remain to be
convinced that such lavish use of oak was necessary.

Cellaring 2–3 years. **Best Vintages** '90, '92, '94
Current Vintage '93
Matching Food Pasta with salmon.
Tasting Note 1993 Medium yellow-green; the bouquet is of light
to medium intensity and, like the palate, is presently dominated by
oak. Prior vintages have shown far more fruit, and the wine may
improve given further time in bottle.

BREAM CREEK

★★★☆ 12–14.50 ML AUS14
East Coast Tasmania **Est.** 1975
Marion Bay Road, Bream Creek, Tas 7175
Ph (002) 31 4646 **Fax** (002) 31 4646
Open By appt **Production** 2500
Winemaker(s) Steve Lubiana (Contract)

Until 1990 the Bream Creek fruit was sold to Moorilla Estate, but
since that time has been independently owned and managed under
the control of Fred Peacock, legendary for the care he bestows on
the vines under his direction. The site has proved very difficult, but
trellis improvements and additional plantings should see a significant
increase in production from 1995 onwards.

Principal Wines Riesling, Chardonnay, Pinot Noir, Cabernet
Sauvignon in two styles: Soft Dry Red (Cabernet-Pinot blend) and
Traditional.

BREAM CREEK TRADITIONAL CABERNET SAUVIGNON
●●● ▶ $13.50

An interesting wine which shows just what can be achieved at this
most difficult of vineyard sites. It would seem probable that some

juice was run off to concentrate the must, and possibly used in the Soft Dry Red Cabernet of the same year.

Cellaring To 1997. **Best Vintages** NA **Current Vintage** '91
Matching Food Venison.

Tasting Note 1991 Medium to full red-purple; concentrated cassis berry aromas and flavours, almost into Ribena on the palate, with a generous mid palate and slightly furry finish.

BREMERTON LODGE WINES *

★★★★ 9–13 CD AUSSD
Langhorne Creek **Est.** 1988
Strathalbyn Road, Langhorne Creek, SA 5255
Ph (085) 32 3093 **Fax** (085) 32 3109
Open Thur–Mon 10–5 **Production** 2300
Winemaker(s) Craig Willson

The Willsons have been grape growers in the Langhorne Creek region for some considerable time, with 22 hectares of cabernet sauvignon, 18 of shiraz, 2 of merlot, and a half hectare each of semillon and sauvignon blanc. They both sell grapes (the major part of the production) and also purchase grapes or wines for the Bremerton Lodge label, which is made under contract — and very competently.

Principal Wines Watervale Riesling, Sauvignon Blanc Semillon, Botrytised Semillon, Old Adam Shiraz, Bremerton Blend (red), Cabernet Sauvignon.

BREMERTON LODGE BREMERTON BLEND
●●●● ▶ $10

A blend of 55% cabernet sauvignon, 33% shiraz and 12% merlot which has been matured in predominantly new American oak. A wine which shows Langhorne Creek at its best.

Cellaring 3–5 years. **Best Vintages** NA **Current Vintage** '92
Matching Food Devilled kidneys.

Tasting Note 1992 Medium red-purple; a complex bouquet with abundant sweet berry fruit and sophisticated spicy vanillin American oak. The palate shows the same combination of luscious fruit and clean, high quality spicy American oak, finishing with soft tannins.

BREMERTON LODGE OLD ADAM SHIRAZ
●●●● $13

One of the two flag-bearers for Bremerton Lodge, the other being the Cabernet Sauvignon (the latter from the '91 vintage not being in the same class). I have not tasted the '92 Cabernet Sauvignon, but if it is as good as the Old Adam Shiraz, it will be very good.

Cellaring 5 years. **Best Vintages** NA
Current Vintage '93
Matching Food Soft ripe cheese.

Tasting Note 1993 Medium to full red-purple; a clean, rich and sweet fruit-driven bouquet with minty aromas and subtle oak. The palate is full-flavoured, with sweet mint, berry and cherry fruit, soft tannins and nicely balanced acidity.

BRIAGOLONG ESTATE

★★☆ 21–25 ML AUSSD
Gippsland **Est.** 1979
Valencia-Briagolong Road, Briagolong, Vic 3860
Ph (051) 47 2322 **Fax** (051) 47 2400
Open Not **Production** 200
Winemaker(s) Gordon McIntosh
This is a weekend hobby for medical practitioner Gordon McIntosh,
who nonetheless tries hard to invest his wines with Burgundian
complexity, with mixed success. He must have established an all-time
record with the 15.4% alcohol in the '92 Pinot Noir.
Principal Wines Chardonnay, Pinot Noir.

BRIAR RIDGE VINEYARD

★★★☆ 15.50–24 CD AUS63
Hunter Valley **Est.** 1972
Mount View Road, Mt View, NSW 2325
Ph (049) 90 3670 **Fax** (049) 90 7802
Open Mon–Fri 9–5, W'ends 9.30–4.30 **Production** 10 000
Winemaker(s) Karl Stockhausen, Neil McGuigan
Semillon and Hermitage, each in various guises, have been the most
consistent performers, underlying the suitability of these varieties to the
Hunter Valley. The Semillon, in particular, invariably shows intense
fruit, and cellars well. In late 1994, Neil McGuigan created a minor
sensation in the industry by leaving the large, public listed McGuigan
Brothers to join the tiny Briar Ridge. As they say, watch this space.
Principal Wines Semillon, Chardonnay, Sauvignon Blanc,
Hermitage, Merlot, Cabernet Sauvignon, Sparkling.

BRIARS, THE See page 438.

BRIDGEWATER MILL

★★★★ 17.75–18.95 R AUS50, 167–170
Adelaide Hills **Est.** 1986
Mount Barker Road, Bridgewater, SA 5155
Ph (08) 339 3422 **Fax** (08) 339 5253
Open Mon–Fri 9.30–5, W'ends 10–5 **Production** 25 000
Winemaker(s) Brian Croser
The second label of Petaluma, which consistently provides wines
most makers would love to have as their top label. The fruit sources
are diverse, with the majority of the Sauvignon Blanc and
Chardonnay coming from Petaluma-owned or managed vineyards,
while the Shiraz is made from purchased grapes.
Principal Wines Sauvignon Blanc, Chardonnay, Millstone Shiraz,
Cabernet Malbec.

BRIDGEWATER MILL SAUVIGNON BLANC

●●●● $17.95
Seemingly the focus of most of the attention of the Bridgewater Mill
label these days; there is not a great deal of activity on other fronts.

The wine is made without oak, and is drawn from a variety of fruit sources, principally the Clare Valley.

Cellaring Drink now. **Best Vintages** NA
Current Vintage '94
Matching Food Smoked trout mousse.
Tasting Note 1994 Light straw-yellow; fragrant passionfruit, peach and gooseberry aromas announce a wine with strongly passionfruit-accented fruit flavours and a crisp, relatively dry finish.

BRINDABELLA HILLS

★★★★ 6–14.50 CD AUS115
Canberra **Est.** 1989
Woodgrove Close, via Hall, ACT 2618
Ph (06) 230 2583
Open W'ends, Public hols 10–5 **Production** 650
Winemaker(s) Dr Roger Harris

Distinguished research scientist Dr Roger Harris has produced a number of excellent wines from Brindabella Hills, none better than the 1992 Shiraz. Unhappily, the 1994 vintage was much reduced by frost, although Brindabella Hills has always supplemented its crush with grapes grown in other Central Tablelands wine regions.
Principal Wines Hilltops Semillon Sauvignon Blanc, Chardonnay, Riesling, Pinot Noir, Cabernet Merlot, Shiraz.

BRINDABELLA HILLS CABERNET MERLOT
●●●● $14.50

Typically a blend of 70% cabernet franc, 20% cabernet sauvignon and 10% merlot, estate-grown at Brindabella Hills. The 1991 vintage (upon which the rating is given) stands head and shoulders ahead of prior years.
Cellaring Now–1996. **Best Vintages** '91
Current Vintage '91
Matching Food Roast lamb.
Tasting Note 1991 Bright medium red-purple; a clean and fresh bouquet with red berry fruits and just a hint of spice. The palate is clean and firm, with clear berry fruit flavours in the mid range of ripeness, finishing with fine tannins and good length. Quite European in style.

BRINDABELLA HILLS HILLTOPS SEMILLON SAUVIGNON BLANC
●●●● $13

Produced from grapes grown at the Moppity Park and Hercynia vineyards in the Hilltops region near Young, but made at Brindabella Hills.
Cellaring Short term; 2–3 years. **Best Vintages** '92
Current Vintage '93
Matching Food Shellfish, prawns.
Tasting Note 1993 Light yellow-green. Crisp, clean, fairly light, gently herbaceous fruit aromas with just a hint of oak. The palate is developing nicely, with hints of lychee and tropical fruit, and again subtle oak. The '93 vintage is not in the same class.

BRINDABELLA HILLS SHIRAZ
●●●●● $14.50
Like the Semillon Sauvignon Blanc, made from grapes grown in the
Hilltops region, coming from the Nioka Ridge vineyard at Young. A
particular feature of the wine is the very sophisticated use of
American (Missouri) oak.
Cellaring 5+ years. **Best Vintages** '90, '92, '93
Current Vintage '92
Matching Food Richer Italian dishes.
Tasting Note 1992 Medium to full red-purple; very stylish, with
rich and sweet red berry fruit and well integrated and balanced oak.
The palate shows dark cherry, plum and blackberry fruit, with
American oak evident but held in appropriate restraint. Delicious
now but will hold.

BRITANNIA CREEK ESTATE

NR NA AUSSD
Yarra Valley **Est.** 1982
Lot 234 Britannia Creek Road, Wesburn, Vic 3799
Ph (03) 9484 3607
Open W'ends 10–6 **Production** 400
Winemaker(s) Charlie Brydon
The wines are made under the Britannia Falls label from 4 hectares
of estate-grown grapes. A very low-profile operation of which I know
nothing.
Principal Wines Sauvignon Blanc, Semillon, Chardonnay,
Cabernet Sauvignon.

BROKE ESTATE

★★★★ 16–18.50 ML AUS111 UK19
Hunter Valley **Est.** 1989
Wollombi Road, Broke, NSW 2330
Ph (065) 79 1065 **Fax** (065) 79 1065
Open By appt **Production** 3200
Winemaker(s) Simon Gilbert (Contract)
The 1991 Cabernets (a blend of cabernet sauvignon and cabernet
franc) was a superlative wine which brought much deserved publicity
to Broke Estate. The Chardonnays have been more variable,
although the '93 is in much the same class.
Principal Wines Chardonnay, Sauvignon Blanc, Cabernets.

BROKE ESTATE CHARDONNAY
●●●● $18.50
Draws upon 8 hectares of estate vineyards, the management of
which is under the direction of the high-profile viticultural consultant
Dr Richard Smart. The quality of the fruit from both the red and white
grape plantings has never been in doubt, although one wishes there
had been a little less extravagant use of oak.
Cellaring Drink now. **Best Vintages** '91, '93, '94
Current Vintage '93

Matching Food Fish in black butter sauce.
Tasting Note 1993 Medium to full yellow-green; a complex, rich bouquet showing strong barrel ferment oak characters over melon and peach fruit. The oak on the palate, while of high quality, tends to dominate; a good, and very nearly great, wine.

BROKEN RIVER WINES

NR 9–12.50 CD AUSSD
Murray River **Est.** 1984
Lemnos-Cosgrove Road, Lemnos, Vic 3631
Ph (058) 29 9486 **Fax** (058) 29 9293
Open By appt **Production** 1500
Winemaker(s) Frank Dawson, Various Contract
The grapes are primarily drawn from 2 hectares of chenin blanc and 1.5 hectares of cabernet franc. As from January 1995 direct sales commenced from the Dawsons' new regional outlet in Shepparton, The Wine Connection.
Principal Wines Chenin Blanc, Cabernet Franc, Cabernets, Chenin Blanc Brut.

BROKENWOOD WINES

★★★★★ 16–22 R AUS36, 137, 167, 168, 170 UK11
Hunter Valley **Est.** 1970
McDonalds Road, Pokolbin, NSW 2321
Ph (049) 98 7559 **Fax** (049) 98 7893
Open 7 days 10–5 **Production** 22 000
Winemaker(s) Iain Riggs, Fiona Purnell
Deservedly fashionable winery producing consistently excellent wines. Unwooded Sauvignon Blanc Semillon has an especially strong following, as has Cabernet Sauvignon; the three Graveyard releases are well worth the extra money, the red wines being exceptionally long-lived. The Graveyard Hermitage is one of the best Hunter reds available today.
Principal Wines Semillon, Sauvignon Blanc Semillon, Chardonnay, Cricket Pitch Cabernet Merlot, Hermitage, Pinot Noir, Cabernet Sauvignon, Graveyard Hermitage.

BROKENWOOD GRAVEYARD HERMITAGE
●●●●● $22
First released under this label from the 1984 vintage, although the 1983 was made entirely from the Graveyard Block (within the Brokenwood estate vineyards) and earlier wines had an essentially similar fruit source. Even taking 1984 as the starting point, the wine has firmly staked its claim to be regarded as an Australian classic.
Cellaring 7–15 years. **Best Vintages** '85, '86, '87, '88, '89, '91, '93, '94 **Current Vintage** '93
Matching Food Roast squab.
Tasting Note 1993 Youthful purple-red; complex and concentrated fruit aromas of liquorice, game and spice dominate the bouquet. The palate is absolutely delicious, with blackberry, liquorice and spice, finely balanced tannins and very well handled oak.

BROKENWOOD SEMILLON
●●●●● $12.95
A wine much appreciated by the Sydney market, which ensures that each release sells out long before the next becomes available. It is made in traditional style: in other words, without the use of oak, and unforced by techniques such as skin contact. Most is drunk young as a crisp, quasi-Chablis style, but as the tastings show, can develop into a Hunter classic.
Cellaring 2–10 years. **Best Vintages** '85, '86, '89, '92, '94
Current Vintage '94
Matching Food Balmain bugs.
Tasting Note 1994 A fragrant and clean bouquet with considerable intensity and lift; both the aromas and flavours show classic herbal/citrus characters, and the wine has the structure and length to guarantee a long future, however enjoyable it may be now. A miracle considering the searing heat (and bushfires) of early summer.

BROOK EDEN VINEYARD *

NR 15–18 CD AUSSD
Pipers Brook **Est.** 1988
Adams Road, Lebrina, Tas 7254
Ph (003) 95 6244
Open W'ends 10–5 **Production** 500
Winemaker(s) Jan Bezemer
Jan and Sheila Bezemer own a 60-hectare Angas beef property which they purchased in 1987, but have diversified with the establishment of 2.5 hectares of vines. Jan Bezemer makes the wine at Delamere, the first vintage being 1993. 1994 was much reduced by storm damage during flowering. The vineyard site is beautiful, with viticultural advice from the noted Fred Peacock.
Principal Wines Chardonnay, Pinot Noir.

BROOKLAND VALLEY

★★★☆ 15.50–17 R AUS101, 122
Margaret River **Est.** 1984
Caves Road, Willyabrup, WA 6284
Ph (097) 55 6250 **Fax** (097) 55 6214
Open Tues–Sun 11–4.30 **Production** 8000
Winemaker(s) Gary Baldwin (Consultant)
Brookland Valley has an idyllic setting, with its Flutes Cafe one of the best winery restaurants in the Margaret River region. Overall, the wines are elegant and technically well made; one simply looks for a little more of the richness present in the 1994 Sauvignon Blanc.
Principal Wines Sauvignon Blanc, Chardonnay, Cabernet Sauvignon Merlot Cabernet Franc.

BROOKLAND VALLEY SAUVIGNON BLANC
●●●● ▶ $16.50
A wine which has consistently impressed, gaining in power and concentration as the vines have matured. The wine is produced from

2 hectares of estate plantings, and is at the richer end of the Margaret River spectrum — an area noted for producing Sauvignon Blanc with excellent varietal character. Winner of a gold medal at the 1994 Perth Sheraton Wine Awards.
Cellaring Drink now. **Best Vintages** '92, '93, '94
Current Vintage '94
Matching Food Calamari.
Tasting Note 1994 Light green-yellow; fresh and crisp aromas with gooseberry fruit untrammelled by oak. The wine has good mouthfeel, with nicely ripened fruit with sweet gooseberry tropical flavours and above-average intensity and length.

BROOKS CREEK VINEYARD

★★☆ 10–15 CD AUSSD
Canberra **Est.** 1973
RMB 209 Brooks Road, Bungendore, NSW 2621
Ph (06) 236 9221 **Fax** (06) 257 4170
Open W'ends 9–5 **Production** 1000
Winemaker(s) Lawrie Brownbill
The Brownbill family purchased what was then known as Shingle House from Max and Yvonne Blake in early 1990, and renamed it Brooks Creek Vineyard. Production varies, as the vineyard can be prone to frost, as in 1994.
Principal Wines Semillon, Chardonnay, Pinot Noir, Cabernet Merlot, Mataro.

BROUSSARDS CHUM CREEK WINERY

NR 8–14 ML AUSSD
Yarra Valley **Est.** 1977
Cunninghams Road, Chum Creek, via Healesville, Vic 3777
Ph (059) 62 5551
Open W'ends, Public hols 10–6 **Production** NFP
Winemaker(s) Contract Made
One of the more remote and smallest of the Yarra Valley wineries, selling most of its grapes to other makers but with small quantities of contract-made wine available at cellar door, principally from the 1991 vintage.
Principal Wines Chardonnay, Pinot Noir, Cabernet Sauvignon, Cabernet Pinot.

BROWN BROTHERS

★★★★☆ 8–25 R AUS14, 15, 103 UK20
North East Victoria **Est.** 1885
Snow Road, Milawa, Vic 3678
Ph (057) 20 5500 **Fax** (057) 20 5511
Open Mon–Sat 9–5, Sun 10–6 **Production** 300 000
Winemaker(s) John Brown, Roland Wahlquist
Brown Brothers draws upon a considerable number of vineyards spread throughout a range of site climates, ranging from very warm

to very cool, with the climate varying according to altitude. It is also known for the diversity of varieties with which it works, and the wines always represent excellent value for money. Deservedly one of the most successful family wineries in Australia.

Principal Wines A very large range of wines available both through retail and cellar door and in various ranges. These include Family Reserve Riesling, Chardonnay, Tarrango, Graciano, Cabernet Sauvignon, Tokay, Sparkling.

BROWN BROTHERS FAMILY RESERVE KING VALLEY RIESLING
●●●● ▶ $14.95

Brown Brothers keep back both white and red wines which the winemakers feel will benefit from cellaring; some of the red wines are released at up to 10 years of age. This Riesling is such a release and offers tremendous value for money.

Cellaring It has already been done for you. **Best Vintages** NA **Current Vintage** '91

Matching Food Fresh asparagus with hollandaise sauce.

Tasting Note 1991 Glowing yellow-green; a rich and smooth bouquet full of tropical lime fruit leads on to a full-flavoured wine, smooth, round and mouthfilling, now at its peak.

BROWN BROTHERS FAMILY SELECTION VERY OLD TOKAY
●●●● ▶ $23.50

While Brown Brothers has always had its own fortified wine programme, and while it is anxious to keep the All Saints programme separate, the quality and complexity of the Brown Brothers releases seems to have increased since the All Saints acquisition. In any event, a lovely wine.

Cellaring NA. **Best Vintages** NA **Current Vintage** NA **Matching Food** After coffee.

Tasting Note NV Medium to full tawny red; very complex tea-leaf/plum pudding/malty aromas. High quality Tokay varietal character on the palate, which is lively and intense, with strong tea-leaf/malt/butterscotch flavours, and good balance.

BROWN BROTHERS GRACIANO
●●●● ▶ $14.30

Brown Brothers is an inveterate experimenter with unusual varieties, looking as far afield as Italy and — in this instance — Spain. Many of these experimental wines are available, as this one is, at cellar door. Brown Brothers indeed has the only plantings in Australia, but has enjoyed sufficient success to cause an increase in those plantings over the past few years.

Cellaring Up to 5 years. **Best Vintages** NA **Current Vintage** '92

Matching Food Steak and kidney pie.

Tasting Note 1992 Dense purple-red; solid, dark chocolate and mint aromas with plenty of power and concentration. The palate has abundant red cherry, mint and plum flavours, with a touch of

American oak, finishing with soft tannins, giving overall generous flavour and texture.

BROWN BROTHERS KING VALLEY PINOT CHARDONNAY
●●●● ▶ $23.40

The big brother of the non vintage wine, and of excellent quality in both 1990 and 1991. It is richer and more complex, but at the significantly higher price, that is as it should be.

Cellaring Has the structure to last for a number of years.
Best Vintages '90, '91 **Current Vintage** '91
Matching Food Shellfish.
Tasting Note 1991 Straw-yellow with a tinge of pink from the pinot; a full, smooth bouquet with sweet, complex fruit. The palate has masses of flavour and complexity, quite French in style; the dosage seems a fraction high.

BROWN BROTHERS NV PINOT CHARDONNAY BRUT
●●●● ▶ $14.20

A non vintage blend of pinot noir and chardonnay grown in the King Valley, much of it at Brown Brothers own Whitlands Vineyard, and which has been consistently good over the last three years. It is overshadowed by better known brands, but always scores well in shows and blind tastings, with numerous gold medals to its credit.
Cellaring Drink now. **Best Vintages** NA **Current Vintage** NA
Matching Food Hors d'oeuvres.
Tasting Note NV Bright, light green-yellow; crisp, clean lemony fruit aromas; lively fresh fruit on the palate, crisp and clean, and very well balanced. Outstanding in its price category and rated accordingly.

BROWN BROTHERS TARRANGO
●●●● $9.50

Yet another example of Brown Brothers' fascination with unusual grape varieties, this one bred by Australia's CSIRO. It makes a wonderful fresh, early-drinking style, which in the bad old days would have been called Beaujolais.
Cellaring Not to be cellared. **Best Vintages** NA
Current Vintage '94
Matching Food Excellent with Asian cuisine.
Tasting Note 1994 Bright medium red-purple; clean and fresh plummy fruit aromas, with a lively, fresh plum and cherry-flavoured palate, finishing crisp and clean.

BULLERS BEVERFORD

★★☆ 7–13 R AUS3, 74
Murray River **Est.** 1952
Murray Valley Highway, Beverford, Vic 3590
Ph (050) 37 6305 **Fax** (050) 37 6803
Open Mon–Sat 9–5 **Production** 25 000
Winemaker(s) Richard Buller (Jnr)
Traditional wines, principally white, which in the final analysis reflect both their Riverlands origin and a fairly low-key approach to style in

the winery. It is, however, one of the few remaining sources of reasonable quality bulk wine available to the public, provided in 25-litre cubes for as little as $60 per cube.

Principal Wines Victoria Classic White and Red; The Magee Dry White and Dry Red; Semillon Chenin Blanc, Spatlese Lexia, Rosé, Cabernet Sauvignon.

BULLERS CALLIOPE

★★★★☆ 13.95–45 R AUS3, 74
North East Victoria **Est.** 1921
Three Chain Road, Rutherglen, Vic 3685
Ph (060) 32 9660 **Fax** (060) 32 8005
Open Mon–Sat 9–5, Sun 10–5 **Production** 3000
Winemaker(s) Andrew Buller
The winery rating is very much influenced by the recent superb releases of museum fortified wines. The Calliope Shiraz is ripe, sweet but tending a little jammy.

Principal Wines Calliope Shiraz, Limited Release Mondeuse Shiraz, Tawny Port, Vintage Port, Muscat, Tokay, Madeira; top fortified releases styled Very Old.

BULLERS CALLIOPE VERY OLD RUTHERGLEN MUSCAT
●●●●● $45
Emerged from the shadows in spectacular fashion at the 1994 Sydney International Winemakers Competition, where it won the trophy for Best Wine of Show. A magnificent wine of great age and complexity.

Cellaring Indefinite. **Best Vintages** NA **Current Vintage** NA
Matching Food Strictly unnecessary, a meal in itself.
Tasting Note NV Deep brown with a touch of olive on the rim; full and deep, almost into chocolate, with intense raisined fruit; richly textured, with great structure to the raisined/plum pudding fruit flavours, and obvious rancio age.

BULLERS CALLIOPE VERY OLD RUTHERGLEN TOKAY
●●●●● $45
The sister wine to the Muscat; the latter covered itself with glory at the 1994 Sydney International Winemakers Competition, while the Tokay came into its own in the 1995 Competition. Both are of extreme quality and of great age.

Cellaring Indefinite. **Best Vintages** NA **Current Vintage** NA
Matching Food Strictly unnecessary, a meal in itself.
Tasting Note NV Medium brown, with a touch of olive; richly concentrated bouquet with strong rancio aged characters and quite bracing spirit; the palate is extremely rich and concentrated, with a voluptuous mid palate, and an appropriately dry finish.

BUNGAWARRA WINES

NR 14–17 CD AUSSD
Granite Belt **Est.** 1975
Bents Road, Ballandean, Qld 4382

Ph (076) 84 1128
Open 7 days 10.30–4.30 **Production** 300
Winemaker(s) Philip Christensen
Now owned by Bruce Humphery-Smith, who also operates Heritage
Wines of Stanthorpe. It draws upon 5 hectares of mature vineyards
which over the years have shown themselves capable of producing
red wines of considerable character.
Principal Wines Traminer, Chardonnay, Shiraz, Cabernet,
Liqueur Muscat.

BURGE FAMILY WINEMAKERS

★★★☆ 10.80–12.50 CD AUSSD
Barossa Valley **Est.** 1928
Barossa Way, Lyndoch, SA 5351
Ph (085) 24 4644 **Fax** (085) 24 4444
Open 7 days 10–5 **Production** 3500
Winemaker(s) Rick Burge
Rick Burge came back to the family winery after a number of years
successfully running St Leonards; there was much work to be done,
but he has achieved much, using the base of very good fortified
wines and markedly improving table wine quality.
Principal Wines Semillon Sauvignon Blanc, Clochmerle,
Grenache; Draycott Shiraz, Merlot; Homestead Cabernet Merlot;
Sparkling.

BURGE FAMILY DRAYCOTT MERLOT
●●● ▶ $11.80
The first release of Draycott Merlot from vines planted in 1987,
and a promising start.
Cellaring Early-drinking style.
Best Vintages NA
Current Vintage '93
Matching Food Mild cheddar.
Tasting Note 1993 Medium to full red-purple; clean, fresh sweet
redcurrant fruit with subtle oak; a crisp, elegant and refreshing
palate with light tannins.

BURGE FAMILY DRAYCOTT SHIRAZ
●●●● $12.50
Produced from the estate-owned Draycott Vineyard (hence the name)
which is hand-pruned and yields 2–3 tonnes per acre, depending on
the vintage. A classic Barossa Shiraz in traditional style.
Cellaring 10+ years.
Best Vintages '84, '88, '91, '94
Current Vintage '92
Matching Food Wild duck or, failing that, domestic duck.
Tasting Note 1992 Medium to full red-purple; dark berry fruit
aromas with a hint of varietal earthy character, and subtle oak.
A supremely honest wine, with soft red berry fruits on the palate,
soft tannins, a touch of vanillin oak, and the capacity to age.

BURNBRAE WINES

★★☆ 9.50–15 CD AUSSD
Mudgee **Est.** 1976
Hargraves Road, Erudgere via Mudgee, NSW 2850
Ph (063) 73 3504 **Fax** (063) 73 3601
Open 7 days 9–5 **Production** 1100
Winemaker(s) Robert Bassel Mace
Robert Mace makes a series of rather rustic but very full-flavoured
wines typically from very ripe grapes. Some of the old oak used
gives rise to technical problems, and the wines will not appeal to
those with a technical approach. The fortified wines are best.
Principal Wines Sauvignon Blanc, Traminer, Rosé, Pinot Noir,
Shiraz; Primavera Red and White; Fortifieds.

CALAIS ESTATES

★★★ 12–17 CD AUS41
Hunter Valley **Est.** 1987
Palmers Lane, Pokolbin, NSW 2321
Ph (049) 98 7654 **Fax** (049) 98 7813
Open Mon–Fri 9–5, W'ends 10–5 **Production** 11 000
Winemaker(s) Alasdair Sutherland
The immensely experienced Alasdair Sutherland, who has long been
connected directly or indirectly with the Hunter Valley, has taken
over winemaking responsibilities. Calais Estates regularly produces
pleasant Chardonnay, the most recent example of which is the yet to
be released 1994 Reserve Chardonnay.
Principal Wines Chenin Blanc, Semillon, Chardonnay, Late
Harvest Riesling, Sauterne, Shiraz Pinot, Shiraz, Cabernet
Sauvignon.

CAMDEN ESTATE

★★★.0 14–16 R AUSSD
Sydney District **Est.** 1980
Lot 32 Macarthur Road, Camden, NSW 2570
Ph (046) 58 1237 **Fax** (02) 369 3986
Open Sat 11–4 and by appt **Production** 2000
Winemaker(s) Norman Hanckel
This historically situated estate has narrowed its production down to
chardonnay and a little pinot noir, the latter grown for the sparkling
wine. Chardonnay flourishes in the warm climate, ripens relatively
early, and has the best chance of standing up to the summer and
vintage rains with which proprietor Norman Hanckel has to contend.
Principal Wines Chardonnay, Sparkling.

CAMDEN ESTATE CHARDONNAY

●●● $14
Produced entirely from vineyards situated on the banks of the
Nepean River at Camden, directly opposite the site of one of
Australia's first commercial vineyards established by John Macarthur

in the early 19th century. In all there are 9 hectares, part of the grape production being sold to others, part going to Camden Estate sparkling wine and with various changing subtle permutations and combinations of the Camden Estate label.

Cellaring Usually quick developing — say 2–3 years.
Best Vintages '83, '88, '89, '91, '93 **Current Vintage** '93
Matching Food Smoked trout mousse.
Tasting Note 1993 Medium to full yellow-green; solid, clean and buttery with peachy fruit and subtle oak aromas. The palate is lighter, and indeed fresher, than the bouquet suggests, with moderate weight and length, and again subtle oak.

CAMPBELLS WINERY

★★★☆ 10.95–60 R AUS84 UK96
North East Victoria **Est.** 1870
Murray Valley Highway, Rutherglen, Vic 3685
Ph (060) 32 9458 **Fax** (060) 32 9870
Open Mon–Sat 9–5, Sun 10–5 **Production** 42 000
Winemaker(s) Colin Campbell
A wide range of table and fortified wines of ascending quality and price, which are always honest; as so often happens in this part of the world, the fortified wines are by far the best, with the extremely elegant Isabella Tokay and Merchant Prince Muscat at the top of the tree.
Principal Wines Chardonnay Semillon, Riesling, Silverburn Dry Graves, Quality Hill Chablis, Bobbie Burns Shiraz, Durif, Malbec, Cabernet Merlot, Isabella Old Rutherglen Tokay, Merchant Prince Muscat.

CAMPBELLS BOBBIE BURNS SHIRAZ
●●●● $14.95
An always interesting wine made from very ripe grapes, typically with alcohol levels of around 14%, and with a relatively high pH which gives the wine softness and roundness in the mouth. 100% estate-grown.
Cellaring Not as long as one might imagine — 3–5 years. **Best Vintages** '86, '88, '90, '91, '92, '93 **Current Vintage** '93
Matching Food Rich game dishes.
Tasting Note 1993 Medium to full red; rich, ripe earthy aromas show pronounced warm-grown varietal fruit. The palate is as powerful as the 14.5% alcohol would suggest, with black cherry and earth flavours, finishing with ample tannins.

CAMPBELLS ISABELLA TOKAY
●●●● ▶ $60
One of a pair of super-premium fortified wines produced by Campbells, the other being Campbells Merchant Prince Muscat. The Campbells wine is, and always has been, lighter and fresher than the other major producers, with more emphasis thrown on the underlying varietal fruit of the wines. It is a question of style rather than quality; these deluxe wines deserve their price.

Cellaring NA. **Best Vintages** NA **Current Vintage** NA
Matching Food As fine an aperitif as it is a digestif.
Tasting Note NV Light tawny gold; fragrant grapey, sweet tea-leaf
aromas with clean spirit; the palate is luscious with sweet juicy berry
and tea-leaf flavours, finishing with good acidity and a very clean
aftertaste.

CAMPBELLS MERCHANT PRINCE MUSCAT
••••• $60
A superbly balanced and constructed Muscat in a distinctly lighter
mould than Baileys, Chambers or Morris, the big names of the
district. For all that, it has an average age of 25 years, with the
oldest component dating back over 60 years. One of those rare
Muscats which actually invites a second glass.
Cellaring NA. **Best Vintages** NA **Current Vintage** NV
Matching Food Coffee, high quality biscuits.
Tasting Note NV Light to medium brown; intense but fragrant
spice and raisin aromas with clean spirit. The palate is remarkably
fresh and light given the age of the wine, with raisin, spice, malt and
toffee flavours all intermingling, followed by cleansing acidity.

CANOBLAS-SMITH WINES

★★★☆ 10–17 CD AUSSD
Central Tablelands **Est.** 1986
Boree Lane, Off Cargo Road, Lidster via Orange, NSW 2800
Ph (063) 65 6113
Open W'ends, Public hols 1–5 **Production** 1200
Winemaker(s) Murray Smith
Wine quality has improved significantly since the first experimental
vintages, and the cellar door (whence most of the wine is sold) is
well worth a visit.
Principal Wines Chardonnay, Pinot Noir, Merlot, Cabernet
Sauvignon.

CANOBLAS-SMITH CHARDONNAY
••• ▶ $15
Produced from 2.2 hectares of estate plantings at an elevation of
820 metres on Mount Canoblas. The vines are not irrigated, and are
grown on red volcanic soils. Each vintage has shown distinct
improvement, although one can see all of the signs of the small
winery.
Cellaring 1–2 years. **Best Vintages** '93 **Current Vintage** '93
Matching Food Pasta.
Tasting Note 1993 Medium yellow-green; a quite complex
bouquet with nutty aromas indicating barrel fermentation at ambient
temperatures. The palate is clean, with soft cashew nut and melon
fruit of medium intensity.

CANOBLAS-SMITH MERLOT
•••• $17
While the major part of the estate plantings are cabernet sauvignon
(2.2 hectares) there is a quarter of a hectare of merlot. One might

have expected Murray Smith to have blended the two, but in 1992 he elected to keep the merlot separate, and it is perhaps not hard to see why. In other years Murray Smith will blend the two grapes together. The wine, incidentally, is graced with one of the most evocative and striking labels imaginable.

Cellaring 2–3 years. **Best Vintages** '92 **Current Vintage** '92
Matching Food Veal kidneys.
Tasting Note 1992 Medium to full red; the bouquet is of medium intensity with quite marked sappy merlot varietal character and subtle oak. The palate is quite European in style, firm, briary and woody, with a relatively long finish and tannins still needing to soften a touch.

CAPE BOUVARD WINERY *

NR 10–14 CD AUSSD
South-west Coastal Plain **Est.** 1990
Mt John Road, Mandurah, WA 6210
Ph (097) 39 1360 **Fax** (097) 39 1360
Open 7 days 10–5 **Production** 400
Winemaker(s) Gary Grierson
Doggerel poet-cum-winemaker Gary Grierson draws upon one hectare of estate plantings, but also purchases grapes from other growers for the new Cape Bouvard label. The '93 Shiraz, tasted at the Mount Barker Show, was rather light, leafy and spicy, but inoffensive.
Principal Wines Chardonnay, Shiraz, Cabernet Sauvignon, Sparkling, Port.

CAPE CLAIRAULT WINES

★★★☆ 13–22 CD AUS61, 86, 144
Margaret River **Est.** 1976
Henry Road, Willyabrup, WA 6280
Ph (097) 55 6225 **Fax** (097) 55 6229
Open 7 days 10–5 **Production** 6000
Winemaker(s) Ian Lewis, Peter Stark
Ian and Ani Lewis have been joined by two of their sons and, in consequence, have not only decided not to sell the business, but to double its size, with winery capacity being doubled from 85 tonnes to 150 tonnes. Notwithstanding increasing production, demand for the wines is so great that Cape Clairault has withdrawn from export to concentrate on the local market.
Principal Wines Cape Clairault label: Sauvignon Blanc, Semillon Sauvignon Blanc, Rhine Riesling, Clairault (Cabernet blend); Cape label: Cape White, Cape Pink, Cape Late Harvest, Cape Red.

CAPE CLAIRAULT CLAIRAULT
●●●● $22
A blend of 50% cabernet sauvignon, 45% merlot and 5% cabernet franc, all estate-grown. The wine characteristically has those faintly earthy/gravelly characters of the region, giving the wine a slightly

austere astringency greatly appreciated by devotees of the style.
Cellaring 3–5 years. **Best Vintages** '82, '85, '86, '90, '91
Current Vintage '91
Matching Food Margaret River Chevre.
Tasting Note 1991 Medium to full red-purple; a concentrated,
powerful bouquet with dark berry fruits and a few more
gamey/earthy notes. The palate is ripe, with lots of flavour, and
that undertone of charry/earthy/gamey regional character.

CAPE CLAIRAULT RHINE RIESLING
●●● ▶ $15.50
Made from a little over half a hectare of estate plantings. Riesling
has always been a temperamental variety in the Margaret River,
producing a range of unpredictable flavours. This wine, however,
seems to have the structure and capacity to develop more in the style
of Mount Barker Rieslings than typical Margaret River Rieslings.
Cellaring 3–5 years. **Best Vintages** '85, '88, '91, '92, '93
Current Vintage '94
Matching Food Avocado.
Tasting Note 1994 Light yellow-green; toasty, dry herbaceous
style with a steely edge. The palate is similarly intense and quite
herbaceous; the finish is firm, and the wine will improve with
bottle age.

CAPE CLAIRAULT SAUVIGNON BLANC
●●● ▶ $17
Cape Clairault has a little over 3 hectares of sauvignon blanc, which
in turn accounts for almost one third of its total plantings. It is, of
course, a variety which does very well in the Margaret River region,
and provides Cape Clairault with its flagship wine. Over the years
some excellent Sauvignon Blancs have been produced under the
Clairault label, notably the '93. Early in its life, the '94 looks lighter
and not quite up to the best.
Cellaring 1–2 years. **Best Vintages** '88, '91, '92, '93
Current Vintage '94
Matching Food Shellfish.
Tasting Note 1994 Light yellow-green; clean, with no winemaking
fault, but relatively neutral in terms of varietal character. The palate
is clean, direct, of light to medium intensity and well balanced. It
may conceivably gain richness and character with another year or
so in the bottle.

CAPE CLAIRAULT SEMILLON SAUVIGNON BLANC
●●●● $15.50
Predominantly semillon (from 1.5 hectares of estate plantings) with a
little sauvignon blanc. The two varieties merge so closely with each
other in the Margaret River, it is often hard to tell where the influence
of one starts and the other finishes in the blend. In 1994 the semillon
component was obviously more concentrated than the sauvignon
blanc, and has provided the better wine.
Cellaring 2–3 years. **Best Vintages** '88, '91, '92, '93
Current Vintage '94

Matching Food Focaccia.
Tasting Note 1994 Light yellow-green; crisp and herbaceous on the bouquet, with hints of spice to the fruit. The palate has good length and intensity, strongly herbal in character, with a lingering finish.

CAPE ESTATE *

NR NA AUSSD
Margaret River **Est.** 1980
PO Box 405, Busselton, WA 6280
Ph NA
Open Not **Production** 500
Winemaker(s) Gavin Berry (Contract)
Cape Estate is owned by Perth architect Peter May. It is in fact the new name for the Shemarin Vineyard established by Rob Bowen in 1980. The 1994 Sauvignon Blanc was made at Capel Vale, the 1994 Chardonnay at Plantagenet, but future wines will all be made at Plantagenet.
Principal Wines Sauvignon Blanc, Chardonnay.

CAPE MENTELLE

★★★★★ 16.25–29.35 R AUS27, 66, 167, 169, 181 UK71
Margaret River **Est.** 1970
Off Wallcliffe Road, Margaret River, WA 6285
Ph (097) 57 3266 **Fax** (097) 57 3233
Open 7 days 10–4.30 **Production** 50 000
Winemaker(s) John Durham
Notwithstanding majority ownership by Veuve Clicquot, David Hohnen remains very much in command of one of Australia's foremost medium-sized wineries. Exceptional marketing skills and wine of the highest quality, with the back-up of New Zealand's Cloudy Bay, are a potent combination.
Principal Wines Chardonnay, Semillon Sauvignon Blanc, Cabernet Sauvignon, Cabernet Merlot, Shiraz, Zinfandel, Trinders Vineyard Cabernet Merlot.

CAPE MENTELLE CABERNET MERLOT TRINDERS VINEYARD

●●●) $17
The inaugural release (in 1992) of the 1990 vintage was simply labelled 'Trinders', the name coming from the long-gone Trinders School which once stood adjacent to the vineyard. The name ultimately proved too obscure, so the wine is now prominently labelled Cabernet Merlot, subtitled Trinders Vineyard. To be honest, I have never been a big fan of the wine, finding it a bit leafy, but the '93 does show greater ripeness.
Cellaring 1–3 years. **Best Vintages** '90, '93
Current Vintage '93
Matching Food Lamb casserole.
Tasting Note 1993 Medium to full red; there is more ripeness

evident in the bouquet than in previous vintages with a mix of dark fruit, cedar and gamey characters. The palate has good extract, with sweet briary/berry fruit, with a faint undertone of earth.

CAPE MENTELLE CABERNET SAUVIGNON
●●●● $29.50

It is ironic that the wine for which Cape Mentelle is most famous should receive a lesser rating than its other top wines, particularly given the fact that the '82 and '83 vintages won consecutive Jimmy Watson trophies, and that the wine is a major part of the Cape Mentelle output. It is not that it is anything other than good; it is, but simply lacks the final excitement or class of the other wines in most years.

Cellaring 10+ years. **Best Vintages** '82, '86, '88, '90, '93
Current Vintage '91
Matching Food Loin of lamb.
Tasting Note 1991 Medium red-purple; solid, concentrated cedary/briary bouquet with little or no berry fruit, and subtle oak. The palate is concentrated and powerful with minerally/briary/dark berry fruit, finishing with firm tannins. A food style needing much time.

CAPE MENTELLE CHARDONNAY
●●●●● $23.50

First made in 1988, and immediately established itself as another classic. The 1990 vintage was selected for British Airways First Class; each succeeding year has reached new heights. These are wines of exceptional complexity, Chardonnays made by a red winemaker (but in the best possible way). The 1993 won the George Mackey Award for best wine exported from Australia in 1994.

Cellaring Typically up to 3 years. **Best Vintages** '90, '91, '92, '93 **Current Vintage** '93
Matching Food Tasmanian salmon.
Tasting Note 1993 Medium to full yellow-green; a rich, complex and intense bouquet with subtle oak and a mix of primary and secondary fruit aromas. In the mouth unusually intense, powerful and long with flavours of melon, fig and citrus, and again with subdued oak.

CAPE MENTELLE SEMILLON SAUVIGNON BLANC
●●●● ▶ $16

A wine which has been part of the Cape Mentelle portfolio since 1985, but which in the early years was not particularly exciting. To what extent the Cloudy Bay skills rubbed off is a moot point, but the fact is that in more recent times this has been another faultless wine combining finesse with power.

Cellaring Not really necessary. **Best Vintages** '85, '88, '91, '93
Current Vintage '94
Matching Food Fish, Asian cuisine.
Tasting Note 1994 Medium to full yellow-green; very smooth, fruit-driven aroma with ripe gooseberry/tropical fruit the dominant force. A well balanced palate in terms of both fruit and oak, seamlessly integrated, but just a little soft on the finish, and not up to the '93.

CAPE MENTELLE SHIRAZ
●●●● ▶ $19.50

Made its debut in 1981, and over the intervening years has
produced some spectacular wines which — to my palate at least —
have not infrequently outclassed the Cabernet Sauvignon. The wines
typically show wonderful spice, game and liquorice characters
reminiscent of the Rhone Valley. Since 1986 a small percentage of
grenache has been included in some years.
Cellaring 3–5 years. **Best Vintages** '86, '88, '90, '91, '93
Current Vintage '93
Matching Food Stir-fried Asian beef.
Tasting Note 1993 Full red-purple; an extremely complex, gamey
Rhone-style with a powerful, concentrated bouquet and palate.
Highly idiosyncratic, but very impressive.

CAPE MENTELLE ZINFANDEL
●●●●● $17.50

Also made its first appearance in 1981, a direct reflection of David
Hohnen's early winemaking experiences in California. Despite its
exceptional quality, remains the only Zinfandel worth mentioning in
Australia; it is most surprising that it has not encouraged others to try.
Cellaring Classic each-way bet. **Best Vintages** '86, '87, '91,
'92, '93 **Current Vintage** '92
Matching Food Rare char-grilled rump steak.
Tasting Note 1992 Medium to full red-purple; classic ripe
cedary/briary/brambly/blackcurrant aromas with the oak
swallowed up. The palate is a classic, big style, faintly jammy
zinfandel which would fit easily into the mainstream of the bigger
Californian style; luscious and striking.

CAPEL VALE

★★★★ 11–27 R AUS15, 16, 17, 29, 70, 75, 123 UK99
South-west Coastal Plain **Est.** 1979
Box 692, Lot 5 Capel North West Road, Capel, WA 6271
Ph (097) 27 2439 **Fax** (097) 91 2452
Open 7 days 10–4 **Production** 35 000
Winemaker(s) Rob Bowen
Notwithstanding the drive of owner Dr Peter Pratten and the
undoubted winemaking skills of Rob Bowen, Capel Vales remains an
enigma. Sometimes the wines show brilliantly (as indeed they
should), and other times they disappoint, given the undoubted
potential. The whites usually live up to one's high expectations, and
the '92 Cabernet Sauvignon and Shiraz mark a return to form.
Principal Wines Chardonnay, Sauvignon Blanc Semillon, Rhine
Riesling, Shiraz, Cabernet Sauvignon, Merlot Cabernet, Pinot Noir;
The CV Cabernet Sauvignon, Chenin Blanc, Classic White are
cheaper, second label wines.

CAPEL VALE CHARDONNAY
●●●● ▶ $20

Sourced from a variety of vineyards spread from the Capel region to
Mount Barker. Initially only one wine was released, but in recent

years the wine comes out in three price and quality categories: CV at the bottom, standard varietal Chardonnay in the middle, and Special Reserve at the top end, with prices ranging from $14.20 to $27.
Cellaring Up to 5 years. **Best Vintages** '86, '87, '91, '92, '93
Current Vintage '92
Matching Food Crab, shellfish.
Tasting Note 1992 Standard: Light to medium yellow-green; intense citrus/grapefruit aromas similar to those we used to see from Padthaway, subtle oak. The palate is fruit-driven, with plenty of flavour and length, again in that citrus/melon spectrum.

CAPEL VALE RHINE RIESLING
●●●● $14.20
A wine with a tremendous track record over the years, with intense fruit and great structure, although occasional vintages have inexplicably disappointed at the start or with bottle age. The grapes come from Capel Vale Stirling Vineyard and from the Whispering Hill Vineyard at Mount Barker. The '91 is currently drinking superbly.
Cellaring 3–7 years. **Best Vintages** '86, '87, '91, '92, '93
Current Vintage '93
Matching Food Caesar salad.
Tasting Note 1993 Glowing yellow-green; very complex aromas with many fruit characters, almost chardonnay-like, with the suggestion of some botrytis. A similarly potent and complex wine on the palate with masses of flavour in a tropical spectrum almost into pineapple. Has developed quickly.

CAPOGRECO ESTATE

NR 8–12 CD AUSSD
Murray River **Est.** 1976
Riverside Avenue, Mildura, Vic 3500
Ph (050) 23 3060
Open Mon–Sat 10–6 **Production** NFP
Winemaker(s) Bruno Capogreco
Italian-owned and run, the wines are a blend of Italian and Australian Riverlands influences; the herb-infused Rosso Dolce is a particularly good example of its kind.
Principal Wines Riesling, Moselle, Shiraz-Mataro, Cabernet Sauvignon, Claret, Rosé, Fortifieds.

CARABOODA ESTATE *

NR 12 CD AUSSD
South-west Coastal Plain **Est.** 1989
297 Carabooda Road, Carabooda, WA 6033
Ph (09) 407 5283
Open 7 days 10–6 **Production** 500
Winemaker(s) Terry Ord
1989 is the year of establishment given by Terry Ord, but it might as well have been 1979 (when he made his first wine) or 1981 (when

he and wife Simonne planted their first vines). But it has been a slowly, slowly exercise, with production from the 3 hectares of estate plantings now supplemented by purchased grapes, the first public release not being made until mid 1994.
Principal Wines Sauvignon Blanc, Shiraz, Cabernet Sauvignon.

CARABOODA ESTATE SHIRAZ
●●●● $12
Principally made from one hectare of estate plantings. When I read Terry Ord's remark, 'I believe too much emphasis has been placed on making wines to a formula', I cringed, for it almost invariably means I am going to taste something that bears not even a passing resemblance to wine. That is certainly not the case with the '93 Carabooda Estate Shiraz.
Cellaring 3–5 years. **Best Vintages** NA **Current Vintage** '93
Matching Food Braised oxtail.
Tasting Note 1993 Medium to full red-purple; earthy, ripe and briary aromas lead on to a rich, ripe, chocolatey/briary/berry fruited palate, with lingering tannins. A generous, well made wine.

CARBUNUP ESTATE *
★★★☆ 12–16 CD AUSSD
Margaret River **Est.** 1988
Bussel Highway, Carbunup, WA 6280
Ph (097) 55 1111
Open 7 days 10–5 **Production** NFP
Winemaker(s) Robert Credaro
A relative newcomer, selling part of the grapes produced from the 18 hectares of vineyards, but keeping part for release under the Cabunup Estate and Vasse River labels — strikingly different in design, and giving no clue that they emanate from the same winery. It has had immediate success with its white wines, and in particular its Chardonnay and Semillon.
Principal Wines Under the premium Vasse River Wines label: Chardonnay, Semillon, Sauvignon Blanc; under Carbunup Estate label: Verdelho, Shiraz.

CARBUNUP ESTATE VASSE RIVER CHARDONNAY
●●● ▶ $15
Made in an unwooded style, and of consistent quality. The 1993 vintage won a silver medal at the Mount Barker Wine Show (the first show entry for Carbunup Estate) and the 1994 won a bronze medal at the 1994 Mount Barker Wine Show.
Cellaring 2–3 years. **Best Vintages** '93, '94
Current Vintage '94
Matching Food Scallop terrine.
Tasting Note 1994 Light green-yellow; made in a fairly elegant, reserved style with citrus and melon aromas. The palate provides more of the same with citrus and herbal fruit on the mid palate, finishing ever-so-slightly sweet. Competent making.

CAROSA VINEYARD

★★ 9.75–19 CD AUSSD
Darling Range **Est.** 1986
Lot 3 Houston Street, Mount Helena, WA 6555
Ph (09) 572 1603
Open W'ends, Hols 11–5 **Production** 300
Winemaker(s) James Elson
Very limited production and small-scale winemaking result in wines
which can only be described as rustic, but which sell readily enough
into the local market. Barrel samples tasted early in the piece were
not in proper condition for judging, while bird damage has restricted
yields from the Carosa vineyards. However, winemaker (and
consultant) Jim Elson has extensive Eastern States winemaking
experience (with Seppelt) so should succeed.
Principal Wines Chardonnay, Semillon, Late Picked Semillon,
Cabernet Merlot, Pinot Noir.

CASELLA WINES

★★ NA AUSSD
Murrumbidgee Irrigation Area **Est.** 1969
Farm 1471, Yenda, NSW 2681
Ph (069) 68 1346
Open Not **Production** 175 000
Winemaker(s) John Casella
Casella makes lush, soft, early-maturing and full-flavoured white
wines, and surprised with a highly-toned, ripe, spicy berry 1990
Cabernet Sauvignon. Most of the wine is sold in bulk to other
producers.
Principal Wines Semillon, Chardonnay, Semillon Chardonnay,
Shiraz, Shiraz Cabernet, Cabernet Sauvignon, Sparkling.

CASSEGRAIN VINEYARDS

★★★☆ 8.95–29 R AUS182 UK39 US9
Hastings Valley **Est.** 1980
Hastings Valley Winery, Pacific Highway, Port Macquarie,
NSW 2444
Ph (065) 83 7777 **Fax** (065) 84 0354
Open 7 days 9–5 **Production** 42 000
Winemaker(s) John Cassegrain, Drew Noon
A very substantial operation based in the Hastings Valley, drawing
some of its more interesting grapes from estate-owned and
associated vineyards there, but also from the Hunter Valley and
elsewhere. The quality of the wines varies significantly from year to
year and from one variety to the next, making it a little difficult to
follow.
Principal Wines Chardonnay, Semillon, Verdelho, Shiraz,
Pinot Noir, Merlot, Chambourcin; Fromenteau Chardonnay;
First Ridge Semillon; Morillon Pinot Noir; Five Mile Hollow Red
and White.

CASSEGRAIN CHAMBOURCIN
●●● ▶ $10.95

A French hybrid cross which is strongly resistant to downy and powdery mildew, and produces incredibly intensely-coloured wines. Its disease resistance is the reason it was chosen for the Hastings Valley, where Cassegrain has the only significant planting in Australia. As the notes indicate, wine quality has varied wildly, and the wine rating is something of a compromise between the extremes. For all that, interesting.

Cellaring 1–3 years. **Best Vintages** '89, '90, '92
Current Vintage '93
Matching Food Italian cuisine.
Tasting Note 1993 Unacceptably marred by what appears to be the results of bacterial infection similar to brettanomyces. Tasted on a number of occasions with identical notes. The '92 by contrast, was very smooth and harmonious with lush red berry fruit flavours and soft tannins.

CASSEGRAIN FROMENTEAU CHARDONNAY
●●●● ▶ $29

Compelling proof that the Hastings Valley, on the north coast of New South Wales, can produce Chardonnay of exceptional quality. From the 2.5-hectare estate-owned Fromenteau Vineyard, planted in 1981, it has always produced very striking wine, hitting a probably never-to-be-repeated peak in the warm dry vintage of 1991. Only 950 cases produced.

Cellaring Quick developing style. **Best Vintages** '89, '91
Current Vintage '91
Matching Food Rich chicken or veal.
Tasting Note 1991 Glowing yellow-green; extremely complex, nutty honeyed fruit with strong barrel ferment influence. A compellingly complex, plush, layered palate with a huge volume of fruit, high class French oak and almost overwhelming impact.

CASSEGRAIN HASTINGS VALLEY SEMILLON
●●● ▶ $15

1993 marked the first Hastings Valley release of Semillon, and a promising start, albeit with limited quantities (only 600 cases made). The style reflects the warm climate, and will be quick maturing.
Cellaring Drink now. **Best Vintages** NA **Current Vintage** '93
Matching Food Pasta marinara.
Tasting Note 1993 Medium to full yellow-green; solid and ripe with honey, melon and peach aromas. The palate is soft and quite rich, although lacking the traditional tightness and length of young semillon.

CASSEGRAIN SHIRAZ
●●● ▶ $13.95

Sourced not from the Hastings Valley, but from the Hunter Valley, whence much of Cassegrain's grapes have come over the years.
Cellaring 3–5 years. **Best Vintages** '89, '91, '93
Current Vintage '93

Matching Food Lamb casserole.
Tasting Note 1993 Full red-purple; a clean, solid fruit-driven bouquet with minimal oak. The palate has abundant and very pleasant dark cherry fruit with soft tannins running throughout, making the structure attractive.

CASTLE ROCK ESTATE

★★★☆ 10–15.15 CD AUS85
Great Southern **Est.** 1983
Porongurup Road, Porongurup, WA 6324
Ph (098) 53 1035 **Fax** (098) 53 1010
Open Wed–Sun, Public hols 10–5 **Production** 3000
Winemaker(s) Various Contract
An exceptionally beautifully sited vineyard and cellar door sale area with sweeping vistas from the Porongurups, operated by the Diletti family. The standard of viticulture is very high, and the site itself ideally situated (quite apart from its beauty). It is a little puzzling why the wines other than the Riesling do not have greater intensity of flavour; having visited the estate on a number of occasions, I am none the wiser.
Principal Wines Rhine Riesling, Late Harvest Riesling, Estate White, Chardonnay, Pinot Noir, Cabernet Sauvignon, Liqueur Muscat.

CASTLE ROCK ESTATE RHINE RIESLING

●●●● $12.50
Consistently the best of the Castle Rock Estate wines, and which ages wonderfully well. It is easy to overlook the wine in its youth, when it is typically very toasty, very crisp and on the lean side, but flowers with age. Tasted in late 1994, the '89 was just entering the prime of its life, with youthful lime flavours, a hint of toast, and a long, fine finish.
Cellaring 5–10 years. **Best Vintages** '86, '89, '90, '91, '94
Current Vintage '93
Matching Food Seafood salad.
Tasting Note 1993 Light green-yellow; clean, crisp, tight and reserved at 18 months of age. The palate is crisp and elegant, neither particularly aromatic nor fruity, but has structure and length, with toast and mineral notes. Its entire life lies in front of it.

CATHCART RIDGE ESTATE

★★☆ 10–17 CD AUSD
Great Western **Est.** 1977
Byron Road, Cathcart via Ararat, Vic 3377
Ph (053) 52 1997 **Fax** (053) 52 1558
Open 7 days 10–5 **Production** 1200
Winemaker(s) David Farnhill
Now owned and operated by the Farnhill family; it remains to be seen whether the high reputation which Cathcart Ridge enjoyed in the early 1980s can be restored, although a recent tasting of '93 Merlot did not impress.

Principal Wines Grampians Riesling, Chardonnay, Shiraz, Cabernet Merlot, Merlot; second label is Mount Ararat Estate, with Victorian White, Red and Late Picked White.

CHALK HILL WINES

NR 5.90–13 CD AUSSD
Southern Vales **Est.** 1973
Brewery Hill Road, McLaren Vale, SA 5171
Ph (08) 323 8815
Open 7 days 1–5 **Production** NFP
Winemaker(s) Nancy Benko
The retirement hobby of distinguished research scientist Dr Nancy Benko; wines from numerous vintages back to 1978 were, on last report, available at very low prices.
Principal Wines Riesling, Rosé, Shiraz, Cabernet Sauvignon, Port.

CHAMBERS ROSEWOOD WINERY *

★★★★☆ 6–40 R AUSSD
North East Victoria **Est.** 1864
Barkley Street, Rutherglen, Vic 3685
Ph (060) 32 8641 **Fax** (060) 32 8101
Open Mon–Sat 9–5, Sun 10–5 **Production** 5000
Winemaker(s) Bill Chambers
Bill Chambers is one of the great characters of the industry, but is not given to correspondence or to filling out forms. Entirely inadvertently, the winery was dropped from the 1994 (and earlier) Pocket Guides. It remains a matter of record, however, that Bill Chambers makes some of the very greatest, albeit nearly unprocurable, Special Old Liqueur Muscat and Special Old Liqueur Tokay to be found in the north east.
Principal Wines A range of modestly-priced and modestly-made table wines, but the real forte of the winery is its Tokay and Muscat, also old Amontillado Sherries and Ports.

CHAPEL HILL WINERY

★★★★★ 11.50–32 R AUS112 UK11
Southern Vales **Est.** 1979
Chapel Hill Road, McLaren Vale, SA 5171
Ph (08) 323 8429 **Fax** (08) 323 9245
Open Mon–Fri 9–5, W'ends 11–5 **Production** 27 000
Winemaker(s) Pam Dunsford
A winery of the highest quality which goes from strength to strength, much expanded, and luxuriously equipped. Consultant winemaker Pam Dunsford is in complete control, producing a range of consistently superlative wines, drawing upon grapes grown in the Southern Vales, Coonawarra and Padthaway.
Principal Wines Riesling, Chardonnay, Unwooded Chardonnay, Cabernet Shiraz, Cabernet Sauvignon; Reserve Chardonnay and Cabernet Sauvignon are limited release, top-end wines.

CHAPEL HILL CABERNET SAUVIGNON
●●●●● $18

A blend of Southern Vales and Coonawarra cabernet, matured in a
mix of quality French and American oak. Consistently good over the
years, but the 5-star rating is very much a tribute to the glorious '92
vintage, which capped a distinguished show career by winning
three trophies at the 1994 National Wine Show in Canberra,
including Best Table Wine of Show.

Cellaring Now–10 years. **Best Vintages** '88, '90, '91, '92
Current Vintage '92
Matching Food Full-flavoured cheddar, red meats.
Tasting Note 1992 Strong purple-red; a complex, concentrated
bouquet with perfectly ripened cabernet, and immaculately
balanced and integrated oak. An outstanding palate, with luscious
blackcurrant fruit showing great length, balance and concentration.

CHAPEL HILL RESERVE CABERNET SHIRAZ
●●●●● $32

The Reserve appellation is kept for the best red wine of the year; in
1992 it was a blend of 67% Coonawarra cabernet sauvignon and
33% McLaren Vale shiraz. Superb oak handling and premium
quality fruit have produced a wine of the highest quality.

Cellaring 15–20-year potential. **Best Vintages** NA
Current Vintage '92
Matching Food Rich game or meat.
Tasting Note 1992 Medium to full purple-red; a wonderfully rich,
complex bouquet redolent of cassis fruit and vanillin oak. The palate
is concentrated and powerful with great texture; there is a seductive
mix of ripe blackcurrant and slightly more herbal fruit; the finish is
long, with fine tannins.

CHAPEL HILL RESERVE CHARDONNAY
●●●●● $19.95

Fully deserves the Reserve label. It is sourced from premium
vineyards in McLaren Vale and the Eden Valley and barrel
fermented in high quality French oak to produce a wine of great
style which is a consistent medal winner in shows.

Cellaring 1–5 years. **Best Vintages** '91, '92, '93
Current Vintage '93
Matching Food Slow-cooked fresh salmon.
Tasting Note 1993 Medium yellow-green; an exceptionally
complex, rich and stylish bouquet with striking barrel ferment oak
characters. The palate has intense melon and citrus fruit interwoven
with gently spicy oak, and an almost creamy texture. Totally
seductive.

CHAPEL HILL UNWOODED CHARDONNAY
●●●● $13

One of the new wave of unwooded Chardonnays, and one of the
better examples. Taking the oak out of Chardonnay is not a magic
solution which, through some process of alchemy, produces a better

wine. It simply produces a different, more direct style, and the fruit base has to be there. A blend of McLaren Vale, Padthaway and Barossa Valley fruit.

Cellaring Best to drink young. **Best Vintages** NA
Current Vintage '94
Matching Food Pasta, salads.
Tasting Note 1994 Medium yellow-green; the aroma is clean and smooth with melon/citrus/tropical fruits, and has the requisite richness. The palate shows the same fig/melon/citrus flavours, finishing with good acidity.

CHARLES CIMICKY WINES

★★★★ 13.50–18.50 CD AUS34, 111
Barossa Valley **Est.** 1972
Gomersal Road, Lyndoch, SA 5351
Ph (085) 24 4025 **Fax** (085) 24 4772
Open 7 days 10.30–4.30 **Production** 7000
Winemaker(s) Charles Cimicky
These wines are of very good quality, thanks to the lavish (but sophisticated) use of new French oak in tandem with high quality grapes. The intense, long-flavoured Sauvignon Blanc has been a particularly consistent performer, as has the rich, voluptuous American oaked Signature Shiraz.
Principal Wines Sauvignon Blanc, Chardonnay, Cabernet Sauvignon, Signature Shiraz, Old Fireside Tawny Port.

CHARLES MELTON WINES

★★★★☆ 9.50–15.90 R AUSSD UK11, 66, 101
Barossa Valley **Est.** 1984
Krondorf Road., Tanunda, SA 5352
Ph (085) 63 3606 **Fax** (085) 63 3422
Open 7 days 11–5 **Production** 6000
Winemaker(s) Charlie Melton
Charlie Melton, one of the Barossa Valley's great characters, with wife Virginia by his side, makes some of the most eagerly sought à la mode wines in Australia. It will be interesting to see whether they ignore the pressure to expand the tiny winery.
Principal Wines Rosé of Virginia, Cabernet Franc, Pinot Hermitage, Shiraz, Cabernet Sauvignon, Nine Popes (Shiraz Grenache Mourvedre), Sparkling.

CHARLES MELTON CABERNET SAUVIGNON
●●●● $15.90
Made from carefully selected Barossa Valley vineyards, with the accent on fresh berry fruit, and the wine released well before most Cabernet Sauvignons of its weight. Whether a little more time in barrel, and a little more time on cork before release might improve the wine further is a question which has to be asked.
Cellaring 5+ years. **Best Vintages** '90, '91, '92, '93
Current Vintage '93

Matching Food Roast duck, hare.
Tasting Note 1993 Medium red-purple; youthful, zippy, fresh
berry fruit with just a hint of American oak. The palate has
abundant, bright, juicy red berry fruit with a hint of mint, and
minimal tannins. Is however, a fraction callow on the finish.

CHARLES MELTON GRENACHE
●●●● ▶ $16
It should come as no surprise that, having recognised the virtues of
dry-grown, low-yielding Barossa grenache over five years ago when
he introduced Nine Popes, Charlie Melton should now be making a
straight varietal. The style of the wine is not unlike Nine Popes, with
slightly more fresh red berry fruit flavours. Very much à la mode.
Cellaring Now–2 years. **Best Vintages** '93
Current Vintage '93
Matching Food High-class hamburger.
Tasting Note 1993 Medium to full red; the bouquet is of medium
intensity with gamey Rhone-like aromas to the red berry fruit. The
palate is complex with a spectrum of game, mint and berry fruit
flavours, the oak subtle and restrained.

CHARLES MELTON NINE POPES
●●●●● $16
A label which is Australia's answer to California's Bonny Doon,
where Randall Grahm is the genius pulling the strings. Charlie
Melton is no slouch either, as this blend of low-yielding, dry-grown
shiraz, grenache and mourvedre handsomely shows. Melton realised
the supreme quality of these vines well before most others, and the
market has now caught up with his vision.
Cellaring Each way; now or in 5 years.
Best Vintages '90, '91, '92, '93
Current Vintage '93
Matching Food Full-blooded Italian cuisine.
Tasting Note 1993 Medium to full red-purple; rich dark cherry
and briary fruit with masses of creamy, vanillin oak on the bouquet.
The palate shows the same abundant creamy vanillin American oak
with wonderfully rich, ripe fruit, and good structure.

CHARLES MELTON ROSÉ OF VIRGINIA
●●●● ▶ $9.95
One of the most interesting Rosés currently made in Australia,
produced from grenache, and presumably a partial by-product of
Nine Popes juice run-off. It has much more fruit flavour than a
standard Rosé, at least being more a cross between a standard
Rosé and a Beaujolais style. Tremendous summer drinking.
Cellaring Drink now. **Best Vintages** NA
Current Vintage '94
Matching Food Light Mediterranean dishes.
Tasting Note 1994 Vivid purple-red of medium depth; abundant
red and black cherry fruit aromas, clean and vibrant. The palate is
fresh and fruitily exuberant with a sweet middle palate and a dry
finish. They don't come much better.

CHARLES STURT UNIVERSITY WINERY

★★★☆ 10–16.50 R AUS3, 72
Hilltops **Est.** 1977
Boorooma Street, North Wagga Wagga, NSW 2650
Ph (069) 22 2435 **Fax** (069) 22 2107
Open 7 days 10–4 **Production** 12 000
Winemaker(s) Rodney Hooper
A fully functioning commercial winery with wines made by Rodney
Hooper, which also acts as a teaching institution. Inevitably there
are some tensions between the two roles, but since the arrival of
Rodney Hooper, there has been a noticeable lift in wine quality
and consistency.
Principal Wines Cowra Chardonnay, Traminer Riesling,
Sauvignon Blanc Semillon, Botrytis Semillon, Coonawarra Cabernet
Sauvignon, Sparkling, Fortified.

CHARLES STURT UNIVERSITY COONAWARRA CABERNET SAUVIGNON

●●● ▶ $16.50
Another slightly sporadic release, invariably well made, although
from time to time one suspects an element of high cropping in the
vineyard, as in 1992.
Cellaring 2–4 years. **Best Vintages** '88, '90, '91, '92
Current Vintage '92
Matching Food Lamb fillets.
Tasting Note 1992 Medium to full red; cool-grown, slightly
leafy/gamey edges to the red berry fruit of the bouquet. The palate
is pleasant with well balanced fruit in the leaf/minty spectrum, and
appropriately subtle oak. Soft tannins.

CHARLES STURT UNIVERSITY COWRA CHARDONNAY

●●●● ▶ $14.50
Charles Sturt University has only limited vineyards of its own, the
primary function of which is for teaching and experimental purposes.
It purchases fruit from various parts of Australia, often on an irregular
basis, so that the Chardonnays come and go — frustratingly at
times. It would be nice to think that this wine becomes a regular part
of the roster.
Cellaring Short term. **Best Vintages** NA **Current Vintage** '93
Matching Food Prawns, creamy pasta.
Tasting Note 1993 Medium yellow-green; a complex bouquet
with a range of buttery/peachy/grapefruit aromas allied with
sophisticated use of oak. A stylish and surprisingly elegant wine for
the region, with a fine, long palate and good barrel ferment
characters.

CHARLEY BROTHERS WINES *

★★★☆ 7.50–12 CD AUSSD
Hastings Valley **Est.** 1988
The Ruins Way, Inneslake, Port Macquarie, NSW 2444
Ph (065) 81 0381 **Fax** (065) 81 0391

Open Mon–Fri 2.30–4.30, W'ends 10–5 **Production** 1000
Winemaker(s) John Cassegrain, Drew Noon (Contract)
The property upon which the Charley Brothers vineyards are
established has been in the family's ownership since the turn of the
century, but in fact had been planted to vines by a Major Innes in
the 1840s. After carrying on logging and fruit growing at various
times, the Charley family planted vines in 1988 with the
encouragement of John Cassegrain, who acts as contract
winemaker. A little over 9 hectares of vines have been established.
Principal Wines Semillon, Chardonnay, Pinot Noir, Cabernet
Merlot; second Innerslake label: Summer White and Dry Red.

CHARLEY BROTHERS CABERNET MERLOT
●●● ▶ $ NA
A blend of 91% cabernet sauvignon and 9% merlot, made from the
first crop of the estate plantings. No longer available, but interesting
because it indicates just what can be achieved if the vintage
conditions are right.
Cellaring 4–6 years. **Best Vintages** '91, '93
Current Vintage NA
Matching Food Chinese duck with mushrooms.
Tasting Note 1991 Medium to full red-purple; showing mature
bottle-developed characters, but attractive and fragrant nonetheless,
with earthy berry aromas. There is plenty of richness and weight on
the palate with soft blackcurrant fruit, and nice tannins on the finish.

CHARLEY BROTHERS CHARDONNAY
●●● $11
Produced from 2.2 hectares of estate plantings. The style is not
dissimilar to that of the Hunter Valley, reflecting the warm growing
conditions, and is relatively fast maturing, although the no-longer-
available '91 vintage still shows fairly crisp, melon fruit.
Cellaring 1–3 years. **Best Vintages** '91, '93
Current Vintage '93
Matching Food Moreton Bay bugs.
Tasting Note 1993 Medium to full yellow-green; a big, ripe
peachy bouquet with lots of tropical aromas. A generously-flavoured
wine with nutty/peachy fruit which toughens off slightly on the finish.

CHARLEY BROTHERS SHIRAZ
●●● ▶ $10
With the high humidity and high rainfall of the region, viticulture
(and winemaking) will always pose challenges — particularly in
years such as 1992. But in years such as 1991 and 1993, very
pleasant wines can be made, as this Shiraz demonstrates. It comes
from 2 hectares of estate plantings.
Cellaring 3–4 years. **Best Vintages** NA **Current Vintage** '93
Matching Food Firm cheddar.
Tasting Note 1993 Strong red-purple; a fairly firm style with
earthy varietal fruit, and a hint of vanillin American oak. The palate
is firm and fresh, seemingly showing some young vine characters but
with pleasant, clean shiraz fruit, finishing with soft tannins.

CHATEAU DORÉ

NR 9–14 CD AUSSD
Bendigo **Est.** 1860
Mandurang Road, via Bendigo, Vic 3551
Ph (054) 39 5278
Open Tues–Sun 10–6 **Production** 1000
Winemaker(s) Ivan Gross
Has been in the ownership of the Gross family since 1860 with the
winery buildings dating back respectively to 1860 and 1893. All
wine is sold through cellar door.
Principal Wines Riesling, Shiraz, Cabernet Sauvignon, Tawny
Port.

CHATEAU DORRIEN

NR 7.90–9.90 CD AUSSD
Barossa Valley **Est.** 1983
Cnr Seppeltsfield Road & Barossa Valley Way, Dorrien, SA 5352
Ph (085) 62 2850
Open 7 days 10–5 **Production** 1000
Winemaker(s) Fernando Martin
Unashamedly and successfully directed at the tourist trade.
Principal Wines Riesling, Chablis, Chardonnay, Semillon,
Auslese Riesling, Hermitage, Cabernet Sauvignon, Fortified.

CHATEAU FRANCOIS

★★★ 10 ML AUSSD
Hunter Valley **Est.** 1969
Broke Road, Pokolbin, NSW 2321
Ph (049) 98 7548
Open W'ends 9–5 or by appt **Production** 800
Winemaker(s) Don Francois
The retirement hobby of former NSW Director of Fisheries, Don
Francois. Soft-flavoured and structured wines which frequently show
regional characters, but which are modestly priced and are all sold
through the cellar door and mailing list to a loyal following. The
tasting room is available for private dinners for 12 to 16 people.
Principal Wines Pokolbin Mallee, Semillon, Chardonnay, Shiraz,
Pinot Noir.

CHATEAU HORNSBY *

NR 12–18 CD AUSSD
Northern Territory **Est.** 1976
Petrick Road, Alice Springs, NT 0870
Ph (089) 55 5133 **Fax** (089) 55 5133
Open 7 days 11–4 **Production** NFP
Winemaker(s) Gordon Cook
Draws in part upon 3 hectares of estate plantings, and in part from
grapes and wines purchased from other regions. Very much a tourist-
oriented operation, with numerous allied entertainments on offer.

Principal Wines Riesling, Semillon, Chardonnay, Shiraz, Cabernet Sauvignon.

CHATEAU LEAMON

★★☆ 10–16 CD AUS17, 28, 72
Bendigo **Est.** 1973
Calder Highway, Bendigo, Vic 3550
Ph (054) 47 7995 **Fax** (054) 47 0855
Open Wed–Sun 10–5 **Production** 3000
Winemaker(s) Ian Leamon
Has produced some wonderful wines over the years; the 1980
Hermitage Cabernet drunk in 1994 was as fresh as a daisy, with
wonderful mint and cherry fruit. It is to be hoped that Ian Leamon
(the son of the founders Phil and Alma) can put the winery back on
track.
Principal Wines Riesling, Semillon Chardonnay, Pinot Noir,
Shiraz, Cabernet Sauvignon.

CHATEAU LEAMON PINOT NOIR
●●● $15
A new departure for Chateau Leamon, using grapes grown by
Christopher Bennett, high in the Strathbogie Ranges of Central
Victoria. Much of the pinot noir from this area presently goes to
sparkling wine, and there is obvious potential for table wine usage.
Cellaring Drink now. **Best Vintages** NA **Current Vintage** '92
Matching Food Quail, duck.
Tasting Note 1992 Medium to full red; a quite stylish bouquet
with a mixture of strawberry, tobacco and stalky aromas. The palate
has good structure and length, although the fruit has already altered
to secondary characteristics. Finishes a fraction too firm for my taste.

CHATEAU PATO

★★★☆ 8.50–25 CD AUSSD
Hunter Valley **Est.** 1978
Thompson's Road, Pokolbin, NSW 2321
Ph (049) 98 7634
Open By appt **Production** 300
Winemaker(s) Nicholas Paterson, Roger Paterson
Nicholas and Roger Paterson have taken over responsibility for this
tiny winery following the death of their father David Paterson during
the 1993 vintage. It is a much loved, if tiny, Hunter landmark, with
vintages back to 1986 available at the microscopic cellar door.
Principal Wines Gewurztraminer, Hermitage.

CHATEAU REMY

★★★ 8.50–22 R AUS97, 128 UK79
Pyrenees **Est.** 1963
Vinoca Road, Avoca, Vic 3467
Ph (054) 65 3202 **Fax** (054) 65 3529
Open 7 days 10–4.30 **Production** 42 500

Winemaker(s) Vincent Gere

Notwithstanding its distinguished French ownership, the perseverance of winemaker Vincent Gere, a very well-equipped winery, and lavish marketing expenditure, Chateau Remy has struggled. However, the move to table wine production is sensible, and the Fiddlers Creek label often represents great value for money.

Principal Wines Sparkling; Blue Pyrenees Chardonnay, Cabernet Sauvignon, Sparkling; Fiddlers Creek Chardonnay, Sauvignon Blanc, Semillon, Pinot Noir, Cabernet Shiraz.

CHATEAU REMY BLUE PYRENEES BRUT
●●● $17

Chateau Remy has had a long struggle to convert from its original function of brandy production to sparkling and table wine. Notwithstanding the substitution of chardonnay and pinot noir for the original trebbiano, the sparkling wines have failed to inspire. Vincent Gere perseveres, and this is the best release yet.

Cellaring None required. **Best Vintages** NA
Current Vintage NA
Matching Food Aperitif style.
Tasting Note NV Light to medium green-yellow; a restrained, tight and clean bouquet, but not terribly complex. The palate has citrussy, slightly green fruit, perhaps reflecting the tightrope the winemaker has to walk in an area a little too warm for quality sparkling wine production.

CHATEAU REMY BLUE PYRENEES CHARDONNAY
●●● ▶ $21

A new direction for the premium Blue Pyrenees label of Chateau Remy, and which may well point the way for the future. 1993 is the first release of the wine (which, to avoid confusion, is a table wine, not sparkling).

Cellaring Short term. **Best Vintages** NA **Current Vintage** '93
Matching Food Lightly-sauced fish.
Tasting Note 1993 Light green-yellow; fragrant white peach and melon fruit with good oak handling and integration. The palate is rather lighter than the bouquet suggests, but is well structured, with clear varietal fruit and a good finish.

CHATEAU REYNELLA

★★★★☆ 6.95–19.95 R AUS20–24 UK18 US8
Southern Vales **Est.** 1838
Reynella Road, Reynella, SA 5161
Ph (08) 381 2266 **Fax** (08) 381 1968
Open 7 days 10–4.30 **Production** 12 500
Winemaker(s) David O'Leary (Red), Tom Newton (White)
A splendidly economical range of four wines with an equally laudably consistent winery style. The only thing that puzzles me is the ridiculously low price at which the wines are sold.
Principal Wines Chardonnay, Basket Pressed Shiraz, Basket Pressed Cabernet Sauvignon, Basket Pressed Cabernet Merlot.

CHATEAU REYNELLA BASKET PRESSED CABERNET MERLOT

●●●● ▶ $13.95

Winemaker David O'Leary is very enamoured of the soft pressing obtained through the use of traditional basket press; it is interesting to note that the $10 million Opus One winery in the Napa Valley has opted for a press of this kind, often seen as old-fashioned. The blend of cabernet and merlot works as well as ever, much of the fruit coming from the vines around the winery.

Cellaring 4–7 years. **Best Vintages** '88, '90, '92, '92, '94
Current Vintage '92
Matching Food Barbecued rack of lamb.
Tasting Note 1992 Medium to full red; a very strong bouquet with briary, bramble, cedary fruit and a considerable charred oak input. On the palate very powerful with plenty of fruit and abundant oak impact, and a long finish.

CHATEAU REYNELLA BASKET PRESSED CABERNET SAUVIGNON

●●●● $13.95

As with the other reds in the Basket Pressed range, there is a very substantial oak input. It may just be the vagaries of vintage, but the wine does not have quite the same volume of fruit as the other two reds, and hence not quite enough to carry that oak input. With all, an impressive wine at the price.

Cellaring 5 years. **Best Vintages** '88, '90, '91, '92, '94
Current Vintage '92
Matching Food Strongly-flavoured cheese.
Tasting Note 1992 Medium to full red-purple; dense, solid fruit which is fairly ripe in the dark berry spectrum, with substantial oak. The palate is similar, dense and fractionally extractive, with a finish which needs to soften, and may well do so given time.

CHATEAU REYNELLA BASKET PRESSED SHIRAZ

●●●● ▶ $13.95

Made from McLaren Vale grapes and handled in very much the same way as its two red stablemates. Like those other wines, is very complex, and is an great bargain at the price.

Cellaring 5+ years. **Best Vintages** '88, '90, '91, '92, '94
Current Vintage '92
Matching Food Kangaroo fillet.
Tasting Note 1992 Medium to full red-purple; elegant fruit with hints of dark cherry and chocolate, and sophisticated oak handling. The wine is fragrant and intense, with chocolate and cherry flavours, and a long, intense finish. The tannins and oak are interwoven.

CHATEAU REYNELLA CHARDONNAY

●●●● $13.95

May play second fiddle to the three red wines from Chateau Reynella, but is nonetheless a consistently impressive wine. Made from McLaren Vale grapes, often underestimated for their quality, and skilfully made with a blend of 50% American and 50% French

oak, the wine is invariably rich and complex, even if in a moderately oaky style.
Cellaring 1–3 years. **Best Vintages** '85, '90, '91, '93, '94
Current Vintage '93
Matching Food Grilled spatchcock.
Tasting Note 1993 Medium to full yellow-green; intense citrus, peach and melon fruit with complex barrel ferment oak aromas. The palate shows rather more oak influence than the bouquet, but finishes with good fruit and acidity. Plenty going on here.

CHATEAU TAHBILK

★★★★ 10.95–49.95 R AUS27, 167–170, 186 UK75
Goulburn Valley **Est.** 1860
Goulburn Valley Highway, Tabilk, Vic 3607
Ph (057) 94 2555 **Fax** (057) 94 2360
Open Mon–Sat 9–5, Sun 11–5 **Production** 95 000
Winemaker(s) Alister Purbrick
A winery steeped in tradition (with high National Trust classification) which should be visited at least once by every wine-conscious Australian, and which makes wines — particularly red wines — utterly in keeping with that tradition. The essence of that heritage comes in the form of the tiny quantities of now beautifully packaged Shiraz made entirely from vines planted in 1862.
Principal Wines Riesling, Chardonnay, Marsanne, Shiraz, Cabernet Saubignon.

CHATEAU TAHBILK CABERNET SAUVIGNON
●●●● $12.95
As with all of the Tahbilk wines, estate-grown, produced from a significant percentage of old vines. This is terroir speaking, the hand of the maker being deliberately withdrawn.
Cellaring Typically 15 or more years. **Best Vintages** '81, '83, '86, '91, '94 **Current Vintage** '91
Matching Food Strong mature cheddar, stilton.
Tasting Note 1991 Medium to full red-purple; solidly ripe, with sweet blackcurrant fruit and slightly earthy undertones. The palate is very concentrated with masses of fruit and tannins in abundance, yet (potentially) balanced.

CHATEAU TAHBILK MARSANNE
●●●● $10.95
The best known of Chateau Tahbilk's wines, with an illustrious history. Made in a very simple and direct fashion, in total contrast to neighbour Mitchelton, and in particular without the use of oak. Like young traditional semillon, frequently needs time to come into its own.
Cellaring 1–20 years. **Best Vintages** '86, '90, '92, '94
Current Vintage '93
Matching Food Lighter Italian or Asian dishes.
Tasting Note 1993 Light yellow-green; light but crisp aromas in the straw/honeysuckle spectrum expected of the variety. There is

power and length to the mid to back palate, with those distinctive
and yet hard to define marsanne flavours. Much lighter than the
more powerful '92.

CHATEAU TAHBILK RHINE RIESLING
●●●● $10.95
Chateau Tahbilk is not particularly well known for its Rhine Riesling,
yet has accumulated a trophy, 11 gold, 26 silver and 51 bronze
medals for this wine since its introduction in 1980. As with all the
Tahbilk wines, estate-grown, and again, as with all Tahbilk wines,
particularly generous in flavour.
Cellaring Early-developing style. **Best Vintages** '86, '90, '92,
'94 **Current Vintage** '94
Matching Food Seafood salad.
Tasting Note 1994 Light green-yellow; full and rich with lots of
limey fruit aromas, generous and slightly broad. In the mouth, a big,
powerful wine with lots of fruit flavour and quite good length.

CHATEAU TAHBILK SHIRAZ
●●● ▶ $11.95
A rock of ages, deliberately made by Alister Purbrick in precisely the
same way as the wines of 10, 20, 30 and 40 years ago. There is
invariably tremendous colour, flavour and extract, with little or no
oak influence. The only question about the wines is whether they
need five, 10 or 20 years in the cellar.
Cellaring Long term. **Best Vintages** '81, '83, '86, '91, '94
Current Vintage '91
Matching Food Barbecued T-bone steak.
Tasting Note 1991 Medium to full red; abundant ripe, earthy
shiraz varietal fruit reflecting the warm vintage. A huge wine on the
palate with earthy/berry fruit and lots of tannins. Needs a decade.

CHATEAU XANADU
★★★★ 12–33.50 R AUS17, 111 UK55, 100
Margaret River **Est.** 1977
Railway Terrace off Wallcliffe Road, Margaret River, WA 6285
Ph (097) 57 2581 **Fax** (097) 57 3389
Open 7 days 10–5 **Production** 13 500
Winemaker(s) Jürg Muggli
Samuel Taylor Coleridge would thoroughly approve of the current
crop of labels on the Chateau Xanadu wines, and one imagines
would be equally pleased with wine quality — quality which can
be excitingly variable, but is currently good.
Principal Wines Semillon, Chardonnay, Secession Semillon
Sauvignon Blanc, Noble Semillon, Featherwhite Rosé, Cabernet
Sauvignon.

CHATEAU XANADU CABERNET SAUVIGNON
●●●● $19.50
Extraordinary packaging has been a feature of the Chateau Xanadu
wines in recent years, but the label of the '92 Cabernet Sauvignon is

an absolutely outstanding piece of graphic design. The wine itself, released under both a standard and Reserve label, is in the typical Margaret River style, edged with astringency and needing time. The Reserve can be outstanding.

Cellaring 5 years. **Best Vintages** '83, '84, '86, '90, '91, '93
Current Vintage '93
Matching Food Strong, aged cheddar.
Tasting Note 1993 Strong red-purple; much more fruit sweetness than was evident in the '92, with nicely ripened red berry fruits which are most harmonious on the bouquet. An attractive wine on the palate, perhaps less concentrated than the '91, which it resembles, but with excellent fruit flavour and well weighted tannins.

CHATEAU XANADU RESERVE CABERNET SAUVIGNON
●●●● ▶ $33.50
Can be absolutely outstanding, as it was in 1991. This wine won the trophy for best Margaret River Red at the 1993 SGIO WA Wine Awards, and it is not hard to see why.

Cellaring 10 years. **Best Vintages** '83, '84, '86, '90, '91
Current Vintage '91
Matching Food Roast lamb.
Tasting Note 1991 Medium to full red; a supremely elegant bouquet with fragrant cedary/briary/chocolate aromas. The palate has classic cabernet varietal fruit with cedary oak and soft but persistent tannins on a long finish.

CHATEAU XANADU SECESSION
●●●● $14.50
A new label with the startling innovative design found on most of the Chateau Xanadu wines. Although the label is not specific on the issue, the wine quite evidently is primarily semillon and sauvignon blanc.

Cellaring Now–2 years. **Best Vintages** '93, '94
Current Vintage '94
Matching Food Ultimate seafood style.
Tasting Note 1994 Brilliant, light green-yellow; a powerful wine on the bouquet with lots of grip to the grass/hay aromas. The palate, too, has plenty of power, particularly on the mid palate, finishing with an ever-so-slightly-oily character.

CHATEAU YALDARA

★★★☆ 5.80–83 R AUS38–40 UK86
Barossa Valley **Est.** 1947
Gomersal Road, Lyndoch, SA 5351
Ph (085) 24 4200 **Fax** (085) 24 4678
Open 7 days 9–5 **Production** 550 000
Winemaker(s) Robert Thumm, Jim Irvine
A thriving operation with a turnover in excess of $15 million and which employs 145 people nationally, now successfully entering the export market with the Lakewood and Acacia Hill brands. The wines are all carefully styled for their market niches, and are made with a high degree of technical and production expertise.

Principal Wines A kaleidoscopic array of wines under (in ascending order) the Lyndoch Valley, Millstream, Acacia Hill, Ducks Flat, Yaldara, Lakewood and recently released super-premium The Farms labels. The Lakewood range is the largest, covering all major wine styles and varietals. There is also a substantial range of sparkling, non-alcoholic and fortified wines.

CHATEAU YALDARA LAKEWOOD SAUVIGNON BLANC SEMILLON
●●● $9.95

A blend of 55% sauvignon blanc and 45% semillon. It is made in archetypal Lakewood style with plenty of fruit and with significant sweetness from residual sugar. There is no question that this is what the legion of Lakewood consumers want, and it is what they will get.

Cellaring Drink now. **Best Vintages** '94
Current Vintage '94
Matching Food Paella.
Tasting Note 1994 Light green-yellow; a fruity, tropical passionfruit and gooseberry-accented bouquet leads on to a full-flavoured palate with rather cloying sweetness.

CHATEAU YALDARA LAKEWOOD WHITMORE GRENACHE
●●● ▶ $12.95

One would have been surprised if Lakewood had not capitalised on the sudden popularity of grenache, and likewise had it not been able to source an old dry-grown vineyard. Mark Whitmore's vineyard is just that, producing dry-grown 14 baume grenache, fermented in open fermenters under heading boards. The emphasis is on the ripe fruit, not oak, which is as it should be.

Cellaring Drink now. **Best Vintages** '94
Current Vintage '94
Matching Food Stir-fried beef.
Tasting Note 1994 Medium red-purple; lush, slightly jammy berry fruit with a hint of mulberry. The palate has abundant sweet berry flavours and soft tannins, but a slightly hard finish deriving from the alcohol.

CHATEAU YALDARA THE FARMS MERLOT
●●●● $83

Jim Irvine believes in making a statement with Merlot, and has certainly done so with this wine. You can buy a 6-litre double magnum for $480 if you wish. The Merlot achieved 15 baume, with the fruit said to be in perfect physiological condition.

Cellaring 10+ years. **Best Vintages** NA
Current Vintage '91
Matching Food Best left in the cellar.
Tasting Note 1991 Medium to full red; immensely ripe, chocolatey sweet fruit aromas, bearing as much resemblance to the Merlot of France as the Sahara Desert does to the South Pole. The palate has a curious empty entry to the mouth, filling out to massive chocolatey fruit and oak on the mid palate, finishing with full tannins.

CHATEAU YALDARA THE FARMS MERLOT CABERNET SAUVIGNON

●●●● ▶ $26.60

The new super-premium flagship, with four wines in the range: this wine, a straight Merlot, a Semillon and a Tawny Port. The Merlot Cabernet is by far the best of the table wines; 500 cases were produced, packaged in 750-ml, 1.5-litre and 6-litre bottles. The grapes come from a single vineyard in the Lyndoch Valley, although the name 'The Farms' is that of a newly-acquired 100-hectare vineyard property adjacent to the Lakewood winery.

Cellaring Up to 10 years. **Best Vintages** NA
Current Vintage '91
Matching Food Beef bourguignon.
Tasting Note 1991 Dark red; powerful, ripe berry and chocolate aromas with rich vanillin oak, said to be French. The palate is a nicely balanced combination of extremely generous, lush berry and chocolate fruit flavours counterbalanced by soft, dusty tannins, the latter coming from the Cabernet component. Good wine.

CHATSFIELD WINES

★★★★☆ 13.95–17 AUS56, 74, 127, 168
Great Southern **Est.** 1976
O'Neil Road, Mount Barker, WA 6324
Ph (098) 51 1704 **Fax** (098) 51 1704
Open Tues–Sun, Public hols 10–5 **Production** 2600
Winemaker(s) Various Contract

Irish-born medical practitioner Ken Lynch and daughter Siobhan can be very proud of their achievements at Chatsfield, as can the various contract winemakers who have taken the high quality estate-grown material and made such impressive wines.

Principal Wines Mount Barker Riesling, Gewurztraminer, Chardonnay, Cabernet Franc, Shiraz.

CHATSFIELD CABERNET FRANC

●●●● ▶ $13.95

Provocatively made and released as an early-drinking style, and so attractive (and unusual) that I had no hesitation in including it in my Top 100 for 1994 in *The Weekend Australian Magazine*. The wine is challenging, because it is fermented in tank and taken straight to bottle, without any wood maturation at any stage.

Cellaring Drink now. **Best Vintages** '94 **Current Vintage** '94
Matching Food Breast of duck.
Tasting Note 1994 Vivid, youthful purple; the bouquet is vibrant, with dark earthy berry aromas, the palate lush and soft, and surprisingly mouthfilling. The flavours are in the juicy red and blackcurrant spectrum.

CHATSFIELD CHARDONNAY

●●●● $15.95

By no means a flashy wine, made in a reserved style, and unequivocally showing its cool-climate background, often seeming

more like a cross between sauvignon blanc and chardonnay than anything else. Will mature well with age.
Cellaring Up to 5 years. **Best Vintages** '87, '89, '90, '93
Current Vintage '93
Matching Food Smoked salmon.
Tasting Note 1993 Medium yellow-green; the bouquet is quite concentrated and firm, in a tight, cool style with the suggestion of a touch of botrytis somewhere at work. The palate has an unusual array of flavours, with citrussy/herbal notes along with the more conventional peach and melon.

CHATSFIELD GEWURZTRAMINER
●●● ▶ $13.95
While it may not be the most trendy variety, this wine shows exemplary varietal character in a light mould. It has not been propped up with residual sugar, and ages remarkably well, as the 1990 vintage showed at the 1994 Mount Barker Wine Show.
Cellaring Up to 5 years. **Best Vintages** '90, '93
Current Vintage '94
Matching Food Asian.
Tasting Note 1994 Light yellow-green; spotlessly clean bouquet with marked spice and lychee aromas. The palate is a little lighter than the bouquet suggests it may be, with crisp spice and lime flavours, and a clean, delicate finish.

CHATSFIELD MOUNT BARKER RIESLING
●●●● ▶ $13.95
A classic Riesling which, like the best of its region, ages superbly. The '94 is a very good wine, and unlucky not to do much better at the 1994 Mount Barker Wine Show, and with a guaranteed future.
Cellaring 5–8 years. **Best Vintages** '85, '87, '89, '90, '93
Current Vintage '94
Matching Food Mild Thai soup.
Tasting Note 1994 Medium yellow-green; a fine and fragrant bouquet with hints of passionfruit and lime. The palate is intense with finely structured citrus and herbal flavours; the only possible criticism is a slightly firm, peppery finish which will soften with time.

CHATSFIELD SHIRAZ
●●●●● $17
A glorious wine, one of the best from Mount Barker, rivalled only by Plantagenet. I tasted three vintages (blind, of course) at the 1994 Mount Barker Wine Show, and every one received a gold medal on my score sheet. It is hard to choose between the '90, '91 and '92 for quality, and the style is remarkably consistent.
Cellaring 5–7 years. **Best Vintages** '88, '90, '91, '92
Current Vintage '92
Matching Food Mature cheddar, finer red meat dishes.
Tasting Note 1992 Medium red-purple; an extremely fragrant bouquet of cherry, spice and liquorice, with subtle oak. The palate is quite marvellous, with flesh and weight, loaded with Rhone character, and all of the liquorice and cherry flavours promised by the bouquet.

CHESTNUT GROVE *

NR NA AUSSD
Warren Valley **Est.** 1988
Perrup Road, Manjimup, WA 6258
Ph (097) 71 1557
Open By appt **Production** 1000
Winemaker(s) Alkoomi (Contract)
A joint venture between the Lange family of Alkoomi and Vic Kordic
and his family, through to grandson Darren Cook. The first wines
were released in April 1993; young vine characters are evident,
and as yet the wines lack intensity.
Principal Wines Chardonnay, Verdelho, Pinot Noir, Cabernet
Merlot.

CHESTNUT GROVE CHARDONNAY

●●● ▶ $14.95
One of a trio of new releases for this recently established winery.
The '94 is very competently made, although a combination of young
vine character and the suspicion of relatively high yields gives an
impression that the wine is fractionally dilute. For all that, the best of
the three.
Cellaring 1–2 years. **Best Vintages** NA **Current Vintage** '94
Matching Food White-fleshed fish.
Tasting Note 1994 Light green-yellow; the bouquet is spotlessly
clean, with gentle citrus and melon fruit and subtle oak. The palate is
similar, with clean, fresh, crisp citrus and melon fruit finishing with
good acid. The wine simply lacks intensity.

CHESTNUT GROVE VERDELHO

●●● $12.95
Verdelho has always been a favourite son of the west, but whether it
is truly suited to all of Western Australia's wine regions remains to
be seen. There is a school of thought which suggests it needs a
warmer rather than a cooler climate to show its best. Perhaps once
the vines are mature, it will prove its ability to perform well in a
range of climates, just as chardonnay does.
Cellaring 1–3 years. **Best Vintages** NA **Current Vintage** '94
Matching Food Asian prawns.
Tasting Note 1994 Light yellow-green; a faintly floral/honeysuckle
aroma leads the bouquet, which is fresh and crisp, albeit light. There
is no sign of oak on either the bouquet or palate; the latter is clean,
faintly sweet with gentle tropical fruit.

CHITTERING ESTATE

★★☆ 9.50–19.50 R AUS102, UK25
Darling Range **Est.** 1982
PO Box 280, Chittering Valley Road, Chittering WA 6084
Ph (09) 237 6250 **Fax** (09) 273 6251
Open Not **Production** 12 000
Winemaker(s) Francois Jacquard
Burgundian-trained Francois Jacquard, ex-Domaine Dujac and then

Bannockburn, is now in charge of winemaking at Chittering Estate.
Vintages up to and including 1992 are, however, way out of
Australian mainstream style, and much of the wine is exported.
Principal Wines Chardonnay, Sauvignon Blanc, Pinot Noir,
Cabernet Merlot.

CIAVARELLA WINES *

NR 7–15 CD AUSSD
North East Victoria **Est.** 1978
Evans Lane, Oxley, Vic 3678
Ph (057) 27 3384
Open 7 days 10–6 **Production** NFP
Winemaker(s) Cyril Ciavarella
The Ciavarellas have been grape growers in the King Valley for
almost 20 years, selling their grapes to wineries such as Brown
Brothers. Changes in the grape marketplace led to Ciavarella
deciding to make limited quantities of wines, which were first
offered for sale from the cellar door in early 1994.
Principal Wines Chenin Blanc, Chardonnay, Shiraz, Cabernet
Sauvignon.

CLARENDON HILLS WINERY

★★★★★ 18–24 R AUS50, 144 UK65
Southern Vales **Est.** 1989
Brookmans Road, Blewitt Springs, SA 5171
Ph (08) 364 0227 **Fax** (08) 364 1484
Open By appt **Production** 1500
Winemaker(s) Roman Bratasiuk
After a period of partnership instability and the industry rumour-mill
hard at work, Clarendon Hills is back doing what it has done from
the outset: producing some of the most startlingly concentrated, rich
and full-bodied red wines to be found in Australia, rivalled in this
respect only by Wendouree. The winery rating is given for power
and, if you like, effrontery.
Principal Wines Chardonnay, Pinot Noir, Merlot, Grenache,
Cabernet Sauvignon.

CLARENDON HILLS CABERNET SAUVIGNON
●●●● ▸ $22
Whether the much-touted comparisons with '92 Chateau Pichon-
Laland and '61 Chateau Latour are or were justified is not terribly
important. The fact is that since 1990, Clarendon Hills has come up
with powerful wines of impressively consistent style.
Cellaring 10–15 years. **Best Vintages** '90, '91, '92
Current Vintage '92
Matching Food Leave it alone.
Tasting Note 1992 Dark purple-red; a massively concentrated,
briary/berry bouquet with some leafy notes; the fruit swallows up
the oak. A big, almost brutal wine on the palate with cedary/briary
fruit, finishing with marked acidity.

CLARENDON HILLS MERLOT
●●●● $22
The '91 Merlot was a marvellous wine with lots of concentration but undeniably varietal character. The '93 vintage is almost a caricature of Merlot, so powerful and essency one can only imagine where it might head with age.
Cellaring 10+ years. **Best Vintages** '90, '91
Current Vintage '93
Matching Food Char-grilled rare rump.
Tasting Note 1993 Full red-purple; the bouquet is potent and intense with quite pronounced herbal, varietal merlot fruit. The palate is simply too powerful and extractive to be enjoyed at this stage.

CLARENDON HILLS OLD VINES GRENACHE
●●●● $18
This wine goes seriously over the top, and will have its fierce adherents simply for that reason.
Cellaring 20 years. **Best Vintages** NA
Current Vintage '93
Matching Food Impossible to conceive.
Tasting Note 1993 Medium to full purple; the bouquet is so concentrated it is almost impossible to find any fruit there, even suggesting it may be fractionally aldehydic. The palate is terrifying in its power on the palate, with massive extract, spicy fruit and all-pervading tannins.

CLARENDON HILLS SHIRAZ
●●●●● $24
By far the best of the current releases of Clarendon Hills, for while it is immensely concentrated and powerful, it is possible both to see the superb varietal fruit which has gone to make the wine, and not impossible to consider drinking it.
Cellaring 7–12 years. **Best Vintages** '90, '91, '92, '93
Current Vintage '93
Matching Food Venison, game.
Tasting Note 1993 Full red-purple; a rich and dense liquorice, chocolate and berry bouquet. The palate is eerily like a top Cotes Rotie, with abundant liquorice and cherry flavours, rich in the mouth, finishing with soft tannins.

CLEVELAND VINEYARD & WINERY

★★★☆ 10.95–22.95 R AUS144
Macedon **Est.** 1985
Shannon's Road, Lancefield, Vic 3435
Ph (054) 29 1449 **Fax** (054) 29 2017
Open 7 days 9–6 **Production** 2000
Winemaker(s) Keith Brien
The Cleveland homestead was built in 1889 in the style of a Gothic Revival manor house, but had been abandoned for 40 years when purchased by the Briens in 1983. It has since been painstakingly

restored, and 3.5 hectares of surrounding vineyard established. Cleveland has done best with Pinot Noir and Chardonnay, but the occasional Cabernet Sauvignon attests to an unusually favourable vineyard site in a very cool region.
Principal Wines Chardonnay, Pinot Noir, Cabernet Sauvignon, Sparkling; Brien Chardonnay.

CLEVELAND CABERNET SAUVIGNON
●●● ▶ $17.50
A far more difficult variety in the cool Macedon region, but flourishes in warm vintages such as 1991, albeit with unusual fruit flavours. In less favourable years, most vineyard sites (though not all) produce wines which are much leafier and tarter than most cool climate Australian Cabernets.
Cellaring 3–5 years. **Best Vintages** '91, '92
Current Vintage '91
Matching Food Ripened brie or camembert.
Tasting Note 1991 Bright red-purple; a fresh, sweet almost strawberry-accented aroma, which is most unusual. The palate also shows extremely sweet and ripe, almost into hyper-ripeness, fruit flavours. Altogether an unusual wine.

CLEVELAND PINOT NOIR
●●●● $17.50
The cool climate of the Macedon Ranges is clearly suited to pinot noir, but even this early-ripening variety has to be grown (and made) with skill to give the appropriate results. The steady progression from '90 to '91 to '92 in the quality and style of the Cleveland Pinot Noir shows that Keith Brien is mastering this most difficult grape.
Cellaring Drink now. **Best Vintages** '91, '92, '94
Current Vintage '92
Matching Food Char-grilled fresh salmon.
Tasting Note 1992 Light to medium red; quite scented, and hints of oriental spices; of medium weight and intensity overall, with plums and a touch of spice on the palate. Well made, and has good structure.

CLIFF HOUSE WINES
★★★ 15 R AUSSD
Tamar Valley **Est.** 1983
RSD 457, Kayena, Tas 7270
Ph (003) 94 7454 **Fax** (003) 94 7419
Open By appt **Production** 2500
Winemaker(s) Julian Alcorso (Contract)
Geoff and Cheryl Hewitt established 4 hectares of vineyard in the Tamar Valley area in 1983. The wines are made at Moorilla Estate and, as one would expect, are usually technically sound. The site, however, produces wines which are less robust than many of the Tamar Valley producers.
Principal Wines Riesling, Chardonnay, Pinot Noir, Cabernet Sauvignon.

CLONAKILLA VINEYARD

★★★★ 10–15 CD AUS62
Canberra **Est.** 1971
Crisps Lane, Off Gundaroo Road, Murrumbateman, NSW 2582
Ph (06) 251 1938
Open W'ends, Hols 11–5 **Production** 500
Winemaker(s) Dr John Kirk

Distinguished scientist Dr John Kirk (among other things, the author of some interesting papers on the measurement of vineyard climate) presides over this tiny winery. Shiraz is the shining star of Clonakilla, leaving the other wines — adequate though they are — in its wake. Production in 1994 was reduced by the frost which affected the entire Canberra district.

Principal Wines Riesling, Chardonnay, Semillon Sauvignon Blanc, Brown Muscat, Shiraz, Cabernets.

CLONAKILLA RIESLING

●●● ▶ $14

While not in the same class as the Shiraz, this estate-grown wine is both durable and reliable, even if the level of sweetness is specifically aimed at cellar door sales.

Cellaring Now–3 years. **Best Vintages** '90, '92, '94
Current Vintage '94
Matching Food Honey-glazed ham.
Tasting Note 1994 Light yellow-green; the bouquet has strong lime juice aromas with some faintly powdery aspects. A rich and full wine on the palate with lots of weight and extract, verging on heavy, with sweet, tropical fruit.

CLONAKILLA SHIRAZ

●●●●● $15

In the majority of years, Clonakilla makes superlative Shiraz, doing so in '90, '92, and '93. Quite why the wine should be so strikingly different from any other Canberra district Shiraz is one of those mysteries; most of the wine is sold through cellar door and mailing list, and is well worth the effort.

Cellaring An each-way proposition. **Best Vintages** '90, '92, '93
Current Vintage '93
Matching Food Jugged hare.
Tasting Note 1993 Dense purple-red; very concentrated liquorice briary fruit aromas with minimal oak influence. In the mouth, classic shiraz of the highest quality; liquorice, dark cherry, spice and briary flavours all present in a very concentrated wine.

CLOVER HILL *

★★★★ 28 R AUS27, 84, 85, 167, 179 UK87
Pipers Brook **Est.** 1986
Clover Hill Road, Lebrina, Tas 7254
Ph (003) 95 6114 **Fax** (003) 95 6257
Open Not **Production** 4000

Winemaker(s) Chris Markell

Clover Hill was established by Taltarni in 1986 with the sole purpose of making a premium sparkling wine. Its 20 hectares of vineyards, comprising 12 hectares of chardonnay, 6.5 of pinot noir and 1.5 of pinot meuniere, are still coming into bearing, and production is steadily increasing.

Principal Wines Clover Hill (Sparkling).

CLOVER HILL
●●●● $28

The 100% Chardonnay Blanc de Blancs style is matured on yeast lees for 24 months. Future releases will incorporate increasing amounts of pinot noir and a little pinot meuniere, but the 1991 vintage wine — although fairly acid — has attracted much favourable comment.

Cellaring Not necessary. **Best Vintages** NA

Current Vintage '91

Matching Food Caviar, shellfish.

Tasting Note 1991 Brilliant light green-yellow; a highly floral perfumed nose with some bready/yeasty aromas, leading on to a palate with pronounced acidity, and zesty, lively citrus and lemon flavours.

CLYDE PARK

NR 16–23 R AUS170 UK43

Geelong **Est.** 1980

Midland Highway, Bannockburn, Vic 3331

Ph (052) 81 1363 **Fax** (052) 81 1349

Open Not **Production** 1200

Winemaker(s) Scott Ireland

Purchased in late 1994 by leading Melbourne hotelier and restaurateur Donlevy Fitzpatrick who has recruited Scott Ireland (formerly winemaker at Dromana Estate) to take over winemaking. Fitzpatrick has big plans for Clyde Park, which will become much more visible in the future.

Principal Wines Chardonnay, Pinot Noir, Cabernet Sauvignon.

COBANOV WINERY *

NR 6–10 CD AUSSD

Swan Valley **Est.** 1960

Stock Road, Herne Hill, WA 6056

Ph (09) 296 4210

Open Wed–Sun 9–5.30 **Production** 10 000

Winemaker(s) Steve Cobanov

A substantial family-owned operation producing a mix of bulk and bottled wine from 21 hectares of estate grapes. Part of the annual production is sold as grapes to other producers, including Houghton; part is sold in bulk; part sold in 2-litre flagons, and the remainder in modestly-priced bottles.

Principal Wines Chenin Blanc, Chardonnay, Sauvignon Blanc, Verdelho, Shiraz, Grenache, Cabernet Sauvignon.

COBAW RIDGE WINERY

★★★★ 16–17 ML AUS94
Macedon **Est.** 1985
Perc Boyer's Lane, East Pastoria via Kyneton, Vic 3444
Ph (054) 23 5227
Open W'ends 10–5, or by appt **Production** 350
Winemaker(s) Alan Cooper
Nelly and Alan Cooper have established Cobaw Ridge's 4-hectare
vineyard at an altitude of 610 metres in the hills above Kyneton
complete with self-constructed pole-framed mud-brick house and
winery. Wine quality has been variable, but overall Alan Cooper
has done extremely well. Yield was severely curtailed during the
abnormal weather conditions of 1994.
Principal Wines Chardonnay, Shiraz, Cabernet Sauvignon.

COBBITTY WINES *

NR 5–14 CD AUSSD
Sydney District **Est.** 1964
Cobbitty Road, Cobbitty, NSW 2570
Ph (046) 51 2281 **Fax** (046) 51 2671
Open Mon–Sat 10–5, Sun 12–6 **Production** 5000
Winemaker(s) Giovanni Cogno
Draws upon 10 hectares of estate plantings of muscat, barbera,
grenache and trebbiano, relying very much on local and ethnic
custom.
Principal Wines A full range of generic table, fortified and
sparkling wines under the Cobbitty Wines label; also cocktail wines.

COFIELD WINES

★★★ 9.50–17.50 CD AUSSD
North East Victoria **Est.** 1986
Distillery Road, Wahgunyah, Vic 3687
Ph (060) 33 3798 **Fax** (060) 33 3798
Open Mon–Sat 9–5, Sun 10–5 **Production** 2500
Winemaker(s) Max Cofield
District veteran Max Cofield, together with wife Karen, is developing
a strong cellar door sales base by staging in-winery functions with
guest chefs, and also providing a large barbecue and picnic area.
The wine style is somewhat rustic.
Principal Wines Riesling, Chenin Blanc, Semillon Chardonnay,
Chardonnay, Cabernet Sauvignon, Cabernet Shiraz, Sparkling,
Fortified.

COLDSTREAM HILLS

NR 14.95–29.95 R AUS27, 167–170, 186 UK15
Yarra Valley **Est.** 1985
31 Maddens Lane, Coldstream, Vic 3770
Ph (059) 64 9388 **Fax** (059) 64 9389

Open Mon–Fri 12–2, W'ends, Public hols 10–5
Production 22 000
Winemaker(s) James Halliday, Philip Dowell
The author's own winery, and hence not rated, but has often been
described as one of Australia's foremost producers of Pinot Noir,
and generally accepted as an outstanding producer of Chardonnay,
Cabernet Sauvignon and Cabernet Merlot. Up to the end of 1994 it
has won 42 trophies, 94 gold medals, 90 silver medals and 146
bronze medals in wine shows principally in Australia, but also
overseas.
Principal Wines Fumé Blanc, Chardonnay, Reserve Chardonnay,
Pinot Noir, Reserve Pinot Noir, Cabernet Merlot, Reserve Cabernet
Sauvignon. Also, for export only, the James Halliday range of
Chardonnay, Botrytis Semillon, Grenache Shiraz and Cabernet
Sauvignon, made at Coldstream Hills but from grapes purchased
from premium regions outside the Yarra Valley.

COLDSTREAM HILLS CABERNET MERLOT

NR $17.95
A blend of cabernet sauvignon, cabernet franc and merlot (with an
occasional touch of malbec) which varies somewhat from year to
year, but which is usually in the range of 60% cabernet sauvignon
and cabernet franc, and 40% merlot. As with the other wines, part
estate-grown, part purchased from other Yarra Valley growers. It is
matured in a mix of new and used French oak (predominantly
Nevers and Allier, with lesser amounts of Troncais) for 18 to 20
months before bottling.
Cellaring 4–10 years. **Best Vintages** '88, '90, '91, '92, '93
Current Vintage '92
Matching Food Lamb with redcurrant sauce.
Tasting Note 1992 Medium full purple-red. Perfectly ripened
redcurrant and blackberry fruit is dominant on the bouquet with
cedary French oak harmoniously integrated. Exceptionally well
balanced and structured, with fine-grained, soft tannins complexing
the sweetly ripe red berry fruit and harmonious oak.

COLDSTREAM HILLS CHARDONNAY

NR $17.95
Made from Yarra Valley grapes, part estate-grown (from 6 hectares
of producing vineyard) and part purchased from other Yarra Valley
growers. Largely barrel fermented in a mix of new and used French
oak under strictly controlled temperatures. Prolonged lees contact but
no malolactic fermentation.
Cellaring 5–10 years. **Best Vintages** '86, '88, '91, '92, '93,
'94 **Current Vintage** '94
Matching Food Oven roasted Blue Eye fish.
Tasting Note 1994 Light to medium yellow-green; a fragrant
and unusually aromatic and full bouquet early in its life, largely
reflecting the very low yields and fruit concentration of the '94
vintage. There are aromas and flavours in the passionfruit, peach
and grapefruit spectrum; the spicy oak is in restraint, but can be
detected.

COLDSTREAM HILLS PINOT NOIR
NR $17.95

Part estate-grown (from 6 hectares of producing vineyard) and part sourced from other Yarra Valley growers, with a range of site climates. It is made using the full gamut of Burgundian techniques, including substantial use of whole bunches; even a percentage of 100% whole bunches, foot stamped and macerated, is included. The primary fermentation is completed in a mix of new and used Troncais (French) oak.

Cellaring 2–6 years. **Best Vintages** '87, '88, '91, '92, '94
Current Vintage '94
Matching Food Seared or slow-cooked salmon, Asian.
Tasting Note 1994 Medium red-purple; strong plum, stone fruit and dark cherry aromas, closest to the '91 in style on the bouquet. The palate shows the same plum and dark cherry fruit flavours, with subtle oak woven through the wine. Will develop into one of the best Coldstream Hills Pinots with two to three years in bottle.

COLDSTREAM HILLS RESERVE CABERNET SAUVIGNON
NR $29.95

First introduced in 1992, and in fact will only be made in those years in which the quality of the cabernet sauvignon is outstanding. Entirely estate-produced, and a blend of 90% cabernet sauvignon and 10% merlot, matured in a high percentage of new Allier and Nevers oak barriques for 20 months.

Cellaring Up to 20 years. **Best Vintages** '92, '93
Current Vintage '92
Matching Food Rump steak.
Tasting Note 1992 Deep purple-red. Complex, powerful and concentrated, with blackcurrant and mulberry fruit, subtle oak. On the palate, an extremely concentrated wine with briary/blackcurrant fruit, fine but persistent tannins and a hint of sweet French oak.

COLDSTREAM HILLS RESERVE CHARDONNAY
NR $29.95

Made primarily, though not exclusively, from estate-grown grapes which are 100% barrel fermented in a mix of new (over 50%) and used French oak barriques, principally Vosges but with Troncais and Allier also used. Six months lees contact; 20% malolactic fermentation.

Cellaring 5–10 years. **Best Vintages** '88, '91, '92, '93, '94
Current Vintage '93
Matching Food Veal, chicken.
Tasting Note 1993 Bright yellow-green; a very fragrant bouquet, with melon and citrus fruit, spicy oak and a hint of nuttiness from the partial malolactic fermentation. Both powerful and very long on the palate, with refreshing acidity. Once again, spicy French oak adds a dimension to the melon/citrus fruit.

COLDSTREAM HILLS RESERVE PINOT NOIR
NR $29.95

Produced almost entirely from estate-grown grapes, in turn coming

from the Amphitheatre Block established in 1985. The same making techniques are used with the Reserve wine as with the standard, the difference being fruit selection and a much higher percentage of new Dargaud & Jaegle Troncais oak barriques.
Cellaring 3–6 years. **Best Vintages** '87, '88, '91, '92, '94
Current Vintage '93
Matching Food Quail, Asian.
Tasting Note 1993 Medium red, slightly deeper than the standard wine of the same year. The bouquet already shows some Burgundian characters, with plum and cinnamon predominating. An harmonious and balanced palate, yet deceptively light — the finish is long, the aftertaste lingers. The flavours are those of the bouquet, with a slight carbonic maceration influence evident.

CONSTABLES *

NR 10–15 CD AUSSD
Warren Valley **Est.** 1988
Graphite Road, West Manjimup, WA 6258
Ph (097) 72 1375
Open 7 days 9–5 **Production** NFP
Winemaker(s) Houghton (Contract)
Father John and son Michael, together with other members of the Constable family, have established an 11-hectare vineyard at Manjimup. Most of the grapes are sold to Houghton under a long-term contract, and limited quantities are made for the Constable label for Houghton under contract.
Principal Wines Riesling, Sauvignon Blanc, Chardonnay, Cabernet Sauvignon.

COOINDA VALE

★★★ 14–15 R AUSSD
Coal River **Est.** 1985
Bartonvale Road, Campania, Tas 7026
Ph (002) 62 4227
Open By appt **Production** 150
Winemaker(s) Andrew Hood (Contract)
The tiny production means that the wines are not widely known, even in southern Tasmania. However, the crisp, lifted 1992 Riesling, and the concentrated, minty/essency 1992 Pinot Noir hold considerable promise.
Principal Wines Riesling, Pinot Noir.

COOLANGATTA ESTATE *

★★★☆ 10.90–13.90 CD AUSSD
South-west Coastal Plain **Est.** 1988
1335 Bolong Road, via Berry, NSW 2535
Ph (044) 48 7131 **Fax** (044) 48 7997
Open 7 days 10–4 **Production** 1400
Winemaker(s) Tyrrell's (Contract)

Coolangatta Estate is part of a 150-hectare resort with
accommodation, restaurants, golf course, etc, with some of the oldest
buildings convict-built in 1822. It might be thought that the wines are
tailored purely for the tourist market, but in fact the standard of
viticulture is exceptionally high (immaculate Scott Henry trellising)
and the winemaking is wholly professional (contract by Tyrrell's).
The net result is comprehensively the best wines of the four producers
in the Shoalhaven region.
Principal Wines Sauvignon Blanc, Semillon Sauvignon Blanc,
Chardonnay, Alexander Berry Chardonnay, Verdelho,
Chambourcin, Cabernet Shiraz, Merlot, Cabernet Sauvignon.

COOLANGATTA ESTATE ALEXANDER BERRY CHARDONNAY

●●●● $13.90

Named after Alexander Berry, who with Edward Wollstonecraft
obtained a grant of 10,000 acres and 100 convicts in 1822,
building their settlement on the foothills of a mountain named
Coolangatta, an aboriginal word meaning 'fine view'.
Cellaring Up to 5 years. **Best Vintages** '91, '94
Current Vintage '94
Matching Food Avocado and seafood.
Tasting Note 1994 Medium yellow-green; the bouquet is full, with
abundant high quality oak with ample peach and melon fruit to carry
the oak. The palate is substantial and chewy, with a range of
cashew, melon and peach flavours, and a full finish. Should develop
like the excellent '91, the latter now a wine at its peak.

COOLANGATTA ESTATE SEMILLON SAUVIGNON BLANC

●●● ▶ $10.90

The Scott Henry Trellis system used at Shoalhaven is ideal for high
vigour vineyards, particularly where (as in the case of Shoalhaven)
the risk of summer rainfall is high. The canopy is split vertically,
allowing sunlight and wind penetration, optimising air movement
and reducing disease. For all that, the tempering effect of the nearby
Shoalhaven River delays maturity, for vintage typically does not get
under way until mid March.
Cellaring 1–2 years. **Best Vintages** '91, '94
Current Vintage '93
Matching Food Whitebait.
Tasting Note 1993 Glowing yellow-green; the bouquet is of
medium to full intensity, clean, with the semillon component
dominant. The palate is likewise clean and well made with attractive
passionfruit and peach flavours, finishing with soft acid.

COOLART VALLEY

NR 11–15 CD AUSSD
Mornington Peninsula **Est.** 1981
Thomas Hill Rd, Red Hill South, Vic 3937
Ph (059) 89 2087
Open All W'ends Nov–Mar, First W'end Mth April–Oct

Production 450
Winemaker(s) Peter Cumming (Contract)
Made an outstanding Cabernet Sauvignon in 1989, with unusual
weight and depth for the year, and perfect balance; a tangy, smoky
1990 Chardonnay rounded off an impressive debut. However, I
have not tasted the '91 or '92 vintage wines in bottle.
Principal Wines Riesling, Chardonnay, Semillon, Cabernet
Sauvignon.

COOMBEND WINERY

★★★★ 7.75–16.50 ML AUSSD
East Coast Tasmania **Est.** 1985
Coombend via Swansea, Tas 7190
Ph (002) 57 8256 **Fax** (002) 57 8484
Open By appt **Production** 300
Winemaker(s) Freycinet (Contract)
John Fenn Smith has established 1.75 hectares of cabernet
sauvignon (together with a little cabernet franc) on his 2600-hectare
sheep station, choosing that part of his property which is
immediately adjacent to Freycinet.
Principal Wines Cabernet Sauvignon.

COOMBEND CABERNET SAUVIGNON
●●●● $16.50
Situated adjacent to Freycinet, and shares the same remarkable site
climate, proving yet again how difficult it is to generalise about the
Tasmanian climate. Both the 1990 and 1991 Cabernets have won
trophies in Tasmanian Shows; it is arguably the best Cabernet
Sauvignon in Tasmania.
Cellaring 4–7 years. **Best Vintages** '90, '91, '92, '94
Current Vintage '92
Matching Food Ragout of lamb.
Tasting Note 1992 Medium to full red, with a touch of purple;
potent leafy/briary/cassis aromas with slightly medicinal overtones;
typical cool-climate fruit. Similar spicy/herbal/medicinal flavours on
the palate, with some spicy/cedary French oak, finishing with soft
tannins.

COORINJA VINEYARD

★★☆ 8–10.50 CD AUSSD
Darling Range **Est.** 1870
Toodyay Road, Toodyay, WA 6566
Ph (096) 26 2280
Open Mon–Sat 8–5 **Production** 3200
Winemaker(s) Michael Wood
An evocative and historic winery nestling in a small gully which
seems to be in a time-warp, begging to be used as a set for a film.
A recent revamp of the packaging accompanied a more than
respectable 1990 Hermitage, with lots of dark chocolate and
sweet berry flavour, finishing with soft tannins.

Principal Wines Dry White, Claret, Hermitage, Burgundy,
Fortifieds; the latter account for 50% of Coorinja's production.

COPE WILLIAMS

★★★★ 9.50–23 R AUSSD
Macedon **Est.** 1977
Glenfern Road, Romsey, Vic 3434
Ph (054) 29 5428 **Fax** (054) 29 5655
Open 7 days 10–5 **Production** 6500
Winemaker(s) Michael Cope Williams
One of the high country Macedon pioneers, specialising in sparkling
wines which are full flavoured, but also producing excellent
Chardonnay and Pinot Noir table wines in the warmer vintages. A
traditional 'English Green'-type cricket ground is available for hire
and booked out most days of the week from spring through till
autumn.
Principal Wines Chardonnay, Cabernet Merlot; d'Vine is second
label: Riesling, Chardonnay and Cabernet Sauvignon; winery
specialty sparkling wine Macedon R.O.M.S.E.Y. Brut.

COPE WILLIAMS R.O.M.S.E.Y. BRUT

●●●● ▶ $23
Made from estate-grown chardonnay and pinot noir, and now fully
made at the property. The high altitude, very cool vineyard site
produces exceptional quality base wine, and this has been reflected
in the illustrious show record of the Cope-Williams sparkling wines
over the past few years — a record undimmed by the limited number
of entries available to it because of restricted production.
Cellaring None required. **Best Vintages** NA
Current Vintage NA
Matching Food Oysters.
Tasting Note NV Bright full yellow with particularly good mousse;
complex bready/yeasty autolysis over fresh citrussy fruit; the palate
is complex with a nice blend of crisp fruit and yeast autolysis. The
finish is long and the dosage low.

CORIOLE

★★★★ 10.50–18 CD AUS27, 48, 75, 184, 187 UK89
Southern Vales **Est.** 1967
Chaffeys Road, McLaren Vale, SA 5171
Ph (08) 323 8305 **Fax** (08) 323 9136
Open Mon–Fri 9–5, W'ends 11–5 **Production** 22 000
Winemaker(s) Stephen Hall
Justifiably best known for its Shiraz, which, both in the very rare
Reserve, and also like standard form, is extremely impressive. It has
spread its wings in recent years, being one of the first wineries to
catch onto the Italian fashion with its Sangiovese, but in wine quality
terms has had more success with its white wines.
Principal Wines Semillon, Semillon Sauvignon Blanc, Chenin
Blanc, Sangiovese, Cabernet Sauvignon; Lloyd Reserve Shiraz.

CORIOLE SEMILLON
●●● ▶ $13

A very interesting wine which over the past few years has shown strong passionfruit/gooseberry aromas when young, presumably due at least in part to the use of aromatic yeast during fermentation, but is possibly also partly vineyard character. Whatever the answer, it produces wines which are striking and attractive in their youth.
Cellaring Hard to tell. **Best Vintages** '93, '94
Current Vintage '94
Matching Food Salad, seafood.
Tasting Note 1994 Light yellow-green; strong smoky passionfruit aromas; similar passionfruit/gooseberry flavours are evident on the palate, which is both striking and vibrant.

CORIOLE SHIRAZ
●●●●● $16.95

One of McLaren Vale's most distinguished Shiraz wines, with a track record going back to the establishment of Coriole in 1967, based upon 1.3 hectares of vines then 60 years old. Those vines provided the core of fruit over the intervening decades until additional plantings came first into bearing and then into maturity, allowing the introduction of a Reserve Shiraz from 1989 using only those original plantings.
Cellaring 5–15 years. **Best Vintages** '70, '74, '84, '88, '89, '90, '91, '92 **Current Vintage** '92
Matching Food Ragout of lamb.
Tasting Note 1992 Full red-purple, with clean, rich, ripe pepper-spice-black cherry aromas. In the mouth, full-bodied, potent and powerful with lots of fruit and well structured tannins.

COSHAM WINES

NR 11–16 ML AUSSD
Perth Hills **Est.** 1989
Lot 44 Union Road, Carmel via Kalamunda, WA 6076
Ph (09) 293 5459
Open Not **Production** 120
Winemaker(s) Anthony Sclanders
The newest of the Perth Hills ventures, with a microscopic amount of wine available. Both the 1991 Chardonnay and 1991 Pinot Noir spent two years in French oak barriques before bottling — a long time by any standards.
Principal Wines Chardonnay, Pinot Noir.

COWRA ESTATE, THE See page 438.

CRABTREE OF WATERVALE

★★★ 10–13 CD AUS17, 68, 98, 178, 183 UK5
Clare Valley **Est.** 1979
North Terrace, Watervale SA 5452
Ph (088) 43 0069 **Fax** (088) 43 0144
Open 7 days 11–5 **Production** 4000
Winemaker(s) Robert Crabtree

The gently eccentric Robert Crabtree is one of the numerous great characters who inhabit the beautiful Clare Valley: the mixture of people, wine, history and beauty is a potent elixir, and you will not regret a visit to the winery, nor tasting the chewy, minty Shiraz Cabernet and full-flavoured lime/toast Riesling.
Principal Wines Riesling, Semillon, Grenache, Shiraz Cabernet, Cabernet Sauvignon, Muscat.

CRABTREE OF WATERVALE GRENACHE
●●● ▶ $12
A new wine for Robert Crabtree, picking up both on the popularity of grenache and the reasonably ready availability of this variety in the Clare Valley. It is not hard to see why the grape has suddenly found such popularity.
Cellaring Best drunk young. **Best Vintages** NA
Current Vintage '94
Matching Food Grilled calf's liver.
Tasting Note 1994 Vivid purple-red; clean, with solid, ripe dark berry fruit aromas and minimal oak influence. The palate shows some minty flavours, not apparent on the bouquet, with plenty of weight, but avoiding over-extraction, and finishing with soft tannins.

CRAIG AVON VINEYARD

★★★☆ 19–23 CD AUSSD
Mornington Peninsula **Est.** 1986
Craig Avon Lane, Merricks North, Vic 3926
Ph (059) 89 7465
Open Not **Production** 900
Winemaker(s) Ken Lang
All of the wines are sold cellar door and by mailing list. No recent tastings, but the last wines assessed (from the 1991 vintage) were well made with good flavour.
Principal Wines Chardonnay, Pinot Noir, Cabernet Sauvignon.

CRAIGIE KNOWE VINEYARD

★★★ 15–16 ML AUS177
East Coast Tasmania **Est.** 1979
Glen Gala Road, Cranbrook, Tas 7190
Ph (002) 23 5620
Open W'ends or by appt **Production** 250
Winemaker(s) Dr John Austwick
Makes a small quantity of full-flavoured, robust Cabernet Sauvignon in a tiny winery as a weekend relief from a busy metropolitan dental practice.
Principal Wines Cabernet Sauvignon, Pinot Noir.

CRAIGLEE

★★★★★ 17–18 CD AUS80
Macedon **Est.** 1976
Sunbury Road, Sunbury, Vic 3429

Ph (03) 9744 4489 **Fax** (03) 9744 7905
Open Sun, Public hols 10–5, or by appt **Production** 2000
Winemaker(s) Patrick Carmody
An historic winery with a proud nineteenth century record which
recommenced winemaking in 1976 after a prolonged hiatus.
Widely recognised as one of the finest producers of Shiraz in
Australia, with marvellously consistent style and quality.
Principal Wines Chardonnay, Pinot Noir, Shiraz, Cabernet
Sauvignon.

1872 CRAIGLEE SHIRAZ

●●●●● $ NA
Over a 20-year span I have been privileged to taste the 1872
Craiglee Shiraz on several occasions, the most recent at a dinner at
Labassa House in Melbourne on 13 February 1994 organised by
Andrew Wood and Darren Harris, noted Melbourne connoisseurs. It
is the oldest Australian wine I have tasted. 10.1% alcohol; nine-year-
old vines.
Cellaring NA. **Best Vintages** NA **Current Vintage** 1872
Matching Food Loin of milk-fed lamb poached in stock.
Tasting Note 1872 Some browning evident, as one would expect;
an ethereal, complex bouquet of gum leaf and dry grass with both
spice and mint progressively emerging. The palate was remarkably
complex with flavours of cardamom, spice and again a touch of dry
gum leaf. The structure was superb, the finish good.

CRAIGLEE SHIRAZ

●●●●● $18
Produced from 4 hectares of estate plantings, almost invariably
producing wines of the highest imaginable quality, with wonderful
cherry, pepper and spice aromas and flavours. The wines are fruit-,
rather than oak-driven; they are immaculately structured, having the
fruit weight and vinous sweetness to balance the peppery/spicy
tang.
Cellaring Conservatively, 7–10 years. **Best Vintages** '88, '99,
'91, '92, '93 **Current Vintage** '93
Matching Food Italian.
Tasting Note 1993 Medium to full purple-red; spotlessly clean intense
pepper/spice/cherry/plum aromas of medium intensity. Archetypal
Craiglee Shiraz palate, showing the same pepper, spice and cherry
flavours of the bouquet. Trophy winner 1994 Lilydale Show.

CRAIGMOOR WINERY

★★★ 10.95–13.95 R AUS117
Mudgee **Est.** 1858
Craigmoor Road, Mudgee, NSW 2850
Ph (063) 72 2208 **Fax** (063) 72 4464
Open Mon–Fri 9–4, W'ends 10–4 **Production** NFP
Winemaker(s) Robert Paul
One of the oldest wineries in Australia to remain in continuous
production, now subsumed into the Orlando/Wyndham group,

with an inevitable loss of identity and individuality of wine style,
although the technical quality of the wines cannot be faulted.
Principal Wines Semillon, Chardonnay, Shiraz, Cabernet
Sauvignon.

CRAIGMOOR CHARDONNAY
●●● ▸ $12.50
In 1971 Craigmoor, together with Tyrrell's, vintaged a wine which
was subsequently released and labelled Chardonnay. These two
wines from that vintage were the first in Australia to be so labelled
this century. Craigmoor in fact acted as the source block for much of
the spread of Chardonnay around Australia; it seems that the stock
can be traced back to the original early 19th century importations of
Busby and Macarthur.
Cellaring 1–3 years. **Best Vintages** '89, '91, '93, '94
Current Vintage '93
Matching Food Smoked chicken.
Tasting Note 1993 Medium yellow-green; smooth melon/fig fruit
with just a hint of oak; falls away slightly on the palate, but smooth
and pleasant, and good value at the price.

CRAIGMOOR SHIRAZ
●●●● $12.95
Part of the Montrose Group, which is in turn owned by Orlando
Wyndham. Could legitimately be regarded as a second label of
Montrose, but offers the same value for money and supremely
honest regional style.
Cellaring Up to 5 years. **Best Vintages** '89, '91, '93
Current Vintage '93
Matching Food Pizza.
Tasting Note 1993 Strong, bright and deep red-purple; abundant
plummy/berry fruit with varietal earthy overtones. On the palate
there is all of the rich earthy/berry fruit promised by the bouquet,
with oak barely perceptible.

CRANEFORD WINES
★★☆ 11–15 CD AUS16, 17, 26, 123
Adelaide Hills **Est.** 1978
Main Street, Springton, SA 5235
Ph (085) 68 2220 **Fax** (085) 68 2538
Open Wed–Mon 11–5 **Production** 2400
Winemaker(s) Colin Forbes
Wine quality has varied widely from a superlative '89 Shiraz
through to the '91 which appeared to suffer from elevated levels of
volatile acidity. Other wines, too, have varied from mediocre to
good.
Principal Wines Riesling, Chardonnay, Shiraz, Cabernet
Sauvignon.

CRANEFORD RIESLING
●●● ▸ $14.95
Re-released as a fully mature wine in March 1995, elegantly

demonstrating the capacity of Eden Valley to develop with bottle age.
Cellaring Now–3 years. **Best Vintages** NA
Current Vintage '90
Matching Food Asparagus salad.
Tasting Note 1990 Medium to full yellow-green; there are attractive toasty bottle-developed aromas with that substrate of Eden Valley lime juice. The palate is quite fine, notwithstanding the bottle age, with toasty flavours, good length and acid balance, and finishing pleasantly dry.

CRANSWICK ESTATE

★★☆ 4.95–9.95 R AUSSD UK12
Murrumbidgee Irrigation Area **Est.** 1976
Walla Avenue, Griffith, NSW 2680
Ph (069) 62 4133 **Fax** (069) 62 2888
Open Mon–Fri 10–4.30 **Production** 1 000 000
Winemaker(s) Ian Honcell
Cranswick Estate has aggressively — and successfully — focused on the export market, offering light-bodied but technically sound wines at highly competitive prices.
Principal Wines Semillon, Semillon Chardonnay, Chardonnay, Traminer Riesling, Sauvignon Blanc, Shiraz Cabernet, Shiraz Merlot, Cabernet Sauvignon, Merlot, Sparkling; Barramundi Semillon Chardonnay, Shiraz Merlot; Jabiru Valley Chardonnay, Sauvignon Blanc, Cabernet Sauvignon.

CRAWFORD RIVER WINES

★★★★ 13–16 ML AUS48, 66
Western Victoria **Est.** 1982
Crawford via Condah, Vic 3303
Ph (055) 78 2267 **Fax** (055) 78 2267
Open 7 days 9–5 **Production** 2500
Winemaker(s) John Thomson
Some exemplary Rieslings, Botrytis Rieslings and Cabernet Sauvignons have been made by full-time grazier, part-time winemaker John Thomson who clearly has the winemaker's equivalent of the gardener's green thumb.
Principal Wines Riesling, Semillon Sauvignon Blanc, Cabernet Sauvignon.

CRAWFORD RIVER CABERNET SAUVIGNON

●●● ▶ $16
Grown at the extreme edge for Cabernet Sauvignon, and always presents a rather austere, minerally, European cast, but in most years redeems itself with the length of its finish, and the way the flavour builds up with the second glass.
Cellaring 5–8 years. **Best Vintages** '86, '88, '90, '91, '93
Current Vintage '90

Matching Food Roast veal.
Tasting Note 1990 Medium red; the bouquet is of light to medium intensity with minerally/herbal aromas. The palate has an interesting European, almost Italianate structure, with nice red berry fruit on the finish and echoes of mint. A wine which creeps up on you. (Tasted June 1994.)

CRAWFORD RIVER RIESLING
●●●● $13
A wine of consistently good quality over the years, tight and reserved, and fully reflecting the very cool climate in which it is grown. It is 100% estate-grown (as are all of the Crawford River wines).
Cellaring Up to 5 years. **Best Vintages** '86, '88, '89, '91, '94
Current Vintage '93
Matching Food Antipasto.
Tasting Note 1993 Light yellow-green; fine, elegant lime fruit with just a hint of volatile acidity, but acceptable. The palate has firm, faintly citrussy, dry/toasty fruit, with a long finish, and structured to age.

CRESTVIEW WINES *

★★★ 5.50–18 CD AUS64, 72, 96, 163 UK26, 36
Southern Vales **Est.** 1989
49 Fraser Avenue, Happy Valley, SA 5159
Ph (08) 322 3611 **Fax** (08) 322 3610
Open Mon–Fri 9–5, W'ends 11–5 **Production** 85 000
Winemaker(s) Robert Dundon
A kaleidoscopic array of brand and varietally identified wines aimed chiefly, but not exclusively, at the export market. Echo Point is the most commonly encountered in Australia.
Principal Wines Arunda, Beacon Hill, Crystal Brook, Bosanquet, Stony Vale, Katherine Hills and Echo Point brands in various varietal configurations.

CRUICKSHANK-CALLATOOTA ESTATE

★★☆ 10–15 CD AUSSD
Upper Hunter Valley **Est.** 1972
Wybong Road, Wybong, NSW 2333
Ph (065) 47 8149 **Fax** (065) 47 8144
Open 7 days 9–5 **Production** 5500
Winemaker(s) Andrew Cruickshank
Owned by Sydney management consultant John Cruickshank and family. It typically produces fairly light-bodied and extremely regional (tarry) wines, but the 1991 vintage provided wines with more weight and fruit than previously, the best for many years.
Principal Wines Rosé, Cabernet Sauvignon, Cabernet Franc blend.

CULLEN WINES

★★★★☆ 15–27 CD AUS17, 111, 150, 161, 168 UK43
Margaret River **Est.** 1971
Caves Road, Cowaramup, WA 6284
Ph (097) 55 5277 **Fax** (097) 55 5550
Open 7 days 10–4 **Production** 10 000
Winemaker(s) Vanya Cullen
One of the pioneers of Margaret River which has always produced
long-lived wines of highly individual style from the substantial and
now mature estate vineyards. Winemaking is now in the hands of
Vanya Cullen, daughter of the founders, and possessed of an
extraordinarily good palate.
Principal Wines Cabernet Merlot, Chardonnay, Sauvignon Blanc,
Pinot Noir.

CULLEN CABERNET MERLOT

●●●●● $25
An estate-grown wine of the highest quality which since 1990 has
been arguably the best Margaret River Cabernet Merlot blend. The
1992, in particular, is a majestic wine. A blend of estate-grown 60%
cabernet sauvignon, 30% merlot and 10% cabernet franc matured
for two years in French oak.
Cellaring A decade or more. **Best Vintages** '77, '84, '86, '90,
'91, '92 **Current Vintage** '92
Matching Food Lamb, strong cheddar.
Tasting Note 1992 Dense impenetrable purple; fine and clean,
yet concentrated bouquet with perfectly ripened fruit and subtle oak.
The palate is similarly concentrated yet fine, with supple tannins
running through dark red berry fruit (and echoes of dark chocolate
and mint), giving the wine great structure and length.

CURRENCY CREEK WINES

★★★ 5–21.25 CD AUS48, 63, 90, 91, 119, 184
Langhorne Creek **Est.** 1969
Winery Road, Currency Creek, SA 5214
Ph (085) 55 4069 **Fax** (085) 55 4100
Open 7 days 10–5 **Production** 8000
Winemaker(s) Phillip Tonkin
Constant name changes (Santa Rosa, Tonkins have also been tried)
did not help the quest for identity or recognition in the marketplace,
but the winery has nonetheless produced some outstanding wood-
matured whites and pleasant, soft reds selling at attractive prices.
Principal Wines Fumé Blanc, Sauvignon Blanc, Chardonnay,
Pinot Noir, Shiraz, Cabernet Sauvignon, Sparkling, Fortified.

CURTIS WINES *

NR NA AUSSD
Southern Vales **Est.** 1988
Foggo Road, McLaren Vale, SA 5171

Ph (08) 323 8389
Open W'ends 11–5 **Production** 1500
Winemaker(s) P Curtis
A small and relatively new producer in McLaren Vale, whose wines I have not tasted.
Principal Wines Semillon, Shiraz, Fortifieds.

D'AQUINO'S WINES

NR 4.99–6.99 CD AUSSD
Orange **Est.** 1952
129 Bathurst Road, Orange, NSW 2800
Ph (063) 62 7381 **Fax** (063) 62 6183
Open 7 days 9.30–8 **Production** 3000
Winemaker(s) Rex D'Aquino
An interesting outpost of the industry: Rex D'Aquino graduated from Roseworthy in 1981 and makes wines from grapes purchased in various parts of Australia, as well as operating a bonded-spirit store and bottling plant and a large retail shop offering wines from most well-known Australian wineries.
Principal Wines Table wines, Fortified, Sparkling.

D'ARENBERG WINES

★★★★☆ 6–15 R AUS14, 86, 110, 126, 182, 185 US2
Southern Vales **Est.** 1912
Osborn Road, McLaren Vale SA 5171
Ph (08) 323 8206 **Fax** (08) 323 8423
Open Mon–Fri 9–5, Sat, Hols 10–5, Sun 12–4
Production 100 000
Winemaker(s) Chester Osborn
A rock of ages, yet showing some signs of moving with the times, flirting with avant-garde packaging while continuing to make soft, velvety McLaren Vale red wines which age with grace, and in recent years doing very nicely indeed with Barrel Fermented Chardonnay and Noble Riesling. D'Arry's Original Burgundy is not only a classic, but a sentimental favourite.
Principal Wines Riesling, Sauvignon Blanc/Chenin Blanc, Barrel Fermented Chardonnay, White Ochre Classic Dry White, Old Vine Shiraz, High Trellis Cabernet Sauvignon, d'Arry's Original Burgundy, Ironstone Pressings, Red Ochre Shiraz, Noble Riesling, Muscat of Alexandria, Port.

D'ARENBERG BARREL FERMENTED CHARDONNAY
●●●● $11
Made from estate-grown chardonnay which often reaches high sugar levels and is invariably rich in flavour, but which can surprise with its crisp, tangy fruit. Matured in a mix of French, American and German oak, typically spending eight months on yeast lees.
Cellaring 2–4 years. **Best Vintages** '90, '93, '94
Current Vintage '93
Matching Food Creamed scallops.

Tasting Note 1993 Light green-yellow; fresh, crisp and tangy fruit with some charry oak aromas on the bouquet. Very fresh and crisp on the palate, seemingly less ripe than 13.5% alcohol, and with good acid on the finish.

D'ARENBERG D'ARRY'S ORIGINAL BURGUNDY
●●●●● $10

A classic wine style with an illustrious show record dating back to 1961. Made from low-yielding old vine shiraz and grenache. Note that the current vintage (1992) is in fact one of the lesser vintages; the wine rating is given for the best wines.

Cellaring 20 years or more. **Best Vintages** '63, '76, '86, '87, '88 **Current Vintage** '92

Matching Food Jugged hare.

Tasting Note 1992 Medium to full red; a complex, ripe bouquet with some regional cow-shed aromas. The palate has abundant ripe, sweet berry fruit, with just a hint of spice in the background.

D'ARENBERG NOBLE RIESLING
●●●● ▶ $14

A wine of exceptional and unusual quality, made from grapes picked at between 26 and 29 baume, heavily infected by botrytis. Interestingly, all come from McLaren Vale, not a region noted for this style. Trophy-winning wine.

Cellaring Now–10 years. **Best Vintages** '92, '93
Current Vintage '92

Matching Food Virtually any rich dessert.

Tasting Note 1992 Glowing yellow-green; intense lime, mandarin and apricot aromas with a hint of vanilla; the palate is very powerful, lingering, and intense with lime, mandarin and apricot flavours, finishing with good acidity to balance the sweetness.

D'ARENBERG OLD VINE SHIRAZ
●●●● $11

Produced from vines dating back as far as 1890 but harvested over a long period to achieve differing flavour and sugar levels. Made traditionally in open fermenters, basket pressed, and aged in small oak for one year.

Cellaring Up to 15 years. **Best Vintages** '82, '88, '90, '91, '94
Current Vintage '92

Matching Food Smoked lamb with red currant sauce.

Tasting Note 1992 Medium to full red; the bouquet shows very ripe, juicy red fruit, a fraction on the jammy side. On the palate there is intense fruit with spicy elements coming through, the finish freshened by acidity.

DALFARRAS

★★★☆ 11.95–14.95 R AUS42, 45, 163
Goulburn Valley **Est.** 1991
PO Box 123, Nagambie, Vic 3608
Ph (057) 94 2637 **Fax** (057) 94 2360

Open Not **Production** 8000
Winemaker(s) Alister Purbrick
The personal project of Alister Purbrick and artist-wife Rosa Dalfarra, whose paintings adorn the labels of the wines. Alister, of course, is best known as winemaker at Chateau Tahbilk, the family winery and home, but this range of wines is intended to (in Alister's words) 'allow me to expand my winemaking horizons and mould wines in styles different to Chateau Tahbilk'.
Principal Wines Riesling, Chardonnay, Semillon, Sauvignon Blanc, Marsanne, Shiraz, Cabernet Sauvignon.

DALFARRAS SAUVIGNON BLANC
●●● ▶ $16.95
Not all of the Dalfarras wines seem as different in style from those of Chateau Tahbilk as one might expect, but this wine does fit that description, being thoroughly modern rather than thoroughly traditional.
Cellaring Drink now. **Best Vintages** NA **Current Vintage** '94
Matching Food Smoked eel.
Tasting Note 1994 Light straw-green; crisp smoky/herbal/gooseberry fruit aromas which are moderately rich and intense. The palate starts crisp and clean, and swells out with some sweetness on the mid to back palate. A well made, fresh wine.

DALRYMPLE VINEYARD

★★★★ 16 ML AUSSD
Tamar Valley **Est.** 1987
Heemskerk/Lebrina Road, Pipers Brook, Tas 7250
Ph (003) 31 3179 **Fax** (003) 31 3179
Open Sat–Sun 10–5 **Production** 1280
Winemaker(s) Various Contract makers
A partnership between Jill Mitchell and her sister and brother-in-law, Anne and Bertel Sundstrup, inspired by father Bill Mitchell's establishment of the Tamarway Vineyard in the late 1960s. In 1991 Tamarway reverted to the Sundstrup and Mitchell families, and it too, will be producing wine in the future, probably under its own label but sold ex the Dalrymple cellar door.
Principal Wines Chardonnay, Sauvignon Blanc, Pinot Noir.

DALRYMPLE CHARDONNAY
●●●● ▶ $16
Produced from 4.8 hectares of estate plantings, and a wine which always stands out amongst its Tasmanian fellows. The '92 vintage, currently available, won the trophy for Best Tasmanian Wooded White Wine at the 1994 Tasmanian Wine Show.
Cellaring Long-lived — 5–7 years. **Best Vintages** '91, '92
Current Vintage '92
Matching Food Tasmanian salmon.
Tasting Note 1992 Light to medium green-yellow; the bouquet is complex with mineral and nut aromas, rather than primary fruit. In the mouth it is discrete and crisp, showing its cool-grown origins, again with more stony/minerally flavours, but a long and intense finish.

DALWHINNIE WINERY

★★★★☆ 21–23 R AUS66, 188, UK89

Pyrenees **Est.** 1976

Taltarni Road, Moonambel, Vic 3478

Ph (054) 67 2388 **Fax** (054) 67 2237

Open 7 days 10–5 **Production** 350

Winemaker(s) David Jones

Owned by distinguished architect Ewan Jones and family, Dalwhinnie goes from strength to strength, making outstanding wines right across the board. The wines all show tremendous depth of fruit flavour, reflecting the relatively low-yielding but very well maintained vineyards.

Principal Wines Chardonnay; Moonambel Shiraz, Cabernet.

DALWHINNIE CHARDONNAY

●●●● ▶ $21

Produced from a little under 4 hectares of low-yielding, un-irrigated estate-grown vines, with an ancestry going back to the clone introduced in the 19th century and discovered at Mudgee in the late 1960s. Barrel fermentation adds to the richness to produce an invariably extremely complex wine.

Cellaring Develops early but will hold. **Best Vintages** '87, '88, '90, '92, '93 **Current Vintage** '93

Matching Food Turkey.

Tasting Note 1993 Medium to full yellow-green; a very rich, fully-developed bouquet showing some evidence of botrytis. All in all, a high-toned wine with plenty of power and punch, some botrytis influence throughout, augmented by buttery/nutty oak.

DALWHINNIE MOONAMBEL CABERNET

●●●● $28.95

Predominantly cabernet sauvignon, but with a small percentage of estate-grown cabernet franc and merlot. Every bit as powerful and concentrated as the Shiraz, and likewise needing many years in bottle.

Cellaring Up to 20 years. **Best Vintages** '86, '88, '90, '91, '92 **Current Vintage** '93

Matching Food Rare char-grilled rump steak.

Tasting Note 1993 Full red-purple; a rich, concentrated dark berry, game and chocolate-accented bouquet with some volatile lift. The palate is high-toned, showing some of the same lifted characters of the bouquet, with dark chocolate and berry flavours, and mid-weight tannins.

DALWHINNIE MOONAMBEL SHIRAZ

●●●● ▶ $23

An exceptionally concentrated and powerful wine, fully reflecting the low yields and the influence of the quartz, clay and gravel soils. These are not wines for the faint-hearted, positively demanding long cellaring, but having the balance to repay patience.

Cellaring Up to 20 years. **Best Vintages** '86, '88, '90, '91, '92 **Current Vintage** '92

Matching Food Potent cheeses, strong red meats.
Tasting Note 1992 An impenetrable red-purple colour heralds a
hugely concentrated bouquet with briary, chocolate and cedar
aromas, yet paradoxically a European feel to it. The tannins run right
through the palate, with cedary flavours from the fruit and oak.

DALYUP RIVER ESTATE

NR 10–12 CD AUSSD
Great Southern **Est.** 1987
Murrays Road, Esperance, WA 6450
Ph (090) 76 5027 **Fax** (090) 76 5027
Open W'ends 10–4 **Production** 500
Winemaker(s) Gavin Berry (Plantagenet)
Light but fresh 1990 vintage white wines were a quiet debut, but
with contract-making by Plantagenet the future seems assured.
Principal Wines Dry Riesling, Medium Sweet Riesling, Fumé
Blanc, Dry Red (Burgundy Style), Port.

DARGO VALLEY WINERY *

NR 9–14 CD AUS25
South Gippsland **Est.** 1992
Lower Dargo Road, Dargo, Vic 3862
Ph (051) 40 1228
Open Mon–Thur 12–8, W'ends, Hols 10–8 **Production** NFP
Winemaker(s) Hermann Bila
Situated in mountain country north of Maffra and looking towards
the Bogong National Park. Hermann Bila comes from a family of
European winemakers; there is also an on-site restaurant, and
Devonshire teas and ploughman's lunches are provided — very
useful given the remote locality.
Principal Wines Traminer Riesling, Sauvignon Blanc, Cabernet
Sauvignon.

DARLING ESTATE

NR 9–14 ML AUSSD
North East Victoria **Est.** 1986
Whitfield-Cheshunt Road, Cheshunt, Vic 3678
Ph (057) 29 8396 **Fax** (057) 29 8396
Open By appt **Production** 500
Winemaker(s) Guy Darling
A long-term grape grower in the King Valley, until 1991 a major
supplier to Brown Brothers, but with a parallel vineyard operation on
the family tobacco farm.
Principal Wines Riesling, Chardonnay, Chenin Blanc, Pinot Noir.

DARLING PARK VINEYARDS

★★★★ 12.50–15.50 CD AUSSD
Mornington Peninsula **Est.** 1986
Red Hill Road, Red Hill, Vic 3937

Ph (059) 89 2732 **Fax** (059) 89 2254
Open see T'Gallant **Production** 600
Winemaker(s) Kevin McCarthy (Contract)
Owned by John and Delys Sargeant. There are two separate
vineyard sites; the T'Gallant winery is situated on the Red Hill Road
Vineyard of Darling Park and it is there that the wines can be tasted.
However, Darling Park was planning to open its own on-site tasting
room in February 1995.
Principal Wines Chardonnay, Rosé Clair (a blend of cabernet,
merlot and pinot gris), Cabernet Merlot.

DARLING PARK CHARDONNAY
●●●● ▶ $15.50
Sourced from a total of one hectare of vineyards on two sites, which
provided two components at markedly different ripeness levels, one
very ripe, the other not so ripe. The result is a complex wine of high
quality.
Cellaring Up to 5 years. **Best Vintages** '94
Current Vintage '94
Matching Food Ragout of sweetbreads.
Tasting Note 1994 Light to medium green-yellow; complex,
powerful and concentrated with intense grapefruit and peach
components. The palate shows many flavours, with lots of white
peach alongside more citrus-like characters; overall fruit sweetness,
with well handled barrel ferment oak.

DARLINGTON ESTATE

NR 9.90–15.50 CD AUS61, 180
Darling Range **Est.** 1983
Lot 39 Nelson Road, Glen Forrest, WA 6071
Ph (09) 299 6268 **Fax** (09) 299 7107
Open Wed–Fri 12–5, W'ends, Hols 10–5 **Production** 2000
Winemaker(s) Balthazar van der Meer
In 1988 and 1989 Darlington showed just what the Perth Hills could
achieve with Chardonnay, Semillon/Sauvignon Blanc and (in 1988)
Cabernet Sauvignon — wines with great style, flavour and length.
Subsequent vintages have disappointed, except for a substantial,
flavoursome 1989 Cabernet Sauvignon; no recent tastings.
Principal Wines Chardonnay, Semillon Sauvignon Blanc, Shiraz,
Cabernet Sauvignon, Port; also cheaper Vin Primeur and Rosé.

DAVID TRAEGER WINES

★★★☆ 14–15.50 R AUS98, 177 UK11
Goulburn Valley **Est.** 1986
399 High Street, Nagambie, Vic 3608
Ph (057) 94 2514 **Fax** (057) 94 2514
Open 7 days 10–5 **Production** 4000
Winemaker(s) David Traeger
David Traeger learnt much during his years as assistant winemaker
at Mitchelton, and knows central Victoria well. The red wines are

solidly crafted, the Verdelho interesting but more variable in quality.
Principal Wines Shiraz, Verdelho, Cabernet.

DAVID TRAEGER CABERNET
●●● ▶ $15.50
Sourced from vineyards in Nagambie and the King Valley.
Predominantly cabernet sauvignon, with lesser amounts of cabernet
franc and merlot, matured in used French oak.
Cellaring 3–5 years. **Best Vintages** '88, '90, '92, '94
Current Vintage '92
Matching Food Lamb casserole.
Tasting Note 1992 Medium to full red-purple; a clean and solid
bouquet with mint and earth aromas, and a touch of oak. The palate
has mint, chocolate and red berry fruit flavours, finishing with soft
tannins, and obvious development potential.

DAVID TRAEGER SHIRAZ
●●●● $15.50
Produced from three vineyards in the Nagambie area, with a total
of 10 hectares under vine. The American oak handling has been
sensibly restrained.
Cellaring 4–6 years. **Best Vintages** '88, '92, '94
Current Vintage '92
Matching Food Wild duck.
Tasting Note 1992 Medium to full red-purple; the bouquet is
complex, ripe but firm with earthy/briary/gamey characters. The
palate has abundant briary/ liquorice fruit, well balanced vanillin
oak, finishing with soft tannins.

DAWSON ESTATE
★★★ 12–14 CD AUS25
Hunter Valley **Est.** 1980
Londons Road, Lovedale, NSW 2325
Ph (049) 90 2904 **Fax** (049) 91 1886
Open 7 days 9–5 **Production** 4000
Winemaker(s) Ben Dawson
A Chardonnay specialist producing wines of somewhat variable
quality, but at their best showing all of the buttery, peachy richness
one could hope for, and which repay cellaring.
Principal Wines Chardonnay, Traminer Riesling.

DE BORTOLI WINES (MURRUMBIDGEE)
★★★★ 4–30 R AUS52–54, 68, 97 UK33
Murrumbidgee Irrigation Area **Est.** 1928
De Bortoli Road, Bilbul, NSW 2680
Ph (069) 63 5253 **Fax** (069) 63 5382
Open Mon–Sat 9–5.30 **Production** 3 400 000
Winemaker(s) Darren De Bortoli
Famous among the cognoscenti for its superb Botrytis Semillon,

which in fact accounts for only a minute part of its total production, this winery turns around low-priced varietal and generic wines which neither aspire to nor achieve any particular distinction. Financial and marketing acumen makes De Bortoli the fastest-growing large winery in Australia today.

Principal Wines Noble One Botrytis Semillon; Premium varietals under Deen De Bortoli label, and a low-priced range of varietal and generic wines under the Sacred Hill label. Substantial exports in bulk.

DE BORTOLI DEEN DE BORTOLI CHARDONNAY
●●● $8

A wine which has on occasions (such as 1993) been astonishingly good given its price, and the volume in which it is made. It is produced almost entirely from Griffith region grapes, but reflects careful selection of the best available material.

Cellaring Drink now. **Best Vintages** '90, '92, '93
Current Vintage '94
Matching Food Pasta marinara.
Tasting Note 1993 Medium to full yellow-green; a surprisingly intense and complex bouquet with both fruit and more nutty aromas, with very cunningly handled oak. Full, soft, rich mouthfilling fruit and just a hint of spicy oak, no doubt from very well handled chips. The '94 is a disappointment in comparison.

DE BORTOLI DRY BOTRYTIS SEMILLON
●●●● $10

In the manner of Chateau d'Yquem, a dry wine made from grapes partially infected by botrytis, and in effect the dry half of Noble One. The '85 (first vintage) was a magnificent wine, the '87 very good indeed.

Cellaring 5–10 years. **Best Vintages** '85, '87, '92, '93
Current Vintage '93
Matching Food Interesting aperitif, prosciutto and melon.
Tasting Note 1993 Medium yellow-green; typical honeyed/honeysuckle aromas with some spicy/chippy oak. The palate needs time to develop weight and complexity, but on the track record of the wine will do so.

DE BORTOLI NOBLE ONE BOTRYTIS SEMILLON
●●●●● $20

A classic wine, without question the foremost example of barrel fermented, wood matured Botrytis Semillon in Australia. Every vintage made has won at least one trophy and innumerable gold medals.

Cellaring 3–10 years. **Best Vintages** '82, '84, '87, '90, '91, '92 **Current Vintage** '92
Matching Food Crème brûlée.
Tasting Note 1992 Deep, glowing yellow-gold; complex apricot and cumquat fruit lifted by an appropriate degree of volatility, and noticeable oak. A very complex wine in the mouth, with the fruit and oak still coming together.

DE BORTOLI WINES (YARRA VALLEY)

★★★★☆ 10–20 R AUS52–54, 68, 97 UK33
Yarra Valley **Est.** 1987
Pinnacle Lane, Dixons Creek, Vic 3775
Ph (059) 65 2271 **Fax** (059) 65 2442
Open Mon–Fri 9–5, W'ends 10–5.30 **Production** 100 000
Winemaker(s) Stephen Webber, David Slingsby-Smith
The former Chateau Yarrinya, now the quality arm of the bustling
De Bortoli group, run by Leanne De Bortoli and husband Stephen
Webber, ex-Lindeman winemaker. Both the top label (De Bortoli)
and the second label (Windy Peak) offer wines of consistently
good quality and excellent value.
Principal Wines Yarra Valley Chardonnay, Pinot Noir, Shiraz,
Cabernet Sauvignon, Cabernet Merlot; Windy Peak Riesling,
Chardonnay, Pinot Noir, Cabernets, Prestige; Montage White
and Red.

DE BORTOLI SEMILLON
●●●●● $17
First made in 1994, with immediate success. Against all the odds,
won the Yeringberg Award and Victorian Wine Centre Trophy at the
1994 Lilydale Show for Best White Wine in all classes other than
Chardonnay. Against all the odds, because young Semillon seldom
shows to advantage against other more obvious varieties.
Cellaring 3–5 years. **Best Vintages** NA **Current Vintage** '94
Matching Food Fresh seafood.
Tasting Note 1994 Intense citrus-tinged fruit, which while strongly
varietal, is not herbaceous in the leaner, drier sense of that term. The
palate shows many fruit flavours, running from citrus through to more
tropical; not oaked, and it does not need to be.

DE BORTOLI WINDY PEAK CHARDONNAY
●●●● $10
Like the Riesling, labelled Southern Victorian, and coming from a
vaiety of fruit sources from the Strathbogie Ranges and south, but
with a substantial Yarra Valley component. As the '93 vintage
proved, can be outstanding value for money.
Cellaring Basically drink now. **Best Vintages** '90, '92, '93, '94
Current Vintage '93
Matching Food Sashimi.
Tasting Note 1993 Light green yellow; clean, crisp melon fruit
aromas with subtle oak; crisp but quite intense melon, fig and citrus
fruit flavours, not propped up by oak, and with a long finish.
Exceptional quality at the price.

DE BORTOLI WINDY PEAK RHINE RIESLING
●●● ▶ $10
Made primarily from riesling grown in the Strathbogie Ranges and
the Yarra Valley, often with a small percentage of Yarra Valley
gewurztraminer included. First made in 1989, the wine has often
excelled.

Cellaring 1–4 years. **Best Vintages** '90, '91, '92
Current Vintage '94
Matching Food Fresh asparagus.
Tasting Note 1994 Light green-yellow; a discrete, and rather tight bouquet; the palate, likewise, is light and crisp, perhaps without the intensity of some of the prior vintages, but nonetheless representing good value.

DE BORTOLI YARRA VALLEY CABERNET SAUVIGNON
●●●● $20
Like the Shiraz, made from both estate-grown and purchased grapes. A 100% Cabernet Sauvignon (a Cabernet Merlot is also marketed) made using what might be described as traditional French techniques, and matured in a mix of new and used French barriques for 18 months before bottling. Can be outstanding; the 1991 vintage won six gold, three silver and seven bronze medals.
Cellaring 5 – 8 years. **Best Vintages** '88, '90, '91, '92, '94
Current Vintage '92
Matching Food Beef casserole.
Tasting Note 1992 Medium to full red-purple; a clean bouquet with gently leafy/minty edges to the berry fruit; the oak well handled and subtle. A relatively soft wine in the mouth with well balanced fruit, oak, acid and tannin.

DE BORTOLI YARRA VALLEY CHARDONNAY
●●●● $17
Made from both estate-grown grapes and grapes purchased from other Yarra Valley vineyards. Usually in a full-bodied style, albeit with restrained oak from partial barrel fermentation.
Cellaring 3–6 years. **Best Vintages** '90, '92, '93, '94
Current Vintage '93
Matching Food Yabbies.
Tasting Note 1993 Light yellow-green; citrus/melon fruit in a restrained, discrete style with subtle oak; the same flavours are evident on a complex yet fairly restrained palate, which finishes with good length.

DE BORTOLI YARRA VALLEY SHIRAZ
●●●● ▶ $17
There are surprisingly few Yarra Valley varietal Shirazs on the market, and the fruit flavours vary significantly from one maker to the next, ranging from strong spice and pepper through to more minty aromas and flavours. The De Bortoli wine is usually in the latter spectrum, but hit the jackpot with the stunning '93.
Cellaring 3–7 years. **Best Vintages** '88, '90, '91, '92, '94
Current Vintage '93
Matching Food Grilled calf's liver.
Tasting Note 1993 Full red-purple; a fragrant, potent bouquet with abundant, fragrant spice and berry fruit aromas interwoven with oak. The palate, too, shows exemplary cool climate varietal shiraz character in the spice/dark cherry/liquorice spectrum, finished off with perfectly balanced tannins and oak.

D'ENTRECASTEAUX *

NR NA AUSSD
Warren Valley **Est.** 1988
Boorara Road, Northcliffe, WA 6262
Ph NA
Open Not **Production** 600
Winemaker(s) Alkoomi (Contract)
Not to be confused with the now moribund Tasmanian winery of the
same name, but likewise taking its name from the French explorer
Admiral Bruni D'Entrecasteaux who visited both Tasmania and the
south west coast of Western Australia. Four hectares of estate
vineyards, planted on rich Karri loam, produce grapes for the
wines which are contract made at Alkoomi.
Principal Wines Chardonnay, Sauvignon Blanc, Pinot Noir,
Cabernet Sauvignon.

DELACOLLINE ESTATE

★★★☆ 10–15 R AUSSD
Port Lincoln **Est.** 1984
Whillas Road, Port Lincoln, SA 5606
Ph (086) 82 5277 **Fax** (086) 82 4455
Open Not **Production** 650
Winemaker(s) Tim Knappstein (White), Neil Pike (Red) (Contract)
Joins Boston Bay as the second Port Lincoln producer; the white
wines are made under contract by Tim Knappstein and the red wines
by Neil Pike. The 3-hectare vineyard, run under the direction of Tony
Bassett, reflects the cool maritime influence, with ocean currents
which sweep up from the Antarctic.
Principal Wines Riesling, Fumé Blanc, Cabernet Sauvignon.

DELAMERE VINEYARD

★★★☆ 20–22 CD AUS129
Pipers Brook **Est.** 1983
Bridport Road, Pipers Brook, Tas 7254
Ph (003) 82 7190
Open 7 days 10–5 **Production** 500
Winemaker(s) Richard Richardson
Richie Richardson produces elegant, rather light-bodied wines which
have a strong following. The Chardonnay has been most successful,
particularly in 1991, with a textured, complex, malolactic-influenced
wine with great, creamy feel in the mouth. The Pinot Noir always
shows distinct varietal fruit, but very consistent tasting notes show
errant aromas deriving from old oak.
Principal Wines Chardonnay, Pinot Noir.

DELATITE WINERY

★★★★ 13.50–21.50 R AUS55, 96, 115, 124, 156, 182, 185
UK9, 11, 17
Central Victoria **Est.** 1982

Stoneys Road, Mansfield, Vic 3722
Ph (057) 75 2922 **Fax** (057) 75 2911
Open 7 days 10–5 **Production** 12 000
Winemaker(s) Rosalind Ritchie
With its sweeping views across to the snow-clad alps, this is
uncompromising cool-climate viticulture, and the wines naturally
reflect the climate. Light but intense Riesling and spicy Traminer
flower with a year or two in bottle, and in years such as '88 and '90
the red wines achieve flavour and mouth-feel, albeit with a distinctive
and all-pervasive mintiness.
Principal Wines Unoaked Chardonnay, Chardonnay, Sauvignon
Blanc, Riesling, Dead Man's Hill Gewurztraminer, Pinot Noir, Devil's
River (Cabernet Sauvignon Malbec Shiraz).

DELATITE CHARDONNAY
●●● ▶ $16.50
The 2 hectares of estate plantings produce a wine in mainstream
Delatite style, far lighter than the usual run of Chardonnays, even
from cool climate regions. But as the '92 vintage shows, can
produce a very attractive Chablis style.
Cellaring 2–4 years. **Best Vintages** '88, '91, '92
Current Vintage '92
Matching Food Crab.
Tasting Note 1992 Medium to full green-yellow; a spotlessly clean
bouquet with smooth, delicate melon fruit and subtle oak. In the
mouth a light, elegant Chablis-weight wine with light melon fruit and
crisp acidity.

DELATITE DEAD MAN'S HILL GEWURZTRAMINER
●●●● $13.50
A wine which has attracted much favourable comment over the
years, particularly from United Kingdom writers. It is exceptionally
delicate, with very low phenolic levels, and at times seems to me to
be just that little bit too delicate. On the other hand, the style is
infinitely better than the heavy, oily versions of Traminer.
Cellaring 1–2 years. **Best Vintages** '82, '86, '87, '93, '94
Current Vintage '94
Matching Food Delicate Chinese dishes.
Tasting Note 1994 Very light green-yellow; light, crisp colour,
floral, faintly spicy fruit on both bouquet and palate; the wine is well
balanced, and Ros Ritchie has resisted the temptation to flesh it out
with residual sugar.

DELATITE DEVIL'S RIVER
●●● ▶ $16.50
A blend of cabernet, merlot, malbec and cabernet franc which, in
most vintages, is by far my most preferred wine from Delatite, simply
because the omnipresent mint aromas and flavours seem to work
best with the wine.
Cellaring 3–5 years. **Best Vintages** '82, '86, '88, '90, '93
Current Vintage '92
Matching Food Leg of lamb.
Tasting Note 1992 Medium to full red-purple; briary/minty

aromas of medium intensity and subtle oak lead on to a palate of light to medium weight with mint and leaf flavours, and soft tannins on the finish.

DELATITE RIESLING
●●●●● $13.50

Delatite has been a leader in the move to the correct labelling of Rhine Riesling as 'Riesling' but has also swept all before it in recent years. The '92 won a gold medal at the National Wine Show in 1993, while the '93 was named as Wine of the Year in the 1994–95 edition of the Good Wine Guide, by Huon Hooke and Mark Shield.
Cellaring Now–5 years. **Best Vintages** '82, '86, '87, '93, '94
Current Vintage '93
Matching Food Grilled fish.
Tasting Note 1993 Bright green-yellow; intense, crisp herb and lime aromas, leading logically on to a palate with good flavour and intensity, with near-identical lime and herb flavours, finishing with delicate acid.

DELATITE SAUVIGNON BLANC
●●●● $15.50

Produced from 1.4 hectares of estate plantings, and made — sensibly enough — without the use of oak. Sometimes lacking fruit intensity and varietal flavour, it comes into its own in better vintages such as 1994.
Cellaring Drink now. **Best Vintages** '82, '86, '87, '93, '94
Current Vintage '94
Matching Food Fresh oysters.
Tasting Note 1994 Bright light green; crisp and elegantly fragrant with some passionfruit yeast esters and gently herbaceous fruit. The palate is similarly crisp, light and elegant in typical Delatite style, with very low phenolic levels.

DENNIS' DARINGA

★★★ 11–25 R AUS28, 183 UK26
Southern Vales **Est.** 1970
Kangarilla Road, McLaren Vale, SA 5171
Ph (08) 323 8665 **Fax** (08) 323 9121
Open Mon–Fri 10–5, W'ends, Hols 11–5 **Production** 10 000
Winemaker(s) Peter Dennis
A low-profile winery which has, from time to time, made some excellent wines, most notably typically full-blown, buttery/peachy Chardonnay.
Principal Wines Sauvignon Blanc, Chardonnay, Shiraz, Cabernet Sauvignon, Merlot Cabernet, Mead, Port.

DEVIL'S LAIR WINES

★★★★☆ 20–23 R AUS3, 11, 55
Margaret River **Est.** 1981
Rocky Road, Forest Grove via Margaret River, WA 6285

Ph (09) 388 1717 **Fax** (09) 381 5423
Open By appt **Production** 10 000
Winemaker(s) Janice McDonald
A relatively new but very substantial operation, with 40 hectares of vineyard, and a 14-hectare lake, stocked with trout and yabbies to service that vineyard and to beautify the landscape. It is the project of Philip Sexton, who started Redback Brewery, and his wife Alli; it seems bound to play a major role in the development of Western Australian wine.
Principal Wines Pinot Noir, Chardonnay, Cabernet Merlot.

DEVIL'S LAIR CABERNET MERLOT
●●●● $20
Fashioned from an estate-grown blend of 64% cabernet sauvignon, 23% merlot, 7% petit verdot and 6% cabernet franc, and the first such release from Devil's Lair. The wine spent over two years in French barriques, yet is far from over-wooded.
Cellaring Up to 7 years. **Best Vintages** NA
Current Vintage '92
Matching Food Roast veal.
Tasting Note 1992 Dark red-purple; a complex bouquet showing cool climate characters with leafy/minty fruit and just a touch of blood plum. The wine has good feel in the mouth, with soft tannins and a pleasing finish, the flavours again running a cool climate mould.

DEVIL'S LAIR CHARDONNAY
●●●●● $24
A 100% estate-grown, barrel fermented and taken through malolactic fermentation. Devil's Lair believes the '94 to be the best wine to so far come from the estate, and I can but agree. The most remarkable feature of the wine is the ease with which it carries its 14.5% alcohol: one would never guess the alcohol content simply by tasting the wine.
Cellaring 4–7 years. **Best Vintages** '91, '92, '94
Current Vintage '94
Matching Food Milk-fed veal.
Tasting Note 1994 Medium yellow-green; there is classic melon/citrus fruit on the bouquet married with complex and stylish barrel ferment character. The palate is mouthfilling, with fig and melon fruit surrounded by lashings of toast and butter, balanced by crisp acid on the finish.

DEVIL'S LAIR PINOT NOIR
●●●●● $23
The rating is given on the basis of the 1993 wine, of which a mere 260 cases were produced. Fruit thinning reduced the yield to 2 tonnes to the acre, and the wine was harvested at 14û baume, although it does not show overripe characters.
Cellaring Up to 5 years. **Best Vintages** NA
Current Vintage '93
Matching Food Game.

Tasting Note 1993 Medium to full red-purple, unusually deep for a Pinot. A stylish, very aromatic bouquet with lush strawberry fruit, with some sappy overtones and superb use of oak. On the palate, very complex, strongly Burgundian in style, again with superb oak balance and integration. Long finish.

DIAMOND VALLEY VINEYARDS

★★★★☆ 10.45–28.90 ML AUS17, 75, 177
Yarra Valley **Est.** 1976
Kinglake Road, St Andrews, Vic 3761
Ph (03) 9710 1484 **Fax** (03) 9710 1369
Open Not **Production** 3500
Winemaker(s) David Lance
One of the Yarra Valley's finest producers of pinot noir, and an early pacesetter for the variety, making wines of tremendous style and crystal-clear varietal character. They are not Cabernet Sauvignon look-alikes, but true Pinot Noir, fragrant and intense. Much of the wine is sold through an informative and well-presented mailing list.
Principal Wines Estate Riesling, White Diamond, Chardonnay, Pinot Noir, Cabernet; Blue Label Chardonnay, Pinot Noir, Cabernet Sauvignon.

DIAMOND VALLEY ESTATE CABERNET
●●● ▶ $19
Made from a blend of estate-grown cabernet sauvignon, merlot, cabernet franc and malbec. As with all the Diamond Valley red wines, the oak is held in restraint, and the overall texture is soft.
Cellaring 3–6 years. **Best Vintages** '80, '82, '86, '90, '93
Current Vintage '90
Matching Food Yearling steak.
Tasting Note 1990 Medium to full red; complex aromas with leafy/gamey/spicy aspects, all typical of the Yarra Valley. There is surprising weight and sweetness on the palate with red berry fruits, finishing with some more leafy/herbal notes, and soft tannins.

DIAMOND VALLEY ESTATE CHARDONNAY
●●●● ▶ $20.25
Produced in very limited quantities from a little over one hectare of estate vines, and first released in 1990. Typically intense, the wine is fruit-, rather than oak-driven. The wine has won numerous gold medals since its first release in 1990.
Cellaring 2–5+ years. **Best Vintages** '90, '92, '94
Current Vintage '92
Matching Food Cold smoked trout.
Tasting Note 1992 Bright, light yellow-green; a clean, fresh, smooth and supple melon-accented bouquet; on the palate absolutely delicious, bright and lively fruit which will age superbly.

DIAMOND VALLEY ESTATE PINOT NOIR
●●●●● $30
Deserves its recognition as one of the greatest of the Yarra Valley Pinot Noirs, invariably generously flavoured, and invariably showing

strong varietal character, often (as in '91 and '93) in a ripe mould. A prolific trophy winner over the years, with the '93 continuing the tradition by winning the Wine Press Club Trophy at the 1994 Royal Melbourne Wine Show — the 24th trophy won by Diamond Valley Pinot Noir in the last 10 years.

Cellaring 2–4 years. **Best Vintages** '86, '90, '91, '92, '93
Current Vintage '93
Matching Food Wild duck.
Tasting Note 1993 Medium to full red-purple; extremely ripe, concentrated plummy fruit aroma, almost into muscat in its sweetness. Ripe and generous in the mouth, with far more weight than any other Yarra Valley Pinot of the vintage, with a long finish.

DOMAINE A

★★★☆ 14–27 CD AUSSD
Coal River **Est.** 1973
Campania, Tas 7202
Ph (002) 62 4174 **Fax** (002) 62 4390
Open By appt **Production** 1300
Winemaker(s) Peter Althaus
The striking new black label, dominated by the single, multicoloured 'A', signifies the change of ownership from George Park to Swiss businessman Peter Althaus. The much expanded vineyard is of undoubted quality, a harbinger of the great potential of the Coal River region. The Domaine A Cabernet Sauvignon is made in a relatively forbidding, heavily-oaked style with abundant tannins.
Principal Wines Domaine A is the top label with Cabernet Sauvignon and Pinot Noir; second label is Stoney Vineyard with Aurora (wood matured Sylvaner), Sauvignon Blanc, Cabernets, Cabernet Sauvignon.

DOMAINE A STONEY VINEYARD CABERNET SAUVIGNON
●●● $20.95
It is paradoxical that a wine predominantly composed of cabernet sauvignon, normally regarded as the latest ripening of the Bordeaux varieties, should be slightly sweeter and more luscious than the 'Cabernets' blend from the same vineyard of the same year. For all that, it is uncompromisingly cool climate, which will appeal strongly to those with a European bent.
Cellaring 3–5 years. **Best Vintages** '88, '90, '92, '93
Current Vintage '93
Matching Food Marinated beef.
Tasting Note 1993 Light to medium red-purple; a clean and smooth bouquet of light to medium intensity, with redcurrant/raspberry fruit aromas and subtle oak. The palate is firm, tending more to herbaceous and with the expected firm acidity of cool-grown cabernet. Not over oaked.

DOMAINE A STONEY VINEYARD CABERNETS
●●● $20.95
An estate-grown blend of the classic Bordeaux varieties, including cabernet sauvignon, cabernet franc and merlot. Fastidious attention

to detail in the vineyard only partially overcomes the impact of such a cool region on these basically late-maturing varieties. In the state-of-the-art winery, no less care is lavished, with a pleasing retreat from excessive oak in both the '93 vintage reds.

Cellaring 2–5 years. **Best Vintages** '88, '90, '92, '93
Current Vintage '93
Matching Food Surprise Bay Cheddar.
Tasting Note 1993 Strong, youthful red-purple; there are very typical ultra-cool grown juicy/leafy fruit aromas on the bouquet, with oak in restraint. The palate is potent, with slightly raspy/leafy blackcurrant fruit. A wine with 12% alcohol which really needed 13%.

DOMAINE CHANDON

★★★★★ 14–29 R AUS151–155 UK63
Yarra Valley **Est.** 1986
Maroondah Highway, Coldstream, Vic 3770
Ph (03) 9739 1110 **Fax** (03) 9739 1095
Open 7 days 11–4.30 **Production** 70 000
Winemaker(s) Dr Tony Jordan, Wayne Donaldson
Wholly owned by Moet et Chandon, and by far the most important wine facility in the Yarra Valley, superbly located with luxurious tasting facilities (a small tasting charge is levied). The wines are exemplary, thought by many to be the best produced by Moet et Chandon in any of its overseas subsidiary operations, a complex blend of French and Australian style.

Principal Wines Sparkling (Methode Champenoise) specialist with 5 sparkling wines: Brut, Blanc de Blancs, Blanc de Noir, Rosé, Yarra Valley, Cuvée Riche; Green Point is export label, also used for still Pinot Noir and Chardonnay; Colonnades is third label for table wines.

DOMAINE CHANDON (CUVÉE RICHE)
●●●●● $23
Just as the Rosé is the only serious example of its kind in Australia, so is the Cuvée Riche, an even rarer style, based on pinot noir and with 50 g/l dosage — a sugar level which is swallowed up by the wine, and seems far less on tasting.

Cellaring None required. **Best Vintages** NA
Current Vintage NA
Matching Food Light cake-type desserts.
Tasting Note NV Straw-yellow; a highly fragrant spicy/strawberry bouquet with very complex spicy nutmeg flavours, with a long finish and barely showing its sugar.

DOMAINE CHANDON BLANC DE BLANCS (CUVÉE 90-2)
●●●●● $23
Made entirely from chardonnay sourced from all over Australia, with a significant contribution from Coonawarra and the Yarra Valley. The Cuvée 90-2 was not disgorged until March 1994, and released at the end of that year. Only Domaine Chandon makes a Blanc de

Blancs in such an elegant, fine style. Will henceforth be vintage
dated.
Cellaring Not required. **Best Vintages** NA
Current Vintage '90
Matching Food Aperitif, shellfish.
Tasting Note 1990–1992 Brilliant green-yellow; intense, lingering
citrus/lemon aromas tinged with toast lead on to a superbly elegant
and fine palate, long, delicate and crisp.

DOMAINE CHANDON BLANC DE NOIR
●●●●● $23
The converse of the Blanc de Blancs, made entirely from pinot noir;
like the Blanc de Blancs, held on lees for over three years before
disgorgement, with the 90–3 (1990 vintage) released early in 1995.
Sourced from numerous southern Australian vineyards, notably the
Yarra Valley and Tasmania.
Cellaring None required. **Best Vintages** NA
Current Vintage '90
Matching Food Hors d'oeuvres.
Tasting Note 1990 Light straw; the aromas are more nutty and
toasty than strawberry fruit, the palate structured and bready, with
bite and length. Has none of the bitter, stemmy characters often
associated with pinot noir used in this fashion.

DOMAINE CHANDON BRUT
●●●●● $23
Formerly labelled Cuvée 91–1, but since the amendment to the laws
allowing 15% of other vintage components in a vintage wine, now
released as such. Typically a blend of 48% chardonnay, 50% pinot
noir and 2% pinot meuniere, sourced from the cooler parts of
Australia. Up to 50 individual components are used in the blend
to produce a wine of exceptional style and complexity.
Dosage 6.5 g/l.
Cellaring Not required. **Best Vintages** '88, '90, '91, '92
Current Vintage '92
Matching Food Ideal aperitif.
Tasting Note 1992 Some faint pink tinges which will age to straw
colour; a clean, fine bouquet with a faint echo of nutmeg from the
pinot noir, and honey from the chardonnay. Lovely sweet flavours,
more fruity than the '91, and more in the style of the '90.

DOMAINE CHANDON ROSÉ (CUVÉE-4)
●●●●● $23
Made from a blend of 58% pinot noir and 42% chardonnay, again
sourced from vineyards across southern Australia. Without question,
it is by far the most serious Rosé, albeit made in tiny quantities, and
hard to find. Indeed, none was made in 1991, so the next release
will be from 1992.
Cellaring None required. **Best Vintages** NA
Current Vintage '90
Matching Food Poached salmon, Asian cuisine.
Tasting Note 1990 Straw pink; a distinctly fruity aroma, in

marked contrast to the Blanc de Noir. The palate, too, shows full fruit flavours, yet is dry and exceptionally well balanced. The dosage is the same (5.5 g/l) as for other wines.

DOMAINE CHANDON YARRA VALLEY (CUVÉE 90-5)
●●●●● $23
Made entirely from Yarra Valley grapes, partially estate-grown and partially from other major valley growers. Typically a blend of 85% pinot noir and 15% chardonnay, and disgorged after three years on lees.
Cellaring None required. **Best Vintages** NA
Current Vintage '90
Matching Food Fish, white meats.
Tasting Note 1990 Light straw-yellow; a very discrete bouquet, with the pinot noir not at all stemmy or stalky; a quite delicious palate with strawberry and nut flavours, arguably the most rounded of all of the wines, but finishing with a dry delicacy.

DONNELLY RIVER WINES

★★★☆ 14 CD AUSSD
Warren Valley **Est.** 1986
Lot 159 Vasse Highway, Pemberton, WA 6260
Ph (097) 76 2052 **Fax** (097) 76 2053
Open 7 days 9.30–4.30 **Production** 3500
Winemaker(s) Blair Mieklejohn, Kim Oldfield
Donnelly River Wines draws upon 6 hectares of estate vineyards, planted in 1986 and which produced the first wines in 1990. It has performed consistently well with its Chardonnay.
Principal Wines Chardonnay, Semillon, Sauvignon Blanc, Pinot Noir, Cabernet Sauvignon.

DONNELLY RIVER CHARDONNAY
●●●● $14
An elegant wine which has performed well in shows, the 1991 vintage being a Sheraton Award winner, the 1993 a bronze medal winner at the 1994 Mount Barker Show (scoring strong silver medal points on my score sheet).
Cellaring 3–5 years. **Best Vintages** '91, '93
Current Vintage '93
Matching Food Calamari.
Tasting Note 1993 Light green-yellow; a fine, elegant citrus/melon bouquet showing its cool-grown origins. The palate has length and intensity, with citrus and melon flavours; a fruit-driven wine which may build greater complexity with bottle age.

DONOLGA WINES

★★☆ 3.80–7.80 CD AUSSD
Southern Vales **Est.** 1979
Main South Road, Aldinga, SA 5173
Ph (085) 56 3179

Open 7 days 10–5 **Production** 4000
Winemaker(s) Nick Girolamo
Almost an anachronism in this day and age, selling entirely from
cellar door to a local, largely ethnic clientele at prices which
compete with the supermarket specials. Flagons and bulk wine
(fill your own container) also available.
Principal Wines Chardonnay, Sauvignon Blanc, Riesling,
Cabernet Sauvignon, Shiraz.

DONOVAN WINES

★★★ 8–12.50 CD AUSSD
Great Western **Est.** 1977
Pomonal Road, Stawell, Vic 3380
Ph (053) 58 2727
Open Mon–Sat 10–4 **Production** 2000
Winemaker(s) Peter Donovan
Donovan quietly makes some attractively fragrant Riesling (an
excellent crisp, toasty '91) and concentrated, powerful Shiraz,
most of which is sold cellar door and by mail order.
Principal Wines Riesling, Classic Dry White, Shiraz, Crouchen
Moselle.

DOONKUNA ESTATE

★★★★ 12–15 CD AUSSD
Canberra **Est.** 1973
Barton Highway, Murrumbateman, NSW 2582
Ph (06) 227 5885 **Fax** (06) 227 5085
Open Mon–Fri 1–4 **Production** 800
Winemaker(s) Karen Leggett
With judicious help from consultants, Lady Janette Murray will
continue the work of the late Sir Brian Murray, former Victorian
Governor-General, in making some of the best white wines in the
Canberra district, and forceful reds of somewhat lesser finesse.
1994 production severely curtailed by October '93 frost.
Principal Wines Chardonnay, Riesling, Pinot Noir, Shiraz,
Cabernet Sauvignon.

DOONKUNA CHARDONNAY

●●●● ▸ $15
The best of the two Doonkuna wines, and usually the best
Chardonnay made in the Canberra district, though sometimes
shaded by Lark Hill. Invariably well made, with skilled use of
barrel fermentation.
Cellaring 3–5 years. **Best Vintages** '88, '90, '91, '92, '93
Current Vintage '92
Matching Food Snowy Mountains trout.
Tasting Note 1992 Light yellow-green; a crisp and clean
bouquet with smoky/tangy aromas, the palate light but elegant,
showing sensibly restrained use of oak, and attractive melon and
citrus fruit.

DOONKUNA ESTATE CABERNET SAUVIGNON
●●●● $18.50

The red wines of Doonkuna, and in particular the Cabernet
Sauvignon, are generously-flavoured wines with slightly rustic notes
which do, however, improve with age. The currently available 1991
Cabernet Sauvignon won a strong bronze medal at the 1994
Australian National Wine Show in Canberra.
Cellaring 5–7 years. **Best Vintages** '90, '91, '92
Current Vintage '91
Matching Food Strongly-flavoured cheese.
Tasting Note 1991 Medium to full red-purple; a luscious bouquet
with full sweet berry and mint fruit, and just a hint of gaminess
lurking on the edge. The palate is likewise big and luscious, with
mint and dark berry fruit flavours, finishing with fairly persistent
tannins. A fraction rough on the finish.

DOONKUNA RIESLING
●●●● $12

As Doonkuna Madew and Lark Hill most consistently, and Helms
occasionally, show, riesling is well suited to the Canberra district
climate. This wine, produced from low-yielding, hand-pruned and
picked vines, is invariably well made with consultancy advice from
Gary Baldwin of Oenotech.
Cellaring Up to 5 years. **Best Vintages** '88, '90, '91, '92, '93
Current Vintage '92
Matching Food Green bean salad with hazelnut oil.
Tasting Note 1992 Light to medium yellow-green; clean, firm
and well constructed, not particularly aromatic, and with a hint of
herbaceousness. The palate has more flavour than the bouquet
suggests, with solid lime fruit which carries through to the back
palate and finish.

DRAYTON'S WINERY

★★★★ 7.50–22 R AUS73 UK67
Hunter Valley **Est.** 1853
Oakey Creek Road, Cessnock, NSW 2321
Ph (049) 98 7513 **Fax** (049) 98 7743
Open 7 days 9–5 **Production** 100 000
Winemaker(s) Trevor Drayton
A family-owned and run stalwart of the Valley, producing honest,
full-flavoured wines which sometimes excel themselves, and are
invariably modestly priced. The size of the production will come as a
surprise to many, but it is a clear indication of the good standing of
the brand.
Principal Wines Semillon, White Burgundy, Riesling, Chardonnay
Semillon, Verdelho, Sauternes, Hermitage, Pinot Noir, Cabernet
Merlot, Cabernet Sauvignon; Oakey Creek Semillon Chardonnay,
Semillon Sauvignon Blanc, Traminer Riesling, Hermitage, Shiraz
Cabernet.

DRAYTON'S BIN 5555 HERMITAGE
●●●● $12.80

Year in, year out, this wine offers the best value in the Drayton
range, as honest as the day is long, and with real depth to the fruit.
In its youth it shows good varietal fruit characters, but will slowly
change with age into a typically regional style, pleasing those who
like old Hunter reds.

Cellaring Up to 15 years. **Best Vintages** '81, '83, '85, '88, '91
Current Vintage '93
Matching Food Lamb casserole.
Tasting Note 1993 Medium to full red-purple; full and solid dark
cherry fruit aromas with minimal oak influence. On the palate, lots of
cherry and berry fruit, soft tannins and nice acid balance.

DRAYTON'S CABERNET SAUVIGNON
●●●● $12.80

A quiet performer with Cabernet Sauvignon, part estate-grown and
part purchased, but all from relatively low-yielding, lower Hunter
vineyards. Vinification is straightforward, and the wine is driven by
its fruit, rather than oak.

Cellaring Up to 10 years. **Best Vintages** '81, '83, '85, '88, '91
Current Vintage '93
Matching Food Soft ripened cheese.
Tasting Note 1993 Medium to full red, with just a touch of purple;
clean red berry and chocolate fruit aromas, with abundant ripe, but
not overripe, red berry fruits and a faint hint of Hunter earth,
finishing with soft tannins. Excellent cellaring potential.

DRAYTON'S SEMILLON
●●● $10.50

Made in traditional Hunter style, without resorting to oak and in
particular to oak chips. It thus requires both patience and
understanding to give of its best.

Cellaring 7–10 years. **Best Vintages** '84, '85, '86, '88, '94
Current Vintage '93
Matching Food Pasta.
Tasting Note 1993 Light to medium yellow-green; clean and
smooth, with light honey and herbal aromas; the palate is pleasant,
of medium weight and a little short, but should fill out with time.

DRAYTON'S VERDELHO
●●● ▶ $11.80

Verdelho was a highly favoured variety in the Hunter Valley around
the turn of the century, subsequently to all but disappear from view.
In recent years it has enjoyed a renaissance, with significant new
plantings, although it is hard to see it challenging the dominant
position of either Semillon or Chardonnay.

Cellaring 3–5 years. **Best Vintages** NA
Current Vintage '94
Matching Food Sweetbreads.
Tasting Note 1994 Medium yellow-green; smooth fruit aromas
with hints of honeysuckle and no obvious oak influence. The palate
has some real life and length, auguring well for medium-term
cellaring.

DRAYTON'S WILLIAM SHIRAZ
●●● ▸ $25

Made from a single block of old vines, and named in honour of William Drayton, the founder of the company, now carried on by his great- grandchildren. The packaging of the wine, and to a lesser degree, its quality, are a little disappointing.

Cellaring 7–10 years. **Best Vintages** NA
Current Vintage '90
Matching Food Rich red meats.
Tasting Note 1990 Medium to full red; ripe, earthy hay/straw aromas in old-fashioned Hunter style; the palate has plenty of weight and power, with some attractive liquorice earth and chocolate flavours, and finely integrated tannins.

DROMANA ESTATE
★★★★ 11–20 R AUS13, 63, 64, 66, 67, 116

Mornington Peninsula **Est.** 1982
Cnr Harrison's Road and Bittern-Dromana Road, Dromana, Vic 3936
Ph (059) 87 3800 **Fax** (059) 81 0714
Open 7 days 11–4 **Production** 12 000
Winemaker(s) Garry Crittenden

The first of the Mornington Peninsula wineries to take a wholly commercial approach to winemaking and marketing. Intriguingly, having had great success in the United Kingdom, has withdrawn from there to concentrate its efforts in Australia, relying in part on a much enlarged and very attractive cellar door sales area.

Principal Wines Dromana Estate Chardonnay, Pinot Noir, Cabernet Merlot; Second label Schinus Delicato, Riesling, Chenin Blanc, Sauvignon Blanc, Chardonnay, Rosé, Pinot Noir, Dolcetto, Nebbiolo, Cabernet, all the latter sourced from diverse regions.

DROMANA ESTATE CHARDONNAY
●●●● $22

As with all of the Dromana Estate wines, estate-grown. It is entirely barrel fermented in a mixture of new and one-year-old French barriques, and — in line with common Mornington Peninsula practice — around 60% is usually taken through malolactic fermentation.

Cellaring Up to 5 years. **Best Vintages** '90, '91, '92, '94
Current Vintage '94
Matching Food Shellfish, prawns.
Tasting Note 1994 Light green-yellow; the bouquet is quite complex, with melon fruit and attractive spicy oak. The palate is elegant, still reserved and tight, with good acidity and the promise of development in bottle.

DROMANA ESTATE PINOT NOIR
●●●● $18

Dromana Estate was one of the first Mornington Peninsula producers to consistently produce distinctive Pinot Noir. Most have proved to

be fairly short lived; notwithstanding the ripeness and the low yield
of the '94 vintage, it seems to be made in the same mould.
Cellaring Drink now. **Best Vintages** '91, '94
Current Vintage '94
Matching Food Char-grilled seafood.
Tasting Note 1994 Light to medium red-purple; a fragrant
bouquet with carbonic maceration characters giving a range of
spicy/tangy/leafy characters. The same flavours are apparent on
the palate which, while seemingly relatively light bodied, is quite
intense, with a mixture of spicy/tangy and more gamey aspects.

DROMANA ESTATE SCHINUS RIESLING
●●● ▶ $14
Made entirely from grapes grown in Victoria's Western District,
and made using the typical Australian approach of bright and clear
juice, cold fermented. Available only from cellar door or mailing list.
Cellaring 1–2 years. **Best Vintages** NA
Current Vintage '94
Matching Food Grilled fish.
Tasting Note 1994 Light green-yellow; fresh and crisp aromas
with citrus/herbaceous notes and just a touch of lightly browned
toast. The palate is of light to medium weight, clean and crisp, with
identical flavours to those of the bouquet.

DROMANA ESTATE SCHINUS ROSÉ
●●● ▶ $11
A most interesting wine, sourced from the Mornington Peninsula
and King Valley, comprising 85% cabernet sauvignon and 15%
nebbiolo, with an amazing 13.5% alcohol.
Cellaring Drink now. **Best Vintages** NA **Current Vintage** '94
Matching Food Any Asian cuisine.
Tasting Note 1994 Bright, light red; a light, crisp and clean
bouquet faintly herbal, but with zest and life. The palate is very well
balanced, particularly given the alcohol, which does, however,
invest the wine with unexpected richness. Finishes dry.

DULCINEA VINEYARD
NR 9.15 ML AUSSD
Ballarat **Est.** 1983
Jubilee Road, Sulky, Ballarat, Vic 3352
Ph (053) 34 6440
Open By appt **Production** 800
Winemaker(s) Various Contract
Rod Stott is a part-time but passionate grape grower and winemaker
who chose the name Dulcinea from 'The Man of La Mancha' where
only a fool fights windmills. With winemaking help from various
sources, he has produced a series of very interesting and often
complex wines, all of which have had show success at one point or
another in their career.
Principal Wines Chardonnay, Sauvignon Blanc, Pinot Noir,
Cabernet Sauvignon.

DUNCAN ESTATE

★★★☆ 10–13 AUS3, 87
Clare Valley **Est.** 1968
Spring Gully Road, Clare, SA 5453
Ph (088) 43 4335 **Fax** (088) 43 4335
Open 7 days 10–4 **Production** 1000
Winemaker(s) John Duncan
The Duncan family has been growing grapes in the Clare Valley since 1968, and first produced wines from its 7.4 hectares of vineyards in 1984. Over the years some attractive wines have been produced, with the Cabernet Merlot and Shiraz usually very good.
Principal Wines Riesling, Chardonnay, Late Picked Traminer Riesling, Shiraz, Cabernet Sauvignon Shiraz Merlot.

DUNCAN ESTATE RIESLING

●●● ▶ $10
As with all of the Duncan Estate wines, made entirely from estate-grown grapes, with the 1994 production severely reduced by frost (the first in 11 years). In the mainstream of Clare Valley style, showing just why this region is so highly regarded for the wine. Both 1992 and 1991 vintages available at the end of 1994.
Cellaring 7–10 years. **Best Vintages** '84, '85, '89, '90, '91
Current Vintage '92
Matching Food Salad niçoise.
Tasting Note 1992 Light to medium yellow-green; of medium intensity, not particularly floral, but with good weight. Some herbal notes evident on the palate, along with more traditional lime and toast; needs time. The '91 is fuller, richer and fractionally sweeter.

DYSON MASLIN BEACH

NR 8.50–12.50 AUS68
Southern Vales **Est.** 1984
Sherriff Road, Maslin Beach, SA 5170
Ph (08) 386 1092
Open 7 days 10–5 **Production** 1600
Winemaker(s) Allan Dyson
Owned by district veteran Allan Dyson. Typically for the district, Sauvignon Blanc has been one of the more consistent performers in the Maslin Beach portfolio, showing good varietal character and depth of flavour. No recent tastings.
Principal Wines Chardonnay, Sauvignon Blanc, Pinot Noir, Cabernet Sauvignon, Sparkling.

EAGLEHAWK ESTATE

★★★☆ 8.95 R AUS104
Clare Valley **Est.** 1856
Main North Road, Watervale, SA 5452
Ph (088) 43 0003 **Fax** (088) 43 0096
Open Mon–Fri 9–5, W'ends 12–4 **Production** 100 000
Winemaker(s) Chris Hatcher

This great legacy of the nineteenth century heyday of the Clare Valley has seen its name changed from Quelltaler to Eaglehawk, and at the time of writing, was being threatened a further name change to Black Opal. Long-term winemaker Stephen John has departed, and the future is uncertain.
Principal Wines Fumé Blanc, Riesling, Chardonnay, Shiraz Merlot Cabernet Sauvignon.

EAGLEHAWK ESTATE CHARDONNAY
●●● $9.95
Made in an unashamedly commercial mould, with skin contact and what appears to be American oak. Given the limitations of the Clare Valley with this variety, a creditable effort.
Cellaring Drink now. **Best Vintages** NA **Current Vintage** '93
Matching Food Pasta carbonara.
Tasting Note 1993 Medium to full yellow-green; rich yellow peach aromas with sweet oak; a big, peachy-flavoured wine with plenty of flavour and not quite so much finesse; finishes soft.

EAGLEHAWK ESTATE FUMÉ BLANC
●●● ▸ $9.95
A blend of sauvignon blanc and semillon, made in a thoroughly commercial mould, aided by skin contact, and quick developing.
Cellaring Drink now. **Best Vintages** NA **Current Vintage** '93
Matching Food Chicken or veal.
Tasting Note 1993 Medium to full yellow green; developed toasty honeyed aromas, almost Hunter-like, with semillon rather than sauvignon blanc dominant. There is a hint of spice on the palate, which is fleshy but a little on the short side.

EASTBROOK ESTATE *

NR 10–12 CD AUSSD
Warren Valley **Est.** 1990
Lot 3 Vasse Highway, Eastbrook, WA 6260
Ph (097) 76 1251 **Fax** (097) 76 1008
Open Fri–Sun, Public hols 11–3 **Production** 200
Winemaker(s) Kim Skipworth
Established on part of the same former grazing property which also accommodates Salitage, Phoenicia, and Dr Bill Pannell's vineyard. A jarrah pole, limestone and cedar weatherboard winery and restaurant have been built on the site by former Perth real estate agent Kim Skipworth, who is also a shareholder in one of the major Margaret River cheese factories. The wines come from 2 hectares each of pinot noir and chardonnay which are still coming into bearing; 2 hectares of shiraz are planned.
Principal Wines Chardonnay, Pinot Noir.

EDEN VALLEY WINES

NR 8.50–20 CD AUSSD UK91
Adelaide Hills **Est.** 1990
Main Street, Eden Valley, SA 5235

Ph (085) 64 1111 **Fax** (085) 64 1110
Open 7 days 10–5 **Production** Nil 1994
Winemaker(s) Peter Thompson
At the end of 1994 the only wines being offered were from the
1989 and 1990 vintages, with no wines made in 1994 or
apparently in the intervening years. The main focus of the operation
is a 300-seat restaurant.
Principal Wines Riesling, Traminer, Spatlese Frontignac,
Chardonnay, Pinot Noir, Shiraz Cabernet, Shiraz, Cabernet
Sauvignon, Sparkling; Eden Springs Wines Riesling, Fumé Blanc,
Port.

ELAN VINEYARD

NR 12 CD AUSSD
Mornington Peninsula **Est.** 1980
17 Turners Road, Bittern, Vic 3918
Ph (059) 83 1858 **Fax** (059) 83 2321
Open First w'end of month, Public hols 11–5 **Production** 200
Winemaker(s) Selma Lowther
Selma Lowther, fresh from Charles Sturt University (as a mature-age
student) made an impressive debut with her spicy, fresh, crisp 1990
Chardonnay. Most of the grapes from the 2.5 hectares of estate
vineyards are sold; production remains minuscule.
Principal Wines Chardonnay, Shiraz, Cabernet Merlot.

ELDERTON WINES

★★★☆ 10.65–29.50 R AUS15, 68, 74, 137, 148, 156, 184
UK6
Barossa Valley **Est.** 1984
3 Tanunda Road, Nuriootpa, SA 5355
Ph (085) 62 1058 **Fax** (085) 62 2844
Open Mon–Fri 8.30–5, W'ends, Hols 11–4 **Production** 32 000
Winemaker(s) Neil Ashmead
Relentlessly driven by the marketing skills of Neil Ashmead, and
given a great boost by the winning of the 1993 Jimmy Watson
Trophy at the Royal Melbourne Show with the recently released
1992 Cabernet Sauvignon.
Principal Wines Riesling, Semillon Chardonnay, Sparkling, Pinot
Noir, Shiraz, Shiraz Cabernet, Cabernet Sauvignon, Cabernet
Merlot, Hermitage; the Elderton Domain range is in fact the second
label.

ELDERTON CABERNET SAUVIGNON
●●●●● $29
The Elderton red wines have always been full-flavoured, and have
been consistent medal winners across the national show system, but
it nonetheless must have come as a pleasant surprise to the Elderton
team to win the 1993 Jimmy Watson Trophy. The wine now
marketed is, without question, very similar to the wine as it tasted
at the show.

Cellaring 10 years. **Best Vintages** NA **Current Vintage** '92
Matching Food Venison.
Tasting Note 1992 Deep purple-red; rich, full and ripe chocolate
and red berry fruits together with abundant, sweet vanillin American
oak on the bouquet, and a similar array of flavours on the palate.
The wine is still coming together, but has all of the ingredients for a
long life.

ELDERTON SHIRAZ
●●●● $14.95
Elderton's strength lies in its 30 hectares of prime Barossa Valley
vineyards, which produce consistently rich red wines which are
made elsewhere under contract. Right from the outset, these wines
have been consistent medal winners.
Cellaring 5–7 years. **Best Vintages** '86, '88, '90, '91, '92
Current Vintage '91
Matching Food Rack of lamb.
Tasting Note 1991 Full red; a rich and full bouquet with
pronounced dark chocolate fruit and subtle oak. There are pleasant
chocolate and vanilla flavours on the palate with well balanced
tannins; should age nicely.

ELDREDGE WINES *

★★★ 9.99–24.95 CD AUSSD
Clare Valley **Est.** 1993
Spring Gully Road, Clare, SA 5453
Ph (088) 42 2750 **Fax** (088) 42 2750
Open 7 days 11–5 **Production** 2000
Winemaker(s) Leigh Eldredge, Tim Adams (Consultant)
Leigh and Karen Eldredge have established their winery and cellar
door sales area in the Sevenhill Ranges, at an altitude of 500
metres, above the town of Watervale. Contract winemaking by Tim
Adams has ensured a solid start to the business.
Principal Wines Riesling, Semillon Sauvignon Blanc, New Age
Grenache, Cabernet Sauvignon.

ELDREDGE WINES NEW AGE GRENACHE
●●● $11.50
I do not know the derivation of the 'New Age' name, but the style is
certainly that, incorporating as it does American oak with the rich
grenache fruit.
Cellaring 1–3 years. **Best Vintages** NA **Current Vintage** '94
Matching Food Stir-fried beef.
Tasting Note 1994 Medium to full purple-red; a clean bouquet
with plenty of rich fruit and abundant, vanillin American oak. At the
moment that vanillin American oak tends to dominate the palate, but
the fruit is there; finishes with appropriately soft tannins.

ELDREDGE WINES RIESLING
●●● $9.99
Made in a rich, full-bodied style, ideally suited to the requirements of
cellar door.

Cellaring Drink now. **Best Vintages** NA **Current Vintage** '94
Matching Food Asian.
Tasting Note 1994 Medium yellow-green; already showing lots
of bottle development, full and soft with tropical/lime aromas. The
palate, too, is full-bodied and soft, with flavours of lime and honey,
finishing slightly sweet.

ELGEE PARK WINES

★★★★ 11–30 R AUS72
Mornington Peninsula **Est.** 1972
Wallaces Road, Merricks North, Vic 3926
Ph (059) 89 7338 **Fax** (059) 89 7553
Open Not **Production** 650
Winemaker(s) Tod Dexter (Contract)
The pioneer of the Mornington Peninsula in its twentieth-century rebirth,
owned by Baillieu Myer and family. The wines are now made at
Stoniers Merricks, Elgee Park's own winery having been closed.
Principal Wines Riesling, Chardonnay, Cabernet Merlot,
Cabernet Franc, Sparkling.

ELMSLIE WINES

★★☆ 15 ML AUSSD
Tamar Valley **Est.** 1972
Upper McEwans Road, Legana, Tas 7277
Ph (003) 30 1225 **Fax** (003) 30 2161
Open By appt **Production** 3000
Winemaker(s) Ralph Power
A small, specialist red winemaker, from time to time blending pinot
noir with cabernet. The fruit from the now fully mature vineyard has
depth and character, but operational constraints mean that the style
of the wine is often somewhat rustic.
Principal Wines Pinot Noir, Cabernet Sauvignon.

ELSEWHERE VINEYARD

★★★★★ 16–20 CD AUSSD
Huon Valley **Est.** 1984
RSD 558 Glaziers Bay, Tas 7112
Ph (002) 95 1509
Open By appt **Production** 2000
Winemaker(s) Andrew Hood (Contract)
Eric and Lette Phillips' evocatively-named Elsewhere Vineyard jostles
for space with a commercial flower farm also run by the Phillips. It is
a mark of the success of the wines that in 1993 some of the long-
established flower areas made way for additional chardonnay and
riesling, although it is Elsewhere's Pinot Noirs that are so stunning.
Principal Wines Pinot Noir, Riesling, Chardonnay, Sparkling.

ELSEWHERE VINEYARD PINOT NOIR
●●●●● $18
The 1991 and 1993 vintages of this wine rank among the best

made anywhere in Australia in those vintages, and certainly in
Tasmania. They both exhibit extraordinary colour, aroma and
richness of fruit, attesting to the superb site climate enjoyed by
Elsewhere.
Cellaring 3–5 years. **Best Vintages** '89, '91, '93
Current Vintage '93
Matching Food Breast of duck with demi-glace.
Tasting Note 1993 Vivid purple-red; very youthful, rich almost
essency yet not jammy pinot; a vivid and youthful wine in the mouth,
redolent of plums and cherries, and with just a hint of oak.
Altogether voluptuous and sensual.

ELTHAM VINEYARDS

★★★☆ 14.95–18.95 ML AUS135
Yarra Valley **Est.** 1990
225 Shaws Road, Arthurs Creek, Vic 3099
Ph (03) 9439 4688 **Fax** (03) 9439 5121
Open By appt **Production** 850
Winemaker(s) George Apted, John Graves
Drawing upon vineyards at Arthurs Creek and Eltham, John Graves
(brother of David Graves of the illustrious Californian Pinot producer
Saintsbury) produces tiny quantities of quite stylish Chardonnay and
Pinot Noir, the former showing nice barrel-ferment characters.
Principal Wines Chardonnay, Pinot Noir, Cabernet Sauvignon.

EPPALOCK RIDGE WINERY

NR 13.50–15.50 CD AUS94
Bendigo **Est.** 1979
Metcalfe Pool Road, Redesdale, Vic 3444
Ph (054) 25 3135
Open W'ends 10–6 **Production** 600
Winemaker(s) Rod Hourigan
A low-key operation with no recent information provided, but a
tasting mid 1993 of the 1990 Shiraz showed a rich, sweet dark
chocolate and plum fruited wine of very acceptable quality.
Principal Wines Chardonnay, Semillon, Shiraz.

ERINACEA WINES

NR 14 CD AUSSD
Mornington Peninsula **Est.** 1988
Devonport Dve, Rye, Vic 3941
Ph (059) 88 6336
Open By appt **Production** 350
Winemaker(s) Ron Glyn Jones
Medical practitioner Dr Ron Jones added a winemaking and
viticulture degree to his qualifications in 1988, and as well as
making tiny quantities of wine, acts as a consultant to others in the
region.
Principal Wines Chardonnay, Cabernet Sauvignon, Cabernet
Merlot.

ETTAMOGAH WINERY

NR 4.50–10.50 CD AUSSD
Southern New South Wales **Est.** 1978
Tabletop Road, Tabletop via Albury, NSW 2640
Ph (060) 26 2366 **Fax** (060) 26 2394
Open Mon–Sat 9–5, Sun 9–4 **Production** 3500
Winemaker(s) Brendan Dalton
Catering for the tourist trade, and apparently now owned by
De Bortoli, which takes the major part of the production from the
15 hectares of vineyards.
Principal Wines Riesling, Semillon, Chardonnay, Cabernet
Sauvignon, Muscat.

EURUNDEREE FLATS WINERY

NR 9–12 CD AUSSD
Mudgee **Est.** 1985
Henry Lawson Drive, Mudgee, NSW 2850
Ph (063) 73 3954 **Fax** (063) 73 3750
Open Sun–Fri 10–4, Sat 9–5 **Production** 1650
Winemaker(s) Peter Knights
Formerly Knights Vines, now called Eurunderee Flats, although under
the same ownership. A small producer making whites of variable
quality, and rather better dry red table wines.
Principal Wines Chardonnay, Semillon Chardonnay, Sauvignon
Blanc, Gordo Riesling, Grenache Rosé, Shiraz Merlot, Fortified.

EURUNDEREE FLATS SHIRAZ MERLOT
●●● $11.50
A blend of 60% shiraz and 40% merlot, matured in a mixture of new
and old American oak for 12 months. A massive, rustic wine, but
with plenty of flavour. Graced with the observation, 'Our
reputation's on the vine'.
Cellaring 10 years. **Best Vintages** NA **Current Vintage** '93
Matching Food Barbecued ox.
Tasting Note 1993 Dense red-purple; immensely concentrated
and powerful bouquet with rustic, earthy overtones to the very rich
fruit. A big, brawny wine with a high level of flavour and extract,
and just a touch of volatility.

EVANS & TATE WINEMAKERS

★★★★★ 14.95–22 R AUS48, 59, 60, 107, 115, 163, 164
UK23
Swan Valley & Margaret River **Est.** 1972
Metricup Road, Willyabrup, WA 6280
Ph (09) 296 4666 **Fax** (09) 296 1148
Open Mon–Fri 10.30–4.30 **Production** 40 000
Winemaker(s) Brian Fletcher, Fee Purnell
Single-handedly changed perceptions of the Swan Valley red wines
in the '70s before opening its highly successful Margaret River

operation which goes from strength to strength. The arrival of the immensely talented and experienced Brian Fletcher as winemaker should guarantee the continuation of its success, supported by Fiona Purnell, who followed Fletcher from the Yarra Valley.

Principal Wines With three exceptions (Western Australia Classic Semillon Sauvignon Blanc, Two Vineyards Chardonnay and Gnangara Shiraz Cabernet) the range is now based on the Margaret River vineyards which produce Semillon, Sauvignon Blanc, Shiraz, Merlot and Cabernet Sauvignon.

EVANS & TATE BARRIQUE 61 CABERNET MERLOT
●●●● $18.95
A new label for Evans & Tate, made from cabernet sauvignon and merlot grown in the Margaret River, Manjimup and Mount Barker regions.
Cellaring 5–7 years. **Best Vintages** NA **Current Vintage** '93
Matching Food Loin of lamb.
Tasting Note 1993 Medium to full red-purple; multi-faceted aromas ranging through berry, spice and earth, interwoven with subtle oak. A wine of considerable richness on the palate, with a range of dark berry fruits, well balanced and integrated oak, and finishing with fine tannins.

EVANS & TATE MARGARET RIVER CABERNET SAUVIGNON
●●●●● $22.15
A blend of 92% cabernet sauvignon and 8% merlot produced mainly from Evans & Tate's Redbrook Vineyard in the Margaret River. Whether coincidence or not, the arrival of Brian Fletcher seems to have lifted this wine into another class and dimension. The '91 vintage was of quite outstanding quality, and the '92 is in the same class. It is matured, incidentally, in French oak.
Cellaring 8 years. **Best Vintages** '86, '88, '90, '91, '92
Current Vintage '92
Matching Food Braised ox cheek in red wine sauce.
Tasting Note 1992 Medium red-purple; fragrant, complex bouquet with a mix of briary aromas and sweeter cassis/blackcurrant. The palate is fruit- rather than oak-driven; its outstanding feature is its structure, compellingly Bordeaux-like with the fine-grained tannins which run throughout.

EVANS & TATE MARGARET RIVER HERMITAGE
●●●● ▶ $22
A 100% estate-grown wine from the Redbrook Vineyard, still using the Hermitage name but, of course, made from shiraz. The Margaret River region has not done a great deal with shiraz overall, preferring to concentrate on other varieties, but this wine shows the potential that the region has for this variety. Matured in a mix of French and American oak.
Cellaring 7 years. **Best Vintages** '86, '88, '90, '91, '92
Current Vintage '92
Matching Food Strong red meat dishes.

Tasting Note 1992 Excellent purple-red; still very youthful with black cherry fruit and oak still integrating on the bouquet. The palate is packed with flavour and extract, with both fruit and oak tannins there in abundance; needs at least three years to come out of its shell and show its best.

EVANS & TATE MARGARET RIVER SEMILLON
●●●●● $19.75

Vies with Moss Wood for the position of top Semillon from the Margaret River, albeit of a quite different style, being more lively, lighter in fruit weight, but more intense in flavour — due in part to barrel fermentation in 100% new oak, half French, half American. 1994 is a multiple gold medal winner.

Cellaring Now or up to 5 years. **Best Vintages** '91, '92, '93, '94 **Current Vintage** '94

Matching Food Marron, yabbies.

Tasting Note 1994 Light to medium yellow-green; intense, fragrant lemony fruit and spicy/nutmeg oak aromas, and a fine, lingering stylish palate with beautifully integrated oak, and a long, slightly smoky finish.

EVANS & TATE TWO VINEYARDS CHARDONNAY
●●●●● $18

As the name indicates, the wine has a mixed regional source, although not strictly from two vineyards: while its base is from estate vineyards at Perth and Margaret River, it also extends to grapes sourced from other south west regions. Interestingly, it is fermented entirely in American oak barrels, principally new; American oak does not always work as well with Chardonnay as it does in this instance.

Cellaring Up to 4 years. **Best Vintages** '91, '92, '93, '94 **Current Vintage** '94

Matching Food Sugar-cured tuna.

Tasting Note 1994 Light green-yellow; smooth bouquet with spicy oak and quite intense melon fruit, and intriguing hints of mint and nettle. The palate shows the typical intense, lingering fruit one comes to expect from these wines, with high-flavoured, aromatic citrus, melon and mint flavours, with spicy oak on the finish.

EVANS & TATE WESTERN AUSTRALIA CLASSIC
●●●● $16.80

At one time called Margaret River Classic, the wine has now been renamed Western Australia Classic, indicating a broadened geographic base for the sauvignon blanc and semillon which go to make up the blend. Interestingly, the wine is said to be unwooded, yet has a definite spicy flavour which adds to the complexity.

Cellaring Best young. **Best Vintages** '91, '92, '93, '94 **Current Vintage** '94

Matching Food Spicy Thai dishes.

Tasting Note 1994 Light green-yellow; fresh, fragrant and distinctly spicy nutmeg overtones to the bouquet; the palate is deliciously fresh, lively and crisp, again with those spicy overtones to the slightly herbaceous fruit.

EVANS FAMILY WINERY

★★★★☆ 15–17.50 ML AUSSD
Hunter Valley **Est.** 1979
Palmers Lane, Pokolbin, NSW 2321
Ph (049) 98 7333 **Fax** (049) 98 7798
Open By invitation **Production** 2900
Winemaker(s) Rothbury (Contract)
Sold chiefly through the extended Evans family and friends — who
are invited to regular no-charge lunches with Len and Trish Evans,
who (in Len's words) 'are aiming to create a gentle wine-house
feeling'. The Chardonnay is the house style — sometimes even the
house wine.
Principal Wines Chardonnay, Sparkling, Gamay, Pinot Noir.

EVANS FAMILY CHARDONNAY

●●●● $19.95
Produced from the 4 hectares of estate plantings which surround Len
and Trish Evans' marvellous Hunter Valley home. The vines are low-
yielding, and the flavour of the wine is always concentrated, and in
mainstream Hunter Valley style — the '92 fleshy and peachy; the
'93 concentrated and tangy; the '94 more citrussy and lighter-
bodied in its extreme youth.
Cellaring 3–5 years. **Best Vintages** '82, '84, '86, '88, '91, '93
Current Vintage '93
Matching Food Leek and onion tart.
Tasting Note 1993 Medium yellow-green; solid fruit aromas with
hints of mineral and some tangy complexity. The palate is richer than
the bouquet suggests it might be, full-bodied and concentrated with
melon and peach fruit, and echoes of the tangy aspects of the
bouquet. Subtle oak.

EYTON-ON-YARRA *

NR 18.95–32.95 R AUSSD
Yarra Valley **Est.** 1991
Lot 7 Maroondah Highway, Coldstream, Vic 3370
Ph (059) 62 2119 **Fax** (059) 62 5319
Open 7 days 9–5 **Production** 3500
Winemaker(s) Tony Royal
The former Yarra Vale property now owned by the Cowan family
and which has been very extensively (and expensively) refurbished.
It has two very large supporting vineyards, and the arrival of former
senior Seppelt winemaker Tony Royal, and the 1995 opening of the
on-site restaurant, heralds the end of a long gestation.
Principal Wines Chardonnay, Shiraz, Methode Champenoise.

EYTON-ON-YARRA CHARDONNAY

●●● ▶ $19.50
One of the first releases from the new ownership, albeit with diverse
winemaking input from a number of transient occupants in the job.
Produced from estate-grown grapes, and has plenty of weight, if not
a great deal of finesse.

Cellaring 2–3 years. **Best Vintages** NA **Current Vintage** '93
Matching Food Crispy-skin chicken.
Tasting Note 1993 Medium yellow-green; yellow peach and
tropical fruit aromas, ripe and honeyed; subtle oak. The palate is
rich and ripe, showing fairly substantial alcohol, and is quite
developed; finishes fractionally short.

EYTON-ON-YARRA SHIRAZ
●●●● ▶ $30
From estate-grown shiraz, and from the cool 1993 vintage. An
exciting wine, and significantly the best in the portfolio. Holds
considerable promise for the future.
Cellaring 2–4 years. **Best Vintages** NA
Current Vintage '93
Matching Food Moroccan lamb.
Tasting Note 1993 Medium to full red; clean, attractive and
potent spicy/peppery varietal fruit aromas, with minimal oak input.
The palate shows similar clearly defined varietal fruit flavours in the
spice and pepper spectrum; the wine has vinosity and flesh, with a
long finish.

FAIRFIELD VINEYARD

NR 8.50–15 CD AUSSD
North East Victoria **Est.** 1959
Murray Valley Highway, Browns Plains via Rutherglen, Vic 3685
Ph (060) 32 9381
Open Mon–Sat 10–5, Some Sun 12–5 **Production** NFP
Winemaker(s) Stephen Morris
Specialist in red and fortified wines made with nineteenth-century
wine equipment housed in the grounds of the historic Fairfield
Mansion built by G F Morris. A tourist must. In late 1994 offered a
range of wines from the 1986 to 1990 vintages.
Principal Wines White Hermitage, Riesling, Moselle, Rosé,
Light Red, Shiraz, Durif, Cabernet Sauvignon, Fortified.

FARRELL'S LIMESTONE CREEK VINEYARD *

NR 10–14 CD AUSSD
Hunter Valley **Est.** 1982
Mount View Road, Mount View, NSW 2325
Ph (049) 91 2808 **Fax** (02) 817 2476
Open W'ends, Public hols 10–5 **Production** 500
Winemaker(s) McWilliam's (Contract)
John and Camille Farrell purchased 50 acres on Mount View in
1980, and gradually established 18 acres of vineyards planted to
semillon, verdelho, chardonnay, shiraz, cabernet sauvignon and
merlot. Most of the grapes are sold to McWilliam's, which contract
makes a small amount for cellar door sales. The quality of the wines
is as good as one would expect.
Principal Wines Semillon, Chardonnay, Shiraz.

FELSBERG VINEYARDS

NR 9.50–12 CD AUSSD
Granite Belt **Est.** 1983
Townsends Road, Glen Aplin, Qld 4381
Ph (076) 83 4332 **Fax** (076) 83 4332
Open Thur–Mon 9.30–4.30 **Production** 1500
Winemaker(s) Otto Haag
After a prolonged gestation, opened for business in 1991. The
wines are made by former brewer Otto Haag. The first few wines
could best be described as experimental; no recent tastings.
Principal Wines Riesling, Traminer, Semillon, Chardonnay,
Sylvaner, Traminer Rosé, Merlot, Shiraz.

FERGUSSON WINERY

★★★★☆ 8.50–17.50 CD AUS183
Yarra Valley **Est.** 1968
Wills Road, Yarra Glen, Vic 3775
Ph (059) 65 2237 **Fax** (059) 65 2405
Open 7 days 11–5 **Production** 5000
Winemaker(s) Christopher Keyes
Best known as a favoured tourist destination, particularly for tourist
coaches, and offering hearty fare in comfortable surroundings
accompanied by wines of non-Yarra Valley origin. For this reason
the limited quantities of its estate wines are often ignored, but should
not be: the current releases are quite excellent.
Principal Wines There are two basic ranges: the lower-priced
Tartan Range sourced from grapes grown outside the Yarra Valley,
with Sauvignon Blanc, Chardonnay, Late Harvest Lexia, Shiraz, Port,
Sparkling; and three wines in the Estate Range, Victoria
Chardonnay, Jeremy Shiraz and Benjamin Cabernet Sauvignon.

FERGUSSON BENJAMIN CABERNET SAUVIGNON
●●●● ▶ $16.85
Named after the third of the Fergusson children, and produced from
estate-grown grapes. Winemaker Chris Keyes has done a wonderful
job with these three estate-produced wines, particularly given the
difficult 1993 vintage for red wines in the Yarra Valley.
Cellaring 7–10 years. **Best Vintages** '88, '91, '92, '93, '94
Current Vintage '93
Matching Food Scotch fillet.
Tasting Note 1993 Medium to full purple-red; the bouquet has
abundant ripe blackcurrant/cassis fruit with vanillin American oak.
The palate shows similarly smooth and sweet ripe cassis fruit on the
mid palate, although it falls away fractionally on the finish. Should
come together with time.

FERGUSSON JEREMY SHIRAZ
●●●●● $16.85
Named after Peter and Louise Fergusson's son Jeremy, and made
from estate-grown grapes. The '93 vintage is a knockout: when the

subject of Yarra Valley Shiraz comes up, Fergusson is more often than not forgotten. It should not be.

Cellaring Up to 10 years. **Best Vintages** '88, '91, '92, '93, '94
Current Vintage '93
Matching Food Osso bucco.
Tasting Note 1993 Dense purple-red; wonderful varietal spice and dark cherry fruit aromas of the highest quality. The palate is similarly driven by superb varietal fruit; while having weight and concentration, it is extremely supple, and perfectly balanced.

FERGUSSON VICTORIA CHARDONNAY

●●●● $16.85

Confusingly, Victoria Chardonnay does not indicate an appellation — in other words, that the wine comes from various regions within Victoria — but is named after the Fergussons' daughter, and is made from estate-grown grapes.

Cellaring Up to 5 years. **Best Vintages** '90, '92, '93, '94
Current Vintage '94
Matching Food Seafood salad.
Tasting Note 1994 Light green-yellow; fragrant citrus/melon fruit in classic Yarra Valley style is evident on both bouquet and palate; the oak influence is subtle, the wine crisp and delicate.

FERMOY ESTATE

NR 13.50–17 CD AUS49
Margaret River **Est.** 1985
Metricup Road, Willyabrup, WA 6280
Ph (097) 55 6285 **Fax** (097) 55 6251
Open 7 days 11–4.30 **Production** 6500
Winemaker(s) Michael Kelly

Over the past year I have tasted Fermoy Estate wines at the Small Winemakers Show in Canberra, the Sydney Wine Show and in separate (unmasked) tastings. I cannot come to grips with the style of either the white or red wines including the 1991 Cabernet Sauvignon, which won the top gold medal at the 1994 Sheraton Perth West Australian Wine Awards, Full Bodied Category. Wine is a contrary thing.

Principal Wines Sauvignon Blanc, Semillon, Pinot Noir, Cabernet Sauvignon.

FISHBURN & O'KEEFE WINES

★★★☆ 13.50–15 CD AUS37, 122
Derwent River **Est.** 1991
c/o Meadowbank Vineyard, Glenora, Tas 7140
Ph (002) 86 1238 **Fax** (002) 86 1168
Open 7 days Richmond Wine Centre, 27 Bridge Street, Richmond
Production 1500
Winemaker(s) Greg O'Keefe

Wine consultant and contract winemaker Greg O'Keefe, formerly winemaker at Normans, has joined forces with Hutchins

schoolteacher Mike Fishburn to produce wines made from grapes purchased from various growers across Tasmania, but with an estate vineyard in the course of establishment. More frequent tastings might encourage a higher rating.
Principal Wines Riesling, Chardonnay, Pinot Noir, Cabernet Sauvignon, Sparkling.

FLYNN & WILLIAMS

★★★★☆ 14 ML AUSSD
Macedon **Est.** 1979
Flynns Lane, Kyneton, Vic 3444
Ph (054) 22 2228
Open Not **Production** 600
Winemaker(s) Laurie Williams, John Flynn
Produces a sought-after, single wine made from 100% cabernet sauvignon grown at Kyneton, a sub-district of Macedon able to produce wonderful red wines in warmer vintages, exemplified by the '88 and '91 vintages. The rating is given on sentiment and prior extensive tastings, but without any recent exposure.
Principal Wines Cabernet Sauvignon.

FRANKLAND ESTATE

★★★★☆ 15–24 R AUS111, 121, 177
Great Southern **Est.** 1988
RMB 705 Frankland, WA 6396
Ph (098) 55 1555 **Fax** (098) 55 1583
Open By appt 10–4 **Production** 12 000
Winemaker(s) Jenny Dobson, Gary Baldwin
(Consultant)
A rapidly-growing Frankland River operation, situated on a large sheep property owned by Barrie Smith and Judi Cullam. The 14-hectare vineyard has been established progressively since 1988, and a winery built on the site for the 1993 vintage (prior to which time the wines were made at Alkoomi).
Principal Wines Riesling, Sauvignon Blanc, Isolation Ridge (predominantly Shiraz), Olmo's Reward (Bordeaux-blend of Cabernet Franc, Merlot, Malbec, Cabernet Sauvignon, with Petit Verdot in future vintages), Cabernet Sauvignon.

FRANKLAND ESTATE CABERNET SAUVIGNON
●●●● $21
The strongest of the Frankland Estate reds, though not necessarily the richest. It is a wine which consistently reflects the cool growing conditions, and which is quite European (ie French) in style. It will be interesting to see what Jenny Dobson, winemaker at Chateau Senejac in Bordeaux for over 10 years, makes with the grapes from the 1995 vintage.
Cellaring 5–7 years. **Best Vintages** '92, '93
Current Vintage '93
Matching Food Matured cheddar.

Tasting Note 1993 Medium to full red-purple; clean, firm berry fruit showing good ripeness and subtle oak. A well balanced palate with blackberry/briary fruit, fine tannins, and overall of light to medium body.

FRANKLAND ESTATE ISOLATION RIDGE
●●●● ▶ $15.30
First made in 1991, Isolation Ridge is predominantly made from estate-grown shiraz, with small components of cabernet franc, cabernet sauvignon, malbec and merlot. It is the richest and strongest of the Frankland Estate reds, and in my view the best.
Cellaring Up to 10 years. **Best Vintages** '92, '93
Current Vintage '92
Matching Food Braised lamb shanks.
Tasting Note 1992 Full purple-red; complex, bottle developed game, liquorice and cherry aromas which are strongly varietal. The palate is unexpectedly fresh and lively, with spicy/peppery notes and finishing with good acidity. The '93 will be a worthy successor, with similar bright cherry and spice flavours.

FRANKLAND ESTATE OLMO'S REWARD
●●●● $24
Named in honour of Dr Harold Olmo, the viticulturist to point to the potential of the Frankland River as far back as 1955. Now in his 80s, Dr Olmo lives in retirement in California, and it is fitting that his contribution to viticulture should be so remembered. The wine is a blend of cabernet franc, merlot, malbec and cabernet sauvignon, all estate-grown; this is the first vintage.
Cellaring 5–7 years. **Best Vintages** NA
Current Vintage '92
Matching Food Veal chops.
Tasting Note 1992 Strong purple-red; the bouquet is of medium intensity with firm dark berry/briary fruit, and subtle oak. A well structured and weighted wine, though not particularly lush or fruity.

FRANKLAND ESTATE RIESLING
●●●●● $14.50
Consistently outstanding over the '92, '93 and '94 vintages, and — in relative terms — the best of the Frankland Estate wines. Its consistency has shone through notwithstanding that it has been made by different winemakers at different wineries, and will have a third winemaker as from the 1995 vintage. As always, meticulous viticulture is the key, with viticultural consultancy advice from Dr Richard Smart.
Cellaring Now to 6 years. **Best Vintages** '92, '93, '94
Current Vintage '94
Matching Food Antipasto.
Tasting Note 1994 Light to medium yellow-green; potent lime and toast aromas of considerable style, typical of the estate. A powerful wine, with good mouthfeel and abundant lime-flavoured fruit, and a long finish.

FRASER VINEYARD

★★★ 12 CD AUSSD
Hunter Valley **Est.** 1987
Lot 5 Wilderness Road, Rothbury, NSW 2321
Ph (049) 30 7594 **Fax** (049) 33 1100
Open 7 days 10–5 **Production** 1850
Winemaker(s) Peter Fraser
A small, 100% estate operation which offers accommodation at the
Claremont Country House recently built on the property, and
accommodating groups of up to 10 people. Has from time to time
made some wonderfully generous and fleshy white wines.
Principal Wines Chardonnay, Semillon Sauvignon Blanc,
Malbec, Shiraz.

FRASER CHARDONNAY
●●● $12
Made with meticulous attention to detail, and some of the early
vintages outstanding. The wines always need time to settle down,
typically showing the impact of new oak when released, and with
that oak needing time to integrate and soften.
Cellaring 3–4 years. **Best Vintages** '87, '91, '92, '93, '94
Current Vintage '94
Matching Food Smoked chicken.
Tasting Note 1994 Glowing yellow-green; abundant barrel
ferment oak aromas and flavours, a little hessiany, and very typically
needing considerable time in bottle to come together, when it will
evolve into a full-bodied White Burgundy style.

FREYCINET VINEYARDS

★★★★★ 14–23 R AUS48, 112
East Coast Tasmania **Est.** 1980
Tasman Highway via Bicheno, Tas 7215
Ph (002) 57 8384 **Fax** (002) 57 8454
Open Mon–Fri 9–5, W'ends 11–5 **Production** 4000
Winemaker(s) Claudio Radenti
The 4-hectare Freycinet vineyards are beautifully situated on the
sloping hillsides of a small valley. The soils are podsol and decaying
granite with a friable clay subsoil, and the combination of aspect,
slope, soil and heat summation produce red grapes of unusual depth
of colour and ripe flavours. One of Australia's foremost producers of
Pinot Noir.
Principal Wines Riesling, Chardonnay, Pinot Noir, Cabernet
Sauvignon, Cabernet Franc.

FREYCINET PINOT NOIR
●●●●● $23
The remarkable site climate of the Freycinet Vineyard is primarily
responsible for the outstanding quality of the pinot noir, although the
experience and skills of Geoff Bull, daughter Lindy Bull and Claudio
Radenti ensure that the potential quality is maximised. Interestingly,

the only red fermenter the winery possesses is a rotary fermenter, which in turn helps in the extraction of both colour and flavour. Unhappily, I have not tasted either the '93 or '94 vintages.
Cellaring Up to 5 years. **Best Vintages** '91, '92
Current Vintage '93
Matching Food Duck, hare, venison.
Tasting Note 1992 Medium to full red; an exceptionally stylish wine with tight, not overripe varietal fruit in a spicy/plummy spectrum. The palate has lots of plummy fruit with fine tannins and well handled oak.

FYFFEFIELD WINES *

NR NA AUSSD
Murray River **Est.** 1993
Murray Valley Highway, Burramine, Vic 3730
Ph (057) 48 4282 **Fax** (057) 48 4282
Open Mon–Sat 10–6, Sun 12–6 **Production** 1000
Winemaker(s) Graeme Diamond
Fyffefield has been established near the Murray River between Cobram and Yarrawonga in a mud brick and leadlight tasting room opposite an historic homestead. A highlight is the ornamental pig collection on display.
Principal Wines A range of table and fortified wines produced from Shiraz, Touriga, Marsanne, Verdelho, Chardonnay.

GALAFREY WINES

★★★★ 11–15.95 R AUS101, 106
Great Southern **Est.** 1977
145 Lower Sterling Terrace, Albany, WA 6330
Ph (098) 41 6533 **Fax** (098) 51 2022
Open Mon–Sat 10–5 **Production** 4000
Winemaker(s) Ian Tyrer
Recently relocated to a new purpose-built but utilitarian winery after previously inhabiting the exotic surrounds of the old Albany wool store, Galafrey makes good and often underrated wines, drawing grapes in the main from 12 hectares of estate plantings at Mount Barker.
Principal Wines Riesling, Chardonnay, Muller Thurgau, Pinot Noir, Shiraz, Cabernet Sauvignon.

GALAFREY CHARDONNAY
●●●● $13.95
Consistent with winemaker Ian Tyrer's approach to Riesling, made in a generous mould with just a touch of sweetness adding to the weight and texture. From time to time budgetary constraints have lead to the use of indifferent oak, and in 1993 botrytis got to work, but the '94 is a very pleasant wine.
Cellaring 1–2 years. **Best Vintages** '88, '90, '91, '94
Current Vintage '94
Matching Food Avocado with seafood.

Tasting Note 1994 Light to medium yellow-green; attractive, albeit relatively developed, bouquet with a tangy melon and citrus fruit, subtle oak and a slight Burgundian pong. Full and rich in the mouth, with round, sweet fruit flavour and texture.

GALAFREY RIESLING
●●●● ▸ $11
Invariably one of the richer and fuller Mount Barker Rieslings, and commensurately quicker developing. A hint of sweetness adds to the commercial appeal, and in my view is justified by the weight of the fruit, but not all judges necessarily agree with that view.
Cellaring 2–3 years. **Best Vintages** '85, '88, '90, '91, '94
Current Vintage '94
Matching Food Sweet and sour pork.
Tasting Note 1994 Light to medium yellow-green; generous fruit aromas in the lime/tropical/passionfruit spectrum. In the mouth an extremely attractive wine, with abundant sweet fruit and a hint of residual sugar carried by that fruit richness and sweetness.

GALAFREY SHIRAZ
●●●● $12.95
Much of the attention to date has been focused on Mount Barker Cabernet Sauvignon and Riesling, but there is every indication that it can regularly produce Shiraz of equally impressive quality. Inevitably, styles vary from lighter to fuller; that of Galafrey varies in weight according to the vintage.
Cellaring 4–8 years. **Best Vintages** '85, '90, '91, '92
Current Vintage '92
Matching Food Washed rind cheese.
Tasting Note 1992 Medium red-purple; vibrant pepper/spice aromas with an underlying hint of gaminess which seems to recur in the Galafrey Shirazs. On the palate, light, fresh and crisp with pepper/spice and red cherry flavours, finishing with soft tannins.

GALAH WINES

★★★★ 9.50–15 ML AUSSD UK11
Adelaide Hills **Est.** 1986
Tregarthen Road, Ashton, SA 5137
Ph (08) 390 1243 **Fax** (08) 390 1243
Open Not — wines available at Ashton Hills **Production** 1000
Winemaker(s) Stephen George
Over the years, Stephen George has built up a network of contacts across South Australia from which he gains some very high quality small parcels of grapes or wine for the Galah label. These are all sold direct at extremely low prices for the quality.
Principal Wines Wood matured Semillon Sauvignon Blanc, Coonawarra Late Harvest Riesling, Clare Valley Shiraz, Clare Valley Cabernet Sauvignon, Port, Sparkling.

GALAH WINES CLARE VALLEY SHIRAZ
●●●● ▸ $12
Although the label makes no mention of it, Stephen George is

consultant winemaker at Wendouree, and it is well known that he has first option on any small parcels not required by Wendouree for its own label. All the hallmarks of having come from that marvellous source.

Cellaring 10–15 years. **Best Vintages** '86, '88, '90, '91, '92
Current Vintage '92
Matching Food Venison, kangaroo.
Tasting Note 1992 Dark red-purple; concentrated dark, briary/blackberry fruit is the dominant force, with a very concentrated palate, high in tannins. A very powerful wine, still fairly raw; a touch of new oak might have lifted it into Olympian class.

GARBIN WINES *

NR 8–9 CD AUSSD
Swan Valley **Est.** 1956
209 Toodyay Road, Middle Swan, WA 6056
Ph (09) 274 1747 **Fax** (09) 274 1747
Open Mon–Sat 8.30–5.30, Sun 12–5.30 **Production** 500
Winemaker(s) Peter Garbin
Peter Garbin, winemaker by weekend and design draftsman by week, decided in 1990 that he would significantly upgrade the bulk fortified winemaking business commenced by his father in 1956. The vineyards have been replanted, the winery re-equipped, and the first of the new generation wines produced in 1994.
Principal Wines Chenin Blanc, Shiraz, Cabernet Sauvignon, Dessert Wine, Port.

GARDEN GULLY VINEYARDS

★★★☆ 10.50–16.90 CD AUS101
Great Western **Est.** 1987
Garden Gully, Great Western, Vic 3377
Ph (053) 56 2400 **Fax** (053) 56 2400
Open Mon–Fri 10.30–5.30, W'ends 10–6 **Production** 2500
Winemaker(s) Brian Fletcher, Warren Randall
Given the skills and local knowledge of the syndicate which owns Garden Gully, it is not surprising that the wines are consistently good across the entire range: an attractive stone cellar door sales area is an additional reason to stop and pay a visit.
Principal Wines Riesling, Shiraz, Sparkling Burgundy, Sparkling Chardonnay.

GARRETT FAMILY WINES *

★★★☆ 10.95–14.95 R AUSSD
Southern Vales **Est.** 1993
151 Main Road, McLaren Vale, SA 5171
Ph (08) 323 8656 **Fax** (08) 323 9096
Open Mon–Fri 10–5, W'ends 12–4 **Production** NFP
Winemaker(s) Andrew Garrett
Having parted company with Andrew Garrett Wines (owned by Suntory of Japan) Andrew and Averil Garrett have commenced a

new wine business based at The Vales Wine Company, which also produces The Vales and Tatachilla labels. As one would expect, all of the wines are competently made, although not much seen in the marketplace.

Principal Wines Riesling, Chardonnay, Sauvignon Blanc, Wooded Semillon, Shiraz, Cabernet Sauvignon Cabernet Franc.

GATEWAY ESTATE

NR NA AUSSD
Hunter Valley **Est.** 1989
Cnr Broke & Branxton Roads, Pokolbin, NSW 2321
Ph (049) 98 7844
Open 7 days 10.30–4 **Production** 3000
Winemaker(s) Colin Peterson
A new, principally cellar door operation; the wines are made by Colin Peterson at Wollundry, but quality is unknown.

Principal Wines Chardonnay, Semillon, White Burgundy.

GEHRIG BROS

★★☆ 7–15 CD AUS72
North East Victoria **Est.** 1858
Cnr Murray Valley Hwy & Howlong Road, Barnawartha, Vic 3688
Ph (060) 26 7296
Open Mon–Sat 9–5, Sun 10–5 **Production** 5000
Winemaker(s) Brian Gehrig
An historic winery (and adjacent house) are superb legacies of the nineteenth century. Progressive modernisation of the winemaking facilities and operations has seen the quality of the white wines improve significantly, while the red wines now receive a percentage of new oak.

Principal Wines Chenin Blanc, Riesling, Sauternes, Pinot Noir, Shiraz, Cabernet Sauvignon.

GEMBROOK HILL

★★★★ 18–22 R AUS144
Yarra Valley **Est.** 1983
Launching Place Road, Gembrook, Vic 3783
Ph (03) 9818 5633 **Fax** (03) 9818 5633
Open By appt **Production** 950
Winemaker(s) Dr Ian Marks, David Lance
The 6-hectare Gembrook Hill Vineyard is situated on rich, red volcanic soils 2 kilometres north of Gembrook in the coolest part of the Yarra Valley. The vines are not irrigated, with consequent natural vigour control. Pinot Noir will join the range of wines produced in late 1993.

Principal Wines Chardonnay, Sauvignon Blanc, Pinot Noir.

GEMBROOK HILL CHARDONNAY

●●●● $22
Immaculate viticulture, with great attention to detail and to canopy

management and manipulation, neatly offsets the ultra-cool site
climate at Gembrook. The Chardonnay always shows its cool
climate origins, but is never thin or herbal.
Cellaring 3–5 years. **Best Vintages** '90, '91, '93
Current Vintage '93
Matching Food Crab, prawns.
Tasting Note 1993 Light green-yellow; a clean and elegant wine
with melon and fig fruit aromas and minimal oak. A classic,
restrained Chablis-style with some textural softness (perhaps partial
malolactic fermentation) which should age well.

GEMBROOK HILL PINOT NOIR
●●● ‣ $22
Tends to reflect the very cool climate, and the rich, red volcanic soils,
rather more than the two white wines, but nonetheless has style and
genuine appeal in a lighter mould.
Cellaring Drink now. **Best Vintages** NA
Current Vintage '93
Matching Food Asian seafood dishes.
Tasting Note 1993 Medium red; highly aromatic, lifted aroma
with edges of wintergreen; the palate does have length, but is on the
cusp of ripeness, with similar herbal characters to those of the
bouquet.

GEMBROOK HILL SAUVIGNON BLANC
●●●● ‣ $18
The wine for which Gembrook Hill first came into prominence, and
suited (in terms of wine style) both to the site and climate. It has
proved to be a very difficult variety to grow, or at least to crop well,
with a tiny production from the 2 hectares of vines. Devotees of the
style are pleased that Dr Ian Marks has persevered.
Cellaring 1–2 years. **Best Vintages** '90, '92, '93, '94
Current Vintage '94
Matching Food Lobster bisque.
Tasting Note 1994 Light to medium yellow-green; pristine
gooseberry/herbal aromas with just a faint touch of yeast influence
giving some passionfruit characters. The palate is similarly intense,
with pronounced herbaceous fruit, but is neither leafy nor mean.

GEOFF MERRILL
★★★★ 9.99–22 R AUS27, 167–170, 186 UK75
Southern Vales **Est.** 1980
Cnr Pimpala & Byards Roads, Reynella, SA 5161
Ph (08) 381 6877 **Fax** (08) 322 2244
Open Mon–Fri 10–4, Sun 12–5 **Production** 7000
Winemaker(s) Geoff Merrill
The premium label of the three wines made by Merrill (Mount Hurtle
(see separate entry) and Cockatoo Ridge being the other two);
always given bottle age, the wines reflect the desire of this otherwise
exuberant winemaker for elegance and subtlety.
Principal Wines Semillon Chardonnay, Cabernet Sauvignon.

GEOFF MERRILL CABERNET SAUVIGNON

●●●● $22

Although simply labelled Cabernet Sauvignon, the wine in fact
contains 14% merlot. Usually two-thirds come from Coonawarra and
one-third from McLaren Vale; the wine is aged in American oak
puncheons for over two years before bottling. The 1989 has won
two gold, six silver and 20 bronze medals in Australian shows.
Cellaring Medium term — to 5 years. **Best Vintages** '80, '83,
'85, '86, '87, '90 **Current Vintage** '89
Matching Food Veal scaloppine.
Tasting Note 1989 Light red; now fully developed in terms of
both bouquet and palate, but will no doubt hold its form for some
time yet. There is an interesting combination of aromas and flavours
ranging from leafy berry through to sweet vanilla, due to the
combination of relatively early-picked fruit and sweet American oak.

GEOFF MERRILL SEMILLON CHARDONNAY

●●●● ▸ $16

A blend of roughly 55% semillon and 45% chardonnay grown in the
McLaren Vale and Barossa Valley, fermented in a combination of
American and French oak puncheons, and aged on lees before
bottling. Always sold with an unusual number of years bottle age,
developing tremendous richness. Multiple gold medal winner.
Cellaring Ready when sold. **Best Vintages** '84, '85, '86, '87,
'89 **Current Vintage** '89
Matching Food Poultry, rabbit.
Tasting Note 1989 Full golden-yellow; toasty, honeyed, nutty
bottle development; fully aged, but at the peak of its power with
masses of buttery/toasty/oaky flavours. A great Australian White
Burgundy style.

GIACONDA WINES

★★★★★ 22–28 ML AUS11, 112
Central Victoria **Est.** 1985
McClay Road, Beechworth, Vic 3747
Ph (057) 27 0246 **Fax** (057) 27 0246
Open By appt **Production** 900
Winemaker(s) Rick Kinzbrunner
Wines which have a super-cult status and which, given the tiny
production, are extremely difficult to find, sold chiefly through
restaurants and mail order. All have a cosmopolitan edge befitting
Rick Kinzbrunner's international winemaking experience. The
Chardonnay and Pinot Noir are made in contrasting styles: the
Chardonnay tight and reserved, the Pinot Noir opulent and ripe.
Principal Wines Chardonnay, Pinot Noir, Cabernet Sauvignon
Merlot Cabernet Franc.

GIACONDA CHARDONNAY

●●●●● $28

450 cases of handcrafted wines are produced from a little under
one hectare of estate vineyard every year. The style of the wine is

entirely different from mainstream Australian Chardonnay, relying far more on texture and structure, and far less on primary fruit. An exceptionally distinguished and consistent wine which is the very deliberate product of Rick Kinzbrunner's winemaking philosophy.
Cellaring 4–7 years. **Best Vintages** '86, '88, '90, '92, '93
Current Vintage '93
Matching Food Slow-roasted Tasmanian salmon.
Tasting Note 1993 Light to medium yellow-green; the aromas are stony/minerally rather than overtly fruity, yet fresh as always; the oak is well balanced and integrated with vanillin hints. The palate is youthful and fresh, still settling down when tasted in November 1994, and absolutely in the Giaconda mainstream, and will build texture and richness as it ages.

GIACONDA PINOT NOIR
●●●●● $28
As fastidiously produced and as full of character as the Chardonnay. It comes from a little over half a hectare of estate plantings, and is made in tiny quantities. The style is quite different from the Pinot Noirs of southern Victoria, being much fuller and more robust, with the obvious potential to age well.
Cellaring 4–6 years. **Best Vintages** '85, '86, '88, '90, '91, '92
Current Vintage '92
Matching Food Saddle of hare.
Tasting Note 1992 Medium red-purple; a complex wine which progressively opens up as it is allowed to breathe in the glass, with stemmy/gamey/plummy characters all apparent. In the mouth, chewy and complex, with flavours running from plum through to dark chocolate. A firm finish needing time to soften.

GILBERT WINES
★★★★ 11–13 CD AUSSD
Great Southern **Est.** 1980
RMB 438 Albany Highway, Kendenup via Mt Barker, WA 6323
Ph (098) 51 4028 **Fax** (098) 51 4021
Open 7 days 9–5 while wine available **Production** 1120
Winemaker(s) Plantagenet (Contract)
The now mature vineyard, coupled with contract winemaking at Plantagenet, has produced small quantities of high quality Rhine Riesling and Chardonnay; the tiny production sells out quickly each year.
Principal Wines Riesling, Late Harvest Riesling, Chardonnay, Shiraz, Port.

GILBERTS RIESLING
●●●● $11
As with so many of the small Mount Barker wineries, dependent on contract winemaking, and the part-time viticultural occupation for owners Beverly and Jim Gilbert. The '92 Riesling was a particularly good wine which is ageing superbly; the '94 is in a rather more advanced mould.

Cellaring 2–7 years. **Best Vintages** '90, '92
Current Vintage '94
Matching Food Asparagus with prosciutto.
Tasting Note 1994 Glowing yellow-green; the bouquet is solid and rich, of medium to full intensity with strong lime fruit, leading on to a rich, full-bodied style with plenty of flavour and developing relatively quickly.

GLEN ERIN GRANGE *

NR 9.80–19 CD AUSSD
Macedon **Est.** 1993
Woodend Road, Lancefield, Vic 3435
Ph (054) 29 1041 **Fax** (054) 29 2053
Open W'ends, Public hols 10–6 **Production** 2000
Winemaker(s) Brian Scales
Brian Scales acquired the former Lancefield Winery and has renamed it Glen Erin Grange. The accompanying restaurant is open on Friday and Saturday evenings â la carte and for Saturday and Sunday lunch.
Principal Wines Traminer Riesling, Chardonnay, Pinot Noir, Cabernet Merlot, Shiraz, Sparkling.

GLENARA WINES

★★★ 9–16 ML AUSSD
Adelaide Hills **Est.** 1971
126 Range Road, North Upper Hermitage, SA 5131
Ph (08) 380 5056 **Fax** (08) 380 5056
Open 7 days 11–5 **Production** 6000
Winemaker(s) Trevor Jones
Glenara has been owned by the Verrall family since 1924; the first vines were planted in 1971, the first wine made in 1975, and the winery built in 1988. Between 1983 and 1988 the wines were made under contract at Kellermeister.
Principal Wines Riesling, Chardonnay, Unwooded Chardonnay, Shiraz, Cabernet Sauvignon Rosé, Cabernet Merlot, Cabernet Shiraz, Cabernet Sauvignon, Sparkling, Port.

GLENARA CABERNET SAUVIGNON
●●● $15
In fact a blend of cabernet sauvignon, merlot and cabernet franc, the latter two varieties having been planted on the estate in 1987 and 1988, respectively, making their first contribution to the wine in 1990.
Cellaring 2–3 years. **Best Vintages** '90, '91, '92
Current Vintage '91
Matching Food Squab.
Tasting Note 1991 Medium to full red-purple; a quite rich and complex bouquet with cassis fruit and cedary oak. On the palate minty notes appear; the texture is smooth and the wine is rather lighter in body than the bouquet might suggest.

GLENARA RIESLING
●●● ▶ $10.90
A range of vintages is available at cellar door, showing significant variation in style and quality from one year to the next. Tasting is strongly recommended.
Cellaring Varies according to vintage. **Best Vintages** '90
Current Vintage Various
Matching Food Braised pork neck.
Tasting Note 1990 Bright green-yellow; a complex bouquet with quasi-Alsatian overtones, rich and limey. In the mouth, the wine is full-blown, nicely developed with smooth, soft and round lime flavours but again just a hint of Alsace in the background.

GLENAYR WINES

★★★☆ 12–16 ML AUSSD
Coal River **Est.** 1975
Back Tea Tree Road, Richmond, Tas 7025
Ph (002) 60 2388 **Fax** (002) 44 7234
Open Not **Production** 200
Winemaker(s) Chris Harrington (at Domaine A)
The principal occupation of Chris Harrington is as viticultural manager of the substantial Tolpuddle Vineyard, the grapes of which are sold to Domaine Chandon. Tiny quantities of wine are made from a small adjacent vineyard for mailing list sales under the Glenayr label.
Principal Wines Pinot Noir, Riesling, Cabernet Sauvignon.

GLENAYR PINOT NOIR
●●●● $16
The Coal River region rivals the Tamar Valley in its capacity to produce full-flavoured red wines of a style one does not traditionally associate with Tasmania.
Cellaring 2–4 years. **Best Vintages** NA **Current Vintage** '91
Matching Food Braised duck.
Tasting Note 1991 Medium red; very ripe, strong varietal plummy fruit with minimal oak influence. The flavours are ripe with tastes of both plum and mint, and a difficult to pinpoint character which is to be found in many Coal River reds, perhaps due to the high natural acids.

GLENAYR RIESLING
●●●● $12
The Coal River region is a relatively new arrival on the scene in Tasmania, having been opened up in the wake of the supply of essential irrigation water, for the summers are exceptionally dry. This wine shows why the region holds such interest.
Cellaring Drink now. **Best Vintages** NA **Current Vintage** '91
Matching Food Tofu.
Tasting Note 1991 Medium to full yellow-green; a full and rich bouquet, with powerful developed toasty aromas. The palate is round, almost luscious, with lovely weight. (Tasted February 1994.)

GLENFINLASS WINES

NR 8 CD AUSSD
Wellington **Est.** 1971
Elysian Farm, Parkes Road, Wellington, NSW 2820
Ph (068) 45 2011 **Fax** (068) 45 3329
Open Sat 9–5 or By appt **Production** 500
Winemaker(s) Brian G Holmes
The weekend and holiday hobby of Wellington solicitor Brian
Holmes, who has wisely decided to leave it at that. I have not tasted
the wines for many years, but the last wines I did taste were
competently made.
Principal Wines Sauvignon Blanc, Shiraz, Cabernet Sauvignon.

GLOUCESTER RIDGE VINEYARD

★★★☆ 12–17 CD AUSSD
Warren Valley **Est.** 1985
Burma Road, Pemberton, WA 6260
Ph (097) 76 1035 **Fax** (097) 76 1390
Open 7 days 10–4 **Production** 3000
Winemaker(s) Various Contract
Gloucester Ridge is the only vineyard located within the Pemberton
town boundary, within easy walking distance. It is owned and
operated by Don and Sue Hancock; quality has varied, but as the
Sauvignon Blanc shows, can be good.
Principal Wines Riesling, Late Harvest Riesling, Sauvignon Blanc,
Pemberton Aurora, Reserve Chardonnay, Unwooded Chardonnay,
Pinot Noir, Cabernets.

GLOUCESTER RIDGE SAUVIGNON BLANC
●●●● $14
A lot of questions still remain to be answered about the Pemberton-
Manjimup region, many turning on fruit intensity. Time alone will tell
whether this is a young vine problem, or whether there are other
factors at work. This wine neatly poses the question, however well it
has been made.
Cellaring Drink now. **Best Vintages** '94 **Current Vintage** '94
Matching Food Delicate seafood.
Tasting Note 1994 Light yellow-green; very light, clean and crisp
herbal fruit with lifted, estery aromas. The flavours are crisp, clean
and direct, showing good varietal character in an uncompromisingly
light mould; does have length, and the wine creeps up on you.

GNADENFREI ESTATE

NR 8–12.50 CD AUSSD
Barossa Valley **Est.** 1979
Seppeltsfield Road, Marananga via Tanunda, SA 5353
Ph (085) 62 2522 **Fax** (085) 62 3470
Open 7 days 10–5.30 **Production** 8000
Winemaker(s) Malcolm Seppelt

A strictly cellar door operation, which relies on a variety of sources for its wines, but has a core of 2 hectares of estate shiraz and one hectare of grenache. A restaurant is open for morning teas, lunches and afternoon teas.

Principal Wines Riesling, Semillon, Traminer Riesling, Muscat Blanc, Cabernet Sauvignon, Cabernet Malbec, Shiraz Grenache, Port, Sparkling.

GOLDEN GRAPE ESTATE

NR 13.95–25.95 CD AUSSD
Hunter Valley **Est.** 1985
Oakey Creek Road, Pokolbin, NSW 2321
Ph (049) 98 7588 **Fax** (049) 98 7730
Open 7 days 10–5 **Production** NFP
Winemaker(s) Michael Jensen
German-owned and unashamedly directed at the tourist, with a restaurant, barbecue and picnic areas, wine museum and separate tasting room for bus tours. Golden Grape Estate is established on the site of the old Barrie Drayton Happy Valley Winery. The substantial range of wines are of diverse origins and style.

Principal Wines Premier Chablis, Fumé Blanc, Chardonnay, Alsacienne (semi sweet), Five Star (light fruity), Frizzante Rosé, Mt Lenonard Cabernet Sauvignon, Shiraz, Cabernet Hermitage, Classic Red, Sparkling, Fortified.

GOLDEN RISE *

NR NA AUSSD
Great Southern **Est.** 1988
Scotsdale Road, Denmark, WA 6333
Ph (098) 48 1821
Open 7 days 10–5 **Production** 800
Winemaker(s) Ron Cocking, Peter Cocking
Ron and Peter Cocking make Chardonnay and Pinot Noir from 4 hectares of estate plantings in the lush surrounds of the Denmark region, not far from Karriview and Tinglewood. The '94 Chardonnay is an excellent wine, rich, full and with lavish oak.

Principal Wines Chardonnay, Pinot Noir.

GOLVINDA WINERY

NR 10–12 CD AUSSD
Gippsland **Est.** 1971
RMB 4635 Lindenow Rd, Lindenow South via Bairnsdale, Vic 3865
Ph (051) 57 1480
Open 7 days 10–5 **Production** NFP
Winemaker(s) Robert Guy
Robert Guy pioneered the Gippsland area, and produced some attractive wines in the late '70s, but the spark faded thereafter; by no means all of the wines now sold are of Gippsland origin. Said to be the only Victorian winery which is part of a golf course, and

offers ploughman's lunches and spit-roasted lamb (bookings for the latter).
Principal Wines Riesling, Chenin Blanc, Semillon Chardonnay, Cabernet Merlot.

GOONA WARRA VINEYARD

★★★★ 10–17 R AUS112
Macedon **Est.** 1863
Sunbury Road, Sunbury, Vic 3429
Ph (03) 9740 7766 **Fax** (03) 9744 7648
Open 7 days 1–5 **Production** 2500
Winemaker(s) John Barnier
An historic stone winery, established under this name by a nineteenth-century Victorian premier. Excellent tasting facilities; an outstanding venue for weddings and receptions; Sunday lunch also served. Situated 30 minutes drive from Melbourne (10 minutes north of Tullamarine airport).
Principal Wines Cabernet Franc, Semillon, Chardonnay, Cabernets.

GOONA WARRA CABERNET FRANC

●●●● ▶ $16
As with all of the Goona Warra wines, estate-grown, but noteworthy both for its rarity as a straight varietal and also for its quality over the past four or five years. A very interesting wine for the wine student.
Cellaring 2–4 years. **Best Vintages** '88, '91, '92, '93
Current Vintage '93
Matching Food Cannelloni.
Tasting Note 1993 Medium to full red-purple; a clean bouquet with moderately intense spicy/cassis fruit aromas and subtle oak. There is plenty of attractive ripe, dark berry/currant fruit on the palate, with an ever so slightly furry finish.

GOUNDREY WINES

★★★★☆ 12.95–18.95 R AUS112 UK86 US2
Great Southern **Est.** 1978
Muir Highway, Mount Barker, WA 6324
Ph (098) 51 1777 **Fax** (098) 51 1997
Open Mon–Sat 10–4.30, Sun 11–4.30 **Production** 33 500
Winemaker(s) Brenden Smith
Having weathered the recession and benefiting from national distribution by Negociants, Goundrey seems likely to achieve the lofty goals it set for itself in the late 1980s. With over 100 hectares of owned or controlled vineyards it has an impressive base to work from, and there is no doubting the quality and potential of the Great Southern region as a whole.
Principal Wines Recently simplified by deleting the Langton and Windy Hill ranges, and substituting two re-labelled ranges: Goundrey Unwooded Chardonnay, Chenin Blanc, Classic White,

Cabernet Sauvignon, Cabernet Merlot; Goundrey Reserve Riesling,
Chardonnay, Sauvignon Blanc, Shiraz, Cabernet Sauvignon, the
latter group under minimalist labels.

GOUNDREY RESERVE CABERNET SAUVIGNON
●●●● $18.95

Over the past 20 years, the wine which has performed most
consistently has been Goundrey Cabernet Sauvignon. Generous,
rich and long-lived, it typifies the region.
Cellaring 5–10 years. **Best Vintages** '81, '85, '87, '90, '92
Current Vintage '92
Matching Food Barbecued beef.
Tasting Note 1992 Medium to full red-purple; in the mould of the
'92 reds from Goundrey, with very ripe cassis/blackcurrant fruit
aromas and flavours; the palate is round and generous, with that
very ripe fruit to the fore.

GOUNDREY RESERVE SAUVIGNON BLANC
●●●●● $14.95

The 10 hectares of sauvignon blanc are spread over a number of
sites providing differing fruit characters. Overall, the Sauvignon
Blancs of the Mount Barker/Frankland region tend to be a little thin
and light, but no such complaint could be directed at this wine.
Cellaring Drink now. **Best Vintages** '89, '91, '94
Current Vintage '94
Matching Food Queensland mud crab.
Tasting Note 1994 Light to medium yellow-green; powerful,
intense, pristine varietal character running the gamut from
herbaceous to gooseberry. A powerful wine in the mouth with herb,
grass, asparagus and snow pea flavours all present, yet not bitter
or astringent.

GOUNDREY RESERVE SHIRAZ
●●●●) $14.95

At the 1994 Perth Wine Show the 1992 Reserve won two trophies
for Best Western Australian Shiraz and best Western Australian Dry
Red. It comes from 11 hectares of estate plantings, and is yet further
evidence of the suitability of the variety to the Mount Barker region.
Cellaring 5–8 years. **Best Vintages** '81, '85, '87, '91, '92
Current Vintage '92
Matching Food Osso bucco.
Tasting Note 1992 Medium to full red-purple; ripe, voluptuous red
berry/red cherry fruit aromas with subtle oak. A striking, vibrant and
very fruity wine on the palate with clean, luscious red berry fruit
flavours.

GOUNDREY UNWOODED CHARDONNAY
●●●● $12.95

One of the principal weapons in the Goundrey armoury and priced
on a par with its Chenin Blanc and Classic White, which of itself
should guarantee very substantial sales volume for what is a good
wine. Draws upon 16 hectares of estate plantings of the variety.

Cellaring Now to 4 years. **Best Vintages** '89, '91, '94
Current Vintage '94
Matching Food Richer seafood, ham.
Tasting Note 1994 Medium yellow-green; plenty of character to
the bouquet which shows quite strong tropical fruit aromas. The
palate, too, has a spectrum of fruit flavours running through from
peach to tropical and showing a hint of botrytis which adds to
rather than detracts from the wine.

GRALYN CELLARS *

NR 10–18 CD AUSSD
Margaret River **Est.** 1979
Caves Road, Willyabrup, WA 6280
Ph (097) 55 6245 **Fax** (097) 55 6245
Open 7 days 10.30–4.30 **Production** 1200
Winemaker(s) Graham Hutton, Merilyn Hutton
The Huttons have been quietly making wine in the Margaret River
region for many years, selling all of the wine from the cellar door
and a little by mailing list, and not seeking publicity. Right from the
outset they have concentrated on fortified wines, but in recent years
have switched the focus back somewhat to table wines made in
what might be called cellar door style.
Principal Wines Riesling, Shiraz, Cabernet Nouveau, and an
extensive range of fortifieds including White Port and Tawny Port.

GRAND CRU ESTATE

★★★☆ 13.50–22 R AUSSD
Adelaide Hills **Est.** 1981
Ross Dewell's Road, Springton, SA 5235
Ph (085) 68 2378 **Fax** (085) 68 2799
Open 7 days 10–5 **Production** 2500
Winemaker(s) Karl Seppelt
Karl Seppelt successfully orchestrates his contract winemakers
(Petaluma makes the white and sparkling wines) but, despite his
prior position as Seppelt marketing director, has been less successful
in obtaining the recognition (and the distribution) these often good
wines deserve.
Principal Wines Riesling, Chardonnay, Cabernet Sauvignon,
Shiraz, Sparkling Brut, Sparkling Shiraz.

GRANITE CELLARS

★★ 7–12.50 CD AUSSD
Granite Belt **Est.** 1991
Lot 9 New England Highway, Glen Aplin, Qld 4381
Ph (076) 83 4324 **Fax** (076) 83 4335
Open Thurs–Mon 9–5 **Production** 1000
Winemaker(s) Robert Gray
A new venture of Rumbalara partner Bob Gray, with the first wines

released end 1991; also incorporates a BYO restaurant. The few
wines tasted to date are hard to recommend.
Principal Wines Semillon, Shiraz, Cabernet Sauvignon.

GRANT BURGE WINES

★★★★☆ 11.95–31.95 R AUS32 UK37
Barossa Valley **Est.** 1988
Jacobs Creek, Tanunda, SA 5352
Ph (085) 63 3700 **Fax** (085) 63 2807
Open 7 days 10–5 **Production** 50 000
Winemaker(s) Grant Burge
As one might expect, this former Krondorf wunderkind makes
consistently good, full-flavoured and smooth wines chosen from the
pick of the crop of his extensive vineyard holdings, which total an
impressive 200 hectares; the immaculately restored/rebuilt stone
cellar door sales buildings are another attraction.
Principal Wines Has recently moved to a series of vineyard-
designated varietal wines including Thorn Vineyard Riesling, Kraft
Vineyard Sauvignon Blanc, Zerk Vineyard Semillon, Barossa Ranges
Chardonnay, Lily Farm Frontignac, Filsell Shiraz, Hillcott Merlot, and
Cameron Vale Cabernet Sauvignon. Top-of-the-range red is
Meshach; Oakland is cheaper second label.

GRANT BURGE BAROSSA RANGES CHARDONNAY
●●●● ▸ $17.95
First released under this label in 1993, and made an immediate
impact, winning a cascade of gold medals and a number of major
trophies. Intense fruit and sophisticated oak handling were, and
remain, the key, even if the '94 vintage does not have the same
early impact of the prior vintage.
Cellaring 3–5 years. **Best Vintages** '93, '94
Current Vintage '94
Matching Food Char-grilled octopus.
Tasting Note 1994 Medium yellow-green; a stylish bouquet with
tangy lemon/citrus fruit and subtle oak. The oak is rather less well
integrated on the palate, but time will see it come together with the
fresh, crisp tangy fruit. Has a touch of sweetness on the finish which
will add to its commercial appeal.

GRANT BURGE CAMERON VALE CABERNET SAUVIGNON
●●●● $13.95
The first Cabernet Sauvignon to be released from Grant Burge to
carry the Cameron Vale name, but by no means the first wine
produced by him from the vineyard, which was planted by Grant
Burge and his parents in 1971–72 in the low hills behind Lyndoch at
the southern end of the Barossa Valley.
Cellaring 5–7 years. **Best Vintages** '92 **Current Vintage** '92
Matching Food Roast beef.
Tasting Note 1992 Medium to full red-purple; a solid bouquet
with an array of minty, spicy and vanillin aromas. The palate belies
its 13.5% alcohol, with a complex array of red berry, spice and mint
flavours, and subtle French oak.

GRANT BURGE KRAFT VINEYARD SAUVIGNON BLANC
●●●● ▶ $9.95

Grant Burge has been purchasing grapes from Dennis Kraft for 15 years, but it was not until 1994, with the new vineyard identification policy of Grant Burge, that the Kraft Vineyard Sauvignon Blanc made its appearance under that name. It was an auspicious beginning for this vineyard, situated outside Tanunda towards the northern end of the Barossa Valley, and which produced a wine which has won an impressive number of show medals in a short period of time. For the record, around 20% was barrel fermented in used American oak.

Cellaring Drink now. **Best Vintages** NA **Current Vintage** '94
Matching Food Fish terrine.
Tasting Note 1994 Light to medium yellow-green; an opulent, highly aromatic bouquet with potent gooseberry and passionfruit aromas. The palate likewise has abundant flesh and weight, at the full end of the spectrum, though retaining varietal character.

GRANT BURGE LILY FARM FRONTIGNAC
●●●●● $11.95

It is impossible not to award this wine five stars, so perfect is the rendition of the grape. As Grant Burge says, "No grape variety produces a wine which tastes so much like crushed, ripe grapes in a glass". It comes from the Lily Farm Vineyard, on the eastern slopes of the Barossa Ranges, appropriately situated next to Grant Burge's front door.

Cellaring Drink now. **Best Vintages** '93, '94
Current Vintage '94
Matching Food A summer's morning.
Tasting Note 1994 Light yellow-green; intensely fragrant, grapey, piercingly pure and clean aromas lead on to a wine with a lively, intense, essence-of-grape flavour, finishing with cleansing acidity.

GRANT BURGE MESHACH SHIRAZ
●●●● $31.95

First made in 1988, and the signature wine of the Grant Burge range. Named in honour of Meshach William Burge, Grant Burge's great-grandfather. It is produced from 65-year-old vines grown on the Filsell Vineyard, which also gives its name to the gold and trophy-winning varietal wine which sits alongside Cameron Vale.

Cellaring 10+ years. **Best Vintages** '88, '90, '91, '92
Current Vintage '92
Matching Food Mungabareena cheese.
Tasting Note 1992 Like the Filsell Vineyard Shiraz, only more so, driven throughout with rich, vanillin American oak. However, there is a lot of concentrated fruit deriving from the old vines, giving plenty of flesh and sweetness to the mid palate, finishing with soft, chewy tannins.

GRANT BURGE THORN VINEYARD RIESLING
●●●● $11.95

The Thorn Vineyard is situated in the Eden Valley, one of South Australia's two classic Riesling areas. Traditionally, Eden Valley

Rieslings took many years to develop their characteristic lime aroma and flavour, but modern winemaking seems to be bringing out those characters earlier in the life of the wines.
Cellaring Now–4 years. **Best Vintages** '88, '90, '92, '93, '94
Current Vintage '94
Matching Food Smoked trout mousse.
Tasting Note 1994 Medium yellow-green; full, tropical fruit aromas make the wine immediately attractive. The same richness and fullness is evident on the palate, already showing abundant regional lime fruit.

GRANTON VINEYARD

NR 15–20 CD AUS179
Tamar Valley **Est.** 1991
Rowbottoms Road, Granton, Tas 7030
Ph (002) 63 7457 **Fax** (002) 63 7457
Open Will open at the end of 1995 **Production** 1500
Winemaker(s) Steve Lubiana
Steve Lubiana has moved from one extreme to the other, having run Lubiana Wines at Moorook in the South Australian Riverlands for many years before moving to the Tamar Valley region of Tasmania to set up a substantial winery which will act as both contract maker and maker for its own label wines.
Principal Wines Chardonnay, Pinot Noir, Sparkling, with strong emphasis on the latter.

GREEN VALLEY VINEYARD

NR 11.50–17.50 CD AUSSD
Margaret River **Est.** 1980
Sebbes Road, Forest Grove via Margaret River, WA 6286
Ph (09) 384 3131
Open Sat, Pub hols 10–6, Sun 10–4 **Production** 2500
Winemaker(s) Clive Otto (Contract)
Owners Ed and Eleanore Green commenced the development of Green Valley Vineyard in 1980. It is still a part time operation, with the wines made by contract, but production has grown steadily, and the Cabernet Sauvignon ('91 and '92) has been a consistent medal winner.
Principal Wines Chardonnay, Riesling, Muller Thurgau, Dolce (Chenin Blanc), Cabernet Sauvignon.

GREENOCK CREEK CELLARS *

NR 13–16.50 CD AUSSD
Barossa Valley **Est.** 1978
Radford Road, Seppeltsfield, SA 5360
Ph (085) 62 8103 **Fax** (085) 62 8259
Open Wed–Mon 11–5 **Production** 1500
Winemaker(s) Michael Waugh
Michael and Annabelle Waugh are disciples of Rocky O'Callaghan of Rockford Wines, and have deliberately accumulated a series of

old dryland, low-yielding Barossa vineyards, aiming to produce wines of unusual depth of flavour and character. They have handsomely succeeded in this aim. They also offer superior accommodation in the ancient but beautifully restored two-bedroom cottage 'Miriam's'; Michael Waugh is a highly-skilled stonemason.
Principal Wines Chardonnay, Shiraz, Cabernet Sauvignon.

GREVILLEA ESTATE

NR 9–13 CD AUSSD
South Coast New South Wales **Est.** 1980
Buckajo Road, Bega, NSW 2550
Ph (064) 92 3006 **Fax** (064) 92 3006
Open 7 days 9–5 **Production** 2100
Winemaker(s) Nicola Collins
A tourist-oriented winery which successfully sells all of its surprisingly large production through cellar door and to local restaurants.
Principal Wines Chardonnay, Fumé Blanc, Riesling, Traminer Riesling, Spatlese, Merlot, Cabernet Sauvignon.

GROSSET WINES

★★★★★ 12.50–19 R AUS28, 70, 144, 161 UK62
Clare Valley **Est.** 1981
King Street, Auburn, SA 5451
Ph (088) 49 2175 **Fax** (088) 49 2292
Open Wed–Sun 10–5 **Production** 6500
Winemaker(s) Jeffrey Grosset
Jeffrey Grosset served part of his apprenticeship at the vast Lindeman Karadoc winery, moving from the largest to one of the smallest when he established Grosset Wines in its old stone winery. He now crafts the wines with the utmost care from grapes grown to the most exacting standards; all need a certain amount of time in bottle to achieve their ultimate potential, not the least the Rieslings and Gaia.
Principal Wines Watervale Riesling, Polish Hill Riesling, Semillon Sauvignon Blanc, Chardonnay, Gaia, Noble Riesling.

GROSSET CHARDONNAY
●●●● $19
The wine tends to be a chameleon, with the character changing from one vintage to the next, and also often developing at an unexpected rate or in an unexpected direction. In all of this it conforms to the schizophrenic nature of Clare Valley chardonnay, the one constant being the precision of the winemaking.
Cellaring 2–3 years. **Best Vintages** '86, '87, '90, '93, '94
Current Vintage '93
Matching Food Wiener schnitzel.
Tasting Note 1993 Light yellow-green; clean and fresh fruit, still light and evolving slowly, with subtle oak. The palate replicates the bouquet, still fresh and delicate, and — at least at this juncture — developing slowly.

GROSSET GAIA

••••• $19.50

A blend of 85% cabernet sauvignon, 10% cabernet franc and 5% merlot, typically made in amounts of less than 1000 cases — 950 cases were made of the '92. Shot to stardom with the initial vintage of 1990, and has not faltered since.

Cellaring 4–10 years. **Best Vintages** '90, '91, '92,
Current Vintage '92
Matching Food Game pie.
Tasting Note 1992 Deep purple-red; spotlessly smooth, sweet and clean, with classic dark berry/cassis fruit with very good oak handling. The palate is everything the bouquet promises, beautifully balanced with dark briary/berry/cassis flavours, soft but persistent tannins and subtle oak. Truly outstanding.

GROSSET POLISH HILL RIESLING

••••• $16

A finer, crisper and more elegant wine than the Watervale, with more lime and citrus fruit, albeit less generous. Since 1985 the Molloy Vineyard has been the major source, but as from 1994 estate plantings also contribute. Like the Watervale, made with neutral yeasts and without the use of enzymes.

Cellaring 7–10 years. **Best Vintages** '82, '86, '87, '90, '93, '94 **Current Vintage** '94
Matching Food Grilled South Australian whiting.
Tasting Note 1994 Classic, youthful Riesling, light green in colour, with tangy lime aromas tinged with herbaceousness. A very intense, lingering palate with toast and lime flavours and a minimum of five years in front of it.

GROSSET SEMILLON SAUVIGNON BLANC

•••• ▶ $16

Other than the Tim Knappstein Fumé Blanc, which incorporates Lenswood fruit from the Adelaide Hills, this is by far the best example of its kind from the Clare Valley. Immaculate winemaking produces a very fine, elegant, crisp seafood style.

Cellaring Drink now. **Best Vintages** '93, '94
Current Vintage '94
Matching Food Shellfish.
Tasting Note 1994 Very pale green-yellow; a crisp, clean direct bouquet of light to medium intensity. The palate has rather more power and length than the bouquet suggests, with cleansing lemony acid on the finish.

GROSSET WATERVALE RIESLING

•••• ▶ $12.50

Made from hand-picked grapes grown on a single vineyard established on red clay over limestone at an altitude of 450 metres. It is a richer, fuller style than the Polish Hill River wine, and tends to be slightly earlier maturing. All of the recent vintages have been made bone dry, with deliberately neutral yeast influence.

Cellaring 5–7 years. **Best Vintages** '81, '86, '90, '93, '94
Current Vintage '94
Matching Food Thai soup.
Tasting Note 1994 Light green-yellow; fragrant, elegant with
faintly spicy/toasty edges to the bouquet. On the palate, elegant,
crisp and lively again showing that touch of nutmeg spice, though
it is fruit- rather than enzyme-derived.

JEFFREY GROSSET PICCADILLY
●●●●● $24
Simply labelled 'Piccadilly' but (as the back label indicates) is
chardonnay from the Piccadilly vineyard in the Adelaide Hills. Only
900 cases were produced; it is made with the fastidious attention to
detail which Jeffrey Grosset always shows, and with equally
impressive skill.
Cellaring 3–6 years. **Best Vintages** NA **Current Vintage** '94
Matching Food Crustacea.
Tasting Note 1994 Light green-yellow; a fine, elegant bouquet
with melon fruit and immediately obvious but not oppressive high
quality French oak integrated through barrel ferment. The wine has a
beautifully sculpted palate with excellent oak and fruit balance and
integration. Restrained but certainly not lean or mean, and will
develop superbly.

HAIG *

NR NA AUSSD
Coonawarra **Est.** 1982
Square Mile Road, Mount Gambier, SA 5290
Ph (087) 25 5414 **Fax** (087) 25 0252
Open 7 days 10–5 **Production** NFP
Winemaker(s) Katnook (Contract)
The 4 hectares of estate vineyards are planted on the rich volcanic
soils near the slopes of the famous Blue Lake of Mount Gambier. I
have neither seen nor tasted the wines.
Principal Wines Chardonnay, Pinot Noir, Fortifieds.

HAINAULT VINEYARD

★★☆ 11–15 CD AUSSD
Darling Range **Est.** 1980
255 Walnut Road, Bickley, WA 6076
Ph (09) 293 8339 **Fax** (09) 293 8339
Open Thurs–Sun 10–5 **Production** 2200
Winemaker(s) Peter Fimmel
Peter Fimmel has been the guiding force in the Perth Hills, and his
commitment to wine is absolute. I simply wish I could be more
enthusiastic about his wines or believe the Perth Hills is the right
area for Pinot Noir, Fimmel's particular love.
Principal Wines Gewurztraminer, Semillon, Chardonnay,
Cabernet Merlot, Pinot Noir.

HALCYON DAZE

★★★ 14–20 ML AUSSD
Yarra Valley **Est.** 1982
Lot 15 Uplands Road, Lilydale, Vic 3140
Ph (03) 9726 7111 **Fax** (03) 9726 7111
Open By appt **Production** 800
Winemaker(s) Richard Rackley
One of the lower-profile wineries with a small, estate-grown
production which in fact sells the major part of its output of grapes
to others. Immaculate viticulture ensures that the grapes have a
strong market.
Principal Wines Riesling, Chardonnay, Pinot Noir, Cabernet
Blend; also Sparkling.

HANGING ROCK WINERY

★★★☆ 7.95–29.95 R AUS107, 161
Macedon **Est.** 1982
The Jim Jim, Jim Road, Newham, Vic 3442
Ph (054) 27 0542 **Fax** (054) 27 0310
Open 7 days 10–5 **Production** 15 000
Winemaker(s) John Ellis
The Macedon area has proved very marginal in spots, and the
Hanging Rock vineyards, with their lovely vista towards the Rock,
are no exception. John Ellis has thus elected to source additional
grapes from various parts of Victoria, to produce an interesting and
diverse style of wines. The low-priced Picnic White and Picnic Red,
with the striking label, have been particularly successful.
Principal Wines Macedon Sparkling, Jim Jim Sauvignon Blanc,
Victoria Chardonnay, Cabernet Merlot, Pinot Noir, Heathcote
Shiraz, Picnic Red and White.

HANKIN ESTATE *

NR 6–14 CD AUSSD
Goulburn Valley **Est.** 1975
Johnsons Lane, Northwood via Seymour, Vic 3660
Ph (057) 92 2396
Open W'ends 10–5 **Production** 1000
Winemaker(s) Dr Max Hankin
Hankin Wines is a strictly weekend and holiday operation for
Dr Max Hankin. Intermittent tastings over the years have revealed
full-bodied if somewhat rustic reds typical of the Central Goulburn
Valley.
Principal Wines Sauvignon Blanc, Semillon Chardonnay, Rosé,
Shiraz, Shiraz Cabernet Merlot.

HANNS CREEK ESTATE

★★★☆ 16–19 CD AUSSD
Mornington Peninsula **Est.** 1987
Kentucky Road, Merricks North, Vic 3926

Ph (059) 89 7266 **Fax** (059) 89 7500
Open 7 days 11–5 **Production** 600
Winemaker(s) Kevin McCarthy (Contract)

Denise and Tony Aubrey-Slocock have established a 3-hectare vineyard on the slopes of Merricks North. After an uncertain start, with contract winemaking moving around, Kevin McCarthy has taken control, and the bronze medals won by the Pinot Noir and Chardonnay at the 1994 Lilydale Wine Show point the way for the future.

Principal Wines Chardonnay, Chardonnay Riesling, Rosé, Pinot Noir, Cabernet Shiraz, Cabernet Sauvignon.

HAPPS

★★★☆ 6–25 CD AUS10
Margaret River **Est.** 1978
Commonage Road, Dunsborough, WA 6281
Ph (097) 55 3300 **Fax** (097) 55 3846
Open 7 days 10–5 **Production** 10 000
Winemaker(s) Erl Happ

Former schoolteacher turned potter and winemaker Erl Happ is an iconoclast and compulsive experimenter. Many of the styles he makes are very unconventional, the future likely to be even more so: the Karridale vineyard planted in 1994 has no less than 22 different varieties established.

Principal Wines Dry table wines are Semillon, Chardonnay, Margaret River Red, Shiraz, Merlot and Cabernet Merlot; sweet table wines are Fuschia, Topaz and Verdelho; fortifieds are Fortis (Vintage Port), 10 Year Fortis (Tawny), Garnet (from Muscat a petit grains), Pale Gold (White Port) and Old Bronze (Muscat). In 1994 a Preservative Free Red was also made.

HAPPS CABERNET MERLOT
●●●● $15

I have to confess to having very longstanding and very consistent problems with the style of many of the Happs Merlots and Cabernet Merlots, with persistent gamey characters showing through, perhaps due to some degree of bacterial activity, possibly to sulphides. The '92 is the best wine for years, even if it does have a hint of that gaminess.

Cellaring 4–6 years. **Best Vintages** '92 **Current Vintage** '92
Matching Food Game pie.
Tasting Note 1992 Medium to full red-purple; there are strong cassis berry fruit aromas on the bouquet with just a faintly gamey edge. The palate is powerful, with blackberry fruit and attractive rustic edges, finishing with soft tannins.

HAPPS CHARDONNAY
●●● ▶ $16

Produced from 1.7 hectares of grapes on the Dunsborough Vineyard, and barrel fermented, even though the oak influence is minimal, and the oak quite evidently had only a small (if any) percentage of new barrels.

Cellaring 3–4 years. **Best Vintages** '91, '94
Current Vintage '93
Matching Food Scallop mousseline.
Tasting Note 1993 Light to medium yellow-green; crisp and clean with melon, fig and peach fruit aromas. The palate is soft, with peachy flavours predominant, and the oak influence barely perceptible.

HAPPS FUSCHIA

●●● ▶ $11

Typical of the adventuresome nature of Erl Happ, made from equal quantities of cabernet sauvignon, merlot and shiraz run off skins very early in the fermentation, and fortified to 14.6% alcohol.
Cellaring Drink now. **Best Vintages** NA **Current Vintage** '94
Matching Food Aperitif, Asian.
Tasting Note 1994 Light, bright pink; the bouquet is fresh and clean with spicy/grapey aromas. The palate is likewise grapey and spirity, with a clean, fruity finish.

HAPPS PRESERVATIVE FREE RED

●●●● $15

Made from an unstated varietal blend, but quite evidently ripe given the 13.5% alcohol. Notwithstanding the absence of sulphur dioxide, there are no aldehydes; an unqualified success.
Cellaring Drink immediately. **Best Vintages** NA
Current Vintage '94
Matching Food Pasta.
Tasting Note 1994 Medium to full red-purple; warm, juicy berry aromas with minimal or no oak evident. The palate is very ripe with lots of clean, juicy, berry fruit flavours and soft tannins.

HARCOURT VALLEY VINEYARDS

NR 9.50–14.50 CD AUSSD
Bendigo **Est.** 1976
Calder Highway, Harcourt, Vic 3453
Ph (054) 74 2223
Open 7 days 10–6 **Production** 2000
Winemaker(s) John Livingstone
Traditional producer of rich, full-bodied red wines typical of the district, but sporadic (and largely outdated) tastings since ownership changed preclude evaluation other than a lovely spicy '91 Barbara's Shiraz tasted in 1993.
Principal Wines Chardonnay, Riesling, Shiraz, Cabernet Sauvignon.

HARDYS

★★★★☆ 5.59–22.95 R AUS20–24 UK18 US8
Southern Vales **Est.** 1853
Reynella Road, Reynella, SA 5161
Ph (08) 381 2266 **Fax** (08) 381 1968

Open 7 days 10–4.30 **Production** NFP
Winemaker(s) Peter Dawson, David O'Leary, Tom Newton, Ed Carr

1992 marked the end of a family dynasty as Thomas Hardy became part of the publicly listed BRL Hardy Limited group, it being no secret that it was Berri Renmano (hence the BRL in the corporate name) which was the groom and Hardy the reluctant bride. The merged group is extremely powerful in terms of volume, edging the Orlando Wyndham group out of second place in the hierarchy.

Principal Wines Starts with Old Castle Rhine Riesling, St Vincent Chablis; then McLaren Vale Hermitage, Classic Dry White; Nottage Hill Riesling, Chardonnay, Cabernet Sauvignon; then the generic Bird series, followed by Siegersdorf Chardonnay and Rhine Riesling. At the top end progressively come Regional Collection Chardonnay, Cabernet Sauvignon, Pinot Noir; at the very top Eileen Hardy Chardonnay, Shiraz and Thomas Hardy Cabernet Sauvignon. There is a full range of sparkling wines, superior quality brandies and ports including Australia's finest Vintage Port.

HARDYS EILEEN HARDY CHARDONNAY
●●●●● $22

One can argue whether or not the wine has a sufficient track record or distinction to justify its rating as a classic, but is a more than usually elegant wine, and some of the early vintages have aged with far greater distinction than most Australian Chardonnays. Moreover, the shift from Padthaway to a Yarra Valley base, coupled with refinements to the winemaking used, will lead to even better wines in the future.

Cellaring 3–6 years. **Best Vintages** '85, '87, '90, '91, '93
Current Vintage '93
Matching Food Fresh Atlantic salmon.
Tasting Note 1993 Light to medium green-yellow; tighter, yet more complex than any of the wines which preceded it, with some citrus aromas and subtle oak on the bouquet. The palate is fresh and crisp, with melon, citrus and a hint of cashew nut. Limited bottling owing to the vintage; 50% Yarra Valley, 50% Padthaway.

HARDYS EILEEN HARDY SHIRAZ
●●●●● $22

If one includes the 1970 in the range, a wine with a proud history. As is the case with Wynns Michael Hermitage, the reincarnation bears little or no resemblance to the original model, but in common with Michael Hermitage, reflects a determination to produce the best (some would say the biggest) possible wine.

Cellaring 10+ years. **Best Vintages** '70, '88, '91, '93
Current Vintage '93
Matching Food Game pie.
Tasting Note 1993 Medium to full red-purple; a ripe and concentrated bouquet with rich essency/rose petal berry aromas with a background of high-toned oak. The palate is bursting with black cherry and blackcurrant fruit with great vinosity, matched by high-toned French oak; better balanced than the '92.

HARDYS EILEEN HARDY VINTAGE PORT
●●●●● $22

Made from very ripe, low-yielding McLaren Vale shiraz, fortified using a very particular brandy spirit made by Hardys. Just as with Portuguese Vintage Port, there is much debate about the relative input and importance of the base wine on the one hand and the fortifying spirit (and fortifying techniques) on the other. What is certain is that this is Australia's finest Vintage Port, the best vintages of which age superbly.

Cellaring Up to 30 years or more. **Best Vintages** '45, '51, '54, '56, '71, '73, '75, '81 **Current Vintage** '82

Matching Food Coffee.

Tasting Note 1982 The product of a relatively cool vintage, and in a lighter style than the '81. Medium to full red; chocolate, earth prune aromas with quite potent brandy spirit. On the palate sweet chocolate and berry fruit balanced by fine tannins, finishing pleasantly dry.

HARDYS SIEGERSDORF CHARDONNAY
●●●● $7.95

A relatively recent extension of the Siegersdorf range, which was for so many years restricted to the Riesling. Has in fact produced some very worthwhile wines, particularly in 1993 and 1994. A blend of McLaren Vale and Padthaway grapes; the Hardy winemakers have resisted the temptation to fill the wine up with oak chips.

Cellaring 1–2 years. **Best Vintages** '92, '93, '94

Current Vintage '94

Matching Food Stir-fried chicken.

Tasting Note 1994 Light yellow-green; the bouquet is of light to medium intensity with citrussy fruit and subtle oak. The palate is fruit-driven, not particularly rich but with pleasant citrus and melon fruit flavours, just the barest flick of oak, and nicely balanced acidity.

HARDYS SIEGERSDORF RHINE RIESLING
●●● ▶ $7.95

A wine with a long and distinguished pedigree, going back to the early 1970s when a youthful Brian Croser briefly served as chief white winemaker. Then one of Hardys premium wines, it is now mainstream commercial, but holds its market share simply because it is a good wine at the price. It is made from Clare Valley and Padthaway grapes, both premium regions, the Clare Valley particularly noted for its riesling.

Cellaring 2–4 years. **Best Vintages** '88, '90, '92, '93, '94

Current Vintage '94

Matching Food Scallop and vegetable terrine.

Tasting Note 1994 Light green-yellow; soft but spicy, with lime/tropical aromas to the bouquet. The palate is clean and crisp, refreshingly made bone-dry, unusual these days in commercial Rieslings, with more of the citrus flavours of the bouquet.

HARDYS THOMAS HARDY CABERNET SAUVIGNON
●●●●● $25

Launched in 1994, with the 1989 vintage. A blend of 87%

Coonawarra cabernet sauvignon and 13% McLaren Vale cabernet
sauvignon matured in 80% French Nevers and 20% American oak
for 18 months. Made at Chateau Reynella (the Hardy corporate
headquarters) using traditional open fermenters and a basket press.
It, together with the '90, '91 and '92 vintages are at the opulent end
of the scale, not unlike Wynns John Riddoch in style. The '89 has
won a trophy, four gold, eight silver and four bronze medals.
Cellaring 10+ years. **Best Vintages** NA **Current Vintage** '89
Matching Food Rich red meat dishes.
Tasting Note 1989 Medium to full red-purple; an extremely
complex, oak-driven style, with masses of cedary oak on both the
bouquet and palate. The latter has lots of soft red berry fruits and
fine tannins to go along with the cedary oak, and is a singularly
impressive achievement from a difficult vintage.

HAREWOOD ESTATE *

NR 20.85 ML AUSSD
Great Southern **Est.** 1988
'Binalong', Scotsdale Road, Denmark, WA 6333
Ph (098) 40 9078 **Fax** (098) 40 9053
Open By appt **Production** 200
Winemaker(s) John Wade (Contract)
Keith and Margie Graham have established a showpiece vineyard
at Binalong. The majority of the grapes are sold to Howard Park and
Domaine Chandon, but gradually increasing amounts of wine will be
made under the Harewood Estate label.
Principal Wines Pinot Noir, Chardonnay.

HAREWOOD ESTATE PINOT NOIR

●●●● $20.85
The first wine to be made for Harewood Estate in anything
approaching a commercial quantity, although smaller amounts of
various wines have been made in prior years for the
library/museum.
Cellaring 1–2 years. **Best Vintages** NA **Current Vintage** '94
Matching Food Hare, of course.
Tasting Note 1994 Medium red-purple; the bouquet is of light to
medium intensity with cherry fruit and hints of spice and earth; subtle
oak. The palate is moderately intense with cherry fruit flavours, a hint
of vanilla, finishing with soft tannins.

HARTZVIEW WINE CENTRE

★★★ 18 CD AUSSD
Huon Valley **Est.** 1988
RSD 1034 Off Cross Road, Gardners Bay, Tas 7112
Ph (002) 95 1623
Open 7 days summer, Wed–Sun autumn, Weekends Winter 10–5
Production NFP
Winemaker(s) Andrew Hood (Contract)
A combined wine centre offering wines from a number of local Huon

Valley wineries and also newly-erected and very comfortable
accommodation for 6 people in a separate, self-contained house.
Hartzview table wines (produced from 3 hectares of estate plantings)
are much to be preferred to the self-produced Pig and Whistle Hill
fruit wines.
Principal Wines Chardonnay, Pinot Noir; also a range of Pig
and Whistle Hill fruit wines.

HASELGROVE WINES

★★★ 7.90–22.50 R AUSSD UK91
Southern Vales & Coonawarra **Est.** 1981
Foggo Road, McLaren Vale, SA 5171
Ph (08) 323 8706 **Fax** (08) 323 8049
Open Mon–Fri 9–5, W'ends 10–5 **Production** 16 000
Winemaker(s) Nick Haselgrove
An over-reliance on the use of oak chips shows up in many of the
red wines which is a pity, given that much of the underlying fruit
does not need such assistance.
Principal Wines Sauvignon Blanc, Chardonnay, Cabernet Merlot,
Futures Shiraz, Grenache Shiraz; premium releases under 'H'
Reserve label.

HASELGROVE GRENACHE SHIRAZ

●●●● $12
A new arrival on the scene for Haselgrove, and very much a sign of
the times, as McLaren Vale grenache comes into its own, making
fleshy, full-bodied, yet early-maturing wines.
Cellaring Best young. **Best Vintages** NA
Current Vintage '93
Matching Food Kangaroo fillet.
Tasting Note 1993 Medium to full purple-red; very ripe full, dark
blood plum fruits with some spicy overtones to the bouquet, and
similar super-ripe cherry, plum and spice fruit on the palate, finishing
with soft tannins.

HAY SHED HILL WINES

★★★☆ 12–14 CD AUS174, 182 UK62
Margaret River **Est.** 1987
RSM 398 Harmans Mill Road, Willyabrup, WA 6280
Ph (097) 55 6234 **Fax** (097) 55 6305
Open Weekends, Hols 10–5 **Production** 5000
Winemaker(s) Peter Stanlake, John Smith
(Consultant)
A landmark on the Margaret River scene, with a striking new
120-tonne winery, a carefully devised business plan by the Morrison
family, energetic marketing, and innovative label design. The white
wines have been erratic, the Cabernet Sauvignon very good.
Principal Wines Sauvignon Blanc, Semillon, Chardonnay,
Pitchfork Pink Rosé, Group 20 Cabernet Sauvignon (light,
unwooded), Cabernet Sauvignon, Pinot Noir.

HAY SHED HILL CABERNET SAUVIGNON
●●●● ▶ $14

Made from estate-grown grapes produced from vines which are now almost 20 years old, and indicative of the quality to be expected from the winery under this label after an erratic start with the '90, and to a lesser degree, '91, vintages.

Cellaring 5–8 years. **Best Vintages** '92 **Current Vintage** '92
Matching Food Beef casserole.
Tasting Note 1992 Medium to full red-purple; a complex bouquet with abundant fresh redcurrant fruit and an obvious new oak input which is not yet entirely integrated. A similarly complex, multiflavoured and multifaceted palate with lots of ripe fruit and strong oak influence. Should age extremely well.

HAYWARD'S WHITEHEAD CREEK

★★ 5–8.50 CD AUSSD
Goulburn Valley **Est.** 1975
Lot 18A Hall Lane, Seymour, Vic 3660
Ph (057) 92 3050
Open Mon–Sat 9–6, Sun 10–6 **Production** Nil
Winemaker(s) Sid Hayward
Production at Hayward's has gone into recess, with grapes from the 5-hectare vineyards currently being sold to others. Older vintages of fairly rustic wines are available from cellar door at very low prices.
Principal Wines Shiraz, Cabernet Sauvignon, Shiraz Port.

HEATHCOTE WINERY

NR 12–14.50 CD AUS87
Bendigo **Est.** 1982
183–185 High Street, Heathcote, Vic 3523
Ph (054) 33 2595 **Fax** (054) 33 3081
Open 7 days 10–6 **Production** 5000
Winemaker(s) Nicholas Simon Butler
A once very visible but now low-profile operation. Former winemaker Nigel Sneyd has departed to France; it will be interesting to see what legacies he has left, but I have not come across the wines in any forum in recent times.
Principal Wines Viognier, Shiraz, Chardonnay; Deschamps Chardonnay Chenin Blanc, Pinot Noir Shiraz.

HEEMSKERK VINEYARDS

★★★☆ 15.95–28 R AUS66
Pipers Brook **Est.** 1967
Pipers Brook, Tas 7254
Ph (003) 82 7133 **Fax** (003) 82 7242
Open Nov–Apr 10–5 **Production** 12 000
Winemaker(s) Garry Ford
In July 1994 Heemskerk was acquired by the JAC Group, which simultaneously acquired Rochecombe Vineyard and the Loira

Vineyard of Buchanan Wines. The new, diversified, publicly listed owners intend to significantly increase group production to 500 tonnes over the next few years.
Principal Wines Chardonnay, Botrytis Riesling, Pinot Noir, Cabernet Sauvignon, Jansz Methode Champenoise.

HEEMSKERK CHARDONNAY
●●● ▶ $28
The combination of climate and soil in the Pipers Brook region has proved to be a very interesting but even more demanding one. Immaculate viticulture and canopy control is essential, and even with this, the wines tend to be very delicate and European in style. This wine is no exception.
Cellaring 3–5 years. **Best Vintages** '84, '88, '91, '94
Current Vintage '92
Matching Food Tasmanian salmon.
Tasting Note 1992 Light to medium yellow-green; a discrete bouquet, bordering on the austere, with some dusty malolactic fermentation characters. The palate is crisp and fairly acidic on the palate, distinctly European in style.

HEEMSKERK JANSZ METHODE CHAMPENOISE
●●●● $25.30
Conceived as a now-terminated collaboration of Heemskerk and Roederer (of France), and made with lofty ambitions. The base wine is made at Heemskerk, but has been tiraged, aged and bottled at Domaine Chandon in the Yarra Valley. The wine is razor sharp, liked by some and not by others; by way of postscript, as it were, it is a blend of pinot noir and chardonnay.
Cellaring 2–4 years. **Best Vintages** NA **Current Vintage** '91
Matching Food Oysters.
Tasting Note 1991 Medium straw with just a tinge of pink from the pinot noir component which will diminish as the wine ages in bottle. A dusty, nutty bouquet, with similar nutty, pinot noir-derived flavours on the palate, finishing with bracing acidity.

HEGGIES

★★★★ 12–16.95 R AUS138–142 UK38
Adelaide Hills **Est.** 1971
Heggies Range Road, Eden Valley, SA 5235
Ph (085) 65 3203 **Fax** (085) 65 3380
Open Not **Production** 12 500
Winemaker(s) Simon Adams
Heggies was the second of the high altitude (570 metres) vineyards established by S Smith & Sons (Yalumba), with plantings on the 120-hectare former grazing property commencing in 1973. The red wines are typically rather lean, but the white wines are never less than good, sometimes outstanding. The Viognier is a most interesting addition.
Principal Wines Riesling, Viognier, Chardonnay, Botrytis Riesling, Cabernets.

HEGGIES CHARDONNAY
●●●● $16.95
Made, needless to say, from 100% estate-grown grapes, barrel
fermented and always given time in bottle before it is brought onto
the market. The result is a complex, rich wine, often sweet and
toasty.
Cellaring 2–4 years. **Best Vintages** '86, '91, '93
Current Vintage '92
Matching Food Veal, turkey.
Tasting Note 1992 Medium to full yellow-green; solid, toasty
aromas with secondary fruit characters and well integrated oak. A
well balanced wine in the mouth, with nutty/oaky flavours and a
relatively soft finish. Good food style.

HEGGIES VIOGNIER
●●●● $16.95
While viognier has been grown on the Mornington Peninsula, at
Elgee Park, for many years, Yalumba (with a separate importation of
clonal material) has been the first to commercialise viognier in
Australia. The early vintages produced rather thin, ordinary wines,
but increasing vine maturity seems to be bringing results, with a
marked improvement in the quality of the '93.
Cellaring Drink now. **Best Vintages** '93 **Current Vintage** '93
Matching Food Prosciutto and figs.
Tasting Note 1993 Light yellow-green; the bouquet shows much
more bouquet and fruit than in prior vintages with flowery
passionfruit overtones. On the palate, distinctively viognier with
flowery pastille/honeysuckle fruit flavours of medium intensity.

HELM'S WINES

★★★☆ 11–18 CD AUS2
Canberra **Est.** 1974
Butt's Road Murrumbateman, NSW 2582
Ph (06) 227 5536 **Fax** (06) 227 5953
Open Thur–Mon 10–5 **Production** 2000
Winemaker(s) Ken Helm
Ken Helm is well known as one of the more stormy petrels of the
wine industry, and is an energetic promoter of his wines and of the
Canberra district generally.
Principal Wines Rhine Riesling, Premium Dry White, Cowra
Chardonnay, Cabernet Shiraz, Cabernet Merlot.

HELM'S CABERNET MERLOT
●●● ▶ $18
First produced in 1989, and has been the most successful of the
Helm's wines since that time, having won 38 show awards including
two gold medals.
Cellaring 3–4 years. **Best Vintages** '83, '86, '88, '90, '92, '93
Current Vintage '93
Matching Food Lamb fillets.
Tasting Note 1993 Medium red-purple; a fairly light,
leafy/tobacco/stemmy-accented bouquet which leads on to a lean

wine on the palate, though possessing some attractive red berry fruit
on the mid palate.

HELM'S COWRA CHARDONNAY
●●●● $15

First produced in 1984, and intermittently thereafter. In 1990 it
moved from a wooded to an unwooded style, Ken Helm being one
of the innovators. The '94 vintage was largely destroyed by frost, so
this wine is a blend of 80% Cowra and 20% Canberra district fruit.
A silver and bronze medal winner.

Cellaring Drink now. **Best Vintages** NA **Current Vintage** '94
Matching Food Snowy Mountains trout.
Tasting Note 1994 Light green-yellow; a clean, firm citrus and
melon bouquet leads on to a well made wine with good fruit
intensity, and length to the finish.

HENKE WINERY

★★★ 10–14 CD AUSSD
Goulburn Valley **Est.** 1974
175 Henke Lane, Yarck, Vic 3719
Ph (057) 97 6277
Open By appt **Production** 250
Winemaker(s) Tim Miller, Caroline Miller
Produces tiny quantities of deep-coloured full-flavoured, minty red
wines known only to a chosen few; in 1993 reds from the 1988
vintage were still available at cellar door. 1994 production from the
2-hectare vineyard was said to be 'not much'.
Principal Wines Shiraz, Shiraz Cabernet.

HENLEY PARK WINES

NR 7.50–16.50 CD AUSSD
Swan Valley **Est.** 1935
149 Swan Street, West Swan, WA 6055
Ph (09) 296 4328 **Fax** (09) 296 1313
Open Mon–Sat 9–6, Sun 10–6 **Production** 3500
Winemaker(s) Claus Petersen
Henley Park was founded by a Yugoslav, a Dane and a Malaysian
businessman (since 1987), had a French winemaker (until recently),
and nestles in the heartland of the Yugoslavian wineries of the Swan
Valley, indeed a tribute to multiculturalism. I have not tasted any of
the wines recently.
Principal Wines Chenin Blanc, Chardonnay, Verdelho
Chardonnay, Frontignac, Mousse (Sparkling), Cabernet Sauvignon,
Fortifieds.

HENSCHKE

★★★★★ 10.95–55 R AUS13, 27, 37, 167–170 UK52 US10
Adelaide Hills **Est.** 1868
264 Moculta Road, Keyneton, SA 5353

Ph (085) 64 8223 **Fax** (085) 64 8294
Open Mon–Fri 9–4.30, Sat 9–12 **Production** 35 000
Winemaker(s) Stephen Henschke

Unchallenged as one of the top half-dozen wineries in Australia, and
has gone from strength to strength over the past 13 years or so
under the guidance of Stephen and Prue Henschke. The red wines
fully capitalise on the very old, low-yielding, high-quality vines, and
are superbly made with sensitive but positive use of new small oak;
the same skills are evident in the white
winemaking.

Principal Wines Henschke Eden Valley sources: Sauvignon Blanc,
Chardonnay, Chenin Blanc, Dry White Frontignac, Gewurztraminer,
Semillon, Tilly's Vineyard, Rhine Riesling, Keyneton Estate, Mount
Edelstone Cyril Henschke Cabernet Sauvignon, Hill of Grace;
Lenswood Vineyard in the Adelaide Hills: Green's Hill Riesling, Croft
Chardonnay, Giles Pinot Noir, Abbott's Prayer Cabernet Merlot.

HENSCHKE ABBOTT'S PRAYER CABERNET MERLOT
●●●●● $28

The evocatively named Abbott's Prayer links the history, religion and
pioneers of the Adelaide Hills. Right from the first vintage, this blend
of 60% merlot, 38% cabernet sauvignon and 2% cabernet franc (as
at 1992) has been of exceptional quality, the '89 winning the trophy
as best wine of the 1991 Sydney International Winemakers
Competition. Unusually for Henschke, it is matured entirely in French
oak.

Cellaring 3–6 years. **Best Vintages** '89, '90, '91, '92
Current Vintage '92
Matching Food Guineafowl in red wine sauce.
Tasting Note 1992 Medium red-purple, showing some signs
of development. The bouquet is strongly reminiscent of Bordeaux,
with fragrant leafy/tobacco aromas interwoven with blackberry
fruit. The supple, almost silky palate shows an intriguing mixture of
tobacco and berry fruit flavours finishing with fine-grained tannins.
Very Bordeaux-like; probably doesn't need too many years
maturation.

HENSCHKE CYRIL HENSCHKE CABERNET SAUVIGNON
●●●●● $31

The 1978 vintage was the first release in 1980, made by Stephen
Henschke in memory of his father who had died the previous year.
Now a blend of 90% cabernet sauvignon, 5% merlot and 5%
cabernet franc sourced from the Eden Valley. A prolific trophy and
gold medal winner at national wine shows.

Cellaring 6–12 years. **Best Vintages** '78, '80, '85, '86, '88,
'90, '91 **Current Vintage** '91
Matching Food Roast lamb.
Tasting Note 1991 Medium to full red-purple; a complex bouquet
with ripe cassis/berry fruit married with charry/lemony oak, and
overtones of Bordeaux from a ripe year. A marvellous wine on the
palate, elegant, yet concentrated with dark briary/berry/cassis fruit
of perfect ripeness, very good tannin balance.

HENSCHKE GREEN'S HILL RIESLING
●●●● ▶ $16.50

In the year 1982 the Henschke family acquired a 14-hectare apple orchard at Lenswood, high in the southern end of the Adelaide Hills at an altitude of 550 metres. The first significant vintage was 1989, but production overall is limited. The Green's Hill Riesling, which overlooks apple orchards operated by the Green family since 1893, is a marvellous example of cool-climate riesling, intense yet generous.

Cellaring 2–5 years. **Best Vintages** NA **Current Vintage** '94
Matching Food Smoked trout pâté.

Tasting Note 1994 Light yellow-green; a very rich, relatively forward wine with intense lime juice aromas. The palate is rich to the point of being luscious, with wonderful smooth and generous lime-accented fruit. Very Germanic, although Germanic from a ripe year.

HENSCHKE HILL OF GRACE
●●●●● $55

Made entirely from 100-year-old shiraz vines on the Hill of Grace Vineyard, planted in the late 1860s by a Henschke ancestor, Nicholas Stanitzki. Is second only to Penfolds Grange, which it rivals in terms of quality, scarcity and (almost) price. The wine has never been entered in wine shows, nor will it ever be: it has its own standards.

Cellaring 10–20+ years. **Best Vintages** '59, '61, '62, '66, '78, '82, '85, '86, '88, '90, '91
Current Vintage '91
Matching Food Rich casserole dishes.

Tasting Note 1991 Medium to full red-purple, with abundant, smooth and sweet dark cherry fruit aromas; the oak is subtle but there is some lift. In the mouth a potent wine with some striking similarities to Grange Hermitage, not the least being the degree of lift, and also the tremendous length on the palate. Strikingly different from the '90, but may simply be the impact of the ripe year.

HENSCHKE KEYNTON ESTATE SHIRAZ CABERNET MALBEC
●●●● ▶ $19.30

Not, as the label might half suggest, a single vineyard or estate wine in the classic sense of that term, but rather a blend of 70% shiraz, 25% cabernet sauvignon and 5% malbec grown in the Eden and Barossa Valleys. It is made in the traditional Henschke fashion in open fermenters, and matured in new and used American and French oak for 12 months. It may not be the greatest of the Henschke red wines, but frequently offers the best value for money.

Cellaring 5–8 years. **Best Vintages** '82, '84, '86, '88, '90
Current Vintage '92
Matching Food Veal chops.

Tasting Note 1992 Medium to full red-purple. A clean, noticeably ripe red berry/raspberry bouquet with subtle oak. The palate is fruit-driven, generous and fleshy; both the oak and tannin contributions are soft.

HENSCHKE MOUNT EDELSTONE
●●●●● $27.50
Made entirely from shiraz grown on the Mount Edelstone Vineyard,
planted in the 1920s and acquired by Henschke in 1974, although
the wine was first made (and labelled as such) in 1952. A wine of
tremendous character and quality.
Cellaring 7–15 years. **Best Vintages** '52, '56, '61, '66, '67,
'78, '82, '86, '88, '90, '92 **Current Vintage** '92
Matching Food Beef bourguignon.
Tasting Note 1992 Youthful purple-red; fresh, scented
cherry/berry/spice aromas, reflecting a relatively cool vintage but
showing lovely varietal character. There is delicious
spicy/cherry/berry fruit on the palate with sweet vanillin oak. A
luscious wine with everything going for it.

HERCYNIA WINES

NR 7–14 CD AUSSD
Hilltops **Est.** 1979
RMB 97 Prunevale Road, Kingsvale, NSW 2587
Ph (063) 84 4243 **Fax** (063) 84 4292
Open W'ends 9–5 **Production** 300
Winemaker(s) Keith John Doldissen (Consultant)
The Doldissen family commenced the development of their 8-hectare
vineyard in 1979, producing the first wines in 1985. Much of the
production is sold to other makers, notably in the Canberra district.
Principal Wines Riesling, Chardonnay, Sauvignon Blanc, Pinot
Noir, Muscat, Port.

HERITAGE FARM WINES

NR 4–10.50 CD AUSSD
Murray River **Est.** 1987
RMB 1005 Murray Valley Highway, Cobram, Vic 3655
Ph (058) 72 2376
Open 7 days 9–5 **Production** 4000
Winemaker(s) Kevin Tyrrell
Heritage Farm claims to be the only vineyard and orchard in
Australia still using horse power, with Clydesdales used for most of
the general farm work. The winery and cellar door area also boasts
a large range of restored horse-drawn farm machinery and a bottle
collection.
Principal Wines Riesling and Chardonnay are the only two
varietal releases; there are a considerable number of generic
releases and fortified wines on sale at cellar door.

HERITAGE WINES

★★★★ 12–17 R AUSSD UK11
Barossa Valley **Est.** 1984
Seppeltsfield Road, Marananga via Tanunda, SA 5352
Ph (085) 62 2880 **Fax** (085) 62 2692
Open 7 days 11–5 **Production** 6000

Winemaker(s) Stephen Hoff
A little-known winery which deserves a far wider audience, for
Stephen Hoff is apt to produce some startlingly good wines. At
various times the Chardonnay, Rhine Riesling (from old Clare Valley
vines) and Rosscos Shiraz (now the flagbearer) have all excelled, at
other times not.
Principal Wines Riesling, Semillon, Chardonnay, Shiraz,
Cabernet Franc, Cabernet Malbec, Rosscos Shiraz.

HERITAGE WINES OF STANTHORPE

NR 8.50–11.50 CD AUSSD
Granite Belt **Est.** 1992
New England Highway, Cottonvale, Qld 4375
Ph (076) 85 2197 **Fax** (076) 85 2172
Open 7 days 9–7 **Production** 2000
Winemaker(s) Bruce Humphery-Smith
A tourist-oriented venture, as are many of the Stanthorpe region
wineries. The estate plantings comprise one hectare each of
chardonnay and verdelho, but the initial offerings come from other
sources.
Principal Wine Semillon, Semillon Chardonnay, Traminer Riesling,
Cabernet Sauvignon, Fortified and flavoured wines.

HERONS RISE VINEYARD

NR 12.50–15 CD AUSSD
Southern Tasmania **Est.** 1984
Saddle Road, Kettering, Tas 7155
Ph (002) 67 4339 **Fax** (002) 67 4245
Open By appt **Production** 85
Winemaker(s) Andrew Hood, Leigh Gawith.
Sue and Gerry White run a small stone country guesthouse in the
D'Entrecasteaux Channel area, and basically sell the wines from
the surrounding one hectare of vineyard to those staying at the
guesthouse. The postal address for bookings is PO Box 271,
Kettering, Tas 7155.
Principal Wines Muller Thurgau Riesling, Pinot Noir.

HICKINBOTHAM WINEMAKERS

★★★ 17–21 R AUS174 UK80
Mornington Peninsula **Est.** 1981
Cnr Wallaces Road & Nepean Highway, Dromana, Vic 3936
Ph (059) 81 0355 **Fax** (059) 81 0355
Open By appt **Production** 2100
Winemaker(s) Andrew Hickinbotham
After a peripatetic period, and a hiatus in winemaking,
Hickinbotham has established a permanent vineyard and winery
base at Dromana. It now makes only Mornington Peninsula wines,
drawing in part on 10 hectares of estate vineyards, and in part on
contract-grown fruit.

Principal Wines Chardonnay, Merlot, Shiraz, Cabernet
Sauvignon, all sourced from the Mornington Peninsula.

HICKINBOTHAM CHARDONNAY
●●● ▶ $19.95
From the Hickinbotham estate plantings which include an unusual
number of clones of chardonnay taken from the CSIRO collection at
Merbein. Fruit-driven, and very much in the mainstream of
Mornington Peninsula style.
Cellaring 3–4 years. **Best Vintages** '86, '92, '93, '94
Current Vintage '94
Matching Food Chinese prawns with cashew nuts.
Tasting Note 1994 Light to medium yellow-green; a fragrant
bouquet with peach, passionfruit and nut aromas. The palate is fresh
and crisp with melon/straw/cashew flavours, finishing with crisp
acidity.

HIGH WYCOMBE WINES

NR NA AUSSD
Barossa Valley **Est.** 1975
Bethany Road, Bethany via Tanunda, SA 5352
Ph (085) 63 2776
Open 7 days 9–4.30 **Production** NFP
Winemaker(s) Colin Davis
Colin and Angela Davis run what they describe as the smallest
winery in the Valley and a holiday cottage complex, selling all of
their wine on site. I have no recent information on the operation.
Principal Wines Riesling, Frontignac, Moselle, Shiraz, Cabernet
Sauvignon, Muscat, Port.

HIGHBANK VINEYARDS

★★★★ 15.90 CD AUSSD
Coonawarra **Est.** 1986
Coonawarra, SA 5263
Ph (087) 36 3311
Open W'ends 9–5 **Production** 700
Winemaker(s) Dennis Vice, Trevor Mast
Mount Gambier lecturer in viticulture Dennis Vice makes a tiny
quantity of smooth, melon-accented Chardonnay and stylish
Coonawarra Cabernet Blend of good quality which are sold through
local restaurants and cellar door, with limited Melbourne distribution.
Principal Wines Coonawarra Cabernet Blend, Chardonnay.

HIGHBANK COONAWARRA CABERNET BLEND
●●●● $15.90
A blend of 55% cabernet sauvignon, 35% merlot and 15% cabernet
franc made for Dennis Vice by Trevor Mast of Mount Langi Ghiran.
A new entry onto the roster, adding to the very attractive
Chardonnay tasted in previous years.
Cellaring 7–10 years. **Best Vintages** '92 **Current Vintage** '92

Matching Food Stuffed shoulder of lamb.

Tasting Note 1992 Medium red; a clean, smooth bouquet of light to medium weight, not especially complex, but nicely balanced. The palate shows rather more, with pleasant briary/berry fruit, and a reasonably firm tannin structure which will ensure that it ages gracefully.

HIGHLAND HERITAGE ESTATE *

NR 15–25 CD AUS58
Orange **Est.** 1982
Mitchell Highway, Orange, NSW 2800
Ph (06) 62 6183 **Fax** (06) 62 6183
Open 7 days 8–3 **Production** 2000
Winemaker(s) John Hordern

Highland Heritage Estate draws upon 3.5 hectares of sauvignon blanc, 3.5 hectares of chardonnay and 2 hectares of pinot noir, the planting of which commenced way back in 1982. However, the first wines were not made until 1990, and the tasting room only fairly recently opened in a converted railway carriage overlooking the vineyard.

Principal Wines Under the Mount Canobolas label: Chardonnay, Sauvignon Blanc, Pinot Noir; Old Tawny Port.

HIGHLAND HERITAGE ESTATE MOUNT CANOBLAS SAUVIGNON BLANC

●●● ▶ $19.95

Believed to be the first release of this wine to hit the retail shelves, albeit in minuscule quantities. Strikingly labelled and packaged, and very competently made, with particularly interesting flavours.

Cellaring Drink now. **Best Vintages** NA **Current Vintage** '94

Matching Food Calamari.

Tasting Note 1994 Medium yellow-green; a clean bouquet with pronounced gooseberry fruit aromas in the mould of riper New Zealand Sauvignon Blanc. The palate is multi-flavoured, with gooseberry through to riper honeyed characters, finishing with firm acid.

HIGHWAY WINES *

NR 5–14.50 CD AUSSD
Swan Valley **Est.** 1954
Great Northern Highway, Herne Hill, WA 6056
Ph (09) 294 4354
Open Mon–Sat 8.30–6 **Production** 4000
Winemaker(s) Tony Bakranich

A survivor of another era, when literally dozens of such wineries plied their business in the Swan Valley. It still enjoys a strong local trade, selling much of its wine in fill-your-own-containers, and 2-litre flagons, with lesser quantities sold by the bottle.

Principal Wines Exclusively Fortified wines, of which 20 are available, including 6 different styles of Sherry, 6 Muscats, 3 Ports, and so forth.

HILL-SMITH ESTATE

★★★★ 13.95 R AUS138–142 UK38
Adelaide Hills **Est.** 1973
c/o Yalumba Winery, Angaston, SA 5353
Ph (085) 61 3200 **Fax** (085) 61 3393
Open Not **Production** 10 000
Winemaker(s) Paul Bowden
Part of the Yalumba stable, drawing upon its own particular estate
vineyards. Has been a particularly strong performer in recent years,
with each one of the three wines in the portfolio deserving a 5-star
rating in one vintage or another. Very much an underrated label,
offering outstanding value for money.
Principal Wines Sauvignon Blanc, Chardonnay, Cabernet Shiraz.

HILL-SMITH ESTATE CABERNET SHIRAZ
●●●●● $13.95
Made from 10 hectares of cabernet sauvignon and 2 hectares of
shiraz grown on the 'Terra Rossa Block', 380 metres above sea
level, and with an annual rainfall of just over 600 mm compared to
just under 800 mm for the 'Air Strip Block' — highlighting the
climatic differences of blocks only a few kilometres apart, differences
due to altitude. As with the Chardonnay, a wine which from time to
time has excelled itself, 1990 being a conspicuous example.
Cellaring 5–8 years. **Best Vintages** '87, '88, '90, '91, '92
Current Vintage '91
Matching Food Shepherd's pie.
Tasting Note 1991 Medium red; a powerful bouquet with a lot of
character with aromas of berry, leaf and earth. The palate is well
structured, with a touch of charry oak and quite pronounced tannins
on the finish.

HILL-SMITH ESTATE CHARDONNAY
●●●●● $13.95
Chardonnay occupies the lion's share of the 'Air Strip Block' with
17 hectares of grapes in production. The wine is barrel fermented in
Vosges oak and given extended lees contact. Vintages such as 1993
and 1990 show just what can be achieved from this Adelaide Hills
vineyard.
Cellaring 2–3 years. **Best Vintages** '87, '88, '90, '93
Current Vintage '93
Matching Food Yabbies in hollandaise sauce.
Tasting Note 1993 Light to medium yellow-green; exuberant,
clean and fresh fruit aromas in the melon and white peach spectrum.
Fruit, rather than oak, likewise drives the palate, with a range of
flavours running from white peach to citrus to passionfruit, with an
excellent finish.

HILL-SMITH ESTATE SAUVIGNON BLANC
●●●● ▶ $13.95
Made from estate-grown sauvignon blanc produced from the 'Air
Strip Block' situated at the northern end of the Adelaide Hills,

650 metres above sea level. From time to time the wine has been piercingly intense in varietal character, in other years a little more subdued. Some will prefer one extreme, some the other.
Cellaring Drink now. **Best Vintages** '82, '84, '86, '92, '93
Current Vintage '94
Matching Food Fresh mussels.
Tasting Note 1994 Light green-yellow; herbal/grassy varietal fruit aromas with no oak input. A reasonably powerful but not particularly pungent mid palate; the overall impression is of a food style wine in the best sense of that term.

HILLSTOWE

★★★★☆ 12–22 R AUS56, 126, 184, 188 UK28
Southern Vales **Est.** 1980
104 Main Road, Hahndorf SA 5245
Ph (08) 388 1400 **Fax** (08) 388 1411
Open Not **Production** 10 000
Winemaker(s) Martin Shaw (Contract)
A relatively new venture founded by renowned viticulturist David Paxton and Chris Laurie, but now controlled by the latter, and employing the contract winemaking skills of Martin Shaw, drawing upon vineyard sources in varying regimens of soil and climate with great effect.
Principal Wines A range of vineyard and varietal-designated wines of ascending price and quality, being McLaren Vale Sauvignon Blanc, Chardonnay, Buxton Cabernet Merlot; and at the top end Adelaide Hills Udy's Mill Chardonnay, Adelaide Hills Carey Gully Pinot Noir, Yarra Valley Hoddles Pinot Noir.

HILLSTOWE BUXTON CABERNET MERLOT
●●●● $15
Ten hectares of cabernet sauvignon and a rather smaller amount of merlot are planted at the Hillstowe vineyards in McLaren Vale on deep alluvial soils, producing wines which are typically rather more elegant than the fuller-bodied McLaren Vale reds. The 1991 vintage won a silver and eight bronze medals in national shows, and the '93 should follow in its footsteps.
Cellaring Short term — 3–4 years. **Best Vintages** '91, '93, '94
Current Vintage '93
Matching Food Veal scaloppine.
Tasting Note 1993 Medium red-purple; leafy, cedary aromas with a hint of mint lead on to a palate of light to medium weight with similar leafy/cedary/minty flavours, finishing with soft tannins. Subtle oak throughout.

HILLSTOWE MCLAREN VALE CHARDONNAY
●●●● $15.50
Drawn from various vineyard sources in McLaren Vale, principally from the 10 hectares planted at the Hillstowe vineyard. Made in the modern Australian style, with anaerobic juice handling, and partial barrel fermentation in French oak.

Cellaring 2–4 years. **Best Vintages** '90, '92, '93, '94
Current Vintage '93
Matching Food Avocado.
Tasting Note 1993 Medium to full yellow; a big, rich and fairly developed aroma in a peach/tropical mould. The palate is similarly sweet with generous honeyed fruit flavours, and a soft finish. Drink this wine now.

HILLSTOWE MCLAREN VALE SAUVIGNON BLANC
●●●● $12
McLaren Vale and its adjacent hills have proved to be the most consistent producers of quality Sauvignon Blanc in Australia. The maritime-cooled climate produces wines which retain good varietal character, grassier in the cooler vintages, and more tropical in the warmer years. This wine is a good example of the district style.
Cellaring Drink now. **Best Vintages** '90, '93, '94
Current Vintage '94
Matching Food Light seafood, oysters.
Tasting Note 1994 Light straw-yellow; clean, crisp and direct, with fruit of light to medium intensity showing pristine varietal character. A no-frills palate, fresh, clean and direct, finishing with crisp acidity.

HILLSTOWE UDY'S MILL CHARDONNAY
●●●●● $22
Produced from 3.2 hectares of chardonnay grown in the Carey Gully subdistrict of the Adelaide Hills, adjacent to McLaren Vale. The climate is distinctly cooler, the grapes harvested later, and clearly reflect the climate. The '92 vintage had spectacular international show success at the 1994 Los Angeles New World International Wine Competition.
Cellaring 3–5 years. **Best Vintages** '90, '92, '93, '94
Current Vintage '93
Matching Food Trout or salmon mousse.
Tasting Note 1993 Light to medium yellow-green; potent, stylish, tangy grapefruit aromas with textured barrel ferment and malolactic fermentation aspects. A tangy, stylish palate with lingering citrus/grapefruit flavours, and well integrated oak. Note some bottles of this wine have been corked.

HJT VINEYARDS
★★★☆ 10.50–12.90 CD AUSSD
North East Victoria **Est.** 1979
Keenan Road, Glenrowan, Vic 3675
Ph (057) 66 2252
Open Fri, Sat, Hols 10–5 **Production** 500
Winemaker(s) Harry Tinson
Harry Tinson, ex-Bailey's winemaker and revered for his Muscats and Tokays, produced a legendary HJT Chardonnay in 1984 and (to a degree) deservedly lives off the reputation of that wine; it and subsequent Chardonnays have been the pick of the crop. As of late 1994 wines from the 1990 to 1992 vintages were on offer.

Principal Wines A varietal range, with occasional use of bin numbers denoting winemaking approaches, Bin 4 being more delicate, Bin 19 fuller bodied. Wines include Riesling Bins 4 and 19, Chardonnay, Chenin Blanc Bin 19, Late Picked Riesling, Pinot Noir, Cabernet Pinot, Shiraz, Cabernet Sauvignon, Merlot, Tawny Port.

HOLLICK WINES

★★★★ 11–40 R AUS80 UK69
Coonawarra **Est.** 1983
Racecourse Road, Coonawarra, SA 5263
Ph (087) 37 2318 **Fax** (087) 37 2952
Open 7 days 9–5 **Production** 23 000
Winemaker(s) Pat Tocaciu, Ian Hollick

Hollick has, if it were possible, added to the reputation of Coonawarra since it released its first wines in the mid '80s. Winner of many trophies (including the most famous of all, the Jimmy Watson), its wines are invariably well crafted and competitively priced.

Principal Wines A very disciplined array of products with Terra White and Red at the bottom end of the price range; Chardonnay and Coonawarra (Cabernet Blend) in the middle, along with Cornel Methode Champenoise; Ravenswood, the deluxe Cabernet Sauvignon at the top end. Limited special cellar door releases known as Cellar Reserve Range.

HOLLICK CHARDONNAY

●●●● $15

A wine which reflects the white winemaking skills of Pat Tocaciu, with a range of winemaking techniques employed including barrel fermentation and malolactic fermentation. Tends more to elegance than power in style.

Cellaring Short term. **Best Vintages** '90, '91, '92, '94
Current Vintage '93
Matching Food Antipasto, grilled fish.
Tasting Note 1993 Light to medium yellow-green; a clean bouquet of light to medium intensity, driven primarily by peach and melon fruit, with subtle oak. The palate is clean and fresh, with wonderfully subtle, light fruit and a creamy texture from the combination of making techniques.

HOLLICK COONAWARRA CABERNET BLEND

●●●● $16

A blend of 75% cabernet sauvignon, 15% merlot and 10% cabernet franc, matured in a mix of French and American oak barrels. A vertical tasting in June 1993 of this wine and its predecessors showed remarkably consistent style, even though the varietal composition has changed over the years since the first release of straight Cabernet in 1992.

Cellaring 4–7 years. **Best Vintages** '84, '88, '90, '91
Current Vintage '92

Matching Food Gently-spiced Asian meat dishes.
Tasting Note 1992 Medium red-purple; a quite complex bouquet with cedary/leafy aromas mixed with red berry fruits. The palate shows similar cedary/leafy flavours with subtle oak; of mid weight and length.

HOLLICK RAVENSWOOD
●●●●● $40
First made in 1988, and without any question, scrupulously selected from the very best material available from the estate vineyards. It is much more concentrated, rich and powerful than the Coonawarra, and is immaculately made.
Cellaring 10+ years. **Best Vintages** '88, '90, '91
Current Vintage '91
Matching Food Scotch fillet.
Tasting Note 1991 Dark red; concentrated, ripe briary fruit and oak with hints of chocolate. In the mouth, powerful and concentrated with strong berry fruit, well handled French oak, and ample tannins to support the wine as it ages.

HOLLICK TERRA WHITE
●●● ▶ $11
A brilliant piece of label design and name introduced in September 1993. An unusual blend of riesling and sauvignon blanc, made without the use of oak, and well positioned as a straightforward drinking style.
Cellaring Drink now. **Best Vintages** NA
Current Vintage '94
Matching Food Light brasserie-type dishes.
Tasting Note 1994 Light green-yellow; quite aromatic, with some sauvignon blanc varietal character evident, although riesling is dominant; a crisp, clean and fresh palate balanced by a deliberate touch of residual sugar. Hard to dislike.

HOLM OAK WINERY

★★★☆ 18.50 R AUS14
Tamar Valley **Est.** 1983
RSD 256 Rowella, West Tamar, Tas 7270
Ph (003) 94 7577 **Fax** (003) 94 7350
Open 7 days 12–5 **Production** 1800
Winemaker(s) Nick Butler
The Butler family produces tremendously rich and strongly-flavoured red wines from the vineyard situated on the banks of the Tamar River, and which takes its name from the grove of oak trees planted around the turn of the century and originally intended for the making of tennis racquets. Together with Marion's Vineyard, it suggests that this section of the Tamar Valley may even be too warm for pinot noir; certainly it is best suited to cabernet sauvignon and chardonnay.
Principal Wines Pinot Noir Chardonnay (still table wine), Pinot Noir, Cabernet Sauvignon.

HOPPERS HILL VINEYARDS

NR 10–12 CD AUSSD
Central Tablelands **Est.** 1990
Googodery Road, Cumnock, NSW 2867
Ph (063) 67 7270
Open W'ends 11–5 **Production** NFP
Winemaker(s) Robert Gilmore
The Gilmores planted their vineyard in 1980, using organic growing
methods and using no preservatives or filtration in the winery which
was established in 1990. Not surprisingly, the wines cannot be
judged or assessed against normal standards, but may have
appeal in a niche market.
Principal Wines Chardonnay, Sauvignon Blanc, Dry White,
Cabernet Franc Merlot, Cabernet Sauvignon.

HORSESHOE VINEYARD

NR 13–18 CD AUS70
Upper Hunter Valley **Est.** 1986
Horseshoe Road, Horseshoe Valley via Denman, NSW 2328
Ph (065) 47 3528
Open W'ends 9–5 **Production** NFP
Winemaker(s) John Hordern
Seems to have fallen by the wayside after a wonderful start in 1986.
Principal Wines Classic Hunter Semillon, Chardonnay Semillon,
Chardonnay, Pinot Noir.

HOTHAM VALLEY ESTATE *

★★★★ 10.95–16.95 CD AUS103
Darling Range **Est.** 1987
South Wandering Road, Wandering, WA 6308
Ph (098) 84 1525 **Fax** (098) 84 1079
Open By appt **Production** 5000
Winemaker(s) James Pennington, Gary Baldwin
(Consultant)
An impressive newcomer to the scene, situated in a region of its
own making, 120 kilometres south east of Perth. It has a continental
climate with cold winters and hot summer days, but cool nights,
tempered by the altitude of 350 metres. Some exceptionally good
wines have been made by former science teacher and now Charles
Sturt University graduate James Pennington, on whose family
property Hotham Valley Estate is established, albeit by way of a
subdivision with outside investment. A state-of-the-art winery was
built in 1993.
Principal Wines Semillon, Chenin Blanc, Classic Dry White,
Chardonnay, Cabernets.

HOTHAM VALLEY ESTATE CHARDONNAY

●●●● $16.95
James Pennington has learnt his craft at an extraordinarily impressive
rate, no doubt assisted by the consultancy of Gary Baldwin. While I

find the Chardonnay a little oaky, others will in all probability like it
for precisely this reason; it was one of a quartet of medal-winning
wines at the 1994 Mount Barker Show, winning a silver medal,
second highest pointed wine in its large class.
Cellaring 1–3 years. **Best Vintages** '92 **Current Vintage** '94
Matching Food Chicken with cashew nuts.
Tasting Note 1994 Medium to full yellow-green; complex
nutty/toasty barrel ferment aromas with some secondary fruit
characters starting to emerge. The palate is a very full-bodied
oaky/nutty/toasty style, needing a touch more fruit to carry the oak
and the obvious winemaking which has gone into it.

HOTHAM VALLEY ESTATE CHENIN BLANC
●●●● $10.95
Yet another success at the 1994 Mount Barker Wine Show, on this
occasion topping the small class of Chenin Blancs, but in so doing,
besting both Moondah Brook and Houghton. Here the boot was on
the other foot, with my fellow judges liking it rather more than I; it no
doubt deserved its silver medal.
Cellaring Drink now. **Best Vintages** NA **Current Vintage** '94
Matching Food Pork.
Tasting Note 1994 Bright green-yellow; a big wine with some
honeyed peach aromas, and a little heavy on both the bouquet and
palate, but nonetheless possessing considerable depth of flavour.

HOTHAM VALLEY ESTATE CLASSIC DRY WHITE
●●●● $10.95
An unspecified blend of what I take to be chenin blanc, riesling and
possibly a little semillon and chardonnay which, like the Semillon,
was also a bronze medal winner at the 1994 Mount Barker Show.
Once again, I was rather more generous in my points.
Cellaring 1–2 years. **Best Vintages** NA **Current Vintage** '94
Matching Food Pasta with creamy sauce.
Tasting Note 1994 Light to medium yellow-green; an interesting
bouquet with tropical/honeysuckle fruit, clean and well made. The
palate shows rich honeysuckle and spice fruit flavours, showing a
warm climate.

HOTHAM VALLEY ESTATE SEMILLON
●●●●● $12.95
I thought this was one of the outstanding 1994 white wines at the
Mount Barker Wine Show, although it is fair to say that my fellow
judges did not altogether share my enthusiasm, the wine ultimately
being given a strong bronze medal. It was not a flash in the pan;
the 1993 vintage was judged the Outstanding White Wine from
the Perth Hills Region at the Annual State SGIO Wine Competition.
Cellaring Up to 5 years. **Best Vintages** '93, '94
Current Vintage '94
Matching Food Salads, cold meats.
Tasting Note 1994 Light to medium yellow-green; a well balanced
and stylish bouquet, gently herbaceous but with good intensity. The
palate shows a lovely young classic semillon with intense varietal

character, great length and outstanding potential. In my view they
don't come much better than this.

HOUGHTON WINES

★★★★★ 8.99–16.50 R AUS20–24 UK73
Swan Valley **Est.** 1836
Dale Road, Middle Swan, WA 6056
Ph (09) 274 5100 **Fax** (09) 274 5372
Open 7 days 10–5 **Production** 300 000
Winemaker(s) Paul Lapsley
The 5-star rating may seem extreme, but is very deliberate and is in
no small measure justified by Houghton White Burgundy, one of
Australia's largest selling white wines, almost entirely consumed
within days of purchase, but which is superlative with 7 or so years
bottle-age. To borrow a phrase of the late Jack Mann, 'There are no
bad wines here'.
Principal Wines Bottom end: Wildflower Ridge range; then
White Burgundy, Chablis, Frankland River Rhine Riesling, Semillon
Sauvignon Blanc, Cabernet Sauvignon; top end: Gold Reserve
Verdelho, Chardonnay and Cabernet Sauvignon, occasional
special release 6-year-old Show Reserve White Burgundy.

HOUGHTON CHABLIS
●●●● $8.95
An unfortunate name no doubt directed at the Sydney market, but
which can readily enough be phased out because the wine is in fact
made from chenin blanc grown in the Swan Valley. Not by any
means a great wine, but as the '94 vintage shows, can be very
attractive in its youth.
Cellaring Drink now. **Best Vintages** NA
Current Vintage '94
Matching Food Seafood salad.
Tasting Note 1994 Light green-yellow; a fragrant, faintly spicy
aroma with tropical fruit and passionfruit (yeast-influenced) aromas,
repeated in a tropical and passionfruit-flavoured palate with a hint
of spice, possibly deriving from the subtle use of oak chips.

HOUGHTON FRANKLAND RIVER RIESLING
●●●● $8.99
Without question, the best wine produced year in, year out from
Houghton's large Frankland River vineyard. Vintages such as the '86
stand among the best white wines ever produced in the State, still
drinking superbly when eight years old.
Cellaring Up to 7 years. **Best Vintages** '83, '86, '87, '91, '93
Current Vintage '94
Matching Food Antipasto.
Tasting Note 1994 Light yellow-green; clean, fine citrus and lime
fruit aromas with just a touch of lift. The intensity and length of
flavour to the palate is unexpected after the relatively light bouquet,
and the wine should develop superbly, with flavours in the typical
citrus/lime spectrum.

HOUGHTON GOLD RESERVE CABERNET SAUVIGNON
●●●● $13.95

Sourced primarily from the Margaret River region, with a proportion of Great Southern grapes also included. Matured for 24 months in French oak. A wine which is never less than good, sometimes rising to spectacular heights, as it did with the '92 vintage.
Cellaring 4–8 years. **Best Vintages** '82, '88, '90, '92, '94
Current Vintage '93
Matching Food Rack of lamb.
Tasting Note 1993 Medium to full red; a clean, solid wine on the bouquet with nicely ripened fruit in a blackcurrant/raspberry spectrum. The palate shows similar bright, fresh berry and leaf fruit flavours, lacking the richness promised by the bouquet, but pleasant enough.

HOUGHTON GOLD RESERVE CHARDONNAY
●●●● ▶ $14

A very stylish wine, and a bargain at the price. Produced from grapes grown in the Margaret River, Frankland River, Pemberton and Mount Barker regions, and fermented and matured in high quality oak from one of the best French coopers, Dargaud & Jaegle.
Cellaring 3–5 years. **Best Vintages** '86, '87, '91, '93
Current Vintage '93
Matching Food Marron, prawns.
Tasting Note 1993 Medium yellow-green; an elegantly complex bouquet with tangy, cool-grown melon and citrus fruit woven with subtle barrel ferment oak. The palate has marked length, again showing citrus and melon fruit and similar smoky/spicy subtle oak. High quality.

HOUGHTON GOLD RESERVE VERDELHO
●●●● $13.95

Made from estate-grown grapes from Houghton's Gingin vineyard sourced from a single vine found by Jack Mann in 1945 and first propagated in commercial quantities in the Swan Valley in 1950, in turn providing the stock used in establishing the Gingin vineyard. Legitimately regarded as one of the special varieties of the Swan Valley/Gingin area, and which ages particularly well.
Cellaring 5+ years. **Best Vintages** '83, '87, '89, '91, '93
Current Vintage '94
Matching Food Lobster mornay.
Tasting Note 1994 Light yellow-green; tangy, lively fruit aromas with some mixed citrus and tropical fruit aromas. A very lively palate with citrus and melon flavours, with a long, clean and crisp finish.

HOUGHTON SEMILLON SAUVIGNON BLANC
●●●● $8.99

A hugely underrated wine, which has also suffered from something of an identity crisis, sometimes effectively being released as Semillon, others as a Semillon Sauvignon Blanc. The blend has now settled down as a 50% semillon, 50% sauvignon blanc blend from the Margaret River, Manjimup and Mount Barker regions.

Cellaring Best drunk young. **Best Vintages** NA
Current Vintage '94
Matching Food Coquilles St Jacques.
Tasting Note 1994 Light to medium yellow-green; a full-blown style with lots of very cleverly handled spicy nutmeg oak, which does not, however, overwhelm the wine. On the palate the same voluptuous spicy oak flavours are perfectly integrated with substantial fruit. A bargain at the price.

HOUGHTON WHITE BURGUNDY
●●●●● $8.99
A wine with an extraordinary pedigree over its 60-year history, made from a blend of chenin blanc, muscadelle, semillon, verdelho and chardonnay primarily grown in the Swan Valley and at Gingin. Released and almost entirely consumed within 12 months of vintage, it invariably matures wonderfully well in bottle over a six to eight-year period, leading to tiny releases of the Show Reserve Wines which accumulate innumerable gold medals and trophies.
Cellaring 5–7 years. **Best Vintages** '83, '87, '89, '91, '93
Current Vintage '94
Matching Food Fish, chicken, veal.
Tasting Note 1994 Medium yellow-green; fruit-driven with abundant white peach and passionfruit aromas. The palate is clean and smooth, with gently peachy fruit, and a hint of melon; well weighted, well balanced, not too sweet and will develop well, if relatively quickly.

HOWARD PARK

★★★★★ 15–35 R AUS11, 47 UK3
Great Southern **Est.** 1986
Lot 11, Little River Road, Denmark, WA 6333
Ph (098) 48 1261 **Fax** (098) 48 2064
Open Not **Production** 7000
Winemaker(s) John Wade
John Wade, one of the most talented winemakers in Western Australia, is poised on the edge of a new venture; together with wife Wendy he has joined forces with Jeff and Amy Birch to build a winery which will make the Howard Park and Madfish Bay wines, but also act as contract winemaker to a dozen Great Southern vignerons. It will be a singularly important centre of winemaking for the region.
Principal Wines Madfish Bay Premium Dry White and Red provide low-priced volume; limited quantities of Howard Park Riesling, Chardonnay and Cabernet Sauvignon Merlot.

HOWARD PARK CABERNET SAUVIGNON MERLOT
●●●●● $35
Like the Riesling, first made in 1986. The regional and varietal mix has changed a little over the years, with the cabernet component ranging from between 70% and 80% over the last three vintages, and the regional source of the merlot likewise moving around from

Margaret River to Pemberton. Whatever the blend, a wine of the highest quality.
Cellaring 10–15 years. **Best Vintages** '86, '88, '89, '90, '92
Current Vintage '92
Matching Food Lamb fillets, mature cheddar.
Tasting Note 1992 Medium to full purple-red; a powerful, classic wine in the mainstream of the Howard Park style, spotlessly clean and with less opulent fruit than the '91. On the palate, immaculately balanced and structured, with near-perfect berry fruit ripeness in a highly disciplined style, finishing with lingering tannins.

HOWARD PARK CHARDONNAY
●●●●● $29.95
John Wade long resisted the temptation to make a Chardonnay, arguing that he was not happy to do so until he was assured of grapes of the highest quality. In 1993 he realised that a component of Madfish Bay met his requirements, and the wine was made from a blend of 50% chardonnay grown in the Denmark region, and 50% at Pemberton. The 1994 is the second release.
Cellaring 4–6 years. **Best Vintages** NA
Current Vintage '93, '94
Matching Food Pan-fried veal.
Tasting Note 1994 Medium yellow-green; a discreet bouquet with nicely balanced melon and fig fruit interwoven with oak and some malolactic fermentation characters. There is tremendous length and focus to the palate which is beautifully balanced, with fine fruit and perfect acid.

HOWARD PARK MADFISH BAY PREMIUM DRY RED
●●●● $15
The red wine brother of the Dry White, made from a blend of 55% cabernet franc, 30% merlot and 15% pinot noir grown in the Great Southern region and the Warren Valley, Western Australia. Like the white, made to be consumed while young and fresh — a bright, modern bistro style.
Cellaring Drink now. **Best Vintages** NA **Current Vintage** '93
Matching Food Pasta, most Italian-accented dishes.
Tasting Note 1993 Light to medium red-purple; clean, fresh gentle red berry fruit aromas of light to medium intensity. The palate is clean, quite soft, gently fruity with subtle oak and minimal tannins.

HOWARD PARK MADFISH BAY PREMIUM DRY WHITE
●●●● $15
The strikingly labelled and named Madfish Bay label was designed by Maxine Fumagalli, a Noongar artist who lives in Denmark, Western Australia. The name itself comes from a favourite fishing spot 15 kms west of Denmark. The white is an unwooded blend of 85% chardonnay, 10% semillon and 5% sauvignon blanc from the Great Southern region.
Cellaring Drink now. **Best Vintages** NA **Current Vintage** '94
Matching Food All shellfish, fish, light white meat dishes.
Tasting Note 1994 Light to medium yellow-green; floral lime fruit

salad aromas with a similar, attractive melange of fruit flavours on
the palate, with peach, melon and citrus interwoven.

HOWARD PARK RIESLING
●●●●● $16
First made in 1986, and in my view the greatest Riesling made in
the Great Southern region, itself home of many of Australia's finest
examples of the style. It ages superbly, the '86 still with years in front
of it.
Cellaring 10+ years. **Best Vintages** '86, '87, '88, '91, '93, '94
Current Vintage '94
Matching Food Fresh asparagus, Asian seafood.
Tasting Note 1994 Light green-yellow; intense, powerful and
fragrant with toasty and lime fruit; no apparent yeast influence. A
very powerful, intense and long flavour with those tightly structured
lime flavours, and grip on the finish.

HUGH HAMILTON FINE WINES *

★★★☆ 10.50–15.50 R AUS58
Southern Vales **Est.** 1992
Recreation Road, McLaren Vale, SA 5171
Ph (08) 323 8689 **Fax** (08) 323 9488
Open Not **Production** 5500
Winemaker(s) Hugh Hamilton
Hugh Hamilton is a member of the famous Hamilton winemaking
family, there being an intensely (and well known) competitive spirit
existing between those various members — notably between
Richard and Hugh — which can only be good for the consumer.
Principal Wines Chenin Blanc, Chardonnay, Shiraz, Merlot,
Cabernet Sauvignon, Sparkling Shiraz.

HUGH HAMILTON CHARDONNAY
●●● ▶ $15.50
Made in the modern unwooded style, and cool fermented. When
tasted at the Sydney International Winemakers Competition in
September 1994, shortly after it had been bottled, it still showed a
lot of fermentation esters, but there was marvellous fruit underneath,
and the wine may well improve over 1995.
Cellaring 2–3 years. **Best Vintages** NA **Current Vintage** '94
Matching Food Smoked salmon.
Tasting Note 1994 Light green-yellow; intense passionfruit and
grapefruit aromas, slightly sweaty and partially fermentation derived.
Similarly powerful, intense citrus and melon fruit on the palate,
showing the cool vintage.

HUGO WINES

★★★☆ 8–12.50 CD AUS111, 163 UK43
Southern Vales **Est.** 1982
Elliott Road, McLaren Flat, SA 5171
Ph (08) 383 0098 **Fax** (08) 383 0446

Open 7 days 10.30–5 **Production** 5000
Winemaker(s) John Hugo
A winery which came from relative obscurity to prominence with
some lovely ripe, sweet '88 reds which, while strongly American oak
influenced, were quite outstanding. Subsequent red releases have
continued in the same style, albeit slightly less exciting.
Principal Wines Shiraz, Riesling, Chardonnay, Cabernet
Sauvignon, Port.

HUGO SHIRAZ
●●●● $12.50
The 12 hectares of estate vineyards drawn upon for the label are
situated in the foothills of the Mount Lofty Ranges, and were
established in 1950 by Colin Hugo. The vineyard is not irrigated,
and the fruit flavours are intense.
Cellaring 4–6 years. **Best Vintages** '86, '88, '90, '92, '94
Current Vintage '92
Matching Food Lamb shashlik.
Tasting Note 1992 Medium to full red, with a touch of purple;
bright, fresh cherry/berry fruit with powerful vanillin American oak.
The palate shows lots of charry American oak, perhaps too much
and unnecessary given the excellent underlying fruit. A faintly
phenolic finish from the oak is the problem.

HUNGERFORD HILL
★★★☆ 8.50–12 R AUS147
Hunter Valley **Est.** 1967
Cnr McDonalds & Broke Roads, Pokolbin, NSW 2321
Ph (049) 98 7666 **Fax** (049) 98 7682
Open Mon–Fri 9–4, W'ends 10–4.30 **Production** 18 000
Winemaker(s) Ian Walsh
Now purely a brand owned by Southcorp, with the winery having
been sold to McGuigan Brothers, and the wines being made at
Tulloch. As the product range indicates, it is no longer purely Hunter
based, but takes its fruit from all over New South Wales.
Principal Wines Cowra Chardonnay, Mudgee Semillon, Hunter
Valley Semillon Chardonnay, Show Reserve Chardonnay, Cabernet
Merlot, Shiraz, Show Reserve Shiraz.

HUNGERFORD HILL COWRA CHARDONNAY
●●● ▶ $12
First made in 1993. Cowra has long been recognised as a high
quality producer of chardonnay, with many famous labels starting off
with this base, including Petaluma. The wine has very substantial,
and presumably expensive, oak input from barrel fermentation,
surprising given the price (and one must say, the weight of the fruit).
Cellaring Drink now. **Best Vintages** NA **Current Vintage** '93
Matching Food Chicken, turkey.
Tasting Note 1993 Medium to full yellow-green; abundant,
sophisticated oak makes an immediate impact on both the bouquet
and palate. There is peach and melon chardonnay fruit, but one

wonders whether this would not have been better had a little more
money been spent on fruit, and a little less on oak.

HUNGERFORD HILL HUNTER VALLEY SEMILLON CHARDONNAY
●●●● $8.50
As the name suggests, a blend of semillon and chardonnay drawn
from sources across the Lower and Upper Hunter Valley. Given the
price of the wine, an extraordinary amount of effort (and cost) has
gone into the oak handling, and it succeeds in this wine very well.
Cellaring Drink now. **Best Vintages** '91, '93, '94
Current Vintage '93
Matching Food Pasta carbonara.
Tasting Note 1993 Glowing yellow-green; striking use of high
quality oak invests the wine with great complexity on the bouquet
and the palate, but there is plenty of luscious fruit there to support
the oak. So rich and multiflavoured, best drunk while fresh.

HUNGERFORD HILL MUDGEE SEMILLON
●●●● $8.50
First made in 1993, with the emphasis on the fruit, and no oak used
either in fermentation or maturation. It is made in a pleasantly
contrasting style to the Chardonnay and Semillon Chardonnay,
and should cellar well if you are so inclined.
Cellaring 3–5 years. **Best Vintages** NA **Current Vintage** '93
Matching Food Asian cuisine, pasta.
Tasting Note 1993 Light yellow-green; a smooth and clean
bouquet with nicely weighted, faintly herbaceous, varietal fruit. The
palate has good fruit weight with a mix of herbal and honey notes
in classic Semillon style.

HUNT'S FOXHAVEN ESTATE
NR 9–15 CD AUSSD
Margaret River **Est.** 1978
Canal Rocks Road, Yallingup, WA 6282
Ph (097) 55 2232 **Fax** (09) 291 6052
Open W'ends, Hols 11–5 **Production** 450
Winemaker(s) David Hunt
Has not long commenced commercial operations, and is still tiny,
albeit with 4.5 hectares of vines coming into production. The only
wines tasted suggest that David Hunt is still learning the trade.
Principal Wines Riesling, Semillon Sauvignon Blanc, Cabernet
Sauvignon, Cabernet Merlot.

HUNTINGTON ESTATE
★★★★★ 9–18 CD AUSSD UK48
Mudgee **Est.** 1969
Cassilis Road, Mudgee, NSW 2850
Ph (063) 73 3825 **Fax** (063) 73 3730
Open Mon–Fri 9–5, W'ends 9–4 **Production** 20 000

Winemaker(s) Susan Roberts

The remarkable Roberts family members have a passion for wine which is equalled only by their passion for music, with the Huntington Music Festival a major annual event. The red wines of Huntington Estate are outstanding, and sell for absurdly low prices.

Principal Wines Semillon, Semillon Sauvignon Blanc, Chardonnay, Pinot Rosé, sundry sweet whites; red wines are released under bin numbers (FB = full bodied, MB = medium bodied) comprising Shiraz, Cabernet Merlot and Cabernet Sauvignon.

HUNTINGTON ESTATE CABERNET MERLOT

●●●● ▶ $11.50

One of the first producers of Cabernet Merlot in Australia, with 1.2 hectares of merlot alongside 12.3 of cabernet sauvignon — most of the cabernet going into the wine under that label. First made in 1977, it ages very well, which is exactly as one would expect.

Cellaring 10–12 years. **Best Vintages** '77, '79, '84, '89, '90, '93 **Current Vintage** '89

Matching Food Game.

Tasting Note 1989 Bin FB25. Medium to full red-purple; cedary/leafy aromas with subtle oak. On the palate there is plenty of sweet berry fruit with well balanced, soft tannins and, as ever, minimal oak input.

HUNTINGTON ESTATE CABERNET SAUVIGNON

●●●●● $11.50

As with all of the Huntington Estate wines, made entirely from estate-grown grapes. Yields are low, and the fruit is tremendously powerful and concentrated, producing wines which age slowly but majestically. There is no particular artifice in the making, with American oak playing a minor role.

Cellaring 10–20 years. **Best Vintages** '74, '79, '81, '84, '89, '90, '91 **Current Vintage** '90

Matching Food Grilled rump steak.

Tasting Note 1990 Bin FB23. Dense purple-red in colour, with a clean, smooth and stylish bouquet redolent of chocolate and mint. The powerful palate has the balance for long cellaring and needs much time, with lots of fruit and persistent tannins.

HUNTINGTON ESTATE SHIRAZ

●●●●● $10.50

In very much the same style and quality class as the Cabernet Sauvignon, made from estate-grown grapes and producing wines of great longevity. As the wines age, the cherry/berry fruits gradually soften and take on that typically, gently earthy shiraz character, and the tannins soften at the same rate as the fruit rounds off and develops. Thus the balance of the wine is never threatened, and patience is rewarded.

Cellaring 10–15 years. **Best Vintages** '74, '75, '78, '79, '84, '90, '91 **Current Vintage** '91

Matching Food Kangaroo fillet.

Tasting Note 1991 Bin FB33. Strong, deep-purple red; fresh, sweet and ripe cassis berry fruit with subtle oak; abundant sweet fruit on the palate, not dissimilar to the superb 1990 Bin FB34 which preceded it, but with slightly more tannins.

HUNTLEIGH VINEYARDS

★★★ 10–12 CD AUSSD
Bendigo **Est.** 1975
Tunnecliffes Lane, Heathcote, Vic 3523
Ph (054) 33 2795
Open 7 days 10–5.30 **Production** 400
Winemaker(s) Leigh Hunt
A retirement hobby, with robust, rather astringent red wines which need time in bottle to lose some of the rough edges.
Principal Wines Riesling, Traminer, Shiraz, Cabernet Sauvignon; Leckie Shiraz.

IBIS WINES *

NR NA AUSSD
Orange **Est.** 1988
Kearneys Drive, Orange, NSW 2800
Ph (063) 62 3257 **Fax** (063) 61 3355
Open Late 1995 **Production** 250
Winemaker(s) Phil Stevenson
A winery was under construction for the 1995 vintage, and Phil Stevenson hopes to obtain his vigneron's licence and open for business some time later in the year, drawing upon a little of over one hectare of estate plantings.
Principal Wines Chardonnay, Pinot Noir, Cabernet Sauvignon, Cabernet Franc.

IDYLL VINEYARD

★★★☆ 11.95–14.95 R AUS35, 96, 148 UK55
Geelong **Est.** 1966
265 Ballan Road, Moorabool, Vic 3221
Ph (052) 76 1280 **Fax** (052) 76 1537
Open Tues–Sun, Hols 10–5 **Production** 4500
Winemaker(s) Dr Daryl Sefton
A stalwart of the region, producing wines in an individual style (pungent, assertive Traminer, long-vatted reds) which are almost as well known and appreciated overseas as they are in Australia.
Principal Wines Idyll Blush, Gewurztraminer Chardonnay, Bone Idyll Rosé, Shiraz, Cabernet Shiraz; with Sefton Estate as budget-priced second label Dry White and Cabernet Shiraz.

INGLEWOOD VINEYARDS *

★★★ 7–14.50 R AUS86
Upper Hunter Valley **Est.** 1988
Yarrawa Road, Denman, NSW 2328
Ph (065) 47 2556

Open Not **Production** 15 500
Winemaker(s) Arrowfield (Simon Gilbert)
Contract

A very significant addition to the viticultural scene in the Upper Hunter Valley, with almost 170 hectares of vineyards established, or in the course of establishment, involving a total investment of around $7 million. Much of the fruit is sold to Lindemans under long-term contracts, but part is made under contract at Arrowfield for the rapidly-expanding winemaking and marketing operations of Inglewood. The emphasis is on Chardonnay and Semillon, and in 1993 and 1994 the wines have been consistent bronze medal winners at national shows.

Principal Wines Bottom level: Rivers Classic Red and White; then Two Rivers label: Chardonnay, Unwooded Chardonnay, Semillon Sauvignon Blanc, Verdelho, Cabernet Sauvignon; top end: Inglewood Show Reserve Chardonnay, Semillon, Verdelho.

INGLEWOOD SHOW RESERVE CHARDONNAY
●●●● $14.50

Only 750 cases of this wine were made; it really is a Show Reserve wine in every respect. There is abundant barrel ferment character evident in the wine, which has been well made, and which draws upon the best of 80 hectares of estate plantings.
Cellaring 1–2 years. **Best Vintages** NA **Current Vintage** '93
Matching Food Chinese pork.
Tasting Note 1993 Medium to full yellow-green; a rich and complex bouquet with abundant ripe yellow peach fruit. The palate is rich to the point of being opulent, with full-blown barrel ferment oak, and a soft, creamy finish.

INGLEWOOD TWO RIVERS SEMILLON SAUVIGNON BLANC
●●●) $9.95

An interesting wine which has a Padthaway component (or at least, did so in 1993). The '93 won several bronze medals, and the '94 is of similar style and quality. It may receive a brief flick of oak, but it is not evident in the wine, which happily survives on its fruit.
Cellaring Drink now. **Best Vintages** '93, '94
Current Vintage '94
Matching Food Sautéed prawns.
Tasting Note 1994 Light green-yellow; the bouquet is clean, with quite intense fruit, without any particular varietal character or component dominating. The palate, too, has good weight and intensity, the flavours smooth to the point of being slightly amorphous.

INGOLDBY WINES

★★★★☆ 9.50–16 CD AUS36, 137
Southern Vales **Est.** 1972
Ingoldby Road, McLaren Flat, SA 5171
Ph (08) 383 0005 **Fax** (08) 383 9467
Open Mon–Fri 9–5, W'ends 11–5 **Production** 10 000

Winemaker(s) Bill Clappis

Bill Clappis is a larger-than-life character who does not allow his irreverence to overshadow the serious business of successfully marketing wines which are consistently very good, none more so than the Cabernet Sauvignon.

Principal Wines Colombard, Hugo's Hill Riesling, Sauvignon Blanc, Shiraz, Grenache, Cabernet Sauvignon, Meteora Tawny Port.

INGOLDBY CABERNET SAUVIGNON

●●●●● $16

A wine that has been consistently outstanding over the years, drawing in part from 8 hectares of estate-grown grapes and in part from other notable McLaren Vale vineyards. It is a paradigm of McLaren Vale cabernet, loaded with dark berry and chocolate fruit, and built to last.

Cellaring 7–12 years. **Best Vintages** '85, '86, '87, '88, '91
Current Vintage '92
Matching Food Oxtail.
Tasting Note 1992 Dark red-purple; a very solid bouquet with ripe berry and dark chocolate fruit aromas. An exceptionally generous palate, with blackcurrant/briary fruit and well handled oak.

INNISFAIL VINEYARDS

NR 11–16.50 CD AUS72
Geelong **Est.** 1980
Cross Street, Batesford, Vic 3221
Ph (052) 76 1258 **Fax** (052) 21 8442
Open Not **Production** 1500
Winemaker(s) Ron Griffiths

This 4-hectare vineyard released its first wines in 1988, made in a small but modern winery on site with a chewy, complex Chardonnay from both 1989 and 1990 attesting to the quality of the vineyard. No recent tastings, however.

Principal Wines Riesling, Chardonnay, Cabernet Sauvignon.

IRAMOO PLAINS VINEYARD *

NR 10–18 CD AUSSD
Geelong **Est.** 1980
Farm Road, Werribee (off Princes Highway to Geelong), Vic 3030
Ph (03) 9741 1290 **Fax** (03) 9742 7060
Open First Sun of month May–Sept 1–5 **Production** 500
Winemaker(s) John Ellis (Contract)

This is the only vineyard in the Werribee area, 20 minutes from Melbourne on the way to Geelong. The grapes are produced from 2 hectares of vineyards on the banks of the Werribee River, and sold from an historic homestead on the property owned by Caroline and Don Hume.

Principal Wines Traminer, Chardonnay, Cabernet Sauvignon.

IRON POT BAY VINEYARD

★★★☆ 14.50–15 CD AUSSD
Tamar Valley **Est.** 1988
West Bay Road, Rowella, Tas 7270
Ph (003) 94 7320 **Fax** (003) 94 7346
Open By appt **Production** 900
Winemaker(s) Andrew Hood (Contract)
Rod and Kyra Cuthbert have established an immaculate 8-hectare
vineyard, utilising an open lyre trellis system and a high density
(5,000 vines per hectare) planting. The vineyard takes its name
from a bay on the nearby Tamar River, and is strongly maritime
influenced.
Principal Wines Chardonnay, Sauvignon Blanc.

IRON POT BAY CHARDONNAY

●●●● $14.50
Made from 4 hectares of immaculately tended estate plantings of
chardonnay, part of the grapes being sold, and part made for the
Iron Pot Bay label. It is made with little or no oak influence.
Cellaring 2–3 years. **Best Vintages** '91, '92
Current Vintage '92
Matching Food Tasmanian salmon.
Tasting Note 1992 Light to medium yellow-green; clean, aromatic,
peach-accented fruit of light to medium weight; well balanced acid
and good mouthfeel.

IRONBARK RIDGE VINEYARD

NR 14 ML AUSSD
Ipswich **Est.** 1984
Middle Road Mail Service 825, Purga, Qld 4306
Ph (07) 28 1440 **Fax** (07) 391 1908
Open By appt **Production** 450
Winemaker(s) Peter Scudamore-Smith MW
Ipswich is situated on the coastal side of the Great Dividing Range,
and the high summer humidity and rainfall will inevitably provide
challenges for viticulture here. Style is still to settle down under the
guidance of Peter Scudamore-Smith, for whom Ironbark Ridge is
very much a part-time interest.
Principal Wines Chardonnay.

JACKSON'S HILL WINES

★★★ 12–15 CD AUSSD
Hunter Valley **Est.** 1984
Mount View Road, Mount View, NSW 2321
Ph (049) 90 1273
Open W'ends, Hols 9–5 **Production** 900
Winemaker(s) Mike Winborne
A new arrival on the spectacularly scenic Mount View Road making
tiny quantities of wine sold exclusively through the cellar door. The
'91 Cabernet Franc was very pleasant; a competently made wine.

Principal Wines Semillon, Oak Fermented Semillon, Cabernet Franc Rosé, Cabernet Franc.

JADRAN WINES

NR 6–12 CD AUSSD
Darling Range **Est.** 1967
445 Reservoir Road, Orange Grove, WA 6109
Ph (09) 459 1110
Open Mon–Sat 10–8, Sun 11–5 **Production** NFP
Winemaker(s) Steve Radojkovich
A quite substantial operation which basically services local clientele, occasionally producing wines of quite surprising quality from a variety of fruit sources.
Principal Wines Riesling, Hermitage, generic red and white table wines, Sparkling, Fortifieds.

JANE BROOK ESTATE

★★★☆ 13–14 CD AUSSD
Swan Valley **Est.** 1972
229 Toodyay Road, Middle Swan, WA 6056
Ph (09) 274 1432 **Fax** (09) 274 1211
Open Mon–Fri 10–5, W'ends 12–5 **Production** 7000
Winemaker(s) Lyndon Crocket
An attractive winery which relies in part on substantial cellar door trade and in part on varying export markets, with much work having been invested in the Japanese market in recent years. Wine quality is variable, the best wines good.
Principal Wines Wood Aged Chenin Blanc, Chardonnay, Sauvignon Blanc, Mount Barker Rhine Riesling, Cabernet Merlot, Shiraz, Methode Champenoise.

JANE BROOK ESTATE CABERNET MERLOT
●●● ▶ $14
A blend of 85% cabernet sauvignon and 15% merlot grown in the Swan Valley. Conventionally fermented, albeit pressed before dryness, and matured in French oak hogsheads for 12 months.
Cellaring 1–3 years. **Best Vintages** '82, '88, '90, '91, '92
Current Vintage '92
Matching Food Milk-fed veal.
Tasting Note 1992 Medium red; the bouquet is light, leafy and minty with subtle oak, and the palate comes as something of a surprise, with far more mouthfeel and length than the bouquet promises. The flavours are in the red berry and mint spectrum, finishing with smooth, fine tannins.

JANE BROOK ESTATE MOUNT BARKER RHINE RIESLING
●●●● $14
Jane Brook has always done well with the rhine riesling it purchases from Mount Barker on a regular basis. The wine is made in a bigger than usual style, with some residual sugar. The '93 won the silver

medal at the Sheraton Wine Awards, simply because the fruit is of
sufficient weight to carry the sugar.
Cellaring 3–4 years. **Best Vintages** '89, '91, '93
Current Vintage '93
Matching Food Ginger prawns.
Tasting Note 1993 Medium to full yellow-green; intense, rich
full-blown lime/tropical fruit aromas suggesting a small amount of
botrytis. The palate is full-bodied, with similar lime/tropical flavours,
and a noticeably sweet finish.

JANE BROOK ESTATE WOOD AGED CHENIN BLANC
●●●● ▶ $13
Vintaged from grapes grown in the Swan Valley on mainly sandy
gravel soils, tank fermented and then matured in French oak
hogsheads for six months. The wood is not overdone, and the wine
shows just why Chenin Blanc is so favoured in the Swan Valley.
Cellaring 2–4 years. **Best Vintages** '89, '91, '93
Current Vintage '93
Matching Food Lemon chicken.
Tasting Note 1993 Medium yellow-green; the bouquet is rich and
full, with abundant sweet tropical fruit salad aromas and nicely
balanced, gently spicy oak. The palate is still lively with white peach
and fresh lemon flavours, a hint of spicy oak, and a softly rounded
finish. Ageing nicely.

JASPER HILL VINEYARD

★★★★☆ 15–35 R AUS11, 144 UK53
Bendigo **Est.** 1975
Drummonds Lane, Heathcote, Vic 3523
Ph (054) 33 2528 **Fax** (054) 33 3143
Open W'ends 10–6 **Production** 3000
Winemaker(s) Ron Laughton
The red wines of Jasper Hill are highly regarded and much sought
after, sold chiefly through the cellar door and by mailing list, with the
1992 Emily's Paddock selling out at cellar door within a fortnight of
release. Growing export markets, although small in volume, only
add to the supply pressure.
Principal Wines Georgia's Paddock Riesling, Georgia's Paddock
Shiraz, Emily's Paddock Shiraz, Cabernet Franc.

JASPER VALLEY WINES

NR 4.20–12 CD AUSSD UK10 US2
South Coast New South Wales **Est.** 1976
RMB 880 Croziers Road, Berry, NSW 2535
Ph (044) 64 1596
Open 7 days 9.30–5.30 **Production** 1100
Winemaker(s) Contract
A strongly tourist-oriented winery with most of its wine purchased
as cleanskins from other makers. Features 2 hectares of lawns,
barbecue facilities, and sweeping views.

Principal Wines White Burgundy, Riesling, Traminer Riesling, Moselle, Summer Red, Cabernet Sauvignon, Port; also non-alcoholic fruit wines.

JEIR CREEK WINES

★★★ 10–14 CD AUSSD
Canberra **Est.** 1984
Gooda Creek Road, Murrumbateman, NSW 2582
Ph (06) 227 5999 **Fax** (06) 227 5900
Open Fri–Sun, Hols 10–5 **Production** 2400
Winemaker(s) Rob Howell
Rob Howell came to part-time winemaking through a love of drinking fine wine, and is intent on improving both the quality and consistency of his wines.
Principal Wines Riesling, Late Harvest Riesling, Botrytis Semillon Sauvignon Blanc, Semillon Sauvignon Blanc, Pinot Noir, Cabernet Merlot.

JENKE VINEYARDS

★★★☆ 9–13 CD AUS71, 122
Barossa Valley **Est.** 1989
Barossa Valley Way, Rowland Flat, SA 5352
Ph (085) 24 4154 **Fax** (085) 24 4154
Open 7 days 10–4.30 **Production** 4500
Winemaker(s) Kym Jenke
The Jenkes have been vignerons in the Barossa since 1854, and have over 25 hectares of vineyards; a small part of the production is now made and marketed through a charming restored stone cottage cellar door.
Principal Wines Semillon, Chardonnay, Late Harvest Riesling, Cabernet Franc, Cabernet Sauvignon, Shiraz.

JENKE SEMILLON

●●● ‣ $11
Produced from estate-grown grapes situated adjacent to the North Para River. Slightly less than 4 hectares of semillon in five separate plots.
Cellaring 2–4 years. **Best Vintages** '90, '94
Current Vintage '94
Matching Food Pasta.
Tasting Note 1994 Light to medium green-yellow; a fruit-driven wine with a quite intense bouquet, clean and unforced. The palate has powerful fruit with substance and length; should develop fairly quickly.

JIM BARRY WINES

★★★★☆ 9.50–55 R AUS13, 37, 112, 138–141 UK88
Clare Valley **Est.** 1959
Main North Road, Clare, SA 5453
Ph (088) 42 2261 **Fax** (088) 42 3752

Open Mon–Fri 9–5, W'ends, Hols 9–4 **Production** 30 000
Winemaker(s) Mark Barry
The high rating may come as a surprise to some, but is fully justified
on the strength of the current range of releases, many of which are
outstanding, and represent excellent value for money.
Principal Wines Watervale Riesling, Clare Chablis, Personal
Selection Sauvignon Blanc and Chardonnay, Sauternes, Cabernet
Merlot, Personal Selection Cabernet Sauvignon, McCrae Wood
Shiraz, The Armagh (Shiraz).

JIM BARRY McCRAE WOOD SHIRAZ
●●●●● $20
Ranks second to The Armagh Shiraz in terms of price, and first
released in 1992. As with The Armagh, it is based upon scrupulous
fruit selection, and shows the well handled use of oak. Whereas The
Armagh needs decades, this wine only needs 10 years.
Cellaring 10 years. **Best Vintages** '92, '93
Current Vintage '93
Matching Food Jugged hare.
Tasting Note 1993 Full purple-red; clean and rich minty/berry
fruit with well handled oak on the bouquet. The palate is ripe, full
and rich, with dark fruits, again a touch of mint, and a hint of earth.
Both the oak and the tannins have been kept under tight control.

JIM BARRY PERSONAL SELECTION CABERNET
SAUVIGNON
●●●● $12.50
Produced from the extensive plantings owned by Jim Barry,
amounting to over 120 hectares in all. Always made in a ripe fruit
style with bright flavours which initially seem a little
confection-like but which settle down nicely with a few years in
bottle.
Cellaring 4–7 years. **Best Vintages** '79, '85, '87, '89, '90
Current Vintage '92
Matching Food Spiced beef.
Tasting Note 1992 Medium purple-red; sweet dark chocolate and
berry fruit aromas with well integrated and balanced oak, and just a
hint of mint. The palate is smooth with noticeably sweet berry fruit,
and ripe, soft tannins.

JIM BARRY THE ARMAGH
●●●●● $55
First made in 1985 from very old, un-irrigated, low-yielding vines.
Not produced in 1986, and not exhibited in wine shows until the
1987 vintage was made. Since that time every vintage since the '87
has received at least one gold medal, with numerous trophies
bestowed on the '89 and '90 vintages, respectively. Unashamedly a
Grange pretender, and succeeding well in its aim.
Cellaring 10–20 years. **Best Vintages** '89, '90, '91, '92, '93
Current Vintage '92
Matching Food The richest game dish possible.
Tasting Note 1992 Dense purple-red; very sweet, rich and ripe

liquorice and cherry aromas, with fruit, rather than oak, driving the wine. A voluptuous palate with masses of ripe, rich fruit across the full spectrum of dark fruit flavours, finishing with appropriately balanced, if persistent, tannins.

JIM BARRY WATERVALE RIESLING
●●●●● $9.50
The often outstanding quality of this wine in recent years can be attributed in part to skilled winemaking but more particularly to the acquisition by Jim Barry of the famed Florita Vineyard at Watervale, once a jewel in the Leo Buring crown, and sold during a dark period of the latter's history. Leo Buring's loss has been Jim Barry's gain.
Cellaring 7 years or more. **Best Vintages** '83, '86, '89, '91, '94 **Current Vintage** '94
Matching Food Ginger pork.
Tasting Note 1994 An outstanding wine. Light green-yellow; fragrant, intense lime juice with a hint of toast on the bouquet, with long, intense and lingering citrussy fruit on the palate. Good as it is now, it will become even better with time.

JINGALLA WINES

★★★★ 9.50–17 CD AUS35, 71, 122
Great Southern **Est.** 1979
RMB 114 Bolganup Dam Road, Porongurup, WA 6324
Ph (098) 53 1023 **Fax** (098) 53 1023
Open 7 days 10.30–5 **Production** 2500
Winemaker(s) Brendan Smith (Contract)
Jingalla is a family-run business, owned and run by Geoff and Nita Clarke and Barry and Shelley Coad, the latter the ever-energetic wine marketer of the business. The 8 hectares of hillside vineyards are low yielding, with the white wines succeeding best.
Principal Wines Great Southern White and Red Riesling, Semillon, Verdelho, Cabernet Sauvignon, Semillon Late Harvest.

JINGALLA RIESLING
●●●● $11.50
Produced from 2 hectares of riesling, with two clones, including the so-called geisenheim clone. Consistent performer, always exhibiting abundant fruit flavour.
Cellaring 3–6 years. **Best Vintages** '84, '86, '90, '93
Current Vintage '94
Matching Food Chinese or Thai cuisine.
Tasting Note 1994 Medium yellow-green; full, soft fruit aromas with some tropical overtones. On the palate, rich, full-flavoured easy drinking style with a subliminal touch of sweetness.

JINGALLA SEMILLON
●●● ▶ $13
There are 1.5 hectares of semillon on the hillside vineyard, situated on the northern slopes of the Porongurup Ranges. Over the years, uncertain use of oak (perhaps due to budgetary constraints) has not

helped the quality of the wine, but the '94 represents a distinct turn
for the better.
Cellaring 3–5 years. **Best Vintages** NA **Current Vintage** '94
Matching Food Deep-fried calamari.
Tasting Note 1994 Light green-yellow; precise varietal fruit with
quite distinct herbal notes, and a hint of oak spice. The palate is of
light to medium weight, with clean, crisp fruit and a clever touch of
commercial spicy/charry oak, possibly chips.

JINGALLA VERDELHO
●●●● $15.50
The one hectare of verdelho has produced some of Jingalla's best
wines over the years, wines which age very well. The 1990 vintage
tasted in late '94 was quite delicious, still lively and with years in
front of it. The wine is barrel fermented.
Cellaring 5–7 years. **Best Vintages** '90, '91, '94
Current Vintage '94
Matching Food Richer, spicier Chinese food.
Tasting Note 1994 Light to medium yellow-green; a fragrant and
complex bouquet with tangy, citrus and honey fruit and a hint of
charry/spicy oak. A cleverly made wine, again showing some oak
phenolics on the finish which typically derive from oak chips, but
which certainly add to the overall commercial appeal of the wine.

JOADJA VINEYARDS *
★★★ 12–25.50 CD AUSSD
Central Tablelands **Est.** 1983
Joadja Road, Berrima, NSW 2577
Ph (048) 78 5236
Open W'ends & hols 10–5 **Production** 3000
Winemaker(s) Kim Moginie
The strikingly-labelled Joadja Vineyard wines, first made in 1990,
are principally drawn from 7 hectares of estate vineyards situated in
the cool hills adjacent to Berrima. Both the red and whites have a
very unusual and consistent eucalypt/peppermint character which is
clearly a product of the climate and (possibly) soil. It makes the
wines difficult to assess by conventional standards, but is by no
means unpleasant, and Joadja is well worth a visit.
Principal Wines Classic Dry White, Chardonnay, Classic Dry
Red, Late Harvest Riesling, Sauternes, Christopher Tawny Port.

JOHN GEHRIG WINES
★★★ 8.50–14CD AUS88, 183
North East Victoria **Est.** 1976
Oxley-Milawa Road, Oxley, Vic 3678
Ph (057) 27 3395 **Fax** (057) 27 3395
Open 7 days 9–5 **Production** 5600
Winemaker(s) John Gehrig
Honest, if seldom exciting, wines; the occasional Chardonnay,
Pinot Noir, Merlot and Cabernet Merlot have, however, risen
above their station.

Principal Wines Oxley Dry White, Riesling, Chenin Blanc, Verdelho, Chardonnay, Sparkling, Pinot Noir, King River Red, Merlot, Cabernet Merlot, Fortifieds.

JONES WINERY

NR NA AUSSD
North East Victoria **Est.** 1864
Chiltern Road, Rutherglen, Vic 3685
Ph (060) 32 9496
Open Mon–Sat 9–5, W'ends, Hols 10–5 **Production** NFP
Winemaker(s) Les Jones
An ultra-reclusive and ultra-traditional winery (despite the garish labels) making no-frills wines from 16 hectares of vineyards. Les Jones even regards details of his current wines and prices as 'my business only'. The emphasis is on Port, Sherry and Muscat.
Principal Wines Chablis, Rielsing, White Burgundy, Light Red, Dry Red, Fortifieds.

JUD'S HILL

●●● ▶ 8.99–15.25 R AUS1, 34, 111
Clare Valley **Est.** 1977
Farrell Flat Road, Clare, SA 5343 **Ph** NA
Open Not **Production** NFP
Winemaker(s) Brian Barry
Brian Barry is an industry veteran with a wealth of winemaking and show judging experience. His is nonetheless in reality a vineyard-only operation, with a substantial part of the output sold as grapes to other wineries, and the wines made under contract at various wineries, albeit under Brian Barry's supervision. As one would expect, the quality is reliably good.
Principal Wines Riesling, Chablis, Cabernet Sauvignon, Cabernet Merlot; Gleesons Ridge is second label.

JUD'S HILL BRIAN BARRY CABERNET SAUVIGNON
●●●● $17.95
Like the Riesling, estate-grown and produced from fully mature vines. Again like the Riesling, in mainstream Clare style, deep in colour and strongly flavoured and structured.
Cellaring 10+ years. **Best Vintages** NA **Current Vintage** '92
Matching Food Steak with red wine sauce.
Tasting Note 1992 Dark red-purple; the bouquet is clean and rich with masses of dark berry and dark chocolate fruit; subtle oak. A solidly rich wine on the palate with dark briary/chocolate flavours, persistent tannins and an echo of cigar box oak.

JUD'S HILL RIESLING
●●●● $14.95
Estate-grown Clare Valley Riesling, made in a competent and conventional fashion, really speaks for itself — or will do so given appropriate time in bottle. The quality of the wine lies in the vineyard, which is now fully mature.

Cellaring Up to 10 years. **Best Vintages** '90, '93, '94
Current Vintage '94
Matching Food Seafood salad.
Tasting Note 1994 Light to medium yellow-green; classic Clare on the bouquet, fresh and clean, with toast and lime aromas. The palate is bone dry and fairly reserved, crisply toasty, and with years of improvement in front of it.

KAESLER WINES

★★★☆ 6.30–14.30 CD AUS118
Barossa Valley **Est.** 1990
Barossa Valley Way, Nuriootpa, SA 5355
Ph (085) 62 2711 **Fax** (085) 62 2788
Open 7 days 10–5 **Production** 3000
Winemaker(s) Roger Harbord (Contract)
Toby and Treena Hueppauff purchased Kaesler Farm, with its 12 hectares of vines, in 1985, and since 1990 have had the wines made under contract by Roger Harbord at Basedows. The winery has an â la carte restaurant offering both indoor and outdoor dining.
Principal Wines Bush Vine Grenache, Prestige Semillon, Late Harvest Semillon, Old Vine Shiraz, Beerenauslese, Fortifieds.

KAESLER FARM BUSH VINE GRENACHE

●●● ▶ $9
Yet further evidence of the restoration in the fortunes of grenache, which was in fact the major variety to suffer during the days of the Vine Pull Scheme during the 1980s. Much of the material was previously used in fortified winemaking at one extreme, and a little Rosé at the other. Most now goes to table wine, rather than the Rosé as in this instance.
Cellaring Drink now. **Best Vintages** NA
Current Vintage '94
Matching Food Asian seafood.
Tasting Note 1994 Bright pink; fresh, crisp, clean and lively with bright, fresh tangy fruit on both bouquet and palate. Very good example of Rosé.

KAISER STUHL

★★★ 4.95 R AUS147
Barossa Valley **Est.** 1931
Tanunda Road, Nuriootpa, SA 5355
Ph (085) 62 0389 **Fax** (085) 62 1669
Open Mon–Sat 10–5, Sun 1–5 **Production** 1.3 million
Winemaker(s) Steve Chapman
Part of the Southcorp Wines empire, but a shadow of its former self, with its once-famous Green Ribbon Riesling and Red Ribbon Shiraz no more. Essentially provides flagon quality wines in bottles at competitive prices.
Principal Wines Black Forest, generic whites under bin numbers, Claret Bin 33, Sparkling; also extensive cask and flagon range.

KANGDERAAR VINEYARD *

NR 6.50–11 CD AUSSD
Bendigo **Est.** 1980
Melvilles Caves Road, Rheola, Vic 3517
Ph (054) 38 8292 **Fax** (054) 38 8292
Open Mon–Sat 9–5, Sun 10–5 **Production** 900
Winemaker(s) James Nealy
The 4.5-hectare vineyard is situated at Rheola, near the Melville
Caves, said to the hideout of the bushranger Captain Melville in the
1850s, and surrounded by the Kooyoora State Park. It is owned by
James and Christine Nealy.
Principal Wines Riesling Traminer, Chardonnay, Cabernet
Sauvignon, Merlot Cabernet.

KARA KARA VINEYARD

★★★☆ 12–14 CD AUS173
Pyrenees **Est.** 1987
Sunraysia Highway via St Arnaud, Vic 3478
Ph (054) 96 3294
Open Mon–Fri 10.30–6, W'ends 9–6 **Production** 1400
Winemaker(s) John Ellis (Contract)
Hungarian-born Steve Zsigmond comes from a long line of
vignerons, and sees Kara Kara as the eventual retirement occupation
for himself and wife Marlene. The first step has been the decision to
have their production contract made by Mitchelton (previously the
grapes were sold) with predictably consistent results over the first
few years.
Principal Wines Fumé Blanc, Chardonnay Semillon, Sauvignon
Blanc, Chardonnay, Semillon, Cabernet Shiraz.

KARA KARA CHARDONNAY
●●●● ▶ $14
An interesting wine which starred at the 1994 Small Winemakers
Competition in Canberra, demonstrating the quality of the fruit
grown at the 1.5-hectare vineyard in the northern foothills of the
Pyrenees Ranges, 50 kilometres north of Avoca.
Cellaring 2–3 years. **Best Vintages** '93
Current Vintage '93
Matching Food Tortellini.
Tasting Note 1993 Light green-yellow; quite intense tangy
grapefruit aromas with subtle oak lead on to a fine, fruit-driven wine
on the palate with grapefruit and melon flavours, subtle oak and
good length.

KARA KARA SAUVIGNON BLANC
●●● ▶ $12
Produced from 2 hectares of estate-grown grapes, typically showing
ripe to very ripe fruit flavours running more into the tropical banana
spectrum than the classic herbal gooseberry. Will appeal to some for
this very reason.

Cellaring Drink now. **Best Vintages** NA
Current Vintage '94
Matching Food Seafood risotto.
Tasting Note 1994 Light to medium yellow-green; the bouquet is
ripe with some tropical fruit overtones and a hint of spice, possibly
from oak. The palate is solid, with ripe fruit bolstered by a degree
of residual sugar.

KARINA VINEYARD

★★★★ 11–17.50 CD AUS183
Mornington Peninsula **Est.** 1984
RMB 4055 Harrisons Road, Dromana, Vic 3936
Ph (059) 81 0137 **Fax** (059) 81 0137
Open W'ends 11–5 **Production** 1700
Winemaker(s) Graeme Pinney
A typical Mornington Peninsula vineyard, situated in the
Dromana/Redhill area on rising, north-facing slopes, just
3 kilometres from the shores of Port Phillip Bay, immaculately
tended and with picturesque garden surrounds.
Principal Wines Riesling, Sauvignon Blanc, Chardonnay,
Cabernet Merlot.

KARINA CABERNET MERLOT
●●●● $13.50
The estate has 1.25 hectares of cabernet sauvignon, 0.25 hectares
of merlot. Vintages prior to the '92 have often shown good extract,
but have been slightly tough or undermade. With this,
winemaker/owner Graham Pinney seems to have got everything
together.
Cellaring 3–5 years. **Best Vintages** '92 **Current Vintage** '92
Matching Food Calf's liver.
Tasting Note 1992 Medium red-purple; of light to medium
intensity with clean, cool-grown but neither soapy nor leafy fruit,
rather more in the red fruit spectrum, with subtle oak. The palate lives
up to the promise of the bouquet with well balanced, pleasantly
ripened red berry fruit, soft tannins and subtle oak.

KARINA RIESLING
●●●● ▶ $11
Made from half a hectare of estate plantings employing the neatly
trimmed vertical canopy so necessary to obtain fruit ripeness in this
cool region. While always elegant and crisp, the wine has often
lacked depth, but no such criticism could be levelled at the '94
vintage.
Cellaring 2–3 years. **Best Vintages** '94 **Current Vintage** '94
Matching Food Crab, mussels.
Tasting Note 1994 Light green-yellow; clean and crisp, with
intense lime and citrus fruit aromas. The palate is lively and fresh,
with far more concentration than one often encounters in the region,
with lime and passionfruit flavours, and a long finish.

KARRIVALE WINES

★★★★☆ 12.50 CD AUS178
Great Southern **Est.** 1979
Woodlands Road, Porongurup, WA 6324
Ph (098) 53 1009 **Fax** (098) 53 1129
Open Wed–Sun 10–5 **Production** 350
Winemaker(s) John Wade
A tiny Riesling specialist in the wilds of the Porongurups forced to
change its name from Narang because Lindemans felt it could be
confused with its Nyrang Hermitage brand; truly a strange world.
The viticultural skills of owner Campbell McGready and the
winemaking skills of John Wade combined to produce the multi-
trophy winning 1994 Riesling, one of the stars of 1994 Mount
Barker Wine Show.
Principal Wines Riesling.

KARRIVALE RIESLING
●●●●● $12.50
The vineyard, progressively planted between 1979 and 1989,
principally to riesling (with some recent plantings of chardonnay)
nestles under the Gibraltar Rock of the Porongurup Ranges, on a
gentle slope. Meticulous attention to viticulture has produced
Rieslings which have always been of high quality, reaching a peak
with the '94 vintage, a trophy winner at the 1994 Mount Barker
Show.
Cellaring 3–10 years. **Best Vintages** '90, '92, '94
Current Vintage '94
Matching Food Cold tomato and basil soup.
Tasting Note 1994 Light yellow-green; classically styled with
intense citrus/herbal fruit aromas. A marvellously balanced wine in
the mouth with superb fruit balance and intensity, which is a dyed-in-
the-wool stayer.

KARRIVIEW WINES

★★★★ 17–22 CD AUSSD
Great Southern **Est.** 1986
Scotsdale Road, Denmark, WA 6333
Ph (098) 40 9381 **Fax** (098) 40 9381
Open Summer hols 7 days 10–5, Feb–April Fri–Mon 10–5, Winter
w'ends 10–5 **Production** 700
Winemaker(s) John Wade (Contract)
One hectare each of immaculately tended pinot noir and
chardonnay on ultra-close spacing produce tiny quantities of two
wines of remarkable intensity, quality and style. Available only from
the winery, but worth the effort.
Principal Wines Chardonnay, Pinot Noir.

KARRIVIEW CHARDONNAY
●●●●● $18
Due to the ultra-close spacing of the vineyard, with exceedingly
narrow rows, all of the work is done by hand, but the quality of the

wine makes the effort worthwhile, even if the price asked is far too
low. The '90, '92 and '93 vintages, tasted in late 1994, were
uniformly outstanding.
Cellaring 5+ years. **Best Vintages** '90, '92, '93
Current Vintage '93
Matching Food Marron, yabbies.
Tasting Note 1993 Medium yellow-green; wonderful ripeness to
the melon, passionfruit and citrus fruit, complexed by a hint of either
barrel ferment or malolactic characters. The palate is supremely
elegant, with understated flavours, yet intensely fruit-driven, with
tremendous length to the finish. Less rich than the multi-trophy-
winning '90 wine, but could develop every bit as well.

KARRIVIEW PINOT NOIR
●●●● ▶ $17
As at late 1994, four vintages were available for sale at the winery,
with each of the '90, '91 and '92 having won gold medals. These
are relatively fast developing styles, but as the '91 vintage shows,
can possess great flavour at three or four years of age. Overall, the
quality and style is very like that of the far-better-known Wignalls.
Cellaring 3–4 years. **Best Vintages** '90, '91, '92
Current Vintage '93
Matching Food Quail salad.
Tasting Note 1993 Has already browned off in the manner of a
lighter-year Burgundy. The bouquet is complex, sappy and stemmy,
with real style, but is disconcertingly advanced. The palate, too,
lacks the richness of fruit one would look for, but certainly has true
Burgundian characters.

KATNOOK ESTATE
★★★★☆ 12.20–28.40 R AUS81–85 UK16
Coonawarra **Est.** 1979
Penola-Naracoorte Road, Coonawarra, SA 5263
Ph (087) 37 2394 **Fax** (087) 37 2397
Open Mon–Fri 9–4.30, W'ends 10–4.30 **Production** 60 000
Winemaker(s) Wayne Stehbens
The changes have been ringing fast at Katnook, the brand name of
Coonawarra Machinery Company. CMC, as it is known, has sold a
large part of its vineyards to Southcorp, but is busy replanting,
having retained an all-essential core of more than 100 hectares.
Principal Wines Premium Katnook label: Riesling, Sauvignon
Blanc, Chardonnay, Cabernet Sauvignon, Merlot, Chardonnay Brut;
second Riddoch label: Riesling, Chardonnay, Sauvignon Blanc,
Cabernet Shiraz.

KATNOOK ESTATE CABERNET SAUVIGNON
●●●● ▶ $26
Made from the very best selection from 70 hectares of estate
vineyards, but over the years has tended to be relatively lean. More
recent vintages have shown better fruit richness and balance,
exemplified by the '91 and '92 vintages.

Cellaring Up to 10 years. **Best Vintages** '88, '90, '91, '92, '94
Current Vintage '91
Matching Food Prime rib of beef.
Tasting Note 1991 Medium to full red-purple; the bouquet is clean and relatively soft, with aromas of blackcurrant and soft, gently spicy vanillin oak. The palate shows the same blackcurrant fruit, allied with some dark chocolate flavours; the tannins are fine; the oak perfectly balanced and integrated.

KATNOOK ESTATE CHARDONNAY
●●●● ▶ $25
Stands alongside Sauvignon Blanc as Katnook's most consistent wine, always elegant, and always long-lived. Produced from the pick of 18 hectares of mature vineyards.
Cellaring Up to 10 years. **Best Vintages** '84, '86, '90, '92, '94
Current Vintage '92
Matching Food Poached salmon.
Tasting Note 1992 Medium to full yellow-green; a complex bouquet with melon fruit and some honeyed/nutty barrel ferment/malolactic characters. The palate is long, with echoes of the caramel-tinged malolactic/barrel ferment characters of the nose, finishing with well balanced acidity.

KATNOOK ESTATE RIDDOCH CABERNET SHIRAZ
●●● ▶ $12
The '92 is a blend of two-thirds Cabernet Sauvignon and one-third Shiraz, which was not bottled until August 1994 and released March 1995. 100% Coonawarra, and from a good vintage.
Cellaring 2–5 years. **Best Vintages** '88, '90, '91, '92
Current Vintage '92
Matching Food Beef casserole.
Tasting Note 1992 Medium to full red; a rich, warm and earthy bouquet with plenty of dark berry fruit and some vanillin oak. A solidly constructed wine on the palate with obvious American oak input, finishing with soft tannins. A traditional, hearty wine.

KATNOOK ESTATE RIESLING
●●●● $15
Held by Katnook for 6 years before its release in March 1995, and an excellent illustration of the capacity of Riesling to age well in bottle regardless of its region of origin. This estate-grown wine from Coonawarra had won one gold, four silver and four bronze medals at the time of its release.
Cellaring None required. **Best Vintages** NA
Current Vintage '89
Matching Food Antipasto.
Tasting Note 1989 Medium to full yellow, but still bright; there are most attractive rounded, toasty, bottle-developed characters on the bouquet, and the palate shows similarly attractive toasty, honeyed fruit flavours, nicely balanced by a twist of acid on the finish.

KATNOOK ESTATE SAUVIGNON BLANC
●●●● ▸ $20

One of the signature wines of Katnook Estate, now made from 8
remaining hectares of plantings of this variety. A chance tasting of
the '82 vintage in late 1994 emphasised how well the wines can
age, even if the change in character is quite radical. On balance,
best drunk young.

Cellaring Attractive young, but does cellar remarkably well.
Best Vintages '84, '86, '90, '92, '94 **Current Vintage** '94
Matching Food Grilled whiting.
Tasting Note 1994 Light green-yellow; fresh and crisp in a direct,
basically herbal style. Well balanced and structured in the mouth,
with good length, and a pleasing echo of fruit sweetness deriving
from more tropical characters.

KAY BROS AMERY

★★★ 9–13.95 R AUS25
Southern Vales **Est.** 1890
Kay Road, McLaren Vale, SA 5171
Ph (08) 323 8211 **Fax** (08) 323 9199
Open Mon–Fri 9–5, W'ends 12–5 **Production** 6500
Winemaker(s) Colin Kay

A traditional winery with a rich history and some priceless old vines;
while the white wines are not recommended, the red wines and
fortified wines can be very good. Of particular interest is Block 6
Shiraz, made from 100-year-old vines.
Principal Wines Sauvignon Blanc, Late Harvest Frontignac, Pinot
Noir, Block 6 Shiraz, Cabernet Sauvignon, Cabernet Shiraz, Port;
Liqueur Muscat.

KELLERMEISTER WINES

★★★ 7–25 CD AUSSD
Barossa Valley **Est.** 1970
Barossa Valley Highway, Lyndoch, SA 5351
Ph (085) 24 4303 **Fax** (085) 24 4880
Open 7 days 9–6 **Production** 8000
Winemaker(s) Trevor Jones

Specialises in older vintage wines made in traditional fashion, an
extraordinary array of which are on offer at enticing prices. As at
late 1994; table wines from 1984, 1986 and 1988 were on sale in
addition to numerous offerings from the cellar door (or by mail
order) with no retail sales.
Principal Wines Chardonnay, Sauvignon Blanc, Riesling,
Gewurztraminer, Semillon White Burgundy, Shiraz, Cabernet
Sauvignon, Sparkling, Fortifieds.

KELLYBROOK WINERY

★★★☆ 10–36 CD AUS17, 87, 166
Yarra Valley **Est.** 1960
Fulford Road, Wonga Park, Vic 3115

Ph (03) 9722 1304 **Fax** (03) 9722 2092
Open Mon–Sat 9–6, Sun 11–6 **Production** 4000
Winemaker(s) Darren Kelly
Situated at Wonga Park at the entrance to the principal
winegrowing regions of the Yarra Valley, replete with picnic area
and a full-scale restaurant. As well as table wine, a very competent
producer of Cider and Apple Brandy (in Calvados style).
Principal Wines Chardonnay, Riesling, Traminer, Methode
Champenoise, Pinot Noir, Shiraz, Cabernet Sauvignon,
Champagne Cider, Apple Brandy.

KELLYBROOK SHIRAZ
●●●● ▶ $15
A lovely wine made during the brief tenure as winemaker of Peter
Draper. Quantities are limited, as there is less than one hectare of
shiraz grapes on the estate, but the wine is yet further proof of the
suitability of the Yarra Valley to this grape, which is in fact relatively
sparsely grown in the region.
Cellaring 3–5 years. **Best Vintages** '90, '93, '94
Current Vintage '93
Matching Food Rack of lamb.
Tasting Note 1993 Bright red; the bouquet has cherry/berry fruit
with peppery notes and a touch of spicy oak. The flavours focus on
red cherry, again with a touch of varietal spice, and soft tannins.
Fruit-, rather than oak-driven.

KEVIN SOBELS WINES

NR 12–13 CD AUSSD
Hunter Valley **Est.** 1992
Cnr Broke & Halls Roads, Pokolbin, NSW 2321
Ph (049) 98 7766 **Fax** (049) 98 7766
Open 7 days 10–5 **Production** 4500
Winemaker(s) Kevin Sobels
Veteran winemaker Kevin Sobels has found yet another home,
drawing upon 8 hectares of vineyards (originally planted by the Ross
Jones family) to produce wines sold almost entirely through cellar
door and mail order, with limited retail representation. The cellar
door offers light meals and picnic and barbecue facilities.
Principal Wines Chardonnay, Semillon, Traminer, Pinot Noir.

KILLAWARRA

★★★★ 9–18 R AUS147 UK83
Barossa Valley **Est.** 1975
Tanunda Road, Nuriootpa, SA 5355
Ph (085) 62 0389 **Fax** (085) 62 1669
Open See Penfolds **Production** NFP
Winemaker(s) John Duval
Purely a Southcorp brand, without any particular presence in terms
of either vineyards or winery, but increasingly styled in a mode
different from the Seaview or Seppelt wines. As one would expect,
the wines are competitively priced.

Principal Wines Only sparkling wines: Non Vintage Brut, Vintage Brut, Premier Brut and Reserve Brut; also Non Vintage Sparkling Burgundy.

KILLAWARRA PREMIER BRUT
●●●● $12.50

A very interesting wine in that the current vintage is made almost entirely from pinot noir (98%) with a token 2% chardonnay, sourced primarily, but not exclusively, from Padthaway and Coonawarra. It spends two years on yeast lees before disgorgement. The trophy-winning '90 vintage was a more conventional blend of Pinot Noir and Chardonnay.
Cellaring Drink now. **Best Vintages** '90, '91
Current Vintage '91
Matching Food Hors d'oeuvres, Asian food.
Tasting Note 1991 Medium to full straw-yellow; a creamy, toasty bouquet with attractive yeast autolysis characters, and not showing its pinot noir base. The palate has very attractive creamy textures and flavours, with some biscuity yeast characters, with good acid on the finish.

KILLAWARRA VINTAGE BRUT
●●● ▶ $9

A somewhat amorphous blend of grapes including pinot noir and chardonnay, but also with others drawn from regions across South Australia, including Coonawarra, Barossa Valley, Padthaway, Riverlands and McLaren Vale.
Cellaring Drink now. **Best Vintages** NA **Current Vintage** '92
Matching Food Hors d'oeuvres, oysters.
Tasting Note 1992 Medium straw-yellow; a clean bouquet with some bready yeasty aromas and the fruit softened by malolactic fermentation, making it a little plain. Well enough balanced on the palate with some pinot noir influence evident, and not too sweet.

KILLERBY VINEYARDS

★★★☆ 12–17 R AUS72, 102
Margaret River **Est.** 1973
Minninup Road off Lakes Road, Gelorup, WA 6230
Ph (097) 95 7222 **Fax** (097) 95 7835
Open 7 days 10–5 **Production** 8500
Winemaker(s) Matt Aldridge
The members of the Killerby family are long-term residents of the south west; Anna Killerby, herself a Roseworthy graduate, is the fourth generation, and is married to Matt Aldridge, formerly of Rosemount and now chief winemaker at Killerby. The 16 hectares of vines were established by Anna's father, the late Dr Barry Killerby in 1973, and are now fully mature.
Principal Wines Semillon, Chardonnay, Shiraz, Cabernet Sauvignon and budget-priced April Classic White (Traminer Semillon Chardonnay Blend) and April Classic Red (Shiraz Pinot Cabernet Blend).

222

KILLERBY CHARDONNAY
●●●● ▶ $17

In recent years, consistently the best of the Killerby wines, not
surprising given winemaker Matt Aldridge's apprenticeship at
Rosemount Estate. Produced from 2.5 hectares of estate vineyards, it
is 100% barrel fermented in French oak, and matured in oak for five
months before bottling and typically released at the end of the year
of vintage. The '94 had not been released at the time of writing, but
is reported to be as good as the excellent '92 and '93 vintages.
Cellaring 3–5 years. **Best Vintages** '92, '93, '94
Current Vintage '93
Matching Food Chicken supreme.
Tasting Note 1993 Medium to full yellow-green; complex, rich
barrel ferment characters with tangy, stylish melon fruit. At the
moment the complex, barrel ferment characters tend to dominate the
fruit a little, as the wine goes through a phase in its development, but
should come out of it given more time.

KINGS CREEK VINEYARD

★★★★☆ 15–19.50 R AUS56
Mornington Peninsula **Est.** 1981
237 Myers Road, Bittern, Vic 3918
Ph (059) 82 2101
Open W'ends, Public hols 12–5 **Production** 1400
Winemaker(s) Penny Gluyas, Kevin McCarthy
Kings Creek is owned and operated by the Bell, Glover and Perraton
families. Planting commenced in 1981, and the vines are now fully
mature. Since 1990 the quality of the wines, particularly of the Pinot
Noir and Chardonnay, has been beyond reproach.
Principal Wines Chardonnay, Pinot Noir, Cabernet Sauvignon.

KINGS CREEK CHARDONNAY
●●●● ▶ $19.50

Predominantly sourced from the Kings Creek vineyards, but from time
to time incorporating up to one-third purchased from an adjoining
grower, and the wines are of greater than usual complexity and
intensity. The wine is barrel fermented, and matured in French oak
for 8–9 months before bottling.
Cellaring 3–4 years. **Best Vintages** '88, '91, '93, '94
Current Vintage '93
Matching Food Stir-fried chicken.
Tasting Note 1993 Richly complex with toasty French oak over
melon and peach fruit. A silver medal winner at the '94 Lilydale
Wine Show. The '94, tasted from barrel, showed similar richness
and complexity.

KINGS CREEK PINOT NOIR
●●●● ▶ $19.50

Estate-grown, and vinified using a range of Burgundian techniques
including 20% whole bunches in the fermentation. Matured for 10
months in French oak and, like the Chardonnay from Kings Creek, a
wine of real complexity and style, with many medals to its credit.

Cellaring Drink now. **Best Vintages** '88, '89, '91, '92, '94
Current Vintage '94
Matching Food Chinese duck with mushrooms.
Tasting Note 1994 Medium purple-red; extremely fragrant, sappy, spicy fruit aromas with subtle oak. The palate has similar spicy/sappy/stemmy flavours, reminiscent of Paringa Estate. The oak is nicely balanced and integrated.

KINGSLEY WINES

★★★☆ 10–12 CD AUSSD
Western Victoria **Est.** 1983
50 Bancroft Street, Portland, Vic 3305
Ph (055) 23 1864
Open 7 days 1–4 **Production** 580
Winemaker(s) Seppelt (Contract)
Only a small part of the 12 hectares is made under contract, the remainder being sold as grapes. As at the end of 1994, '90 and '91 Cabernet Sauvignon and Rieslings from '90 to '93 were available for sale at low prices.
Principal Wines Riesling, Botrytis Riesling, Cabernet Sauvignon.

KNIGHT GRANITE HILLS

★★★☆ 10.50–17 R AUS48, 72, 88
Macedon **Est.** 1979
Burke & Wills Track, Baynton RSD 391, Kyneton, Vic 3444
Ph (054) 23 7264 **Fax** (054) 23 7288
Open Mon–Sat 10–6, Sun 12–6 **Production** 5000
Winemaker(s) Lew Knight
Knight's Granite Hills is one of the early pacesetters, indeed the pacesetter, for cool climate, spicy Shiraz and intense Riesling. Sales have slowed dramatically in recent years, and the wines seemed to suffer somewhat from spending too long in tank before being bottled.
Principal Wines Dry White, Riesling, Chardonnay, Spatlese Shiraz, Cabernet Sauvignon.

KNIGHT GRANITE HILLS RIESLING
●●●● $12.95
Produced from 2 hectares of low-yielding vines which invariably produce grapes with great concentration of flavour. The wines can be superb, developing powerful, idiosyncratic characters as they age, exemplified by the currently available '91 vintage.
Cellaring 4–7 years. **Best Vintages** '81, '82, '86, '88, '90
Current Vintage '91
Matching Food Salad niçoise.
Tasting Note 1991 Bright green-yellow; powerful, concentrated old-style riesling with a touch of that famed kerosene character. On the palate, intense and powerful in a style reminiscent of the wines of 20 or 30 years ago.

KNIGHT GRANITE HILLS SHIRAZ
●●● ▶ $17

The fact that the vineyard is called Granite Hills, and is situated on the Burke & Wills Track gives some idea of the remoteness, if not the high elevation, of this vineyard. The winds which blow incessantly, and the granite soils, keep yields low and flavours generally high. In most years, the Shiraz is very spicy, but occasionally, as with the current release, spicy notes are less evident.

Cellaring 4–6 years. **Best Vintages** '81, '82, '88, '91, '92
Current Vintage '91
Matching Food Lasagne.
Tasting Note 1991 Medium red; smooth, gently sweet berry fruit and subtle oak on the bouquet. The palate has pleasant red cherry fruit, soft tannins and little or no oak impact, finishing just a little short.

KNOWLAND ESTATE WINES

NR NA AUSSD
Mudgee **Est.** 1990
Mount Vincent Road, Running Stream, NSW 2850
Ph (063) 58 8420 **Fax** (063) 58 8423
Open By appt **Production** 80
Winemaker(s) Peter Knowland
The former Mount Vincent Winery which sells much of its grape production from the 3.5 hectares of vineyards to other makers, but which proposes to increase production under its own label.
Principal Wines Shiraz, Pinot Noir.

KOMINOS WINES

★★★☆ 10–14 CD AUSSD
Granite Belt **Est.** 1976
New England Highway, Severnlea, Qld 4352
Ph (076) 83 4311 **Fax** (076) 83 4291
Open 7 days 9–4.30 **Production** 4000
Winemaker(s) Tony Comino
Tony Comino is a dedicated viticulturist and winemaker; and together with his father, battled hard to prevent ACI obtaining a monopoly on glass production in Australia, foreseeing many of the things which have in fact occurred. However, Kominos keeps a very low profile, selling all of its wine through cellar door and mailing list.
Principal Wines Chenin Blanc, Semillon, Chardonnay, Light Red, Shiraz, Cabernet Sauvignon.

KOPPAMURRA WINES

★★★★ 5.60–9.60 ML AUSSD
Coonawarra **Est.** 1973
Joanna via Naracoorte, SA 5271
Ph (08) 271 4127 **Fax** (08) 271 0726
Open By appt **Production** 2000

Winemaker(s) John Greenshields

Koppamurra has come back out of the shadows in recent years, during which time much of its grapes were sold to major Coonawarra producers. It is situated at Joanna, outside the proposed Coonawarra boundary, but the wines are very much in mainstream Coonawarra style. The current mailing list offering is representing exceptional value for money.

Principal Wines Riesling, Autumn Pick Riesling, Pinot Meunier, Naracoorte Ranges Dry Red, Cabernet Merlot, Merlot.

KOPPAMURRA CABERNET MERLOT

●●●● ▶ $10

Made from a varying blend of cabernet sauvignon, cabernet franc and merlot, with the cabernet component ranging between a low of 60% in 1993 and a high of 88% in 1991. The 1990, considered by architect turned winemaker John Greenshields to be somewhat lighter than the other years, is still available at the end of 1994, and an extraordinary bargain at $9.50. The '91 is very flavoursome but more rustic in nature.

Cellaring Up to 10 years. **Best Vintages** '82, '90, '91, '93
Current Vintage '93
Matching Food Topside steak.
Tasting Note 1993 Medium to full red-purple; a complex bouquet with a range of aromas from very ripe blackcurrant fruit to earth, to slightly spicy/chippy oak. The palate has luscious sweet berry fruit, the only question mark being that slightly resinous oak.

KOPPAMURRA MERLOT

●●●● $5.50

The label of these wines adds to the geographic confusion by describing the location of Koppamurra as in the Naracoorte Ranges, one of the possible names which may be given to the Joanna area. Be that as it may, the 1.2 hectares of merlot were planted way back in the 1970s, and this wine (released only in 375 ml bottles) is a bargain.

Cellaring 4–6 years. **Best Vintages** NA **Current Vintage** '91
Matching Food Veal shanks.
Tasting Note 1991 Medium to full red-purple; a solid, quite concentrated bouquet with leafy/briary aromas. The palate shows good varietal character of medium intensity, with leafy/earthy flavours, finishing with soft tannins.

KROEMER ESTATE

NR 6.50–15.50 CD AUSSD
Barossa Valley **Est.** 1986
Tanunda, SA 5352
Ph (085) 63 3375 **Fax** (085) 63 3758
Open 7 days 10–5 **Production** 2000
Winemaker(s) Roger Harbord (Contract)
Opened its doors on 30 June 1990 specialising with — of all unlikely grapes — sylvaner; the '86 vintage (first) has matured

surprisingly well, but subsequent attempts have been less convincing.
On the other side of the ledger, an elegant, toasty 1990 Rhine
Riesling showed Roger Harbord's skill.
Principal Wines Sylvaner, Riesling, Sparkling, Shiraz, Cabernet
Sauvignon.

KRONDORF WINES

★★★★ 9.95–14.95 R AUS104
Barossa Valley **Est.** 1978
Krondorf Road, Tanunda, SA 5352
Ph (085) 63 1245 **Fax** (085) 62 3055
Open 7 days 9–5 **Production** 120 000
Winemaker(s) Nick Walker
Part of the Mildara Blass group, with a tightly focused and controlled
range of wines. The Show Reserve Chardonnay is of exceptional
merit, but all of the wines exhibit the technical gloss and represent
the value-for-money expected of one of Australia's foremost wine-
producing groups.
Principal Wines Barossa Valley Riesling, Barossa Valley Chablis,
Chardonnay, Frontignac Spatlese, Coonawarra Hermitage, Shiraz
Cabernet; Show Reserve Chardonnay and Cabernet Sauvignon are
top-end wines.

KRONDORF CHARDONNAY

●●● ▶ $9.95
A multi-district blend made in the manner Krondorf has always made
its Chardonnays, with prolonged skin contact prior to pressing,
which leads to considerable colour and flavour development early in
the wine's life, and which can be described as 'fly now, pay later'
winemaking. It does, however, present a full-flavoured, ready-to-drink
style immediately on release.
Cellaring Drink now. **Best Vintages** NA **Current Vintage** '94
Matching Food Pasta with a creamy sauce.
Tasting Note 1994 Full yellow, with just a touch of green; lots of
broad, rich, peach, butter and melon aromas on the bouquet; full-
flavoured, ripe canned peach flavours on the palate with
toasty/buttery overtones.

KRONDORF COONAWARRA HERMITAGE

●●● ▶ $9.95
As the label says, made from Coonawarra hermitage sourced from
parent Mildara and contract growers. While not in the same league
as Wynns Coonawarra Estate or Penfolds Bin 128, it is certainly
competitively priced, well made and does show clean, if somewhat
light regional/varietal characteristics.
Cellaring Drink now. **Best Vintages** '88, '90, '91, '92
Current Vintage '92
Matching Food Pizza.
Tasting Note 1992 Medium red-purple; clean cherry and plum
fruit aromas of light to medium intensity, with subtle oak. A pleasant,
smooth cherry-flavoured wine with a soft finish, unforced by oak,
whether chips or otherwise.

KRONDORF SHOW RESERVE CABERNET SAUVIGNON
●●● ▶ $14.95

Obviously enough, the brother to the Show Reserve Chardonnay.
The style has varied somewhat over recent years, the '90 being
elegant and cedary, the '91 riper, and much more influenced by
American oak.
Cellaring 3–5 years. **Best Vintages** '88, '90
Current Vintage '91
Matching Food Beef Wellington.
Tasting Note 1991 Medium red-purple; soft, textured red berry
fruit is present, but the predominant aromas are of tangy lemon and
vanilla oak. The same American oak influence is very evident on the
palate, which finishes with soft tannins.

KRONDORF SHOW RESERVE CHARDONNAY
●●●●● $14.95

Made from a blend of McLaren Vale, Barossa Valley and Eden
Valley chardonnay which is given some skin contact before
fermentation is initiated in tank. Part way through fermentation the
wine is transferred to a mix of new Nevers, Limousin, Allier and
Vosges hogsheads. The '93 vintage is a multiple gold medal winner.
Cellaring 2–3 years. **Best Vintages** '90, '92, '93
Current Vintage '93
Matching Food Smoked breast of turkey.
Tasting Note 1993 Medium to full yellow-green; rich, full peach,
fig and melon fruit aromas with an obvious toasty barrel ferment oak
contribution to the bouquet. The palate is rich, but not excessively
forced, with abundant melon and peach flavours, finishing with
good intensity and length. Very much a show stopper style.

KYEEMA ESTATE

★★★★ 10–14 CD AUSSD
Canberra **Est.** 1986
PO Box 282, Belconnen, ACT 2616
Ph (06) 254 7557 (AH)
Open 7 days 10–5 The Wine Press tel (06) 230 2430
Production 450
Winemaker(s) Andrew McEwin
Part-time winemaker, part-time wine critic (with *Winewise* magazine)
Andrew McEwin had a golden year in 1994, winning four trophies
in regional shows for his 1992 red wines. Every wine made since
1986 has won a show award of some description.
Principal Wines Chardonnay, Semillon, Cabernet Merlot.

KYEEMA ESTATE CABERNET MERLOT
●●● ▶ $14

Although it only received a silver medal at the 1994 Yass Show,
accumulated three trophies for the Best Table Wine of Show,
Best Red Table Wine of Show and Best Bordeaux Blend of Show.
Cellaring 3–5 years. **Best Vintages** '87, '88, '89, '90, '92
Current Vintage '92

Matching Food Steak and kidney pie.
Tasting Note 1992 Medium red-purple; a clean bouquet with
solid dark berry/briary fruit and subtle oak. A chunky, briary wine
on the palate with blackberry and blackcurrant on the mid palate
before dipping slightly on the finish.

KYEEMA ESTATE CHARDONNAY
●●● ▶ $14
As with all the Kyeema wines, sourced from vineyards in the
Canberra region. The '93 vintage is ageing gracefully and was a
silver medal winner at the 1994 Yass Show, and the second highest
pointed wine at that show.
Cellaring 3–4 years. **Best Vintages** '88, '89, '91, '92, '93
Current Vintage '93
Matching Food Dim sim.
Tasting Note 1993 Light yellow-green; the bouquet is fairly light
with faintly minty characters, with a hint of slightly raw oak in the
background. The palate, however, has good mouthfeel and balance,
showing competent winemaking, with the promise of further
improvement as the wine ages.

KYEEMA ESTATE SHIRAZ
●●●● $14
By far the best credentialled of the Kyeema wines, being the top
gold in the Open Shiraz Class at the 1994 Cowra Wine Show
(which is effectively a national show) and being the highest pointed
wine from the Canberra region, thus winning the trophy for Best
Regional Red Table Wine.
Cellaring 5 years. **Best Vintages** '87, '88, '89, '90, '92
Current Vintage '92
Matching Food Braised beef.
Tasting Note 1992 Medium to full red-purple; the bouquet is very
strong, with earthy/briary/chocolate aromas, with similar rich and
concentrated flavours on the palate. There seems to me to be a touch
of aldehyde in the wine, but clearly other judges do not agree.

LA PROVENCE VINEYARDS

NR 17–21 CD AUSSD
Tamar Valley **Est.** 1956
407 Lalla Road, Lalla, Tas 7267
Ph (003) 95 1290
Open By appt **Production** 200
Winemaker(s) Andrew Hood (Contract)
La Provence incorporates the pioneer vineyard of Frenchman Jean
Miguet, now owned by Stuart and Kay Bryce who purchased it in
1980 and who have expanded the original 1.3-hectare vineyard to
a little over 3 hectares as well as grafting over unsuitable grenache
and cabernet (left from the original plantings) to chardonnay, pinot
noir and semillon.
Principal Wines Semillon, Chardonnay, Pinot Noir.

LAANECOORIE

★★★☆ 16.95 R AUS1
Pyrenees **Est.** 1982
Bendigo Road, Betley, Vic 3472
Ph (054) 68 7260 **Fax** (054) 68 7388
Open Not **Production** 1500
Winemaker(s) John Ellis (Contract)
John McQuilten's 4-hectare vineyard produces grapes of consistently
high quality, and competent contract winemaking by John Ellis at
Hanging Rock has done the rest.
Principal Wines A single Bordeaux-blend dry red of Cabernet
Franc, Cabernet Sauvignon and Merlot in roughly equal proportions.

LADBROKE GROVE WINES

NR 8–14 CD AUS68, 173
Coonawarra **Est.** 1982
Coonawarra Road, Penola, SA 5277
Ph (087) 37 2997 **Fax** (087) 62 3236
Open 7 days 9–4 **Production** 800
Winemaker(s) Ken Ward
Has been relaunched with the Blue Label and Gold Label Shiraz
after a hiatus; wine quality has been variable, but it does have
2 hectares of hand-pruned shiraz planted by John Redman in the
1960s upon which to draw.
Principal Wines Riesling, Late Picked Riesling, Blue Label Shiraz,
Gold Label Shiraz.

LAKE BARRINGTON ESTATE *

NR 14–18 CD AUSSD
Northern Tasmania **Est.** 1988
Old Wilmot Road, Sheffield, Tas 7306
Ph (004) 91 1249 **Fax** (003) 34 2892
Open W'ends 10–5 **Production** 1000
Winemaker(s) Steve Lubiana (Contract)
Lake Barrington Estate is owned by Roger and Marie Taylor, and
takes its name from the adjacent Lake Barrington, 30 kilometres
south of Devonport, on the northern coast of Tasmania. There are
picnic facilities at the vineyard, and, needless to say, the scenery
is very beautiful.
Principal Wines Riesling, Chardonnay, Pinot Noir, Cabernet
Sauvignon.

LAKE BREEZE WINES

★★★★☆ 8–14 CD AUSSD
Langhorne Creek **Est.** 1987
Step Road, Langhorne Creek, SA 5255
Ph (085) 37 3017 **Fax** (085) 37 3267
Open 7 days 10–5 **Production** 3500

Winemaker(s) Greg Follett
The Folletts have been farmers at Langhorne Creek since 1880, grape growers since the 1930s. Since 1987 a small proportion of their grapes has been made into wine, and a cellar door sales facility was opened in early 1991. The quality of the early releases has been exemplary.
Principal Wines Chardonnay, White Frontignac, Cabernet Sauvignon, Cabernet Merlot, Shiraz, Bernoota (Cabernet Shiraz), Tawny Port.

LAKE BREEZE BERNOOTA
●●●●● $11
A blend of 60% cabernet sauvignon and 40% shiraz, drawn from the large Follett family vineyards. Strong American oak has tended to dominate the '89 and '90 vintages, but the '92 is a superb wine in which the lush fruit more than stands up to the oak.
Cellaring 10+ years. **Best Vintages** '87, '88, '90, '92, '93
Current Vintage '92
Matching Food Rich game or steak.
Tasting Note 1992 Dense purple-red; very concentrated, powerful briary, earthy, minty aromas lead on to a powerful yet classically structured and balanced palate with lots of berry fruit of perfect ripeness, with soft, fine-grained tannins running throughout.

LAKE BREEZE CABERNET SAUVIGNON
●●●● $14
The pick of the crop from 20 hectares of cabernet sauvignon, most of which is sold to leading winemakers such as Mildara Blass. The yet-to-be-released '92 vintage had won six gold medals at major wine shows as at the end of 1994, and promises even better things in store.
Cellaring 5–10 years. **Best Vintages** '87, '88, '90, '92, '93
Current Vintage '90
Matching Food Smoked kangaroo fillet.
Tasting Note 1990 Medium red-purple; fairly potent vanillin/coconut American oak drives the bouquet with some quite rich blackcurrant fruit in the background. An extremely generous, full-bodied soft wine in the mouth with rich, essency fruit and oak, finishing with soft tannins.

LAKE GEORGE WINERY
★★★☆ 15–20 R AUSSD
Canberra **Est.** 1971
Federal Highway, Collector, NSW 2581
Ph (048) 48 0039
Open Not **Production** 700
Winemaker(s) Dr Edgar F Riek
Dr Edgar Riek is an inquisitive, iconoclastic winemaker who is not content with his role as Godfather and founder of the Canberra district, forever experimenting and innovating. His fortified wines, vintaged in North East Victoria but matured at Lake George, are

very good. A 1991 Pinot Noir tasted in 1994 showed attractive and
quite complex strawberry fruit.
Principal Wines Chardonnay, Semillon, Pinot Noir, Cabernet
Sauvignon, Merlot, fortifieds.

LAKE'S FOLLY

★★★★★ 29 CD AUS51, 173, 175, UK52
Hunter Valley **Est.** 1963
Broke Road, Pokolbin, NSW 2321
Ph (049) 98 7507 **Fax** (049) 98 7322
Open Mon–Sat 10–4 **Production** 4800
Winemaker(s) Stephen Lake
The first of the weekend wineries to produce wines for commercial
sale, long revered for its Cabernet Sauvignon and thereafter its
Chardonnay. Very properly, terroir and climate produce a distinct
regional influence, and thereby a distinctive wine style. Some find
this attractive, others are less tolerant.
Principal Wines Chardonnay, Cabernet Sauvignon.

LAKE'S FOLLY CABERNET SAUVIGNON
●●●● ▶ $29
Like Max Lake himself, never far from controversy; again like Max
Lake, full of earthy personality. It is not a wine which can or should
be judged by conventional standards; if it were to be so treated, the
judgment would not do the wine justice.
Cellaring 4–15 years. **Best Vintages** '69, '75, '81, '87, '89,
'91, '93 **Current Vintage** '93
Matching Food Rabbit, hare.
Tasting Note 1993 Medium red-purple; clean and smooth, with a
characteristic vineyard dark plum fruit character; elegant and of light
to medium intensity. The palate is spotlessly clean, with plummy fruit,
subtle oak and soft tannins.

LAKE'S FOLLY CHARDONNAY
●●●● ▶ $29
Only 1200 cases a year (with some seasonal variation) are made
from estate-grown grapes. The wine is invariably correct in style, and
— unlike the Cabernet — should cause no discussion or argument.
Cellaring 3–6 years. **Best Vintages** '81, '82, '83, '84, '86, '89,
'92, '94 **Current Vintage** '93
Matching Food Sweetbreads.
Tasting Note 1993 Medium yellow-green; a quite tight and
powerful bouquet with toasty/smoky fermentation aromas
reminiscent of the Tyrrell's '93 Vat 47. The palate is generous with
similar peachy fruit, a hint of toast and vanillin oak.

LALLA GULLY VINEYARD

NR 16–18 R AUSSD
Northern Tasmania **Est.** 1988
Brooks Road, Lalla, Tas 7250
Ph (003) 31 2325

Open By appt **Production** 300
Winemaker(s) Andrew Hood (Contract)
Owners Rod and Kim Ascui have established one hectare each of
pinot noir, chardonnay and sauvignon blanc, producing the first tiny
crop in 1992; Sauvignon Blanc was due to come into production in
1995.
Principal Wines Chardonnay, Pinot Noir.

LAMONT WINES

★★★★ 6–12 CD AUSSD
Swan Valley **Est.** 1978
Bisdee Road, Millendon, WA 6056
Ph (09) 296 4485 **Fax** (09) 296 1663
Open Wed–Sun 10–4 **Production** 4000
Winemaker(s) Corin Lamont
Corin Lamont is the daughter of the late Jack Mann, and makes her
wines in the image of those her father used to make, resplendent in
their generosity. Lamont also boasts a superb restaurant, with a
gallery for the sale and promotion of local arts.
Principal Wines White Burgundy, Chardonnay, Sweet White,
Cabernet Rosé, Cabernet Merlot, fortifieds, including Flor Fino,
Amontillado and Reserve Sherry (Oloroso style).

LARK HILL WINERY

★★★★☆ 12–18 CD AUSSD
Canberra **Est.** 1978
RMB 281 Gundaroo Road, Bungendore, NSW 2621
Ph (06) 238 1393 **Fax** (06) 238 1393
Open Thurs–Mon 10–5 **Production** 2500
Winemaker(s) Dr David Carpenter, Sue Carpenter
The Lark Hill Vineyard is situated at an altitude of 860 metres, level
with the observation deck on Black Mountain Tower, and offering
splendid views of the Lake George Escarpment. Right from the outset,
David and Sue Carpenter have made wines of real quality, style and
elegance.
Principal Wines Riesling, Chardonnay, Auslese Riesling, Pinot
Noir, Sparkling, Cabernet Merlot.

LARK HILL CABERNET MERLOT

●●●●● $16
A blend of cabernet sauvignon, cabernet franc and merlot which
does best in warmer vintages such as 1991; the wine rating is
given for this specific vintage, indeed. Overall, the move at Lark Hill
is towards the earlier-ripening varieties, but it has produced some
lovely Cabernet Merlots over the years, this being one of the
best.
Cellaring 4–7 years. **Best Vintages** '88, '91, '92, '93, '94
Current Vintage '91
Matching Food Rabbit, hare.

Tasting Note 1991 Medium red-purple; moderately ripe, chocolate and red berry fruit marry with dusty, sweet oak on the bouquet. The palate is complex and mouthfilling, with abundant ripe blackcurrant fruit rounded off with quite lovely soft and round tannins. Just delicious.

LARK HILL CHARDONNAY
●●●● $18
Chardonnay occupies a major portion of the 4-hectare estate vineyard (with a 2-hectare satellite on a neighbouring property). The wines are barrel fermented, and are taken through malolactic fermentation to produce a textured, complex style away from primary fruit flavours.
Cellaring 3–6 years. **Best Vintages** '88, '91, '92, '93, '94
Current Vintage '93
Matching Food Crispy chicken.
Tasting Note 1993 Medium yellow-green; strong, textured malolactic and barrel ferment secondary aromas lead logically on to a palate with pronounced stony/minerally/mealy flavours which work very well. A wine with a more European than Australian feel to it.

LARK HILL RIESLING
●●●● ▶ $14
Over the past four years the Lark Hill Rieslings have accumulated a trophy, two gold, two silver and six bronze medals in wine shows. The 1994 was the top gold medal against Australia's best Rieslings in Class 1 at the Cowra Wine Show (open nationally). The tasting note is for the wine as at that show; note that some bottles show a slightly pink tinge.
Cellaring 3–5 years. **Best Vintages** '88, '91, '92, '93, '94
Current Vintage '94
Matching Food Gazpacho.
Tasting Note 1994 Light straw-green; clean citrus and passion fruit aromas of light to medium intensity. The intensity steps up markedly on the palate, which has excellent length to the dry crisp finish.

LATARA WINES
NR 9.50–11 CD AUSSD
Hunter Valley **Est.** 1979
Cnr McDonalds & Deaseys Roads, Pokolbin, NSW 2320
Ph (049) 98 7320
Open Sat 9–5, Sun 9–4 **Production** 250
Winemaker(s) Iain Riggs (Contract)
The bulk of the grapes produced on the 5-hectare Latara vineyard, which was planted in 1979, are sold to Brokenwood. A small quantity is vinified for Latara and sold under its label. As one would expect, the wines are very competently made, and are of show medal standard.
Principal Wines Semillon, Cabernet Sauvignon, Shiraz.

LAUREN BROOK WINERY *

★★★☆ 12–12.50 CD AUSSD
Warren Valley **Est.** 1993
Eedle Terra, Bridgetown, WA 6255
Ph (097) 61 1676
Open W'ends, Public hols 11–5 **Production** 250
Winemaker(s) Stephen Bulleid
Lauren Brook is established on the banks of the beautiful Blackwood
River, and is the only commercial winery in the Bridgetown
subregion of Mount Barker. An 80-year-old barn on the property
has been renovated to contain a micro winery and a small gallery.
There is one hectare of estate chardonnay coming into bearing,
supplemented by grapes purchased locally.
Principal Wines Riesling, Bridgetown Blend (Riesling, Taminga,
Traminer).

LAUREN BROOK RIESLING

●●●● $12.50
Where Stephen Bulleid learnt his winemaking I do not know, but
wherever, he has learnt it well, for this is a very well made wine
which shows Mount Barker riesling to best effect.
Cellaring 3–5 years. **Best Vintages** NA **Current Vintage** '94
Matching Food Chinese stir-fry.
Tasting Note 1994 Very light green-yellow; a fine, highly
aromatic bouquet with passionfruit/lime aromas. There is lovely fruit
on the palate, with similar lime and passionfruit flavours; it does
finish with a fair degree of residual sugar sweetness, no doubt
deliberate given the cellar door clientele.

LAWSON HILL WINES

★★☆ 5–14 CD AUS51
Mudgee **Est.** 1985
Henry Lawson Drive, Eurunderee, Mudgee, NSW 2850
Ph (063) 73 3953 **Fax** (063) 73 3948
Open 7 days 9.30–5.30 **Production** 2000
Winemaker(s) Various Contract & José Grace
Former music director and arranger (for musical acts in Sydney
clubs) José Grace and wife June run a strongly tourist-oriented
operation situated next door to the Henry Lawson Memorial, offering
a kaleidoscopic array of wines, produced from 8 hectares of
vineyard, and made under contract.
Principal Wines Chardonnay, Verdelho, Sauvignon Blanc,
Riesling, Traminer Riesling, Gewurztraminer, Merlot, Pinot Noir,
Port.

LEASINGHAM WINES

★★★★☆ 5.95–18 R AUS20–24 US8
Clare Valley **Est.** 1893
7 Dominic Street, Clare, SA 5453
Ph (088) 42 2555 **Fax** (088) 42 3293

Open Mon–Fri 8.30–5.30, W'ends 10–4 **Production** 95 000
Winemaker(s) Richard Rowe

Successive big-company ownerships and various peregrinations in labelling and branding have not resulted in any permanent loss of identity or quality. With a core of high-quality, aged vineyards to draw on, Leasingham is in fact going from strength to strength under BRL Hardys direction.

Principal Wines Top end: Classic Clare Shiraz, Classic Clare Cabernet Sauvignon; mid range: Bin 37 Chardonnay, Bin 56 Cabernet Malbec, Bin 61 Shiraz; main range: Riesling, Semillon; low-priced: Hutt Creek Riesling, Sauvignon Blanc, Shiraz Cabernet, Riesling.

LEASINGHAM BIN 56 CABERNET MALBEC
●●●● $9.95

The blend of cabernet sauvignon and malbec has been a Clare Valley specialty for decades; anyone lucky enough to have the '71 Bin 56 or virtually any of Wendouree's Cabernet Malbecs will need no persuasion of the merits of the blend. The '92 vintage of this wine has won three gold medals, and continues the line.
Cellaring 7–12 years. **Best Vintages** '88, '90, '91, '92, '94
Current Vintage '92
Matching Food Jugged hare.
Tasting Note 1992 Medium red-purple; a solid bouquet crammed with dark plum and berry fruit, with lots of vanillin oak. In the mouth, a big, dense chewy wine with dark briary/berry fruit, a touch of plum but threatened by the vanillin American oak which needs to come back into the wine.

LEASINGHAM BIN 61 SHIRAZ
●●●● $9.95

A junior brother to the Classic Clare, with less weight and extract, and seemingly relying upon the use of some oak chips as well as barrels. The quality of Clare Valley shiraz is still very evident, and the wine is exceptionally well priced.
Cellaring 5–10 years. **Best Vintages** '88, '90, '91, '92, '94
Current Vintage '92
Matching Food Spiced lamb kebabs.
Tasting Note 1992 Medium to full red-purple; concentrated, rich briary/plum pudding dark fruits with spicy oak on the bouquet. An extremely rich and concentrated palate, with lush fruit, a chewy mid palate, finishing with slightly resinous oak.

LEASINGHAM CLASSIC CLARE CABERNET SAUVIGNON
●●●● ▸ $18

Like peas in a pod with the Classic Clare Shiraz, a massively — at times dauntingly — powerful wine with layer upon layer of fruit and layer upon layer of American oak, bound together with lashings of tannin and extract. In many ways, a throwback to older times. Trophy winner at the 1994 Rutherglen Wine Show.
Cellaring 10–20 years. **Best Vintages** '88, '90, '91, '92, '94
Current Vintage '92
Matching Food Leave it in the cellar.

Tasting Note 1992 Medium to full red-purple; dense blackberry fruit with very potent lemon and vanilla American oak. A massive wine on the palate with red berry fruits and chewy vanillin oak, finishing with formidable tannins.

LEASINGHAM CLASSIC CLARE SHIRAZ
●●●● ▶ $18

The best Clare Valley shiraz available to Leasingham is matured in (real) new American oak barrels, consistently producing a wine of tremendous depth and richness. Even though the '93 vintage is not rated by Leasingham as among the best five of the past two decades, it won the trophy for Best Dry Red table wine from the 1993 vintage (against all varieties) at the 1994 National Wine Show of Australia.

Cellaring 10–15 years. **Best Vintages** '88, '90, '91, '92, '94
Current Vintage '92
Matching Food Kangaroo, strong red meat, strong cheese.
Tasting Note 1992 Dense purple-red; concentrated fruit running the full gamut through dark berry, dark chocolate and mint backed by masses of vanillin oak. The palate is as potent as the bouquet suggests, with an enormous depth of fruit and oak, with chewy tannins running throughout. Needs a decade.

LEASINGHAM RIESLING
●●●● ▶ $9

Always a steady and honest performer, as one would expect from a Clare Valley Riesling, the wine hit the high spots with the '94 vintage, which won the top gold medal in Class 1 at the 1994 Canberra National Wine Show of Australia.

Cellaring Up to 7 years. **Best Vintages** '84, '86, '87, '90, '94
Current Vintage '94
Matching Food Blue swimmer crab.
Tasting Note 1994 Light straw-green; classic Clare style with refined toasty aromas and a hint of spice, the latter coming from the fruit and not from enzymes. Crisp, clean and toasty on the palate, with just a hint of lime and passionfruit lurking in the background; should develop superbly.

LECONFIELD

★★★★ 12–18 R AUS11, 56, 61, 64, 111, 116
Coonawarra **Est.** 1974
Main Penola-Naracoorte Road, Coonawarra, SA 5263
Ph (087) 37 2326 **Fax** (087) 37 2285
Open 7 days 9–5 **Production** 38 000 (including contract)
Winemaker(s) Ralph Fowler

The rating is something of a compromise between the best and the least of the Leconfield wines, which seem to reflect in no uncertain fashion the swings and roundabouts of vintage variation. This, it must be said, has not slowed down sales, which have forced early release of many of the wines.

Principal Wines Riesling, Chardonnay (Wooded and Unwooded), Shiraz, Cabernet Sauvignon.

LECONFIELD CABERNET SAUVIGNON
●●●● $18

Many great Leconfield Cabernet Sauvignons have appeared over the years, the '78 and '80 vintages being landmarks of the time (made by octogenarian Sydney Hamilton, Leconfield's founder). The vintages throughout the '90s tend to show pronounced herbaceous/dimethyl sulphide characters which will appeal to some more than others.

Cellaring 5–7 years. **Best Vintages** '80, '82, '88, '90
Current Vintage '93
Matching Food Yearling steak, mild cheddar.
Tasting Note 1993 Medium to full red-purple; distinct leafy/cedary/gamey fruit aromas with nicely balanced French and American oak. The palate is in the same fairly pungent, leafy mode with soft tannins and nicely modulated oak.

LECONFIELD SHIRAZ
●●●● $16

A wine which is not produced every vintage, but only in those years in which the fruit is judged to have gained sufficient ripeness and depth. It is said to be matured in mature oak casks, but they appear to have retained a lot of their punch, and a little less American oak influence might make for an even better wine.

Cellaring 4–6 years. **Best Vintages** '88, '90, '91, '93
Current Vintage '93
Matching Food Beef casserole.
Tasting Note 1993 Medium to full red-purple; abundant sweet vanillin aromas, predominantly oak-driven, lead on to the rich palate with some sweet berry fruit and full-throated American oak.

LECONFIELD UNWOODED CHARDONNAY
●●● ▸ $14.95

Made in very much a sign of the times, released earlier than the barrel fermented (and typically elegant) wooded version from Leconfield. It will be interesting to see how the better of the current crop of unwooded Chardonnays mature in bottle, even though they are undoubtedly intended for consumption immediately upon release.

Cellaring Drink now. **Best Vintages** NA **Current Vintage** '94
Matching Food Robe lobster.
Tasting Note 1994 Light yellow-green; a clean, light and crisp bouquet, uninfluenced by aromatic yeasts. On the palate, crisp and clean, with light melon and white peach fruit, with good acidity and length.

LEEUWIN ESTATE

★★★★★ 12.85–45 R AUS63, 64, 113, UK32 US2
Margaret River **Est.** 1974
Gnarawary Road, Margaret River, WA 6285
Ph (09) 430 4099 **Fax** (09) 430 5687
Open 7 days 10.30–4.30 **Production** 35 000

Winemaker(s) Bob Cartwright

Leeuwin Estate's Chardonnay is, in my opinion, Australia's finest example based on the wines of the last 15 years. The Cabernet Sauvignon, too, is an excellent wine with great style and character. Almost inevitably, the other wines in the portfolio are not in the same Olympian class.

Principal Wines Art Series Chardonnay, Riesling, Sauvignon Blanc, Pinot Noir, Cabernet Sauvignon; Prelude Chardonnay, Pinot Noir, Cabernet Sauvignon are significantly lower-priced alternatives, with a non-vintage Prelude blended white the cheapest wine on the list.

LEEUWIN ESTATE ART SERIES CABERNET SAUVIGNON

●●●●● $26.50

Invariably lean and elegant wines which take many years to show their best, making no concessions to the more typical softly fruity Australian commercial red wine styles.

Cellaring 10+ years. **Best Vintages** '79, '86, '87, '89, '90
Current Vintage '90
Matching Food Eye fillet of lamb.
Tasting Note 1990 Full red-purple; the bouquet is of medium ripeness with blackcurrant and cherry fruit aromas. The palate has lots of sweet blackcurrant/cassis and plum fruit balanced by fine, cedary tannins. Gives the impression that it will mature slightly quicker than its predecessors, but be none the worse for that, and is the product of an unusually good vintage.

LEEUWIN ESTATE ART SERIES CHARDONNAY

●●●●● $45

The core of the Art Series Chardonnay is Block 20 (one of five blocks on the estate) with yields never exceeding 2.5 tonnes to the acre, and frequently less than 2 tonnes. Barrel fermentation in the finest French oak, and prolonged bottle maturation do the rest.

Cellaring 7–12 years. **Best Vintages** '80, '81, '82, '83, '85, '87, '89, '90, '92 **Current Vintage** '92
Matching Food Richer veal, chicken dishes.
Tasting Note 1992 Light to medium yellow-green; a wonderfully elegant yet intense bouquet with hallmark Burgundian overtones to the citrus and melon fruit. The palate is extraordinarily intense, powerful and long, with potent grapefruit and melon fruit interwoven with subtle oak. Leeuwin at its best.

LEFROY BROOK WINES

NR 21.95 R AUSSD
Warren Valley **Est.** 1986
Glauder Road, Pemberton, WA 6260
Ph (09) 386 8385
Open Not **Production** 600
Winemaker(s) Peter Fimmel (Contract)
Owned by Perth residents Pat and Barbara Holt, the former a graduate in biochemistry and microbiology working in medical

research, but with a passion for Burgundy. The 1.5 hectares of vines are now both netted and fenced with steel mesh, producing wines which, on tastings to date, are outside the mainstream.
Principal Wines Chardonnay, Pinot Noir.

LELAND ESTATE

NR 10–19 CD AUSSD
Adelaide Hills **Est.** 1986
PO Lenswood, SA 5240
Ph (08) 389 6928
Open Not **Production** 750
Winemaker(s) Rob Cootes
Former Yalumba senior winemaker Rob Cootes, with a Master of Science Degree, deliberately opted out of mainstream life when he established Leland Estate, living in a split-level, one-roomed house built from timber salvaged from trees killed in the Ash Wednesday bushfires.
Principal Wines Sauvignon Blanc (piercingly pure and fragrant), Pinot Noir, Neudorf Adele (Sparkling).

LENNARDS BROOK ESTATE *

★★★★ NA AUSSD
Darling Range **Est.** 1993
Lennards Road, Gingin, WA 6503 **Ph** NA
Open By appt **Production** 750
Winemaker(s) Barbara Potter
Former nurse Barbara Potter and son-in-law Ian Atkinson run Lennards Brook Estate, which produces 40 tonnes a year of grapes, two-thirds of which are sold to Houghton under long-term contract. In 1993 the decision was taken to make one-third of the output into wine, and the beautiful labels came into being. The Late Harvest Verdelho caused much comment on debut in late 1993, but it was the dry Verdelho which swept all before it at the 1994 Mount Barker Show.
Principal Wines Chardonnay, Verdelho, Fine White, Late Harvest Verdelho.

LENNARDS BROOK ESTATE VERDELHO
●●●●● $NA
One of two very good wines made by Lennards Brook entered in the 1994 Mount Barker Wine Show, the other being its 1994 Fine White. The Verdelho received the ultimate accolade from Swan Valley veteran John Kosovich, who knows more about the variety than most, and received a gold medal competing against both Houghton and Moondah Brook, to which is sells much of its grapes.
Cellaring Up to 5 years. **Best Vintages** '94
Current Vintage '94
Matching Food Pan-fried veal.
Tasting Note 1994 Light green-yellow; intense, fragrant tropical/honeysuckle aromas with a little free sulphur dioxide which

blew off. A very concentrated wine on the palate with more of the fruit salad flavours of verdelho, with a particularly rich mid palate and long finish.

LENSWOOD VINEYARD *

★★★★★ 18.50–28.90 R AUS14, 93, 103, 110, 112, 113, 164, 184

Adelaide Hills **Est.** 1981

c/o Tim Knappstein Wines, 2 Pioneer Avenue, Clare, SA 5453

Ph (088) 42 2600 **Fax** (088) 42 3831

Open 7 days 9–5 at Tim Knappstein **Production** 3000

Winemaker(s) Tim Knappstein

With new labels introduced in 1994, Lenswood Vineyard has been given its own distinct identity, which it most certainly deserves. While owned by Tim and Annie Knappstein, it has an entirely distinct vineyard base (with part of the grapes being sold back to Tim Knappstein Wines) and is separately distributed.

Principal Wines Chardonnay, Semillon, Pinot Noir (and under Tim Knappstein label Fumé Blanc).

LENSWOOD VINEYARD CHARDONNAY

●●●●● $27.25

Produced from 2.2 hectares of estate vineyards planted in 1981 and 1984. Only the best wine is chosen for release under the new Lenswood Vineyard label, the remainder being used to support the Tim Knappstein-labelled Chardonnay. The few releases to date have been of very high quality.

Cellaring Up to 5 years. **Best Vintages** '93, '94

Current Vintage '93

Matching Food Terrine of smoked salmon.

Tasting Note 1993 Light to medium yellow-green; a complex bouquet with fig, melon, white peach and cashew all intermingling, with subtle barrel ferment oak input. The palate is unusually elegant and textured, with creamy notes showing an obvious malolactic fermentation influence; finishing with gently toasty oak and good acidity.

LENSWOOD VINEYARD PINOT NOIR

●●●●● $28.90

Since a stellar debut in 1990 has been quite outstanding, significantly outperforming other producers in the region, and leaving no doubt that the Lenswood area will in time become a most important producer of Pinot Noir. As Tim Knappstein himself observes, the style is fuller than that of the Yarra Valley, more akin to Geelong and Bannockburn. Nonetheless it is unmistakably varietal.

Cellaring 2–5 years. **Best Vintages** '91, '93, '94

Current Vintage '93

Matching Food Quail, hare.

Tasting Note 1993 Medium to full red-purple; very concentrated, stylish with briary/sappy overtones, obvious whole bunch component, and very good use of oak. The palate is immense by the standards of Pinot Noir, yet is not forced or extractive. There are lots of plum, spice and briar flavours, the finish firm but long. Outstanding.

LENTON BRAE ESTATE

NR 13.50–16.50 CD AUS70, 166
Margaret River **Est.** 1983
Willyabrup Valley, Margaret River, WA 6285
Ph (097) 55 6255 **Fax** (097) 55 6268
Open 7 days 10–6 **Production** 6500
Winemaker(s) William Shields
Former architect and town planner Bruce Tomlinson has built a strikingly beautiful winery, but will not stand for criticism of his wines. The 1994 Sauvignon Blanc, clean, crisp and typical of the Margaret River, does not need any criticism.
Principal Wines Chardonnay, Semillon Sauvignon Blanc, Sauvignon Blanc, Cabernet Sauvignon, Cabernet Merlot.

LENTON BRAE SEMILLON SAUVIGNON BLANC
●●● ▶ $13.95
An estate-grown made in mainstream Margaret River style with fruit rather than oak dominant.
Cellaring 1–3 years. **Best Vintages** NA **Current Vintage** '94
Matching Food Fresh asparagus.
Tasting Note 1994 Medium yellow-green; the bouquet is of medium to full intensity with clean, clearly articulated fruit, gently herbaceous. The palate is of medium weight with the Semillon component dominant, finishing crisp, clean and dry.

LEO BURING

★★★★★ 8.30–17 R AUS147, UK83
Barossa Valley **Est.** 1931
Seppeltsfield via Tanunda, SA 5352
Ph (085) 63 2184 **Fax** (085) 63 2804
Open Mon–Fri 8.30–5, Sat 10.30–4.30, Sun 11–4
Production NFP
Winemaker(s) Geoff Henriks
Earns its 5-star rating by virtue of being Australia's foremost producer of Rieslings over a 30-year period, with a rich legacy left by former winemaker John Vickery. But it also has the disconcerting habit of bobbing up here and there with very good wines made from other varieties, even if not so consistently.
Principal Wines A complicated, indeed Byzantine, mix of sub-brands, varieties and bin numbers. Apart from Class Aged Releases, top wines are Leonay Watervale Riesling and Eden Valley Riesling with changing Bin numbers; next come a range of varietal wines, some with Bin numbers, some without, most with a regional base, including Barossa Valley Riesling, Eden Valley Sauvignon Blanc, Eden Valley Chardonnay, Coonawarra Chardonnay, Coonawarra/Barossa Cabernet Sauvignon; then Semillon Chardonnay and Bin number Cabernet Sauvignon.

LEO BURING BIN DR505 CABERNET SAUVIGNON
●●●● $14.95

A blend of 57% Coonawarra and 43% Barossa Valley cabernet, the latter component grown on an estate-owned vineyard in the Valley. It is matured in a mix of new and one-year-old American and French oak hogsheads for 15 months, maturation which imparts a great deal of oak character to the wine, with the American portion predominant. The current vintage of 1991 won five gold medals in shows between 1992 and 1993.

Cellaring 5–8 years. **Best Vintages** '86, '88, '90, '91, '92
Current Vintage '91
Matching Food Mature cheddar.
Tasting Note 1991 Medium to full red-purple; a generous, full bouquet with lots of sweet, chocolatey fruit with lashings of vanillin oak. An extremely ripe, full-flavoured wine on the palate, with abundant fruit matched by abundant coconut vanillin oak.

LEO BURING BIN DW33 WATERVALE RIESLING
●●● ▶ $8.30

The basic Riesling in the Leo Buring range sourced from the Clare Valley, and in particular the Watervale subdistrict. While not in the class of the best Leo Buring wines, is extremely honest, with generous flavour, and will in fact repay medium-term cellaring.

Cellaring Up to 5 years. **Best Vintages** NA
Current Vintage '94
Matching Food Char-grilled octopus.
Tasting Note 1994 Light to medium yellow-green; solid, fractionally heavy lime and toast aromas lead on to a generously flavoured wine with plenty of riesling fruit and well balanced residual sugar to flesh the wine out.

LEO BURING BIN DWT18 RIESLING
●●●● $9.50

Bin DWT18 is a constant bin number, which does not change from one year to the next, but its regional source can and does. Thus the 1991 was a blend of 55% Eden Valley and 45% Barossa Valley material, while the '92, '93 and '94 vintages are pure Eden Valley wines. The '92 won the Collotype Trophy at the Adelaide Wine Show for Best Varietal White Table Wine in 1992, a remarkable performance for a wine selling for less than $10.

Cellaring 3–7 years. **Best Vintages** '90, '91, '92, '94
Current Vintage '94
Matching Food Sugar-cured tuna.
Tasting Note 1994 Light green-yellow; clean, crisp, youthful and fresh, with gentle lime fruit leads on to a firm, long and relatively unevolved palate with good ageing potential.

LEO BURING LEONAY EDEN VALLEY RIESLING
●●●●● $16.50

Classic Eden Valley Rieslings have been made by Leo Buring for many decades, but it was not until 1991 that the decision was taken to release the two top Rieslings of each year — one from Watervale

and one from the Eden Valley — under the Leonay label. The grapes
come from long-term contract growers throughout the Eden Valley.
Cellaring 10–15 years. **Best Vintages** '70, '72, '75, '77, '79,
'90, '92 **Current Vintage** '90
Matching Food Asparagus and salmon salad.
Tasting Note 1990 Bin DWT17. Light to medium yellow-green; a
firm, tight, fresh and crisp bouquet in classic style. The palate is
bright and fresh, with quite intense lime flavours, a hint of
passionfruit; good balance and length.

LEO BURING LEONAY WATERVALE RIESLING
●●●●● $16.50
Leonay is the flagship release of the Leo Buring Rhine Riesling range
(other than the classic aged Show Releases). Once sourced from the
Florita Vineyard, which in a moment of corporate distraction was
sold (to Jim Barry Wines), the wine now comes from contract grape
growers in the same region, and the inheritance of John Vickery lives
on. The wine had won two gold and five silver medals early in its
career.
Cellaring 10–15 years. **Best Vintages** '72, '75, '88, '90, '91
Current Vintage '91
Matching Food Scallop and crab terrine.
Tasting Note 1991 Bin DWU13. Medium yellow-green; clean,
well balanced, tight and intense aromas of herb, lime and mint. An
outstanding palate with weight and mouthfeel similar to the '88, with
generous flavours and a soft finish.

LESNIK FAMILY WINERY

NR 9.95–14.95 CD AUSSD
Hunter Valley **Est.** 1986
Branxton Road, Pokolbin, NSW 2321
Ph (049) 98 7755 **Fax** (049) 98 7750
Open 7 days 9–5 **Production** 3500
Winemaker(s) Josef Lesnik
A no-holds-barred tourist-oriented cellar door operation, offering
wines from estate-grown grapes; quality has been variable but an
outstanding, stylish 1991 barrel-fermented Chardonnay justifiably
topped the Small Producers Class at the 1992 Royal Sydney Wine
Show. Subsequent show success at the Hunter Valley Wine Show
suggests this performance was not a fluke.
Principal Wines Semillon Chardonnay, Chardonnay, Verdelho,
Shiraz, Cabernet Merlot and generic Rougelais and Kiewa red
wines.

LIEBICHWEIN *

NR 6.50–9.70 CD AUSSD
Barossa Valley **Est.** 1992
Narrow Road, Rowland Flat, SA 5352
Ph (085) 24 4543
Open W'ends 11–5, Mon–Fri by appt **Production** 200

Winemaker(s) Ron Liebich

Liebichwein is Barossa Deutsch for "Love I wine". Members of the Liebich family have been grape growers and winemakers at Rowland Flat since 1919, with Ron "Darky" Liebich one of the great local characters. He himself commenced making wine in 1969, but it was not until 1992 that together with wife Janet he began selling wine under the Liebichwein label. The '89 Riesling Traminer, still available at $7.80, was a trophy winner at the 1993 Barossa Wine Show.

Principal Wines Riesling of the Valleys (a blend of Barossa and Clare Valley Riesling), Riesling Traminer, Cabernet Sauvignon, Classic Old Barossa Tawny Port, Benno Port; bulk port constitutes major sales.

LILLYDALE VINEYARDS

★★★☆ 10–20 CD AUS100
Yarra Valley **Est.** 1976
Lot 10, Davross Court, Seville, Vic 3139
Ph (059) 64 2016 **Fax** (059) 62 3009
Open 7 days 10–5 **Production** 9000
Winemaker(s) Alex White

Acquired by McWilliam's Wines in 1994, an acquisition which in due course will mean considerable change and ultimately expansion of Lillydale Vineyards. In the short term, it is business as usual, with Alex White continuing to fill the winemaking role.

Principal Wines Riesling, Sauvignon Blanc, Gewurztraminer, Chardonnay, Pinot Noir, Cabernet Sauvignon; second label is Yarra Range.

LILLYDALE VINEYARDS CHARDONNAY

●●● ▶ $13.50

One of the pioneers of Chardonnay, with Alex White always making a fruit-driven rather than oak-driven style. The early vintages were very good by the standards of their time, but were outpaced by many others in the latter part of the 1980s. The current vintage is typical of more recent years, being somewhat dilute in flavour.
Cellaring 2–3 years. **Best Vintages** '86, '88, '90, '91
Current Vintage '93
Matching Food Avocado.
Tasting Note 1993 Medium to full yellow-green, with considerable dissolved carbon dioxide. Light peachy/tropical/passionfruit aromas hinting at some botrytis, characters which reappear on the palate with some canned fruit flavours; finishes light.

LILLYDALE VINEYARDS PINOT NOIR

●●●● $16.50

Not known as a major producer of pinot noir, but the low-yielding 1994 vintage produced a wine of considerable style and character.
Cellaring Drink now. **Best Vintages** '94 **Current Vintage** '94
Matching Food Chinese seafood.
Tasting Note 1994 Light to medium red-purple; tangy, intense fruit

aromas with spicy peppery characters on both bouquet and palate. Has above average length and intensity, particularly on the finish.

LILLYDALE VINEYARDS SAUVIGNON BLANC
●●●● $13.50
Lillydale Vineyards was one of the first producers of sauvignon blanc in the Yarra Valley, finding the variety very difficult to handle from a viticultural viewpoint, with inconsistent and often very low yields. Production has increased somewhat in recent years, the wine being made (as one would expect given Alex White's overall philosophy) without the use of oak.
Cellaring Drink now. **Best Vintages** NA **Current Vintage** '92
Matching Food Shellfish.
Tasting Note 1992 Light green-yellow; a fairly potent and full bouquet with herbal/gooseberry fruit aromas. The palate is very correct, firm and with good length, showing similar flavours to the bouquet.

LILLYPILLY ESTATE
★★★☆ 8.50–19.95 CD AUSSD
Murrumbidgee Irrigation Area **Est.** 1982
Lillypilly Road, Leeton, NSW 2705
Ph (069) 53 4069 **Fax** (069) 53 4980
Open Mon–Sat 10–5.30, Sun by appt **Production** 6000
Winemaker(s) Robert Fiumara
Apart from occasional Vintage Ports (the '85 a gold medal winner at the 1992 Canberra National Wine Show) the best wines by far are the botrytised white wines, with the Noble Muscat of Alexandria unique to the winery; these wines have both style and intensity of flavour, and can age well. The Noble Semillon and Noble Traminer add new strings to the bow of the winery.
Principal Wines Riesling, Chardonnay, Fumé Blanc, Tramillon® (Traminer Semillon), Noble Riesling, Noble Traminer, Noble Semillon, Noble Muscat of Alexandria, Red Velvet® (medium sweet red), Cabernet Sauvignon, Hermitage, Shiraz, Vintage Port.

LILLYPILLY ESTATE CHARDONNAY
●●● $8.85
A modest enough wine, but then so is the price. Robert Fiumara has always known how to make white wines well, and any lack of varietal fruit is a reflection of the vineyards, not winery technique.
Cellaring Drink now. **Best Vintages** NA **Current Vintage** '92
Matching Food White-fleshed fish.
Tasting Note 1992 Medium to full yellow-green; clean and smooth, with a hint of vanilla oak on the bouquet. The palate shows similar vanillin oak influences (the wine was briefly cask fermented) with light fruit and a clean finish.

LILLYPILLY ESTATE NOBLE MUSCAT OF ALEXANDRIA (375 ML)
●●●● $15.95
A Lillypilly specialty, and one of the few botrytised Muscats made in

the country. Even then, it is only made in exceptional vintages, the only releases to date being from '85, '87 and '90.

Cellaring Now–3 years. **Best Vintages** '85, '97, '90
Current Vintage '90
Matching Food Tarte Tatin.
Tasting Note 1990 Full yellow-orange; complex, tangy apricot and raisin aromas lead on to an intensely-flavoured palate with peach, honey, mead, spice, apricot and toffee running riot across the tongue, finishing with good acidity.

LILLYPILLY ESTATE NOBLE TRAMINER
●●●● ▶ $19.95
Another relatively rare wine, although De Bortoli has made a botrytised Traminer from time to time from the same region. A striking and stylish wine.

Cellaring Drink now. **Best Vintages** NA
Current Vintage '91
Matching Food Pecan pie.
Tasting Note 1991 Glowing yellow-green; penetrating spice, lychee and peach aromas. The palate is concentrated, with similar flavours to those of the bouquet, although of auslese sweetness, finishing with good acidity.

LILLYPILLY ESTATE SHIRAZ
●●● $10.95
Like most Griffith producers, Lillypilly is far better known for its white and fortified wines than for its dry, red table wines. I have tasted the latter over the years, and have never been particularly impressed. Usually the wines are light bodied, ageing quickly, and seldom attaining cask quality. The '92 is an exception. The wine was matured in French oak for 10 months prior to bottling.

Cellaring 1–3 years. **Best Vintages** NA **Current Vintage** '92
Matching Food Osso bucco.
Tasting Note 1992 Surprisingly deep colour; a solid bouquet which tends more to briary/leathery than aromatic or fruity, but is satisfying. The palate, likewise, has surprising depth and structure with briary/woodsy flavours and a nice touch of oak.

LILLYPILLY ESTATE TRAMILLON
●●● $9.95
Tramillon® is a trade-marked, proprietary name for a blend of Traminer and Semillon which propelled winemaker Robert Fiumara and Lillypilly Estate to overnight fame when the first vintage won the gold medal and trophy for Small Producers White Wine at the Royal Sydney Show in the early 1980s. It is, to put it mildly, an unusual blend, but does make a very pleasant cellar door style.

Cellaring Drink now. **Best Vintages** NA **Current Vintage** '94
Matching Food Gently spiced Asian dishes.
Tasting Note 1994 Medium yellow-green; an appropriately fragrant and fresh bouquet with spicy traminer to the fore. The palate has distinct sweetness, with some slightly heavy notes often encountered with traminer, but works well enough.

LINDEMANS (COONAWARRA & PADTHAWAY)

★★★★★ 11.95–27 R AUS147 UK83 US11

Coonawarra and Padthaway **Est.** 1908

Main Penola–Naracoorte Road, Coonawarra SA 5263

Ph (087) 36 3205 **Fax** (087) 36 3250

Open 7 days 10–4 **Production** NFP

Winemaker(s) Phillip John, Greg Clayfield

Lindemans is clearly the strongest brand other than Penfolds in the Southcorp group, with some great vineyards and a great history. The Padthaway and Coonawarra vineyards are of ever-increasing importance because of the increasing move towards regional identity in the all-important export markets, and one is already seeing the emergence of a new range of regional/varietal labels.

Principal Wines Padthaway label: Semillon Blanc, Verdelho, Chardonnay, Cabernet Merlot; new Coonawarra Vineyard label: Riesling, Sauvignon Blanc; premium red trio: Pyrus (Cabernet Blend), Limestone Ridge (Shiraz Cabernet), St George (Cabernet Sauvignon).

LINDEMANS COONAWARRA VINEYARD RIESLING

●●●● $12.95

Lindemans has had a stop-start relationship with riesling in Coonawarra, for a considerable period of time consigning the wine to the anonymity of blend proprietary products. However, wines such as the extraordinary 1975 Nursery Rhine Riesling, still as fresh as a daisy, leave the fundamental merit of the wine in no doubt. Here, too, it is likely that this newly-introduced label will be the first of a long series.

Cellaring 5+ years. **Best Vintages** NA **Current Vintage** '94

Matching Food Artichoke salad.

Tasting Note 1994 Light green-yellow; a firm, crisp, faintly herbaceous, faintly spicy bouquet leads on to a dry, crisp, lime and herb-flavoured palate, with good length. The acid and the structure are there for long ageing.

LINDEMANS COONAWARRA VINEYARD SAUVIGNON BLANC

●●●● $12.95

Lindemans' first release of Sauvignon Blanc from Coonawarra, and forming part of the new Coonawarra Vineyard range. Made without oak in a modern, crisp style.

Cellaring Drink now. **Best Vintages** NA **Current Vintage** '94

Matching Food South Australian whiting.

Tasting Note 1994 Light green-yellow; fragrant, herbaceous and gooseberry fruit aromas on the bouquet lead on to a palate with pleasantly austere grassy fruit, with a crisp and lively finish.

LINDEMANS PADTHAWAY VERDELHO

●●● ▶ $12.95

Lindemans has had verdelho planted in its Padthaway vineyards right from the outset, but there have been only intermittent releases over the years. It is reasonable to expect that this wine will now be a

permanent part of the range. It is barrel fermented in new and one-year-old French oak hogsheads, and given two months oak maturation, strongly influencing the shape of the wine.
Cellaring 1–2 years. **Best Vintages** NA **Current Vintage** '94
Matching Food Rich chicken or veal dishes.
Tasting Note 1994 Medium to full yellow-green; strong spicy/nutty barrel ferment oak drives the bouquet with underlying honeysuckle varietal fruit aromas. The palate, too, is essentially oak-driven, although there are crisp, tropical fruit flavours evident, balanced by good acidity.

LINDEMANS PYRUS
●●●● ▶ $27
A label conjured up in the heat of the moment when the 1985 vintage bobbed up with the Jimmy Watson Trophy when Lindemans was least expecting it. It is a blend of cabernet sauvignon, merlot, malbec and cabernet franc; since 1985 the percentage of cabernet sauvignon has increased from 35% in the early days to 70% in the '91 vintage. It has come of age with the latter wine, with the fruit and 18 months new French oak maturation working to great effect. A trophy and six gold medals.
Cellaring 5 years. **Best Vintages** '88, '90, '91
Current Vintage '91
Matching Food Entrecote of beef.
Tasting Note 1991 Full red-purple; concentrated briary/berry fruit, a fuller and sweeter version of the '90. The palate is rich and ripe with masses of chocolate and dark berry fruit, finishing with soft, lingering tannins. Far better than any Pyrus which preceded it.

LINDEMANS ST GEORGE
●●●●● $27
Made entirely from cabernet sauvignon grown on the 12-hectare St George Vineyard, first produced in 1973. A very distinguished label with an at-times brilliant show record, but which has seen both style vary and quality fluctuate over the years. It has fully lived up to its reputation since 1986.
Cellaring 5–10 years depending on vintage. **Best Vintages** '86, '88, '90, '91, '92 **Current Vintage** '91
Matching Food Shoulder of lamb.
Tasting Note 1991 Medium to full red-purple; a smooth, clean, fine and elegant bouquet with well balanced and integrated oak. The palate is full-bodied with ripe plum and berry fruit, showing above average concentration, and the same very well integrated and balanced oak evident on the palate. The tannin structure, too, is good. Four gold medals.

LINDEMANS (HUNTER VALLEY)
★★★★★ 11.95–35 R AUS147 UK83 US11
Hunter Valley **Est.** 1870
McDonalds Road, Pokolbin, NSW 2321
Ph (049) 98 7501 **Fax** (049) 98 7682
Open 7 days 9–5 **Production** 60 000

Winemaker(s) Phillip John

There has been a definite renaissance in the fortunes of Lindemans Hunter River wines over the past few years, although I am still puzzled at Southcorp's overall strategy which has some of the Lindemans Hunter River products priced at the same level as those of Tulloch and Hungerford Hill. The label deserves better, and the rating I have given in fact relates to the best of the wines, which are as good as all of the wines under the label should be.

Principal Wines Standard wines under annually changing Bin numbers of Semillon, Chablis, White Burgundy, Semillon Chardonnay, Chardonnay, Burgundy, Hermitage; deluxe releases under Reserve Bin label; individual vineyard labels (e.g. Steven) and revitalised older Classic Release label.

LINDEMANS HUNTER RIVER BURGUNDY
●●●●● $19

As with the Semillon, something of a moving feast, albeit less confusing. At the end of 1994 there were two wines on release, 1991 Bin 8203 ($15) and 1988 Reserve Bin 7600 ($19). Each is outstanding in its price range.

Cellaring Up to 30 years for the best vintages.
Best Vintages '59, '65, '67, '73, '83, '86, '87, '88, '90, '91
Current Vintage '88, '91
Matching Food Game.
Tasting Note 1988 Bin 7600. Medium to full red; a quite rich bouquet with traditional earth and chocolate aromas. On the palate, an interesting throwback to some of the older wines in the tasting, with attractive chocolate and earth edges to red berry fruits, finishing with well balanced tannins. Outstanding for a relatively unfashionable vintage.

LINDEMANS HUNTER RIVER CLASSIC RELEASE SEMILLON
●●●●● $35

As from 1986, a special selection has been made of the best semillon, and held back for maturation and shows. The 1986 Bin 6855 was released as part of the Classic Release programme in 1994, and the trophy-winning 1987 Bin 7055 is due for release in 1995. Produced principally from the School Block Vineyard adjacent to the winery.

Cellaring 10–15 years. **Best Vintages** '86, '87
Current Vintage '86
Matching Food Lobster, crab.
Tasting Note 1986 Light to medium green-yellow; an amazingly youthful bouquet, intense with firm citrus-tinged fruit and some smoky aspects starting to develop. The palate is well balanced, with intense lime and herb fruit, with a long, crisply acid finish.

LINDEMANS HUNTER RIVER SEMILLON
●●●●● $11.95

At its best (as it was in the 1960s and as it has the potential to be in the future) one of Australia's great classics. Labels, times and wine styles are all changing, making the link between present and past tenuous, hence separate entries for two strands of the wine. Since 1992, indeed, around 15% of semillon from the Central Tablelands near Young.

Cellaring 5–30 years. **Best Vintages** '63, '65, '68, '70, '79, '86, '87, '91, '93, '94 **Current Vintage** '93

Matching Food Strictly depends on the age.

Tasting Note 1993 Bin 8255. Light yellow-green; an interesting and complex floral/herbal bouquet showing intense varietal character. The palate, too, shows clearly defined herbaceous/lemony varietal character, having grip and intensity to the finish.

LINDEMANS LIMESTONE RIDGE

●●●●● $27

Arguably the most distinguished of the Coonawarra trio. Typically a blend of 80% shiraz and 20% cabernet sauvignon made from grapes grown on the 20 hectares of shiraz and 4 hectares of cabernet sauvignon on the Limestone Ridge Vineyard. Matured in a mix of American and French oak, with American oak predominating.

Cellaring 4–10 years depending on the vintage.

Best Vintages '86, '88, '90, '91, '92 **Current Vintage** '91

Matching Food Beef casserole.

Tasting Note 1991 Medium to full red-purple; clean, concentrated plum, cherry and spice fruit aromas with perfectly balanced and integrated oak. On the palate, exceptionally concentrated in comparison to all others in the line-up, with lots of round, mouthfilling plum cherry and raspberry fruit, finishing with good tannins.

LINDEMANS STEVEN HERMITAGE

●●●● ▸ $17.95

From the long established Lindemans-owned Steven Vineyard, which is a consistent producer of very typical but generously-flavoured Shiraz (or Hermitage as it is still called on the label). The wine is matured in American oak hogsheads for 12 months, but typically shows little impact from the oak.

Cellaring 7–12 years. **Best Vintages** '79, '83, '86, '87, '90, '91 **Current Vintage** '90

Matching Food Mild mature cheese.

Tasting Note 1990 Medium to full red-purple; the bouquet is rich, with ripe, luscious sweet fruit in abundance, without compromising the strong regional underlay. The palate is similarly ripe and regional, with some of the earth, hay and straw characters evident on the bouquet. Nicely balanced tannins round off a very good regional wine.

LINDEMANS (MURRAY RIVER)

★★★★ 5–8.50 R AUS147 UK83 US11

Murray River **Est.** 1963

Nangiloc Road, Karadoc via Mildura, Vic 3500

Ph (050) 24 0303 **Fax** (050) 24 0324

Open Mon–Sat 10–4.30 **Production** 3.5 million

Winemaker(s) Phillip John (Chief)

Now the production centre for all of the Lindeman and Leo Buring
wines, with the exception of special lines made in the Coonawarra
and Hunter wineries. The biggest and most modern single facility in
Australia allowing all-important economies of scale, and the major
processing centre for the beverage wine sector (casks, flagons and
low-priced bottles) of the Southcorp empire. Its achievement in
making 4 million bottles of Bin 65 Chardonnay a year is
extraordinary given the quality and consistency of the wines.
Principal Wines Bin 23 Rhine Riesling, Bin 65 Chardonnay (one
of the largest-selling Chardonnay brands in the world), Bin 95
Sauvignon Blanc, Bin 50 Shiraz Cabernet, Bin 60 Merlot are the
most important in terms of volume; Cawarra Homestead range of
Colombard Chardonnay and Shiraz Cabernet introduced as budget
specials in 1994; a large range of varietals under Matthew Lang
label; also Nyrang Hermitage. Karadoc also produces the great
fortified wines, including the premium Fino, Amontillado and
Oloroso Sherries, Old Liqueur Muscat, Tokay and Madeira and
fine Tawny Ports.

LIRRALIRRA ESTATE

★★★☆ 9–15 CD AUSSD
Yarra Valley **Est.** 1981
Paynes Road, Lilydale, Vic 3140
Ph (03) 9735 0224
Open W'ends, Public hols 10–6 **Production** 500
Winemaker(s) Alan Smith
Off the beaten track, and one of the lesser-known Yarra Valley
wineries; owner Alan Smith originally intended to make a Sauternes-
style wine from semillon, sauvignon blanc and muscadelle, but has
found the conditions do not favour the development of botrytis, and
is hence producing dry red and white wines.
Principal Wines Semillon, Sauvignon Blanc Semillon, Sauvignon
Blanc Semillon Muscadelle, Pinot Noir, Yarra Valley Cabernets.

LIRRALIRRA ESTATE SAUVIGNON BLANC
●●● ▶ $12
Like its sister wine from the '94 vintage, made without the use of
oak, and hence much improved. It comes from half a hectare of
estate plantings.
Cellaring 1–2 years. **Best Vintages** '94 **Current Vintage** '94
Matching Food Crab.
Tasting Note 1994 Light straw-green; a crisp, light herbal bouquet
showing distinctive varietal character. The palate is clean but lacks
the fruit intensity of the Semillon.

LIRRALIRRA ESTATE SEMILLON
●●●● $12
Produced from three-quarters of a hectare of estate-grown grapes.
Vintages prior to 1994 were sometimes blended with sauvignon
blanc, but, more importantly, put in indifferent oak. In 1994 the wine
was allowed to speak for itself, and is much the better for that.

Cellaring 3–4 years. **Best Vintages** '94 **Current Vintage** '94
Matching Food Asparagus salad.
Tasting Note 1994 Light yellow-green; clean, crisp and fresh with
pleasant herbaceous varietal fruit on the bouquet, the palate
following precisely on from the bouquet, finishing crisp and clean.

LIRRALIRRA ESTATE YARRA VALLEY CABERNETS

●●●● $15

A blend of 75% cabernet sauvignon, 15% cabernet franc and 10%
merlot, 50% coming from the half a hectare of cabernet sauvignon
at Lirralirra and 50% from Halcyon Daze vineyard.
Cellaring 3–4 years. **Best Vintages** '88, '90, '91, '92, '94
Current Vintage '93
Matching Food Roast lamb.
Tasting Note 1993 Strong red-purple; a clean bouquet with ripe,
dark berry fruits, a hint of fruit spice, and subtle oak. The palate is
distinctively Yarra Valley in style with minty/gamey undertones to
the firm red berry fruit.

LITTLE RIVER WINES

NR 5–8 CD AUSSD
Swan Valley **Est.** 1934
Cnr West Swan & Forest Roads, West Swan, WA 6055
Ph (09) 296 4462 **Fax** (09) 296 1022
Open 7 days 10–5.30 **Production** 5000
Winemaker(s) Bruno de Tastes
Following several quick changes of ownership (and of consultant
winemakers) the former Glenalwyn has gone through a period of
change. It now has as its winemaker the eponymously-named Count
Bruno de Tastes.
Principal Wines Chenin Blanc, Sauvignon Blanc, Chardonnay,
Cabernet Sauvignon, Shiraz, Florial Rosé, Vin Doux Late Harvest,
Noble Classic.

LITTLE'S WINERY

★★★ 13–15 CD AUSSD
Hunter Valley **Est.** 1984
Lot 3 Palmers Lane, Pokolbin, NSW 2321
Ph (049) 98 7626 **Fax** (049) 98 7867
Open 7 days 10–4.30 **Production** 4200
Winemaker(s) Ian Little
A successful cellar door operation with friendly service and friendly
wines: aromatic, fresh and sometimes slightly sweet white wines and
light, inoffensive red wines.
Principal Wines Chardonnay, Semillon, Gewurztraminer, Late
Harvest Semillon, Pinot Noir Blanc de Noir, Cabernet Sauvignon,
Vintage Port.

LITTLE'S GEWURZTRAMINER

●●● ▶ $13

Gewurztraminer is a relatively rare grape in the Hunter Valley, but suits Ian Little's style of winemaking which enhances the aromatics and leaves enough residual sugar to attract those who like a touch of distinct sweetness to their white wines.

Cellaring Drink now. **Best Vintages** NA **Current Vintage** '94
Matching Food Rockmelon, cakes.
Tasting Note 1994 Light to medium yellow-green; intense, spicy rich aromatics to the bouquet. There are lots of tutti-frutti flavours on the palate which is appreciably sweet, but fresh and nicely balanced. Good example of the style.

LITTLE'S SEMILLON
●●● ▶ $13
Like all the Little's white wines, cold fermented to emphasise the fruit aromas and with some interesting tropical characters emerging. The French oak stipulated on the label does not appear to be of particularly distinguished origin, and makes only a minor contribution to the wine.

Cellaring 2–3 years. **Best Vintages** '85, '86, '88, '91, '94
Current Vintage '93
Matching Food Quiche Lorraine.
Tasting Note 1993 Medium to full yellow-green; a smooth, clean bouquet of medium weight and gently tropical fruit, with subliminal oak. The palate is quite weighty, with quite strong tropical fruit flavours, finishing with slightly oily oak.

LITTLE'S VINTAGE PORT (375 ML)
●●● ▶ $11
Ian Little learnt his winemaking at Chateau Reynella in the days of Geoff Merrill, and amongst other things witnessed first-hand the making of some of Australia's best Vintage Ports. Thus Little's has always produced interesting wines in this style, even if the current release is of indeterminate style.

Cellaring 2–3 years. **Best Vintages** '86, '87, '88, '91, '94
Current Vintage '91
Matching Food Petits fours.
Tasting Note 1991 Medium red; a solid and sweet bouquet, more tawny in style than vintage, but clean and commercial. On the palate sweet chocolate flavours predominate in what is a quite appealing tawny and vintage cross.

LOCHVIE WINES

NR 9.50 CD AUSSD
Yarra Valley **Est.** 1985
28 Lavender Park Road, Eltham, Vic 3095
Ph (03) 9439 9444 **Fax** (03) 9439 3694
Open W'ends 9.30–5.30, Weekdays by appt **Production** NFP
Winemaker(s) John Lewis
A tiny home winery producing a single 65%/35% cabernet merlot blend. The grapes were sold in 1993 and 1994 and no wine made; the 1990 to 1992 vintages are currently on sale.
Principal Wines Cabernet Merlot.

LONG GULLY ESTATE

★★★☆ 16–19.50 R AUS74, 96, 122, UK80

Yarra Valley **Est.** 1982

Long Gully Road, Healesville, Vic 3777

Ph (03) 9807 4246/(018) 361 020

Fax (03) 9807 2213

Open W'ends, Hols 11–5 **Production** 12 000

Winemaker(s) Peter Florance

One of the larger (but by no means largest) of the Yarra Valley producers which has successfully established a number of export markets over recent years. Wine quality is consistent rather than exhilarating.

Principal Wines Riesling, Chardonnay, Semillon, Sauvignon Blanc, Merlot, Cabernets, Pinot Noir, Shiraz.

LONG GULLY ESTATE CHARDONNAY

●●● ▶ $19.50

Produced from estate-grown grapes from gentle north-facing slopes and matured in 100% French oak of various ages. A typical elegant Yarra Valley style, but might benefit from a touch more new wood.

Cellaring 3–5 years. **Best Vintages** '88, '89, '91, '92, '93

Current Vintage '92

Matching Food Abalone.

Tasting Note 1992 Medium yellow-green; clean and smooth melon and fig fruit aromas with just a hint of oak. There are similar melon and fig flavours on the palate, the oak again subtle, the finish slightly soapy.

LONGLEAT WINES

★★★☆ 9–14.50 CD AUS183

Goulburn Valley **Est.** 1975

Old Weir Road, Murchison, Vic 3610

Ph (058) 26 2294 **Fax** (058) 26 2510

Open Mon–Sat 9–5, Sun 10–5 **Production** 2000

Winemaker(s) Mark Schulz, Alister Purbrick (Consultant)

Longleat has long had a working relationship with Chateau Tahbilk, which makes the Longleat wines under contract, and buys significant quantities of grapes surplus to Longleat's requirements. The wines are always honest and full flavoured.

Principal Wines Riesling, Sauvignon Blanc, Chardonnay, Spatlese, Shiraz, Cabernet Sauvignon, Liqueur Muscat.

LONGLEAT CABERNET SAUVIGNON

●●●● $14.50

Produced from 7 hectares of cabernet sauvignon grown on the 'home' vineyard situated at Murchison on the banks of the Goulburn River. The relatively warm climate produces wines of great depth of colour, flavour and extract.

Cellaring 5–10 years. **Best Vintages** '82, '84, '86, '91, '92

Current Vintage '91

Matching Food Lamb casserole.
Tasting Note 1991 Medium red-purple; smooth, ripe soft berry fruits of medium intensity on the bouquet lead on to a soft palate with berry/briary/chocolate flavours, finishing with soft tannins. More restrained than many prior vintages.

LONGLEAT CHARDONNAY
●●● ▶ $14
Grown not at Murchison, but in the cooler King Valley region, and matured in a mix of French and American oak barrels. Typically fruit- rather than oak-driven, and again with plenty of flavour notwithstanding the cooler growing conditions.
Cellaring 2–3 years. **Best Vintages** '88, '91, '93, '94
Current Vintage '92
Matching Food Chinese lemon chicken.
Tasting Note 1992 Medium yellow-green; complex with quite strong fruit and some spicy oak influence on the bouquet. The palate is full-blown, ripe and with some sweetness, possibly deriving from alcohol.

LONGLEAT RIESLING
●●● ▶ $9
Produced from grapes grown on the estate vineyard which totals 25 hectares, situated near Murchison on the banks of the Goulburn River.
Cellaring 3–6 years. **Best Vintages** '85, '86, '87, '93, '94
Current Vintage '93
Matching Food Full-flavoured Asian dishes.
Tasting Note 1993 Light green-yellow; intense fruit ranging through lime and citrus to tropical, starting to show some classic kerosene bottle development. A very full-flavoured, solid wine with plenty of weight and a touch of residual sugar on the finish.

LONGMILE ESTATE *

NR 6–10 CD AUSSD
Barossa Valley **Est.** 1976
Langmeil Road, Tanunda, SA 5352
Ph (085) 62 2595 **Fax** (08) 295 6365
Open Wed–Sun 10–5 **Production** 30 000
Winemaker(s) Ross Fassina
A very substantial business, but principally directed to the bulk trade with sales to other wineries.
Principal Wines Riesling, Shiraz, Cabernet Sauvignon, fortifieds.

LOVEGROVE OF COTTLES BRIDGE

★★★☆ 15–22 CD AUSSD
Yarra Valley **Est.** 1988
1420 Heidelberg-Kinglake Road, Cottles Bridge, Vic 3099
Ph (03) 9718 1569 **Fax** (03) 9718 1028
Open W'ends, Hols 11.30–6 **Production** 1000

Winemaker(s) Various Contract
A recently opened cellar door gives visitors to the pretty and distinctively different Diamond Valley subregion a chance to taste some very well made wines. Not a high-profile operation, with much of the estate-grown grapes being sold to others.
Principal Wines Chardonnay, Pinot Noir.

LOWE FAMILY WINES

NR 11.40 CD AUS69
Mudgee **Est.** 1987
Ashbourne Vineyard, Tinja Lane, Mudgee, NSW 2850
Ph (063) 72 1762
Open Not **Production** 1000
Winemaker(s) David Lowe
The family vineyard of former Rothbury winemaker David Lowe, making typically rich, full-bodied Chardonnay, albeit in tiny quantities. I have not tasted recent vintages.
Principal Wines Chardonnay.

LYRE BIRD HILL WINES

★★★☆ 12.50–18 CD AUSSD
South Gippsland **Est.** 1986
Inverloch Road, Koonwarra, Vic 3594
Ph (056) 64 3204 **Fax** (056) 64 3204
Open W'ends, Hols 12–5 **Production** 800
Winemaker(s) Owen Schmidt
Former Melbourne professionals Owen and Robyn Schmidt make small quantities of estate-grown wine, offering accommodation for three couples (RACV 4-star rating) in their newly-built spacious house. Shiraz has been by far the most successful wine to date.
Principal Wines Riesling, Traminer, Chardonnay, Pinot Noir, Cabernet Sauvignon, Shiraz.

LYRE BIRD HILL SHIRAZ
●●●● $18
This South Gippsland location is clearly ideally suited to shiraz. The half hectare of shiraz has produced a vibrantly peppery wine each vintage since 1991, with quite startling flavour.
Cellaring 3–5 years. **Best Vintages** '91, '92, '93
Current Vintage '93
Matching Food Wild duck.
Tasting Note 1993 Full purple-red; potent spicy bouquet still opening up; the palate has masses of vibrant peppery/spicy fruit, finishing with good acidity.

MACEDON RIDGE

NR 35 ML AUSSD
Macedon **Est.** 1985
'Brook Farm', McDonalds Lane, Hesket, Vic 3442
Ph (054) 27 0524

Open Not **Production** 500
Winemaker(s) John Ellis (Contract)
Macedon Ridge is the venture of well known radio and television
personality Derryn Hinch. The immaculate vineyard was established
in 1985, producing its first commercial crop in 1991. The tiny
quantity of sparkling wine produced is sold direct to the wide circle
of friends and acquaintances of Derryn and Jacqueline Hinch.
Principal Wines Sauvignon Blanc, Pinot Noir, Sparkling.

MADDENS LANE WINERY

NR 15 ML AUSSD
Yarra Valley **Est.** 1989
Maddens Lane, Gruyere via Coldstream, Vic 3770
Ph (059) 64 9279
Open By appt. **Production** 150
Winemaker(s) Various Contract
A small and intermittent producer, selling its grapes in some years,
and in others having the wine vinified. It is the former Prigorjie
Winery, now owned by Geoffrey Norris.
Principal Wines Sauvignon Blanc, Semillon, Chardonnay.

MADEW WINES

★★★☆ 13–14.50 CD AUSSD
Canberra **Est.** 1984
Furlong Road, Queanbeyan, ACT 2620
Ph (06) 299 2303
Open W'ends, Public hols 11–5 **Production** 700
Winemaker(s) Greg Tilbrook
Madew Wines has bowed to the urban pressure of Queanbeyan,
and purchased the Westering Vineyard from Captain G P Hood
from where its future wines will come. Those currently being sold
are from the original vineyard, which is in the course of becoming
another suburban subdivision.
Principal Wines Riesling, Late Picked Riesling, Semillon
Chardonnay, Shiraz Cabernet Merlot.

MADEW RIESLING
●●● ▶ $12.95
Produced in both conventional and late picked modes, the latter with
expected sweetness (nicely balanced by acidity), the former with an
unexpected touch of sweetness which is no doubt directed to the
substantial Canberra-based tiny winery.
Cellaring Short term. **Best Vintages** '93, '94
Current Vintage '93
Matching Food Antipasto.
Tasting Note 1993 Brilliant green-yellow; the bouquet is redolent
of classic toasty riesling, strongly reminiscent of the Clare Valley,
and the pronounced residual sugar on the finish of the palate comes
as something of a surprise, both in terms of texture and flavour. The
'92 Late Picked Riesling works rather better, in fact.

MAGLIERI WINES

★★★ 4.50–13 CD AUS68, 73, 115
Southern Vales **Est.** 1972
Douglas Gully Road, McLaren Flat, SA 5171
Ph (08) 383 0177 **Fax** (08) 383 0136
Open Mon–Sat 9–4, Sun 12–4 **Production** 110 000
Winemaker(s) John Loxton

One of the better-kept secrets among the wine cognoscenti, but not among the many customers who drink thousands of cases of White and Red Lambrusco every year. An example of niche marketing at its profitable best. Its dry red wines may be a little rustic but are invariably generously proportioned and full of character.

Principal Wines Prolific Italian-accented range of generic and varietal table wines, spearheaded by White and Red Lambrusco and Spumante; fortified and flavoured wines; also Riesling, Semillon, Semillon Chardonnay, Shiraz and Cabernet Sauvignon.

MAIN RIDGE ESTATE

★★★★ 14–25 ML AUSSD
Mornington Peninsula **Est.** 1975
Lot 48 William Road, Red Hill, Vic 3937
Ph (059) 89 2686 **Fax** (059) 89 2686
Open Mon–Fri 12–4, W'ends 12–5 **Production** 800
Winemaker(s) Nat White

Nat White gives meticulous attention to every aspect of his viticulture and winemaking, doing annual battle with one of the coolest sites on the Peninsula. The same attention to detail extends to the winery and the winemaking.

Principal Wines Chardonnay, Pinot Noir, Pinot Meunier, Cabernet Sauvignon.

MAIN RIDGE ESTATE CABERNET SAUVIGNON

●●●● $18.50

A blend of 90% cabernet sauvignon, 5% merlot and 5% cabernet franc; as with all of the Main Ridge wines, estate-grown. Post fermentation maceration was extended for a month, and the wine spent two years in a mix of new to three-year-old French oak barriques. The warm vintage of 1991 also helped make the best Main Ridge Cabernet to date.

Cellaring 4–6 years. **Best Vintages** '88, '91, '92, '93, '94
Current Vintage '91
Matching Food Roast squab.
Tasting Note 1991 Medium to full red-purple; the bouquet is smooth and clean, with pleasantly ripe berry fruits of medium intensity. The palate is light- to medium-bodied, with a nice touch of spicy oak married with sweet red and blackcurrant fruits, with no herbaceous characters.

MAIN RIDGE ESTATE CHARDONNAY

●●●● ▶ $25

Since 1991 Nat White has moved away from conventional

Australian techniques to a far more French-influenced regimen, using barrel fermentation, malolactic fermentation and lees contact. The 1992 wine was a stand-out success, toasty, buttery and rich, scoring highly in the 1992 Great Chardonnay Challenge conducted by Duke & Lynch. The '93 is not quite in the same class, but is a good wine.

Cellaring Up to 5 years. **Best Vintages** '91, '92, '93, '94
Current Vintage '93
Matching Food Sweetbreads.
Tasting Note 1993 Medium to full yellow-green; rich and textured, with a marked but very successful malolactic input which seems to give unique characters in the Mornington Peninsula. The palate, likewise, is wholly distinctive, with strong hazelnut and cashew flavours, and a pleasantly mealy texture.

MAIR'S COALVILLE VINEYARD

★★★☆ 15 ML AUSSD
Gippsland **Est.** 1985
Moe South Road, Moe South, Vic 3825
Ph (051) 27 4229 **Fax** (051) 27 2148
Open By appt **Production** 250
Winemaker(s) Dr Stewart Mair
Dr Stewart Mair has fashioned a remarkably consistent wine from his small vineyard, on the lean side perhaps, but with the elegance which comes from very cool-grown fruit.
Principal Wines A single wine, predominantly cabernet sauvignon with a little cabernet franc, malbec and merlot, labelled Coalville Red.

MAJELLA WINES *

★★★★ 15 CD AUSSD
Coonawarra **Est.** 1969
Lynn Road, Coonawarra, SA 5263
Ph (087) 36 3293 **Fax** (087) 36 3293
Open Not **Production** 1300
Winemaker(s) Brian Lynn
Majella is one of the more important contract grape growers in Coonawarra, with 36 hectares of shiraz and cabernet sauvignon in production and now fully mature. Common gossip has it that much of the production finds its way into the Wynns John Riddoch Cabernet Sauvignon and Michael Hermitage, or their equivalent within the Southcorp group. Production under the Majella label will increase in future years as long-term supply contracts expire.
Principal Wines Shiraz (Cabernet Sauvignon for future release).

MAJELLA SHIRAZ
●●●● ▶ $15
The 1992 is the second commercial release of the only wine so far produced under the Majella label. The '91 was Champion Medium Bodied Dry Red at the 1992 Adelaide Wine Show. The style is rich, with abundant oak.

Cellaring 5–8 years. **Best Vintages** '91, '92, '93, '94
Current Vintage '92
Matching Food Braised kangaroo.
Tasting Note 1992 Deep red-purple; the bouquet shows strong
vanillin and spice oak intermingling with black cherry and spice
varietal fruit. The palate is rich, full-bodied and fairly tannic, again
with marked oak influence. Needs time.

MALCOLM CREEK WINES

★★★☆ 14.95 R AUSSD
Adelaide Hills **Est.** 1982
Bonython Road, Kersbrook, SA 5231
Ph (08) 389 3235
Open W'ends, Public hols 10–5 **Production** 500
Winemaker(s) Reg Tolley
The tiny hobby vineyard of Tolley's chief Reg Tolley, the vinous
equivalent of a bus conductor's holiday; the wines are smooth, clean
and somewhat simple, but are released with significant bottle age.
Principal Wines Chardonnay, Cabernet Sauvignon.

MANNING PARK WINES

NR 9.50–12.50 CD AUSSD
Southern Vales **Est.** 1979
Cnr Olivers & Chalk Hill Roads, McLaren Vale, SA 5171
Ph (08) 323 8209
Open 7 days 9–5 **Production** NFP
Winemaker(s) Allan McLean
A low-key cellar door operation which places special emphasis on
old (and expensive) tawny ports.
Principal Wines Riesling, Fumé Blanc, White Burgundy,
Sauternes, Hermitage, Cabernet Sauvignon, Port, Muscat.

MARIENBERG WINES

★★★ 9.50–14.95 R AUS76–79
Southern Vales **Est.** 1966
2 Chalk Hill Road, McLaren Vale, SA 5171
Ph (02) 630 5429 **Fax** (02) 583 2729
Open 7 days 10–5 **Production** 27 000
Winemaker(s) Grant Burge
The Marienberg brand was purchased by the Hill group of
companies in late 1991 following the retirement of Ursula Pridham.
Releases under the new regime have been honest, full-flavoured
wines.
Principal Wines Cottage Classic, Lavinia Classic Dry White,
Riesling, Semillon Chardonnay, Chardonnay, Shiraz, Cabernet
Sauvignon, Sparkling, Port.

MARIENBERG CHARDONNAY

●●● ▶ $11.95
Marienberg does not have any vineyards of its own, relying upon a

spread of contract growers over the Barossa Valley and McLaren Vale. The wines are now made by Grant Burge, and, as one would expect, are invariably competently handled, and deliberately aimed at the commercial market. The '93 was a bronze medal winner at the 1994 Adelaide Wine Show.

Cellaring Drink now. **Best Vintages** NA **Current Vintage** '93 **Matching Food** Creamy pasta.

Tasting Note 1993 Medium yellow-green; clean, fruit-driven wine of medium intensity with gently peachy/tropical fruit aromas which carry through on to a soft, full-flavoured, fruit-driven palate, finishing ever so slightly sweet.

MARION'S VINEYARD

★★★ ☆ 15–18 ML AUS154
Tamar Valley **Est.** 1980
Foreshore Drive, Deviot, Tas 7275
Ph (003) 94 7434 **Fax** (003) 94 7434
Open 7 days 10–5 **Production** 2100
Winemaker(s) Mark Semmens, Marion Semmens
The irrepressible Mark Semmens and indefatigable wife Marion have one of the most beautifully situated vineyards and wineries in Australia on the banks of the Tamar River. As well as an outdoor restaurant and accommodation, there is a jetty and a stage — indeed, life is a stage for Mark Semmens. Production is increasing, with Zinfandel and Pinot Gris in the planning pipeline.
Principal Wines Chardonnay, Muller Thurgau, Pinot Noir, Cabernet Sauvignon.

MARKEITA CELLARS

NR NA AUSSD
Central West New South Wales **Est.** 1974
Mitchell Highway, Neurea, NSW 2820
Ph (068) 46 7277
Open 7 days 9–6 **Production** 1600
Winemaker(s) Keith Reinhard
Full-bodied red wines and fortifieds, some purchased elsewhere, are dispensed in containers of all shapes and sizes to both locals and passing tourists.
Principal Wines Frontignac, Shiraz, Cabernet Sauvignon, Port.

MARKWOOD ESTATE

NR 10–18 CD AUSSD
North East Victoria **Est.** 1971
Morris Lane, Markwood, Vic 3678
Ph (057) 27 0361
Open 7 days 9–5 **Production** 900
Winemaker(s) Rick Morris
A member of the famous Morris family, Rick Morris shuns publicity, and relies virtually exclusively on cellar door sales for what is a small output.

Principal Wines Chardonnay, Cabernet Sauvignon, Shiraz, Muscat, Tokay, Port.

MARRON VIEW WINES

NR 12.50 ML AUSSD
Great Southern **Est.** 1988
Frankland-Rocky Gully Road, Frankland, WA 6396
Ph (098) 55 2278
Open Not **Production** 400
Winemaker(s) Alkoomi (Contract)
Kim Hart has sold the former Marron Creek vineyard after moving east to Chateau Remy; the wines, however, continue to be made at Alkoomi (where Hart was winemaker) under their new label of Marron View.
Principal Wines Chardonnay, Cabernet Sauvignon.

MARSH ESTATE

★★★☆ 12.50–16.50 CD AUSSD
Hunter Valley **Est.** 1971
Deasey Road, Pokolbin, NSW 2321
Ph (049) 98 7587 **Fax** (049) 98 7884
Open Mon–Fri 10–4.30, W'ends 10–5 **Production** 5000
Winemaker(s) Peter Marsh
Through sheer consistency, value-for-money and unrelenting hard work, the Marsh family (who purchased the former Quentin Estate in 1978) has built up a sufficiently loyal cellar door and mail list clientele to allow all of the considerable production to be sold direct. Wine style is always direct, with oak playing a minimal role, and prolonged cellaring paying handsome dividends.
Principal Wines Semillon (variously labelled as Chablis, Burgundy and Fumé Blanc), Semillon Chardonnay, Chardonnay, Traminer, Semillon Sauternes, Hermitage (labelled Vat S, Vat R and PM Private Bin), Cabernet Merlot, Cabernet Sauvignon Vat N, James II Tawny Port.

MASSONI MAIN CREEK

★★★★☆ 26 R AUS72
Mornington Peninsula **Est.** 1984
Mornington-Flinders Road, Red Hill, Vic 3937
Ph (059) 89 2060 **Fax** (059) 89 2348
Open By appt **Production** 1560
Winemaker(s) Contract
Highly regarded former Melbourne restaurateur Leon Massoni has formed a joint venture with Yellowglen founder Ian Home which will lead to a significant increase in the output of the Massoni wines, as well as the release of a sparkling wine under the 'Home' brand. One of the stated objectives is also to increase the complexity of the Chardonnay — a wine which in many vintages has been impressively complex in any event.
Principal Wines Chardonnay, Pinot Noir.

MASSONI MAIN CREEK CHARDONNAY
●●●●● $26
Produced from 1.5 hectares of estate plantings, and made using the
full gamut of barrel fermentation, malolactic fermentation and lees
contact. In many ways the most striking example of Mornington
Peninsula Chardonnay, with tremendous character, body and
richness.
Cellaring 3–6 years. **Best Vintages** '89, '90, '91, '92, '93
Current Vintage '93
Matching Food Veal, pork.
Tasting Note 1993 Medium to full yellow-green; a very complex
bouquet with strong, buttery/hazelnut malolactic characters. The
palate is richly textured with full-blown buttery fruit, tremendous
mid palate richness, and a succulent finish.

MASSONI MAIN CREEK PINOT NOIR
●●●● ▶ $26
The mirror image of the Chardonnay, always rich, full-bodied and
opulent, where so many of the Mornington wines — Pinot and
Chardonnay alike — tend to be prettier and more elegant.
Cellaring 2–4 years. **Best Vintages** '91, '92, '93
Current Vintage '93
Matching Food Breast of duck.
Tasting Note 1993 Medium to full red; complex aromas with fresh
cherry fruit, hints of earth, and soft oak. The palate is typically rich,
particularly on the mid palate, with flavours ranging from cherry to
plum; does not have the length on the finish of the best of the
Massoni Pinots.

MATILDA'S MEADOW*

★★★☆ 14–16.50 CD AUSSD
Great Southern **Est.** 1990
Eladon Brook Estate, RMB 654 Hamilton Road, Denmark, WA 6333
Ph (098) 48 1951 **Fax** (098) 48 1957
Open 7 days 10–4 **Production** 1000
Winemaker(s) John Wade (Contract)
Former hotelier Don Turnbull and oil industry executive Pamela
Meldrum have quickly established a thriving business at Matilda's
Meadow, based on 6 hectares of estate plantings, and with a
restaurant offering morning and afternoon teas and lunches every
day.
Principal Wines Chardonnay, Sauvignon Blanc Semillon, Pinot
Noir, Cabernet Sauvignon.

MATILDA'S MEADOW SAUVIGNON BLANC SEMILLON
●●●● $NA
Very competently made by John Wade, and in an unoaked, dry style
which Pamela Meldrum favours. A bronze medal winner at the
1994 Mount Barker Wine Show.
Cellaring Drink now. **Best Vintages** NA **Current Vintage** '94
Matching Food Cold seafood salad.

Tasting Note 1994 Light green-yellow; a firm and crisp aroma with gently herbaceous fruit. The palate has excellent mouthfeel, flavour and balance, with the semillon smoothing over the more herbaceous notes of the sauvignon blanc.

MAXWELL WINES

★★★☆ 11–16 R AUS17, 156, 172, 175
Southern Vales **Est.** 1979
26 Kangarilla Road, McLaren Vale, SA 5171
Ph (08) 323 8200 **Fax** (08) 323 8900
Open 7 days 10–5 **Production** 6000
Winemaker(s) Mark Maxwell
Full-flavoured, rather traditional wines (and excellent mead) are the order of the day, although Mark Maxwell is forever experimenting, dropping some styles and introducing others. Ellen Street Shiraz and Mount Bold Shiraz are convincing blends of old and new: old shiraz vines and modern winemaking techniques.
Principal Wines Maxwell Wines brand: Semillon, Sauvignon Blanc, Chardonnay, Cabernet Merlot, Ellen Street Shiraz, Cabernet Sauvignon; premium Mount Bold label: Chardonnay, Cabernet Sauvignon; excellent Honey Mead, Spice Mead and Liqueur Mead.

MAXWELL WINES CABERNET MERLOT
●●● ▶ $11
Maxwell was one of the early experimenters with merlot in McLaren Vale, blending it with cabernet sauvignon to produce a wine which is often powerful and full-flavoured, although the '93 is rather lighter and more elegant, reflecting the cool growing season. Matured in a mix of French and American oak, but a fruit- rather than oak-driven, style.
Cellaring 3–7 years. **Best Vintages** '82, '88, '91, '92, '94
Current Vintage '93
Matching Food Scotch fillet.
Tasting Note 1993 Medium red; the bouquet is of medium intensity, with clean minty fruit and just a hint of spicy oak. The palate is driven by fresh dark cherry and redcurrant fruit, finishing with subtle tannins.

MAXWELL WINES ELLEN STREET SHIRAZ
●●●● ▶ $12.50
There is in fact a Reserve Shiraz, which is in theory superior to the Ellen Street, but I have often preferred the latter wine for its outstanding varietal character. Once again, high quality fruit does the work, with oak playing a pure support role.
Cellaring 6–9 years. **Best Vintages** '82, '88, '91, '92, '94
Current Vintage '92
Matching Food Kangaroo.
Tasting Note 1992 Medium to full red; a very attractive bouquet with clean spicy varietal fruit which leads on to a wonderful palate with potent, classic liquorice and spice flavours, subtle oak and a long, well balanced finish.

MAXWELL WINES SEMILLON

●●●● $11

As with all of the Maxwell wines, sourced primarily from grapes grown on Maxwell's own vineyards. A full-flavoured style which neither needs nor is given any oak input, and should age very well.
Cellaring 2–6 years. **Best Vintages** '86, '88, '91, '92, '94
Current Vintage '93
Matching Food Char-grilled octopus.
Tasting Note 1993 Bright yellow-green; intense varietal fruit aromas ranging from grassy through to sweeter, more honeyed characters. The same strong varietal definition and rich fruit is evident on the palate, which has plenty of flesh and mouthfeel, and is sure to develop well.

McALISTER VINEYARDS

★★★☆ 26 ML AUS173
Gippsland **Est.** 1975
Golden Beach Road, Longford, Vic 3851
Ph (051) 49 7229 **Fax** (051) 49 7229
Open By appt **Production** 500
Winemaker(s) Peter Edwards
The McAlister Vineyards are situated on the most easterly finger of the Strzelecki Hills, and the climate is strongly maritime influenced both by sea breezes and by the Gippsland lake system.
Principal Wines A single wine, The McAlister, a blend of cabernet sauvignon, cabernet franc and merlot.

McALISTER VINEYARDS THE McALISTER

●●● ▶ $26

A blend of 70% cabernet sauvignon and cabernet franc and 30% merlot produced from low-yielding vines. The intention was to produce a Bordeaux-style wine, and Peter Edwards has succeeded in his aim. The wines are invariably sinewy and tight, sometimes a little astringent, and very different from the mainstream lush Australian red style.
Cellaring 10 years. **Best Vintages** '84, '87, '90, '91, '92
Current Vintage '92
Matching Food Roast lamb.
Tasting Note 1992 Bright medium purple-red; a complex bouquet with some leafy notes, a hint of earth, a touch of game and briar. The palate is sinewy and tight, with fine-grained tannins and minerally flavours.

McGUIGAN BROTHERS

★★★ 9.50–12.50 R AUS13, 67, 76, UK93
Hunter Valley **Est.** 1992
PO Box 31, Branxton, NSW 2335
Ph (049) 98 7400 **Fax** (049) 98 7401
Open 7 days 10–5 **Production** 120 000
Winemaker(s) Brian McGuigan

A public-listed company which is the ultimate logical expression of Brian McGuigan's marketing drive and vision, on a par with that of Wolf Blass, even if the wines are not. Highly successful in its chosen niche market. What impact the recent departure of Neil McGuigan to the tiny Briar Ridge winery will have, remains to be seen.
Principal Wines Bottom price, export range: First Harvest Semillon Chardonnay, Night Harvest Graves, Autumn Harvest Traminer Riesling, Black Shiraz; then the Bin range 2000 Hermitage, 3000 Merlot, 4000 Cabernet Sauvignon, 6000 Verdelho, 7000 Chardonnay; finally, Shareholder Reserve Chardonnay, Cabernet Merlot, Sauternes; also Personal Reserve.

McGUIGAN BROTHERS BIN 2000 HERMITAGE
●●● ▶ $9.95
A very high-flavoured style, always released very early, and which gained considerable attention when it won a trophy at the 1994 Hunter Valley Wine Show, following earlier success at the New World International Wine Show in the United States.
Cellaring Drink now. **Best Vintages** NA **Current Vintage** '93
Matching Food Spiced lamb.
Tasting Note 1993 Medium red-purple; vibrant fresh juicy red berry fruit and charry oak aromas lead on to a high-flavoured, juicy fruit palate, finishing with very charry/chippy oak.

McIVOR CREEK WINERY
NR 9.50–14.95 CD AUSSD
Bendigo **Est.** 1973
Costerfield Road, Heathcote, Vic 3523
Ph (054) 33 3000 **Fax** (054) 33 2609
Open 7 days 10–5.30 **Production** 10 000
Winemaker(s) Peter Turley
The beautifully situated McIvor Creek Winery is well worth a visit, and does offer wines in diverse styles of which the red wines are the most regional. Peter Turley has 5 hectares of cabernet sauvignon together with 2.5 hectares of cabernet franc and merlot (the latter coming into bearing) and supplements his intake with grapes from other growers. No recent tastings.
Principal Wines Riesling, Semillon, Sauvignon Blanc, Auslese Riesling, Shiraz, Cabernet Shiraz, Cabernet Sauvignon, fortifieds.

McMANUS WINES
NR 4–8 CD AUSSD
Murrumbidgee Irrigation Area **Est.** 1972
Rogers Road, Yenda, NSW 2681
Ph (069) 68 1064
Open 7 days 9–5 **Production** 700
Winemaker(s) Dr David McManus
An extremely idiosyncratic winery run by Griffith GP Dr David McManus, his sister and other family members. Natural winemaking methods lead to considerable variation in quality, but the prices are

from another era, some of the vintages likewise. Thus in late 1994 a 1981 Chardonnay was still available at $5 a bottle.

Principal Wines Chardonnay, Dry White, Malbec, Merlot, Shiraz, Pinot Malbec Shiraz; many named after family members.

McWILLIAM'S HANWOOD

★★★★ 4.95–39.95 R AUS100, 186 UK98 US3
Murrumbidgee Irrigation Area **Est.** 1877
Winery Road, Hanwood, NSW 2680
Ph (069) 62 0001 **Fax** (069) 63 0002
Open Mon–Sat 9–5.30, Sun 10–4 **Production** NFP
Winemaker(s) Jim Brayne

Some of the best wines to emanate from the Hanwood winery are from other regions, notably the Barwang vineyard at Hilltops in New South Wales, Coonawarra and Eden Valley; on the other side of the coin as it were, the critical mass of the business continues to come from the Murrumbidgee Irrigation Area, which provides the bulk of the rapidly growing export business of the company.

Principal Wines A disciplined and easy-to-follow product range (all varietally identified), commencing with Hillside casks; Inheritance range; Hanwood; Charles King; Barwang Chardonnay, Shiraz and Cabernet Sauvignon; finally, Limited Release Hunter Valley Chardonnay, Eden Valley Riesling and Riverina Botrytis Semillon. Also superb fortified wines including MCWII Liqueur Muscat and 10-Year-Old Hanwood Tawny Port, heading a much larger range of Sherries, which still form an important part of the business.

McWILLIAM'S BARWANG CABERNET SAUVIGNON

●●●●● $13.95

The continental climate of the Barwang Vineyard, marked by cold nights and warm summer days, but with the growing season finishing much later than it does in either the Hunter Valley or Mudgee, produces red wines of considerable flavour, power and extract, exemplified by this wine with its 14% of alcohol.

Cellaring 15 years. **Best Vintages** '89, '91, '92, '93
Current Vintage '93
Matching Food Beef Wellington.
Tasting Note 1993 Medium to full red-purple; a fragrant and arresting bouquet, tangy and lively with mint aromas running into citrus, sweetened by a touch of vanillin oak. The palate has abundant rich, sweet blackcurrant fruit with good tannins and nicely handled oak.

McWILLIAM'S BARWANG CHARDONNAY

●●●● ▶ $13.95

From the Barwang Vineyard in the Hilltops region, near Young, New South Wales, purchased from Peter Robertson some years ago, and now significantly expanded. After a slightly uncertain and unconvincing start, these Barwang Chardonnays have gone from strength to strength. The '93 was good, the '94 better still.

Cellaring 3–4 years. **Best Vintages** '93, '94

Current Vintage '94
Matching Food Calamari.
Tasting Note 1994 Light green-yellow; a fragrant and stylish bouquet with melon fruit and excellent oak balance and integration. The palate is no less stylish than the bouquet, with first-class mouthfeel, melon/fig fruit and subtle oak. Substantial but not overblown, and will age well, helped by good acidity.

McWILLIAM'S BARWANG SHIRAZ
●●●●● $13.95
Although the Cabernet Sauvignon from Barwang is of high quality, it is the Shiraz which really shines. Each vintage has been extremely good, with very clear varietal character, the only problem being a slight hardness in the mouth in the lesser years. Another wine to go from strength to strength, and a great bargain at the price. The '93 vintage won a gold medal at the Royal Melbourne Show in 1994.
Cellaring 5–8 years. **Best Vintages** '90, '91, '92, '93
Current Vintage '93
Matching Food Kraft Australian parmesan.
Tasting Note 1993 Medium to full red-purple; a briary/woodsy bouquet, not overtly fruity, but nonetheless complex and interesting. The palate is firm, reserved and tight, with faint cherry and spice fruit flavours and oak in restraint. Will develop.

McWILLIAM'S EDEN VALLEY RIESLING
●●●●● $13.95
Part of a range of wines which appear sporadically, utilising small parcels of premium quality fruit produced from top regions. This wine received the trophy for Best Dry White Riesling at the 1993 Australian National Wine Show in Canberra, and continues to develop very well.
Cellaring Up to 10 years. **Best Vintages** NA
Current Vintage '90
Matching Food Caesar salad.
Tasting Note 1990 Light yellow-green; attractive and immediately identifiable regional lime bottle-developed aromas. The palate shows an attractive combination of lime and toast, marrying elegance with flavour, and should continue to develop.

McWILLIAM'S INHERITANCE SHIRAZ CABERNET
●●● $4.95
An interesting wine which reflects changing attitudes within the McWilliam's management and winemaking group. Hitherto the accent was on wines with long periods of bottle maturation, even if the wines themselves did not merit this. This is a non vintage blend of some old and some much younger material, and works exceptionally well at the price.
Cellaring Drink now. **Best Vintages** NA **Current Vintage** NV
Matching Food Pasta.
Tasting Note NV Light to medium red; fresh juicy berry fruit, with just a hint of spice. On the palate a fresh, cherry-flavoured wine with soft tannins, a hint of charry/chippy oak but thoroughly commendable at the price.

McWILLIAM'S LOVEDALE SEMILLON
●●●●● $24.50

The first release of this wine under the Lovedale label, although
intermittent prior releases have occurred under the former Anne
Riesling name — Riesling meaning Hunter River Riesling, in other
words, Semillon. A single-vineyard wine which is held back for even
longer than Elizabeth, and only released in exceptional years.
Cellaring Now–10 years. **Best Vintages** '75, '79, '84
Current Vintage '84
Matching Food Seafood pasta.
Tasting Note 1984 Glowing yellow-green; a zesty/lemony
bouquet with complex, slightly vegetal undertones. The palate has
extraordinary power and intensity, verging on grippy, but with
great character and verve.

McWILLIAM'S MCW11 LIQUEUR MUSCAT
●●●●● $39.95

This wine, blended to a constant quality and style, has amassed four
trophies and 42 gold medals in its show career. Very long ageing in
barrel is the secret; the wines do not have the intense muscat fruit
character of those of North East Victoria when young, but do attain
tremendous complexity with age.
Cellaring None required. **Best Vintages** NA
Current Vintage NV
Matching Food A winter's night.
Tasting Note NV Very deep dark mahogany brown; extreme
wood age shows with concentrated plum pudding aromas leading
on to a multiflavoured palate ranging from malt to toffee to plum
pudding, finishing with cleansing acidity to balance the intense
sweetness of the mid palate.

McWILLIAM'S RIVERINA BOTRYTIS SEMILLON (375 ML)
●●●●● $18.95

McWilliam's winemaker Jim Brayne has mastered the technically
very difficult production of this style of wine, and the releases pose
a serious challenge to the supremacy of De Bortoli. They are slower
developing, which is a good thing, and the current release has won
a large string of trophies and gold medals in national shows.
Cellaring Up to 10 years. **Best Vintages** '90, '91, '92
Current Vintage '92
Matching Food Rich, sweet fruit-based desserts.
Tasting Note 1992 Brilliant yellow-green; very clean, fresh and
seductive peachy fruit with excellent oak integration. The palate is
very intense, showing strong botrytis influence, but is not abrasive
or phenolic, finishing long and clean. Outstanding.

McWILLIAM'S MOUNT PLEASANT

★★★★★ 9–40 R AUS100, 186 UK98 US3
Hunter Valley **Est.** 1880
Marrowbone Road, Pokolbin, NSW 2321
Ph (049) 98 7505 **Fax** (049) 98 7761

Open Mon–Fri 9–4.30, W'ends, Public hols 10–4
Production 80 000
Winemaker(s) Phillip Ryan

McWilliam's Elizabeth (a pure Hunter wine) is now the only mature
Hunter Semillon generally commercially available, and is an under-
valued and underpriced treasure, with a consistently superb show
record. The three individual vineyard wines, together with the Maurice
O'Shea memorial wines, add to the lustre of this proud name.
Product Range Much simplified and rationalised over the past
year. The base range now comprises Mount Pleasant Elizabeth,
Philip, Late Harvest Dessert Wine and Chardonnay; then individual
vineyard wines, Rosehill Shiraz, Old Paddock & Old Hill Hermitage,
Lovedale Semillon (previously known as Anne), then Maurice
O'Shea Chardonnay and Shiraz; finally, Museum releases of
Elizabeth.

McWILLIAM'S MAURICE O'SHEA
●●●●● $NA

These are notes accumulated over a far wider span of time than most
in this work. In each case I indicate the year in which the wines were
tasted; because of the long time-frame involved, the passage of time
is unlikely to have altered the character of the wine to any noticeable
degree. However, cellar conditions may well have done so;
remember the adage, that there are no great old wines, only
great old bottles.
Cellaring NA. **Best Vintages** NA **Current Vintage** NA
Matching Food NA
Tasting Note 1954 OP Hermitage. Light tawny red in colour; two
bottles tasted, the lesser bottle still showing good fruit under slight
break-up characters, with the better wine showing classic, gentle
tarry/earthy Hunter aromas and flavours, and good tannins on the
finish. As the name indicates, from the Old Paddock. (Tasted June
1991.)

McWILLIAM'S MOUNT PLEASANT ELIZABETH
●●●●● $9.95

A wine with an exceptional pedigree and deserved reputation for
consistency, yet chronically underpriced and hence underrated
(or the reverse, I am not sure which). Changes to the packaging,
notably the bottle shape, and the hand of McWilliam's chief
executive Kevin McLintock may well see the wine gradually being
repositioned in the market to assume its rightful place. Even without
this, an undoubted classic, having won eight trophies and 75 gold
medals since 1981.
Cellaring 7–15 years. **Best Vintages** '75, '81, '82, '83, '86,
'89, '90 **Current Vintage** '89
Matching Food Rich seafood.
Tasting Note 1989 Medium yellow; a very complex bouquet with
some of the slightly vegetal/French characters of the Tyrrell's Vat 1
of the same year. The most complex, multiflavoured wine in the
entire range, with unusual herbaceous characters, which are
deceiving because they must be derived from the grapes, but give all

the appearance of having come from changed fermentation
techniques (they did not).

McWILLIAM'S MOUNT PLEASANT OP & OH HERMITAGE
●●●●● $26.95

OP & OH is the sort of obscure designation which so delighted
Maurice O'Shea. The letters in fact stand for Old Paddock and Old
Hill, planted respectively, in 1880 and 1920, and which provide the
bulk of the grapes which go into this distinguished wine. To confuse
matters a little, since 1987 it has been sold as O'Shea Hermitage, in
honour of Maurice O'Shea, in outstanding vintage years. So
sometimes you will see it sold as O'Shea, sometimes as OP & OH.
Cellaring 7–20 years. **Best Vintages** '65, '66, '67, '79, '85,
'87, '90, '91 **Current Vintage** '90
Matching Food Roast veal.
Tasting Note 1990 O'Shea. Light to medium red-purple; clean,
fresh, gentle red berry fruit aromas with a hint of vanilla and mint.
The palate is nicely structured, with a perfect balance between fruit
tannins and oak, and plenty of length to the finish.

MEADOWBANK WINES

★★★★ 10.50–20 CD AUS16, 35, 48, 92, 122, UK43
Derwent River **Est.** 1974
'Meadowbank', Glenora, Derwent Valley, Tas 7410
Ph (002) 86 1269 **Fax** (002) 86 1133
Open 7 days 11–5 **Production** 6500
Winemaker(s) Greg O'Keefe (Contract)
The Meadowbank vineyard is now one of the larger in Tasmania,
with 10 hectares of vines, but is only a tiny part of the diversified
agricultural and horticultural enterprise of the Ellis family, carried on
on a very large and historic grazing property with the Derwent River
running through the middle. Wine quality can be very good.
Principal Wines Riesling, Chardonnay, Grace Elizabeth
Chardonnay, Pinot Noir, Cabernet Sauvignon.

MEADOWBANK CABERNET SAUVIGNON
●●● $20.95

Produced from the Meadowbank Estate vineyard situated on a
picturesque escarpment immediately above the Derwent River.
Meadowbank is better known for its Pinot Noir, Chardonnay and
Riesling, but this is a creditable effort in a lighter, cool-grown style.
Cellaring 2–4 years. **Best Vintages** NA **Current Vintage** '93
Matching Food Nut of veal.
Tasting Note 1993 Medium red-purple; a very high toned
bouquet with leafy aromas in a pronounced varietal cool climate
mode; some tobacco and briar notes. On the palate a pungent,
leafy Chinon (Loire Valley, France) style with some tannins and
relatively pronounced acidity.

MEADOWBANK GRACE ELIZABETH CHARDONNAY
●●●● ▶ $20

A small quantity of the grapes harvested from the 4 hectares of estate plantings is set aside for the Grace Elizabeth Chardonnay. It is barrel fermented in new French (Dargaud & Jaegle) oak, taken through malolactic fermentation, and left on lees for nine months. A distinguished wine.

Cellaring 3–5 years. **Best Vintages** NA **Current Vintage** '93
Matching Food Fresh Tasmanian salmon.

Tasting Note 1993 Light to medium yellow-green; youthful apple, pear and peach aromas, with the oak still a fraction assertive on the bouquet. The palate is elegant, with apple, nut and melon flavours, and a creamy texture from the malolactic fermentation. Well balanced, and will age well.

MEADOWBANK PINOT NOIR
●●●● ▶ $20
One of the wines to fulfil the promise for so long held out by Tasmania. The wine has come of age under the direction of former Normans' winemaker Greg O'Keefe, who acts as contract winemaker for Meadowbank as well as a number of other growers throughout Tasmania. Made from estate-grown grapes, with 4 hectares of pinot in production.

Cellaring 2–4 years. **Best Vintages** NA **Current Vintage** '93
Matching Food Tasmanian venison.

Tasting Note 1993 Bright medium red-purple. An elegant style, fruit-driven with attractive dark morello cherry aromas and flavours. The palate is very supple, as befits pinot noir, with nice length to the finish.

MEADOWBANK RIESLING
●●● ▶ $16.50
Produced from just under one hectare of estate-grown riesling, which constituted the first plantings at Meadowbank, and which were initially sold to Hickinbotham Winemakers (in the late 1970s), transported across the Bass Strait in styrene containers.

Cellaring 3 years. **Best Vintages** NA **Current Vintage** '94
Matching Food Asparagus.

Tasting Note 1994 Light green-yellow; a powerful bouquet with herb, mineral and toast aromas. The palate is clean and dry, with more toasty/minerally notes, and not particularly fruity. Could develop nicely in bottle, however.

MERRICKS ESTATE

NR 16.50–17.50 CD AUS177
Mornington Peninsula **Est.** 1977
Thompsons Lane, Merricks, Vic 3916
Ph (059) 89 8416)
Open First w'end month 12–5 **Production** 1600
Winemaker(s) Alex White
Melbourne solicitor George Kefford, together with wife Jacquie, runs Merricks Estate as a weekend and holiday enterprise as a relief from professional practice. Right from the outset it has produced very distinctive, spicy, cool-climate Shiraz which has accumulated an

impressive array of show trophies and gold medals. No recent tastings.
Principal Wines Chardonnay, Shiraz, Cabernet Sauvignon, Pinot Noir.

MIDDLEBROOK WINERY*

NR 12–16 CD AUSSD
Southern Vales **Est.** 1947
Sand Road, McLaren Vale, SA 5171
Ph (08) 383 0004 **Fax** (08) 383 0470
Open Mon–Fri 9–5, W'ends 10–5 **Production** 1500
Winemaker(s) Walter Clappis
Middlebrook is best known for its restaurant which provides lunch every day and dinner on Saturday night, particularly catering for functions and wedding receptions. As a winery it has had a chequered career, but has recently been purchased by Walter (Bill) Clappis of Ingoldby, and things should take a turn for the better.
Principal Wines Sauvignon Blanc, Chardonnay, Shiraz, Merlot, Cabernet Sauvignon.

MIDDLETON ESTATE

NR 7.50–10 CD AUS74
Southern Vales **Est.** 1979
Flagstaff Hill Road, Middleton, SA 5213
Ph (085) 55 4136 **Fax** (085) 55 4108
Open Fri–Sun 10–5 **Production** 5000
Winemaker(s) Nigel Catt
Nigel Catt has demonstrated his winemaking skills at Andrew Garrett and elsewhere, so wine quality should be good; despite its decade of production, I have never seen or tasted its wines.
Principal Wines Riesling, Sauvignon Blanc, Semillon Sauvignon Blanc, Cabernet Hermitage.

MILDARA (COONAWARRA)

★★★★ 10.95–25.95 R AUS104, UK51
Coonawarra **Est.** 1955
Penola–Naracoorte Road, Coonawarra, SA 5263
Ph (087) 36 3339
Open 7 days 9–5 **Production** 150 000
Winemaker(s) Gavin Hogg
Mildara Managing Director Ray King knows better than most that brands have natural life cycles. Having prospered mightily with Jamiesons Run, and having extended it to include a Chardonnay, he has now introduced Robertson's Well, and is said to be hard at work reshaping the top end, with a new face pending for what was once the lead brand, the White Label Cabernet Sauvignon.
Plus ça change.
Principal Wines The volume is driven by Jamiesons Run Red and Jamiesons Run Chardonnay; Robertson's Well Cabernet Sauvignon

has been recently introduced, with the Coonawarra Cabernet to be repositioned. Alexanders remains the top-end wine for the time being.

1963 MILDARA COONAWARRA CABERNET SAUVIGNON
●●●●● $NA

Arguably the most famous Coonawarra red of the past 30 years, and certainly the best from Mildara. Tasted at the 'Legends of Coonawarra' dinner held in Sydney in late 1994, still drinking superbly and still showing those hallmark flavours. Long nicknamed 'Peppermint Pattie'.

Cellaring Drink now. **Best Vintages** NA **Current Vintage** NA
Matching Food Fine cheddar, parmesan.
Tasting Note 1963 Still holding its colour incredibly well, with bright red-purple hues. The bouquet is very intense, with pronounced leaf and peppermint aromas. The palate has more sweet fruit than the bouquet promises, though again that peppermint character is there in abundance. Still remarkably fresh; a unique wine which marches to the tune of its own drum.

MILDARA ALEXANDERS
●●●● $25.95

The premium Bordeaux blend from Mildara, utilising estate-grown cabernet sauvignon, merlot and cabernet franc. The oak treatment in the wine has always been positive, but I personally have always had some degree of difficulty with it. The '90 has developed nicely, however, and is the product of a very distinguished Coonawarra vintage.

Cellaring 5–10 years. **Best Vintages** '86, '88, '90, '91
Current Vintage '90
Matching Food Lamb loin.
Tasting Note 1990 Medium red; secondary fruit characters now starting to appear in a complex briary/cedary bouquet. The palate has a melange of flavours ranging from leafy to briary to redcurrant, with a fairly firm, oaky finish.

MILDARA COONAWARRA CABERNET SAUVIGNON
●●●● $13.95

A wine made famous by the 1963 vintage, immediately and forever nicknamed 'Peppermint Pattie' because of its intense eucalypt aromas and flavours. A separate wine entry is given for this wine because it remains a landmark. There have been some other excellent vintages over the years, but nothing to challenge the '63, and the wine is apparently due to be repositioned within the Mildara framework.

Cellaring 4–7 years. **Best Vintages** '63, '86, '88, '90, '91
Current Vintage '92
Matching Food Beef casserole.
Tasting Note 1992 Medium red-purple; solid, dark briary fruit with slightly hard, charry oak. There is lots of good dark berry fruit on the palate, but with some fairly hard, varnish tannins, possibly oak derived.

MILDARA JAMIESONS RUN COONAWARRA RED
●●●● $10.95
A blend of cabernet sauvignon, shiraz, merlot and cabernet franc,
the last two in lesser quantities, sourced from Mildara's extensive
Coonawarra vineyards. Has enjoyed extraordinary show success,
and held its quality, notwithstanding vast increases in volume,
although it no longer pretends to any great complexity or weight.
Cellaring 3–4 years. **Best Vintages** '86, '88, '90, '91, '92
Current Vintage '92
Matching Food Mediterranean, Italian.
Tasting Note 1992 Medium red-purple. An aromatic bouquet
with some cedary/leafy aromas, subtle oak and of light to medium
intensity. The palate is light, lacking structural complexity, but with a
pleasant mix of red berry fruit and cedary American oak.

MILDARA ROBERTSON'S WELL CABERNET SAUVIGNON
●●●● ▶ $14.95
Introduced in 1992, and named after a local landmark which
(slightly embarrassingly) turned out to be outside the tentative
boundaries for Coonawarra. The problem was resolved by
bestowing the name on one of the Coonawarra vineyards within the
boundary. Had an auspicious start winning the Stodart Trophy and
three gold medals in national wine shows. A similar blend to
Jamieson's Run but with more weight.
Cellaring 3–7 years. **Best Vintages** NA **Current Vintage** '92
Matching Food Roast beef.
Tasting Note 1992 Medium to full red-purple; complex, elegant
fragrant cedary aromas with substantial oak input, said to be
French. The palate shows lots of stylish cedary, lemony oak and
has a long finish with lingering tannins.

MILDARA (MURRAY RIVER)

★★★☆ 8–10 R AUS104, UK51
Murray River **Est.** 1888
Wentworth Road, Merbein, Vic 3505
Ph (050) 25 2303 **Fax** (050) 25 3300
Open 7 days 9–5 **Production** 1 million
Winemaker(s) Alan Harris
A somewhat antiquated Merbein facility remains the overall group
production centre following its acquisition of Wolf Blass, although
all of its premium wines are sourced from and made at Coonawarra.
The Church Hill range is dependable, the sherries good.
Principal Wines Church Hill Chardonnay, Fumé Blanc, Cabernet
Merlot; Sherries (Chestnut Teal, George, Supreme), Pot Brandy.

MILLINUP ESTATE

NR 11–14.50 CD AUSSD
Great Southern **Est.** 1989
RMB 1280 Porongurup Road, Porongurup, WA 6324
Ph (098) 53 1105
Open Mon–Fri 10–4 **Production** 220

Winemaker(s) John Wade (Contract)
The Millinup Estate vineyard was planted in 1978, when it was
called Point Creek. Owners Peter and Lesley Thorn purchased it in
1989, renaming it and having the limited production vinified by
John Wade at Plantagenet.
Principal Wines Riesling, Cabernet Merlot.

MILNATHORT WINES

NR 10–11 CD AUSSD
Southern Tasmania **Est.** 1983
Channel Highway, Birchs Bay, Tas 7162
Ph (002) 67 4750 **Fax** (002) 67 4601
Open Not **Production** 80
Winemaker(s) Andrew Hood (Contract)
Although production is minuscule, quality has been consistently high.
The Riesling is well made, but the interesting wine from this far
southern vineyard is Cabernet Sauvignon: clearly, the vineyard
enjoys favourable ripening conditions.
Principal Wines Riesling, Cabernet Sauvignon.

MINTARO WINES

★★★ 9–12 CD AUSSD
Clare Valley **Est.** 1986
Leasingham Road, Mintaro, SA 5415
Ph (088) 43 9046
Open 7 days 9–5 **Production** 2000
Winemaker(s) James Pearson
Has produced some very good Rhine Riesling over the years,
developing well in bottle. The Cabernet Sauvignon, by contrast,
has tended to dullness and/or bitterness.
Principal Wines Riesling, Cabernet Sauvignon.

MINYA WINERY, THE See page 439.

MIRAMAR WINES

★★★★ 8.50–16 CD AUSSD
Mudgee **Est.** 1977
Henry Lawson Drive, Mudgee, NSW 2850
Ph (063) 73 3874 **Fax** (063) 73 3854
Open 7 days 9–5 **Production** 8000
Winemaker(s) Ian MacRae
Miramar won the Open Dry White Trophy at the Mudgee Wine
Show eight times between 1982 and 1992, adding the Museum
Class Trophy in 1990 and 1993. As this record indicates, its white
wines (particularly its Chardonnay) are particularly good, but the
aged reds on offer are also full of character.
Principal Wines Semillon Chardonnay, Semillon, Chardonnay,
Fumé Blanc, Riesling, Rosé, Pinot Noir, Cabernet Sauvignon, Shiraz,
Vintage Port; Wilbertree is second label.

MIRAMAR CABERNET SAUVIGNON
●●●● $12.95

At the end of 1994, Ian MacRae was still offering the 1988
Cabernet Sauvignon, which in his words, 'Has been a slow learner
but in the last year or so has really come together'. Only in Mudgee
could one find a Cabernet of this quality and age at this price.

Cellaring 7–12 years. **Best Vintages** '82, '84, '85, '86, '91
Current Vintage '88
Matching Food Mild cheddar.
Tasting Note 1988 Medium red; fully aged, with caramel, vanilla
and cedar aromas. The palate has softened and developed well,
with similar cedary/briary/vanillin characters to those of the
bouquet, finishing with very soft, fine tannins.

MIRAMAR CHARDONNAY
●●●● ▶ $14.50

Miramar has been one of the leading producers of Chardonnay in
the Mudgee district for many years. What is more, the wines are
unusually long-lived, winning trophies and gold medals at up to 10
years of age. The wine is sometimes delicate when young, peachy
and rich when old.

Cellaring Up to 10 years. **Best Vintages** '81, '82, '84, '86, '87,
'91 **Current Vintage** '91
Matching Food Deep-fried calamari.
Tasting Note 1991 Youthful, light to medium yellow-green; clean
and firm, still largely unevolved aromas. The palate, too, is fresh and
youthful, more like a youngish Semillon than a Chardonnay.

MIRAMAR SHIRAZ
●●● ▶ $12.95

Another slow-developing wine made from estate-grown grapes,
moving progressively earthy, cedary characters as it ages. The oak
contribution is typically subtle.

Cellaring 5–8 years. **Best Vintages** '82, '84, '85, '86, '91
Current Vintage '91
Matching Food Braised oxtail.
Tasting Note 1991 Medium red; still quite firm with mint and red
berry fruits on the bouquet, leading on to a moderately fruit wine on
the palate, with cedary oak, finishing with dusty tannins.

MIRANDA WINES

★★★☆ 3.99–15.95 AUS105
Murrumbidgee Irrigation Area **Est.** 1939
57 Jondaryan Avenue, Griffith, NSW 2680
Ph (069) 62 4033 **Fax** (069) 62 6944
Open 7 days 9–5 **Production** Over 1 million
Winemaker(s) Shayne Cunningham

In recent years, Miranda has produced some startlingly good wines,
no doubt due to its purchases of Clare Valley and Barossa Valley
grapes, followed by its acquisition of the Rovalley winery. Some of
the Chardonnays in particular have scored very highly in shows, but

it is not always easy to tell which wine ends up under which label; seemingly, both Mirrool Creek and Wyangan ranges have done extremely well.

Principal Wines Wyangan Estate is the premium label, then comes Mirrool Creek, then Somerton and, finally, generics under the Miranda label.

MIRANDA MIRROOL CREEK CHARDONNAY
●●● $6.99
Sourced from the Riverina, with lesser a percentage from the Hunter and Barossa Valleys. Part of the wine was barrel fermented and given some oak ageing. You certainly get more than you pay for.
Cellaring Drink now. **Best Vintages** NA **Current Vintage** '93
Matching Food Seafood pasta.
Tasting Note 1993 Bright yellow-green; fresh, crisp citrussy fruit aromas of light to medium intensity, with just a touch of lift. The palate is not quite as exciting as the bouquet suggests it might be, but does have some pleasant peachy fruit, with just a hint of vanillin oak.

MIRANDA WYANGAN ESTATE CHARDONNAY
●●●● $10.99
The 1992 vintage was sourced from the Riverina (40%), Eden Valley (20%), Barossa Valley (17%), King Valley (13%), and Hunter Valley (10%). Just to add further complexity, it is 85% chardonnay, 13% semillon and 2% sauvignon blanc. Surprisingly, given a wine of this price, it was barrel fermented in new American oak barriques and aged in those barrels for seven months. The wine has won four medals in national shows.
Cellaring Drink now. **Best Vintages** NA **Current Vintage** '93
Matching Food Ginger pork.
Tasting Note 1993 Deep yellow; complex bottle-developed aromas with lots of intensity and weight; the fruit is in the grapefruit/peach spectrum, and there is obvious barrel ferment oak. The palate is already starting to tire a little, not surprising given the ancestry of the wine, and emphasising that this style should be consumed sooner rather than later.

MITCHELL

★★★★☆ 11.95–14.95 CD AUS27, 65, 67, 74, 82, 83, 137, UK58
Clare Valley **Est.** 1975
Hughes Park Road, Sevenhill via Clare, SA 5453
Ph (088) 43 4258 **Fax** (088) 43 4340
Open 7 days 10–4 **Production** 18 000
Winemaker(s) Andrew Mitchell
For long one of the stalwarts of the Clare Valley, producing long-lived Rieslings and Cabernet Sauvignons in classic regional style, but having extended the range with very creditable Semillon and Shiraz.
Principal Wines Rieslings and Cabernet Sauvignons; also Old Liqueur Riesling, Semillon, Peppertree Vineyard Shiraz, Sparkling Peppertree.

MITCHELL CABERNET SAUVIGNON

●●●● ▶ $14.95

First made in 1976; from then to 1983 fashioned entirely from cabernet sauvignon, but between then and 1985 first cabernet franc and then merlot were added, now contributing 5-15% of the finished wine, which is aged in a mix of new and older French oak.

Cellaring 7–15 years. **Best Vintages** '78, '80, '84, '86, '90, '92 **Current Vintage** '92

Matching Food Roast lamb.

Tasting Note 1992 Great depth to the purple-red colour; the bouquet is very concentrated, with a range of earthy, briary, berry and cassis aromas, with a hint of lift. The palate is likewise concentrated with ripe blackcurrant fruit and good tannin balance, and just a faint whisper of gaminess lurking somewhere in the depths.

MITCHELL PEPPERTREE VINEYARD SHIRAZ

●●●● $14.95

Like the Semillon, first made in 1984, and which takes its name from the old pepper tree which grows in the shiraz vineyard at Watervale. The wine is aged for 18 months in small French and American oak; in some years it shows minty characters, in other years more spice and cherry.

Cellaring 5–7 years. **Best Vintages** '84, '86, '87, '94 **Current Vintage** '93

Matching Food Devilled kidneys.

Tasting Note 1993 Medium red-purple; attractive berry fruits with a hint of spice and subtle oak to a bouquet of light to medium intensity. The palate is fresh with spicy cherry fruit, finishing with soft tannins.

MITCHELL SEMILLON

●●●● ▶ $12.50

First made in 1984, initially with very pronounced French oak, but in latter years with a less generous hand — which is all to the good. An each-way drinking style, good when young, but even better with some age.

Cellaring 2–5 years. **Best Vintages** '84, '87, '93, '94 **Current Vintage** '94

Matching Food Abalone.

Tasting Note 1994 Light to medium green-yellow; clean, direct herbaceous varietal fruit with good weight and very subtle oak on the bouquet. It has attractive fruit flavours with hints of passionfruit, with a long, clean finish. Once again, the oak is barely perceptible.

MITCHELL WATERVALE RIESLING

●●●●● $11.50

First made in 1977 and produced from the estate vineyards in the Watervale region. This is a classic Clare Riesling which, as the classic tasting shows, ages magnificently for up to 15 years in good vintages.

Cellaring 5–10+ years. **Best Vintages** '78, '84, '90, '92, '93, '94 **Current Vintage** '94

Matching Food Grilled fish.
Tasting Note 1994 Light green-yellow; the bouquet is solid, with lime, herb and toast aromas with a strong core of fruit. The same fruit comes through on a long, well balanced palate with strong regional lime and toast flavours.

MITCHELTON

★★★★☆ 9.95–23.95 R AUS66 UK47 US9
Goulburn Valley **Est.** 1974
Mitchellstown via Nagambie, Vic 3608
Ph (057) 94 2710 **Fax** (057) 94 2615
Open 7 days 9–5 **Production** 230 000
Winemaker(s) Don Lewis

Acquired by Petaluma in 1994, having already put the runs on the board in no uncertain fashion with the gifted team of Stephen Shelmerdine, Christopher Anstee and winemaker Don Lewis. Boasts an extraordinarily impressive array of wines across a broad spectrum of style and price, but each carefully aimed at a market niche.

Principal Wines Top of the range Print Label Shiraz, then Reserve Chardonnay, Cabernet Sauvignon, Marsanne; next comes Mitchelton III wines, White (Marsanne, Grenache, Viognier), Red (Shiraz, Grenache Mourvedre); Chinaman's Bridge Merlot, Blackwood Park Riesling and MCM (formerly Cab Mac). Preece Chardonnay and Cabernet Sauvignon are volume sellers, as is the Thomas Mitchell range of Chardonnay, Riesling, Chablis, Semillon Chardonnay and Cabernet Shiraz Malbec. Finally, intermittent aged classic releases.

MITCHELTON BLACKWOOD PARK RIESLING
●●●●● $9.95

Over the past few years Blackwood Park has laid claim to being the best commercial Riesling in Australia, even though its origins go back to 1978 under different labels. Since that time various vintages have won 8 trophies, 51 gold, 66 silver and 102 bronze medals, with the '94 vintage adding to both the trophy and gold medal records.
Cellaring Classic each way. **Best Vintages** '81, '85, '90, '91, '92 **Current Vintage** '94
Matching Food Sashimi.
Tasting Note 1994 Light green-yellow; tight lime juice and passionfruit aromas with distinctly Germanic overtones. An elegant, lime-accented palate which is flavourful but not the least phenolic, with a long, clean finish. Has the structure to age.

MITCHELTON CHINAMAN'S BRIDGE MERLOT
●●●● $11.95

Another addition to the Mitchelton range; the 1992 vintage was the first release. It is named for an old bridge located between Nagambie and Mitchelton built in 1890, so named because of the many Chinese market gardens in the region. Interestingly, the wine is

estate-grown, and is intended for immediate consumption.
Cellaring None required. **Best Vintages** NA
Current Vintage '92
Matching Food Pizza.
Tasting Note 1992 Medium to full red; fragrant leaf, mint, herb
and cherry aromas with little oak impact. The palate has interesting
flavours and textures, with earthy/cherry fruit, and a pleasing finish.

MITCHELTON III RED
●●●● $13.95
First made in 1992 as a partner to the Mitchelton III White and,
like its partner, a Rhone-inspired blend of shiraz, grenache and
mourvedre. The precise regional base of the wine is not given,
but it seems probable it will have a substantial South Australian
component.
Cellaring 3–5 years. **Best Vintages** NA **Current Vintage** '92
Matching Food Braised duck.
Tasting Note 1992 Dense, dark red-purple; a concentrated
bouquet with a complex array of dark berry, mint and game
aromas. The palate is similarly multiflavoured with genuine style,
even if for some palates it may be a little over the top.

MITCHELTON III WHITE
●●●● ▶ $13.95
Introduced in 1993 with a very distinctive oval label, yet another
demonstration of the skills of graphic design artist Brian Sadgrove.
Made from a blend of marsanne, grenache and viognier, principally
grown in the Goulburn Valley, with marsanne the major component.
Cellaring 2–3 years. **Best Vintages** NA **Current Vintage** '93
Matching Food Mediterranean-style seafood.
Tasting Note 1993 Medium yellow-green; rich, tropical
honeysuckle fruit aromas with both the marsanne and viognier
making their mark. On the palate, an interesting wine with real
Rhone fruit characters, likened by Don Lewis to jasmine, ripe citrus
and a hint of thyme. The oak is subtle.

MITCHELTON PREECE CABERNET SAUVIGNON
●●●● $10.95
Named in honour of Colin Preece, one of the great winemakers of
the 20th century, and for decades chief winemaker at Seppelt Great
Western. He came out of a 10-year retirement to help found
Mitchelton in 1973. The wine is 100% cabernet sauvignon, made
predominantly from fruit grown in the Goulburn Valley of Victoria.
Cellaring 2–3 years. **Best Vintages** NA **Current Vintage** '93
Matching Food Spaghetti with pesto.
Tasting Note 1993 Medium red-purple; pronounced peppermint
aromas give the bouquet an almost citrussy character, and herald a
palate with similarly pronounced peppermint and leaf flavours of
medium weight, finishing with soft tannins.

MITCHELTON PRINT LABEL SHIRAZ
●●●● ▶ $23.95
In 1981 Mitchelton conceived the idea of staging a Print Exhibition

and making an annual purchase of the best print in the exhibition for subsequent use as the label of the best red wine of the vintage. Both the '90 and '91 vintages were outstanding, the former winning the Jimmy Watson Trophy; notwithstanding the 2 gold, 2 silver and 3 bronze medals garnered by the '92, it is of somewhat lesser quality.
Cellaring Up to 10 years. **Best Vintages** '81, '82, '90, '91
Current Vintage '92
Matching Food Marinated venison.
Tasting Note 1992 Dense red-purple; a concentrated, ripe essency bouquet with some slightly sweaty/gamey aromas. On the palate, extremely concentrated and powerful, but again with gamey/minty aspects. One suspects the presence of some imperfectly ripened fruit.

MITCHELTON VICTORIA CHARDONNAY
●●●●● $22.95
No region of origin is claimed for the wine, nor is any given in the PR material. Instead Don Lewis says, 'over several years I have identified a number of vineyard sites producing chardonnay grapes of extraordinary quality'. It is a reasonable assumption that these include sites in both the Goulburn River and the Yarra Valley. As with the Marsanne, the 1993 heralds the name change from Reserve to Victoria.
Cellaring 4–7 years. **Best Vintages** '81, '85, '90, '91, '92
Current Vintage '93
Matching Food Crumbed brains.
Tasting Note 1993 Medium yellow-green; softly sweet melon fruit is matched with well-balanced and integrated oak. A pleasantly complex wine on the palate, with similar melon fruit intermingling with cashew notes, partly oak and partly fruit derived. Trophy and gold medal winner.

MITCHELTON VICTORIA MARSANNE
●●●● $19.95
Initially made in a very oaky style (and not under a Reserve label) which made it difficult, if not impossible, to see the delicate varietal fruit underneath the oak. Over the years, the oak has been pulled back to the point where now the wine is entirely fruit-driven. The 1993 vintage continues the trend away from oak and towards fruit, and also signifies a change in name from Reserve to Victoria.
Cellaring Up to 7 years. **Best Vintages** '85, '90, '91, '92, '93
Current Vintage '93
Matching Food Delicate white meat dishes.
Tasting Note 1993 Medium yellow; the bouquet is soft, with some secondary bottle-developed aromas now starting to appear. The palate shows authentic honeysuckle fruit with minimal oak input.

MOLLY MORGAN VINEYARD *

NR 10–12.50 CD AUSSD
Hunter Valley **Est.** 1984
Talga Road, Allandale, NSW 2321
Ph (049) 30 7695 **Fax** (02) 221 4168

Open W'ends, Public hols 10–5 **Production** 600
Winemaker(s) Bill Sneddon and Geoffrey Broadfield (Contract)
The weekend retreat of Sydney barrister Geoff Petty; much of the
production from the 10-hectare plantings of semillon, chardonnay,
shiraz and riesling are sold elsewhere. Tastings over the years have
always shown rich, well-flavoured wines. No recent tastings.
Principal Wines Non-Wooded Semillon, Barrel Fermented
Semillon, Joe's Black Semillon, Chardonnay, Shiraz.

MONBULK WINERY

★★☆ 8.50–14.90 CD AUSSD
Yarra Valley **Est.** 1984
Macclesfield Road, Monbulk, Vic 3793
Ph (03) 9756 6965 **Fax** (03) 9756 6965
Open W'ends 12–5, by appt **Production** 1000
Winemaker(s) Paul Jabornik
Originally concentrated on Kiwifruit wines, but now extending to
table wines; the very cool Monbulk subregion should be capable
of producing wines of distinctive style, but the table wines are
(unfortunately) not of the same standard as the Kiwifruit wines,
which are quite delicious.
Principal Wines Chardonnay, Riesling, Pinot Noir, Cabernet
Sauvignon, Shiraz; also Kiwifruit wines.

MONICHINO WINES

★★★ 9–21 CD AUS173
North Goulburn River **Est.** 1962
1820 Berrys Road, Katunga, Vic 3640
Ph (058) 64 6452 **Fax** (058) 64 6538
Open Mon–Sat 9–5, Sun 10–5 **Production** 11 000
Winemaker(s) Carlo Monichino
An altogether surprising winery which quietly makes very clean,
fresh wines in which the fruit character has been carefully preserved.
Principal Wines Monichino premium label: Chardonnay,
Sauvignon Blanc, Cabernet Malbec Shiraz, Shiraz, Shiraz Malbec
and various Ports and fortifieds; Monichino Karunga Estate label:
Sauvignon Blanc, Semillon, Dry White, Spatlese Frontignac, Orange
Muscat, Lexia, Botrytis Semillon, Dry Red. Bulk sales also available.

MONTARA WINES

★★★ 10–18 CD AUS51, 72, UK43
Great Western **Est.** 1970
Chalambar Road, Ararat, Vic 3377
Ph (053) 52 3868 **Fax** (053) 52 4968
Open Mon–Sat 9.30–5, Sun 12–4 **Production** NFP
Winemaker(s) Mike McRae
Achieved considerable attention for its Pinot Noirs during the 1980s,
but other regions (and other makers) have come along since. Recent
tastings across the board show wines of serviceable quality.

Principal Wines Chardonnay, Riesling, Ondenc, Chasselas, Pinot Noir, Shiraz, Cabernet Sauvignon, Port; second label is 'M' range of Riesling, Ondenc and Pinot Noir Shiraz.

MONTARA 'M' PINOT SHIRAZ
●●● $10.95
Pinot Shiraz blends were used by the famous winemaker Maurice O'Shea at Mount Pleasant in the Hunter Valley in the 1940s and 1950s, but have never been widely employed. That alone gives the wine interest; likewise, Montara's early success with a fairly full-flavoured style of Pinot Noir back in the 1970s has ensured continued interest in the wine.
Cellaring 1–3 years. **Best Vintages** NA
Current Vintage '94
Matching Food Spiced quail.
Tasting Note 1994 Medium to full red-purple; a potent bouquet with many fruit aromas ranging from juicy blackcurrant through to more leafy/spicy characters. A similarly interesting juicy/spicy wine on the palate with lots of fruit flavour, though far from conventional Pinot in style.

MONTROSE ESTATE WINES
★★★★ 8.95–13.95 R AUS117
Mudgee **Est.** 1974
Henry Lawson Drive, Mudgee, NSW 2850
Ph (063) 73 3853 **Fax** (063) 73 3795
Open Mon–Fri 9–4, W'ends 10–4 **Production** 50 000
Winemaker(s) Robert Paul
A small piece of the Orlando/Wyndham empire, acting partly as a grape and bulk wine source for that empire, and partly as a quality producer in its own right, making typically full-flavoured whites and deep-coloured reds.
Principal Wines Poet's Corner Classic Dry White and Classic Dry Red are at the inexpensive end; premium varietals are Chardonnay, Cabernet Merlot and Cabernet Sauvignon.

MONTROSE ESTATE CHARDONNAY
●●●● ▶ $11.95
Montrose followed closely in the footsteps of neighbour Craigmoor (both now being part of the Wyndham empire, but not then) in producing some of the first Chardonnays in Australia. From the outset, the quality has been high, with then winemaker Carlo Carino anticipating the future in first making unwooded Chardonnay (in the 1970s). The '91 vintage of this wine amassed four trophies.
Cellaring 3–6 years. **Best Vintages** '84, '86, '89, '90, '91
Current Vintage '93
Matching Food Fillet of pork.
Tasting Note 1993 Light yellow-green; fragrant, fresh, lively citrus and melon fruit drives the bouquet, with similar lively, fresh and crisp flavours on the palate, with a background of subtle oak (and no oak chips). Good acidity. Has won two gold medals at local shows.

MONTROSE ESTATE POET'S CORNER CLASSIC DRY RED
●●● ▶ $11.95

A blend of shiraz, cabernet sauvignon and cabernet franc produced from the various vineyards owned by the Montrose interests (part of Orlando Wyndham). Always an honest, full-flavoured red at a bargain price.

Cellaring 1–5 years. **Best Vintages** '86, '87, '91, '93
Current Vintage '93
Matching Food T-bone steak.
Tasting Note 1993 Medium red-purple; a clean and rich bouquet with lots of dark plum and dark cherry fruit together with a touch of mint. The palate is fresh and lively with minty/berry fruit, finishing with soft tannins. The oak influence is barely discernible.

MOONDAH BROOK

★★★★ 12.95–13.95 R AUS20–24, UK18
North Perth **Est.** 1968
c/o Houghton, Dale Road, Middle Swan, WA 6056
Ph Fax (09) 274 5372
Open Not **Production** 90 000
Winemaker(s) Paul Lapsley

Part of the Houghton Wine Group which has its own special character as it draws part of its fruit from the large Gingin vineyard, 70 kilometres north of the Swan Valley, and part from the Margaret River and Great Southern. In recent times it has excelled even its own reputation for reliability with some quite lovely wines.

Principal Wines Chardonnay, Chenin Blanc, Verdelho, Sauvignon Blanc, Cabernet Sauvignon; also occasional Show Reserve releases of Chenin Blanc and Verdelho.

MOONDAH BROOK CABERNET SAUVIGNON
●●●● $13.95

The Moondah Brook label is something of a misnomer, as fruit sources have gradually extended across the State of Western Australia. So it is with the Cabernet Sauvignon, which burst into prominence with the '91 vintage, winning gold medals at national shows, made from Margaret River and Great Southern fruit, while the '92 is not up to the '91, it is a pleasant wine.

Cellaring Short term only. **Best Vintages** '82, '88, '91, '94
Current Vintage '92
Matching Food Veal chops Italian style.
Tasting Note 1992 Medium to full red-purple; fresh, bright red and blackcurrant fruit with slightly raw oak on the bouquet. The palate is light, fresh and elegant with similar bright fruit flavours. Early-drinking style.

MOONDAH BROOK CHARDONNAY
●●● ▶ $12.95

With the skills of white winemaker Paul Lapsley, and the reputation of the variety, one might have expected this to be the star of the range, but in fact it is less interesting than the other white wines. Drawn from vineyard sources across the State.

Cellaring 2–3 years. **Best Vintages** NA **Current Vintage** '93
Matching Food Marron.
Tasting Note 1993 Light to medium green-yellow; the bouquet has
good, concentrated, tangy fruit marred by some sweaty fermentation
characters. The palate shows the same excellent fruit, both
concentrated and long, but again some fermentation/yeast
characters intrude.

MOONDAH BROOK CHENIN BLANC
●●●● ▶ $12.95
Stakes a strong claim as Australia's best Chenin Blanc. Produced
entirely from Moondah Brook's Gingin Vineyard, the '92 won the
White Wine of the Year Award in the 1993 *Wine Magazine*
International Wine Challenge in London. The '93, by contrast, came
from a perfect vintage. The wines are cold fermented and then
matured in new American oak for six months. As the '87 Show
Reserve demonstrated in 1994, ages into a buttery, unctuous wine.
Cellaring Up to 7 years. **Best Vintages** '80, '87, '89, '91, '93
Current Vintage '93
Matching Food Prosciutto and figs.
Tasting Note 1993 Light to medium yellow-green; clean and
smooth with attractive, tropical passionfruit aromas and a barely
perceptible hint of vanilla from the oak. The palate is very attractive,
smooth and harmonious, with a long and balanced finish. Exemplary
oak handling, subtle in the extreme.

MOONDAH BROOK SAUVIGNON BLANC
●●●● ▶ $12.95
A new addition to the roster, drawn primarily from fruit grown in the
southern regions of Western Australia (as is the Cabernet
Sauvignon). The initial vintage from 1994 displayed a very
interesting array of aromas and tastes.
Cellaring Drink now. **Best Vintages** NA
Current Vintage '94
Matching Food Coquilles St Jacques.
Tasting Note 1994 Light to medium green-yellow; highly aromatic,
pungent fruit salad aromas, composed of half fresh and half canned
fruit. The palate is also striking, although more conventional
Sauvignon Blanc in the gooseberry/tropical range, with overall fruit
weight and richness.

MOONDAH BROOK VERDELHO
●●●● $12.95
Sourced predominantly from the Gingin Vineyard, but with a smaller
contribution from the Margaret River. It is cold fermented in stainless
steel, and not given any oak maturation. The '90 Show Reserve,
tasted in 1994, shows how well the wine matures, with attractive
tropical and citrus fruit aromas and flavours.
Cellaring Up to 6 years. **Best Vintages** '80, '87, '89, '90, '91,
'93 **Current Vintage** '93
Matching Food Sugar-cured tuna.
Tasting Note 1993 Light to medium yellow-green; a spotlessly

clean bouquet of light to medium intensity with tropical pineapple
and peach aromas. The palate is quite rich, with round, mouthfilling
tropical spicy fruit.

MOONSHINE VALLEY WINERY *

NR 8–12 CD AUSSD
Granite Belt **Est.** 1985
3 Forest Court, Forest Glen, Buderim, Qld 4556
Ph (074) 45 1198 **Fax** (074) 45 2052
Open 7 days 10–5 **Production** 1000
Winemaker(s) Frederick Houweling
Frederick Houweling brings a European background to his making
of these fruit-based wines. The winery is situated on a large property
among natural lakes and forest, and also offers a restaurant,
cafeteria and souvenir shop.
Principal Wines A kaleidoscopic array of basically fruit-based
wines, including Le Dry (mulberries and blueberries, oak matured),
Moonlight White (West Indian limes), Sunshine Nouveau (locally-
grown jaboticabas), Old Buderim Ginger (fortified base with honey
and ginger added), Strawberry Wine, Exporto (mulberry and
blueberry-based port wine).

MOOREBANK ESTATE

NR 15–23 CD AUS174
Hunter Valley **Est.** 1977
Palmers Lane, Pokolbin, NSW 2321
Ph (049) 98 7610 **Fax** (049) 98 7367
Open Wed–Sun 10–4 **Production** 1300
Winemaker(s) Iain Riggs (Contract)
Ian Burgess and Debra Moore operate a newly-opened winery
with contract winemaking by Iain Riggs of Brokenwood. They
have 45 hectares of vines, which are now mature.
Principal Wines Chardonnay, Semillon, Gewurztraminer, Merlot,
Liqueur Muscat.

MOORILLA ESTATE

★★★★☆ 17.50–24 R AUS1, 14, 42
Derwent River **Est.** 1958
655 Main Road, Berriedale, Tas 7011
Ph (002) 49 2949 **Fax** (002) 49 4093
Open 7 days 9–5 **Production** 12 000
Winemaker(s) Julian Alcorso
While Julian Alcorso remains as winemaker, majority ownership of
Moorilla has passed out of the family. The good news, as it were,
of the change of ownership has been the injection of substantial
additional equity which, among other things, has allowed the
purchase of the St Matthias Vineyard which will henceforth supply
grapes to Moorilla.
Principal Wines Riesling, Chardonnay, Gewurztraminer, Pinot
Noir, Cabernet Sauvignon, Vintage Brut.

MOORILLA ESTATE CHARDONNAY
●●●● ▶ $21
A complex wine which is, as one would expect, very much in cool climate style. It is produced from 2.5 hectares of immaculately trained estate vineyards, and given what might loosely be called 'the full treatment' in the winery. Sometimes, as in 1993, botrytis makes an impact on the wine.
Cellaring 4–6 years. **Best Vintages** '81, '82, '90, '91, '92
Current Vintage '93
Matching Food Tasmanian salmon.
Tasting Note 1993 Medium to full yellow-green; rich citrus and melon fruit aromas with a strong botrytis influence apparent in both the bouquet and palate. The latter follows the track of the bouquet with rich, high-toned, intense fruit, strongly botrytis-influenced.

MOORILLA ESTATE PINOT NOIR
●●● ▶ $17.50
For many years Moorilla Estate harboured the ambition to produce great Pinot Noir, and indeed to become a Pinot Noir specialist. For whatever reason, and despite the immaculate tending of the 4 hectares of estate grapes, it has been a reluctant performer — a fact recognised by Moorilla in the pricing of the wine at the bottom end of the scale.
Cellaring 3–4 years. **Best Vintages** '84, '86, '90, '91, '92
Current Vintage '92
Matching Food Quail.
Tasting Note 1992 Light to medium red, with just a touch of purple; a clean, light bouquet with faintly minty aspects, packing varietal character. The palate shows some cherry and strawberry fruit with minty overtones; the finish is harder than one would like.

MOORILLA ESTATE RIESLING
●●●●● $17.50
In my view, consistently the best of the Moorilla Estate wines, reaching a high point in 1994, but with a long track record of excellence. Produced from 1.5 hectares of estate vineyards. In addition, the occasional releases of botrytised Riesling (by mailing list and through cellar door), are sensational.
Cellaring 5–7 years. **Best Vintages** '81, '82, '90, '91, '93, '94
Current Vintage '94
Matching Food Asparagus.
Tasting Note 1994 Light green-yellow; a very fine, elegant and intense bouquet with lime and faintly herbaceous aromas. The palate is finely balanced and structured, with green lime flavours, finishing long and dry. Highest quality.

MOOROODUC ESTATE
★★★★☆ 23.50 R AUS144
Mornington Peninsula **Est.** 1983
Derril Road, Moorooduc, Vic 3936
Ph (03) 9696 4130 **Fax** (03) 9696 2841

Open First w'end each month 12–5 **Production** 900
Winemaker(s) Dr Richard McIntyre

Dr Richard McIntyre, with help from consultant Nat White, produces one of the richest and most complex Chardonnays in the region, with grapefruit/peach fruit set against sumptuous spicy oak; the '88, '89 and '90 Chardonnays are all of the highest quality. The 1990 Cabernet Sauvignon, too, was an excellent wine for the year, but was surpassed as a young wine by the great 1991 Cabernet Sauvignon with its lush, perfectly ripened, cassis-accented fruit.
Principal Wines Chardonnay, Pinot Noir, Cabernet Sauvignon.

MOOROODUC ESTATE CABERNET SAUVIGNON
●●● ▶ $23.50

The least of the three Moorooduc Estate wines, produced from one hectare of estate vineyards. The site is a cool one, and — as is so often the case on the Mornington Peninsula — only in exceptional years does the cabernet gain real richness and weight.
Cellaring 3–4 years. **Best Vintages** '88, '90, '91, '92, '93
Current Vintage '92
Matching Food Italian, brasserie.
Tasting Note 1992 Medium red-purple; the bouquet is clean and light with minty/leafy aromas in typical Peninsula style. The palate, too, is in the sappy/leafy/minty spectrum, finishing with soft tannins.

MOOROODUC ESTATE CHARDONNAY
●●●● $23.50

Produced from 2.5 hectares of estate plantings, and made by Dr Richard McIntyre in a very consistent style, which is always strongly influenced by the secondary malolactic fermentation. The resultant nutty/buttery wine tends to stand out even in the background of the Mornington Peninsula, and certainly against other wine styles.
Cellaring 2–4 years. **Best Vintages** '88, '90, '91, '92, '93
Current Vintage '94
Matching Food Grilled spatchcock.
Tasting Note 1994 Medium to full yellow; a typically complex bouquet with buttery/nutty/oaky aromas. The palate is rich and textured, with buttery/butterscotch flavours, and tremendous depth and feel in the mouth.

MOOROODUC ESTATE PINOT NOIR
●●●● $23.50

Produced from one hectare of estate plantings with two clones: D2V5 and D5V12. Typically very fragrant, sappy and spicy, excelling in vintages such as 1992.
Cellaring 2–4 years. **Best Vintages** '88, '91, '92, '93
Current Vintage '94
Matching Food Asian meat dishes.
Tasting Note 1994 Medium red-purple; the bouquet is of light to medium intensity, with complex gamey maceration characters, along with red berry. The palate is long, with gamey/berry flavours, soft tannins and relatively high acidity.

MORNING CLOUD WINES *

NR 14–16 R AUSSD
Mornington Peninsula **Est.** 1983
RMB 1880, Red Hill-Shoreham Road, Red Hill South, Vic 3937
Ph (059) 89 2044 **Fax** (059) 89 2700
Open By appt **Production** 400
Winemaker(s) Tod Dexter (Contract)
Morning Cloud Wines (previously Cloud Valley) is a joint venture
between Kathy and Bill Allen and Peter and Judy Maxwell. Each
family has its own vineyard at Red Hill South, and the grapes are
pooled and the wine made under contract at Stonier's Winery. The
Cabernet Sauvignon tends to be very leafy in Chinon style; the
Chardonnay light, fresh, crisp and citrus-tinged.
Principal Wines Chardonnay, Cabernet Sauvignon.

MORNINGSIDE WINES

NR 10–13 ML AUSSD
Southern Tasmania **Est.** 1980
RMB 3002 Middle Tea Tree Road, Tea Tree, Tas 7017
Ph (002) 68 1748
Open Not **Production** 200
Winemaker(s) Peter Bosworth
The name 'Morningside' was given to the old property on which the
vineyard stands because it gets the morning sun first. The property
on the other side of the valley was known as 'Eveningside', and,
consistently with the observation of the early settlers, the Morningside
grapes achieve full maturity with good colour and varietal flavour.
Production is as yet tiny, but will increase as the 1.5-hectare
vineyard matures.
Principal Wines Riesling, Pinot Noir, Cabernet Sauvignon.

MORNINGSIDE PINOT NOIR

●●● ▸ $13
Produced from ultra-close-planted vines, with 1.8 metres between
the rows, and 1.25 metres between the vines. The concentration of
flavour no doubt partially reflects this very close planting, but also
the northeast-facing slopes, which are only 100 metres above sea
level, and which have a limestone-based subsoil.
Cellaring 2–3 years. **Best Vintages** NA **Current Vintage** '93
Matching Food Hare.
Tasting Note 1993 Strong red-purple; potent black cherry fruit
aromas with subtle oak. There is a great volume of cherry fruit on the
palate with quite high acid to balance that fruit. A hint of earth or
mushroom lurks in the background.

MORNINGTON VINEYARDS

★★★☆ 14–19 R AUS173
Mornington Peninsula **Est.** 1989
Moorooduc Road, Mornington, Vic 3931
Ph (059) 74 2097 **Fax** (059) 74 2097

Open By appt **Production** 1000
Winemaker(s) Hugh Robinson, Kevin McCarthy (Contract)
As with so many Mornington Peninsula vineyards, a high degree of
viticultural expertise, care and attention, coupled with skilled contract
winemaking has paid dividends. If there is to be a criticism, it is in
the lack of concentration of flavour, something which will come as
the vineyards mature.
Principal Wines Chardonnay, Pinot Nouveau.

MORNINGTON VINEYARDS CHARDONNAY
●●●●● $19
Produced from a little over 3 hectares of estate-grown grapes,
and made by Kevin McCarthy at T'Gallant Winery. One of the
outstanding 1994 Chardonnays from the Mornington Peninsula.
Cellaring 3–5 years. **Best Vintages** '91, '93, '94
Current Vintage '94
Matching Food Garnished lobster.
Tasting Note 1994 Medium to full green-yellow; an unusually
complex and concentrated bouquet with ripe citrus and melon fruit
interwoven with subtle oak. The palate is elegant and well balanced,
with a long, tangy citrus and melon flavoured finish. Tighter and
more focused than many Mornington Peninsula Chardonnays.

MORRIS WINES

★★★★★ 9.95–29.95 R AUS117
North East Victoria **Est.** 1859
Mia Mia Road, Rutherglen, Vic 3685
Ph (060) 26 7303 **Fax** (060) 26 7445
Open Mon–Sat 9–5, Sun 10–5 **Production** 32 000
Winemaker(s) David Morris
One of the greatest of the fortified winemakers, some would say the
greatest. If you wish to test that view, try the Old Premium Muscat
and Old Premium Tokay, which are absolute bargains given their
age and quality. The table wines are dependable, the white wines
all being made by owner Orlando.
Principal Wines A limited range of table wines, sparingly
distributed, the most important of which is the red wine Durif; then
fortified wines, comprising Mick Morris Old Tawny Port, Liqueur
Tokay, Old Premium Liqueur Tokay, Mick Morris Muscat, Old
Premium Liqueur Muscat, Mick Morris Commemorative Liqueur
Muscat, Old Premium Liqueur Muscat at the top end of the range;
tiny quantities of Show Reserve are released from time to time,
mainly ex winery.

MORRIS DURIF
●●●● $13.95
Durif is an exceedingly obscure variety closely related to another
grape of similar ilk, pelourisin. It may not be the same as
California's petite syrah; if it is not, Australia is the only country in
the world producing wines from it. It is as much for its rarity and for
its individuality as its ultimate quality that it is considered a classic.

Cellaring 10–20 years. **Best Vintages** '70, '72, '74, '80, '83, '86, '88, '90 **Current Vintage** '90
Matching Food Biltong.
Tasting Note 1990 Dark, dense red; a massively concentrated bouquet, ripe, earthy and chocolatey. The palate is equally massive, with prune and chocolate flavours, and tannins under control. 14.3% alcohol.

MORRIS LIQUEUR MUSCAT
●●●●● $13.95
As with the Tokay in the same range, the accent is thrown onto the varietal character of muscat, otherwise known as brown frontignac. The style differs from that of Baileys, which tends to be sweet and in some ways more complex, but with less clarity of varietal character. Which one prefers is very much a matter of personal taste.
Cellaring NA. **Best Vintages** NA **Current Vintage** NA
Matching Food Aperitif or digestif.
Tasting Note NV Light to medium red-brown; clearly articulated, lively, raisiny muscat varietal aromas. In the mouth you can literally taste the grapes, as if one were chewing on an explosively rich raisin; great length, and perfect balance.

MORRIS LIQUEUR TOKAY
●●●●● $13.95
Made from the muscadelle grape, used as a minor component in Sauternes, but nowhere else in the world used to make fortified dessert wines. In this version, which contains a greater percentage of younger material (two-four years old) than the premium labels, the accent is thrown firmly on to the very distinctive varietal character of muscadelle.
Cellaring NA. **Best Vintages** NA **Current Vintage** NA
Matching Food Either aperitif or at the end of the meal.
Tasting Note NV Light to medium golden brown; a fragrant bouquet with fresh tea-leaf varietal aroma. There is masses of flavour on the palate, yet the wine is quite fresh with archetypal cold tea and butterscotch flavours, with the mid palate sweetness followed by a cleansing, crisp finish.

MORRIS OLD PREMIUM LIQUEUR MUSCAT
●●●●● $29.95
Here the component of old material is much greater than in the less expensive standard Liqueur range. The blending of young, middle-aged and very old wines lies at the heart of the style, with a tiny percentage of 30- and 40-year-old wood aged material having a disproportionate impact on the blend.
Cellaring NA. **Best Vintages** NA **Current Vintage** NA
Matching Food Coffee, petit fours.
Tasting Note NV Medium to full tawny, with a hint of olive on the rim. A rich bouquet with complex caramel, toffee and coffee aromas intermingling with the raisins. The palate shows more of the raisiny varietal fruit, although the complexity of the bouquet does repeat itself. A great example of blending.

MOSS BROTHERS

NR 12–23 R AUS87
Margaret River **Est.** 1984
Caves Road, Willyabrup, WA 6280
Ph (097) 55 6270 **Fax** (097) 55 6298
Open 7 days 9–5.30 **Production** 5600
Winemaker(s) Jane Moss, David Moss
Established by long-term viticulturist Jeff Moss and his family, notably
sons Peter and David and Roseworthy graduate daughter Jane. A
100-tonne rammed-earth winery was constructed in 1992, and
draws upon both estate-grown and purchased grapes. Early tastings
did not impress, but the winery has done well in some more recent
wine shows.
Principal Wines Semillon, Semillon Sauvignon Blanc,
Chardonnay, Sauvignon Blanc, Cabernet Merlot, Pinot Noir, Moses
Rock Red.

MOSS BROTHERS CABERNET MERLOT

●●● ▶ $19.50
A blend of cabernet sauvignon, merlot and cabernet franc, all estate-
grown, which spent 20 months in small oak before bottling. A wine
with plenty of character.
Cellaring 3 years. **Best Vintages** NA **Current Vintage** '91
Matching Food Beef Wellington.
Tasting Note 1991 Medium to full red-purple; lifted, briary, dark
fruit aromas and hints of vanillin oak. The palate is rich and
concentrated, with dark briary/berry fruit, soft tannins and subtle
oak; again there is some of the volatile lift apparent on the bouquet,
but was in the bounds of commercial acceptability.

MOSS WOOD WINERY

★★★★★ 20–29 R AUSS17, 63, 123, 150, 168, UK85
Margaret River **Est.** 1969
Metricup Road, Willyabrup, WA 6280
Ph (097) 55 6266 **Fax** (097) 55 6303
Open By appt **Production** 4500
Winemaker(s) Keith Mugford
Widely regarded as one of the best wineries in the region, capable
of producing glorious Semillon (the best outside the Hunter Valley) in
both oaked and unoaked forms, unctuous Chardonnay and elegant,
gently herbaceous, superfine Cabernet Sauvignon which lives for
many years.
Principal Wines Semillon, Wood Matured Semillon, Chardonnay,
Cabernet Sauvignon, Pinot Noir.

MOSS WOOD CABERNET SAUVIGNON

●●●●● $29
First made in 1973, and has established itself as one of the classic
wine styles not only of the Margaret River, but of Australia. The
wines have a distinctive suppleness and softness which sets them

apart from other Margaret River Cabernets, and which Dr John Gladstones firmly attributes to the particular terroir of the vineyard. **Cellaring** 7–15 years. **Best Vintages** '77, '80, '86, '87, '90, '91, '92 **Current Vintage** '92
Matching Food Beef with olives.
Tasting Note 1992 Medium to full purple-red; the bouquet is clean, of medium intensity with sweet blackcurrant and redcurrant fruits, and even a touch of violets; gentle oak. Tasted early in its life, and may rate even higher with bottle maturation; medium to full fruit style with good tannins and overall elegance.

MOSS WOOD CHARDONNAY
●●●● ▶ $26
First made in 1930 from 1.3 hectares of estate plantings. Over the years both the viticulture (a new Scott Henry trellis system installed in 1990) and the winemaking have seen numerous changes as Keith Mugford has strived for more intensity and complexity. For all this, the wine has always been in a distinctive, rich style, upholding the high reputation of Moss Wood.
Cellaring 2–6 years. **Best Vintages** '80, '85, '90, '92, '93
Current Vintage '93
Matching Food Free-range chicken.
Tasting Note 1993 Medium yellow-green; tasted relatively early in its life, still showing some attractive yeast influences with strong underlying citrus and melon fruit. Full-flavoured, intense and with a real tang to the flavour and finish; the oak is well integrated and balanced.

MOSS WOOD SEMILLON
●●●●● $20
Both the wooded and unwooded versions of this wine are now a yearly release. On occasions the unwooded wine emerges as the best, on others it is the turn of the wood matured wine. However, while the style is quite different, the quality differences are minuscule.
Cellaring 5–12 years. **Best Vintages** '81, '82, '83, '84, '86, '87, '92, '94 **Current Vintage** '94
Matching Food Crab, lobster.
Tasting Note 1994 Light green-yellow; a complex, concentrated and intense bouquet with some faintly herbal notes, more to White Bordeaux in style. The palate is as powerful and concentrated as the bouquet promises, again with those overtones of White Bordeaux, and the richness so particular to Moss Wood.

MOUNT ALEXANDER VINEYARD
★★ 10–14 CD AUSSD
Bendigo **Est.** 1984
Calder Highway, North Harcourt, Vic 3453
Ph (054) 74 2262 **Fax** (054) 74 2553
Open 7 days 10–5.30 **Production** 6000
Winemaker(s) Keith Walkden
A substantial operation with large vineyards with 12 hectares of

vineyards planted to all the right varieties. It is several years since
I have tasted the wines, but I have no reason to suppose they have
changed much.
Principal Wines A wide range of various table wines, sparkling,
fortifieds, meads and liqueurs.

MOUNT ANAKIE WINES

★★☆ 10–18 R AUSSD
Geelong **Est.** 1968
Staughton Vale Road, Anakie, Vic 3221
Ph (052) 84 1452 **Fax** (052) 84 1405
Open Tues–Sun 11–6 **Production** 8000
Winemaker(s) Otto Zambelli
Also known as Zambelli Estate, and has produced some excellent
wines (under its various ownerships and winemakers), all
distinguished by their depth and intensity of flavour. The most
recently tasted wines were unconvincing, but none tasted from the
1992 vintage.
Principal Wines Riesling, Chardonay, Semillon, Dolcetto,
Cabernet Sauvignon, Cabernet Franc, Shiraz, Tawny Port.

MOUNT AVOCA VINEYARD

★★★ 12–18 CD AUS142, UK56
Pyrenees **Est.** 1970
Moates Lane, Avoca, Vic 3467
Ph (054) 65 3282 **Fax** (054) 65 3544
Open Mon–Fri 9–5, W'ends 10–5 **Production** 10 000
Winemaker(s) Rodney Morrish
A substantial winery which has for long been one of the stalwarts of
the Pyrenees region, and steadily growing, increasing its plantings in
1994 by 4 hectares, with a further 1.5 hectares projected for 1995.
Principal Wines Pyrenees Dry White, Semillon, Chardonnay,
Autumn White, Shiraz, Cabernet Sauvignon, Port.

MOUNT AVOCA CABERNET SAUVIGNON
●●● $15
Produced from 4 hectares of estate-grown grapes. Along with the
Sauvignon Blanc, has been a signature wine of the estate for many
years, with a distinctive vineyard character.
Cellaring 5–7 years. **Best Vintages** '88, '90, '91, '92, '93
Current Vintage '91
Matching Food Char-grilled steak.
Tasting Note 1991 Medium to full red-purple; a concentrated
bouquet with minty/earthy/gamey characters intertwined. The
palate is full-bodied, with earth and mint flavours, finishing with
pronounced tannins.

MOUNT AVOCA SAUVIGNON BLANC
●●● ▶ $15
Produced from 5 hectares of existing plantings, with further vineyard
area to come on stream in future vintages. Is always made in a

concentrated style, and has from time to time been quite outstanding.
Cellaring 2–3 years. **Best Vintages** '87, '89, '92, '93, '94
Current Vintage '94
Matching Food Blanquette of veal.
Tasting Note 1994 Light yellow-green; potent, herbaceous
bouquet with just a suspicion of bitterness. The palate is concentrated
and powerful with ripe varietal fruit; no oak evident.

MOUNT CHALAMBAR WINES

★★★☆ 12.50–15.50 R AUS56
Great Western **Est.** 1978
Tatyoon Road, Ararat, Vic 3377
Ph (053) 54 3207
Open See Mount Langi Ghiran **Production** 1200
Winemaker(s) Trevor Mast
These days a small addendum to the far larger and far more
visible Mount Langi Ghiran, although the two brands are run quite
separately. The Riesling is full-flavoured and lime-accented, the
Chardonnay barrel fermented and complex.
Principal Wines Riesling, Chardonnay.

MOUNT DUNEED

★★☆ 14–17 CD AUS72
Geelong **Est.** 1970
Feehan's Road, Mount Duneed, Vic 3216
Ph (052) 64 1281
Open Sat 9–5, Sun 12–5 **Production** 1000
Winemaker(s) Ken Campbell
Rather idiosyncratic wines are the order of the day, some of which
can develop surprisingly well in bottle; the Botrytis Noble Rot
Semillon has, from time to time, been of very high quality.
Principal Wines Semillon, Sauvignon Blanc, Riesling, Botrytis
Semillon, Cabernet Malbec, Cabernet Sauvignon.

MOUNT HELEN

★★★ 14.50–19.50 R AUS104, UK64
Goulburn Valley **Est.** 1978
Strathbogie Ranges (vineyard only), Vic 3666
Ph (054) 82 1911
Open See Tisdall **Production** 6500
Winemaker(s) Toni Stockhausen
Now part of the Mildara Blass group, with much of the extensive
grape production used for other brands, and with a low commercial
profile.
Principal Wines Chardonnay, Riesling, Cabernet Merlot.

MOUNT HELEN CABERNET MERLOT
●●●● ▶ $18.95
This wine formed part of the re-launch of the Mount Helen label in
early 1995, and it is easy to see why it was selected for this

purpose. An estate-grown wine, now reaching the peak of its development.

Cellaring Now–4 years. **Best Vintages** NA
Current Vintage '91
Matching Food Yearling beef.
Tasting Note 1991 Still retains bright red-purple hues to the colour; a complex yet elegant array of spicy fruit and French oak on the bouquet leads on to a most attractive wine on the palate with fine, dark berry fruits, a hint of bitter chocolate and just a touch of oak to round things off.

MOUNT HORROCKS WINES

★★★★ 12.99–15.99 R AUS113, 130, 161
Clare Valley **Est.** 1982
Mintaro Road, Leasingham, SA 5452
Ph (088) 49 2243 **Fax** (088) 49 2243
Open W'ends 11–5 **Production** 3000
Winemaker(s) Jeffrey Grosset (Contract)
Mount Horrocks was purchased several years ago by Stephanie Toole, Jeffrey Grosset's partner. Not surprisingly, Jeffrey Grosset has continued to make the wines, although the fruit sources are quite separate from those of his own winery and label.
Principal Wines Watervale Riesling, Unwooded Chardonnay, Semillon, Cordon Cut Riesling, Cabernet Merlot.

MOUNT HORROCKS CORDON CUT RIESLING (375 ML)
●●●● $14.50
Cordon cut describes a winemaking technique almost as old as winemaking itself. The fruit-bearing canes are cut but not removed, and the grapes are left to hang, partially desiccating and, as they do so, gaining in sugar and acidity. The resultant wines are different from botrytised sweet wines, where the action of the mould adds an extra layer of complexity.
Cellaring 2–3 years. **Best Vintages** NA **Current Vintage** '94
Matching Food Lemon and vanilla mille-feuille.
Tasting Note 1994 Medium yellow-green; intense lime and tropical fruit aromas, clean and powerful. The palate shows similar intense, firm lime-flavoured fruit, with the riesling varietal character unmodified by botrytis. The finish is a fraction firm.

MOUNT HORROCKS WATERVALE RIESLING
●●●● ▸ $12.99
Mount Horrocks was originally the wine production end of the Ackland Brothers' extensive vineyard holdings. The two have now effectively been split, and Mount Horrocks is dependent on contract-grown grapes through the Watervale region. The sources are good, and the quality of the wine is high, as one would expect with Jeffrey Grosset as winemaker.
Cellaring 5–7 years. **Best Vintages** '86, '87, '90, '93, '94
Current Vintage '94
Matching Food Vegetable salad.

Tasting Note 1994 Light green-yellow; a firm, crisp and direct bouquet of medium to full intensity with slight herbaceous edges to the fruit. The palate is lively, fresh and crisp, with very good mouthfeel and a particularly well balanced finish. Certain to age well.

MOUNT HURTLE WINES

★★★★ 9.99–12.99 R AUS27, 167–170, 186, UK75
Southern Vales **Est.** 1897
Cnr Pimpala & Byards Roads, Reynella, SA 5161
Ph (08) 381 6877 **Fax** (08) 322 2244
Open Mon–Fri 10–5, Sun 12–5 **Production** 47 000 (total group production)
Winemaker(s) Geoff Merrill
The current release wines reflect the joint ownership of Mount Hurtle by Geoff Merrill and Chateau Tahbilk. The fruit sources for all of the wines have diversified considerably, and the volume increased significantly in consequence. The result is wines of very consistent quality which are competitively priced.
Principal Wines Sauvignon Blanc, Chardonnay, Cabernet Merlot, Shiraz, Grenache Shiraz, Grenache.

MOUNT HURTLE CABERNET MERLOT
●●● ▶ $12.99
A blend of 54% Goulburn Valley, 27% McLaren Vale and 13% Coonawarra cabernet sauvignon, rounded off with 6% of merlot from McLaren Vale. A wine deliberately fashioned in a drink-now style.
Cellaring None required. **Best Vintages** NA
Current Vintage '92
Matching Food Risotto.
Tasting Note 1992 Medium red-purple; a clean, fresh and smooth bouquet with some dark cherry and blackberry aromas. The palate is well balanced and very smooth; both the oak and tannins are subtle; a wine which soothes rather than challenges.

MOUNT HURTLE CHARDONNAY
●●● ▶ $12.99
As is the case with the Sauvignon Blanc, drawing upon a wide variety of fruit sources and regions, and tailored to the needs and requirements of a particular market sector.
Cellaring Drink now. **Best Vintages** NA **Current Vintage** '93
Matching Food Grilled spatchcock.
Tasting Note 1993 Medium yellow-green; soft, bready/nutty aromas to the bouquet with slightly creamy/vanilla overtones. The palate shows rather more lively, fresh fruit with some citrussy flavours, finishing with good acidity. The oak influence is minimal.

MOUNT HURTLE SAUVIGNON BLANC
●●●● $12.99
Made in an unwooded style with grapes sourced primarily from the McLaren Vale region. The style is direct, bright and fresh, directly aimed at the brasserie/cafe market.

Cellaring Drink now. **Best Vintages** NA
Current Vintage '94
Matching Food Calamari.
Tasting Note 1994 Light to medium green-yellow; a clean bouquet
with nicely ripened, soft gooseberry fruit aromas. The palate is clean
and crisp, pleasantly balanced in a slick commercial style, and with
a soft, ever so faintly sweet finish.

MOUNT HURTLE SHIRAZ
●●●● $12.99
Yet more of the same from Mount Hurtle; am immaculately made
wine which is sufficiently light and fresh to be enjoyed immediately
upon release, and which is not intended to be cellared, but simply
enjoyed.
Cellaring Drink now. **Best Vintages** NA
Current Vintage '92
Matching Food Italian cuisine.
Tasting Note 1992 Medium red-purple; fresh cherry fruit aromas
of light to medium intensity, with minimal oak. The palate is lively
and fresh with some spice and cherry flavours, a bare flick of oak
and minimal tannins. A snappy cafe red.

MOUNT IDA

★★★★ 16.50 R AUS104
Bendigo **Est.** 1978
Northern Highway, Heathcote, Vic 3523
Ph (054) 82 1911
Open At Tisdall **Production** 1500
Winemaker(s) Toni Stockhausen
Established by the famous artist Leonard French and Dr James
Munro, but purchased by Tisdall after the 1987 bushfires. Up to
the time of the fires, wonderfully smooth, rich red wines with
almost voluptuous sweet, minty fruit were the hallmark. After a
brief period during which the name was used as a simple brand
(with various wines released) has returned to a single estate-
grown wine.
Principal Wines Shiraz.

MOUNT IDA SHIRAZ
●●●●● $16.95
A single-vineyard wine produced from an estate established by
noted Australian artist Leonard French, but which was acquired by
Tisdall in the 1980s. Produced in limited quantities, but well worth
the search.
Cellaring Now–5 years. **Best Vintages** NA
Current Vintage '91
Matching Food Australian parmesan.
Tasting Note 1991 Youthful red-purple; a clean and fragrant
bouquet with attractive cedar and red berry fruits, quite European in
style. The palate, too, is elegant with cedary/spicy berry fruit and
fine-grained tannins.

MOUNT LANGI GHIRAN WINERY

★★★★★ 14–19 R AUS48, 63, 66, 95, 125, 145, UK101
Great Western **Est.** 1969
Warrak Road, Buangor, Vic 3375
Ph (053) 54 3207 **Fax** (053) 54 3277
Open Mon–Fri 9–5, W'ends 12–5 **Production** 12 000
Winemaker(s) Trevor Mast

A maker of outstanding cool climate peppery Shiraz, crammed with
flavour and vinosity, and very good Cabernet Sauvignon. The Shiraz
points the way for cool climate examples of the variety, for weight,
texture and fruit richness all accompany the vibrant pepper-spice
aroma and flavour.

Principal Wines Cabernet Sauvignon, Shiraz; Langi label:
Riesling, Chardonnay, Cabernet Merlot; Circa (a regional blend red
and white).

MOUNT LANGI GHIRAN LANGI CABERNET MERLOT

●●●● $19.90

A new direction for Mount Langi Ghiran, dressed in a somewhat
stridently labelled bottle featuring a yellow and black cockatoo.
While the packaging may be gauche, the wine is not.

Cellaring 5+ years. **Best Vintages** NA **Current Vintage** '92
Matching Food Moroccan lamb.

Tasting Note 1992 Medium to full red-purple; a ripe, sweet, with
lots of luscious blackcurrant fruit aromas and well handled oak. The
palate is very complex, with a melange of flavours ranging from
sweet berry through to herb and then mint.

MOUNT LANGI GHIRAN SHIRAZ

●●●●● $19.90

One of the top half-dozen Shirazs in Australia. The site climate
of the Mount Langi Ghiran vineyards produces wines which have
tremendous depth and complexity: there are pepper and spice notes,
but there are also all of the lush ripe fruit flavours running from
cherry to liquorice which a top Rhone Valley maker would
immediately recognise and appreciate.

Cellaring 4–10+ years. **Best Vintages** '86, '88, '90, '92, '93
Current Vintage '93
Matching Food Kangaroo, venison.

Tasting Note 1993 Vivid, dense red-purple; the bouquet is
redolent of spice, pepper, supple black cherry fruit of considerable
intensity. The palate is super rich and concentrated, chewy but not
excessively tannic, and the fruit has swallowed up the oak.

MOUNT MAGNUS WINES

NR 7.50–20 CD AUSSD
Granite Belt **Est.** 1933
Donnellys Castle Road, Pausieres, Qld 4352
Ph (076) 85 3313 **Fax** (076) 85 3313
Open 7 days 9–5 **Production** NFP

Winemaker(s) Peter Scudamore-Smith MW (Contract)
One of the oldest vineyards in the district, which has had a
chequered history and numerous changes of ownership and
winemakers. The label proudly proclaims Mount Magnus to be
Australia's highest altitude winery.
Principal Wines Semillon, Semillon Chardonnay, Granite Hills
(Dry White), Western Hills (Traminer Riesling), Shiraz Cabernet,
Cabernet Merlot, fortifieds.

MOUNT MARTHA VINEYARD

NR 11–14 ML AUSSD
Mornington Peninsula **Est.** 1986
Range Road, Mount Martha, Vic 3934
Ph (059) 74 2700 **Fax** (059) 74 4007
Open Not **Production** 750
Winemaker(s) Kevin McCarthy (Contract)
The 2-hectare Mount Martha Vineyard is owned by the Matson
and Scalley families, overlooking Port Phillip Bay on undulating
loam. Competent contract winemaking should ensure the quality
of the wines.
Principal Wines Chardonnay, Sauvignon Blanc, Cabernet
Sauvignon.

MOUNT MARY VINEYARD

★★★★★ 20–24 ML AUSSD US2
Yarra Valley **Est.** 1971
Coldstream West Road, Lilydale, Vic 3140
Ph (03) 9739 1761 **Fax** (03) 9739 0137
Open Not **Production** NFP
Winemaker(s) Dr John Middleton, Mario Marson, Peter Draper
Superbly refined, elegant and intense Cabernets, and usually
outstanding and long-lived Pinot Noirs, fully justify Mount Mary's
exalted reputation. The Triolet blend is very good, more recent
vintages of Chardonnay likewise.
Principal Wines Chardonnay, Triolet (Sauvignon Blanc, Semillon,
Muscadelle), Pinot Noir, Cabernets Quintet (Bordeaux blend).

MOUNT MARY CABERNETS QUINTET
●●●●● $31.75
First made in 1977; one of few wines in Australia to include in its
make-up the five classic grape varieties of Bordeaux: cabernet
sauvignon, merlot, cabernet franc, malbec and petit verdot. This
wine is Mount Mary's finest; at its best the ultimate expression of the
style, at its least showing that the climate of the Yarra Valley can
treat the later-ripening varieties with harshness.
Cellaring 5–15 years. **Best Vintages** '78, '79, '84, '88, '90,
'91 **Current Vintage** '91
Matching Food Boned loin of lamb.
Tasting Note 1991 Medium red-purple; lush, ripe fruit with cassis
and mint, and some most attractive spicy characters, possibly fruit

derived, possibly oak derived; these spicy characters continue on the palate along with cassis and dark berry fruits; silky smooth texture and a long finish.

MOUNT MARY PINOT NOIR
●●●●● $31.75
The first Yarra Valley Pinot Noir I tasted, and was largely responsible for my move to the Yarra Valley seven or eight years later. The wine remains one of the classics of the region, deceptively elegant when young, and with a totally surprising capacity to age if the vintage conditions have been kind.
Cellaring 3–7 years. **Best Vintages** '79, '85, '86, '89, '91
Current Vintage '91
Matching Food Breast of squab.
Tasting Note 1991 Light red-purple; clean, firm with some cherry fruit but relatively unevolved. The palate shows medium concentration with good weight, mouthfeel and balance. Still tied up, and could well improve for a decade.

MOUNT PRIOR VINEYARD

NR 7–18 CD AUSSD
North East Victoria **Est.** 1860
Cnr River Road & Popes Lane, Rutherglen, Vic 3685
Ph (060) 26 5591 **Fax** (060) 26 7456
Open 7 days 10–5 **Production** 8000
Winemaker(s) Garry Wall
Re-established in 1989 after a disastrous foray into exports to the United States; the experience of Garry Wall should ensure quality. The historic homestead and winery offer a restaurant 'Kitchen in the Cellar', and grand-scale accommodation at 'The House at Mount Prior'. Much of the wine is sold cellar door.
Principal Wines Chardonnay, Chenin Blanc, Cabernet Merlot, Shiraz, Durif, Carignane, Malbec; also Australian Classic Dry Red and White.

MOUNT VIEW ESTATE

★★★ 14–16 CD AUSSD
Hunter Valley **Est.** 1971
Mount View Road, Mount View, NSW 2325
Ph (049) 90 3307 **Fax** (049) 91 1289
Open Mon–Fri 10–4, W'ends, Hols 9–5 **Production** 2000
Winemaker(s) Harry Tulloch
Some new oak would help the table wines immeasurably; the range of fortified wines is distinctly better. The fortified and late harvest styles have been largely responsible for Mount View winning four trophies, six gold medals and three silver medals at the Hunter Valley Small Winemakers Show between 1991 and 1993.
Principal Wines Verdelho, Chardonnay, Verdelho Chardonnay, Cabernet Sauvignon, Shiraz, Liqueur Verdelho, Trophy Muscat.

MOUNT VINCENT MEAD

★★★★ 12.90–27.80 CD AUSSD
Mudgee **Est.** 1980
Common Road, Mudgee, NSW 2850
Ph (063) 72 3184 **Fax** (063) 72 3184
Open Mon–Sat 10–5, Sun 10–4 **Production** 2000
Winemaker(s) Jane Nevell
Forget the table wines, and concentrate on the Meads, which can be
absolutely outstanding, as a recent tasting of the '93 Stringy Bark
Mead demonstrated.
Principal Wines Does make a Shiraz and a Liqueur Muscat, but is
essentially a meadery, with White Box Honey Wine, Napunyah Dry
Mead, White Box Dry Mead, Napunyah Medium Sweet, Stringy
Bark Sweet, Thistle Sweet Metheglin and Stringy Bark Liqueur Mead.
Each of these is vintage dated.

MOUNT WILLIAM WINERY

NR 7–20 CD AUS94
Macedon **Est.** 1987
Mount William Road, Tantaraboo, Vic 3764
Ph (054) 29 1595 **Fax** (054) 29 1998
Open 7 days 1–5 **Production** 1000
Winemaker(s) Murray Cousins, Michael
Cope-Williams
Adrienne and Murray Cousins established 4 hectares of vineyards
between 1987 and 1992, planted to pinot noir, cabernet franc,
semillon and chardonnay. The cabernet franc is to be used as part
of a base wine for Sparkling Burgundy, while the chardonnay is not
expected to come into bearing for several years. The wines are
made under contract (Cope-Williams), and are sold through a stone
tasting room cellar door facility.
Principal Wines Chardonnay, Semillon, Rosé, Pinot Noir,
Cabernet Sauvignon, Sparkling Burgundy.

MOUNTADAM VINEYARD

★★★★☆ 10.99–30 R AUS17, 63, 66, 97, 115, 156 UK43 US9
Adelaide Hills **Est.** 1972
High Eden Road, High Eden Ridge, SA 5235
Ph (085) 64 1101 **Fax** (085) 64 1064
Open 7 days 11–4 **Production** 45 000
Winemaker(s) Adam Wynn
One of the leading small wineries, founded by David Wynn and
run by winemaker son Adam Wynn; initially offered only the
Mountadam range at relatively high prices. The subsequent
development of the three ranges of wines has been very successful,
judged both by the winemaking and wine marketing viewpoint.
Principal Wines Premium Mountadam label: Riesling,
Chardonnay, Pinot Noir, The Red (50% merlot, 50% cabernet),
Chardonnay Pinot Noir Methode Champenoise; David Wynn label:
Unwooded Chardonnay, Shiraz, Patriarch Shiraz, Cabernet

Sauvignon; organically-grown Eden Ridge labe: Chardonnay, Sauvignon Blanc, Shiraz, Cabernet Sauvignon.

MOUNTADAM CHARDONNAY
●●●●● $25
The Mountadam Chardonnay accounts for around 70% of the total 10,000 case production under the Mountadam label. It is 100% estate-grown from low-yielding, high-altitude vineyards, the resulting fruit concentration fully expressing itself in the wine. Although Adam Wynn says that the changes in winemaking since 1984 have essentially been limited to fine tuning, there is no doubt that there has been a sea change in the end product since 1989.
Cellaring 3–6 years. **Best Vintages** '86, '89, '90, '91, '92, '93
Current Vintage '93
Matching Food Salmon terrine.
Tasting Note 1993 Medium yellow-green; a spotlessly clean bouquet with fig and melon aromas interwoven with delicate spicy/nutmeg oak. A lovely wine on the palate with good citrus/melon/fig fruit intensity; the oak is a little more up front, but in control, and will come into balance with time.

MOUNTADAM DAVID WYNN CABERNET SAUVIGNON
●●●● $13
The precise source of the cabernet sauvignon is not stated, but does come from the general Eden Valley region. The Shiraz under this label has been consistently outstanding, and the '93 Cabernet is in much the same league. Matured for one year in used French oak, and demands time in the bottle.
Cellaring 3–5 years. **Best Vintages** '88, '90, '91, '92
Current Vintage '93
Matching Food Boned loin of lamb.
Tasting Note 1993 Medium red-purple; a clean bouquet of medium intensity with fragrant mint, dark berry and chocolate aromas. As yet, the wine is rather firm in the mouth, but has the structure and fruit weight to open up and build complexity as it ages.

MOUNTADAM DAVID WYNN PATRIARCH SHIRAZ
●●●●● $19
The '93 vintage of this wine was especially poignant, more or less coinciding with the death of David Wynn. It is an outstanding vintage of what is always a particularly good wine, and is a fitting tribute to one of the most important figures in the Australian wine industry of the past 50 years. The wine is made from old shiraz vines in the Barossa Hills and is matured in French oak, although the power of the fruit makes the oak incidental.
Cellaring 10+ years. **Best Vintages** '88, '90, '91, '93
Current Vintage '93
Matching Food Game.
Tasting Note 1993 Dense red-purple; a marvellously concentrated and intense bouquet, redolent of liquorice and spice. The same exceptional concentration and power is evident on the palate, with almost riotous spice, liquorice and black cherry fruit.

MOUNTAIN CREEK WINES

NR 13.50 CD AUSSD
Pyrenees **Est.** 1973
Mountain Creek Road, Moonambel, Vic 3478
Ph (054) 67 2230
Open W'ends, Hols 10–7 **Production** 720
Winemaker(s) Taltarni (Contract)
Brian Cherry acquired the Mountain Creek Vineyard in 1975 and
has slowly extended it. The first wine was made in 1987, all or part
of the grapes before and in some years since then sold to other
Pyrenees wineries. The wine is made under contract, and shows all
of the substance and weight for which the district is renowned.
Principal Wines Sauvignon Blanc, Cabernet Sauvignon.

MOUNTFORD WINES *

★★★☆ 12–18.50 CD AUS11, 67
Warren Valley **Est.** 1987
Bamess Road, West Pemberton, WA 6260
Ph (097) 76 1439 **Fax** (097) 76 1439
Open 7 days 10–5 **Production** 2500
Winemaker(s) Andrew Mountford
English-born and trained Andrew Mountford and wife Sue migrated
to Australia in 1983, first endeavouring to set up a winery at
Mudgee, and thereafter moving to Pemberton with far greater
success. Their strikingly packaged wines (complete with beeswax
and paper seals) have been well received on Eastern States markets,
being produced from 6 hectares of permanently netted, dry-grown
vineyards.
Principal Wines Sauvignon Blanc Semillon, Chardonnay, Blanco
Alegre, Blanc de Noir, Pinot Noir.

MOUNTFORD WINES PINOT NOIR
●●● $15.50
As from 1994 the red wines have been made at Mountford by
Andrew Mountford, the '92 having been made at Chateau Xanadu.
The prime movers in opening up the Pemberton region were and are
convinced that it can make great Pinot Noir. Time will tell.
Cellaring 2–3 years. **Best Vintages** NA **Current Vintage** '93
Matching Food Spiced chicken.
Tasting Note 1993 Medium red; notwithstanding the difficult
vintage, shows quite rich and ripe cherry fruit with some
spicy/earthy notes. The palate has plenty of flavour, repeating the
characters of the bouquet, but does have definite sharp edges
which detract somewhat.

MOUNTFORD WINES SAUVIGNON BLANC SEMILLON
●●●● $14
The wine is made under contract at Frankland Estate, as the newly-
constructed Mountford winery is only set up for red winemaking.
It incorporates 15% semillon from the Margaret River and is a
particularly pleasant well made wine.

Cellaring 1–2 years. **Best Vintages** NA **Current Vintage** '94
Matching Food Deep-fried calamari.
Tasting Note 1994 Light green-yellow; the bouquet is of moderate
intensity, with earth, mineral and herbal notes all intermingling. A
well constructed and balanced wine in the mouth, with crisp,
herbaceous varietal fruit, and nicely balanced acidity on the finish.

MOUNTILFORD VINEYARD

NR 8–9.50 CD AUSSD
Mudgee **Est.** 1985
Vincent Road, Ilford, NSW 2850
Ph (063) 58 8544
Open 7 days 10–4 **Production** NFP
Winemaker(s) Don Cumming
Surprisingly large cellar door operation which has grown
significantly over the past few years. I have not, however, had the
opportunity of tasting the wines.
Principal Wines Riesling, Gewurztraminer, Chardonnay, Smoky
Red, Vineyard Red, Windamere, Sir Alexander Port.

MOUNTVIEW WINES

★★★☆ 6–20 CD AUSSD
Granite Belt **Est.** 1990
Mount Sterling Road, Glen Aplin, Qld 4381
Ph (076) 83 4316
Open Wed–Sat 9–5, Sun 10–5 **Production** 350
Winemaker(s) David Price
David and Linda Price are refugees from the Sydney rat-race
operating a small, neat, red cedar farm-style winery. Both the 1990
and 1991 Shiraz were clean, well made wines with good varietal
fruit and a pleasant touch of sweet American oak, the '93s better
still, winning medals at the 1994 Courier Mail Queensland Wine
Awards (Best Red Wine) and the Australian Small Winemakers
Show (Best Queensland Shiraz).
Principal Wines Chablis, Sauvignon Blanc, Cerise (light red),
Shiraz, Cabernet Shiraz, Cabernet Merlot.

MUDGEE WINES

NR 7.50–9 CD AUSSD
Mudgee **Est.** 1963
Henry Lawson Drive, Mudgee, NSW 2850
Ph (063) 72 2258
Open Mon–Sat 10–5, Sun 12–5 **Production** 1000
Winemaker(s) Jennifer Meek
All of the wines are naturally fermented with wild yeasts and made
without the addition of any chemicals or substances including sulphur
dioxide, a very demanding route, particularly with white wines. For
some consumers, any shortcoming in quality will be quite acceptable.
Principal Wines Chardonnay, Gewurztraminer, Crouchen,
Riesling, Rosé, Shiraz, Pinot Noir, Cabernet Sauvignon.

MURRINDINDI

★★★★ 17.95 R AUSSD

Southern Victoria **Est.** 1979

Cummins Lane, Murrindindi, Vic 3717

Ph (057) 97 8217 **Fax** (057) 97 8422

Open Not **Production** 1800

Winemaker(s) Alan Cuthbertson, Hugh Cuthbertson

Not quite in the Yarra Valley, nor in Macedon, but in a very cool climate which means that special care has to be taken with the viticulture to produce ripe fruit flavours. In more recent vintages, Murrindindi has succeeded handsomely in so doing.

Principal Wines Chardonnay, Cabernets.

MURRINDINDI CABERNETS

●●●● ▶ $17.95

Just as 1993 was the best vintage for many years for Murrindindi's white wines, so 1992 was the best for its red wines. Here a perfect growing season through the southern part of Victoria brought red wines to a near peak of perfection.

Cellaring 4–7 years. **Best Vintages** '85, '88, '90, '92, '93

Current Vintage '92

Matching Food Rib of beef.

Tasting Note 1992 Medium to full red-purple; a very complex bouquet with briary/berry/faintly earthy fruit, with hints of cool climate spicy characters. The palate is multiflavoured with cassis, leaf, mint and spice all attesting to the cool climate in which it is grown, yet giving abundant flavour.

MURRINDINDI CHARDONNAY

●●●● ▶ $17.95

1993 was a strange vintage in southern Victoria; for the first six months of the growing season it seemed improbable the grapes would ripen properly, then the warmest and driest April on record achieved marvellous ripeness and high sugar levels, as witnessed by the 13% alcohol present in this wine.

Cellaring 3–4 years. **Best Vintages** '84, '90, '91, '92, '93

Current Vintage '93

Matching Food Mussels.

Tasting Note 1993 Light green-yellow; a fine and stylish bouquet with melon and citrus fruit, and subtle barrel ferment oak. The palate is fine, elegant and long with superb melon, fig and citrus fruit flavours, echoing the barrel ferment characters of the bouquet.

MURRUMBATEMAN WINERY

NR NA AUS74

Canberra **Est.** 1972

Barton Highway, Murrumbateman, NSW 2582

Ph (06) 227 5584

Open 7 days 10–5 **Production** 1000

Winemaker(s) Duncan Leslie

Revived after a change of ownership, the Murrumbateman Winery draws upon 2.3 hectares of vineyards, and also incorporates an à la carte restaurant, function room, together with picnic and barbecue areas.

Principal Wines Riesling, Sauvignon Blanc, Chardonnay, Shiraz, Cabernet Sauvignon.

NARKOOJEE VINEYARD *

NR 16.50 CD AUSSD
Gippsland **Est.** 1981
1110 Francis Road, Glengarry, Vic 3854
Ph (051) 92 4257
Open W'ends by appt **Production** 500
Winemaker(s) Harry Friend
Narkoojee Vineyard is set on the foothills of Mount Erica, with views of the Strzeleckie Ranges, and within easy reach of the old gold mining town of Walhalla. The wines are produced from 2.5 hectares of estate vineyards.
Principal Wines Chardonnay, Cabernet Merlot.

NEPEAN WINES

NR 13.50–15 ML AUSSD
Mornington Peninsula **Est.** 1987
'Moonah', Truemans Road, Rosebud, Vic 3939
Ph (069) 28 4638 **Fax** (069) 28 4606
Open Not **Production** 550
Winemaker(s) Various Contract
Nepean Wines is a joint venture between the Leslie and Matear families; the main vineyards are situated on limestone-based soils behind Rye on the southern Mornington Peninsula, in one of the coolest vineyard sites.
Principal Wines Chardonnay, Pinot Noir.

NICHOLSON RIVER WINERY

★★★★ 12–25 CD AUSSD
Gippsland **Est.** 1978
Liddells Road, Nicholson, Vic 3882
Ph (051) 56 8241 **Fax** (051) 56 8433
Open 7 days 10–4 **Production** 2000
Winemaker(s) Ken Eckersley
The fierce commitment to quality in the face of the temperamental Gippsland climate and frustratingly small production has been handsomely repaid by some stupendous Chardonnays.
Principal Wines Chardonnay, Semillon, Sur-Lee Riesling, Pinot Noir, Cabernets; second label is Montview.

NICHOLSON RIVER CABERNETS

●●● ▶ $20
Drawn primarily from one hectare of estate cabernet sauvignon and just under half a hectare of estate merlot, with a little cabernet franc

also included. It usually demonstrates the cool, maritime-influenced
nature of the South Gippsland climate, and certainly did so in 1991.
Cellaring 4–7 years. **Best Vintages** '87, '88, '90, '91, '92
Current Vintage '91
Matching Food Veal shanks.
Tasting Note 1991 Medium to full red-purple; a concentrated
bouquet with briary/leafy aromas predominating. On the palate
there is intense leafy/minty/berry fruit with fairly high acid, and
tannins still to resolve.

NICHOLSON RIVER CHARDONNAY
●●●● ▶ $25
Possibly the most powerful and complex Chardonnay made in
Australia today. The wine has everything: concentrated fruit,
abundant use of French oak, deliberately challenging winemaking
techniques which place the emphasis on structure and weight, and
away from primary fruit characters. It is a style which polarises
opinion.
Cellaring 3–7 years. **Best Vintages** '87, '88, '91, '92, '93
Current Vintage '93
Matching Food Soft, mature Gippsland cheese.
Tasting Note 1993 Deep gold; extreme
honeyed/malty/nutty/buttery aromas and flavours. A wine which
really cannot be marked or judged by conventional standards.

NOON'S
NR 12.50–17.50 CD AUSSD
Southern Vales **Est.** 1976
Rifle Range Road, McLaren Vale, SA 5171
Ph (08) 323 8290 **Fax** (08) 323 8290
Open 7 days 10–5 **Production** 2000
Winemaker(s) David Noon
Massive wines made in wholly idiosyncratic style, which are
marketed exclusively through the cellar door (and mailing list), and
drawing in part on 3 hectares of estate grenache. The cellar door
includes a barbecue and picnic area.
Principal Wines Cabernet Sauvignon, Burgundy, Dry Red, Shiraz,
Shiraz Cabernet, Port.

NORMANS WINES
★★★★☆ 7–20 R AUS43–46, 61 UK33 US4
Southern Vales **Est.** 1851
Grant's Gully Road, Clarendon, SA 5157
Ph (08) 383 6138 **Fax** (08) 383 6089
Open Mon–Sat 10–5, Sun 11–5 **Production** 110 000
Winemaker(s) Brian Light
In late 1994 Normans issued a prospectus seeking to raise
$6 million in new share capital preparatory to joining the lists
of Australian Associated Stock Exchanges. The issue was not

underwritten, but reflected the considerable success Normans has enjoyed in recent years in establishing its brand both in domestic and export markets.

Principal Wines At the bottom: Chandlers Hill Fumé Blanc, Chardonnay Semillon, Chenin Blanc, Spatlese, Fine Hermitage; then Family Reserve Riesling, Chardonnay, Cabernet Sauvignon; at the top: Chais Clarendon Chardonnay, Shiraz, Cabernet Sauvignon.

NORMANS CHAIS CLARENDON CABERNET SAUVIGNON
●●●● ▶ $20

Like the Chais Clarendon Shiraz, primarily sourced from the Clarendon region high in the southern end of the Adelaide Hills. All of the wines in the Chais Clarendon range receive some new oak which adds a dimension not possessed by the other Normans wines.
Cellaring 6–8 years. **Best Vintages** '82, '86, '90, '91, '92
Current Vintage '91
Matching Food Fillet of beef with bone marrow.
Tasting Note 1991 Bright red-purple; softly ripe red and black berry fruits with oak still to fully integrate on the bouquet. The palate shows strong redcurrant and blackcurrant fruit flavours with warm, spicy/vanillin oak rather better integrated than the palate would suggest, finishing with soft tannins and a good aftertaste.

NORMANS CHAIS CLARENDON SHIRAZ
●●●● ▶ $20

Although the Chais Clarendon label is strictly a brand, the majority of the grapes for the wines under the label does come from the Clarendon district at the southern end of the Adelaide Hills. Normans has a 6.6-hectare vineyard here which produces fruit of high quality.
Cellaring 5–8 years. **Best Vintages** '82, '86, '90, '91, '92
Current Vintage '92
Matching Food Shoulder of lamb.
Tasting Note 1992 Medium red-purple; a clean and smooth bouquet with some minty edges to the cherry-accented fruit, and subtle oak. A smooth palate with red cherry fruit, good oak integration, ample soft tannins, and a particularly harmonious finish.

NORMANS FAMILY RESERVE CABERNET SAUVIGNON
●●●● ▶ $10

Only 5% of Normans' crush is estate-grown. The remainder (including the grapes for this wine) are supplied by contract growers. It is a wine which can rise way above its station, as it did in 1992, showing the consummate skills of winemaker Brian Light.
Cellaring 3–6 years. **Best Vintages** '82, '86, '90, '91, '92
Current Vintage '92
Matching Food Veal kidneys.
Tasting Note 1992 Medium to full purple-red; fresh, youthful minty/spicy/berry fruit with subtle oak. The same fruit-driven generosity is apparent on the palate, with very attractive spicy berry fruit and soft tannins. Excellent balance.

NOTLEY GORGE VINEYARD

NR 10–14.50 ML AUSSD
Tamar Valley **Est.** 1983
Loop Road, Glengarry, Tas 7275 (vineyard only)
Ph (003) 96 1166 **Fax** (003) 96 1200
Open By appt **Production** 1800
Winemaker(s) Doug Bowen, Andrew Hood (Consultant)
Marine engineer Doug Bowen (no relation to the Doug Bowen of
Coonawarra) spreads his favours around, having his sauvignon
blanc processed at Domaine A, chardonnay at Rochecombe,
and pinot noir crushed at Notley Gorge, pressed at Holm Oak
and then returned to Notley Gorge for maturation in the former
apple orchard coolstore, a building which just happened to be
on the property and which precipitated him into wine
production.
Principal Wines Sauvignon Blanc, Chardonnay, Pinot Noir,
Cabernet Sauvignon, Cabernet Merlot (light red).

OAKRIDGE ESTATE

★★★★☆ 14.95–29.95 R AUS112
Yarra Valley **Est.** 1982
Aitken Road, Seville, Vic 3139
Ph (059) 64 3379 **Fax** (059) 64 2061
Open W'ends, Hols 10–5 **Production** 2000
Winemaker(s) Michael Zitzlaff
After some uncertainty, the future of Oakridge is now assured,
with Michael Zitzlaff at the helm and national distribution
through Negociants. The winery operations are being expanded,
and will continue to produce some of the Yarra Valley's best
Cabernets.
Principal Wines Chardonnay, Cabernet Merlot, Reserve
Cabernet Sauvignon.

OAKRIDGE ESTATE CABERNET MERLOT

●●●● ▶ $14.95
Previously labelled Quercus, but now Cabernet Merlot under a
revamped and significantly improved label. Draws upon
2.7 hectares of estate cabernet sauvignon and 1.7 hectares of
estate merlot, all on the rich red volcanic soils of the Seville
subdistrict of the Yarra Valley. A distinguished producer of
Cabernet wines, and the upcoming 1992 release shows just
why that reputation has been earned.
Cellaring 5–7 years. **Best Vintages** '88, '90, '91, '92
Current Vintage '92 (mid 1995)
Matching Food Yarra Valley venison.
Tasting Note 1992 Medium to full red-purple; a clean bouquet
with complex cedar/cigar box/briary fruit aromas, with subtle oak.
The palate is similarly complex with dark berry/briary/leafy
flavours, all intermingling, woven through with soft tannins. A
good wine with many things going on in terms of flavour.

OAKRIDGE ESTATE CHARDONNAY
●●●● ▶ $14.95
A new addition to the range for Oakridge, but not so for winemaker
Michael Zitzlaff, who has made the Yarra Edge Chardonnay (under
contract) with great distinction for a number of years. The '94
vintage, the first for Oakridge Chardonnay, is an elegant wine in
mainstream Yarra Valley style.
Cellaring 3–5 years. **Best Vintages** NA **Current Vintage** '94
Matching Food Fish quenelles in white sauce.
Tasting Note 1994 Light to medium yellow-green; fresh, clean and
elegant with melon/citrus fruit and hints of cashew on the bouquet.
The palate is correspondingly lively, clean and crisp with lemon,
citrus and gentle cashew flavours.

OAKVALE WINERY

★★★ 11–16.50 CD AUS34, UK45
Hunter Valley **Est.** 1893
Broke Road, Pokolbin, NSW 2321
Ph (049) 98 7520 **Fax** (049) 98 7747
Open 7 days 9–5 **Production** 5000
Winemaker(s) Barry Shields
Former Sydney solicitor Barry Shields seems content with the change
in his lifestyle as he presides over the historic Oakvale Winery which
he purchased from the Elliott family over a decade ago. The
emphasis is on Semillon, Chardonnay and a blend of the two in both
oaked and unoaked versions, most of which are offered with 3 to
5 years bottle age.
Principal Wines Peach Tree Semillon, Oak Matured Semillon,
Chardonnay Semillon, Chardonnay, Peppercorn Shiraz, and a
handful of fortified wines.

OLD BARN WINES

NR 5.70–11.80 CD AUSSD
Barossa Valley **Est.** 1990
Langmeil Road, Tanunda, SA 5352
Ph (085) 63 0111
Open Mon–Fri 9–5, W'ends 10–5 **Production** 2200
Winemaker(s) Trevor Jones
Owned by a partnership of Barry and Elizabeth Chinner and Janet
Hatch, with an honorary establishment date of 1861, being the date
of construction of the old stone barn from which the wines are
exclusively sold.
Principal Wines Riesling, Semillon, Traminer Riesling, Fumé Blanc,
Old Fashioned Hock, Barossa Dry Red, Cabernet Shiraz, Light Sweet
Red, and a range of other sweet and fortified wines.

OLD CAVES WINERY

NR 7.50–13.50 CD AUSSD
Granite Belt **Est.** 1980
New England Highway, Stanthorpe, Qld 4380

Ph (076) 81 1494 **Fax** (076) 81 2722
Open Mon–Sat 9–5, Sun 10–5 **Production** 2200
Winemaker(s) David Zanatta

A range of wines tasted from the 1990 and 1991 vintages showed significant winemaking problems, but over the years Old Caves has produced some pleasant wines.

Principal Wines Chardonnay, Classic Dry White, Light Red, Shiraz, Cabernet Sauvignon, and a range of generic wines in both bottle and flagon, including fortifieds.

OLD KENT RIVER *

★★★☆ 16–20 CD AUSSD
Great Southern **Est.** 1985
Turpin Road, Rocky Gully, WA 6397
Ph (098) 55 1589 **Fax** (098) 55 1589
Open By appt **Production** 400
Winemaker(s) Alkoomi (Contract)

Mark and Debbie Noack have done it tough all of their relatively young lives, but have earned respect from their neighbours and from Eastern States producers, such as Domaine Chandon, now buying over 80% of the 50 tonnes of grapes they produce each year on their sheep property. 'Grapes', they say, 'saved us from bankruptcy'.

Principal Wines Classic White, Chardonnay, Pinot Noir, Diamontina (Sparkling).

OLD KENT RIVER CHARDONNAY
●●●● $10.85

Like the Pinot Noir, made at Alkoomi. Here the oak works much better than it does with the Pinot Noir, producing an attractive barrel ferment-driven style.

Cellaring 3–4 years. **Best Vintages** '92, '94
Current Vintage '94
Matching Food Chicken breast.

Tasting Note 1994 Light to medium yellow-green; a stylish bouquet with nutty barrel ferment aromas and gently tropical fruit. There is both strength and length to the palate, with oak at this stage a little dominant, but likely to settle down as the peachy fruit comes through.

OLD KENT RIVER PINOT NOIR
●●● ▶ $10.85

Replete with the striking label (a photograph of a dead jarrah tree taken by Mark's brother Ken) the wine invariably has strong colour and solid, ripe flavours, notwithstanding the generous yields. Bronze medal winner at the 1994 Mount Barker Show.

Cellaring 2–3 years. **Best Vintages** NA **Current Vintage** '93
Matching Food Pasta, cheese.

Tasting Note 1993 Medium red-purple; good, ripe cherry varietal fruit aromas offset by slightly hard oak. The palate, too, has attractive fruit under somewhat hard/green oak; there is plenty of flavour and substance. The '94 wine is bigger and richer still.

OLIVE FARM WINES

★★★☆ 10–16 CD AUSSD
Swan Valley **Est.** 1829
77 Great Eastern Highway, South Guildford, WA 6055
Ph (09) 277 2989 **Fax** (09) 279 4372
Open Mon–Fri 10–5, Sat 9–3 **Production** 9500
Winemaker(s) Ian Yurisich
The oldest winery in Australia in use today, and arguably the least communicative. The ultra-low profile tends to disguise the fact that wine quality is by and large good.
Principal Wines Verdelho, Chenin Blanc, Chablis, Semillon, Chardonnay, Gewurztraminer, Cabernet Shiraz, Hermitage, Cabernet Sauvignon, Cabernet Shiraz Merlot, Sherry, Port, Sparkling.

OLIVERHILL WINES

NR 5–11 CD AUSSD
Southern Vales **Est.** 1973
Seaview Road, McLaren Vale, SA 5171
Ph (08) 323 8922
Open 7 days 10–5 **Production** 1300
Winemaker(s) Stuart Miller
Oliverhill has changed hands, but otherwise continues an operation aimed almost entirely at the local tourist trade. As far as I know, the restaurant is still open daily.
Principal Wines Great Outdoors White and Red, Chardonnay, Shiraz Cabernet, Port, Muscat.

ORLANDO WINES

★★★★ 5.95–33 R AUS117 UK22 US7
Barossa Valley **Est.** 1847
Sturt Highway, Rowland Flat, SA 5350
Ph (085) 24 4500 **Fax** (085) 21 3100
Open Mon–Fri 9.30–5.30, W'ends 10–4 **Production** NFP
Winemaker(s) Phil Laffer
As befits a group of this size, Jacobs Creek is an enormously successful international brand, which has done particularly well in the United Kingdom, and is doubtless the financial jewel in the Orlando crown.
Principal Wines The table wines are sold in four ranges: first, the national and international best selling Jacobs Creek, Chablis, Chardonnay, Riesling, Nouveau and Shiraz Cabernet Malbec Claret; then the Gramps range of Chardonnay, Botrytis Semillon, Cabernet Merlot; next, the Saint range, St Helga Riesling, St Hilary Chardonnay, St Hewitt Pinot, St Hugo Cabernet Sauvignon; finally, the premium range of Flaxmans Eden Valley Traminer, Steingarten Riesling, Jacaranda Ridge Cabernet Sauvignon and Lawsons Padthaway Shiraz. Also Russet Ridge Coonawarra Cabernet Shiraz Merlot off to one side; sparkling wines under the Trilogy and Carrington labels.

ORLANDO GRAMP'S BOTRYTIS SEMILLON (375 ML)
●●●● $10.95

Sourced from botrytised semillon grown in the Griffith region, and a marked departure in style from the original dessert table wines made from semillon which were released under the briefly famous Goldbeeren label, made from cane-cut, late harvested (and non botrytised) Barossa semillon.

Cellaring 1–2 years. **Best Vintages** NA **Current Vintage** '93
Matching Food Crème brûleé.
Tasting Note 1993 Full yellow orange; soft, rich cumquat and apricot botrytis aromas, and barely perceptible oak. On the palate, the wine is already fully mature, it is complex and quite powerful with the same cumquat and apricot flavours evident in the bouquet.

ORLANDO JACARANDA RIDGE CABERNET SAUVIGNON
●●●● $33

Orlando's top red wine, aimed at the premium end of the market. It is aged for two years in new French and American oak, followed by two years in bottle before release. Like the Lawsons Shiraz, it enjoys significant show success, although one wonders whether a little less oak and a little more fruit might not produce a better wine.

Cellaring Usually ready upon release. **Best Vintages** '86, '88, '90, '91 **Current Vintage** '89
Matching Food Smoked beef.
Tasting Note 1989 Medium to full red-purple; a complex, oak-dominated bouquet with soft berry fruit. The palate is likewise complex with a range of vanilla, briar, leaf and red berry flavours.

ORLANDO LAWSON'S PADTHAWAY SHIRAZ
●●●● $22.95

Named after a 19th century pioneer surveyor, Robert Lawson. It is matured for two years in new Nevers oak hogsheads, with further bottle maturation before release. This expansive oak input makes its mark on the wine: the regular shower of gold and silver medals which descend on the wine shows that many judges do not regard the input as excessive.

Cellaring 4–7 years. **Best Vintages** '88, '90, '91
Current Vintage '91
Matching Food Beef stroganoff.
Tasting Note 1991 Dense red-purple; a very rich and concentrated bouquet with lots and lots of vanillin oak leads on to a ripe, full and fleshy palate with a rather chewy finish, again showing dramatic use of oak and all of the concentration one could expect from the 1991 vintage.

ORLANDO RUSSET RIDGE CABERNET SHIRAZ MERLOT
●●●● ▶ $12.95

First released in 1991, and continuing the move towards rather tighter and more concentrated fruit in the Orlando red wines. It is made entirely from Coonawarra grapes, a blend (in descending order) of approximately 85% cabernet sauvignon, 10% shiraz and 5% merlot. The wine is matured in a mixture of new and used French and American oak hogsheads for between 12 and 18 months.

Cellaring 3–5 years. **Best Vintages** '91, '92
Current Vintage '91
Matching Food Hot, honey-glazed ham.
Tasting Note 1992 Medium to full red; a cedary, elegant bouquet with a fairly pronounced overlay of lemon and vanilla oak. The palate is of light to medium intensity with subtle oak, soft tannins and a nice amalgam of briar, leaf, berry and vanilla flavours. The '91 was a much bigger wine.

ORLANDO ST HELGA EDEN VALLEY RIESLING
●●●● $9.95
Produced from grapes grown on Orlando's St Helga Vineyard in the Eden Valley and first made in 1980. That initial release was not put onto the market until it was four years old, and was initially priced as a premium product. It is now conventionally marketed in the year of production, and in real terms the price has come down significantly.
Cellaring Drink now. **Best Vintages** NA **Current Vintage** '94
Matching Food Asian cuisine.
Tasting Note 1994 Light to medium yellow-green; there is a typical hint of spice to the bouquet with fairly tight lime aromas underneath, and a gently toasty edge. A well made commercial style with some regional lime and passionfruit, soft and nicely balanced for immediate consumption.

ORLANDO ST HUGO CABERNET SAUVIGNON
●●● ▶ $18.95
First made in 1980, and over the years has accumulated 7 trophies and over 60 gold medals at Australian wine shows. The focus has been on ripe grapes to produce a soft, fleshy style, but since 1985 the vinification has been more complex, including barrel ferment components and some given post fermentation maceration. A mix of French and American oak is used.
Cellaring 3–5 years. **Best Vintages** '86, '88, '90, '91
Current Vintage '91
Matching Food Mixed grill.
Tasting Note 1991 Medium to full red-purple; fine, cedary aromas with a hint of leafiness, though not green, and a general character closer to Merlot than Cabernet Sauvignon in style. Elegant on the palate, essentially fruit-driven with soft, fine tannins and subtle oak.

PADTHAWAY ESTATE, THE See page 439.

PALMARA VINEYARD
★★★☆ 14.50 CD AUSSD
Coal River **Est.** 1985
Main Road, Richmond, Tas 7025
Ph (002) 62 2462
Open W'ends Winter 1–4, Summer 10–6 **Production** 200
Winemaker(s) Allan Bird, Andrew Hood
Allan Bird has the Palmara wines made for him by Andrew Hood, all in tiny quantities. The Pinot Noir has performed consistently well

since 1990. The Schoenberger Siegerrebe blend is unchallenged as Australia's most exotic and unusual wine, with amazing jujube/lanolin aromas and flavours.
Principal Wines Pinot Noir; other wines produced in minuscule quantities include an Ehrenfelser Semillon and a Schoenberger-dominated blend.

PALMARA VINEYARD PINOT NOIR
●●●● $14.50
Produced from 2 hectares of estate vineyards, with part of the grapes going to contract winemaker Andrew Hood. Performs as many of the Pinots from the Coal River/Richmond region do, with considerable flavour intensity, varying to plum in the riper years.
Cellaring 2–3 years. **Best Vintages** '91, '92
Current Vintage '93
Matching Food Saddle of hare.
Tasting Note 1993 Light to medium purple-red; the bouquet is of medium intensity, tending slightly firm, and with less plummy fruit than the '92. The palate has some wild thyme/wild herb notes together with red cherry fruit, and a fairly firm finish. Should continue to develop and open up in bottle.

PALMERS WINERY *

★★★★ 15–18 R AUS102
Margaret River **Est.** 1977
Caves Road, Willyabrup, WA 6280
Ph (097) 97 1881 **Fax** (097) 97 2534
Open By appt **Production** 4500
Winemaker(s) Eddie Price, Amberley Estate (Contract)
Stephen and Helen Palmer planted their first hectare of vines way back in 1977, but a series of events (including a cyclone and grasshopper plagues) caused them to lose interest and instead turn to thoroughbred horses. But, with encouragement from Dr Michael Peterkin of Pierro, and after a gap of almost 10 years, they again turned to viticulture, and now have 15 hectares planted to the classic varieties.
Principal Wines Sauvignon Blanc, Semillon, Classic White, Chardonnay, Cabernet Sauvignon.

PALMERS CHARDONNAY
●●●●● $18
The barrel fermented Chardonnay has been enormously successful for Palmer Wines. Up until 1993 it was made by Dr Michael Peterkin, the 1991 vintage winning the Qantas Trophy for Best White Wine at the 1993 Mount Barker Wine Show. Eddie Price of Amberley Estate took over winemaking from 1994, and promptly came up with a gold medal-winning wine of absolutely outstanding quality.
Cellaring Up to 5 years. **Best Vintages** '91, '93, '94
Current Vintage '94
Matching Food Ragout of sweetbreads.
Tasting Note 1994 Light to medium green-yellow; rich, complex barrel ferment oak perfectly interwoven and balanced with tangy,

concentrated fruit on the bouquet. The palate shows the same potent mix, with very sophisticated oak, and great length to the citrus/melon fruit. A gold medal winner in any company.

PANKHURST WINES

NR 10–12 ML AUSSD
Canberra **Est.** 1986
Old Woodgrove, Woodgrove Road, Hall, NSW 2618
Ph (06) 230 2592 **Fax** (06) 273 1936
Open Not **Production** 1000
Winemaker(s) Sue Carpenter (Contract)
Agricultural scientist and consultant Allan Pankhurst and wife Christine (with a degree in pharmaceutical science) have established a 3-hectare, split canopy vineyard. Tastings of the first wines produced showed considerable promise; there have been no recent tastings.
Principal Wines Chardonnay, Semillon, Classic Dry White, Pinot Noir, Cabernet Merlot.

PANORAMA VINEYARD

★★★ 11.50 CD AUS48
Huon Valley **Est.** 1974
193 Waterworks Road, Dynnyrne, Tas 7005
Ph (002) 23 1948
Open 7 days 10–5 **Production** 580
Winemaker(s) Steve Ferencz
The quality of the underlying fruit, particularly with the red wines, is not in doubt. These have great colour and startling richness of flavour in favoured vintages, the '93 Panorama Pinot Noir winning a truckload of trophies at the 1994 Royal Hobart Wine Show.
Principal Wines Chardonnay, Pinot Noir, Cabernet Sauvignon.

PANORAMA VINEYARD PINOT NOIR
●●●●) $11.50
Produced entirely from pinot noir grown on the 3 hectares of estate vineyards, which are close planted and part organic, with no pesticides of any description used.
Cellaring Up to 5 years. **Best Vintages** '90, '91, '92, '93
Current Vintage '93
Matching Food Coq au vin.
Tasting Note 1993 Very deep red-purple; full, ripe curranty fruit with lots of oak, not as yet showing a great of varietal character. The palate is ripe, full and sweet with lots of oak again apparent; a massive wine still hiding its varietal fruit, but with no green characters whatsoever. A gold medal winner.

PARADISE ENOUGH *

NR 11–15 CD AUSSD
Gippsland **Est.** 1987
Stewarts Road, Kongwak, Vic 3951

Ph (056) 57 4241
Open Sun, Public hols 10–5 **Production** 500
Winemaker(s) John Bell
Phillip Jones of Bass Phillip persuaded John Bell to establish his small
vineyard on a substantial dairy and beef cattle property. The
Chardonnay is intensely flavoured, but the wine tasted suffered from
a degree of volatility.
Principal Wines Chardonnay, Pinot Noir, Cabernet Merlot.

PARINGA ESTATE

★★★★★ 16–24 R AUS72
Mornington Peninsula **Est.** 1985
44 Paringa Road, Red Hill South, Vic 3937
Ph (059) 89 2669
Open Mon, Wed–Fri 12–5, W'ends, Public hols 11–5
Production 1000 (abnormally low)
Winemaker(s) Lindsay McCall
No longer a rising star, but a star shining more brightly in the
Mornington Peninsula firmament than any other. Has produced
consistently superlative Pinot Noir and Shiraz over the past few
years, with Chardonnay also in the highest category. What a pity
there is not more of the wine.
Principal Wines Chardonnay, Pinot Noir, Shiraz, Cabernet
Sauvignon.

PARINGA ESTATE CHARDONNAY
●●●●● $19
Produced entirely from half a hectare of estate plantings, and 100%
barrel fermented in 100% new Vosges and Allier French oak
barriques of the highest quality. Typically, 10% (and no more) is
taken through malolactic fermentation, and the wine spends almost
a year on yeast lees before bottling. The style is opulent and
concentrated.
Cellaring 3–6 years. **Best Vintages** '91, '92, '93, '94
Current Vintage '94
Matching Food Pan-fried veal with abalone mushrooms.
Tasting Note 1994 Medium to full yellow-green; intense citrussy
fruit with exotic high toast oak woven throughout the bouquet. The
palate, too, shows very sophisticated oak handling which does not
threaten the tangy grapefruit and citrus flavours. The strength of the
wine is the power and length of the finish.

PARINGA ESTATE PINOT NOIR
●●●●● $20
The most strikingly individual style in the Paringa range, and
arguably the most controversial, although its formidable show
record, strewn with trophies and gold medals, would not suggest
any great element of controversy. It is very pungent, with herb
and spice aromas and flavours attesting to the very cool climate,
yet to my palate it has the requisite vinosity and sweet fruit. The '94
was the only gold medal winner in its class at the 1994 Lilydale
Wine Show.

Cellaring 1–2 years. **Best Vintages** '88, '90, '91, '92, '93
Current Vintage '94
Matching Food Wild duck, game.
Tasting Note 1994 Medium to full red; potent, spicy/earthy/leafy characters run through riper plum and berry fruit on the bouquet. The palate is as powerful, potent and concentrated as the bouquet suggests, with a very interesting amalgam of ripe fruit and spicier characters. It is not over-oaked.

PARINGA ESTATE SHIRAZ
●●●●● $20
There can be no controversy here. The '90, '91 and '92 vintages received a trophy and eight gold medals, while the '93 is arguably the best yet, being a gold medal winner at the 1995 Sydney International Winemakers Competition, and one of the highest pointed wines out of the thousand entries in the show. Spice and liquorice are the keys here; entirely estate-produced (as are all the Paringa wines), in this instance from one hectare of vines.
Cellaring 3–5 years. **Best Vintages** '91, '92, '93
Current Vintage '93
Matching Food Stir-fried beef.
Tasting Note 1993 Medium to full purple-red; incredibly like a high quality wine from the northern Rhone Valley with strong liquorice and spice fruit. On the palate the wine is entirely fruit-driven, with freakish intensity of liquorice, cherry and spice, finishing with soft tannins and crisp acidity.

PARKER COONAWARRA ESTATE

★★★★☆ 16.90–35 R AUS56, 188, UK27
Coonawarra **Est.** 1975
Penola Road, Coonawarra, SA 5263
Ph (02) 357 3376 **Fax** (02) 358 1517
Open Not **Production** 2500
Winemaker(s) Ralph Fowler (Contract)
Parker Coonawarra Estate is a joint venture between the Parker, Fowler and Balnaves families: John Parker, former chairman of Hungerford Hill; Doug Balnaves, long-term viticulturist in Coonawarra; and Ralph Fowler, winemaker at Leconfield and contract maker for Parker Coonawarra Estate. The partnership grows 400 tonnes of fruit a year, and selects the best 30 tonnes for the Parker label. All of the wines released to date have shown very opulent fruit and no less opulent oak, and are at the richest end of the spectrum of Australian wine style.
Principal Wines Cabernet Sauvignon under two labels, Parker Coonawarra Estate and Parker Coonawarra Estate Terra Rossa First Growth.

PARKER COONAWARRA ESTATE TERRA ROSSA FIRST GROWTH
●●●● ▶ $35
First made in 1988, with a consistent style ever since. It is drawn from a little over 50 hectares of vineyards owned by the Parkers,

and without question uses only the highest quality fruit from each
vintage. The '91 vintage has more merlot and cabernet franc than
prior vintages because of the strength of the cabernet sauvignon
component. The time in French and American oak was also
extended to two years because of the power of the wine.
Cellaring 10–15 years. **Best Vintages** '88, '90, '91
Current Vintage '91
Matching Food Prime rib of beef.
Tasting Note 1991 Medium to full red, starting to lose its purple
hues; there is abundant cedary oak, with complex fruit underneath.
The palate precisely tracks the bouquet, with a substantial oak input
but also with a complex array of berry and leaf flavours, and fine,
rounded tannins. Altogether opulent in style.

PARKER WINES

NR 10.40–28 R AUSSD
Hunter Valley **Est.** 1968
McDonalds Road, Pokolbin, NSW 2321
Ph (049) 98 7585 **Fax** (049) 98 7732
Open W'ends, Hols 11–5 **Production** 12 000
Winemaker(s) David Lowe
Established as Tamburlaine, this seemingly ill-starred winery then
became Tamalee, then Sobels and now Parker — named after its
owner Stan Parker. With ex-Rothbury chief winemaker David Lowe in
charge, it is reasonable to hope — and indeed expect — that the
fortunes of what is now Parker Wines will take a turn for the better.
Principal Wines Semillon, Oak Matured Semillon, Chablis, Rhine
Riesling, Sauvignon Blanc, Chardonnay, Pinot Noir, Shiraz,
Cabernet Sauvignon, Sparkling, Ports.

PARKLANE WINES

NR 10–15 CD AUSSD
Canberra **Est.** 1986
Brooklands Road via Hall, ACT 2618
Ph (06) 230 2263 **Fax** (06) 230 2263
Open W'ends 11–5 **Production** 2500
Winemaker(s) Alwyn Lane
Alwyn and Margaret Lane run the 8-hectare vineyard and winery
as a full-time occupation, making only estate-grown wines, and with
plans to increase production to 4500 cases by 1996. In the
meantime, the Lanes have lost no time in stirring local viticultural
politics.
Principal Wines Riesling, Fumé Blanc, Chardonnay, Pinot Noir,
Cabernets.

PASSING CLOUDS VINEYARD

★★★★ 13.50–20 CD AUS11, 173, UK53
Bendigo **Est.** 1974
RMB 440 Kurting Road, Kingower, Vic 3517
Ph (054) 38 8257 **Fax** (054) 38 8246

Open 7 days 10–5 **Production** 3000
Winemaker(s) Graeme Leith
Graeme Leith is one of the great personalities of the industry, with a superb sense of humour, and makes lovely regional reds, with cassis, berry and mint fruit. Intermittent releases of white wines from the cellar door come from grapes grown on an adjoining property.
Principal Wines Red wine specialist; principal wines include Pinot Noir, Shiraz, Shiraz Cabernet, Ben's Blend Shiraz Cabernet, Angel Blend Cabernet, Merlot Cabernet Franc.

PASSING CLOUDS BEN'S BLEND SHIRAZ CABERNET
●●●● ▶ $16.65
A special limited release selected by Tasmanian wine merchant Ben Vaughan, who chose one barrel each of late picked shiraz and middle vintage cabernet sauvignon for their outstanding quality and compatibility. The blend works exceptionally well, underpinning the very high quality of the '92 vintage at Passing Clouds.
Cellaring 10+ years. **Best Vintages** NA
Current Vintage '92
Matching Food Lamb casserole.
Tasting Note 1992 Dense purple-red; rich, full, concentrated dark berry fruits are the first impression, followed by some oak. A big, rich, round, mouthfilling wine with lots of dark berry fruit and extract, finishing with soft tannins.

PASSING CLOUDS SHIRAZ
●●●● ▶ $15
Contrary to what one might expect, 1992 marked the first release of a 100% shiraz from Passing Clouds; prior to that time the shiraz was used in the various shiraz cabernet blends. It is an extremely auspicious start, albeit from a very good vintage.
Cellaring 10+ years. **Best Vintages** '92
Current Vintage '92
Matching Food Cassoulet.
Tasting Note 1992 Dense red-purple; very concentrated Central Victorian style with ripe, dark cherry and mint aromas. The palate is tremendously concentrated, yet not extractive, with layer upon layer of mint and dark berry fruit. Will be very long-lived.

PASSING CLOUDS SHIRAZ CABERNET
●●● ▶ $16
First made in 1980; a blend of 60% shiraz and 40% cabernet sauvignon matured in American oak, and (happily) not too much new oak.
Cellaring 5–9 years. **Best Vintages** '81, '82, '86, '90, '92
Current Vintage '91
Matching Food Rack of lamb with mint sauce.
Tasting Note 1991 Medium to full red; typical eucalypt mint edges to the berry fruit, and just a whisper of vanillin oak. The palate is of medium to full weight, smooth but with pronounced eucalypt mint flavours, finishing with soft tannins.

PATERNOSTER *

★★★ 11–30 CD AUSSD
Yarra Valley **Est.** 1985
17 Paternoster Road, Emerald, Vic 3782
Ph (059) 68 3197
Open W'ends 10.30–5.30 **Production** 600
Winemaker(s) Philip Hession
The densely-planted, non-irrigated vines (at a density of 5000 vines
to the hectare) cascade down a steep hillside at Emerald in one of
the coolest parts of the Yarra Valley. Pinot noir is the specialty of the
winery, producing intensely flavoured wines with a strong eucalypt
mint overlay reminiscent of the wines of Delatite.
Principal Wines Semillon, Chardonnay, Pinot Noir, Shiraz,
Cabernets, Vintage Port.

PATRITTI WINES

★★☆ 4.50–8 CD AUSSD
Adelaide Plains **Est.** 1926
13-23 Clacton Road, Dover Gardens, SA 5048
Ph (08) 296 8261 **Fax** (08) 296 5088
Open Mon–Sat 9–6 **Production** 65 000
Winemaker(s) G Patritti, J Patritti
One of the old-style winemaker-cum-merchant offering wines and
spirits at old-style prices.
Principal Wines A kaleidoscopic array of table, sparkling,
fortified and flavoured wines (and spirits) offered in bottle and
flagon.

PATTERSONS WINES

★★★☆ 14–16 CD AUS150, 175
Great Southern **Est.** 1982
28 Montem Street, Mount Barker, WA 6324
Ph (098) 51 2063
Open By appt **Production** 800
Winemaker(s) John Wade (Contract)
Schoolteachers Sue and Arthur Patterson have grown chardonnay
and grazed cattle as a weekend relaxation for a decade. The cellar-
door is in a recently completed and very beautiful rammed earth
house, and a number of vintages ranging from 1988 to 1992 are
available for sale.
Principal Wines Chardonnay, Pinot Noir, Shiraz.

PATTERSONS CHARDONNAY
●●●● ▶ $16
Planting of the vineyard commenced in the early 1980s, and the
first Chardonnay made in 1986. It is consistently the best of the
Pattersons wines, developing very well with age into a rich, full-
blown style. Tasted in late 1994, the '90 was quite delicious, fruit-
driven and still with a nice tang to the palate. It and the '88 are
still available at cellar door.

Cellaring 5+ years. **Best Vintages** '88, '90, '91, '92, '93
Current Vintage '90, '92, '93
Matching Food Roast pork.
Tasting Note 1993 Medium yellow-green; round, smooth and rich with generous peachy fruit aromas. Full-flavoured palate, smooth and round, again with peachy fruit and nicely integrated vanillin oak.

PATTERSONS SHIRAZ
●●● ▶ $14
The second string to the Pattersons Wines bow, although the Pinot Noir can be good in some years. Both the '90 and '91 vintages were available at cellar door in late 1994.
Cellaring 4–7 years. **Best Vintages** '90, '91
Current Vintage '91
Matching Food Chicken casserole.
Tasting Note 1991 Light to medium red; clean cherry-accented aromas with just a hint of French oak on the bouquet. A stylish wine in a lighter style on the palate, with spice, cherry and liquorice flavours, finishing with fine-grained tannins.

PAUL CONTI WINES
★★★★ 7–12.50 CD AUS56, 103, 124
South-west Coastal Plain **Est.** 1968
529 Wanneroo Road, Wanneroo, WA 6065
Ph (09) 409 9160 **Fax** (09) 309 1634
Open Mon–Sat 9.30–5.30, Sun by appt **Production** 8000
Winemaker(s) Paul Conti
In 1968 Paul Conti succeeded his father in the business the latter had established in 1948, and since assuming responsibility has quietly gone about making some outstanding wines, doing much to help pioneer the Mount Barker region, even though most of the wines are made from grapes grown on the south-west coastal plain around Perth.
Principal Wines Chablis, Chenin Blanc, Chardonnay, Carabooda Chardonnay, Late Picked Frontignac, Mariginiup Hermitage, White Port, Reserve Port.

PAUL CONTI CARABOODA CHARDONNAY
●●●● ▶ $16.95
Paul Conti developed the Carabooda Vineyard in the early 1980s, selecting the site for its unique sand over limestone soil, and close proximity to the Indian Ocean which provides cool coastal sea breezes. The 1994 vintage of the wine was a gold medal winner at the Mount Barker Wine Show, narrowly missing out on several major trophies.
Cellaring 3–5 years. **Best Vintages** '89, '90, '91, '92, '94
Current Vintage '94
Matching Food King prawns.
Tasting Note 1994 Light green-yellow; a complex, tangy and powerful fruit-driven bouquet. The palate is similarly powerful and

concentrated with layers of melon, fig and grapefruit flavours, and
no apparent oak input — and none needed.

PAUL CONTI MARIGINIUP HERMITAGE
●●●● $13.95
Made from vines planted in the Mariginiup Vineyard in 1958, which
have produced many fine vintages over the years stretching back
into the 1960s. The style is not elaborate but does age well,
attesting to the '91 release still on sale at the end 1994.
Cellaring 5–8 years. **Best Vintages** '88, '89, '91, '93, '94
Current Vintage '91
Matching Food Osso bucco.
Tasting Note 1991 Medium red; sweet, dusty/earthy shiraz varietal
aromas with little or no oak influence. The palate is soft with sweet fruit
and gentle, faintly dusty tannins. An early-maturing vintage.

PAUL OSICKA WINES

★★★☆ 12–16 CD AUS173
Goulburn Valley **Est.** 1955
Graytown, Vic 3608
Ph (057) 94 9235
Open Mon–Sat 10–5, Sun 12–5 **Production** NFP
Winemaker(s) Paul Osicka
An ultra-low-profile producer which seems determined to hide its light
under a bushel. The soft, sometimes minty, sometimes spicy Shiraz is
the pick of the wines.
Principal Wines Chardonnay, Riesling, Cabernet Sauvignon,
Shiraz.

PAULETT WINES

★★★★ 10.50–13 CD AUS64, 124, 126, 177, UK49
Clare Valley **Est.** 1983
Polish Hill Road, Polish Hill River, SA 5453
Ph (088) 43 4328 **Fax** (088) 43 4384
Open 7 days 10–5 **Production** 5000
Winemaker(s) Neil Paulett
The recent completion of the winery and cellar door sales facility
marks the end of a development project which began back in 1982
when Neil and Alison Paulett purchased a 47-hectare property with
a small patch of old vines and a house in a grove of trees (which
were almost immediately burnt by the 1983 bushfires). The
beautifully situated winery is one of the features of the scenic Polish
Hill River region.
Principal Wines Riesling, Late Harvest Riesling, Sauvignon Blanc,
Shiraz, Cabernet Merlot, Methode Champenoise.

PAULETT WINES CABERNET MERLOT
●●● ▶ $13
A blend of 75% cabernet sauvignon and 25% merlot, predominantly
coming from estate-grown grapes. Made in a direct style, and
definitely at the lighter edge of the spectrum of Clare Valley reds.

Cellaring 3–5 years. **Best Vintages** '88, '90, '91, '92
Current Vintage '92
Matching Food Beef shashlik.
Tasting Note 1992 Medium red-purple; a wine which comes up slowly in the glass, initially looking a little plain, but then gaining complexity. The palate is well balanced with dark chocolate and dark fruit flavours augmented by coconut oak, finishing with persistent tannins.

PAULETT WINES RIESLING

●●● ▶ $10.50

Produced from 4 hectares of estate plantings on the Polish Hill River slopes. While in classic Clare style, often develops a little more quickly than many of the other Rieslings of the district, which is no bad thing.
Cellaring 2–6 years. **Best Vintages** '84, '90, '92, '93, '94
Current Vintage '94
Matching Food Quiche Lorraine.
Tasting Note 1994 Light to medium yellow-green; quite full and even a fraction broad, with lots of lime and toast aromas. The palate is full-flavoured, particularly on the mid palate, again with lime and toast, and a relatively short finish.

PAULETT WINES SHIRAZ

●●●● ▶ $13

Consistently one of the best of the Paulett range, always full-flavoured but reaching a high point in 1992. It comes from a little over 3 hectares of estate-grown grapes.
Cellaring 5–8 years. **Best Vintages** '90, '91, '92, '93, '94
Current Vintage '92
Matching Food Beef casserole.
Tasting Note 1992 Medium to full red-purple; a rich, full and complex bouquet with liquorice and black fruits married with vanillin oak. The palate is rather more elegant than the bouquet suggests it may be, tending almost to Cabernet in terms of structure, with complex minty/briary/berry fruit and nicely balanced and integrated oak. Very good wine.

PEEL ESTATE

NR 11.95–16.95 R AUS1, 17, 103, 188, UK43
South-west Coastal Plain **Est.** 1974
Fletcher Road, Baldivis, WA 6171
Ph (09) 5241221 **Fax** (09) 524 1625
Open 7 days 10–5 **Production** 5000
Winemaker(s) Will Nairn
Will Nairn has concentrated on wood-matured Chenin Blanc and light but elegant reds, with some success; recent oak handling has not been convincing, but the underlying wine quality is good. Insufficient recent tastings to justify a rating.
Principal Wines Chardonnay, Wood-matured Chenin Blanc, Sauvignon Blanc Semillon, Verdelho, Shiraz, Cabernet Sauvignon.

PEEL ESTATE SHIRAZ
●●● ▶ $19.95
Produced from estate-grown grapes, and very much a hallmark wine
for Peel Estate, with a history going back two decades. Always fine
and soft in style, it can age surprisingly well. This vintage was still
being offered through wholesale channels in mid 1995, and should
be available in selected fine wine retailers.
Cellaring Now–5 years. **Best Vintages** NA
Current Vintage '90
Matching Food Spaghetti Bolognese.
Tasting Note 1990 Medium red-purple; there is a quite
pronounced American oak input, but earthy varietal shiraz is also
present on the bouquet. There is yet more fruit on the palate, with
flavours of black cherry and chocolate, surrounded by some oak
but also fine tannins. Ageing slowly and gracefully.

PENDARVES ESTATE
★★★★ 14–18 CD AUS124
Hunter Valley **Est.** 1986
Lot 10 Old North Road, Belford, NSW 2335
Ph (065) 74 7222
Open W'ends 11–5, Mon–Fri by appt **Production** 3200
Winemaker(s) Tamburlaine (Contract)
The perpetual motion general practitioner and founder of the
Australian Medical Friends of Wine, Dr Philip Norrie, is a born
communicator and marketer, as well as a wine historian of note. He
also happens to be a passionate advocate of the virtues of Verdelho,
inspired in part by the high regard held for that variety by vignerons
around the turn of the century.
Principal Wines An unusual portfolio of Verdelho, Sauvignon
Blanc Semillon, Chardonnay, Pinot Noir, Chambourcin, Shiraz,
Cabernet Merlot Malbec.

PENDARVES ESTATE CABERNET MERLOT MALBEC
●●●● ▶ $18
A star at the 1994 Winewise Small Makers Competition, and
likewise at the 1993 Hunter Valley Small Winemakers Show. The
merlot and malbec components come from estate-grown grapes; the
cabernet sauvignon is purchased from contract growers. The '92
was an exceptionally good wine given the intermediate status of the
vintage across the Hunter Valley for red wines.
Cellaring 2–4 years. **Best Vintages** NA **Current Vintage** '92
Matching Food Steak Diane.
Tasting Note 1992 Youthful purple-red; attractively ripe fruit
aromas with some more briary/earthy regional notes. The palate
has abundant blackcurrant/cassis fruit, with well balanced and
integrated oak, and soft tannins on a long finish. So enjoyable now
it is hard to see what is to be gained from cellaring.

PENDARVES ESTATE VERDELHO
●●● ▶ $14
The flagship wine of Pendarves in the sense that, along with

chardonnay, it occupies pride of place in the vineyard, with just
under 4.5 hectares of vines. Dr Philip Norrie is a tireless advocate of
the variety, which was much in favour around the turn of the century
before largely disappearing, and is now undergoing a substantial
renaissance in the Hunter Valley.

Cellaring 3–5 years. **Best Vintages** NA **Current Vintage** '93
Matching Food Seafood salad.

Tasting Note 1993 Bright green-yellow; the bouquet is of light to
medium intensity, fruit- rather than oak-driven, with a faintly
smoky/toasty overlay. The palate is still building weight which, in the
manner of all Hunter white wines, will certainly come with time.

PENFOLDS WINES

★★★★★ 7–150 R AUS147 UK83 US11

Barossa Valley **Est.** 1844
Tanunda Road, Nuriootpa, SA 5355
Ph (085) 62 0389 **Fax** (085) 62 2494
Open Mon–Fri 9–5, Sat 10–5, Sun 1–5 **Production** 745 000
Winemaker(s) John Duval

Senior among the 14 wine companies or stand-alone brands in
Southcorp Wines, and undoubtedly one of the top wine companies
in the world in terms of quality, product range and exports, the latter
amounting to over $100 million for the year ended 30 June 1994.
The consistency of the quality of the red wines and their value for
money (including even Grange at $100 a bottle) can only be
described as breathtaking. It is working on its white wines, seeking
to develop a Chardonnay to sit alongside Grange.

Principal Wines Kalimna Bin 28 Shiraz, 128 Coonawarra Shiraz,
389 Cabernet Shiraz, 407 Cabernet Sauvignon, 707 Cabernet
Sauvignon and Special Show Bin reds. Brands include Minchinbury
Sparkling; Penfolds Chardonnay and Semillon; Koonunga Hill Shiraz
Cabernet, Semillon Chardonnay and Chardonnay; Magill Estate;
Clare Estate and Clare Estate Chardonnay; St Henri Claret; Grange
Hermitage. Also various export-only labels. Finally, Grandfather Port
and Great Grandfather Port.

PENFOLDS BARREL FERMENTED CHARDONNAY

●●● ▶ $11

Made from chardonnay grown in the Clare Valley, Adelaide Hills
and Eden Valley regions, and now 100% barrel fermented in a
mixture of new and one-year-old French oak, in which it spends eight
months. A fast-maturing style which derives a considerable amount
of its impact from the oak. One cannot quibble about the value of
the wine, but I do wonder whether in this instance more is indeed
better.

Cellaring None required. **Best Vintages** '93
Current Vintage '94
Matching Food Pasta, chicken, turkey.

Tasting Note 1994 Glowing yellow-green; a rich, full, sweet,
buttery/toasty bouquet leads on to a full-flavoured, opulently oaked
and already fully mature style.

PENFOLDS BARREL FERMENTED SEMILLON
●●●● $15

Interestingly, sold for a significantly higher price than the Chardonnay, and arguably a better wine, although it shares many of the same traits. 70% is fermented and matured in new French and American oak barrels, and 30% in one-year-old American oak, spending six months in barrel before bottling. It is made from semillon grown in the Barossa Valley, Clare Valley and McLaren Vale with partial malolactic fermentation.

Cellaring None required. **Best Vintages** '92, '93
Current Vintage '94
Matching Food Rich seafood, veal or ham.
Tasting Note 1994 Medium to full yellow; a full-on bouquet with masses of complex fruit and oak, but the latter is well integrated and does not obscure the varietal character. The wine has full-bodied, mouthfilling flavours which are not excessively phenolic. Nonetheless, an early maturing style.

PENFOLDS BIN 128 COONAWARRA SHIRAZ
●●●● $14

Curiously, the only wine made by Penfolds every vintage from Coonawarra grapes and sold in the Australian market (there are some export labels). No less curious has been the lacklustre performance (by Penfolds standards and given the reputation of Coonawarra) of the wine over the years. However, since 1986 the wine has taken a distinct turn for the better, which is as it should be. It is one of the few wines in the Penfolds range which is matured entirely in French oak, 20% new and 80% one and two years old.

Cellaring 5–7 years. **Best Vintages** '63, '66, '80, '86, '89, '90, '91, '92 **Current Vintage** '92
Matching Food Veal; mild cheddar.
Tasting Note 1992 Medium red-purple; a generous dark-fruited bouquet with fairly pronounced oak, seemingly more American in character than French. Similarly, a wine of presence and power on the palate with concentration, generous red fruits, good tannins, and with the oak evident but not intrusive.

PENFOLDS BIN 389 CABERNET SHIRAZ
●●●●● $18

First made in 1960, and promptly dubbed 'Poor Man's Grange'. A blend of 50% cabernet sauvignon and 50% shiraz from the Barossa Valley, Coonawarra and Padthaway. Matured in a mixture of new (20%) and older American oak barrels.

Cellaring 20 years or more. **Best Vintages** '66, '70, '71, '86, '90, '91, '92
Current Vintage '92
Matching Food Double lamb loin chops.
Tasting Note 1992 Full purple-red; a powerful, rich wine with that inimitable Penfolds oak stamp on the bouquet. The palate is exceptionally concentrated and rich with blackberry and dark chocolate flavours, finishing with tannins derived from both fruit and oak.

PENFOLDS BIN 407 CABERNET SAUVIGNON
●●●● ▶ $17

A recent introduction to the Penfolds range, first made in 1990; now a blend of McLaren Vale, Padthaway and Coonawarra cabernet sauvignon. Matured in a mix of 30% new oak (American and French) and 70% hand-me-downs from Bin 707. Initially conceived as a lower-priced wine, the sheer quality of Bin 407 and its already illustrious show record led to its higher price when released.

Cellaring 10+ years. **Best Vintages** '90, '91
Current Vintage '92
Matching Food Venison, kangaroo fillet.
Tasting Note 1992 Dense red-purple; a powerful, strong wine with massive dark fruit aromas and slightly resinous oak. The palate is similarly massive, with the oak threatening the balance; certainly needs time, and at this stage of its life, not as impressive as the '90 or '91.

PENFOLDS BIN 707 CABERNET SAUVIGNON
●●●●● $50

First made in 1964, with a hiatus between 1969 and 1976 as scarce supplies of cabernet sauvignon were diverted to Bin 389. Now made from a blend of Coonawarra, Barossa and Eden Valley grapes, vinified in a fashion similar to Grange, with the fermentation finished in American oak barrels.

Cellaring 15–25 years. **Best Vintages** '66, '80, '84, '86, '88, '90 '91 **Current Vintage** '91
Matching Food Rare scotch fillet.
Tasting Note 1991 Dense red-purple; luscious, concentrated ripe fruit and vanillin oak bouquet leads on to a palate with a cascade of plum, spice, vanilla and mint flavours, finishing with slightly disjointed tannins still coming together so early in its life. Could well end up in the highest rank.

PENFOLDS CLARE ESTATE
●●●● $14.50

Made from a blend of merlot, cabernet sauvignon, cabernet franc and malbec grown entirely on Penfolds 180-hectare vineyard in the Polish Hill River Valley, east of the main Clare Valley region. The wine is matured in new French oak for one year and invariably shows very well at a relatively early age. First made 1985.

Cellaring 4–7 years. **Best Vintages** '88, '90, '91, '92
Current Vintage '93
Matching Food Yearling steak; mild cheese.
Tasting Note 1993 Full red-purple; a powerful wine, with fairly strong, almost resinous, oak on the bouquet. The palate is similarly powerful and oak dominated; there are red and dark berry fruit flavours, but they are as yet fighting to express themselves.

PENFOLDS CLARE ESTATE CHARDONNAY
●●●● $10.50

In my view the best of the Penfolds white wines, though not the most expensive. Produced entirely from Penfolds Polish Hill River estate, and 100% barrel fermented in new and one-year-old French oak barrels for eight months, the wine has better balance and greater fruit intensity (relative to the oak) than the other white wines.

Cellaring None required. **Best Vintages** '88, '90, '92, '93

Current Vintage '93, '94

Matching Food Lamb's brains.

Tasting Note 1993 Medium yellow-green; stylish barrel ferment characters with some tang and bite to the peach and melon fruit. The palate is, as one would expect, quite oaky, but does have length with attractive figgy fruit and nutty overtones to the pleasantly firm finish.

PENFOLDS GRANDFATHER PORT

●●●● ▶ $60

First released in the 1960s; made from Barossa Valley shiraz and mourvedre which is oak matured in old barrels for decades, and which is finally blended from selection of very old and much younger material. Penfolds has always kept a tight rein on production, thus preserving the all-important old material which forms the base of the wine.

Cellaring None required. **Best Vintages** NA

Current Vintage NA

Matching Food Coffee.

Tasting Note NV Medium to full tawny red; exceedingly complex, with strong barrel-aged rancio characters and attractively earthy spirit. A long and richly flavoured wine, with the cleansing, drying finish which is so essential to the style.

PENFOLDS GRANGE HERMITAGE

●●●●● $100

Australia's greatest red wine, with a turbulent early history chronicled in Huon Hooke's book entitled *Max Schubert Winemaker* (1994). What can be said in a few words? The bare bones are: first made 1955; sourced from low-yielding, old shiraz vines (and up to 15% cabernet sauvignon) chiefly from the Barossa but also from the Clare Valley and McLaren Vale. Fermentation finished in and matured in new American oak.

Cellaring Up to 40 years. **Best Vintages** '52, '53, '55, '62, '66, '67, '71, '76, '78, '80, '85, '86, '90 **Current Vintage** '90

Matching Food Rich game dishes.

Tasting Note 1990 Destined to be one of the greatest Granges. A beautifully weighted and concentrated bouquet, with seamless fruit and oak; masses of dark cherries and plum. In the mouth a superb wine; while the fruit is opulent, it is not excessively so; indeed there is a touch of near austerity to the fine tannins to give the wine both character and balance. The iron fist in a velvet glove.

PENFOLDS GREAT GRANDFATHER PORT

●●●●● $150

First released in 1994 to celebrate the 150th birthday of Penfolds. In a neat marketing gimmick, 1994 bottles were blended and bottled, utilising the very oldest and best stocks, dating back to the early

years of the 20th century. The concentration and power of the wine
is reminiscent of the very old Seppelt Liqueur Tawny Ports.
Cellaring None required. **Best Vintages** NA
Current Vintage NA
Matching Food Coffee.
Tasting Note NV Deep tawny with an olive-green rim; both the
bouquet and palate are extraordinarily concentrated and rich, very
much into the liqueur style of Port which is unique to Australia.
Shows the brandy spirit which was used in the fortifying process,
and which adds yet extra complexity.

PENFOLDS KALIMNA BIN 28 SHIRAZ
●●●● ▶ $14.50
A multi-region blend sourced from the Barossa, Padthaway and
McLaren Vale regions. There is a good argument to be made that it
should be Bin 28, rather than Bin 389, which is 'Poor Man's
Grange'. The emphasis is on the same lush fruit; the oak used is
second- and third-use American barrels handed down through the
Grange and Bin 389 programmes.
Cellaring Typically 10–15 years. **Best Vintages** '64, '66, '71,
'80, '81, '83, '86, '90, '91, '92 **Current Vintage** '92
Matching Food Lamb or beef casserole.
Tasting Note 1992 Medium to full red-purple; the bouquet shows
lots of sweet berry fruit married with obvious but balanced American
oak. A classic Penfolds style on the palate with lots of fruit on a
sweet mid palate surrounded by vanillin oak, and finishing with
good tannins.

PENFOLDS KOONUNGA HILL SHIRAZ CABERNET
●●●●● $8
First made in 1976, it is sourced from premium areas across South
Australia (not including the Riverlands) from a varying blend, with
the cabernet component usually ranging between 30% and 40%, but
with a high of 48% and a low of 5% according to vintage. It is
matured in real oak (no chips) and is not batch-bottled. Outstanding
value for money.
Cellaring Desirably 5–15 years. **Best Vintages** '82, '87, '90,
'91, '92 **Current Vintage** '92
Matching Food Hearty fare.
Tasting Note 1992 Youthful purple-red; spotlessly clean, luscious
red and blackcurrant fruit drives the bouquet. In the mouth youthful
blackcurrant fruit which is very well balanced, and the oak totally
restrained. 52% shiraz, 48% cabernet sauvignon.

PENFOLDS MAGILL ESTATE
●●●●● $35
Made solely from the 5.2-hectare vineyard established on the site
where Dr Christopher Rawson Penfold built his house in 1844. It is
an estate wine in the fullest sense of the term, made at the historic
Magill winery, which is currently being restored and refurbished.
Situated within 10 minutes of the centre of Adelaide, Magill Estate
will become one of Australia's foremost viticultural landmarks.

Cellaring 7–12 years. **Best Vintages** '83, '86, '89, '90, '91
Current Vintage '91
Matching Food Rack of lamb.
Tasting Note 1991 Full red-purple; the bouquet is clean and
smooth, with that seamless oak integration which is the mark of the
line, together with hints of liquorice. The palate is rich and chewy
with mouthfilling plum, spice and liquorice all there; concentrated
and long-lived.

PENFOLDS OLD VINE MOURVEDRE GRENACHE SHIRAZ
●●●● ▶ $16.50
Rumours of the impending release of this wine had been circulating
for some considerable time before it made its appearance in March
1995. A blend of 51% mourvedre (formerly called mataro), 26%
grenache and 23% shiraz from old, low-yielding Barossa Valley
vineyards. It is a testament to the extraordinary rise in popularity of
the Rhone varietals, a rise triggered as much by export as domestic
demand.
Cellaring 5–10 years. **Best Vintages** NA **Current Vintage** '92
Matching Food Rich meat dishes.
Tasting Note 1992 Medium to full red; the bouquet is clean and
smooth, with that seamless oak integration which is the mark of the
line, together with hints of liquorice. The palate is rich and chewy
with mouthfilling plum, spice and liquorice all there; concentrated
and long-lived.

PENFOLDS SPECIAL BIN 920 SHOW RED
●●●●● $100
Penfolds Show red wines have been produced sporadically since
1962, typically in quantities of 500 dozen, and designed
specifically for show purposes. These wines put the lie to those who
sneer at 'show wines', for they include in their number the majority
of the greatest reds made in Australia since 1962 — greater even
than Grange. Current release Bin 920 is a blend of 65% cabernet
sauvignon and 35% shiraz from Coonawarra.
Cellaring Typically 20–30 years. **Best Vintages** '62, '66, '67,
'80, '82, '90 **Current Vintage** '90
Matching Food Depends on the age of the wine.
Tasting Note 1990 The colour is almost impenetrable, so deep is
it. There is amazingly lush, opulent plummy fruit on the bouquet; the
palate has layer upon layer of dark plum, cassis and cherry fruit with
equally layered soft and supple tannins running throughout. Will be
ready long before Bin 90A, though nonetheless has a 20-year future.

PENFOLDS ST HENRI CLARET
●●●● ▶ $22
Born of the vigorous rivalry between and radically different
winemaking philosophies of Max Schubert and John Davoren. With
the exception of emphasis on the highest quality grape sources,
Grange and St Henri are polar opposites. This traditional wine is
made from Barossa, Clare and Eden Valleys, McLaren Vale, and
Langhorne Creek shiraz; and cabernet sauvignon from Coonawarra
and the Barossa Valley. Oak influence is minimal.

Cellaring Up to 20 years for the best vintages. **Best Vintages**
'66, '67, '76, '82, '85, '88, '90, '91 **Current Vintage** '91
Matching Food Steak and kidney pie.
Tasting Note 1991 Medium to full red-purple; a clean, fruit-driven
bouquet with ripe plum/berry fruits intermingling with dark
chocolate. A mouthfilling round and rich, almost luscious, wine,
continuing the change seen in 1990 towards a riper style; good
tannins, too.

PENINSULA ESTATE

NR 10–16 CD AUSSD
Mornington Peninsula **Est.** 1985
Red Hill Road, Red Hill, Vic 3937
Ph (059) 89 2866
Open W'ends, Public hols 11–4 **Production** 5000
Winemaker(s) Daniel Greene
A relative newcomer, but one of the larger operations on the
Mornington Peninsula, now with former Elgee Park winemaker
Daniel Greene in charge of winemaking. The 1992 Point Nepean
Chardonnay is clean and fresh, with a nice touch of spicy oak, even
if a little on the light side.
Principal Wines Chardonnay, Pinot Noir, Cabernet Sauvignon;
Point Nepean Sauvignon Blanc, Chardonnay Cabernet Sauvignon,
Pinot Noir.

PENLEY ESTATE

★★★★☆ 14–32 R AUS70, 113, 123, 161, 164, UK52, 89
Coonawarra **Est.** 1988
McLeans Road, Coonawarra, SA 5263
Ph (08) 231 2400 **Fax** (08) 231 0589
Open W'ends, Hols 10–4 **Production** 10 000
Winemaker(s) Kym Tolley
Owner winemaker Kym Tolley describes himself as a fifth generation
winemaker, the family tree involving both the Penfolds and the
Tolleys. He worked 17 years in the industry before establishing
Penley Estate and has made every post a winner since, producing a
succession of rich, complex, full-bodied red wines and stylish
Chardonnays.
Principal Wines Chardonnay, Hyland Shiraz, Shiraz Cabernet,
Cabernet Sauvignon, Methode Champenoise.

PENLEY ESTATE CABERNET SAUVIGNON
●●●●● $32
Made from the pick of 38 hectares of estate-grown cabernet
sauvignon, matured in a cleverly handled mix of American and
French oak. Like its predecessors from 1989 and 1990, the '91 has
been a prolific winner of accolades in the show ring, winning two
trophies, nine gold, six silver and two bronze medals, as well as
being declared the 1994 Hyatt-Advertiser Wine of The Year for the
Best Commercial Wine Available in South Australia.

Cellaring 5–15 years. **Best Vintages** '89, '90, '91
Current Vintage '91
Matching Food Rare beef.
Tasting Note 1991 Medium purple-red; the bouquet has started to evolve fragrant, briary aromas, the palate likewise showing some evolution towards secondary flavours. All in all, a wine of true breed and elegance, with beautifully balanced oak and a very long finish.

PENNYWEIGHT WINERY*

NR 8–16 CD AUSSD
North East Victoria **Est.** 1982
Pennyweight Lane, Beechworth, Vic 3747
Ph (057) 28 1747
Open Thur–Tues 10–5 **Production** 1000
Winemaker(s) Stephen Newton Morris
Pennyweight was established by Stephen Morris, great-grandson of G F Morris, founder of Morris Wines. The vines are not irrigated, and are moving towards organic certification. The business is run by Stephen; he is assisted by wife Elizabeth and their three sons.
Principal Wines A fortified specialist, but also producing limited table wines, including Trebbiano, Riesling, Shiraz and Cabernet Sauvignon; the primary focus is on Fino and Amontillado Sherries, a range of Ports from Old Tawny to Ruby, Vintage Port, White Port and Muscat.

PENWORTHAM WINE CELLARS

NR 7.50–14.50 CD AUS55, 143
Clare Valley **Est.** 1985
Government Road, Penwortham, SA 5453
Ph (088) 43 4345
Open Sat 10–5, Sun, Hols 10–4 **Production** 1500
Winemaker(s) Richard Hughes
A relatively new arrival on the Clare Valley scene; I have not tasted any of the wines. Not all come from the Valley.
Principal Wines Riesling, Burgundy, Cabernet Sauvignon, Shiraz, Muscat Frontignac, Tawny Port.

PEPPER TREE WINES

★★★ 9–25 CD AUSSD
Hunter Valley **Est.** 1993
Halls Road, Pokolbin, NSW 2321
Ph (049) 98 7539 **Fax** (049) 98 7746
Open 7 days 9–5 **Production** 18 000
Winemaker(s) Chris Cameron
The Pepper Tree winery is situated in the complex which also contains The Convent guesthouse and Roberts Restaurant. Formerly known as Murray Robson Wines, it no longer has any association with Murray Robson who has, it seems, finally departed from the wine industry. The company which now owns Pepper Tree is headed by Chris Cameron, chief winemaker since 1991.

Principal Wines Bottom end: Print Range of Frost Hollow and
Mulberry Row; then Commercial Range: Semillon Sauvignon Blanc,
Chardonnay, Traminer, Shiraz, Merlot Cabernet; top end: Reserve
Range of Semillon, Chardonnay, Traminer, Cabernet Sauvignon,
Merlot. Several fortified wines are also available cellar door.

PEPPER TREE WINES FROST HOLLOW

●●● ▶ $9

A chardonnay-dominant blend made in traditional Hunter style,
rich and generous. It offers particularly good value for money,
particularly when compared to the other Pepper Tree wines.
Cellaring 1–2 years. **Best Vintages** '89, '91, '93
Current Vintage '93
Matching Food Pan-fried pork fillet.
Tasting Note 1993 Medium to full yellow-green; some toasty
regional aromas, faintly medicinal. The palate has good flavour,
weight and richness, with tangy melon fruit, and some toasty
characters which are more fruit- than oak-driven.

PEPPERS CREEK WINES

NR 15 CD AUSSD
Hunter Valley **Est.** 1987
Broke Road, Pokolbin, NSW 2321
Ph (049) 98 7532 **Fax** (049) 98 7531
Open Wed–Sun 10–5 **Production** 700
Winemaker(s) Peter Ireland
A combined winery and antique shop which sells all its wine through
the cellar door. The red wines previously tasted were clean and full
flavoured.
Principal Wines Chardonnay, Shiraz, Merlot.

PERTARINGA VINEYARDS *

★★★★ 14.95–22 R AUS96
Southern Vales **Est.** 1980
Cnr Hunt & Rifle Range Roads, McLaren Vale, SA 5171
Ph (08) 383 6027 **Fax** (08) 383 6497
Open Not **Production** 1400
Winemaker(s) Geoff Hardy
The Pertaringa and Geoff Hardy labels are made from a small
percentage of the grapes grown by leading viticulturists Geoff Hardy
and Ian Leask. The Pertaringa vineyard of 24 hectares was acquired
in 1980 and rejuvenated; establishment of the Kuitpo vineyard
began in 1987 and now supplies leading makers such as Petaluma
and Shaw & Smith.
Principal Wines Pertaringa label: Barrel Fermented Semillon,
Sauvignon Blanc, Cabernet Sauvignon; Geoff Hardy label: Fleurieu
Shiraz, Botrytis, Kuitpo Shiraz.

PERTARINGA BARREL FERMENTED SEMILLON

●●● ▶ $14.95

Produced from 6 hectares of estate semillon grown in the cool

climate of the foothills of the South Adelaide Hills, and as the name suggests, is barrel fermented to produce a robust style.
Cellaring 1–3 years. **Best Vintages** NA **Current Vintage** '94
Matching Food Honeyglazed ham, served warm.
Tasting Note 1994 Light to medium yellow-green; a complex and sophisticated bouquet with American barrel ferment oak. The palate is somewhat crisper and tighter than the bouquet suggests it will be, but is still driven by the barrel ferment oak.

PERTARINGA CABERNET SAUVIGNON
●●●●● $19.95
Pertaringa has some of the finest vineyards in the Southern Vales/Adelaide foothills region, and is a renowned supplier of high quality grapes to others. This wine shows why Pertaringa is held in such regard.
Cellaring 4–10 years. **Best Vintages** '89, '90, '91
Current Vintage '91
Matching Food Barbecued beef or lamb.
Tasting Note 1991 Medium to full red-purple; the bouquet is rich and concentrated, with unmistakable regional chocolate aromas. The palate fulfils the promise of the bouquet, rich but perfectly balanced, with mouthfilling chewy chocolate fruit.

PETALUMA

★★★★★ 15–33 R AUS50, 167–170, UK38
Adelaide Hills **Est.** 1976
Spring Gully Road, Piccadilly, SA 5151
Ph (08) 339 4122 **Fax** (08) 339 5253
Open See Bridgewater Mill **Production** 80 000
Winemaker(s) Brian Croser
The Petaluma empire continues to flourish; in 1994 it acquired Mitchelton, more than doubling group turnover in the process. The quality of the Petaluma wines has never been in question, but does go from strength to strength.
Principal Wines Riesling, Chardonnay, Coonawarra (Cabernet Blend), Croser (Sparkling); second label Sharefarmers White and Red. Bridgewater Mill is another second label — see separate entry.

PETALUMA CHARDONNAY
●●●●● $32
One of the more elegant and refined Australian Chardonnays which has, however, radically changed its geographic base since it was first made in 1977, starting in Cowra then moving to Coonawarra, then partly to the Clare Valley, and ultimately (since 1990) being made from Piccadilly Valley grapes. The style of the wine has been refined over the period, but has remained remarkably consistent given the quite radically changing regional base.
Cellaring 5 years. **Best Vintages** '87, '90, '91, '92, '93
Current Vintage '93
Matching Food Slow-roasted Tasmanian salmon.
Tasting Note 1993 Medium to full yellow-green; a gamut of

aromas with spicy nutmeg oak woven through almost honeyed fruit showing both barrel and malolactic fermentation characters. The palate is structured and textured, with nutty cashew fruit flavours and tremendous length. One of the best yet under this distinguished label.

PETALUMA COONAWARRA
••••• $32
A logical counterpart to the Chardonnay in the sense that it is far more elegant and refined than the more typical South Australian (and in particular, Coonawarra) Cabernet. Its regional base has remained the same since 1979, but the varietal composition has changed significantly, moving from shiraz and cabernet in '79 through to a cabernet dominant blend with around 15% merlot. As with the Chardonnay, the more recent vintages are best.
Cellaring 5–8 years. **Best Vintages** '79, '86, '88, '90, '91, '92
Current Vintage '91
Matching Food Saddle of lamb.
Tasting Note 1991 Full purple-red; luscious ripe blackcurrant/berry aromas, not dissimilar to the '90. The palate is softer, rounder and riper than the '90, with luscious red and blackcurrant fruit, finishing with fine-grained tannins.

PETALUMA CROSER
••••• $32
It was the desire to make a great sparkling wine which primarily drew Brian Croser to the Piccadilly Valley in the first instance. The climate is very cool, and ideally suited to the production of the fine base wine for Croser. First made in 1984 from 100% chardonnay, but quickly moved to its current mix of approximately 50% chardonnay and 50% pinot noir, although the mix between the two varies from 40-60% (either side) according to the vintage.
Cellaring Up to 5 years. **Best Vintages** '86, '88, '90, '92
Current Vintage '92
Matching Food Caviar.
Tasting Note 1992 Medium yellow-green; the bouquet shows more bready pinot influence than any previous wine, but perhaps also some malolactic influence. The palate is complex with spicy/nutty pinot flavours, and a much finer structure than the '91, with excellent length. May not challenge the glorious '90, but otherwise looks the best yet.

PETALUMA RIESLING
••••• $18.95
A 100% estate-produced wine from Petaluma's Hanlins Hill Vineyard in the Clare Valley, one of the classic Australian Riesling regions. The wine is made with iron discipline, and is a crystal-pure reflection of the interaction of climate, soil and variety. As the notes indicate, it ages with grace.
Cellaring 10 years for the best vintages. **Best Vintages** '80, '85, '86, '88, '90, '92, '93, '94 **Current Vintage** '94
Matching Food Sashimi.

Tasting Note 1994 Light green-yellow, still showing lots of green tinges. The bouquet is floral and toasty, with hints of spice; tight and elegant. The palate has delicious lime fruit to the mid palate which the '93 isn't showing at the moment and has excellent length to the finish. Should prove to be one of the great Petaluma Rieslings.

PETER LEHMANN WINES

★★★★☆ 10–19.25 R AUS112, UK75
Barossa Valley **Est.** 1979
Samuel Road off Para Road, Tanunda, SA 5352
Ph (085) 63 2500 **Fax** (085) 63 3402
Open Mon–Fri 9.30–5, W'ends, Hols 10.30–4.30
Production 200 000
Winemaker(s) Peter Lehmann, Andrew Wigan, Peter Scholz, Leonie Lange
1994 was a great year for Peter Lehmann wines. The highlights were its successful entry to the lists of the Australian Associated Stock Exchanges; the release of its Jimmy Watson Trophy-winning 1989 Stonewell Shiraz; and its outstanding success at the 1994 Adelaide Wine Show at which the 1989 and 1990 Stonewell Shiraz respectively accumulated the Wally Ware Trophy for Best Medium Bodied Dry Red (the '89) and the Montgomery Trophy for Best Full Bodied Dry Red and Adelaide Trophy for Best Dry Red Table Wine in Show (the '90).
Principal Wines Varietal Peter Lehmann label: Barossa Eden Riesling, Barossa Semillon, Barossa Chardonnay, Barossa Shiraz, Barossa Cabernet Sauvignon, Clancy's Gold Preference and Bin AD 2001 Vintage Port; premium Cellar Collection label: Eden Valley Riesling, Chardonnay, Cabernet Blend, Stonewell Shiraz, Noble Semillon.

PETER LEHMANN BAROSSA EDEN RIESLING
●●● ▶ $10
What's in a name? Prior to 1993, the Peter Lehmann Riesling was made from 100% Eden Valley fruit, even though the label itself stated Barossa — reflecting the historic view that the Eden Valley district of the eastern Barossa Ranges was part of the Barossa Valley. Then, as from 1993 a component of Barossa floor riesling was introduced into the wine, and the 1994 vintage is a blend of 60% Eden Valley and 40% Barossa Valley material. The label now states this, and has also dropped the word 'Rhine', a move to be applauded. The wine itself is a model of consistency.
Cellaring 2–6 years. **Best Vintages** '82, '87, '91, '93, '94
Current Vintage '94
Matching Food Grilled bream, whiting.
Tasting Note 1994 Light to medium green-yellow; a dry, toasty classically reserved wine with years in front of it. The palate has a steely backbone with flavours running from citrus through to toast and will become more honeyed as it ages.

PETER LEHMANN BAROSSA SHIRAZ
●●● ▸ $11.60

The blood brother, as it were, to the Peter Lehmann Riesling. A traditional Barossa style as honest as the day is long, but also reflecting the multitude of vineyard sources available to Peter Lehmann through his long association with the Valley.

Cellaring Each way — up to 5 years. **Best Vintages** '89, '90, '91, '92 **Current Vintage** '92

Matching Food Spiced Barossa sausage.

Tasting Note 1992 Medium to full red; solid, dark berry and chocolate fruit aromas with spicy oak lead on to a solidly constructed palate with abundant, rich red berry/cherry fruit, finishing with slightly phenolic, charry oak.

PETER LEHMANN CELLAR COLLECTION CABERNET BLEND
●●●● $19.25

This wine is based predominantly on cabernet sauvignon, blended in varying proportions with malbec, merlot and shiraz which fluctuate from year to year. Fermentation is finished in barrel and then matured for a further two and a half years in French and American oak hogsheads prior to bottling. I find the oak handling a little on the heavy side, but others will like it.

Cellaring 5–8 years. **Best Vintages** '80, '89, '91, '92 **Current Vintage** '91

Matching Food Spiced beef.

Tasting Note 1991 Medium to full red-purple; a voluminous bouquet essentially driven by masses of sweet caramel/vanillin American oak. There is more youthful, red berry fruit on the palate, although the oak comes again on the mid to back palate and on the finish.

PETER LEHMANN CLANCY'S GOLD PREFERENCE
●●●● $11.60

A blend of Barossa-grown shiraz, cabernet sauvignon, cabernet franc and merlot, spiced with the American oak which is so much part of the Peter Lehmann style. Right from the outset, an unqualified success in the marketplace simply because it represents such good value for money, and because it is ready to drink when released.

Cellaring Drink now. **Best Vintages** NA **Current Vintage** '92

Matching Food Pasta with tomato or meat sauce.

Tasting Note 1992 Medium to full red-purple; rich, lively berry and mulberry fruit, with a hint of smooth vanillin oak. A nicely balanced and composed wine which is fruit-driven and easy drinking, finishing with just the right amount of tannins.

PETER LEHMANN STONEWELL SHIRAZ (MAGNUM)
●●●●● $100

The wine is made solely from low-yielding old vineyards of the Stonewell, Ebenezer and Moppa subdistricts of the Barossa Valley. The fermentation is finished in new American oak, in which it is then matured for two years prior to bottling. It is then given three years bottle age before release, the '89 Stonewell being released on 1

November 1994, with an illustrious show record, including the 1990 Jimmy Watson Trophy and the Wally Ware Trophy at the 1994 Royal Adelaide Wine Show. The 1990 Stonewell, which won two trophies including Best Red at the same show, is an even better wine.

Cellaring Up to 15 years. **Best Vintages** '80, '89, '91, '92
Current Vintage '89
Matching Food Kangaroo fillet.
Tasting Note 1989 Full red-purple; a very complex bouquet with liquorice and spice aromas interwoven with ripe fruit in a style reminiscent of the Rhone Valley. The palate is multifaceted, soft and supple, with the fruit and high quality American oak beautifully balanced and interwoven. Nine gold medals.

PETERSON CHAMPAGNE HOUSE *

NR NA AUSSD
Hunter Valley **Est.** 1994
Cnr Broke & Branxton Roads, Cessnock, NSW 2325
Ph (049) 98 7844 **Fax** (049) 98 7813
Open 7 days 10–5 **Production** 2000
Winemaker(s) Gary Reed
Prominently and provocatively situated on the corner of Broke and Branxton Roads, as one enters the main vineyard and winery district in the Lower Hunter Valley. It is an extension of the Peterson family empire, and no doubt very deliberately aimed at the tourist. Sooner or later, however, it will have to change its name.
Principal Wines Chardonnay-based Sparkling Wine.

PETERSONS WINES

★★☆ 12.50–18.50 CD AUS41
Hunter Valley **Est.** 1971
Mount View Road, Mount View, NSW 2325
Ph (049) 90 1704 **Fax** (049) 91 1344
Open Mon–Sat 9–5, Sun 10–5 **Production** 10 500
Winemaker(s) Gary Reed
Petersons may have slipped from the high pedestal on which it once sat but retains its marketplace image. A 1985 Semillon drunk (not just tasted) at the end of 1994 confirmed just how high the quality of Petersons once was.
Principal Wines Semillon, Chardonnay, Hunter River Riesling, Pinot Noir, Cabernet Sauvignon, Sauternes, Vintage Port, Sparkling.

PETERSONS BACK BLOCK CABERNET SAUVIGNON

●●●● $33.95
The third of a trio of excellent red wines from Petersons' 1993 vintage, although it will be apparent I prefer both the standard and Back Block Shiraz. For all that, this is a powerful and concentrated wine which will surely repay extended cellaring.
Cellaring 10–15 years. **Best Vintages** NA
Current Vintage '93

Matching Food Whole roasted ox kidney.

Tasting Note 1993 Full red; a concentrated and dense bouquet with briar, blackcurrant and chocolate fruit to the fore. The palate is similarly rich, concentrated and chewy, with the oak a little more evident than it is on the bouquet, but potentially in balance. Just leave it in the cellar for now.

PETERSONS BACK BLOCK SHIRAZ
●●●●● $33.95

Whether this wine is worth its 50% price premium over the standard Shiraz of Petersons of the same year is something which the market will determine. Since it is made in such limited quantities, the issue is almost certainly largely irrelevant. Certainly, both wines share high quality fruit and extremely competent winemaking, and both will be very long lived.

Cellaring 10+ years. **Best Vintages** NA **Current Vintage** '93
Matching Food Rare rump steak.
Tasting Note 1993 Deep red-purple; the bouquet is clean and fragrant, with stylish oak handling and pristine varietal shiraz fruit. The palate is of the highest quality, with spotlessly clean fruit, attractive oak, and finishes with fine-grained tannins.

PETERSONS SHIRAZ
●●●●● $22.95

Some wonderfully concentrated yet balanced red wines were made in the Hunter Valley in 1993, few better than this one. Both it and its more expensive sibling, Back Block Shiraz, show similarities to the Brokenwood Graveyard Hermitage style and to the Rothbury Reserve Shiraz style.

Cellaring Up to 10 years. **Best Vintages** '86, '91, '93
Current Vintage '93
Matching Food Steak and kidney pie.
Tasting Note 1993 Deep red-purple; the bouquet shows strong, earthy varietal shiraz with a pleasant touch of American oak; it is clean, and varietal rather than regional in character. The palate similarly clean, rich and full with masses of sweet, concentrated fruit and sensitively handled oak. Good tannins guarantee a long life.

PEWSEY VALE

★★★☆ 9.95–13.95 R AUS138–142
Adelaide Hills **Est.** 1961
Browne's Road, Pewsey Vale, Adelaide Hills, SA (vineyard only)
Ph (085) 61 3200
Open Not (see Yalumba) **Production** 27 000
Winemaker(s) Alan Hoey

Pewsey Vale was a famous vineyard established in 1847 by Joseph Gilbert, and it was appropriate that when S Smith & Son (Yalumba) began the renaissance of the high Adelaide Hills plantings in 1961, they should do so by purchasing Pewsey Vale. Right from the outset, the decision to seek cooler growing conditions through altitude was proved correct, with a long line of extremely distinguished Rhine Rieslings the result.

Principal Wines Riesling, Botrytis Riesling, Sauvignon Blanc, Cabernet Sauvignon.

PFEIFFER WINES

★★★ 9.90–18.50 CD AUSSD, UK80
North East Victoria **Est.** 1984
Distillery Road, Wahgunyah, Vic 3687
Ph (060) 33 2805 **Fax** (060) 33 3158
Open Mon–Sat 9–5, Sun 11–4 **Production** 10 000
Winemaker(s) Christopher Pfeiffer
Ex-Lindeman fortified winemaker Chris Pfeiffer occupies one of the historic wineries (built 1880) which abound in the north east, and which is worth a visit on this score alone. The fortified wines are good, and the table wines have improved considerably over recent vintages.
Principal Wines Riesling, Auslese Tokay, Chardonnay, Semillon, Chardonnay, Spatlese Frontignac, Pinot Noir, Cabernet Sauvignon, fortifieds.

PIANO GULLY WINES

★★☆ 12–15 CD AUSSD
Warren Valley **Est.** 1987
Piano Gully Road, Manjimup, WA 6258
Ph (097) 723 5583
Open W'ends, Public hols 10–5 **Production** 450
Winemaker(s) Haydon White
The 4-hectare vineyard was established in 1987 on rich Karri loam, 10 kilometres south of Manjimup, with the first wine made from the 1991 vintage. The three 1993 (Chardonnay, Pinot Noir and Cabernet Sauvignon) vintage wines at the 1994 Mount Barker Wine Show did not impress.
Principal Wines Chardonnay, Pinot Noir, Cabernet Sauvignon, Concerto.

PIBBIN WINES

NR 12.50–17 R AUSSD
Adelaide Hills **Est.** 1991
Greenhill Road, Balhannah, SA 5242
Ph (08) 388 7375 **Fax** (08) 388 7685
Open 7 days 10–5 **Production** 1000
Winemaker(s) Roger Salkeld
The 2.5-hectare Pibbin vineyard, near Verdun, is managed on organic principles; owners Roger and Lindy Salkeld explain that the name 'Pibbin' is a corruption of a negro spiritual word for Heaven, adding that while the wines may not have achieved that lofty status yet, the vineyard has. Quality has been variable; the '92 Pinot, massive, slightly sweet and tannic, the '94 Pinot Rosé, dry, crisp, fresh and well made.
Principal Wines Pinot Noir, Pinot Rosé, Pinot Sparkling Burgundy.

PICCADILLY FIELDS WINES

NR 14.90–19.45 ML AUSSD
Adelaide Hills **Est.** 1989
Udy's Road, Piccadilly, SA 5151
Ph (08) 272 2239 **Fax** (08) 232 5395
Open Not **Production** 1000
Winemaker(s) Sam Virgara
A tiny winery which takes its name from that part of the Adelaide
Hills made famous by Petaluma. The only tastings to date were
uninspiring.
Principal Wines Chardonnay, Merlot Cabernet Franc.

PIERRO VINEYARDS

★★★★☆ 17–34 R AUS63, 64, 113, UK62
Margaret River **Est.** 1980
Caves Road, Willyabrup via Cowaramup, WA 6284
Ph (097) 55 6220 **Fax** (097) 55 6308
Open 7 days 10–5 **Production** 5000
Winemaker(s) Dr Michael Peterkin
Dr Michael Peterkin is another of the legion of Margaret River
medical practitioners who, for good measure, married into the
Cullen family. Pierro is renowned for its stylish white wines, which
often exhibit tremendous complexity, although Michael Peterkin is
nervous about any reference to or comparison with French
Burgundies (or their making).
Principal Wines Chardonnay, Semillon Sauvignon Blanc, Pinot
Noir.

PIERRO CHARDONNAY
●●●● ▶ $33
One of the most distinguished of a band of striking wines from the
Margaret River region and which achieved great acclaim during the
second half of the 1980s. The style is invariably complex,
concentrated and powerful, with the emphasis on secondary rather
than primary fruit characters.
Cellaring 2–5 years. **Best Vintages** '86, '87, '89, '90, '92, '93
Current Vintage '93
Matching Food Seafood pasta.
Tasting Note 1993 Medium yellow-green; very complex
nutty/buttery aromas showing both barrel ferment and malolactic (or
ambient temperature) fermentation characters. The rich and powerful
palate does show its 14% alcohol.

PIERRO SEMILLON SAUVIGNON BLANC
●●●● ▶ $17
Made from relatively low-yielding estate-grown grapes, and
originally marketed under the 'Les Trois Cuveés' label, the passing of
which is not to be lamented. The wine tastes as if it may have been
wholly or partially barrel fermented, though no mention of this is
made on the label.

Cellaring 2–4 years. **Best Vintages** '87, '89, '90, '94
Current Vintage '94
Matching Food Veal cutlets.
Tasting Note 1994 Light green-yellow; a rich, concentrated, nutty/toasty bouquet leads on to a powerful yet supple wine in the mouth; again there are toasty notes suggesting some barrel ferment.

PIESSE BROOK WINES

NR 9–15 CD AUS180
Darling Range **Est.** 1974
226 Aldersyde Road, Bickley, WA 6076
Ph (09) 293 3309
Open Sat 1–5, Sun, Public hols 10–5 **Production** 500
Winemaker(s) Di Bray, Ray Boyanich (Michael Davies Consultant)
Surprisingly good red wines made in tiny quantities. The first Chardonnay was made in 1993, but there have been no recent tastings.
Principal Wines Chardonnay, Shiraz, Cabernet Sauvignon, Cabernet Shiraz, Cabernova (early drinking style).

PIETER VAN GENT WINERY

NR 7.50–15.80 CD AUSSD
Mudgee **Est.** 1978
Black Springs Road, Mudgee, NSW 2850
Ph (063) 73 3807 **Fax** (063) 73 3807
Open Mon–Sat 9–5, Sun 11–4 **Production** 5000
Winemaker(s) Pieter van Gent
Many years ago, Pieter van Gent worked for Lindemans, before joining Craigmoor, then moving to his own winery in 1979 where he has forged a strong reputation and following for his fortified wines in particular, although the range extends far wider. The wines are seldom seen outside cellar door.
Principal Wines The only dry wines are the Chardonnay, Muller Thurgau, Cabernet Merlot and Cabernet Sauvignon; the Frontignac, Rivaner, Angelic White and Soft Red all have varying degrees of sweetness; fortified wines are the specialty, including Pipeclay Port, Mudgee White Port, Cornelius Port, Mudgee Oloroso, Pipeclay Muscat, Mudgee Liqueur Frontignac, Pipeclay Vermouth.

PIKES

★★★★☆ 13.10–20.65 R AUS27, 167–170, 186, UK43
Clare Valley **Est.** 1985
Polish Hill River Road, Sevenhill, SA 5453
Ph (088) 43 4249 **Fax** (088) 43 4353
Open W'ends, Public hols 10–4 **Production** 10 000
Winemaker(s) Neil Pike
Owned by the relatively young Pike brothers, one of whom (Andrew) is a senior viticulturist with Penfolds, the other (Neil) a former winemaker at Mitchells. Pikes now has its own winery, with Neil Pike presiding. The current crop of releases is particularly impressive.

Principal Wines Riesling, Sauvignon Blanc, Chardonnay, Shiraz, Cabernet Sauvignon.

PIKES RIESLING
●●●● ▶ $12.95
Produced from a little over 3.5 hectares of estate-grown riesling. In the mainstream of Clare Valley style, crisp, lively and zesty when young, and developing considerable character with bottle age.
Cellaring 3–7 years. **Best Vintages** '86, '90, '92, '93
Current Vintage '92
Matching Food Asparagus.
Tasting Note 1992 Medium yellow-green; full, clean toasty lime aromas with nice weight. While starting to show bottle-developed characters, the fruit flavours are still pristine and fresh, and the wine not the least bit phenolic; has developed beautifully over the last 18 months, and will continue to do for several years at least.

PIKES SAUVIGNON BLANC
●●● ▶ $14.95
Sauvignon blanc has always been an important variety for Pikes: the vineyards have a little over 3.5 hectares each of sauvignon blanc, riesling and shiraz, with lesser quantities of other varieties. There is no question that the wine performs better in some years than in others: the suspicion is that the Clare Valley is not as well suited to the variety as (say) McLaren Vale.
Cellaring Drink now. **Best Vintages** NA **Current Vintage** '94
Matching Food Shellfish, crab.
Tasting Note 1994 Light to medium straw yellow; some smoky/toasty edges to the aroma which slightly blur the varietal character, although the palate is powerful, particularly on the mid to back palate. Not especially varietal, but may have broad appeal as a drier food style.

PIKES SHIRAZ
●●●● ▶ $19.95
Produced from 3.5 hectares of estate plantings. The 1993 is slightly out of the mainstream, and very much the product of a cooler vintage, but is nonetheless particularly attractive as a lighter example of Clare Valley Shiraz.
Cellaring 3–7 years. **Best Vintages** '85, '86, '90, '91, '93
Current Vintage '93
Matching Food Mature cheddar, Kraft parmesan.
Tasting Note 1993 Medium to full purple-red; very distinctive spicy varietal fruit of medium to full intensity which is at once attractive and unusual for the district. The palate, too, is lighter than usual, with very pronounced varietal spice and a touch of mint. The oak is held in restraint throughout.

PINELLI WINES *

NR 5–16 CD AUSSD
Swan Valley **Est.** 1979
18 Bennett Street, Caversham, WA 6055

Ph (09) 279 6818 **Fax** (09) 377 4259
Open 7 days 10–6 **Production** 7000
Winemaker(s) Robert Pinelli
Domenic Pinelli and son Robert — the latter a Roseworthy
Agricultural College graduate — sell 75% of their production in
flagons, but are seeking to place more emphasis on bottled wine
sales in the wake of recent show successes with Chenin Blanc.
Principal Wines Limited table wine range, centred on Chenin
Blanc, Chardonnay, Shiraz and Cabernet Sauvignon, and an
extensive range of fortified wines, including Cabernet-based Vintage
Port. The wines have won a number of medals at the Perth Show in
recent years.

PIPERS BROOK VINEYARD

★★★★☆ 14–22.20 CD AUS82, UK77
Pipers Brook **Est.** 1974
Bridport Road, Pipers Brook, Tas 7254
Ph (003) 82 7197 **Fax** (003) 82 7226
Open Mon–Fri 10–4, W'ends 11–5 Nov–Apr **Production** 25 000
Winemaker(s) Andrew Pirie
Dr Andrew Pirie founded the Pipers Brook region; an immensely
knowledgeable and skilled viticulturist and winemaker, he heads a
progressive and ever-growing company, producing some of the most
beautifully packaged of all Australian wines.
Principal Wines Top label: Pipers Brook Chardonnay, Riesling,
Pellion (Pinot Noir); second label: Ninth Island Chardonnay,
Riesling, Straits Dry White, Cabernet Merlot, Pinot Noir.

PIPERS BROOK CHARDONNAY
●●●● ▶ $22.20
First made in 1981. Pipers Brook is now able to draw upon three
distinct estate-owned vineyard sources: Pipers Brook Vineyard,
Pellion Vineyard and Ninth Island Vineyard. The expanded base has
strengthened an already distinguished wine which is made using the
full range of techniques including barrel fermentation and partial
malolactic fermentation. The style is always elegant, and longer-lived
than Australian Chardonnays grown in warmer regions. Incidentally,
these wines typically achieve high sugar (and hence alcohol) levels
of around 13%.
Cellaring 4–7 years. **Best Vintages** '82, '88, '91, '92, '93
Current Vintage '93
Matching Food Veal in white sauce.
Tasting Note 1993 Medium yellow-green; complex and
concentrated nutty/earthy aromas with citrus and melon fruit married
into subtle oak. The palate is rich, concentrated and strongly
flavoured, with spicy melon and green fig fruit.

PIPERS BROOK NINTH ISLAND CHARDONNAY
●●●● ▶ $16
Ninth Island is the new name for the previous Tasmania Wine
Company second label, which suffered from obvious problems of

anonymity. Ninth Island derives its name from the Bass Strait island which lies just off the coast of northern Tasmania adjacent to the Pipers Brook region. The wine is made from both estate- and contract-grown grapes, and is unwooded.

Cellaring 3–6 years. **Best Vintages** '92, '93, '94
Current Vintage '94
Matching Food Crab, shellfish.
Tasting Note 1994 Light to medium yellow-green; the bouquet is clean and fresh with citrus, melon, passionfruit and apple aromas all intermingling. The palate is likewise crisp, fresh and lively, with apple flavours and a hint of fruit spice.

PIPERS BROOK NINTH ISLAND STRAITS DRY WHITE
●●●● $14.80
One of the most exotic blends to be found in Australia: 80% pinot noir, and 20% semillon and sauvignon blanc. Very much a cafe/brasserie style, crisp, cleansing and, above all else, different.
Cellaring Drink now. **Best Vintages** NA **Current Vintage** '94
Matching Food Seafood salad.
Tasting Note 1994 Bronze-pink derived from the pinot noir content. The aromas are in the herbal/spicy/stemmy spectrum with very obvious pinot noir influence. The palate is intense, with ample flavour and structure, and a long, bone-dry finish with typical cleansing acidity.

PIPERS BROOK PELLION
●●●●) $22.20
First made in 1981 (a bucketful of remarkable wine) but changed its name to Pellion only in 1992. Pellion was an artist on one of the very early voyages of discovery to Tasmania, hence the name; notwithstanding the absence of any varietal claim on the label, the wine is in fact 100% pinot noir. Winemaker Andrew Pirie says, 'the expression of this grape in the red soils and climate of the region is so individual that we do not think we should be constrained by names which lead to preconceived ideas as to the taste of the wine'.
Cellaring 2–4 years. **Best Vintages** '81, '85, '91, '92, '94
Current Vintage '93
Matching Food Ripe King Island brie.
Tasting Note 1993 Medium red; a complex bouquet of light to medium intensity, with some stemmy notes, and not quite as fragrant as the Ninth Island Pinot of the same year. The palate is again quite complex, with spicy fruit, a hint of tobacco, some gamey characters, and finishes well. Early maturing style.

PIPERS BROOK RIESLING
●●●● $17
First made in 1979. The 3 hectares of riesling at the home Pipers Brook Vineyard are situated on the favourable north and northeast-facing aspects, and are now approaching 20 years of age. The wine is reliably good, and invariably develops well with prolonged cellaring.
Cellaring Up to 10 years. **Best Vintages** '82, '91, '92, '93, '94

Current Vintage '94
Matching Food Lemon chicken salad.
Tasting Note 1994 Medium yellow-green; a surprisingly full and developed bouquet which has already gained complexity. The palate is full, showing much more fruit flavour and fruit sweetness than one usually encounters in young Pipers Brook Rieslings.

PIRRAMIMMA WINES

★★★☆ 8.50–18 R AUS26, 143, 177
Southern Vales **Est.** 1892
Johnston Road, McLaren Vale, SA 5171
Ph (08) 323 8205 **Fax** (08) 323 9224
Open Mon–Fri 9–5, Sat 10–5, Sun, Public hols 12–4
Production 40 000
Winemaker(s) Geoff Johnston
A very interesting operation with large vineyard holdings of very high quality, and a winery which devotes much of its considerable capacity to contract processing of fruit for others. While the Pirramimma brand may have lost some of its status, the business is flourishing.
Principal Wines Chablis, Semillon Chardonnay, Classic Riesling, Chardonnay, Centenary Shiraz, Cabernet Sauvignon, Ports.

PIRRAMIMMA CHARDONNAY

●●●● ▶ $12
Pirramimma now has over 66 hectares of chardonnay in production, much of it contracted to major Australian wine producers. That produced under the Pirramimma label relies primarily on its fruit, with minimal oak influence — a style which in today's market is proving increasingly popular, and the currently available vintage ('92) is in fact a very good wine.
Cellaring 5–7 years. **Best Vintages** '82, '84, '86, '88, '92
Current Vintage '92
Matching Food Calamari.
Tasting Note 1992 Light to medium green-yellow; fine, well balanced and quite tight fruit aromas with a lemony citrus edge, and a hint of smokiness. The wine has good intensity and length, with citrus and melon fruit to the fore.

PIRRAMIMMA SEMILLON CHARDONNAY

●●● ▶ $8.50
Not a common blend in the McLaren Vale, drawing upon a little under 3 hectares of estate semillon in addition to the chardonnay component. Like the chardonnay, there is little or no oak influence on the wine, which represents good value.
Cellaring 2–3 years. **Best Vintages** NA
Current Vintage '93
Matching Food Smoked eel.
Tasting Note 1993 Bright green-yellow; crisp, clean and lively citrus and melon fruit aromas lead on to a pleasantly soft citrus and peach flavoured palate, with little or no oak influence evident.

PLANTAGENET WINES

★★★★★ 9.75–19.50 CD AUS63, 137, 181, UK84
Great Southern **Est.** 1974
Albany Highway, Mount Barker, WA 6324
Ph (098) 51 2150 **Fax** (098) 51 1839
Open Mon–Fri 9–5, W'ends 10–4 **Production** 19 000
Winemaker(s) Gavin Berry
The senior winery in the Mount Barker region which has hit an
absolute purple patch over the past few years, making superb wines
across the full spectrum of variety and style.
Principal Wines Riesling, Chenin Blanc, Sauvignon Blanc, Omrah
Vineyard Chardonnay, Mount Barker Chardonnay, Fine White, Fine
Red, Pinot Noir, Shiraz, Cabernet Sauvignon, Mount Barker Brut.

PLANTAGENET CABERNET SAUVIGNON
●●●●● $18.50
First made in 1974 (in fact at Sandalford in the Swan Valley) and has
established itself as one of the West Australian classics over the
intervening years. While primarily based upon estate-grown cabernet
sauvignon, malbec, cabernet franc and merlot have all contributed to
the wine over the last decade, with the core of the wine coming from
the Plantagenet Bouverie Vineyard at Denbarker. The '92 was a gold
medal winner at the 1994 Mount Barker Wine Show.
Cellaring 10+ years for the best vintages. **Best Vintages** '81,
'83, '85, '86, '90, '91 **Current Vintage** '91, '92
Matching Food Rack of lamb.
Tasting Note 1992 Medium to full purple-red; wonderfully bright
and fresh red berry fruit with subtle oak as befits the line. The palate
is already balanced, with powerful dark berry fruit flavours, finely-
grained tannins, and just a hint of oak.

PLANTAGENET MOUNT BARKER BRUT
●●●●● $19.50
Made from the classic blend of chardonnay and pinot noir, the
1990 vintage being entirely made at Plantagenet and deservedly
winning the trophy for Best Sparkling Wine at the 1994 Mount
Barker Wine Show. The quality of the wine is indeed outstanding,
and adds another string to the bow of this fine wine region.
Cellaring Drink now. **Best Vintages** NA **Current Vintage** '90
Matching Food Aperitif.
Tasting Note 1990 Medium straw-yellow, with good mousse; a
very complex bouquet with strong nutty yeast autolysis characters.
The wine has developed tremendous richness in the mouth with
nutty/creamy flavours and an ever-so-slightly sweet finish which
in no way imperils the balance of the wine.

PLANTAGENET MOUNT BARKER CHARDONNAY
●●●● ▶ $17.50
Usually draws upon four different vineyards in the Mount Barker
region deliberately harvested at varying levels of ripeness to
increase the flavour complexity. It is barrel fermented in a mix of
Vosges, Allier and Troncais oak, with a percentage taken through

malolactic fermentation. It is invariably a generously proportioned wine, while still retaining some of the tighter, cool-grown characters one would expect.

Cellaring 3–5 years. **Best Vintages** '81, '83, '86, '92, '94
Current Vintage '93
Matching Food Breast of chicken.
Tasting Note 1993 Glowing yellow-green; fragrant citrus, melon and peach fruit, gently ripe, with subtle oak. The palate combines riper, fleshy peachy characters with high-toned citrussy edges, with a long finish. Fruit- rather than oak-driven throughout.

PLANTAGENET OMRAH VINEYARD CHARDONNAY
●●●● $14.50

The Omrah Chardonnay was one of the first unwooded Chardonnays to catch the eye of the public and wine-writers alike. Although the '94 vintage was a good one, it has to be said that the '94 Omrah was less attractive when released than its predecessors — but that may well be the consequence of a single vineyard source and the lack of protective oak.

Cellaring Short term. **Best Vintages** NA **Current Vintage** '94
Matching Food Scampi.
Tasting Note 1994 Light green-yellow; the bouquet is of light to medium intensity with some smoky/yeasty fermentation aromas showing when released mid 1994. The palate is quite long, but there are some slightly hard, grassy edges which may soften out with time.

PLANTAGENET RIESLING
●●●● ▶ $12.50

Draws upon 6.2 hectares of estate vineyards, all of which are now fully mature, and which (along with a similar amount of cabernet sauvignon) constitute the major estate plantings. First made in 1975, one of the flagships not only for Plantagenet but for the region as a whole.

Cellaring 3–10 years. **Best Vintages** '81, '83, '86, '92, '94
Current Vintage '94
Matching Food Most Asian dishes.
Tasting Note 1994 Bright light green-yellow; a firm and clean bouquet with good fruit weight and depth, not the least bit yeast influenced. A generous, full-flavoured wine with plenty of weight and authority.

PLANTAGENET SHIRAZ
●●●●● $18.50

A quite marvellous wine which was one of the high points of the 1994 Mount Barker Wine Show. It draws upon 4 hectares of estate plantings, the style varying with the vintage. In cooler years the vibrant pepper/spice characters are to the fore, in warmer years it tends more to liquorice, dark cherry and berry. The one consistent feature is the quality of the wine.

Cellaring 5–10 years. **Best Vintages** '82, '83, '85, '90, '91, '94 **Current Vintage** '91
Matching Food Hare, squab.

Tasting Note 1991 Medium red-purple; the bouquet shows absolutely classic varietal fruit with vibrant pepper and spice aromas and a hint of liquorice. The palate is beautifully balanced and flavoured, entirely driven by the spicy black cherry and liquorice fruit, with a long, sustained finish.

PLATT'S WINES

★★☆ 9–12 CD AUSSD
Mudgee **Est.** 1983
Mudgee Road, Gulgong, NSW 2852
Ph (063) 74 1700 **Fax** (063) 72 1055
Open 7 days 9–5 **Production** 4000
Winemaker(s) Barry Platt
Inconsistent and often rather unhappy use of oak prevents many of the wines realising their potential.
Principal Wines Chardonnay, Semillon, Gewurztraminer, Cabernet Sauvignon.

PLATT'S SEMILLON

●●●● $11.95
Cold-fermented in stainless steel and relatively early-bottled, thus (appropriately) placing the focus on the primary fruit flavours. What is slightly unusual is the alcohol of 13%, higher than most Semillons achieve, particularly those from the Hunter Valley. An altogether interesting wine.
Cellaring 5+ years. **Best Vintages** NA **Current Vintage** '92
Matching Food Avocado.
Tasting Note 1992 Light to medium yellow-green; attractive and fresh aromas which run from conventional Australian Semillon through to characters more reminiscent of White Bordeaux, characters which are also evident on the youthful, high-toned palate. There is lots of power and depth to the wine with clean, tangy, citrus-accented fruit.

PLUNKETT WINES

★★★★ 10.95–15.50 CD AUS57
Goulburn Valley **Est.** 1980
Lambing Gully Road, Avenell, Vic 3664
Ph (057) 96 2150 **Fax** (057) 96 2147
Open 7 days 11–5 **Production** 5000
Winemaker(s) Sam Plunkett
The Plunkett family first planted grapes way back in 1968, establishing 3 acres with 25 experimental varieties. Commercial plantings commenced in 1980, with 40 hectares now under vine. While holding a vigneron's licence since 1985, the Plunketts did not commence serious marketing of the wines until 1992, and has since produced a consistently impressive array of wines.
Principal Wines The top-of-the-range wines are released under the Strathbogie Range label (Cabernet Merlot and Chardonnay); standard wines under the Blackwood Ridge brand of Riesling, Sauvignon Blanc Semillon, Cabernet Merlot.

PLUNKETT BLACKWOOD RIDGE CHARDONNAY

●●●● $15.50

The Plunketts have established over 40 hectares of vineyards at an elevation of around 550 metres in the Strathbogie Ranges. These have come from an initial one-hectare planting of 25 varieties in 1968, the ultimate in experimentation. Not surprisingly, chardonnay has emerged as one of the principal varieties on the property. Given that this is the second label, it is a particularly impressive (if forward) wine.

Cellaring Drink now. **Best Vintages** NA **Current Vintage** '94
Matching Food Smoked turkey.
Tasting Note 1994 Glowing yellow-green; there are abundant, sweet yellow peach and melon fruit aromas on the bouquet. The palate shows rather more cool-grown characters, tending more to white peach, melon and citrus.

PLUNKETT BLACKWOOD RIDGE SAUVIGNON BLANC SEMILLON

●●● ▷ $10.95

The commercial sauvignon blanc planting dates back to 1980, no doubt reflecting the success of the variety in the trial plantings and the cool climate. The wine shows the herbal characters one would expect — a little less sweetness on the finish would make it an even better wine.

Cellaring Drink now. **Best Vintages** NA **Current Vintage** '94
Matching Food Mussels.
Tasting Note 1994 Medium to full yellow-green; the bouquet is quite potent, with plenty of depth to the herbaceous fruit. The palate, too, has plenty of flavour and power, but finishes unexpectedly sweet.

POKOLBIN ESTATE

NR 12–17 CD AUSSD
Hunter Valley **Est.** 1980
McDonalds Road, Pokolbin, NSW 2325
Ph (049) 98 7524 **Fax** (049) 98 7765
Open 7 days 10–6 **Production** 1200
Winemaker(s) Trevor Drayton
An unusual outlet, offering its own-label wines made under contract by Trevor Drayton, together with the wines of Lake's Folly, Peacock Hill and Pothana, and with cheap varietal 'cleanskins'. Wine quality under the Pokolbin Estate label is very modest.
Principal Wines Semillon, Traminer Riesling, Riesling, Chardonnay, Shiraz, Shiraz Merlot, Pinot Noir, fortifieds.

POOLE'S ROCK VINEYARD

★★★☆ 17.99 R AUSSD, UK60
Hunter Valley **Est.** 1988
Lot 41 Wollombi Road, Broke, NSW 2330
Ph (065) 79 1251 **Fax** (065) 79 1277
Open Not **Production** 2000

Winemaker(s) Iain Riggs (Contract)
Sydney merchant banker David Clarke has had a long involvement
with the wine industry, ranging from his chairmanship of the Royal
Sydney Wine Show Committee through to partnership with Sydney
retailer Andrew Simon in Wollombi Brook, to directorship of
McGuigan Brothers Limited. The 5-hectare Poole's Rock vineyard,
planted purely to chardonnay, is his personal venture.
Principal Wines Chardonnay.

POOLE'S ROCK CHARDONNAY
●●● ▶ $17.99
Right from the outset, this 100% estate-grown wine has been made
in full-blown fashion by contract winemaker Iain Riggs (of
Brokenwood). The propensity of Hunter Valley chardonnay to
produce a rich, buttery, peachy wine was given free rein,
complexed by partial malolactic fermentation and maturation in
French Vosges oak barriques.
Cellaring 1–2 years. **Best Vintages** '92, '93
Current Vintage '93
Matching Food Full-flavoured chicken or veal dishes.
Tasting Note 1993 Deep yellow; full, buttery peachy fruit aromas
with subtle oak lead on to an even fuller-flavoured, buttery/peachy
palate with a full, slightly cloying finish.

POPLAR BEND

NR 12.50–18 ML AUSSD
Mornington Peninsula **Est.** 1988
RMB 8655 Main Creek Road, Main Ridge, Vic 3928
Ph (059) 89 6046 **Fax** (059) 89 6046
Open Public hols, first w'end each month 10–5 **Production** 350
Winemaker(s) Keith Dunstan
The quasi-retirement venture of Melbourne journalist, author and
raconteur Keith Dunstan and wife Marie. The label depicts Chloe in
all her glory, and would be calculated to send the worthy inhabitants
of the Bureau of Alcohol, Tobacco and Firearms (of the United
States) into a state of cataleptic shock.
Principal Wines Pinot Chloe, Cabernet Chloe, Sparkling Chloe.

PORT PHILLIP ESTATE

★★★★☆ 17.95–19.95 R AUSSD
Mornington Peninsula **Est.** 1987
261 Red Hill Road, Red Hill, Vic 3937
Ph (059) 89 2708 **Fax** (059) 89 2891
Open First w'end each month 12–5 **Production** 2500
Winemaker(s) Alex White (Contract), Lindsay
McCall
The vineyard of leading Melbourne QC Jeffrey Sher, which released
its first wine from the 1991 vintage. The promise of the early wines
was fulfilled in no uncertain fashion by those from the 1993 vintage.
Principal Wines Chardonnay, Pinot Noir, Cabernet Merlot,
Shiraz.

Clare Valley riesling which is either naturally botrytised, or naturally raisined.

Cellaring 2–5 years. **Best Vintages** '91, '92, '93
Current Vintage '93
Matching Food Orange soufflé.
Tasting Note 1993 Medium to full yellow-green; intense apricot botrytis aromas together with varietal lime fruit. The palate is very well balanced, with attractive lime, pineapple and apricot flavours, finishing with crisp acidity.

PRIMO ESTATE COLOMBARD

●●●● ▶ $10

Joe Grilli has always been able to conjure something quite magical from the 4.5 hectares of estate plantings of colombard. The variety is known for its capacity to hold its natural acidity in hot climates (and the Adelaide Plains are hot) but no one else seems to be able to invest the wine with the fruit freshness and crispness — almost sauvignon blanc-like — achieved by Joe Grilli.

Cellaring Emphatically drink now. **Best Vintages** NA
Current Vintage '94
Matching Food Oysters, shellfish.
Tasting Note 1994 Light green-yellow; a clean, fresh and crisp bouquet, although not so sauvignon-like as it is in some years. The palate mirrors the bouquet, fresh, crisp and tangy, best served ice cold on a hot summer's day.

PRIMO ESTATE JOSEPH CABERNET MERLOT

●●●●● $25

Although the front label does not make reference to it, the back label says 'moda amarone' — a modest claim which has brought the wrath of the Italians down on the head of Joe Grilli, and his promise to desist from using it. The wine does in fact use the amarone methods of partially drying the red grapes before fermentation. 20% of this wine came from Coonawarra cabernet, 20% from McLaren Vale merlot, and the remaining portion from McLaren Vale cabernet sauvignon.

Cellaring Up to 15 years. **Best Vintages** '81, '84, '86, '90, '91
Current Vintage '92
Matching Food Bistecca Fiorentina.
Tasting Note 1992 Medium to full red-purple; very concentrated, briary aromas underlaid by sweet fruit. The palate is potent, powerful and chewy with dark fruits and dark chocolate flavours running through a textured finish.

PRINCE ALBERT VINEYARD

★★★★ 13–17 ML AUS148
Geelong **Est.** 1975
100 Lemins Road, Waurn Ponds, Vic 3221
Ph (052) 41 8091 **Fax** (052) 41 8091
Open By appt **Production** 600
Winemaker(s) Bruce Hyett

Australia's true Pinot Noir specialist (it has only ever made the one wine) which also made much of the early running with the variety: the wines always show good varietal character, although some are a fraction simple. The '92 and '93 vintages are the best for many years.
Principal Wines Pinot Noir.

QUEEN ADELAIDE

★★★☆ 6.95–7.95 R AUS147
Barossa Valley **Est.** 1858
181 Flinders Street, Adelaide, SA 5000
Ph (08) 236 3400 **Fax** (08) 224 0964
Open Not **Production** NFP
Winemaker(s) Southcorp (Penfolds)
The famous brand established by Woodley Wines, and some years ago subsumed into the Seppelt and now Penfolds Wine Group. It is a pure brand, without any particular home, either in terms of winemaking or fruit sources, but ironically quality has increased since its acquisition by Seppelt.
Principal Wines A revamped product range with White Burgundy, Chablis and Claret phased out and in their place, Semillon Sauvignon Blanc, Chenin Blanc and Ruby Cabernet/Cabernet Sauvignon added to the range, which also includes Australia's largest-selling wine, Queen Adelaide Chardonnay. Riesling (in the top 10) and Pinot Noir complete the range.

READS WINERY

NR 7.50–13 CD AUSSD
North East Victoria **Est.** 1972
Evans Lane, Oxley, Vic 3678
Ph (057) 27 3386 **Fax** (057) 27 3559
Open Mon–Sat 9–5, Sun 10–6 **Production** 1900
Winemaker(s) Kenneth Read
Limited tastings have not impressed, but there may be a jewel lurking somewhere, such as the medal-winning 1990 Sauvignon Blanc.
Principal Wines Riesling, Chardonnay, Sauvignon Blanc, Crouchen, Cabernet Shiraz, Cabernet Sauvignon, Port.

RED HILL ESTATE

NR 12.95–21.95 R AUSSD
Mornington Peninsula **Est.** 1989
53 Redhill-Shoreham Road, Red Hill South, Vic 3937
Ph (059) 89 2838 **Fax** (059) 89 2855
Open 7 days 12–5 **Production** 2400
Winemaker(s) Jenny Bright
Sir Peter Derham and family completed the construction of an on-site winery in time for the 1993 vintage, ending a period in which the wines were made at various wineries under contract arrangements. The 8-hectare vineyard is one of the larger plantings on the

Mornington Peninsula, and the newly-opened tasting room has a superb view across the vineyard to Westernport Bay and Phillip Island.
Principal Wines Particular emphasis on Methode Champenoise, but also producing Waterholes Creek Chardonnay (Unwooded), Chardonnay, Pinot Noir, Cabernet Sauvignon and Merlot, with Muscat (from Rutherglen material) available cellar door only.

REDBANK WINES

★★★☆ 7.50–44.90 CD AUS112 UK38
Pyrenees **Est.** 1973
Sunraysia Highway, Redbank, Vic 3467
Ph (054) 67 7255 **Fax** (054) 67 7248
Open 7 days 9–5 **Production** 27 000
Winemaker(s) Neill Robb
Neill Robb makes very concentrated wines, full of character; the levels of volatile acidity can sometimes be intrusive, but are probably of more concern to technical tasters than to the general public.
Principal Wines The range centres on a series of evocatively named red wines, with Sally's Paddock the flagship, but including wines such as Hard Hill Cabernet Sauvignon, Fighting Flat Shiraz and various specialties available cellar door. Long Paddock Shiraz and Long Paddock Chardonnay are cheaper, larger-volume second labels.

REDGATE WINES

★★★☆ 8.50–15.30 CD AUS108 109 US10
Margaret River **Est.** 1977
Boodjidup Road, Margaret River, WA 6285
Ph (097) 57 6208 **Fax** (097) 57 6308
Open 7 days 10–5 **Production** 12 000
Winemaker(s) Paul Ullinger
Twenty hectares of vineyard provide the base for one of the larger wineries of the Margaret River region which probably has a lower profile than it deserves. The wines are solid, but a degree of astringency seems to run through many of them. I am not too convinced about the merits of the Reserve range.
Principal Wines Sauvignon Blanc Semillon, Sauvignon Blanc, Chardonnay, Classic Dry White, Chenin Blanc, Spatlese Riesling, Botrytis Riesling, Pinot Noir, Cabernet Sauvignon, Cabernet Franc, White Port; what are classified as the best wines are released under the Reserve label.

REDGATE BOTRYTIS RIESLING (375 ML)

●●●●● $15.30
A freakish wine made in tiny quantities and exceedingly rare in the Margaret River. It stood out in its class at the 1994 Mount Barker Wine Show, winning a unanimous gold medal.
Cellaring 1–3 years. **Best Vintages** NA **Current Vintage** '92
Matching Food Cheesecake.

Tasting Note 1992 Yellow-orange; intense apricot aromas lead on to a powerful and long palate, with abundant cumquat and apricot flavours, finishing with perfectly balanced acidity.

REDGATE CABERNET SAUVIGNON
●●●● $14

Draws upon 5 hectares of estate plantings; the estate merlot and cabernet franc are included in the softer Bin 588 Cabernet. The Cabernet Sauvignon is made in an uncompromising firm, slightly gravelly style which is very typical of the region.
Cellaring 5–10 years. **Best Vintages** '82, '85, '88, '91, '92
Current Vintage '92
Matching Food Mature cheddar.
Tasting Note 1992 Medium red-purple; bright, aromatic cassis/red and blackcurrant fruit on the bouquet leads on to bright, fresh berry fruit on the palate which is, however, firm to the point of hardness, and does need time to soften and evolve.

REDMAN WINES

★★★☆ 8.95–15.95 R AUS20–24
Coonawarra **Est.** 1966
Main Penola-Naracoorte Road, Coonawarra, SA 5253
Ph (087) 36 3331 **Fax** (087) 36 3013
Open Mon–Fri 9–5, W'ends 10–4 **Production** 20 000
Winemaker(s) Bruce Redman, Malcolm Redman
After a prolonged period of mediocrity, the Redman wines are showing distinct signs of improvement, partly through the introduction of modest amounts of new oak, even if principally American. It would be nice to say the wines now reflect the full potential of the vineyard, but there is still some way to go.
Principal Wines Shiraz (formerly labelled as Claret), Cabernet Merlot (the first new wine in 24 years), Cabernet Sauvignon.

REDMAN CABERNET SAUVIGNON
●●● ▶ $15.95

The first three vintages of this wine, made in the '70 to '72 vintages, respectively, and released in magnum, were landmarks at the time. As with the Claret, quality slipped, but is now on the rebound, with the yet to be released '93 wine a reversion to top form.
Cellaring 5–15 years. **Best Vintages** '90, '91, '92, '93
Current Vintage '91
Matching Food Stuffed capsicum.
Tasting Note 1991 Medium red; vanilla bean American oak dominates (there is some French used) and the fruit does not have the concentration one expects from '91. The palate is pleasant, with some berry fruit, but most of the flavour coming from the oak.

REDMAN SHIRAZ
●●● ▶ $8.95

First released in 1966, the wine of that year, 1969 and 1970 all being very good, and still showing well. Those wines were made from the Arthur Hoffman block, planted around the turn of the

century; a number of things happened thereafter which led to a distinctly more diffuse style. There are signs of a recovery since 1990.
Cellaring 5–15 years. **Best Vintages** '90, '91, '92, '93
Current Vintage '92
Matching Food Pasta.
Tasting Note 1992 Medium red; clean, light fresh pepper spice and cherry fruit, with a hint of oak. The palate is light-bodied, the fruit again fresh with spicy characters from both the fruit and a touch of American oak.

RENMANO WINES

★★★ 8.95 R AUS20–24, UK36
Riverlands **Est.** 1914
Sturt Highway, Renmark, SA 5341
Ph (085) 86 6771 **Fax** (085) 86 5939
Open Mon–Sat 9–5 **Production** 1.6 million
Winemaker(s) Fiona Donald (Red), Ann-Marie Wasley (White).
The unctuous, buttery Chardonnay (foremost) and Cabernet Sauvignon lead the Chairman's Selection range, which is remarkable both for its consistency of style and for its value for money. Whether the style of the wine will continue to gain the same acceptance in the future as it has in the past remains to be seen; certainly, it is made for immediate consumption and does not repay cellaring.
Principal Wines Chairman's Selection Chardonnay, Hermitage, Cabernet Sauvignon.

RENMANO CHAIRMAN'S BIN 104 SELECTION CHARDONNAY
●●● $9.95
Made in a totally distinctive and very consistent style which many (myself included) would see as somewhat outmoded. All of the colour, all of the phenolics and all of the flavour are respectively extracted from the grapes, leading to luscious but short-lived wines which need to be consumed immediately they are released. Others, it must be said, are more forgiving of the style which does, at least, have a distinct personality.
Cellaring Drink now. **Best Vintages** NA **Current Vintage** '94
Matching Food Braised pork.
Tasting Note 1994 Medium yellow-green; the bouquet is very typical of the line, though less overtly extracted and oaked than some. While the palate shows pronounced spicy/charry oak, there are definite signs of some fining and tightening of the style.

RENMANO CHAIRMAN'S SELECTION CABERNET SAUVIGNON
●●● $8.95
Very much the red wine equivalent of the Chardonnay, with soft fruit allied with heaps and heaps of American oak. In some years (such as 1991) the fruit achieves sufficient concentration to carry the oak quite well, and the wine then rises above its station.

Cellaring Short term. **Best Vintages** '88, '90, '91, '93
Current Vintage '92
Matching Food Pizza.
Tasting Note 1992 Medium red; appreciably sweet blackberry and blackcurrant fruit with voluminous, aromatic American oak on both bouquet and palate, the latter precisely replicating the former, finishing with soft tannins.

REYNOLDS YARRAMAN

★★★☆ 15–17 CD AUS63, UK69
Upper Hunter Valley **Est.** 1967
Yarraman Road, Wybong, Muswellbrook, NSW 2333
Ph (065) 47 8127 **Fax** (065) 47 8013
Open Mon–Sat 10–4, Sun, Public hols 11–4 **Production** 7000
Winemaker(s) Jon Reynolds
Formerly Horderns Wybong Estate, now owned by talented ex-Houghton and Wyndham winemaker Jon Reynolds and wife Jane. The wines are reliable, but with one or two exceptions (such as the '92 Chardonnay and '91 Cabernet Merlot) are not as exciting as one would expect given the vineyard sources and Jon Reynolds' vast experience.
Principal Wines Semillon (100% estate-grown), Chardonnay (a blend of estate-grown and grapes from the Bloodwood Vineyard at Young, in the Central Highlands), Cabernet Merlot (a blend of 50% merlot, 25% cabernet sauvignon and 25% cabernet franc from Orange, Mudgee and the Upper Hunter), Cabernet Sauvignon, (100% cabernet from the Bloodwood Vineyard and the Augustine Vineyard at Mudgee).

RIBBON VALE ESTATE

★★★ 12–16 CD AUS127, 177
Margaret River **Est.** 1977
Lot 5 Caves Road, Willyabrup via Cowaramup, WA 6284
Ph (097) 55 6272 **Fax** (097) 55 6337
Open W'ends, Hols 10–5 **Production** 3500
Winemaker(s) Mike Davies
When in form, makes crisp, herbaceous Semillon and Sauvignon Blanc (and blends), ideal seafood wines, and austere, very firm Cabernets all in mainstream regional style.
Principal Wines Semillon, Sauvignon Blanc, Cabernet Merlot, Merlot.

RIBBON VALE ESTATE SEMILLON

●●●● $14
Produced from 2 hectares of semillon grown on the uniquely-shaped estate which is only 150 metres wide and 1.5 kilometres long — hence the name. Always herbaceous in style, it comes into its own in years such as 1993.
Cellaring 2–4 years. **Best Vintages** '85, '88, '92, '93, '94
Current Vintage '93

Matching Food Marron or yabbies.
Tasting Note 1993 Light yellow-green; fragrant, herbal/tangy
fruit aromas of considerable intensity and little or no oak evident.
A potent wine in mainstream Margaret River style, with lots of
concentrated herbal/citrus flavours, and a long finish.

RICHARD HAMILTON WINES

★★★★☆ 12–19 R AUS61, 111, 116, 127, 163, UK69
Southern Vales **Est.** 1972
Willunga Vineyards, Main South Road, Willunga, SA 5172
Ph (085) 56 2288 **Fax** (085) 56 2868
Open Mon–Sat 10–5, Sun, Public hols 11–5 **Production** NFP
Winemaker(s) Ralph Fowler
The quality and character of the Richard Hamilton wines have grown
in leaps and bounds over the past five years or so, no doubt due to
the combined skills of winemaker Ralph Fowler and the eccentric
marketing genius of Brian Miller — and of course support from
owner Dr Richard Hamilton.
Principal Wines Chardonnay, Farm Block Semillon, Hut Block
Cabernet Sauvignon, Old Vines Shiraz, Burton's Vineyards
Grenache Shiraz, Lion Heart Old Tawny Port.

RICHARD HAMILTON BURTON'S VINEYARD GRENACHE SHIRAZ
●●●●) $16
Named in honour of Burton Hamilton (1904–1994) Richard
Hamilton's father. It is a blend of 60% grenache and 40% shiraz,
made in a style which suddenly finds itself in huge demand. The '92
had a little too much oak, but no such criticism can be levelled at
the '93.
Cellaring 2–5 years. **Best Vintages** '91, '92, '93
Current Vintage '93
Matching Food Mild Indian curry.
Tasting Note 1993 Medium purple-red; the fresh, fruity/spicy red
berry aromas are immediately obvious. The palate is soft but
generous, with almost juicy spicy berry flavours, soft tannins and the
barest hint of oak.

RICHARD HAMILTON CHARDONNAY
●●●● $14
First produced in 1979 from grapes planted in 1975, and one of
the first wines of its variety made in McLaren Vale, if not the first. The
style has wandered around somewhat over the years, but has really
come into its own since 1992.
Cellaring 2–5 years. **Best Vintages** '86, '91, '92, '93, '94
Current Vintage '94
Matching Food Blue swimmer crab.
Tasting Note 1994 Light green-yellow; a delicate, crisp melon-
accent bouquet with minimal oak influence. The palate is more
powerful and much longer than the bouquet leads one to expect,
with cool-grown melon and citrus fruit driving the flavour.

RICHARD HAMILTON COONAWARRA CABERNET SAUVIGNON MERLOT

●●●● $25

The first release of Cabernet Sauvignon Merlot from the Richard Hamilton Coonawarra vineyard. Matured in new French oak casks for 12 months; only 300 cases of the wine were made.

Cellaring 3–7+ years. **Best Vintages** NA **Current Vintage** '93
Matching Food Roast squab.
Tasting Note 1993 Medium to full red-purple; a fragrant and complex bouquet with aromas of cedar and game. The palate is an interesting combination of blackcurrant fruit with cooler, leafier flavours; of medium weight, finishing with fine tannins and a hint of toasty oak.

RICHARD HAMILTON FARM BLOCK SEMILLON

●●●● $12

Made from grapes grown on loamy soil at Willunga, with the inclusion of a small proportion of sauvignon blanc. An unwooded, modern bright cafe style with plenty of flavour.

Cellaring 1–4 years. **Best Vintages** '86, '87, '88, '90, '93, '94
Current Vintage '94
Matching Food Seafood, Asian.
Tasting Note 1994 Light green-yellow; crisp, fragrant with some fruit salad aromas, partly fruit and partly yeast derived. The palate is crisp, clean and tangy with good length, and again a range of flavours running from herbal through to passionfruit and gooseberry.

RICHARD HAMILTON HUT BLOCK CABERNET SAUVIGNON

●●●● $16

Brian Miller (Richard Hamilton's marketing director) says: 'Hut Block Cabernet Sauvignon 1993 was made from grapes grown on a McLaren Vale vineyard named from the old hut on the property. The original vines of the Hut Block were carefully nurtured by Richard Hamilton's father, Burton Hamilton, who first planted grapes in McLaren Vale in 1947.' Carefully chosen words perhaps.

Cellaring 5–8 years. **Best Vintages** '86, '90, '91, '93
Current Vintage '93
Matching Food Beef Provençale.
Tasting Note 1993 Medium to full red-purple; a complex bouquet with a range of aromas from slightly gamey and leafy through to blackcurrant/cassis. The palate is even more complex, with many things going on, showing blackcurrant/bramble/gamey/leafy flavours and subtle oak.

RICHARD HAMILTON OLD VINES SHIRAZ

●●●● ▶ $19

As the name suggests, the wine is made from vines dating back more than a century, located at the southern fringe of McLaren Vale. In bygone years the grapes went to make port, but now produce a wine full of character, vibrantly spicy/peppery in 1992, but riper in 1993. First made in 1990, with a succession of admirable wines since that time.

Cellaring 2–7 years. **Best Vintages** '90, '91, '92, '93
Current Vintage '93
Matching Food Casserole of venison.
Tasting Note 1993 Dense purple-red; a markedly intense bouquet, more briary than in prior years, with a hint of sweet vanillin American oak in the background. There is a complex array of flavours on the palate with red berry fruits, a touch of vanillin oak and abundant tannins. Will be long-lived.

RICHMOND GROVE WINERY

★★★☆ 8.95–9.95 R AUS117
Hunter Valley and Barossa Valley **Est.** 1977
Hermitage Road, Pokolbin, NSW 2321/Para Road, Tanunda, SA 5352
Ph (049) 98 7792 **Fax** (049) 98 7783
Open Mon–Fri 9.30–5, W'ends 10–4 **Production** NFP
Winemaker(s) Steve Clarkson, John Vickery
Richmond Grove now has two homes, including one in the Barossa Valley, where John Vickery presides. It is owned by Orlando Wyndham, and draws its grapes from diverse sources. Vickery has had immediate success with the Rieslings, which is no more than one would expect.
Principal Wines White Bordeaux, White Burgundy (a legacy of Mark Cashmore, but doomed), Eden Valley Traminer Riesling, Watervale Riesling, Barossa Valley Riesling, Oak Matured Chablis, Cowra Chardonnay, Cowra Verdelho, French Cask Chardonnay, Black Ribbon Hunter Hermitage, Coonawarra Cabernet Sauvignon, Cabernet Merlot.

RICHMOND GROVE COONAWARRA CABERNET SAUVIGNON
●●● ▶ $9.95
The initial release of Coonawarra Cabernet Sauvignon under the Richmond Grove label, matured in a mix of French and American oak casks for 18 months before blending and bottling. It is a wine of light to medium intensity, not surprising given its modest price.
Cellaring Drink now. **Best Vintages** NA **Current Vintage** '92
Matching Food Lamb cutlets.
Tasting Note 1992 Medium to full red; the bouquet is quite developed, with a range of cedary/leafy/briary aromas. The palate shows similar characters; the fruit is neither particularly assertive nor even fresh, but the wine does have some elegance, with fine tannins on the finish.

RICHMOND GROVE FRENCH CASK CHARDONNAY
●●● ▶ $9.95
The name of the wine is strictly a brand, and does not particularly connote either making methods or the extensive use of French oak, whether new or otherwise. The wine is made in traditional Hunter style, rich and fruity, and quick developing.
Cellaring Drink now. **Best Vintages** '89, '91, '93

Current Vintage '93
Matching Food Sweet and sour pork.
Tasting Note 1993 Medium to full yellow; sweet,
honeyed/peachy/buttery aromas denote its warm-grown origin.
A big, sweet peachy/honeyed wine in the mouth, but quite well
balanced overall.

RICHMOND GROVE WATERVALE RIESLING
●●●● ▶ $9.95
With John Vickery's vast experience and impeccable contacts, it is
not surprising that the first Watervale Riesling under the Richmond
Grove label should be as good as it is. Top 100 1995 Sydney
International Winemakers Competition.
Cellaring 3–5 years. **Best Vintages** NA
Current Vintage '94
Matching Food Asparagus with hollandaise sauce.
Tasting Note 1994 Medium to full yellow-green; the bouquet is
firm, with intense lime and herbal fruit, the palate very full-flavoured
with lime, toast and spicy characters running throughout.

RIDDOCH ESTATE *

NR 15 R AUSSD
Coonawarra **Est.** 1972
Wrattonbully Road, Joanna, SA
Ph c/o John Coppins Liquor (09) 384 0777
Open Not (Vineyard only) **Production** 500
Winemaker(s) Ralph Fowler (Contract)
To compound the confusion concerning the Riddoch name, the only
producer entitled to use the name Riddoch Estate (following legal
proceedings) has now appeared on the scene, owned by Melbourne
QC A J Meyers. Most of the grapes are sold; a small portion of the 7
hectares is vinified by Ralph Fowler. Wines are only available through
John Coppins Liquor, 502 Stirling Highway, Cottesloe, WA 6011.

RIDGE WINES, THE See page 439.

RIVENDELL WINES

★★★☆ 10 R AUSSD
Margaret River **Est.** 1987
Lot 328 Wildwood Road, Yallingup, WA 6282
Ph (097) 55 2090 **Fax** (097) 55 2295
Open 7 days 10–5 **Production** 1125
Winemaker(s) Mike Davies, Jan Davies
With 13.5 hectares of vineyards coming into bearing, production for
Rivendell will increase significantly over the coming years. The cellar
door sales facility is in a garden setting complete with restaurant. An
unusual sideline is the sale of 50 types of preserves, jams and
chutneys.
Principal Wines Semillon Sauvignon Blanc, Honeysuckle Late
Harvest Semillon, Verdelho, Shiraz Cabernet.

RIVENDELL SEMILLON SAUVIGNON BLANC
●●● ▶ $10
Made from the initial 2 hectare plantings of semillon and sauvignon
blanc established in 1987, and the first wine made (in 1990) in a
direct style, without the intervention of oak, and typical of the
Margaret River region.
Cellaring 2–3 years. **Best Vintages** NA **Current Vintage** '93
Matching Food Lobster bisque.
Tasting Note 1993 Bright, light green-yellow. The bouquet and
the palate both have a trace of bitterness, redeemed in the case of
the bouquet by crisp, lemon and citrus fruit aromas, and by plenty of
fruit weight and cut on the palate.

RIVENDELL VERDELHO
●●● ▶ $10
The maiden release for the winery, and one full of promise.
Competent contract winemaking by Mike and Jan Davies certainly
helps, but the wine does have real character.
Cellaring 2–3 years. **Best Vintages** NA **Current Vintage** '94
Matching Food Parma ham with figs.
Tasting Note 1994 Very pale colour, almost white; the bouquet is
lightly perfumed with tropical passionfruit and lychee aromas which
carry through on a crisp, lively, tropical-accented palate of light
weight but nice overall character and flavour.

RIVERINA WINES
★★★ 4.50–7.50 CD AUS46, 173
Murrumbidgee Irrigation Area **Est.** 1969
Farm 1305, Hillston Road, Tharbogang via Griffith, NSW 2680
Ph (069) 62 4122 **Fax** (069) 62 4628
Open 7 days 9–5.30 **Production** 80 000
Winemaker(s) John Casella
One of the large producers of the region chiefly selling wine in bulk
to other producers, but the Ballingal Estate label is one to watch,
particularly from the '91 vintage: the wines have won a number of
show medals.
Principal Wines An extensive range of varietal wines under the
Ballingal Estate and Cooper County labels, the former being slightly
higher priced, each including Chardonnay, Semillon, Semillon
Chardonnay, Shiraz, Cabernet Sauvignon and Cabernet Merlot,
with a few additions under the Ballingal Estate label. There is also
a range of sparkling wines and fortifieds in both bottle and cask.

RIVERINA WINES BALLINGAL ESTATE CABERNET SAUVIGNON
●●● $7
Made in the only way possible, with extensive use of stainless steel
tanks and judicious use of oak chips. The result is a very fresh, fruity
wine which, like the Chardonnay, suits its market very well.
Cellaring Drink now. **Best Vintages** NA **Current Vintage** '93
Matching Food Spaghetti bolognaise.

Tasting Note 1993 Medium red; the bouquet is soft, with slightly jammy/berry fruit with considerable fragrance. The palate shows lots of jammy berry fruit of some richness, balanced by reasonable tannins.

RIVERINA WINES BALLINGAL ESTATE CHARDONNAY
●●● $7.50

An unashamedly commercial wine which is modestly priced, which has plenty of flavour, and which has sufficient residual sugar to capture its target audience.

Cellaring Drink now. **Best Vintages** NA **Current Vintage** '94
Matching Food Sweet and sour pork.
Tasting Note 1994 Medium to full yellow-green; soft, sweet peachy fruit of medium intensity on the bouquet, and a fleshy, soft palate finishing with distinct sweetness.

ROBINSONS FAMILY VINEYARDS

★★★☆ 9–18.50 CD AUSSD
Granite Belt **Est.** 1969
Curtins Road, Ballandean, Qld 4382
Ph (076) 84 1216 **Fax** (076) 39 2718
Open 7 days 9–5 **Production** 1100
Winemaker(s) Rod MacPherson, Philippa Hambledon
The conjunction of a picture of a hibiscus and 'cool climate' in prominent typeface on the labels is a strange one, but then that has always been the nature of Robinsons Family Vineyards. The current releases are the best for some time, and deserve to be taken seriously.
Principal Wines Sauvignon Blanc Semillon, Chardonnay, Lyra Dry White, Traminer, Late Harvest Traminer, Shiraz, Shiraz Cabernet, Cabernet Sauvignon, Sparkling.

ROBINSONS FAMILY CHARDONNAY
●●● ▶ $12

Produced from a little over 4 hectares of estate vineyards, which wend their way up hill and down dale, through patches of eucalyptus forest and scrub. An important wine for Robinsons, and won the 1994 Sheraton/Courier Mail award for Best Queensland Dry White.
Cellaring 2–3 years. **Best Vintages** '83, '85, '89, '92, '93
Current Vintage '93
Matching Food Queensland mud crab.
Tasting Note 1993 Light green-yellow; a light, crisp lemon and apple bouquet, with minimal oak influence. The palate has plenty of biscuity/nutty flavour and texture, suggesting either malolactic influence or ambient temperature fermentation in barrel.

ROBINSONS FAMILY SHIRAZ
●●●● ▶ $14

There is only 1.2 hectares of shiraz at Robinsons, which seems a pity given the quality of the wine. Like the Shiraz Cabernet, it is predominantly fruit-driven, and should develop well with bottle age.

Cellaring 5–10 years. **Best Vintages** '81, '82, '83, '85, '93
Current Vintage '93
Matching Food Kangaroo fillet.
Tasting Note 1993 Vibrant red-purple; a clean, youthful bouquet with concentrated red berry and earth aromas. There is abundant cherry essence fruit on the palate with soft tannins and minimal oak; not over extracted, and will age well.

ROBINSONS FAMILY SHIRAZ CABERNET
●●●● $10
The Robinsons Family red wines have always been exceptionally full-flavoured, often overextracted and impossibly tough and tannic. This wine has been designed for early consumption, and was bottled and released early. It has some lovely flavours, but whether it is really ready for early consumption is another matter.
Cellaring 2–4 years. **Best Vintages** NA **Current Vintage** '93
Matching Food Beef shashlik.
Tasting Note 1993 Full purple-red; a firm bouquet with youthful red berry fruits and a hint of earth, a little unformed. The palate is driven by powerful juicy red berry fruit, and again a hint of the earth deriving from the shiraz. Lots of potential.

ROBINVALE WINES

★★★☆ 3.80–11 CD AUS18, UK95
Murray River **Est.** 1976
Sea Lake Road, Robinvale, Vic 3549
Ph (050) 26 3955 **Fax** (050) 26 1123
Open 7 days 9–6 **Production** 3000
Winemaker(s) Bill Caracatsanoudis
Robinvale claims to be the only winery in Australia to be fully accredited with the Biodynamic Agricultural Association of Australia. Most, but not all, of the wines are produced from organically-grown grapes, with certain of the wines made preservative free.
Principal Wines A kaleidoscopic array of wines, including five preservative-free wines, white wines which run from Retsina through to Auslese Muscat Hamburg, Dry Marsanne, red wines which encompass Lambrusco, Scarlet Bliss, Cabernet Sauvignon/Franc, Kokkinelli, Fruity Rosé; and fortified wines ranging from Mavrodaphne to Cream Marsala, with a few Vintage Ports thrown in for good measure.

ROBINVALE CHARDONNAY
●●● $10
Made from certified biodynamic, estate-grown grapes, but vinified using conventional techniques, including the incorporation of American and French oak.
Cellaring Drink now. **Best Vintages** NA **Current Vintage** '94
Matching Food Roast chicken.
Tasting Note 1994 Medium to full yellow-green; a complex bouquet with hints of camphor, hazelnut and honey; plenty going on. The palate is nutty, dry and toasty, with the contribution of American oak evident in the vanillin overtones.

ROBINVALE ZINFANDEL MERLOT

●●● ▶ $10

The provenance of the zinfandel is not stated; it is a very rare grape in Australia, and I have not previously heard of it being grown on the Murray River. The blend with merlot makes the wine even more unusual, the exotic label being matched by the wine in the glass.
Cellaring Drink now. **Best Vintages** NA **Current Vintage** '94
Matching Food Highly-spiced meats.
Tasting Note 1994 Light to medium red-purple; the bouquet is crammed full with bright, fresh juicy cherry fruit aromas, which are even more pronounced on the palate which has the flavours of freshly pressed, unfermented grape juice. An amazing wine, albeit far from conventional.

ROCHECOMBE VINEYARD

★★★☆ 14.10–17.90 CD AUS72, 86, 156
Pipers Brook **Est.** 1985
Baxter's Road, Pipers River, Tas 7252
Ph (003) 82 7122 **Fax** (003) 82 7231
Open 7 days 10–4 **Production** 4500
Winemaker(s) Steve Goodwin
Rochecombe is now ultimately owned by the publicly listed JAC Group of meat exporters. The change of ownership came in the wake of several debilitating frosts, but founders Bernard and Brigitte Rochaix are staying on to make the wines and manage the on-site restaurant.
Principal Wines The wines are now sold in two ranges, Classic and Traditional. The former is the lower priced, comprising Pinot Chardonnay, Chardonnay Pinot Rosé and Pinot Noir; the latter includes Chardonnay, Pinot Noir and Cabernet Sauvignon/Cabernet Franc.

ROCHFORD WINES

★★★☆ 19.50–21.50 R AUS174, 187
Macedon **Est.** 1983
Romsey Park, Rochford, Vic 3442
Ph (054) 29 1428 **Fax** (054) 29 1066
Open By appt **Production** 750
Winemaker(s) Bruce Dowding
Construction engineer-cum-restaurateur-cum-grape grower and winemaker Bruce Dowding (and partner Sheila Hawkins) hit the headlines with their '90 and '91 Pinot Noirs, proving the suitability of the variety to the Macedon region. The Cabernet Sauvignon, however, has fairly consistently lacked ripe fruit.
Principal Wines Pinot Noir, Cabernet Sauvignon.

ROCHFORD PINOT NOIR

●●●● $23

Pinot has consistently been the outstanding wine from Rochford, typically exhibiting both complexity and richness of flavour, and helping establish the reputation of the Macedon region as yet

another area suited to this fickle variety. The '93 carries on a run
of excellent vintages.
Cellaring 2–3 years. **Best Vintages** '91, '92, '93, '94
Current Vintage '93
Matching Food Breast of squab.
Tasting Note 1993 Unusually deep purple-red; full, ripe
briary/plummy/gamey aromas of considerable complexity. A very
concentrated and complex wine on the palate, with quite massive
briary/plummy fruit.

ROCKFORD WINES

★★★★ 8.70–18 CD AUSSD, UK1
Barossa Valley **Est.** 1984
Krondorf Road, Tanunda, SA 5352
Ph (085) 63 2720 **Fax** (085) 63 3787
Open 7 days 11–5 **Production** 18 000
Winemaker(s) Robert O'Callaghan
The wines are sold through Adelaide retailers only (and cellar door),
and are unknown to most Eastern States wine drinkers, which is a
great pity, for these are some of the most individual, spectacularly
flavoured wines made in the Barossa today, with an emphasis on
old low-yielding dry-land vineyards.
Principal Wines Vine Vale Riesling, Eden Valley Riesling, Local
Growers Semillon, Alicante Bouchet, Basket Press Shiraz, Black
Shiraz, Dry Country Grenache, Cabernet Sauvignon.

ROMAVILLA WINES

★★★ 6.50–26 CD AUSSD
West Queensland **Est.** 1863
Northern Road, Roma, Qld 4455
Ph (076) 22 1822 **Fax** (076) 22 1822
Open Mon–Fri 8–5, Sat 9–12, 2–4 **Production** 2000
Winemaker(s) David Wall
An amazing, historic relic, seemingly untouched since its nineteenth-
century heyday, producing eminently forgettable table wines but still
providing some extraordinary fortifieds, including a truly stylish
Madeira, made from riesling and syrian (the latter variety originating
in Persia).
Principal Wines Fourteen varietal and generic table wines and
13 fortified wine styles including Madeira and Tawny Port are on
sale at the winery; the Very Old Tawny Port is made from a blend
of material ranging in age from 10 to 25 years.

ROSABROOK ESTATE

★★★☆ 9.99–15 CD AUS102, 173, UK82
Margaret River **Est.** 1980
Rosa Brook Road, Margaret River, WA 6285
Ph (097) 57 2286 **Fax** (097) 57 3634
Open Summer 7 days 11–4 **Production** 3000
Winemaker(s) Dan Pannell

The 7-hectare Rosabrook Estate vineyards have been established progressively since 1980, with no less than 9 varieties planted. The cellar door facility is housed in what was Margaret River's first commercial abattoir, built in the early 1930s, with a new winery constructed in 1993.

Principal Wines Semillon, Classic Dry White, Chardonnay, Autumn Harvest Riesling, Cabernet Merlot; under Comfort Hill label (no cheaper): Semillon.

ROSABROOK ESTATE CABERNET MERLOT
●●●● ▶ $14

Rosabrook Estate is still in its early days, and Dan Pannell (son of Bill and Margaret Pannell) has not been long in charge of winemaking for Perth-based owners Dr John Shepherd and wife Joan. However, the 1991 and 1992 Cabernet Merlots, made from estate-grown grapes, show considerable promise, particularly the latter wine, which really is outstanding.

Cellaring 4–7 years. **Best Vintages** '91, '92
Current Vintage '92
Matching Food Roast veal.
Tasting Note 1992 Medium to full red with just a touch of purple remaining. The aromas are quite Italianate in style, soft but complex. The same characters appear in an attractive, rounded, supple palate with lovely texture and sweet berry fruit.

ROSEMOUNT ESTATE

★★★★★ 9.95–39.95 R AUS132–136 US12
Upper Hunter Valley **Est.** 1969
Rosemount Road, Denman, NSW 2328
Ph (065) 47 2467 **Fax** (065) 47 2742
Open Mon–Sat 10–4, Sun Summer 10–4, Winter 12–4
Production 700 000
Winemaker(s) Philip Shaw

Rosemount Estate has achieved a miraculous balancing act over the past years maintaining — indeed increasing — wine quality while presiding over an ever-expanding empire and ever-increasing production. The wines are consistently of excellent value; all have real character and individuality; not a few are startlingly good.

Principal Wines A very large range of wines which in almost all instances are varietally identified, sometimes with the conjunction of vineyards at the top end of the range, and which in the case of the lower-priced volume varietals increasingly come from all parts of south east Australia. Names and label designs change regularly but the emphasis remains on the classic varietals. Roxburgh Chardonnay and Balmoral Syrah are the white and red flagbearers; Chardonnay, Shiraz and Cabernet Sauvignon under the standard labels consistently excellent at the price.

ROSEMOUNT ESTATE BALMORAL SYRAH
●●●●● $30

Formerly sold under the Show Reserve Syrah label, the name comes from the 1852 Hunter Valley Homestead of the Oatley family, founders of Rosemount Estate. A tasting of the four vintages of the wine so far released ('89-'92) showed an incredible consistency of style, with the 100-year-old vines at Rosemount's Ryecroft Vineyard in McLaren Vale at the heart of the wine. Less than 2000 cases are made each year, 50% being exported to the United States.

Cellaring 15–20 years. **Best Vintages** '90, '91, '92
Current Vintage '92
Matching Food Char-grilled rump.
Tasting Note 1992 Medium to full red-purple; a very complex bouquet with a savoury/earthy regional substrate to concentrated fruit and oak. Slightly more elegant than its immediate predecessors, the palate runs the gamut of earthy/briary/woodsy/raspberry/bitter chocolate flavours, finishing with moderately full tannins.

ROSEMOUNT ESTATE CABERNET SAUVIGNON
●●●●● $12

With the 1993 vintage of this wine, Rosemount achieved a level of excellence hitherto only consistently achieved by its Shiraz. Even more remarkable (given the price) is the source of the wine: principally from Coonawarra and McLaren Vale, with a small proportion of merlot and cabernet franc included. The wine was fermented warm, given five to seven days extended maceration, and then aged for 12 months in one-year-old and older French barriques. A gold medal winner at the 1994 Adelaide Wine Show in tough competition.

Cellaring 2–5 years. **Best Vintages** '86, '88, '90, '92, '93, '94
Current Vintage '93
Matching Food Rare sirloin steak.
Tasting Note 1993 Bright medium purple-red; an exceedingly complex bouquet with liquorice, spice, redcurrant and chocolate fruit aromas all to be found. Even better is the palate, which has wonderful feel, with softly rounded blackcurrant and chocolate fruit, subtle oak and fine tannins.

ROSEMOUNT ESTATE CHARDONNAY
●●●● $12

The only wine in this large so-called premium varietal range to continue to have and claim a Hunter Valley origin, or, to be precise, Upper Hunter origin. The wine is made to throw maximum emphasis on fairly rapid flavour development; part of the wine underwent malolactic fermentation while ageing in French and American oak, while part was tank fermented and held on lees prior to blending. The American oak is slightly phenolic, but does add flavour.

Cellaring Drink now. **Best Vintages** '84, '86, '87, '90, '93
Current Vintage '94
Matching Food Veal parmigiana.
Tasting Note 1994 Developed, deep yellow; in absolutely typical style for Rosemount, with big, buttery/nutty aromas and flavours already apparent within 12 months of vintage. Very much a drink now style; released in the new Italian bottle.

ROSEMOUNT ESTATE ROSÉ LABEL YARRAWA SAUVIGNON BLANC

●●●● $19

First released in 1994 and symptomatic of the changing mix of labels and designations within the Rosemount stable, but nonetheless a very attractive wine, somewhat surprisingly sourced from estate plantings in the Upper Hunter River region, bordering the Wollombi National Park, and one of the Hunter Valley's most westerly vineyards. Surprising, simply because sauvignon blanc does not normally perform so well in either the Lower or Upper Hunter.

Cellaring Drink now. **Best Vintages** NA **Current Vintage** '94
Matching Food Grilled fish.
Tasting Note 1994 Light yellow-green; clean, crisp, lightly herbaceous but lingering aromas lead on to a wine with good length and mouthfeel, unforced by oak, and lively and fresh.

ROSEMOUNT ESTATE ROXBURGH CHARDONNAY

●●●●● $39.95

Since 1983 the flagship of Rosemount Estate and, at least in some quarters, regarded as the premier Australian white. Throughout the 1980s the style was quite controversial but has become more conventional in the 1990s as more emphasis has been placed on fresh fruit. It is a single vineyard wine, most of the fruit coming from two 9-acre blocks at the top of the Roxburgh Vineyard planted on limestone-impregnated terra rossa soil.

Cellaring 3–5 years. **Best Vintages** '86, '87, '89, '91, '92, '93
Current Vintage '92
Matching Food Veal, pork.
Tasting Note 1992 Medium yellow-green; the bouquet is clean and quite firm, of medium to full intensity with melon and citrus fruit aromas and a hint of oak. The palate is quite firm, indeed elegant, with herb, lime and melon flavours, interwoven with pleasant oak.

ROSEMOUNT ESTATE SEMILLON

●●● ▶ $12

A new departure for Rosemount, being its first unoaked Semillon, stainless steel fermented and bottled early. Intriguingly, an estate-grown wine harvested from Rosemount's Roxburgh and Giant's Creek vineyards.

Cellaring 1–3 years. **Best Vintages** NA **Current Vintage** '94
Matching Food Lobster, crab.
Tasting Note 1994 Medium to full yellow-green; ample fruit intensity and depth, with good varietal character on the bouquet, leading on to a well-flavoured and weighted palate with herbal/citrus fruit flavours dominant, and a few tropical notes also evident.

ROSEMOUNT ESTATE SHIRAZ

●●●● ▶ $12

A wine which has been largely responsible for the phenomenal success of Rosemount Estate in the United States, winning consistently (and at times amazingly) high points from the world's most influential wine magazine, *The Wine Spectator*. Rosemount has never made any secret of the fact that it does subtly alter the balance of its export wines according to the dictates of the market of destination, and in any event, wines in this volume are batch-bottled. Over many years and in many places I have tasted some quite spectacular renditions of the wine, even if the '93 is not quite up to the best (or the Cabernet of that year).

Cellaring 2–3 years. **Best Vintages** '88, '90, '91, '92, '94
Current Vintage '93
Matching Food Lamb shanks.
Tasting Note 1993 Medium to full red-purple; sweet berry/cherry fruit with somewhat phenolic/chippy oak on the bouquet; sweet, ripe fruit on the palate showing hints of liquorice, but overall seemed to have been rushed into bottle.

ROSEMOUNT ESTATE SHOW RESERVE CABERNET SAUVIGNON

●●●● ▶ $19.50

Made entirely from estate-grown grapes produced from Rosemount's Coonawarra Kirri Billi vineyard which was planted in 1982. The Cabernets produced from this vineyard and released under the Show Reserve label have accumulated 47 gold medals to date. The wine spends 20 months in French oak before bottling.

Cellaring 5–8 years. **Best Vintages** '88, '90, '91, '92
Current Vintage '92
Matching Food King Island Cheddar.
Tasting Note 1992 Full red-purple; the bouquet is dominated by dark briary/berry fruit with subtle oak. The palate has plenty of depth with a mix of sweet red berry fruits ranging through to dark chocolate flavours, with well-balanced tannins giving plenty of mouthfeel.

ROSENBERG CELLARS

★★★ 8–10 CD AUSSD
Clare Valley **Est.** 1985
Main North Road, Watervale, SA 5452
Ph (088) 43 0131
Open W'ends 10–5 **Production** NFP
Winemaker(s) Terry Blanden
The wines, basically white and usually with residual sugar, are made under contract at Eaglehawk and Sevenhill; not surprisingly, quality is good, particularly at the price.
Principal Wines Chenin Blanc, Cottage White, Sparkling, Rosé, Shiraz.

ROSEWHITE VINEYARDS

NR 10 CD AUSSD
North East Victoria **Est.** 1983
Happy Valley Road, Happy Valley via Myrtleford, Vic 3737
Ph (057) 52 1077
Open Fri–Mon, Wed 10–5 **Production** 500

Winemaker(s) Joan Mullett

After a career with the Victorian Department of Agriculture, agricultural scientists Ron and Joan Mullett began the establishment of Rosewhite in 1983, and have since established a little over 2 hectares of vineyards at an altitude of 300 metres. A 1989 Pinot Noir indicated that the area had real potential for this variety, but I have not tasted subsequent vintages.

Principal Wines Traminer, Chardonnay, Pinot Noir, Cabernet Sauvignon.

ROSSETTO WINES

★★★ 3.95–22 CD AUSSD

Murrumbidgee Irrigation Area **Est.** 1930

Farm 576, Beelbangera, NSW 2686

Ph (069) 63 5214 **Fax** (069) 63 5542

Open Mon–Sat 8.30–5.30 **Production** NFP

Winemaker(s) Ralph Graham

A winery with an interesting mix of products, with 50% of total sales coming from the Mt Bingar range of 4-litre casks, 40% being provided by fortified wines, cocktail wines and 12,000 cases of Rossetto premium table wines. The latter can offer very good value.

Principal Wines Mt Bingar generic and varietal casks, a kaleidoscopic range of flavoured and fortified wine, premium table wines under Rosetto label.

ROTHBURY ESTATE

★★★★☆ 9.95–30 R AUS176, UK94

Hunter Valley **Est.** 1968

Broke Road, Pokolbin, NSW 2321

Ph (049) 98 7555 **Fax** (049) 98 7870

Open 7 days 9.30–4.30 **Production** 400 000

Winemaker(s) Peter Hall (Chief), Keith Hall (Red)

Rothbury Estate is now the holding company of a range of producers extending across Australia, the most recent acquisition being that of Saltram in the Barossa Valley, which gave Seagrams a 20% holding in Rothbury. Other significant brands include Baileys and St Huberts, while its large Cowra vineyards play a very important role, as do its Upper Hunter vineyards at Denman.

Principal Wines A tightly controlled range with Trident (varietal regional blended white) at the bottom end of the price range, followed by Hunter Valley Semillon, Hunter Valley Verdelho, Hunter Valley Chardonnay, Cowra Chardonnay, South East Australia Shiraz; next come Barrel Fermented Hunter Chardonnay, Hunter Shiraz, Reserve Hunter Valley Chardonnay, with a final large jump (in terms of price) to Reserve Hunter Valley Shiraz.

ROTHBURY ESTATE BARREL FERMENTED CHARDONNAY
●●●● ▶ $15

First made in 1990, and an overnight success, although that particular wine has developed disconcertingly quickly. Initially intended for the export market, it is now sold both domestically and

overseas, achieving great distinction with the 1992 vintage which
won the Bert Bear Trophy for Best One Year Old Table Wine at the
1993 Royal Sydney Wine Show.
Cellaring 2–4 years. **Best Vintages** '91, '92, '93, '94
Current Vintage '94
Matching Food Loin of pork.
Tasting Note 1994 Light green-yellow; complex barrel ferment
aromas with relatively tight, stylish fruit. The palate shows an
attractive amalgam of grapefruit and melon flavours which are still
evolving and balanced with good acidity. The oak has been held
in restraint.

ROTHBURY ESTATE COWRA CHARDONNAY
●●●● $12.95
First made in 1981 (a wine of superb quality which is still drinking
magnificently) and which has since become a very important part of
the Rothbury portfolio. It draws upon 44 hectares of existing
vineyard, much of it mature, but with further plantings projected.
The style is always luscious and full-blown, but has a remarkable
capacity to age.
Cellaring 2–10 years. **Best Vintages** '81, '83, '84, '89, '93
Current Vintage '94
Matching Food Sugar-cured tuna.
Tasting Note 1994 Light green-yellow; a very light and crisp
bouquet, more Semillon-like than Chardonnay, and in radically
different style from most of the Cowra Chardonnays early in its life.
The palate, too, is light and crisp, with some herbaceous overtones.
Uncertain how it will develop.

ROTHBURY ESTATE HUNTER VALLEY CHARDONNAY
●●● ▶ $12.95
Originally sourced from the Lower Hunter Valley, but now
increasingly taken from the Denman plantings. It is not particularly
complex, and does not aspire to greatness or a long life, but is well
made and well flavoured, providing good value.
Cellaring 2–3 years. **Best Vintages** '87, '91, '92, '94
Current Vintage '94
Matching Food Wiener schnitzel.
Tasting Note 1994 Light to medium yellow-green; light, fresh
and youthful citrussy fruit aromas with minimal oak on the bouquet.
A pleasant commercial wine with citrus/melon fruit, subtle oak and
moderate intensity and length to the palate.

ROTHBURY ESTATE HUNTER VALLEY SEMILLON
●●●●● $12.95
The first commercial release was in 1972, of a single estate
semillon. Since that time the wine has appeared in a large number
of different guises, sometimes vineyard identified, sometimes
Director's Reserve, and sometimes Shareholder's Reserve. The latter
has been continued, the other labelling discontinued. The rating is
given for the overall quality of the wines between
1972 and now.

Cellaring 5–20 years. **Best Vintages** '72, '73, '74, '75, '76, '79, '84, '89, '93, '94 **Current Vintage** '94
Matching Food Smoked eel.
Tasting Note 1994 Brilliant green-yellow; the bouquet is crisp and lively with excellent tangy lemon/herbaceous varietal fruit of medium intensity. The palate is lively, fresh, crisp and tangy, with a touch more varietal bite than the '93 but in similar mould. Should develop into a classic.

ROTHBURY ESTATE RESERVE HUNTER VALLEY SHIRAZ
●●●●● $30
Produced only in the very best vintages, with three wines made since its inception in 1989 — that year, 1991 and 1993. Powerful fruit from low-yielding Lower Hunter estate shiraz is cleverly married with quality American oak to produce a wine in radically different style from anything produced by Rothbury prior to 1989.
Cellaring 10+ years. **Best Vintages** '89, '91, '93
Current Vintage '93
Matching Food Entrecote of beef.
Tasting Note 1993 Medium red-purple; the bouquet has some of the spicy characters of the standard '93, suggesting a percentage of other region grapes, with lively cherry and spice fruit. The palate is rich, with cherry/plummy/berry fruit flavours, soft but persistent tannins, and well integrated and balanced oak.

ROTHBURY ESTATE SHIRAZ
●●●● ▶ $15
Another wine to undergo various metamorphoses over the years, the most significant being with the wonderful 1993 vintage which received a gold medal at the 1994 London Wine Challenge in the Rhone Style Dry Red class. Up to that year the label specified that the wine was from the Hunter Valley; no claim is made for the '93 which is, quite evidently, a very classy regional blend incorporating some cool climate shiraz, presumably from Victoria.
Cellaring 5–10 years. **Best Vintages** '81, '83, '89, '91, '93
Current Vintage '93
Matching Food Beef bourguignon.
Tasting Note 1993 Medium red-purple; very fragrant, vibrant cherry, pepper and spice aromas with just a hint of spicy oak. A vibrantly lively palate follows with dark cherry, plum and spice flavours which are beautifully balanced. Arguably best enjoyed while young.

ROTHERHYTHE WINES

NR 15 CD AUSSD
Tamar Valley **Est.** 1969
Hendersons Lane, Gravelly Beach, Exeter, Tas 7251
Ph (003) 34 0188
Open See Delamere **Production** 1300
Winemaker(s) Dr Steven Hyde
The softly-spoken Dr Stephen Hyde is one of the nice guys of the

wine industry, and I simply wish I could be more enthusiastic about
the wines. Sulphide-derived astringency has been a consistent
problem, but the 1992 Chardonnay and 1991 Cabernet Sauvignon
are certainly pointing in the right direction, and suggest that better
things are in store.

Principal Wines Chardonnay, Pinot Noir, Cabernet Merlot.

ROTHERHYTHE CABERNET SAUVIGNON

●●●● $19.95

Grown on the banks of the Tamar River on a site with excellent
exposure which produces far riper flavours in all the Rotherhythe
reds than one finds in most Tasmanian vineyards. A wine seldom
seen on the mainland, but being offered through wholesale channels
in mid 1995 in tiny quantities, of course.

Cellaring Now–5 years. **Best Vintages** NA

Current Vintage '90

Matching Food Braised lamb shanks.

Tasting Note 1990 Medium to full red-purple; complex aromas
of cedar, leaf and tobacco; medium to full intensity. The palate has
many overtones of Bordeaux, with fragrant leafy/cedary flavours
and fine-grained tannins. Subtle oak.

ROUGE HOMME

★★★★ 10.95–14.95 AUS147, UK83

Coonawarra **Est.** 1954

Main Penola-Naracoorte Road, Coonawarra, SA 5263

Ph (087) 36 3205 **Fax** (087) 36 3250

Open Mon–Sat 10–4 **Production** 35 000

Winemaker(s) Paul Gordon

I have previously described Rouge Homme as the warrior brand
of the Lindeman Group Coonawarra operations, and in recent
times it has proved a formidable warrior, most surprisingly with
its Pinot Noir, but also with its newly-introduced Richardson's
Red Block.

Principal Wines Chardonnay, Pinot Noir, Shiraz Cabernet,
Richardson's Red Block, Cabernet Sauvignon.

ROUGE HOMME CABERNET SAUVIGNON

●●● ▶ $14.95

While in price terms the flagship of the range, does not seem to
have the quality edge over the other wines that one might expect.
Certainly it is well made, coming as it does from 100% Coonawarra
cabernet sauvignon, and being matured in French oak hogsheads
for 15 months.

Cellaring 3–6 years. **Best Vintages** '88, '90, '91, '92

Current Vintage '92

Matching Food Roast leg of lamb.

Tasting Note 1992 Medium to full red; a solid bouquet with ripe
fruit and evident oak. A much bigger wine on the palate than the
preceding vintages with plenty of dark fruit flavours; lacks a little
finesse, perhaps.

ROUGE HOMME CHARDONNAY
●●● ▶ $12.95

As with so many of the Southcorp Group wines, you get a surprising amount for your dollars. 70% of the blend was barrel fermented in new French oak hogsheads and matured on its lees for three months before being matured in a mix of those barrels and one-year-old Troncais and Allier barriques for seven months before bottling.

Cellaring 3–5 years. **Best Vintages** '88, '90, '91, '92
Current Vintage '93
Matching Food Pan-fried veal.
Tasting Note 1993 Medium to full yellow; highly scented oak dominates the bouquet and, to a slightly lesser degree, the palate, which has some soft, peachy fruit.

ROUGE HOMME PINOT NOIR
●●●● ▶ $10.95

The influence of chief winemaker Philip John has been instrumental in the development of the style and quality of this wine, the only example of its kind from Coonawarra to have impressed. At the price it is a bargain, although one cannot help but be mildly surprised at the number of trophies and gold medals won by the 1993 vintage at national wine shows. It not that is not a good wine — clearly it is, but it is a fraction on the hard side. The full gamut of winemaking techniques has been used including whole bunch fermentation and subsequent barrel fermentation in new French oak.

Cellaring 2–3 years. **Best Vintages** '93 **Current Vintage** '93
Matching Food Char-grilled salmon, quail.
Tasting Note 1993 Medium to full red; a complex bouquet with sappy, earthy varietal characters and hints of spice together with slightly hard oak. A powerful wine in the mouth with lots of stemmy/sappy fruit showing whole bunch and carbonic maceration characters, and supporting French oak.

ROUGE HOMME RICHARDSON'S RED BLOCK
●●●● $12.50

Named after one of Coonawarra's pioneer viticulturists, and the first of the Rouge Homme red wines to incorporate malbec and merlot together with cabernet sauvignon in the manner of a junior brother to Lindemans Pyrus.

Cellaring 3–4 years. **Best Vintages** NA **Current Vintage** '92
Matching Food Lamb shanks.
Tasting Note 1992 Medium purple-red; a lighter, more elegant style with fragrant sweet berry fruit on both bouquet and palate. The influence of the malbec and merlot is quite pronounced on the palate in particular, which is elegantly fruity rather than powerful.

ROUGE HOMME SHIRAZ CABERNET
●●●● $10.95

This is the descendant of Rouge Homme Claret, for long the mainstay of the Rouge Homme brand. Originally made entirely from shiraz, it is now a 50/50 blend of shiraz and cabernet sauvignon matured in French and American oak barrels for an average period of 12 months. The '92 follows on the excellent '91; if anything it is even better than its formidable predecessor.

Cellaring Up to 5 years. **Best Vintages** '88, '90, '91, '92
Current Vintage '92
Matching Food King Island cheddar.
Tasting Note 1992 Medium to full red; the bouquet is smooth with attractive cherry and plum fruit, and the oak held nicely in restraint. The palate follows the bouquet with good structure and balance; there are smooth cherry fruit flavours, soft but adequate tannins, and subtle oak.

ROVALLEY ESTATE

★★★★ 6.95–20 R AUS105
Barossa Valley **Est.** 1919
Sturt Highway, Rowland Flat, SA 5352
Ph (085) 24 4537 **Fax** (085) 24 4066
Open 7 days 9–4.30 **Production** 150 000
Winemaker(s) Shayne Cunningham, Moss Kaesler
Since its acquisition by Miranda Wines of Griffith, the quality of the Rovalley Estate wines has been transformed. All of the Show Reserve wines have been multiple gold medal and trophy winners, the Grey Series multiple medal winners.
Principal Wines At the bottom end comes the so-called Premium Varietal range of Rovalley Ridge Chardonnay, Riesling, Late Harvest Riesling, Sauvignon Blanc, Dry White Frontignac, Pinot Noir, Cabernet Shiraz; next comes the Grey Label Series Chardonnay, Shiraz, Cabernets; finally top-of-the-range Show Reserve Chardonnay, Shiraz Cabernet and Old Vines Shiraz; Sparkling, Ports.

ROVALLEY ESTATE ROVALLEY RIDGE CHARDONNAY
●●●● $6.95
A complex blend which shows just how far Miranda/Rovalley are prepared to go in sourcing the wines. It is a blend of Hunter Valley (56%), Riverina (35%) with components from the Barossa Valley, King Valley, Mudgee and Cowra making up the balance. What is more, it is a varietal blend of over 90% chardonnay, with a touch of semillon and sauvignon blanc. The wine was cold fermented, given some oak maturation and partial malolactic fermentation. All this in a wine selling for $6.95.
Cellaring Drink now. **Best Vintages** NA
Current Vintage '93
Matching Food Crumbed lamb's brains.
Tasting Note 1993 Medium to full yellow-green; rich, complex, ripe nutty/peachy fruit on the bouquet with a particular Miranda family quality to the flavour which is hard to define, but which is very high-toned and gives a particularly intense finish.

ROVALLEY ESTATE ROVALLEY RIDGE LATE HARVEST RHINE RIESLING

●●●● $7.45

The grapes for this wine came from the long-established and well-known Koombhala Vineyard in the King Valley of north east Victoria. It is a genuine late harvest style, with the fruit intensity and character so often lacking. The grapes were partially botrytis-infected, and the wine cold-fermented and early-bottled. A gold medal winner at the 1994 Royal Sydney Wine Show.

Cellaring 1–4 years. **Best Vintages** NA **Current Vintage** '93
Matching Food Fresh fruit.

Tasting Note 1993 Medium yellow-green; the bouquet is surprisingly intense with strong lime juice aromas. The palate has rich, lime-accented fruit with some tropical overtones, balanced by crisp but not searing acidity.

ROVALLEY ESTATE SHOW RESERVE CHARDONNAY

●●●● ▶ $15.99

Sourced entirely from a single vineyard in the upper Eden Valley and barrel fermented in new American oak barriques, before being given seven months lees contact in the same barrels. A winner of three gold and two silver medals at Australian wine shows, including gold medals at Sydney, Melbourne and Adelaide, three of the toughest shows.

Cellaring Short term. **Best Vintages** NA **Current Vintage** '92
Matching Food Roast turkey.

Tasting Note 1992 Full yellow; concentrated, developed and complex barrel ferment aromas with vanillin oak and peachy fruit. The palate is similarly rich and potent, with yellow peach and citrus fruit flavours allied with creamy vanillin oak.

ROVALLEY ESTATE SHOW RESERVE SHIRAZ CABERNET

●●●●● $20

A blend of 79% shiraz and 21% cabernet sauvignon sourced from two vineyards in the Eden Valley, and matured in new American oak barrels for 16 months prior to bottling. A wine which had phenomenal show success, winning three trophies, six gold medals and innumerable other show medals.

Cellaring Up to 10 years. **Best Vintages** NA
Current Vintage '91
Matching Food Peking duck.

Tasting Note 1991 Medium red-purple; a wine still showing complexity and freshness with beautifully balanced and integrated sweet fruit and oak in September 1994, with excellent acidity. A wine with quite wonderful mouthfeel and balance, and one really wonders whether there is any point in cellaring.

RUKER WINES

NR 10 CD AUSSD
Canberra **Est.** 1991
Barton Highway, Dickson, ACT 2602
Ph (06) 230 2310

Open W'ends, Public hols 10-5 **Production** 500
Winemaker(s) Richard Ruker
Barbara and Richard Ruker, with the assistance of eldest daughter
Niki, planted 2 hectares of riesling and traminer in 1984. The cellar
door-cum-winery is a farmshed, subsequently converted to an office
and then to its present function; it is finished with heavy wooden
beams salvaged from a railway bridge near Tarago and clad with
the remains of an old slab hut, while the tables are made from huge
red and yellow box trees cut down when the vineyard was planted.
The first wines were made in 1991, and I have not tasted them.
Principal Wines Riesling, Gewurztraminer.

RUMBALARA VINEYARDS

NR 6.20–14.50 CD AUSSD
Granite Belt **Est.** 1974
Fletcher Road, Fletcher, Qld 4381
Ph (076) 84 1206 **Fax** (076) 83 4335
Open 7 days 9-5 **Production** 3000
Winemaker(s) Bob Gray
Over the years has produced some of the Granite Belt's finest
honeyed Semillon and silky, red berry Cabernet Sauvignon, but
quality does vary, and has recently disappointed, though the peachy
'91 Semillon showed some character and the '92 Cabernet
Sauvignon plenty of fruit character and weight.
Principal Wines Barrel Fermented Semillon, Granitegolde, Light
Shiraz, Cabernet Sauvignon, Pinot Noir, Cabernet Shiraz and a
range of fortified wines, Cider and Vermouth.

RYECROFT VINEYARDS

★★★★ 7.95–12.95 R AUS132–136 UK82 US12
Southern Vales **Est.** 1888
Ingoldby Road, McLaren Flat, SA 5171
Ph (08) 383 0001 **Fax** (08) 383 0456
Open Mon-Fri 10-5, W'ends 12-5 **Production** 100 000
Winemaker(s) Charles Whish
Following its acquisition by Rosemount Estate in late 1991, wine
quality has become very much more consistent, even if unashamedly
commercial.
Principal Wines At the bottom price bracket: Flame Tree Red and
White; then Flame Tree Chardonnay, Shiraz; at the top:
Contemporary Chardonnay, Traditional Cabernet Shiraz Merlot.

RYECROFT FLAME TREE CHARDONNAY
●●●● $9.95
Sourced predominantly from McLaren Vale, and shows extremely
sophisticated (and successful) winemaking. The wine has performed
with great distinction in masked tastings, outclassing wines costing
far more.
Cellaring 2–3 years. **Best Vintages** '82, '86, '88, '90, '92
Current Vintage '93

Matching Food Sweetbreads.
Tasting Note 1993 Medium yellow-green; a smooth bouquet with well balanced melon fruit and oak. A graceful wine on the palate, with a particularly long finish given its class.

RYECROFT FLAME TREE RED
●●●● $7.95
A blended red wine made with minimal oak and bottled within the year of vintage to capture maximum fruit freshness. The problem with such wines is that they often appear hard and callow, but Ryecroft succeeded brilliantly with the '93.
Cellaring Drink now. **Best Vintages** NA
Current Vintage '93
Matching Food Italian.
Tasting Note 1993 Medium red-purple; attractive fruit aromas in the mint, cherry, plum and spice spectrum. The same flavours appear on the palate, lusciously sweet and minty; made without the use of oak and succeeds brilliantly.

RYECROFT TRADITIONAL CABERNET SHIRAZ MERLOT
●●●● $11.95
When this quaintly named wine was introduced in 1987, it was given a label which won the Benjamin Franklin Trophy in the United States for the Best Label Design in the world, as well as winning most Australian label design competitions. Traditional it could not be accused of being, but beautiful and unusual it is. The wine, too, has been good right from the outset, with French and American oak used with discretion and adding to the complexity of the wine. Why the name? I don't really know.
Cellaring 3-6 years. **Best Vintages** '88, '90, '91, '92
Current Vintage '91
Matching Food Jugged hare.
Tasting Note 1991 Medium to full red; the bouquet is full and soft with ripe, dark chocolate-accented fruit and sweet vanillin oak. The palate is similarly soft and chewy with lots of regional chocolate flavour and style, finishing with soft tannins.

RYLAND RIVER *

NR 10-15 CD AUSSD
Mornington Peninsula **Est.** 1986
Lot 2 Main Creek Road, Main Ridge, Vic 3928
Ph (059) 89 6098
Open W'ends 10-5 **Production** 1000
Winemaker(s) John Bray
Ryland River offers a unique attraction to tourists: called the 'Chardonnay and Trout Lake' it gives you the opportunity to catch and cook your trout and enjoy it with a glass of Ryland River Chardonnay.
Principal Wines Ryland River, Mountain Mist and Arthur's Seat Winery labels: Semillon, Sauvignon Blanc, Chardonnay.

RYMILL WINES

★★★★☆ 13.95–29 R AUS76, 97, 137, 164, UK58, 69
Coonawarra **Est.** 1970
Old Penola Estate, Penola, SA 5277
Ph (087) 36 5001 **Fax** (087) 36 5040
Open Not **Production** 20 000
Winemaker(s) John Innes

The Rymills are descendants of John Riddoch, and have long owned some of the finest Coonawarra soil upon which they have grown grapes since 1970. Peter Rymill has made a small amount of Cabernet Sauvignon since 1987, and has now plunged headlong into commercial production, with winemaker John Innes presiding over the striking winery portrayed on the label.

Principal Wines Basic Riddoch Run label: Sauvignon Blanc, Chardonnay, Shiraz, Cabernet Sauvignon; Rymill label: Chardonnay, Cabernet Sauvignon, Methode Champenoise.

RYMILL CABERNET SAUVIGNON
●●●● ▶ $24

During each vintage, a small quantity of the best fruit is selected for special oak maturation and eventual release under the Rymill label. For many years Rymill sold the grapes from the vineyard, and the label first appeared on a small quantity of experimental wine made under contract. It won instant show success, and persuaded Peter Rymill to enter commercial winemaking on an ever-increasing scale. This wine shows why.

Cellaring 5–7 years. **Best Vintages** '90 **Current Vintage** '90
Matching Food Mushroom risotto.

Tasting Note 1990 Medium to full red; fragrant, cedary, stylish red berry fruit in a lighter mould. A complex, relatively light-bodied palate with red berry mint and leaf flavours, rounded off by fine-grained tannins.

RYMILL RIDDOCH RUN SAUVIGNON BLANC
●●● ▶ $13.95

Made in a deliberately direct, unwooded style, with the gently crisp, faintly herbaceous style one has come to expect from this variety grown on Coonawarra's terra rossa soils.

Cellaring None required. **Best Vintages** NA
Current Vintage '94
Matching Food Seafood, shellfish.

Tasting Note 1994 Light green-yellow; the bouquet is light, clean and crisp, but not particularly intense. The palate is likewise clean and crisp, well made, with just a hint of herbaceousness.

RYMILL RIDDOCH RUN SHIRAZ
●●●● ▶ $13.95

Produced entirely from estate-grown grapes, and matured in a mix of new and used French and American oak barrels. The wine has always been potent and concentrated, showing excellent varietal character and depth.

Cellaring 5–8 years. **Best Vintages** '90, '91, '92
Current Vintage '92
Matching Food Stuffed eggplant.
Tasting Note 1992 Vivid red-purple; a clean, firm bouquet with dark cherry fruit aromas of medium to full intensity and subtle oak. The palate shows similarly fresh and firm dark cherry fruit, with soft but persistent tannins, and oak in restraint.

SADDLERS CREEK WINES

★★★☆ 11.50–15 CD AUSSD
Hunter Valley **Est.** 1989
Marrowbone Road, Pokolbin, NSW 2321
Ph (049) 91 1770 **Fax** (049) 91 1778
Open 7 days 9–5 **Production** 5000
Winemaker(s) Craig Brown-Thomas
An impressive newcomer to the district producing consistently full-flavoured and rich wines, with the 1990 red wines showing lovely fresh, sweet fruit and the 1991 whites having the softness and concentration one expects from this vintage. No recent tastings.
Principal Wines Vosges Chardonnay, Traminer Riesling, Semillon Chardonnay, Semillon Sauvignon Blanc, Fumé Blanc, Hermitage, Cabernet Merlot, Bluegrass Cabernet Sauvignon.

SALISBURY ESTATE

★★★ 4.95–12.95 R AUS75 95, 107, 109, 137 UK101 US5, 6
Murray River **Est.** 1977
Campbell Avenue, Irymple, Vic 3498
Ph (050) 24 6800 **Fax** (050) 24 6605
Open Mon–Sat 10–4.30 **Production** 150 000
Winemaker(s) Bob Shields
The 150,000-case production under the various group labels is but a fraction of the total amount produced each year (around 4 million litres). Alambie has recently acquired a 176-hectare vineyard near Loxton, planted by French interests 25 years ago, with a very interesting varietal mix, and which has produced the two unusual Castle Crossing reds. White wine quality is, however, drug-dependent on the use of American oak chips.
Principal Wines Top-end wines under Milburn Park label: Chardonnay, Cabernet Sauvignon; under the Salisbury Estate label: Show Reserve Chardonnay, Show Reserve Cabernet Sauvignon. Then standard Salisbury Estate range: Rhine Riesling, Chardonnay Semillon, Sauvignon Blanc Semillon, Chardonnay, Cabernet Sauvignon, Cabernet Merlot; cheaper Castle Crossing range: Fumé Blanc, Colombard Chardonnay, Spatlese Rhine Riesling, Chenin Blanc, Chambourcin, Shiraz Malbec Morvedre (sic), Claret; Acacia Ridge non vintage generics bring up the rear, with two wines in the Tennyson Vineyard off to one side.

SALISBURY ESTATE CASTLE CROSSING CHAMBOURCIN
●●● ▸ $5.50
Chambourcin, is a French-bred hybrid hitherto mainly produced by

Cassegrain in the Hastings Valley of northern New South Wales, where its resistance to the mildews comes in very handy. The Castle Crossing wine comes from 4 hectares of contracted shareholder vineyards in north west Victoria. It shares the same vivid colour of the Cassegrain Chambourcins.

Cellaring Drink now. **Best Vintages** NA **Current Vintage** '94
Matching Food Pasta, eggplant.
Tasting Note 1994 Bin CC2. Vivid purple-red; the bouquet is clean with juicy blackcurrant/berry fruit aromas. The palate is ripe, full and juicy, and not extractive, although it does dip slightly on the back palate. Best served slightly chilled.

SALISBURY ESTATE CASTLE CROSSING SHIRAZ MALBEC MORVEDRE
●●●● $5.50

Notwithstanding the inability to spell mourvedre on the label or the supporting press material, this is an interesting wine of real quality and style. It is a blend of 50% shiraz, 33% malbec and 17% mourvedre grown on the newly-acquired Alambie Vineyard at New Residence near Loxton, planted by French owners 25 years ago — hence the Rhone varieties.

Cellaring Drink now. **Best Vintages** NA **Current Vintage** '93
Matching Food Cassoulet.
Tasting Note 1993 Bin CC1. Medium red-purple; a soft, jammy/juicy bouquet with some spicy/chippy notes. The palate is most attractive with genuine echoes of the Rhone Valley, particularly in the feel, balance and fine tannins of the wine.

SALITAGE *

★★★★☆ 19–29.99 R AUSSD US2
Warren Valley **Est.** 1989
Vasse Highway, Pemberton, WA 6260
Ph (097) 76 1195 **Fax** (097) 76 1504
Open 7 days 10–4 **Production** 3500
Winemaker(s) John Wade (Consultant), Patrick Coutts
Salitage is the showpiece of Pemberton. If it had failed to live up to expectations, it is a fair bet the same fate would have befallen the whole of the Pemberton region. After an unconvincing start with its 1992 vintage wines, Salitage has dispelled those doubts with its '93 Chardonnay and Pinot Noir, and with the erection of a state-of-the-art winery in 1994, one can only expect that as the vines mature, already impressive quality will rise higher.
Principal Wines Chardonnay, Sauvignon Blanc, Pinot Noir.

SALITAGE CHARDONNAY
●●●● ▶ $25.99

The chardonnay plantings of just under 12 hectares comprise 60% of the total estate plantings. Various trellis designs are used, including conventional VSP, Scott Henry and Te Kauwhata two-tier. The wine is barrel fermented in new French oak and matured on yeast lees for seven months before bottling.

Cellaring 3–5 years. **Best Vintages** '93, '94
Current Vintage '93
Matching Food West Australian marron.
Tasting Note 1993 Medium to full yellow-green; the bouquet is as complex and stylish as one would expect with nutty barrel ferment characters along with passionfruit and grapefruit aromas. The palate is fine and elegant, of moderate intensity with melon and citrus flavours, and judiciously balanced oak which does not overwhelm the fairly delicate fruit.

SALITAGE PINOT NOIR
●●●● ▶ $29.99
Pemberton has had various prophets, notably Dr John Gladstones and Gerard Potel, co-owner of the distinguished Burgundy producer Domaine De la Pousse d'Or, not to mention Salitage's owner and founder John Horgan. The climate is eerily close to that of Burgundy, while the gravelly ironstone soils of Salitage (as opposed to the deep Karri loams of the region) seem ideally suited to the grape.
Cellaring 3–4 years. **Best Vintages** '93 **Current Vintage** '93
Matching Food Barbecued quail.
Tasting Note 1993 Medium red-purple; obvious varietal character of medium intensity, with cherry/strawberry fruit aromas, and some more spicy/sappy notes. The palate is of moderate intensity with a similar blend of sappy/spicy/strawberry/cherry flavours, with a long finish. Infinitely better than the '92.

SALITAGE SAUVIGNON BLANC
●●● ▶ $19
With less than one hectare planted, the Sauvignon Blanc will not be a major part of the Salitage production. It is tank fermented, neither needing nor, indeed, being able to stand up to oak.
Cellaring Drink now. **Best Vintages** NA **Current Vintage** '94
Matching Food Asparagus salad.
Tasting Note 1994 Light to medium yellow-green; a light, crisp and clean palate with gentle herbaceous fruit. The palate is fairly light; it will be interesting to see whether the fruit weight intensifies as the vines age.

SALTRAM WINERY
★★★★ 8.95–45 R AUS176
Barossa Valley **Est.** 1859
Angaston Road, Angaston, SA 5353
Ph (085) 64 3355 **Fax** (095) 64 3384
Open 7 days 10–5 **Production** 180 000
Winemaker(s) Nigel Dolan
Now part of the Rothbury group with former owner Seagram a major shareholder in Rothbury. With Nigel Dolan as winemaker, and with Rothbury in charge, one can only assume that Saltram will indeed emerge from the deep sleep it entered into during its long ownership by the multinational giant Seagram.

Principal Wines At the top end Pinnacle Chardonnay, Riesling and Coonawarra Cabernet Sauvignon; next Mamre Brook Chardonnay, Cabernet Shiraz; next Private Reserve Eden Valley Chardonnay, Sauvignon Blanc, Cabernet Malbec; then Classic Chardonnay, Rhine Riesling, Sauvignon Blanc, Semillon, Cabernet Sauvignon, Shiraz. Mr Pickwick is deluxe Tawny Port.

SALTRAM CLASSIC SHIRAZ
●●● ▶ $8.95
Since its introduction in 1990, the Classic range of Saltram has always provided excellent value for money, the Chardonnay when young, the Semillon and Shiraz with age. This wine is 100% shiraz from Langhorne Creek and has three show medals to its credit. The oak used is said to be French, but one wonders whether a little American oak did not find its way in through the cracks.
Cellaring 2–3 years. **Best Vintages** '84, '86, '90, '92
Current Vintage '92
Matching Food Barbecued lamb chops.
Tasting Note 1992 Medium to full red-purple; the aromas are clean with dark berry, a hint of anise and creamy/vanillin oak. The palate has abundant cedar and spice flavours, replete with soft tannins. At its peak over the next year or two.

SALTRAM MR PICKWICK TAWNY PORT
●●●●● $45
One of Australia's best known Tawny Ports made from Barossa shiraz and grenache, and judiciously using a blend of very old and much younger material.
Cellaring Not required. **Best Vintages** NA
Current Vintage NV
Matching Food After dinner.
Tasting Note NV Light to medium tawny, with just a hint of red; there is pronounced rancio with a hint of spice and clean, penetrating spirit on the bouquet. The palate is well balanced, showing a range of nutty/nutmeg/spice flavours with a clean, lingering finish, showing the skilled blending of younger and older material. Good acidity.

SALTRAM PINNACLE CHARDONNAY
●●●● ▶ $19.95
A blend of 78% Eden Valley and 22% Barossa Valley chardonnay, given the full treatment of barrel fermentation in new French oak and prolonged lees contact thereafter. The '93 has won two gold, five silver and two bronze medals in national shows and, in my view, is a significantly better wine than the trophy-winning Mamre Brook Chardonnay of the same vintage.
Cellaring 2 years. **Best Vintages** '90, '92, '93
Current Vintage '93
Matching Food Weisswurst.
Tasting Note 1993 Glowing yellow-green; fragrant melon and citrus fruit on the bouquet with subtle barrel ferment oak. The palate is lively with distinct peach and tropical fruit flavours together with

some cashew notes, with the French oak nicely balanced and integrated.

SALTRAM PINNACLE RIESLING
●●●● $14.95

New brand manager, new label; so it is with the Pinnacle range. In this instance, it is a distinct improvement in a modern, minimalist style. That apart, the wine is 100% Eden Valley and the 1994 vintage should develop tremendously well with age.
Cellaring 4–7 years. **Best Vintages** '84, '86, '90, '92, '93
Current Vintage '94
Matching Food Fillet of fish in beurre blanc.
Tasting Note 1994 Light green-yellow; a fragrant, toasty floral bouquet with hints of spice. A reserved style on the palate which needs time to build on the floral, spice and citrus fruit of the palate, which finishes with appropriately balanced acid.

SALTRAM STONYFELL METALA CABERNET SHIRAZ
●●●● ▸ $15

An historic label which has retained extraordinary goodwill notwithstanding years of neglect and inferior vintages. 1993 was the first vintage made by current Saltram chief winemaker Nigel Dolan, and marks a complete reversal in the quality of this Langhorne Creek-based blend of cabernet (68%) and shiraz (32%).
Cellaring Up to 5 years. **Best Vintages** NA
Current Vintage '93
Matching Food Spiced beef.
Tasting Note 1993 Youthful red-purple; a clean, bright and fresh bouquet with lively, spicy berry fruit leads on to a palate showing similar fresh cherry/berry fruit, with good fruit weight and depth. Attractive now but will age well.

SAMPHIRE WINES

NR 7 CD AUSSD
Adelaide Hills **Est.** 1982
Watts Gully Road Cnr Robertson Road, Kersbrook, SA 5231
Ph (08) 389 3183
Open 7 days 9–6 by appt **Production** 67
Winemaker(s) Tom Miller
Next after Scarp Valley, the smallest winery in Australia offering wine for sale; pottery also helps. Tom Miller has one of the more interesting and diverse CVs, with an early interest in matters alcoholic leading to the premature but happy death of a laboratory rat at Adelaide University and his enforced switch from biochemistry to mechanical engineering.
Principal Wines Riesling.

SAND HILLS VINEYARD

★★★ 7–9 CD AUSSD
Central West New South Wales **Est.** 1920
Sandhills Road, Forbes, NSW 2871

Ph (068) 52 1437
Open Mon–Sat 9–5, Sun 12–5 **Production** 435
Winemaker(s) John Saleh
Having purchased Sand Hills from long-term owner Jacques Genet,
the Saleh family have set about replanting the vineyard to
appropriate varieties, with 2.25 hectares of premium varieties
having been established between 1989 and 1993. These are
supplemented by grapes purchased elsewhere.
Principal Wines White Burgundy, Traminer Riesling, Shiraz,
Shiraz Pinot Noir, Pinot Noir.

SAND HILLS SHIRAZ
●● ▸ $9
Received a bronze medal at the 1994 New South Wales Small
Winemakers Wine Show, and is a sound wine, interesting for its
unusual region of origin.
Cellaring 2–3 years. **Best Vintages** NA **Current Vintage** '93
Matching Food Spiced sausage.
Tasting Note 1993 Medium purple-red; the bouquet is direct, of
medium intensity, with faintly earthy/gravelly shiraz fruit. The palate
is sweeter, with berry/strawberry flavours, simple and direct.

SANDALFORD WINES

★★★☆ 11.85–16.80 R AUS76, 130, 137, 185, UK14
Swan Valley & Margaret River **Est.** 1840
West Swan Road, Caversham, WA 6055
Ph (09) 274 5922 **Fax** (09) 274 2154
Open 7 days 10–5 **Production** 83 000
Winemaker(s) Bill Crappsley
The arrival of Bill Crappsley as winemaker and installation of Ted
Avery as general manager, coupled with the refurbishment of the
winery, have heralded major changes at Sandalford. Wine quality
has improved markedly, although as Bill Crappsley himself says,
'We know we've got a long way to go'.
Principal Wines At the bottom end under the Caversham label:
Premium Dry White, Chenin Blanc, Verdelho, Cabernet Shiraz; then
the 1840 Collection: Classic 'R', Classic Dry Red, Classic
Chardonnay; premium range Margaret River label: Riesling, Late
Harvest Riesling, Verdelho, Cabernet Sauvignon, Shiraz; Mount
Barker Riesling; at the top of the range: Margaret River/Pemberton
Chardonnay and Margaret River/Mount Barker Shiraz; also
excellent fortifieds, notably Sandalera.

SANDALFORD 1840 COLLECTION CLASSIC DRY WHITE
●●● ▸ $12.95
The striking 1840 Collection label was introduced in 1993
emphasising that Sandalford was in fact founded in 1840, although
its winemaking activities did not commence until this century. The
Classic Dry White is a Margaret River estate-grown blend of
unspecified varieties, but presumably drawing upon the estate
plantings of sauvignon blanc, chenin blanc, semillon, verdelho
and riesling.

Cellaring Drink now. **Best Vintages** NA
Current Vintage '94
Matching Food West Australian crayfish.
Tasting Note 1994 Light green-yellow; a fragrant bouquet with floral/passionfruit aromas of light to medium intensity. The palate is similarly high-toned and floral, with some herbal and lemony characters also present, all attesting to what is seemingly a complex varietal blend. Finishes with lively acid.

SANDALFORD MARGARET RIVER/MOUNT BARKER SHIRAZ
●●● ▶ $17
As the name indicates, a blend of Margaret River and Mount Barker grapes, and a new label for Sandalford. In common with the other releases made between the end of 1994 and early 1995, shows a distinct lift in quality.
Cellaring 2–4 years. **Best Vintages** NA
Current Vintage '93
Matching Food Rabbit casserole.
Tasting Note 1993 Medium red; intriguing eucalypt/leaf/bark overtones to more traditional spicy/plummy fruit. The palate is clean, with an array of red berry flavours running through to more leafy/minty notes. Oak in restraint.

SANDALFORD MARGARET RIVER PEMBERTON CHARDONNAY
●●●● $15.95
A blend of Mount Barker and Margaret River grapes which have been barrel fermented in high quality oak to produce a wine of real style and substance, worthy of Bill Crappsley's skills as a winemaker, and auguring particularly well for the future.
Cellaring 3–4 years. **Best Vintages** '93, '94
Current Vintage '94
Matching Food Marron.
Tasting Note 1994 Light to medium yellow-green; attractive, lifted fragrant melon and citrus fruit, with subtle barrel ferment oak characters. The palate is harmonious, balanced and stylish, with elegant melon, fig and citrus fruit interwoven with subtle, spicy oak.

SANDALFORD MARGARET RIVER VERDELHO
●●● ▶ $14.95
Produced from 14.5 hectares of estate plantings; next to riesling (56 hectares) and cabernet sauvignon (25 hectares), verdelho is the most important grape in the Margaret River province. It is made without the use of oak to produce a wine which benefits substantially from medium-term cellaring.
Cellaring 3–5 years. **Best Vintages** '87, '88, '91, '93, '94
Current Vintage '94
Matching Food Prosciutto and melon.
Tasting Note 1994 Light to medium yellow-green; a lively bouquet with tropical/ melon/honeysuckle aromas. The palate is similarly lively and crisp, with lemony flavours lingering on the finish.

SANDSTONE WINES

★★★☆ 18.75 R AUS26, 47, 64
Margaret River **Est.** 1988
Lot 5 Caves Road, Willyabrup via Cowaramup, WA 6284
Ph (097) 55 6271 **Fax** (097) 55 6292
Open Not **Production** 1200
Winemaker(s) Mike Davies
The family operation of consultant winemakers Mike and Jan Davies,
who also operate very successful mobile bottling plants. The wines
are made at Ribbonvale, where the Davies work as consultants and
contract winemakers for others.
Principal Wines Semillon, Cabernet Sauvignon.

SANDSTONE SEMILLON

●●● ▶ $20.95
Prior vintages of this wine have often shown pronounced American
oak influence which has added to the impact of the wine but was not
really to my taste. In the '93 vintage the strong varietal fruit has been
allowed to make its own statement.
Cellaring 5+ years. **Best Vintages** '92, '93
Current Vintage '93
Matching Food Avocado with seafood.
Tasting Note 1993 Medium yellow-green; the bouquet has
abundant character and varietal bite, with powerful citrus-accented
fruit and little or no oak influence apparent. The palate, too, is
powerful and concentrated with tangy but ripe semillon fruit driving
a long finish.

SCARBOROUGH WINES

★★★★☆ 18.50 CD AUSSD
Hunter Valley **Est.** 1985
Gillards Road, Pokolbin, NSW 2321
Ph (049) 98 7563 **Fax** (049) 98 7786
Open 7 days 9–5 **Production** 5000
Winemaker(s) Ian Scarborough
Ian Scarborough put his white winemaking skills beyond doubt
during his years as a consultant, and his exceptionally complex and
stylish Chardonnay is no disappt. Marketing and promotion,
however, remain at a low level.
Principal Wines Chardonnay; token quantities of Pinot Noir.

SCARBOROUGH CHARDONNAY

●●●● ▶ $18.50
Produced from 9 hectares of estate plantings, and made in a
deliberately full-blown fashion, with masses of fruit and well handled
and integrated oak. These are big wines, but have the structure to
age remarkably well.
Cellaring 3–7 years. **Best Vintages** '87, '89, '91, '93, '94
Current Vintage '91
Matching Food Pork spare ribs.

Tasting Note 1991 Glowing yellow-green; concentrated peachy/honeyed/buttery fruit with spicy nutmeg oak. A big, ripe honeyed style in the mouth, with a long, smooth lingering finish.

SCARBOROUGH PINOT NOIR
●●●● $18.50
Only 500 cases of Pinot are produced from the one hectare of estate plantings, and are made simply to present some variety at cellar door. Ian Scarborough is a skilled winemaker, and cannot help but make an attractive red wine, even if it does not have a great deal of pinot varietal character.
Cellaring 2–3 years. **Best Vintages** NA
Current Vintage '90
Matching Food Rabbit.
Tasting Note 1990 Red with a tawny rim; a sweet Hunter dry red on the bouquet with good vinosity but little evident varietal character. On the palate a lively wine with a touch of lift, and pleasant tannin grip on the finish; will develop into an attractive regional style.

SCARP VALLEY WINES

NR 15 ML AUSSD
Perth Hills **Est.** 1978
6 Robertson Road, Gooseberry Hill, WA 6076
Ph (09) 454 5748
Open Not **Production** 27
Winemaker(s) Peter Fimmel (Contract)
Owner Robert Duncan presides over what has to be the smallest producer in Australia, with one-quarter acre of shiraz producing a single cask of wine each year if the birds do not get the grapes first. Recently-introduced netting should help alleviate that problem. The 1990 vintage, tasted in March '93, was a pleasant wine, light and clean with gently minty fruit, and can be found in local Perth Hills restaurants and liquor stores.
Principal Wines Hermitage.

SCARPANTONI ESTATES

NR 10.95–17.95 R AUS1, 68, 118 UK76
Southern Vales **Est.** 1979
Scarpantoni Drive, McLaren Flat, SA 5171
Ph (08) 383 0186 **Fax** (08) 383 0490
Open 7 days 10–5 **Production** 10 000
Winemaker(s) Michael Scarpantoni, Filippo Scarpantoni
A somewhat erratic performer; the red wines and Botrytis Riesling are best, and occasionally very good.
Principal Wines Riesling Block One, Sauvignon Blanc, Chardonnay, Gamay, School Block (Cabernet Shiraz Merlot), Shiraz Block Three, Cabernet Sauvignon, Botrytis Riesling.

SCHMIDTS TARCHALICE

NR 7.25–20.60 CD AUSSD
Barossa Valley **Est.** 1984
Research Road, Vine Vale via Tanunda, SA 5352
Ph (085) 63 3005 **Fax** (085) 63 0667
Open Mon–Sat 10–5, Sun 12–5 **Production** NFP
Winemaker(s) Christopher Schmidt
In late 1994 two 1985 vintage Rieslings were on offer at $7.25, with
a range of other wines from the 1980s and only one from 1991.
Principal Wines Barossa Riesling, Eden Valley Riesling, Barossa
Chardonnay, Barossa Semillon, Gewurztraminer, Auslese Riesling,
Shiraz Cabernet/Cabernet Franc, Walter's Blend, Fortifieds.

SCOTCHMANS HILL VINEYARDS

★★★★ 17.95 R AUS11 UK49
Geelong **Est.** 1982
Scotchmans Road, Drysdale, Vic 3222
Ph (052) 51 3176 **Fax** (052) 53 1743
Open 7 days 10.30–4.30 **Production** 14 000
Winemaker(s) Robin Brockett
In fact situated on the Bellarine Peninsula, south east of Geelong,
with a very well-equipped winery and first-class vineyards. Was a
tremendously consistent performer with its Pinot Noir up to 1992, but
for one reason or another, I have not tasted the '93 or '94 vintages.
The '94 Sauvignon Blanc is clean, crisp, direct but light bodied.
Principal Wines Riesling, Sauvignon Blanc, Chardonnay, Pinot
Noir, Cabernet Merlot.

SCOTTS BROOK *

NR 9.95–13.99 CD AUSSD
Warren Valley **Est.** 1987
Scotts Brook Road, Boyup Brook, WA 6244
Ph (097) 65 3014 **Fax** (097) 65 3030
Open W'ends, School hols 10–5 or by appt **Production** 800
Winemaker(s) Elaine Washer (Contract)
Boyup Brook is in fact more or less equidistant between the Margaret
River and Great Southern regions and has been developed by local
schoolteachers Brian Walker and wife Kerry — hence the opening
hours during school holidays. There are 5.5 hectares of vineyards;
contract making to date has given surprisingly variable results, with
the Alsace-like 1993 Riesling being by far the best wine, possessing
lots of character.
Principal Wines Rhine Riesling, Autumn Harvest White,
Chardonnay, Soft Red, Cabernet Sauvignon.

SEAVIEW

★★★★☆ 8.95–24.50 R AUS147 UK83 US11
Southern Vales **Est.** 1850
Chaffey's Road, McLaren Vale, SA 5171

Ph (08) 323 8250 **Fax** (08) 323 9308
Open Mon–Fri 9–4, Sat 11–5, Sun 11–4 **Production** 500 000
Winemaker(s) Mike Farmillo
A maker of sturdy, reliable white wines, red wines which are
frequently absurdly underpriced and perhaps suffer in consequence
and, of course, some of the country's best known sparkling wines,
which have gone from strength to strength over recent years.
Principal Wines Increasingly tied to McLaren Vale, with only the
Riesling and the sparkling wines using fruit from outside the region.
Riesling, Chardonnay, Semillon Sauvignon Blanc, White Burgundy,
Sauvignon Blanc, Shiraz, Cabernet Sauvignon make up the basic
range. Recently introduced super-luxury Edwards & Chaffey range of
Shiraz, Cabernet Sauvignon, Methode Champenoise, the latter
replacing Edmond Mazure.

SEAVIEW CABERNET SAUVIGNON
●●●● $10.50
A vertical tasting of over 20 vintages going back to 1972 carried
out in mid 1993 showed a remarkably consistent wine which does
have the capacity to age without ever aspiring to ultimate greatness.
The '92 vintage moves back predominantly to McLaren Vale with
small components from Coonawarra, Barossa and Padthaway, and
was matured in American and French oak for 12 months.
Cellaring 3–7 years. **Best Vintages** '76, '85, '86, '90, '91
Current Vintage '92
Matching Food Steak and kidney pie.
Tasting Note 1992 Medium to full red-purple; a complex bouquet
with cedar and cigar box aromas over concentrated dark chocolate
fruit. The palate has plenty of concentration with dark berry and
chocolate flavours finishing appropriately firm tannins.

SEAVIEW CHARDONNAY
●●●● $9.95
Made entirely from McLaren Vale chardonnay. Part was barrel
fermented in French oak, and part of the wine was matured on yeast
lees for three months and underwent malolactic fermentation prior to
blending.
Cellaring 1–2 years. **Best Vintages** '90, '92, '93, '94
Current Vintage '94
Matching Food Smoked chicken.
Tasting Note 1994 Medium to full yellow-green; a complex
bouquet showing the making effort which has gone into it, and also
showing a considerable amount of oak influence. The palate is
generous, full-bodied and ripe with tropical peachy fruit and well
handled oak.

SEAVIEW CHARDONNAY METHODE CHAMPENOISE
●●●●● $12.95
First made in 1991, and immediately caught the eye. The 1992 is
made from 100% chardonnay grown in the Adelaide Hills and Eden
Valley, and spends 18 months on yeast lees before disgorgement.
The '92 vintage was a trophy and gold medal winner at national
wine shows.

Cellaring Drink now. **Best Vintages** NA **Current Vintage** '92
Matching Food Aperitif, sweeter seafood dishes.
Tasting Note 1992 Light straw-yellow; a complex bouquet with
attractive yeasty autolysis aromas and creamy fruit. The palate is
fine and tangy with citrussy/lemony fruit and a perfectly-judged
dosage level.

SEAVIEW EDWARDS & CHAFFEY CABERNET SAUVIGNON
●●●●● $24.95
The sister wine to the Edwards & Chaffey Shiraz of the same year,
made from old, low-yielding McLaren Vale Cabernet and matured in
new French oak for 18 months. Won three trophies and three gold
medals in 1994, and shows that anything Wynns or Penfolds can
do, so can Seaview.
Cellaring 10–15 years. **Best Vintages** NA
Current Vintage '92
Matching Food Leave it in the cellar.
Tasting Note 1992 Medium to full red-purple; rich, ripe vanilla
and berry aromas with masses of spicy oak. The palate is dense,
with chocolate, plum and blackberry fruit flavours hiding in the forest
of French oak.

SEAVIEW EDWARDS & CHAFFEY SHIRAZ
●●●● ▶ $24.50
The newly-introduced super premium label of Seaview, honouring its
founders F H Edwards and W B Chaffey, who launched the brand
in 1951. The wine is made from old low-yielding vines and was
matured in new French and American oak for 18 months. It has
won three gold medals at national wine shows.
Cellaring 10–15 years. **Best Vintages** NA
Current Vintage '92
Matching Food Leave it in the cellar.
Tasting Note 1992 Dense red-purple; strongly textured American
oak and concentrated dark berry/briary/chocolatey fruit. A power-
packed, hugely oaky wine with tremendous extract and rather drying
American oak tannins which need years to soften.

SEAVIEW PINOT CHARDONNAY METHODE CHAMPENOISE
●●●●● $12.95
A very complex blend of pinot noir and chardonnay sourced
predominantly from Coonawarra, Padthaway and the Eden Valley
in South Australia, but with small components from the New South
Wales Alps, Strathbogie Ranges of Victoria and Adelaide Hills. It
spends two years on yeast lees before disgorgement.
Cellaring NA. **Best Vintages** NA **Current Vintage** '92
Matching Food Oysters.
Tasting Note 1992 Medium to full straw-yellow; a complex
bouquet with bready/biscuity/toast crumb aromas. A full-blown
wine on the palate with sweet creamy/biscuity/bready mid-palate
flavours and a faintly peppery finish.

SEAVIEW SHIRAZ

●●●● ▶ $9.95

Introduced in 1992 as part of the repositioning and refocusing of the
Seaview range. Prior to 1992 there was a Shiraz Cabernet which
was sourced from many South Australian regions. This wine
effectively replaces it, and is a distinct improvement.

Cellaring 5–7 years. **Best Vintages** NA **Current Vintage** '92
Matching Food Lamb shashlik.

Tasting Note 1992 Full red-purple; the bouquet is solid with plenty
of depth and extract, an authentic hint of varietal gaminess, a touch
of plum and oak in restraint. The palate is similarly well constructed
with plenty of dark berry and chocolate fruit, good tannins and spicy
oak.

SEAVIEW WHITE BURGUNDY

●●●● ▶ $9.95

A blend of 70% semillon and 30% sauvignon blanc from McLaren
Vale. A portion of the blend was barrel fermented in French and
American oak casks, and 60% was oak matured on yeast lees for
three months, with selected components undergoing malolactic
fermentation prior to final blending. Not a bad effort for an
unashamedly commercial wine, and it shows in the quality which is
outstanding for the price.

Cellaring Drink now. **Best Vintages** NA **Current Vintage** '94
Matching Food Sashimi.

Tasting Note 1994 Brilliant green-yellow; a soft bouquet with
gently tropical fruit salad aromas touched with gooseberry. The
palate is hyper-commercial with very attractive sweet fruit and hints
of smokiness providing complexity without aggression.

SELDOM SEEN VINEYARD

NR 11–13 CD AUS75
Mudgee **Est.** 1987
Craigmoor Road, Mudgee, NSW 2850
Ph (063) 72 4482 **Fax** (063) 72 1055
Open 7 days 9.30–5 **Production** 4000
Winemaker(s) Barry Platt

A major grape grower which reserves a proportion of its crop for
making and release under its own label. Quality has been
inconsistent.

Principal Wines Semillon, Chardonnay Semillon, Chardonnay,
Traminer, Cabernet Shiraz.

SEPPELT

★★★★★ 20–2600 R AUS147 UK83 US11
Barossa Valley **Est.** 1850
Seppletsfield via Tanunda, SA 5352
Ph (085) 62 8028 **Fax** (085) 62 8333
Open Mon–Fri 8.30–5, Sat 10.30–4.30, Sun 11–4
Production NFP
Winemaker(s) James Godfrey

A multi-million dollar expansion and renovation program has seen the historic Seppeltsfield winery become the production centre for the Seppelt wines, adding another dimension to what was already the most historic and beautiful major winery in Australia. It is now home to some unique fortified wines.

Principal Wines The great wines of Seppeltsfield are first and foremost Para Liqueur Port, Show Tawny Port DP90, Seppeltsfield Fino Sherry and Dorrien Cabernet Sauvignon. The other wines in the Seppelt portfolio are handled at Great Western. The 1894 Para Liqueur Port is the $2600-a-bottle jewel in the crown.

SEPPELT 100 YEAR OLD PARA LIQUEUR PORT
●●●●● $2600

Every year since 1986 Seppelt has made a tiny release of 100 Year Old Para Port, kept in cask for a century and not diluted or maintained by a solera system of topping up. In other words, it is a true vintage wine. Made from Barossa shiraz and grenache, the analysis of the 1894 vintage tells just how much it has concentrated with age: 16.25° baume, 25.5% alcohol and 10.8 grams per litre of acid, with a pH of 3.68. The baume and acid levels have more than doubled over the years as the wine has become incredibly concentrated.

Cellaring NA. **Best Vintages** 1886, 1887, 1890, 1892, 1894
Current Vintage 1894
Matching Food The finest quality double expresso coffee.
Tasting Note 1894 Deep olive brown in colour; powerful aromas of briar, chocolate, earth, plum pudding and toffee lead on to a wine of almost unbelievable intensity, hugely powerful with dark briary/berry/plum pudding flavours and surprisingly powerful tannins. The acid is a perfect counter-balance to the intensely sweet and rich mid palate.

SEPPELT DORRIEN CABERNET SAUVIGNON
●●●●● $26

Based upon the Seppelt Dorrien Vineyard in the Barossa Valley from which it takes its name, sometimes including small components of Coonawarra and Langhorne Creek, and a dab of merlot here and there. Two years maturation in French Nevers oak always gives the wine tremendous impact. Only released when the quality is considered sufficiently high, once in any two years on average. A prolific trophy and gold medal show winner in recent years.

Cellaring 10+ years. **Best Vintages** '88, '89, '90, '91
Current Vintage '90
Matching Food Rare fillet of beef.
Tasting Note 1990 Medium red, with some purple hues remaining. An exceptionally aromatic and fragrant bouquet with fused fruit and oak cedar, leaf and vanillin aromas. A potent wine with briary, blackcurrant fruit with cedar and vanilla, and a long finish.

SEPPELT PARA LIQUEUR VINTAGE TAWNY PORT
●●●●● $27

Reintroduced as a vintage-dated wine in 1992, when the 1976 wine was released. Henceforth a 15-year-old vintage Para will be released each year, the 1977 being released in late 1993 and the 1979 in early 1995. It is made from shiraz and grenache grown in the Barossa Valley, and is a quite unique style.

Cellaring NA. **Best Vintages** NA **Current Vintage** '77
Matching Food Coffee and petits fours.

Tasting Note 1977 Pale golden-tawny; infinitely complex bouquet of brandysnap biscuit, toffee, nuts and faint tea-leaf run through the bouquet, while the palate is rich and raisiny, with luscious fruit on the mid palate finishing with appropriate acidity.

SEPPELT SHOW FINO SHERRY BIN DP117
●●●●● $27

Made from Barossa-grown palomino and matured in a traditional floor Sherry solera system of small casks. The wine remains under a floor yeast for a minimum of seven years before the long process of final blending takes place. A prolific trophy and gold medal winner at Australian shows.

Cellaring None required. **Best Vintages** NA
Current Vintage NV
Matching Food Consommé.

Tasting Note NV Light straw-yellow; penetrating floor aromas which almost defy description, having a penetrating mineral and nutty aroma. The flavour is almost tingling in its dryness, with a powerful, cleansing finish.

SEPPELT SHOW TAWNY PORT BIN DP90
●●●●● $45

DP90 has an average age of 21 years, blended from the reserve stocks of very old Tawny Port made from Barossa Valley shiraz and grenache, with a little cabernet sauvignon. Between 1968 and 1991 alone DP90 won 30 trophies and 106 gold medals at Australian wine shows, making it the most awarded wine of any style. It is intermittently released in limited quantities.

Cellaring None required. **Best Vintages** NA
Current Vintage NV
Matching Food The ultimate winter aperitif.

Tasting Note NV Light golden-tawny; the bouquet is incredibly penetrating and fine, with intense rancio and an underlay of caramel and spice. The palate is relatively light-bodied, yet piercingly intense, with sweet faintly raisiny fruit on the mid palate, finishing with cleansing acidity.

SEPPELT GREAT WESTERN

★★★★★ 5.95–38 AUS147 UK83 US11
Great Western **Est.** 1866
Moyston Road, Great Western, Vic 3377
Ph (053) 61 2222 **Fax** (053) 61 2200
Open Mon–Sat 9–5, Sun 12–5 **Production** NFP
Winemaker(s) Ian McKenzie (Chief)

Australia's foremost producer of sparkling wine, always immaculate in its given price range, but also producing excellent Great Western-

sourced table wines, especially long-lived Hermitage and Australia's
best Sparkling Burgundies. Now the production centre for many
Southcorp group brands, with a vast new bottling plant and
attendant warehouse facilities.
Principal Wines Methode Champenoise comprising (from the
bottom up) Brut Reserve, Imperial Reserve, Rosé Brut, Fleur de Lys,
Vintage Brut and Salinger; also various varietal and regional
sparkling wines of high quality; also premium regional Chardonnay,
Riesling, Hermitage; finally various brands including the much-
diminished Chalambar and Moyston.

SEPPELT GREAT WESTERN COLIN PREECE DRY RED
●●●●● $NA
Ever so rarely, some of these wines may come up at auctions in
Australia. If ever you see the distinctive white label with its Seppelt
crest and simple black typing, and the wine in the bottle is not
unduly ullaged, be prepared to offer a lot for the wine — and still
expect to get a bargain. These wines are some of the greatest made
this century, standing alongside the masterpieces of Maurice
O'Shea, Roger Warren and Max Schubert.
Cellaring None required. **Best Vintages** NA
Current Vintage NA
Matching Food Australian parmesan.
Tasting Note 1962 CH20 Burgundy. A wine which took almost
30 years to come into full flower, consistently tasting superbly in the
early 1990s. Medium to full red, with sweet, rich, ripe red berry fruit
aromas, and a marvellously supple palate, lush and full of dark
berries and soft dark chocolate flavours.

SEPPELT GREAT WESTERN CORELLA RIDGE CHARDONNAY
●●●●● $11.50
A Victorian-based blend, utilising grapes grown at Great Western
Avoca (in the Pyrenees), Strathbogie Ranges and the Mornington
Peninsula. The wine is 100% barrel fermented and taken through
partial malolactic fermentation, and is of exceptional quality and
style given its price.
Cellaring 2–5 years. **Best Vintages** '92, '93, '94
Current Vintage '94
Matching Food Grilled fish.
Tasting Note 1994 Medium yellow-green; a complex and stylish
bouquet with tangy melon and citrus fruit aromas attesting to the
cool climate origins of the wine. The palate is fine and long-
flavoured with melon, fig and citrus fruit, subtle oak and perfectly
balanced acidity.

SEPPELT GREAT WESTERN HERMITAGE
●●●●● $25
A wine made intermittently by Colin Preece (who was much given
to blending) and which disappeared altogether between 1975 and
1983 inclusive. Since its reappearance, it has been sourced

principally from a very old block of shiraz adjacent to the winery, which produces wine of tremendous style.

Cellaring 5–20 years. **Best Vintages** '54, '56, '60, '63, '71, '84, '85, '86, '91, '92, '93 **Current Vintage** '88

Matching Food Herbed rack of lamb.

Tasting Note 1988 Medium red-purple; the bouquet is fragrant and fresh, with mint and leaf aromas, and subtle oak. The palate is very minty, a character which I personally do not enjoy when it is as dominant as it is here; vanillin oak does provide some counterbalance.

SEPPELT GREAT WESTERN SALINGER METHODE CHAMPENOISE

●●●●● $24.95

Seppelt's flagship Methode Champenoise, made from a blend of pinot noir, chardonnay and pinot meuniere drawn primarily from the Tumbarumba and Tooma vineyards in the Snowy Mountains of New South Wales (at an altitude of 730 metres) and Seppelt's Drumborg Vineyard in southern Victoria, with a small proportion of grapes from New Zealand. There were three separate disgorgements of the 1990 wine, with a minimum of two and a half years and a maximum of four years on yeast lees.

Cellaring None required. **Best Vintages** '88, '89, '90 **Current Vintage** '90

Matching Food Aperitif, oysters, shellfish.

Tasting Note 1990 Bright, light yellow-green colour with good mousse; the bouquet is complex with bready/biscuity aromas indicating the influence of both the pinot noir and pinot meuniere components. The palate is clean, crisp, finely structured, with very good mouthfeel and balance.

SEPPELT GREAT WESTERN SHOW SPARKLING BURGUNDY

●●●●● $38

Made from old vine shiraz grown at Seppelt Great Western, matured in large oak casks for one year before tiraging, and then on yeast lees for nine to 10 years before disgorgement. Always an exceptionally complex wine, which will live for decades.

Cellaring Up to 20 years. **Best Vintages** '44, '46, '54, '61, '64, '67, '84, '85, '86, '87, '90, '91 **Current Vintage** '84

Matching Food Borscht.

Tasting Note 1984 Medium to full red; a distinctly peppery/spicy bouquet with clearcut and spotlessly clean cool-grown varietal shiraz aroma. The palate is lively and fresh, again with pronounced peppery/spicy flavours and a crisp finish. Idiosyncratic, but I personally like the style.

SEPPELT GREAT WESTERN SUNDAY CREEK PINOT NOIR

●●● $17

The maiden release by Seppelt of a Pinot Noir under its Victorian range. It is made from grapes grown on the Mornington Peninsula, at Ballarat and at Drumborg, taking its name from Sunday Creek which flows near the Drumborg vineyard in south western Victoria. It is neither a convincing nor unconvincing addition to the Victorian range.

Cellaring 1–2 years. **Best Vintages** NA **Current Vintage** '93
Matching Food Tortellini.

Tasting Note 1993 Medium red-purple; the bouquet is of medium intensity with ripe, briary/plummy fruit and minimal oak. The palate has reasonable weight, with similar slightly meaty/plummy flavours to those evident on the bouquet; riper and rather more four-square than one might expect from the vintage.

SERENELLA ESTATE

NR 7–22 CD AUSSD
Upper Hunter Valley **Est.** 1981
Mudgee Road, Baerami via Denman, NSW 2333
Ph (065) 47 5168 **Fax** (065) 47 5164
Open W'ends 10–4, Mon–Fri by appt **Production** NFP
Winemaker(s) Letitia Ceccini

A very substantial viticultural enterprise with 60 hectares of vineyards equally divided between sylvaner, semillon, chardonnay, shiraz and cabernet sauvignon. The last wines tasted in 1993 were of modest quality.

Principal Wines Chablis, White Burgundy, Semillon Sauvignon Blanc, White Hunter Late Harvest, Riesling, Sylvaner Chardonnay, Reserve Chardonnay, Serena's Bin Chardonnay, Bin GCC Chardonnay, Shiraz, Shiraz Show Wine, Cabernet Sauvignon, Cabernet Sauvignon Show Wine, Shiraz Cabernet.

SERVENTY WINES *

★★★ 11.60–12.50 CD AUS89, 150, UK95
Margaret River **Est.** 1984
Valley Home Vineyard, Rocky Road, Witchcliffe, WA 6286
Ph (097) 57 7535 **Fax** (097) 57 3541
Open Fri–Sun, Hols 10–4 **Production** 1500
Winemaker(s) Peter Serventy

Peter Serventy is nephew of the famous naturalist Vincent Serventy and son of ornithologist Dominic Serventy. It is hardly surprising, then, that Serventy should practise strict organic viticulture, using neither herbicides nor pesticides. The wines, too, are made with a minimum of sulphur dioxide, added late in the piece and never exceeding 30 parts per million.

Principal Wines Shiraz, Chardonnay, Pinot Noir.

SERVENTY SHIRAZ

●●●● $12.50
Produced from 1.5 hectares of estate shiraz in one of the coolest parts of the Margaret River. The style is very consistent: vibrantly, fragrantly spicy/peppery, intense but fairly light-bodied. The '92 vintage was awarded a gold medal at the 1993 Mount Barker Wine Show.

Cellaring 1–2 years. **Best Vintages** '90, '91, '92, '93
Current Vintage '93
Matching Food Asian beef dishes.
Tasting Note 1993 Light red-purple; the bouquet is fragrant with
light spicy/peppery overtones to cherry fruit. The palate is similarly
fragrant and peppery, it really needs a little more flesh on the bones,
particularly if it is to be cellared.

SEVENHILL CELLARS

★★★★ 9–15 CD AUS72, 76, 77, 123, 175
Clare Valley **Est.** 1851
College Road, Sevenhill via Clare, SA 5453
Ph (088) 43 4222 **Fax** (088) 43 4382
Open Mon–Fri 8.30–4.30, Sat, Public hols 8–4
Production 9300
Winemaker(s) Brother John May, John Monten
One of the historical treasures of Australia; the oft-photographed
stone wine cellars are the oldest in the Clare Valley, and
winemaking is still carried out under the direction of the Jesuitical
Manresea Society and, in particular, Brother John May.
Principal Wines St Aloysius (Chenin Blanc, Chardonnay,
Verdelho blend), Semillon, Riesling, College White, Traminer
Frontignac, St Ignatius (Cabernet Sauvignon, Malbec, Franc and
Merlot blend), Shiraz, Cabernet Sauvignon, Fortifieds,
Sacramental Wine.

SEVENHILL CELLARS CABERNET SAUVIGNON
●●●● ▶ $13
As with all of the Sevenhill reds, made in an heroic style. It is taken
from just under 10 hectares of estate vineyards, with mature and
relatively low-yielding vines adding to the authority of the wine
which needs patience.
Cellaring 10+ years.
Best Vintages '80, '87, '89, '91, '92
Current Vintage '92
Matching Food Leave it in the cellar.
Tasting Note 1992 Dense purple-red; ripe cassis and dark
chocolate fruit aromas with subtle oak. The palate is powerful, with
ripe dark berry and dark chocolate fruit, strong but not excessive
tannins, and oak largely swallowed up by the fruit. Give it another
five years at least.

SEVENHILL CELLARS RIESLING
●●●● $12
Produced from a fraction under 3 hectares of estate-grown riesling,
and more often than not very good, although it is always made with
relatively high levels of residual sugar.
Cellaring 2–5 years. **Best Vintages** '87, '89, '91, '92, '94
Current Vintage '94
Matching Food Antipasto.

Tasting Note 1994 Light to medium green-yellow; quite good floral fruit aromas with a hint of lift to the bouquet. The palate is quite powerful and potent with full lime fruit finishing with appreciable sweetness.

SEVENHILL CELLARS ST ALOYSIUS
●●● ▶ $12
Packaged in the distinctive ceramic glass bottle, and an unusual blend of chenin blanc, chardonnay and verdelho, the latter one of the larger plantings on the Sevenhill Cellars vineyards. The '92, '93 and '94 vintages of this wine have all been good, particularly the '92 and '93, the latter winning a silver medal at the Canberra Australian National Wine Show.
Cellaring Drink now. **Best Vintages** '92, '93
Current Vintage '94
Matching Food Grilled spatchcock.
Tasting Note 1994 Light to medium green-yellow; a full bouquet with fruit salad aromas married with vanillin oak. A full-bodied wine on the palate with rich tropical/fruit salad flavours and ever-so-slightly oily oak.

SEVENHILL CELLARS ST IGNATIUS
●●● ▶ $15
A blend of cabernet sauvignon, malbec, cabernet franc and merlot, all of which are estate-grown. The policy has always been to pick the grapes very ripe, thus producing a densely-coloured and massively-flavoured wine which really needs much time to soften and mature.
Cellaring 10–15 years.
Best Vintages '80, '87, '89, '91, '92
Current Vintage '93
Matching Food Strong cheese or red meat.
Tasting Note 1993 Full purple-red; very ripe, dense jammy/cherry/berry fruit with subtle oak on the bouquet. The palate, too, shows extremely ripe fruit with abundant tannins and extract.

SEVERN BRAE ESTATE *

NR 14–14.50 ML AUSSD
Granite Belt **Est.** 1990
Lot 2 Back Creek Road (Mount Tully Road), Severnlea, Qld 4352
Ph (076) 83 5292
Open Mid-late 1995 **Production** 120
Winemaker(s) Bruce Humphery-Smith
Patrick and Bruce Humphery-Smith have established 2.5 hectares of chardonnay with relatively close spacing and trained on a high two-tier trellis. Winery and cellar door facilities were in the course of construction in 1994, destined to be completed in time for the 1995 vintage. Prior to that time, the Chardonnay was made at Sundown Valley winery.
Principal Wines Chardonnay, Liqueur Muscat.

SEVILLE ESTATE

★★★★★ 15.45–18.10 ML AUS144 UK81
Yarra Valley **Est.** 1970
Linwood Road, Seville, Vic 3139
Ph (059) 64 4556 **Fax** (059) 64 3585
Open Not **Production** 1500
Winemaker(s) Dr Peter McMahon

Sadly, Dr Peter McMahon has given away the battle with botrytis, and there will be no more of his magnificent Botrytised Rieslings. The compensation is the superb Shiraz, which will no longer be threatened by its hostile vineyard neighbour (in other words, the Botrytis Riesling).
Principal Wines Shiraz, Chardonnay, Pinot Noir, Cabernet Sauvignon.

SEVILLE ESTATE SHIRAZ

●●●●● $15.45
Consistently the best of the Seville Estate wines (though the others are very good) and, indeed, one of the best cool climate Shirazs in Australia, but little known outside a select circle simply because production is so limited. It is matured in a mixture of French and American oak, but it is the fruit which really drives the wine.
Cellaring Option to 10 years. **Best Vintages** '88, '90, '91, '92
Current Vintage '92
Matching Food Pot-au-feu.
Tasting Note 1992 Medium to full red-purple; a vibrantly clean spice and black cherry bouquet of medium to full intensity, and minimal oak influence. The palate shows lovely ripe fruit with cherry and spice flavours, fine-grained tannins, balanced acidity and subtle oak.

SHANTELL VINEYARD

★★★★ 12–17 CD AUS173
Yarra Valley **Est.** 1980
Melba Highway, Dixon's Creek, Vic 3775
Ph (059) 65 2264 **Fax** (059) 65 2331
Open W'ends & public hols 10–5 **Production** 940
Winemaker(s) Shan & Turid Shanmugam

The substantial and now fully mature Shantell vineyards provide the winery with a high quality fruit source; part is sold to other Yarra Valley makers, the remainder vinified at Shantell.
Principal Wines Semillon, Chardonnay, Pinot Noir, Cabernet Sauvignon.

SHANTELL VINEYARD CABERNET SAUVIGNON

●●●●● $17
The currently available '91 vintage is an outstanding wine, much the best to come from Shantell to date. It is produced from 2 hectares of estate grapes, and in the warm 1991 vintage, everything came together perfectly.

Cellaring Up to 10 years. **Best Vintages** '91
Current Vintage '91
Matching Food Shoulder of lamb.
Tasting Note 1991 Medium red-purple; clean, fragrant spice, leaf and cassis aromas in perfect harmony. The palate is long and intense, with spicy cassis fruit, very good structure and a long finish. A beautiful example of Yarra Valley cabernet.

SHANTELL VINEYARD SEMILLON
●●●● $12

There is not a great deal of semillon grown in the Yarra Valley, but what there is produces some attractive wines. In most vintages, as one would expect, the wine has a distinctly herbaceous feel akin to sauvignon blanc, but enough intensity not to require oak. The Shantell wine is made in this fashion from half a hectare of estate grapes.
Cellaring Up to 5 years. **Best Vintages** '88, '90, '91, '92, '93
Current Vintage '94
Matching Food Abalone.
Tasting Note 1994 Light green-yellow; clean, crisp, lime and herb aromas lead on to a light, crisp and lively palate with gently herbaceous fruit. The wine has good length and acidity, and is well made.

SHARMANS GLENBOTHY VINEYARD

★★★☆ 12–15 ML AUSSD
Northern Tasmania **Est.** 1987
RSD 282 Glenwood Road, Rilbia, Tas 7258
Ph (003) 43 0773 **Fax** (003) 43 0773
Open By appt **Production** 180
Winemaker(s) Andrew Hood (Contract)
Stylish wines produced in minuscule quantities from the half-hectare vineyard of wine enthusiast Mike Sharman.
Principal Wines Riesling, Chardonnay, Pinot Noir.

SHAW & SMITH

★★★★★ 16–23 R AUS63, 64, 66, 103, 164 UK101
Southern Vales **Est.** 1989
Flaxman Valley Road, Adelaide, SA 5152
Ph (08) 370 9911 **Fax** (08) 370 9339
Open Not **Production** 12 000
Winemaker(s) Martin Shaw
Hitherto, Shaw & Smith has relied upon contract-grown grapes, but has begun the development of a 40-hectare vineyard at Woodside in the Adelaide Hills which will ultimately provide all of the material for the wines. Quality has been exemplary from the outset, and the label has already gained an international reputation.
Principal Wines Sauvignon Blanc, Unoaked Chardonnay, Reserve Chardonnay.

SHAW & SMITH RESERVE CHARDONNAY
●●●●● $23
First made in 1992 and undoubtedly merits the Reserve designation.
Using fruit from Geoff Hardy's vineyard, winemaker Martin Shaw
applies the full gamut of Burgundian techniques of barrel
fermentation, extended time on yeast lees and partial malolactic
fermentation, using only finest French oak.
Cellaring Up to 7 years. **Best Vintages** '92, '93, '94
Current Vintage '93
Matching Food Baked schnapper.
Tasting Note 1993 Medium yellow-green; a complex,
multilayered bouquet with smooth, sweet fruit and hazelnut oak. In
the mouth, the wine is elegant, with fine melon and citrus fruit, a hint
of toasty oak, finishing with great length.

SHAW & SMITH SAUVIGNON BLANC
●●●● ▶ $16
So far produced from grapes grown on Geoff Hardy's Range
Vineyard at Kuitpo in the Adelaide Hills. First produced in 1990,
the wine is unoaked, but has abundant fruit flavour.
Cellaring Not necessary. **Best Vintages** '92, '93, '94
Current Vintage '94
Matching Food Grilled whiting.
Tasting Note 1994 Light green-yellow; clean and crisp
herbal/gooseberry aromas of medium intensity. Bright and fresh on
the palate, with perfectly balanced acidity, and while not having
quite as much fruit as the '93, does have a long finish.

SHAW & SMITH UNOAKED CHARDONNAY
●●●● $16
First made in 1993, and part of the modern trend away from oaky,
high-alcohol Chardonnays. The fruit is sourced primarily from the
Adelaide Hills.
Cellaring Best young. **Best Vintages** NA **Current Vintage** '94
Matching Food Delicate seafood.
Tasting Note 1994 Medium yellow-green; the bouquet is quite
fragrant with citrus, herbal and melon aromas of light intensity. In the
mouth the wine tends towards a traditional Chablis style.

SHOTTESBROOKE WINES

★★★☆ 14–18 R AUS43, 48, 64, 74, 123, 177, 178 UK62
Southern Vales **Est.** 1984
Ryecroft Vineyard, Ingoldby Road, McLaren Flat, SA 5171
Ph (08) 383 0002 **Fax** (08) 383 0222
Open 7 days 12–5 **Production** 5000
Winemaker(s) Nick Holmes
Now the full-time business of former Ryecroft winemaker Nick
Holmes, made from grapes grown on his vineyard at Myoponga, at
their best showing clear berry fruit, subtle oak and a touch of
elegance.
Principal Wines Chardonnay, Sauvignon Blanc, Cabernet Merlot,
Merlot.

SHOTTESBROOKE CABERNET MERLOT
●●●● $18

For many years Shottesbrooke was a busman's holiday for winemaker/proprietor Nick Holmes while he worked for other, larger wineries. During this time he was one of the first to develop a cabernet merlot (from time to time with a little malbec) blend in McLaren Vale for his Shottesbrooke label, and has accumulated considerable experience in dealing with the blend.
Cellaring 3–5 years. **Best Vintages** '84, '86, '88, '92, '93
Current Vintage '91
Matching Food Italian.
Tasting Note 1991 Medium red-purple; a light but quite complex bouquet with aromas of game, herbs and mint. The palate shows similar flavours; the oak has been sensitively handled, and the overall impression is of lightness and elegance.

SHOTTESBROOKE CHARDONNAY
●●● ▶ $14

Produced from 3.6 hectares of estate plantings. The 1994 is a very unusual wine, which seems to have more in common with semillon or sauvignon blanc than chardonnay, but lends itself to the Chablis-style subtle oak treatment, apparently with partial barrel fermentation.
Cellaring Drink now. **Best Vintages** NA **Current Vintage** '94
Matching Food Calamari.
Tasting Note 1994 Light green-yellow; tight lemony/herbal/citrus aromas with little oak evident, followed by a tight, intense palate with the structure of a Semillon. It is just possible that the wine may develop great complexity with bottle age.

SHOTTESBROOKE MERLOT
●●●● $14

Made from 4 hectares of estate-grown grapes, and fashioned in the elegant style which winemaker/proprietor Nick Holmes has always favoured. There are some very interesting varietal characters running throughout the wine, which is fruit-driven.
Cellaring 3–4 years. **Best Vintages** '84, '86, '88, '92, '93
Current Vintage '93
Matching Food Braised ox tongue.
Tasting Note 1993 Medium red-purple; fragrant leafy/minty aromas of some concentration. The palate shows a range of flavours from minty to leafy through to red berry, finishing with soft tannins and subtle oak.

SILOS WINERY, THE See page 439.

SILVAN WINERY *

NR 8 CD AUSSD
Yarra Valley **Est.** 1993
Lilydale-Silvan Road, Silvan, Vic, 3795
Ph (03) 9737 9392

Open W'ends, Public hols 11–6 **Production** 500
Winemaker(s) John Vigliaroni
One of the newest and smallest of the Yarra Valley wineries; tastings are held in the Vigliaronis' spacious Italian villa.
Principal Wines Chardonnay, Pinot Noir, Cabernet, Cabernet Shiraz Merlot, Merlot.

SIMON HACKETT WINES

★★★☆ 10.99–12.99 R AUSSD, UK12
Southern Vales **Est.** 1981
PO Box 166, Walkerville, SA 5081
Ph (08) 232 4305 **Fax** (08) 223 3714
Open Not **Production** 10 000
Winemaker(s) Simon Hackett
Simon Hackett runs a very interesting operation, owning neither vineyards nor winery, but purchasing grapes and then making the wines at various establishments on a lend-lease basis. With considerable industry experience, he is thus able to produce a solid range of wines at highly competitive prices.
Principal Wines Semillon, Barossa Valley Chardonnay, McLaren Vale Chardonnay, Shiraz, Cabernet Sauvignon.

SIMON HACKETT CABERNET SAUVIGNON
●●●● $12.99
As with the white wines, ready to go. There is, indeed, almost a role reversal: whereas the white wines are relatively full-bodied, this is a pleasantly light-bodied McLaren Vale Cabernet.
Cellaring Drink now. **Best Vintages** '88, '90, '91, '92, '94
Current Vintage '92
Matching Food Italian, Mediterranean.
Tasting Note 1992 Medium red-purple; a fragrant bouquet of light to medium intensity with sweet berry and chocolate fruit, rounded off with a nice touch of vanillin oak. The palate is fresh and lively, with red berry fruit, soft tannins and nicely balanced oak.

SIMON HACKETT MCLAREN VALE CHARDONNAY
●●● ▶ $12.99
One of two Chardonnays produced in 1994 by Simon Hackett, the other from Barossa Valley fruit. Both are fairly oaky styles, but the greater fruit intensity of the McLaren Vale version makes it the better of the two.
Cellaring Drink now. **Best Vintages** '92, '93, '94
Current Vintage '94
Matching Food Sweet and sour pork.
Tasting Note 1994 Medium yellow-green; the bouquet is quite oaky and firm, with melon and honey fruit. The palate is quite lively, with peachy fruit flavours coming through, and some freshening acidity, although the American oak certainly makes its presence felt.

SIMON HACKETT SEMILLON
●●● ▶ $10.99
A traditional, reasonably full-bodied Barossa Semillon style, using

skin contact prior to pressing and then fermentation and three
months maturation in American oak.
Cellaring Drink now. **Best Vintages** '92, '93, '94
Current Vintage '94
Matching Food Deep-fried chicken.
Tasting Note 1994 Medium to full yellow-green; a big, rich,
smooth and already developed bouquet showing the effects of skin
contact, and camphor and vanilla American oak. The wine works
well as a drink-now style with attractive lemon and honey fruit, and
well balanced oak in a super-generous mould.

SKILLOGALEE WINES

★★★☆ 11.95–16.50 R AUS2, 48, 56, 70, 123
Clare Valley **Est.** 1970
Off Hughes Park Road, Sevenhill via Clare, SA 5453
Ph (088) 43 4311 (088) 43 4343
Open 7 days 10–5 **Production** 8000
Winemaker(s) Dave Palmer, Stephen John (Contract)
David and Diana Palmer purchased Skillogalee from the George
family several years ago, and have capitalised to the full on the
exceptional fruit quality of the Skillogalee vineyards. The winery
also has a well-patronised lunchtime restaurant.
Principal Wines Riesling, Late Picked Riesling, Gewürztraminer,
Shiraz, The Cabernets.

SKILLOGALEE LATE HARVEST RIESLING

●●● ▶ $11
A cellar door special; it is extraordinary how much wine of this style
is sold ex-cellar door tastings, and how little through the retail trade.
As ever, it would seem people talk dry and drink sweet.
Cellaring 2–3 years. **Best Vintages** NA **Current Vintage** '93
Matching Food Smoked trout mousse.
Tasting Note 1993 Medium yellow-green; clean with
tropical/apricot aromas of light to medium intensity. There are
similar soft tropical and apricot flavours on the palate of a soft,
pleasant cellar door style.

SKILLOGALEE RIESLING

●●●● $12.95
The principal wine of Skillogalee, produced from 8 hectares of
estate grapes which wind up and down the steep hills of the Skilly
Valley, and which are now fully mature. The style is consistently at
the fuller end of the Clare Valley spectrum, honest, generous and
relatively quick maturing.
Cellaring 1–3 years. **Best Vintages** '80, '84, '87, '90, '92
Current Vintage '94
Matching Food Quiche Lorraine.
Tasting Note 1994 Medium yellow-green; the bouquet is powerful
and strongly toasty, with an underlay of lime, and showing some
development. The palate is full-flavoured with abundant lime and
toast fruit, and a soft, almost fleshy finish, without being excessively
phenolic.

SKILLOGALEE THE CABERNETS
●●● ▶ $16.50

Predominantly cabernet sauvignon, with a small percentage of estate-grown cabernet franc and malbec making up the blend. The style is relatively light-bodied, often with distinctly minty overtones, balanced by a touch of American oak.

Cellaring 2–4 years. **Best Vintages** '84, '87, '90, '92
Current Vintage '92
Matching Food Yearling steak.
Tasting Note 1992 Developed medium red; clean, soft and relatively light leafy/minty aromas with just a hint of vanillin oak. A light-bodied wine on the palate, with similar sappy/leafy/minty flavours, finishing with soft tannins.

SMITHBROOK WINES *

★★★★ 25 R AUS168
Warren Valley **Est.** 1988
Smith Brook Road, Middlesex via Manjimup, WA 6258
Ph (097) 72 3557 **Fax** (097) 72 3579
Open Not **Production** 1400
Winemaker(s) John Wade (Contract)

Smithbrook is first and foremost a grape producer for others, with total plantings growing from 27 hectares at the end of 1994 to 48 hectares at the end of 1995. It sells grapes to leading wine producers across Australia including Domaine Chandon in the Yarra Valley (in which region general manager Philip May had worked at Hoddles Creek before moving to Smithbrook).
Principal Wines Chardonnay, Pinot Noir.

SMITHBROOK CHARDONNAY
●●●● $25

Produced from 12 hectares of bearing vineyard. The 1992 vintage won the Best White Wine of Region trophy at the November 1993 SGIO Wine Show Awards. It reflects the very high standard of viticulture on this professionally-run vineyard. The '93 is a worthy follow-on.

Cellaring 2–5 years. **Best Vintages** '92, '94
Current Vintage '93
Matching Food Scampi, marron.
Tasting Note 1993 Light to medium yellow-green; there are discrete melon and fig aromas backed by subtle oak on the bouquet. There are flavours of melon, citrus and citrus peel on the palate, with complex barrel fermentation flavours, finishing with good acidity.

SMITHBROOK PINOT NOIR
●●●● $25

The 1992 Pinot Noir paralleled the success of its sister wine, winning the trophy for Best Red Wine of Region at the November 1993 SGIO Wine Show Awards. The dry-grown pinot noir yields very small bunches of intensely-coloured fruit, and holds out much promise for the variety. The '93 is a worthy follow-on.

Cellaring 1–2 years. **Best Vintages** '91, '92
Current Vintage '93
Matching Food Grilled quail.
Tasting Note 1993 Medium to full red-purple; a clean bouquet of medium intensity showing clear varietal character, though not especially complex. There is more style evident on the palate, even with some overtones of Burgundy; the cherry and plum fruit augers well for the future development of the wine.

SNOWY RIVER WINERY *

NR 10–20 CD AUSSD
Southern Highlands **Est.** 1984
Rockwell Road, Berridale, NSW 2628
Ph (064) 56 5041 **Fax** (064) 56 5005
Open 7 days 10–5 **Production** 2500
Winemaker(s) Geoff Carter
Claims the only Eiswein to have been made in Australia, picked on 8 June 1990 after a frost of –8° Celsius. Also makes a Trocken Beeren Auslese (sic) picked mid-May from the vineyard situated on the banks of the Snowy River, one hour from Mount Kosciusko. One suspects many of the wines are purchased from other makers.
Principal Wines Riesling, Semillon, Sauvignon Blanc, Semillon Chardonnay, Muller Thurgau Sylvaner, Sieger Rebe (sic), Trocken Beeren Auslese, Cabernet Sauvignon, Port.

SORRENBERG WINES

★★☆ 12–19 CD AUS187
North East Victoria **Est.** 1986
Alma Road, Beechworth, Vic 3747
Ph (057) 28 2278
Open Mon–Fri by appt, W'ends 1–5 **Production** 1000
Winemaker(s) Barry Morey
Barry and Jan Morey made their first wines in 1989 from the 2.5-hectare vineyard situated on the outskirts of Beechworth. They are still learning the winemaking craft.
Principal Wines Sauvignon Blanc Semillon, Chardonnay, Gamay, Cabernet Sauvignon Franc Merlot.

SPRING VALE VINEYARDS

★★★☆ 18 CD AUS37, 144
East Coast Tasmania **Est.** 1986
Spring Vale, Swansea, Tas 7190
Ph (002) 57 8208 **Fax** (002) 57 8598
Open W'ends, Hols 10–5 **Production** 1080
Winemaker(s) Andrew Hood (Contract)
Rodney Lyne has progressively established 1.2 hectares of pinot noir and 0.8 hectares of chardonnay (not all in bearing) in the uniquely-favoured climate of Tasmania's east coast, and has produced

wonderfully rich and generous Pinot Noir well worth the search,
although the '93 was fractionally disappointing.
Principal Wines Chardonnay, Pinot Noir.

ST FRANCIS WINES

★★★ 6.20–19.90 CD AUSSD
Southern Vales **Est.** 1869
Bridge Street, Old Reynella, SA 5161
Ph (08) 381 1925 **Fax** (08) 322 6655
Open Mon–Fri 9–5, W'ends 10–5 **Production** 8000
Winemaker(s) Various Contract
A full-blown tourist facility and convention centre with a thriving
cellar door sales facility offering wines purchased in bulk from other
makers (usually bottled or cleanskins). Thanks to the skill and
contacts of its consultants, the average quality is good, especially
at the price.
Principal Wines Riesling, Classic Riesling (aged), Frontignac,
Classic Dry White, Semillon Chardonnay, Sauvignon Blanc,
Chardonnay, Shiraz, Grenache, Cabernet Sauvignon, and a range
of sparkling and fortified wines.

ST GREGORY'S WINES

NR 12 ML AUSSD
Western Victoria **Est.** 1983
Bringalbert South Road, Bringalbert South via Apsley, Vic 3319
Ph (055) 86 5225
Open By appt **Production** 200
Winemaker(s) Gregory Flynn
A strictly weekend hobby of port enthusiast Greg Flynn.
Principal Wines Port.

ST HALLETT WINES

★★★★★ 9.95–25 R AUS81–85 UK11 US10
Barossa Valley **Est.** 1944
St Hallett's Road, Tanunda, SA 5352
Ph (085) 63 2319 **Fax** (085) 63 2901
Open 7 days 10–4 **Production** 15 000
Winemaker(s) Stuart Blackwell, Neil Doddridge
One of the true-blue Aussie success stories, with its Old Block Shiraz
gaining super-cult status in markets as far away and as unlikely as
Ireland and Paris; it is no exaggeration to say that the entire
production could be sold in London. It has driven the development of
the Barossa Valley Shiraz and Poacher's Blend Semillon, which are
cleverly crafted additions to the portfolio.
Principal Wines Poacher's Blend (White), Semillon Sauvignon
Blanc, Chardonnay, Gamekeeper's Reserve (Red), Cabernet
Sauvignon Franc Merlot, Old Block Shiraz, Old Crock
Tawny Port.

ST HALLETT GAMEKEEPER'S RESERVE
●●●● $10.95

Designed as a twin to the Poacher's Blend, and similarly designed for early consumption. The varietal base is not stated, but is no doubt predominantly Barossa shiraz and grenache, with the oak input non-existent. A wine which precisely meets it purpose.

Cellaring Drink now. **Best Vintages** NA **Current Vintage** '93
Matching Food Tandoori chicken.
Tasting Note 1993 Bright red-purple; clean fresh and lively fruit aromas, in a minty/cherry spectrum. The palate is similarly juicy, youthful and bright, with fresh cherry fruit. The wine is not structurally complex, and is not intended to be.

ST HALLETT OLD BLOCK SHIRAZ
●●●●● $25

A wine which has propelled St Hallett into international stardom, and which is responsible for the overall winery rating. Made from 60- to 100-year-old dry-grown Barossa vines, with the addition of new American oak making its impact since 1988.

Cellaring 4–8 years. **Best Vintages** '80, '84, '87, '88, '90, '91, '92 **Current Vintage** '92
Matching Food Kangaroo, game.
Tasting Note 1992 Medium to full red-purple; fragrant, spicy varietal fruit with an abundant sweet cherry core and a hint of vanillin/coconut oak. The palate shows lovely cherry fruit with a hint of liquorice, and more spice than in either the '91 or '90 vintages.

ST HALLETT POACHER'S BLEND
●●● ▶ $8.95

An unoaked blend of Barossa Valley chenin blanc, semillon and chardonnay, deliberately made in a medium dry white style, and intended to be drunk immediately on release.

Cellaring Not required. **Best Vintages** NA
Current Vintage '94
Matching Food Satay.
Tasting Note 1994 Light green-yellow; a voluminous bouquet with strong canned yellow clingstone peach aromas, with similar tropical yellow peach and pineapple flavours on the palate, finishing with appreciable residual sugar.

ST HUBERTS VINEYARD

★★★★☆ 8.90–25.40 R AUS176, UK94
Yarra Valley **Est.** 1966
Maroondah Highway, Coldstream, Vic 3770
Ph (03) 9739 1421 **Fax** (03) 9739 1015
Open Mon–Fri 9–5, W'ends 10.30–6 **Production** 20 000
Winemaker(s) Greg Traught

The changes have come thick and fast at St Huberts, which is now part of the Rothbury Estate group, and with former Rothbury red winemaker Greg Traught in charge. Traught has duly produced some quite lovely wines, none better than the 1994 Chardonnay.

Principal Wines Chardonnay, Pinot Noir, Cabernet Sauvignon, Cabernet Merlot; under the second label Rowan Sauvignon Blanc, Chardonnay, Shiraz, Pinot Noir, Cabernet Merlot.

ST HUBERTS CABERNET SAUVIGNON
●●●● ▶ $24.50
Almost 50% of the 20 hectares of estate plantings at St Huberts are cabernet sauvignon, some of it original plantings, and more grafted over from other varieties. The '77 St Huberts Cabernet caused a sensation at the time, both for its quality and its then astronomically high price of $17 a bottle. The '92, likewise, is a show stopper.
Cellaring 10+ years. **Best Vintages** '88, '90, '91, '92, '94
Current Vintage '92
Matching Food Rich casserole dishes.
Tasting Note 1992 Dense red-purple; very ripe and concentrated blackcurrant fruit with subtle oak on the bouquet. The palate is massively concentrated and rich, with lots of sweet berry fruit, and no minty/gamey characters at all. Unusual style for the Yarra Valley, reflecting the perfect ripening season.

ST HUBERTS CHARDONNAY
●●●●● $24.50
Received the Trophy for Best Chardonnay at the 1994 Lilydale Show, open to all southern Victorian wines. Estate-grown and barrel fermented, this is a superior wine in all respects, although it does no more than confirm the reputation of prior vintages.
Cellaring Up to 5 years. **Best Vintages** '88, '90, '91, '92, '94
Current Vintage '94
Matching Food Yabbies.
Tasting Note 1994 Light yellow-green; fine, elegant and complex with subtle but evident French oak. The palate is of medium to full weight, with harmonious, sweet peach, fig and melon fruit.

ST HUBERTS ROUSSANE
●●●● ▶ $17.50
No doubt partially inspired by neighbour Yerinberg, which was famous for its 19th century Marsanne, and which has since re-established both Marsanne and Roussane. However, the two are blended at Yerinberg, leaving the St Huberts Roussane the only example of its kind available through retail outlets in Australia — and then in minuscule quantities.
Cellaring Uncertain; watch its development. **Best Vintages** NA
Current Vintage '94
Matching Food Pasta.
Tasting Note 1994 Medium to full yellow; a highly scented, floral/honeysuckle bouquet relying entirely on fruit uninfluenced by oak. The palate, too, is fruit-driven, again showing surprisingly intense flavour in a honeysuckle/honey spectrum.

ST LEONARDS VINEYARD
★★★☆ 8.90–25 CD AUS75
North East Victoria **Est.** 1860

Wahgunyah, Vic 3687
Ph (060) 33 1004 **Fax** (060) 33 3636
Open Mon–Sat 9–5, Sun 10–4 **Production** 8000
Winemaker(s) Terry Barnett
An old favourite, producing always-interesting wines cleverly
marketed through an active mailing list and singularly attractive
cellar door at the historic winery on the banks of the Murray.
Principal Wines Semillon, Chardonnay, Sauvignon Blanc, Chenin
Blanc, Late Harvest Semillon, Rosé, Pinot Noir, Cabernet Franc
Merlot, Cabernet Sauvignon.

ST LEONARDS LATE HARVEST SEMILLON
●●●● ▶ $15
St Leonards has come up with some very interesting late harvest
wines over the years, making a spectacular Late Harvest Chenin
Blanc in the early 1980s. This is a wine of similar quality and
style.
Cellaring 3–4 years. **Best Vintages** NA **Current Vintage** '93
Matching Food Stuffed baked apple.
Tasting Note 1993 Medium to full yellow-orange; intense tropical
apricot lime and pineapple aromas with minimal oak influence. The
palate is redolent of apricot and lime, with an acceptable degree of
volatile acidity giving lift and piquancy.

ST MARY'S VINEYARD

NR 14–22.50 CD AUS72
Coonawarra **Est.** 1986
V & A Lane, via Coonawarra, SA 5277
Ph (087) 36 6070 **Fax** (087) 36 6045
Open 7 days 10–4 **Production** 4000
Winemaker(s) Ralph Fowler (Contract)
The Mulligan and Hooper families established St Mary's Vineyard in
1986 on a patch of terra rossa soil 15 kilometres west of the
township of Coonawarra and in the proposed Penola appellation
district. Only part of the production from the 22-hectare vineyard is
made into wine, the remainder of the grapes being sold. Ralph
Fowler (Contract) makes the wine at Leconfield.
Principal Wines Chardonnay, Cabernet Sauvignon.

ST MARY'S CHARDONNAY
●●●● $17
Made in consistent style by Ralph Fowler at Leconfield for St Mary's,
with primary emphasis on the high quality fruit, and less on the oak.
Cellaring 3–5 years. **Best Vintages** '92, '93
Current Vintage '93
Matching Food Prawns.
Tasting Note 1993 Light to medium yellow-green; tangy
grapefruit/citrus fruit with slightly sweeter notes in the background.
A stylish wine on the palate with elegant melon and grapefruit
flavours, a long finish and little or no oak input.

ST PATRICKS WINES *

NR 14–20 R AUS48
Huon Valley **Est.** 1990
c/o PO, Woodbridge, Tas 7162
Ph (002) 67 4483
Open Not **Production** 500
Winemaker(s) Leigh Gawith
When Leigh Gawith sold his vineyard at Pipers Brook to the winery
of that name, he did not sell the St Patricks brand, which migrated
with him to Woodbridge in southern Tasmania. Here he continues to
make wines, sold principally through the Woodbridge Hotel, but
also distributed through Tasmania by David Johnson & Associates.
Principal Wines Chardonnay, Floral Dry White, Pinot Noir.

STAFFORD RIDGE WINES

★★★★☆ 13–19.50 R AUS112, UK4, 11, 62
Adelaide Hills **Est.** 1982
2 Gilpin Lane, Mitcham, SA 5062
Ph (08) 272 2105 **Fax** (08) 271 0177
Open Not **Production** 2500
Winemaker(s) Geoff Weaver
Stafford Ridge is now the full-time business of former Hardy Group
chief winemaker Geoff Weaver. He draws upon a little under
10 hectares of vineyard established between 1982 and 1988; for
the time being, at least, the physical winemaking is carried out by
Geoff Weaver at Petaluma.
Principal Wines Sauvignon Blanc, Riesling, Chardonnay,
Cabernet Merlot.

STAFFORD RIDGE CHARDONNAY

●●●●● $19.50
The low-yielding vines (in 1991 yielding at 2.5 tonnes per acre)
produce very concentrated fruit from the 2.8 hectares planted
between 1983 and 1988. Geoff Weaver then applies the full range
of technique to this material, including barrel fermentation, ageing
on yeast lees for 12 months, and full malolactic fermentation. The
result is an extremely concentrated, long-lived style.
Cellaring Up to 10 years. **Best Vintages** '90, '91, '93, '94
Current Vintage '91
Matching Food Sweetbreads.
Tasting Note 1991 Bright yellow-green; lovely cool-climate
aromas in a floral/jasmine/citrus/melon range. The palate is long
and stylish, with melon and grapefruit flavours interwoven with more
nutty characters from the malolactic fermentation and barrel
fermentation. A wine of very high quality.

STAFFORD RIDGE RIESLING

●●●● $13
Produced from one hectare of riesling planted in 1982 at an altitude
of 540 metres. The 1993 vintage was an unusual one, very cool

throughout much of the growing season, but with a very warm March and April which resulted in wines of greater than usual power and flavour.

Cellaring Up to 7 years. **Best Vintages** '90, '93, '94
Current Vintage '93
Matching Food Antipasto.
Tasting Note 1993 Medium yellow-green; extremely concentrated lime, citrus and honey aromas with tang and lift. The palate, too, shows unusually concentrated flavours, finishing long and crisp.

STAFFORD RIDGE SAUVIGNON BLANC
••••• $17

Produced from 1.8 hectares of close-planted but very low-yielding sauvignon blanc planted in 1987. Right from the outset, the quality of this wine has been exceptional, with a purity and intensity of flavour equalled by few other Australian Sauvignon Blancs. It is not wooded, nor does it need to be.

Cellaring 1–3 years. **Best Vintages** '92, '93, '94
Current Vintage '94
Matching Food Mussels.
Tasting Note 1994 Medium yellow-green; an intense tobacco/herbal/gooseberry bouquet of great purity. The palate has all of the intensity one could wish for, with a mixture of herbal and riper tropical/gooseberry flavours, with a dry, lingering finish.

STANLEY BROTHERS *

★★★ 11–14.50 CD AUS126
Barossa Valley **Est.** 1991
Barossa Valley Way, Tanunda, SA 5352
Ph (085) 63 3375 **Fax** (085) 63 3758
Open 7 days 9–5 **Production** 2500
Winemaker(s) Lindsay Stanley

Former Anglesey winemaker and industry veteran Lindsay Stanley has now established his own business in the Barossa Valley. As one would expect, the wines are competently made.

Principal Wines Cabernet Sauvignon, Semillon, Shiraz.

STANLEY BROTHERS CABERNET SAUVIGNON
••• ▶ $14.50

Made from contract-grown Barossa Valley grapes, and treated in a thoroughly traditional fashion with quite pronounced use of American oak, but still remarkably fresh for its age.

Cellaring 5–7 years. **Best Vintages** NA
Current Vintage '91
Matching Food Mild hard cheese.
Tasting Note 1991 Medium red; fresh, sweet fruit with dusty/vanillin American oak on the bouquet. The palate is of light to medium weight, a little simple, but with clean, fresh berry fruit and soft vanillin oak.

STANTON & KILLEEN WINES

★★★☆ 6.50–25 CD AUS56, UK96
North East Victoria **Est.** 1875
Jacks Road, Murray Valley Highway, Rutherglen, Vic 3685
Ph (060) 32 9457 **Fax** (060) 32 8018
Open Mon–Sat 9–5, Sun 10–5 **Production** 7000
Winemaker(s) Chris Killeen
A traditional maker of smooth, rich reds, some very good Vintage
Ports, and attractive, fruity Muscats and Tokays.
Principal Wines A red wine and fortified wine specialist, though
offering Chardonnay, Riesling, White Frontignac, Dry White as well
as Cabernet Shiraz, Shiraz, Durif, Old Tawny Port, Old Rum Port,
Vintage Port, Liqueur Port, Liqueur Tokay, Liqueur Muscat and top-of-
the-range Special Old Liqueur Muscat.

STANTON & KILLEEN SPECIAL OLD LIQUEUR MUSCAT
●●●●● $25
A blend of all of the great years going back to the early 1960s, and
worth every cent of its price.
Cellaring NA. **Best Vintages** NA **Current Vintage** NV
Matching Food Rich cakes.
Tasting Note NV Dark brown, with an olive rim; strong, complex
aged raisiny muscat fruit with clean, earthy spirit. Tremendous
richness on the palate, yet retaining potent raisin and toffee muscat
varietal character. Totally delicious.

STEINS WINES

★★★ 8.50–12 CD AUSSD
Mudgee **Est.** 1976
Pipeclay Lane, Mudgee, NSW 2850
Ph (063) 73 3991 **Fax** (063) 73 3709
Open 7 days 10–4 **Production** 3000
Winemaker(s) Robert Stein
The sweeping panorama from the winery is its own reward for cellar
door visitors. Wine quality, too, has been very good from time to
time, as witness the 1991 Shiraz (sold out). Rather indifferent, hard
green oak does not help the wooded white wines.
Principal Wines Chablis, Riesling, Semillon Chardonnay, Semillon
Riesling, Traminer, Chardonnay, Rosé, Dry Red, Shiraz, and a range
of Muscats and Ports.

STEVENS CAMBRAI WINES

★★★ 4.90–20 CD AUS17, 99
Southern Vales **Est.** 1975
Hamilton's Road, McLaren Flat, SA 5171
Ph (08) 383 0251 **Fax** (08) 383 0251
Open 7 days 9–5 **Production** 6000
Winemaker(s) Graham Stevens
Graham Stevens knows both his own mind and the district very well;
a challenging mixture of the exotic and the run-of-the-mill, the good

and the not-so-good, has typified the table wines, but the Vintage
Ports have been of consistently high quality.
Principal Wines Chardonnay, Gewurztraminer, Frontignac,
Shiraz, Zinfandel, Cabernet Sauvignon, Vintage Port.

STONE RIDGE VINEYARDS

★★★☆ 11–20 CD AUSSD
Granite Belt **Est.** 1981
Limberlost Road, Glen Aplin, Qld 4381
Ph (076) 83 4211
Open 7 days 10–5 **Production** 1800
Winemaker(s) Jim Lawrie, Anne Kennedy
Spicy Shiraz is the specialty of the winery, but the portfolio has
progressively expanded over recent years to include two whites and
the only Stanthorpe region Malbec.
Principal Wines Stone Ridge label: Semillon, Chardonnay,
Shiraz, Malbec; Mount Sterling label: Dry Red Shiraz.

STONE RIDGE MALBEC
●●● ▶ $20
A wine which shows the typical jammy fruit characters of malbec
with minimal oak influence. A warning is that the wine does appear
to have relatively low sulphur levels.
Cellaring Not certain. **Best Vintages** NA **Current Vintage** '93
Matching Food Goulash.
Tasting Note 1993 Medium red-purple; abundant sweet jammy
berry fruit which is extremely varietal in character, with subtle oak.
There are nearly identical ripe, jammy/berry fruit flavours, with a
whisper of volatile acidity and some of the signs of low sulphur
levels. A striking wine in many respects.

STONE RIDGE SEMILLON
●●● ▶ $14
An interesting wine which has been fully barrel fermented in used
French oak, yet has retained considerable fragrance. It also exhibits
the tropical fruit characters which have been seen from time to time
in the best Semillons from the Granite Belt region.
Cellaring 2–3 years. **Best Vintages** NA **Current Vintage** '93
Matching Food Grilled perch.
Tasting Note 1993 Light green-yellow; fragrant passionfruit and
other tropical aromas intermingling with more herbaceous/straw-like
characters on the bouquet. The palate is of light to medium weight
with light peach and passionfruit flavours again apparent, falling
away slightly on the finish.

STONE RIDGE SHIRAZ
●●●● ▶ $14
This wine usually exhibits marked pepper and spice characters, but
the '92 vintage departs somewhat more towards the sort of sappy
characters one normally associates with Pinot. As ever, these are
fruit- rather than oak-driven wines.

Cellaring 3–4 years. **Best Vintages** '86, '87, '88, '92, '93
Current Vintage '92
Matching Food Pan-fried veal.
Tasting Note 1992 Medium to full red, fractionally dull, clean and soft with sappy Pinotish aromas which developed in the glass. The flavours are in the same spectrum, the texture and feel of the wine quite sweet and supple, all as much reminiscent of Pinot as Shiraz.

STONIER'S WINERY

★★★★★ 15.95–25.95 R AUS112, UK97
Mornington Peninsula **Est.** 1978
362 Frankston-Flinders Road, Merricks, Vic 3916
Ph (059) 89 8300 **Fax** (059) 89 8709
Open 7 days 12–5 **Production** 7000
Winemaker(s) Tod Dexter
1994 was the most successful year ever for Stonier's, with six trophies in three major wine shows, and a cascade of gold medals. Looked at across the range, Stonier's is now the pre-eminent winery in the Mornington Peninsula; its standing is in turn based more or less equally on its Chardonnay and Pinot Noir under the Reserve label.
Principal Wines Chardonnay, Pinot Noir, Cabernet Sauvignon; Reserve label: Chardonnay, Pinot Noir, Cabernet Sauvignon.

STONIER'S RESERVE CHARDONNAY
●●●●● $25
Produced from 3.5 hectares of estate-grown grapes, and made using the full gamut of Burgundian techniques including barrel fermentation, lees contact and malolactic fermentation. The wines are exceptionally complex and stylish; the '93 was selected for Qantas First Class service, won a number of gold medals at national wine shows, and two trophies at the 1994 Ballarat Wine Show, including the trophy for Best Wine of Show (the first time it has been awarded to a white wine).
Cellaring 3–5 years. **Best Vintages** '86, '88, '91, '93
Current Vintage '93
Matching Food Milk-fed veal.
Tasting Note 1993 Medium yellow-green; a very complex wine with outstanding fruit and oak balance and integration, and a teasing degree of volatile lift. The palate is equally complex with lots of tangy/citrus fruit married with more complex nutty barrel ferment/malolactic cashew nut and oak characters.

STONIER'S RESERVE PINOT NOIR
●●●●● $25
If it were possible, the Reserve Pinot Noir has an even more distinguished track record than the Reserve Chardonnay. The 1992 vintage was nominated as the Best Pinot Noir in the 1994/95 *Penguin Good Australian Wine Guide*, by Huon Hooke and Mark Shield, while the 1993 vintage won two major trophies at the 1994 Royal Adelaide Wine Show, including the trophy for Best Varietal

Dry Red Table Wine — Any Variety. The wine is exceedingly
complex and stylish.
Cellaring 2–4 years. **Best Vintages** '90, '91, '92, '93
Current Vintage '93
Matching Food Coq au vin.
Tasting Note 1993 Medium to full red; a tremendous volume of
aroma neatly combining sappy fruit with spicy oak. The palate is
long and intense, with spicy characters from both stems and high
quality French oak, some plummy/briary fruit, and a fine, lingering
finish.

STRATHERNE VALE ESTATE *

NR NA AUSSD
Cuballing **Est.** 1980
Campbell Street, Cuballing, WA 6311
Ph (098) 81 2148 **Fax** (098) 81 3129
Open Not **Production** 600
Winemaker(s) Contract
Stratherne Vale Estate stretches the viticultural map of Australia yet
further. It is situated near Narrogin, which is north of the Great
Southern region and south of the most generous extension of the
Darling Ranges. The closest viticultural region of note is at
Wandering, to the north east.
Principal Wines A single Red Wine made from a blend of
Cabernet Sauvignon, Zinfandel, Merlot and Shiraz.

STUMPY GULLY VINEYARD

★★★★ 12–16 CD AUS144
Mornington Peninsula **Est.** 1988
1247 Stumpy Gully Road, Moorooduc, Vic 3933
Ph (059) 78 8429 **Fax** (059) 78 8429
Open First w'end of month 12–5 **Production** 1000
Winemaker(s) Frank Zantvoort, Wendy Zantvoort
Frank and Wendy Zantvoort have progressively established
9 hectares of vineyard planted to chardonnay, marsanne, sauvignon
blanc, pinot noir, cabernet sauvignon and merlot, electing to sell
80% of the production to local winemakers, and vinifying the
remainder, with impressive results.
Principal Wines Marsanne, Sauvignon Blanc, Merlot.

STUMPY GULLY MARSANNE
●●●● $13
The second vintage of Marsanne from Stumpy Gully, and an
excellent rendition of the variety. Beautifully made, with 30% barrel
fermented, although this does not really show in the finished wine,
which is fruit-driven.
Cellaring 3+ years. **Best Vintages** NA **Current Vintage** '94
Matching Food Spiced Asian seafood.
Tasting Note 1994 Light straw-yellow; a firm bouquet with that
very distinctive varietal straw/dusty/chalky/honeysuckle/mineral

varietal character that is so hard to describe, but is nonetheless
distinctive. The palate is crisp, lively and tangy with a faint hint of
tobacco spice from the oak.

STUMPY GULLY MERLOT
●●●●● $16
The first Merlot from Stumpy Gully, and an absolutely delicious wine,
which sets new standards for Mornington Peninsula reds.
Cellaring 1–3 years. **Best Vintages** NA
Current Vintage '93
Matching Food Peking duck.
Tasting Note 1993 Medium to full red-purple; wonderfully clean,
ripe and juicy fruit aromas with no green characters whatsoever. The
palate is perfection, with juicy redcurrant fruit, subtle oak and soft
tannins.

STUMPY GULLY SAUVIGNON BLANC
●●● ▶ $13
Made in the modern style, without oak and early bottled.
Cellaring Drink now. **Best Vintages** NA **Current Vintage** '94
Matching Food Moreton Bay bugs.
Tasting Note 1994 Light to medium yellow-green; crisp, light
herbal aromas with a faint hint of tobacco leaf. The palate is crisp,
light and lively, with pleasing acidity on the finish.

SUMMERFIELD VINEYARDS

★★★★☆ 9–18 CD AUSSD
Pyrenees **Est.** 1979
Main Road, Moonambel, Vic 3478
Ph (054) 67 2264 **Fax** (054) 67 2380
Open 7 days 9–6 **Production** 2300
Winemaker(s) Ian Summerfield
A specialist red wine producer, the particular forte of which is
Shiraz. The wines since 1988 have been consistently excellent,
luscious and full-bodied.
Principal Wines Trebbiano Chardonnay, Chardonnay Sauvignon
Blanc, Shiraz, Estate Shiraz, Cabernet Shiraz, Cabernet Sauvignon.

SUMMERFIELD CABERNET SHIRAZ
●●●● $18
An unusual and complex blend, unusual in that the two components
provide radically different aroma and flavour components. The 1992
vintage was selected in the Top 100 at the 1994 Sydney
International Winemakers Competition.
Cellaring 3–5 years. **Best Vintages** NA
Current Vintage '92
Matching Food Lamb in filo pastry.
Tasting Note 1992 Medium to full red; a complex bouquet with
mint, leaf, game and spice characters all present. The spicy/peppery
shiraz component dominates the palate, which is rich and finishes
with good mouthfeel.

SUMMERFIELD ESTATE SHIRAZ
●●●●● $18

The 1991 vintage reviewed hereunder may not be released until well into 1995, but is a prime example of the best of the Summerfield Shiraz style, with tremendous concentration, coming from the 1.82 hectares of estate plantings.

Cellaring 7–10 years. **Best Vintages** '80, '83, '88, '90, '91
Current Vintage '91
Matching Food Rare beef.
Tasting Note 1991 Dense red-purple; clean and rich with full, moderately ripe dark berry and mint fruit aromas backed by subtle oak. On the palate there is abundant, luscious minty/berry fruit; soft tannins contribute to good balance and mouthfeel. Top quality wine.

SUMMERFIELD SHIRAZ
●●●● ▶ $16.50

One of the signature wines of Summerfield, although outranked by the Estate Shiraz. After a period during which rather too much American oak was used, the style has settled down with better balance.

Cellaring 5–7 years. **Best Vintages** '80, '83, '88, '90, '91
Current Vintage '92
Matching Food Beef in black bean sauce.
Tasting Note 1992 Medium to full red; strong, penetrating berry fruit with some mint and game characters also present. Spicy cherry fruit comes through on the palate, with some of the leaf and game characters of the bouquet also present. A wine with lots of character.

SUNNYCLIFF ESTATES

★★★★ 5.75–7.50 R AUS84, UK58
North West Victoria **Est.** 1980
Nangiloc Road, Iraak, Vic 3496
Ph (050) 29 1666 **Fax** (050) 29 1528
Open 7 days 10–4 **Production** 100 000
Winemaker(s) Mark Zeppel

Part of the Rentiers-Katnook group, now producing ever-increasing quantities of wine under the Sunnycliff label for both the domestic and export markets, and heading a golden streak with its '93 Chardonnay.

Principal Wines Chardonnay, Sauvignon Blanc, Riesling, Colombard Chardonnay, Cabernet Sauvignon.

SUNNYCLIFF CABERNET SAUVIGNON
●●● ▶ $7.50

Deliberately made in a bright, fresh, light style which does not try to force out of Riverlands cabernet something which is not there in the first place. Most attractive easy-drinking, early-maturing style.

Cellaring Drink now. **Best Vintages** NA **Current Vintage** '93
Matching Food Pasta.
Tasting Note 1993 Medium red-purple; clean, fresh, fragrant red berry fruit and subtle oak. On the palate bright, fresh and lively; only the structure is missing, but that does not matter.

SUNNYCLIFF CHARDONNAY
●●●● ▶ $7.50

A winner of two gold medals in the 1994 show circuit, including a much coveted gold medal at the 1994 Royal Sydney Wine Show. The grapes were picked at varying degrees of ripeness; a portion of the blend received French oak treatment, lees contact and malolactic fermentation. The result is a wine of remarkable finesse at the price.
Cellaring Drink now. **Best Vintages** '93 **Current Vintage** '93
Matching Food Salmon.
Tasting Note 1993 Medium to full yellow-green; strong peachy/buttery fruit with a lively bite and tang. The palate has unexpected intensity with grapefruit, melon and peach, a well integrated touch of oak, and a tangy, crisp acid finish.

SUTHERLAND WINES

★★★☆ 12.50–15 CD AUS173, UK70
Hunter Valley **Est.** 1979
Deasey's Road, Pokolbin, NSW 2321
Ph (049) 98 7650 **Fax** (049) 98 7603
Open 7 days 10–4.30 **Production** 8000
Winemaker(s) Neil Sutherland, Nicholas Sutherland
With substantial and now fully mature vineyards to draw upon, Sutherland is a more or less consistent producer of generous, mainstream Hunter whites and reds.
Principal Wines Chardonnay, Semillon, Semillon Chardonnay, Chenin Blanc, Shiraz, Pinot Noir, Cabernet Sauvignon.

SUTHERLAND CHARDONNAY
●●● ▶ $15

Sutherland always makes big, rich wines, and in drought years such as 1991, big becomes bigger still. The white wines from this vintage were never destined to be long-lived, and this does not break the rules.
Cellaring Drink now. **Best Vintages** '83, '85, '87, '91, '94
Current Vintage '91
Matching Food Pork with ginger.
Tasting Note 1991 Full yellow-orange; complex, toasty, hazelnut and butter aromas lead on to a multi-flavoured wine with some vaguely French characters, though finishes somewhat sweet, due as much to the alcohol as to anything else.

SUTHERLAND SEMILLON CHARDONNAY
●●●● $13.50

The Hunter Valley was the first region in the world to blend semillon and chardonnay (Tyrrell's in 1970, calling it Pinot Riesling, just to confuse matters) and the blend has proved to be an enduring one. The 1991 vintage of this wine has been given the New South Wales Benchmark status, and is indeed ultra-typical of the Hunter Valley.
Cellaring Drink now. **Best Vintages** '83, '85, '87, '91, '94
Current Vintage '91
Matching Food Fried eggplant.

Tasting Note 1991 Deep yellow; big, broad, rich, full-blown White Burgundy style with lots of toast, butter and nuts. A high-flavoured, toasty nutty wine now at its peak. Looks much older than it is, but that doesn't really matter.

T'GALLANT WINES

★★★★☆ 15–25 R AUS36, 66
Mornington Peninsula **Est.** 1990
Red Hill Road, Red Hill, Vic 3937
Ph (059) 89 2203 **Fax** (059) 89 2203
Open 7 days 11–5 **Production** 5000
Winemaker(s) Kathleen Quealy, Kevin McCarthy
Husband and wife consultant winemakers Kathleen Quealy and Kevin McCarthy are starting to carve out an important niche market for the T'Gallant label, noted for its innovative label designs and names. The acquisition of a 15-hectare property, and the already commenced progressive planting of over 10 hectares of pinot gris gives the business a firm geographic base.
Principal Wines Chardonnay, Pinot Grigio, White Pinot, Holystone and Crosstrees Cabernet Malbec.

T'GALLANT CHARDONNAY
●●●● ▶ $16
Quealy and McCarthy are firm believers in the virtues of unwooded Chardonnay, but recognise the paramount necessity of fully ripe grapes which are free from botrytis. Made from selected contract growers across the Peninsula, the wine has 13.5% alcohol which gives it the requisite flesh and character.
Cellaring 2–5 years. **Best Vintages** NA
Current Vintage '94
Matching Food Sweet white-fleshed fish.
Tasting Note 1994 Light yellow-green; lots of white peach, fig and melon fruit to the bouquet. The palate is of medium intensity, long and smooth with similar fruit flavours to those of the bouquet. Oh, for just a touch of oak.

T'GALLANT HOLYSTONE
●●●● ▶ $15
All of the T'Gallant wines feature brilliant packaging and label designs, none more so than the reverse see-through Holystone label featuring its roses. The wine is a blend of whole-bunch pressed pinot noir and 10% chardonnay, very deliberately made in a European food style, and quite different from anything else on the market.
Cellaring 1–2 years. **Best Vintages** NA
Current Vintage '94
Matching Food Asian cuisine of all kinds.
Tasting Note 1994 Pale pink; strawberry and dusty aromas intermingle on the bouquet. The wine is crisp and quite tart in the mouth, notwithstanding the presence of a hint of strawberry, as it finishes bone dry. Very refreshing; serve slightly chilled on a hot day.

T'GALLANT PINOT GRIGIO
●●●● ▶ $20
Pinot grigio (or pinot gris to give its English/French rather than
Italian name) is a mutation of pinot noir. T'Gallant has firmly staked
its future on the variety, and this wine, from the Lyncroft and Pig &
Whistle Vineyards in the Mornington Peninsula, suggests that faith
may be well founded.
Cellaring 1–4 years. **Best Vintages** NA **Current Vintage** '94
Matching Food Smoked salmon.
Tasting Note 1994 Glowing yellow-green; complex and powerful
stone fruit aromas with a distinct varietal smoky edge. The palate is
well balanced and unusually complete and full-bodied for a young,
unwooded white wine, there are stone fruit and faintly herbal
flavours, and richness throughout. 13.6% alcohol.

T'GALLANT RESERVE CHARDONNAY
●●●●● $18
Tasted as a bottled wine, but without the final package, and I am not
sure whether it will be called 'Reserve' or 'Super'. However, it could
as well be called both, for this really is an outstanding wine.
Cellaring Up to 7 years. **Best Vintages** NA
Current Vintage '94
Matching Food Fresh lobster.
Tasting Note 1994 Glowing yellow-green; intense melon and
grapefruit aromas of very high quality. The palate is equally good;
an outstanding example of cool-climate Chardonnay, with a very
long palate, good richness and lingering melon and grapefruit
flavours.

TALIJANCICH WINES
★★★ 12.30–72 CD AUSSD
Swan Valley **Est.** 1932
121 Hyem Road, Herne Hill, WA 6056
Ph (09) 296 4289 **Fax** (09) 296 4289
Open Sun–Fri 11–5 **Production** 4000
Winemaker(s) James Talijancich
A fortified wine specialist also producing a small range of table
wines. The 1961 Liqueur Muscat remains supreme at $72 a bottle.
Principal Wines Verdelho, Semillon, Grenache Rosé, Burgundy,
Ruby Port, Liqueur Hermitage, Liqueur Tokay, Liqueur Muscat.

TALTARNI VINEYARDS
★★★★ 9–18 R AUS27, 84, 85, 167, 179, UK87
Pyrenees **Est.** 1972
Taltarni Road, Moonambel, Vic 3478
Ph (054) 67 2218 **Fax** (054) 67 2306
Open 7 days 10–5 **Production** 60 000
Winemaker(s) Dominique Portet, Greg Gallagher, Chris Markell
The red wines are uncompromising in style; tannin usually teeters on
the edge of acceptability, and sometimes the second label Reserve

de Pyrenees can outperform its betters simply because it is softer.
These are, above all else, wines for the long haul.
Principal Wines Fumé Blanc, Sauvignon Blanc, Blanc des
Pyrenees, Rosé des Pyrenees, Reserve Red des Pyrenees, Merlot
Cabernet, Shiraz, Cabernet Sauvignon, Merlot; Sparkling Blanc de
Blanc Tete de Cuvée, Cuvée Brut, Brut Tache, Clover Hill.

TALTARNI MERLOT

●●●● $18
Typically 85% merlot and 15% cabernet franc, all estate-grown.
Very similar in style to South African and Californian Merlots, with
much more substance than most Australian counterparts.
Cellaring 7–10 years. **Best Vintages** '84, '88, '90, '91, '92
Current Vintage '91
Matching Food Barbecued T-Bone.
Tasting Note 1991 Medium to full red; solid, sweet and deep
aromas in Californian style. The tannins come rocketing through on
the palate with chewy fruit on the mid palate, finishing with slightly
earthy/leathery notes among the tannins.

TALTARNI SHIRAZ

●●●● $18
Produced from a little over 12 hectares of estate-grown grapes, and
has established a track record for its strength and longevity. The
wines are never fruity or fragrant; durability and honesty are their
hallmarks.
Cellaring 10 years. **Best Vintages** '84, '88, '90, '91, '92
Current Vintage '92
Matching Food Gippsland blue cheese.
Tasting Note 1992 Medium red-purple; clean, solid bouquet with
hints of spice, briar, plum and vanillin oak. The palate has the
typical extract and power of the Taltarni reds, but the tannins are in
restraint, giving the wine the necessary balance to age well.

TAMBURLAINE WINERY

★★★☆ 12–20 CD AUSSD
Hunter Valley **Est.** 1966
McDonalds Road, Pokolbin, NSW 2321
Ph (049) 98 7570 **Fax** (049) 98 7763
Open 7 days 9.30–5 **Production** 12 000
Winemaker(s) Greg Silkman, Mark Davidson
One of the longer-established wineries in the Hunter Valley which
has established a solid reputation and following. Overall, the red
wines are more reliable than the whites.
Principal Wines Semillon, Verdelho, Sauvignon Blanc, Petite
Fleur, Chardonnay, Cabernet Merlot Malbec, The Chapel Reserve
Dry Red.

TAMBURLAINE SEMILLON

●●● ▶ $15
Produced from 2 hectares of estate semillon, made without oak, and
fleshed out with a hint of sugar. Notwithstanding bushfires, '94

produced many fine whites in the Hunter Valley, and this wine does
the reputation of the vintage no harm.

Cellaring 3–5 years. **Best Vintages** '86, '89, '91, '93, '94
Current Vintage '94
Matching Food Tripe.
Tasting Note 1994 Bright yellow-green; solid, smooth with some
honey notes, but also herbs. The palate is solid with
grassy/herbaceous notes more evident, but balanced by just a hint
of residual sugar on the finish.

TAMBURLAINE THE CHAPEL RESERVE DRY RED
●●● ▶ $20
One of the most unusual flagship wines imaginable, for it is a non
vintage, non varietal-specific blend.
Cellaring 5+ years. **Best Vintages** NA **Current Vintage** NV
Matching Food Moussaka.
Tasting Note NV Medium to full red-purple; some chocolate
and berry fruit aromas interwoven with strong bluegrass vanillin
American oak. The palate is dense, concentrated and chewy with
rich dark fruit flavours and lots of American bluegrass soak again
evident.

TAMBURLAINE VERDELHO
●●●● ▶ $15
Grown at Belford on soil said to contain limestone. Made without
oak, and shows tremendous depth of fruit flavour.
Cellaring Up to 5 years. **Best Vintages** NA
Current Vintage '94
Matching Food Carpaccio of Tasmanian salmon.
Tasting Note 1994 Brilliant green-yellow; potent fruit aromas in
the tropical peach spectrum. The palate shows similar concentration
and weight with citrus tones alongside more tropical fruit; has
considerable length and acid balance.

TANAMI RED WINES
NR 8–9 CD AUSSD
Southern Vales **Est.** 1990
McMurtrie Road, McLaren Vale, SA 5171
Ph (08) 383 0351
Open W'ends, Public hols 11–4.45 **Production** 340
Winemaker(s) Les Payne
No rating, simply because I have not tasted the wines.
Principal Wines Shiraz, Cabernet Sauvignon.

TANGLEWOOD DOWNS ESTATE
NR 13–19 CD AUSSD
Mornington Peninsula **Est.** 1984
Bulldog Creek Road, Merricks North, Vic 3926
Ph (059) 74 3325 **Fax** (059) 74 4170
Open Sun–Mon 12–5 **Production** 600
Winemaker(s) Ken Bilham

Tanglewood Downs produced a very attractive Chardonnay in 1993, and a rather more minty one in 1994 — both tasted as unfinished wines.
Principal Wines Riesling, Chardonnay, Pinot Noir, Cabernet blend.

TANTEMAGGIE WINES *

NR NA AUSSD
Warren Valley **Est.** 1987
Kemp Road, Pemberton, WA 6260
Ph (097) 76 1164
Open W'ends 9–5 **Production** 400
Winemaker(s) Donnelly River (Contract)
Tantemaggie was established by the Pottinger family with the help of a bequest from a deceased aunt named Maggie. It is part of a mixed farming operation, and by far the greatest part of the 20 hectares is under long-term contract to Houghton. The bulk of the plantings are cabernet sauvignon and verdelho, the former producing the light-bodied style favoured by the Pottingers.
Principal Wines Cabernet Sauvignon.

TAPESTRY WINES

★★★☆ 10–20 R AUS131
Southern Vales **Est.** 1993
Olivers Road, McLaren Vale, SA 5171
Ph (08) 323 9196 **Fax** (08) 323 9476
Open Mon–Thurs 11–3, Fri–Sun 11–5 **Production** 5000
Winemaker(s) Brian Light
Owned by Brian Light (of Normans Wines) and wife Kay as a separate, private venture. Formerly known as Merrivale, the wines are now sold under the Tapestry label. The estate-grown Cabernet and Cabernet Shiraz are the pick of the crop, the Chardonnay and Riesling being honest, straightforward and well made, as one would expect.
Principal Wines Riesling, Chardonnay, Spatlese Muscat of Alexandria, Pinot Noir, Cabernet Shiraz, Cabernet Sauvignon, Tawny Port. Limited back releases under the Merrivale label.

TAPESTRY CABERNET SAUVIGNON
●●● ▶ $16
Again, produced from 2 hectares of estate-grown grapes. It is an extremely powerful wine which borders on toughness, possibly due to low sulphur levels which have led to somewhat inconsistent tasting notes.
Cellaring Uncertain; theoretically up to 10 years.
Best Vintages NA **Current Vintage** '92
Matching Food Strong red meat dishes.
Tasting Note 1992 Dense, full purple-red; a potent, powerful bouquet with lots of weight and extract to the cassis/redcurrant fruit. The palate is complex, full-flavoured but bordering on the extractive. A wine which could go in any direction with age.

TAPESTRY CABERNET SHIRAZ

●●●● ▶ $14

Draws upon 2 hectares of estate cabernet sauvignon and 2 hectares of estate shiraz; the wine has always been full-flavoured, but the '91 vintage in particular seemed to suffer from a surprising degree of neglect. The '92 vintage shows no such problems.

Cellaring 4–7 years. **Best Vintages** NA **Current Vintage** '92
Matching Food Braised lamb shanks.
Tasting Note 1992 Medium red-purple; a complex bouquet with solid dark chocolate aromas together with a touch of sweet earth. A generously flavoured wine on the palate with attractive spicy shiraz fruit together with sweet berry flavours from the cabernet, and well balanced oak.

TARCOOLA ESTATE

NR 8–10 CD AUSSD
Geelong **Est.** 1971
Spillers Road, Lethbridge, Vic 3332
Ph (052) 81 9245 **Fax** (052) 81 9311
Open 7 days 10–5 **Production** 4000
Winemaker(s) Keith Wood

After a period of slow decline, Tarcoola was purchased in 1990 by Keith Wood, who is determined to breathe new life into the vineyard and winery. Old, sub-standard stock has been disposed of, and new labels introduced, emphasising those wines made from estate-grown grapes.

Principal Wines Riesling, Muller Thurgau, Hilltop Shiraz, River Flat Shiraz, Cabernet Sauvignon.

TARRAHILL ESTATE

★★★ 12–13 ML AUS148
Yarra Valley **Est.** 1983
340 Old Healesville Road, Yarra Glen, Vic 3775
Ph (03) 9439 7425 **Fax** (03) 9435 9183
Open Not **Production** 850
Winemaker(s) Dr Ian Hanson

Dental surgeon Ian Hanson planted his first vines in the late 1960s close to the junction of the Yarra and Plenty Rivers; in 1983 those plantings were extended (with 3000 vines), and in 1988 the Tarrahill property at Yarra Glen was established with 10 further acres. The Lower Plenty wines bear the Hanson label; the Yarra Glen bear the Tarrahill Estate label.

Principal Wines Hanson Cabernets, Cabernet Franc, Cabernet Sauvignon.

TARRAHILL ESTATE HANSON CABERNETS

●●●● $13

Draws upon the various estate plantings of Ian Hanson and is the first release of the three principal Bordeaux varieties. Made very much in the fragrant tobacco leaf/cedar mould of all of the Tarrahill

wines; received a silver medal at the 1994 Victorian Wines Show.
60% cabernet sauvignon.
Cellaring 3–5 years. **Best Vintages** NA **Current Vintage** '93
Matching Food Pastrami.
Tasting Note 1993 Medium to full red-purple; fragrant tobacco
leaf and cedar aromas in typical style. The palate has briary fruit
undertones to the same gently leafy/tobacco/herbal characters.

TARRAWARRA VINEYARD

★★★★☆ 15.50–26 R AUS163, 185, UK51
Yarra Valley **Est.** 1983
Healesville Road, Yarra Glen, Vic 3775
Ph (059) 62 3311 **Fax** (059) 62 3887
Open Mon–Fri 10–5 **Production** 8000
Winemaker(s) Martin Williams
Slowly evolving Chardonnay of great structure and complexity is the
winery specialty; robust Pinot Noir also needs time and evolves
impressively if given it. The second label Tunnel Hill wines are more
accessible when young, and better value for those who do not wish
to wait for the Tarrawarra wines to evolve.
Principal Wines Chardonnay and Pinot Noir each released under
the Tarrawarra Vineyard and second label Tunnel Hill.

TARRAWARRA CHARDONNAY
●●●● ▶ $26
Produced from 4.7 hectares of estate-grown grapes in a state-of-the-
art winery using a complex range of viticultural and winemaking
techniques including multiple picking of the grapes at different
maturity levels, barrel fermentation of partly clarified juice, lees
contact and malolactic fermentation. The style is always very
complex with much of the emphasis placed on structure and texture,
the resulting style being quite different from most other wines of the
Yarra Valley.
Cellaring 3–5 years. **Best Vintages** '87, '88, '90, '92, '93
Current Vintage '92
Matching Food Pheasant, turkey.
Tasting Note 1992 Bright, light green-yellow; concentrated
secondary aromas and characters showing malolactic fermentation
and barrel fermentation influences, with the primary fruit down-
played. The palate is complex, almost chewy, with lots of weight,
again showing a range of secondary characters, and should live
for a long time.

TARRAWARRA PINOT NOIR
●●●● ▶ $26
Produced from 6.5 hectares of estate plantings of several different
clones. As with the Chardonnay, much attention is paid to style and
structure: the grapes are picked when very ripe, and the winemaking
techniques are designed to gain maximum extraction of colour and
flavour from the grapes. The wines are often awkward when young,

powerfully impressive with age and have won a significant number of trophies in Australian wine shows in recent years.
Cellaring 3–5 years. **Best Vintages** '88, '90, '91, '92, '94
Current Vintage '92
Matching Food Squab.
Tasting Note 1992 Medium red-purple; clean, sweet, solid plum and cherry fruit with nicely balanced and integrated oak. Sweet, spicy plum fruit is present in abundance on the early and mid palate, firming off on the finish as tannins make their presence felt. Needs time.

TARRAWARRA TUNNEL HILL PINOT NOIR
●●●● $15.50
The second label is not simply a selection of those barrels of Tarrawarra Pinot which have been less successful, but at least part of the wine is deliberately made in a different fashion right from the outset, placing less emphasis on structure, more on fruit and using less new oak. Quite deliberately designed to make a simpler style.
Cellaring 2–3 years. **Best Vintages** '91, '92, '94
Current Vintage '94
Matching Food Poached Tasmanian salmon.
Tasting Note 1994 Light to medium purple; a light and clean bouquet tending simple with hints of Pinot strawberry fruit. There is more weight on the palate with smooth strawberry varietal character; should develop nicely over the next 12 to 18 months.

TARWIN RIDGE WINES

NR 12–13 CD AUSSD
Gippsland **Est.** 1983
Whittles Road, Leongatha South, Vic 3953
Ph (056) 64 3211 **Fax** (056) 64 3211
Open W'ends, Hols **Production** 500
Winemaker(s) Brian Anstee
For the time being Brian Anstee is making his wines at Nicholson River under the gaze of fellow social worker Ken Eckersley; the wines come from 1 hectare of estate pinot and half a hectare each of cabernet and sauvignon blanc.
Principal Wines Sauvignon Blanc, Pinot Noir, Cabernet Merlot.

TAYLORS WINES

★★★★ 7.95–13.95 R AUS27, 115, 157–160
Clare Valley **Est.** 1972
Mintaro Road, Auburn, SA 5451
Ph (088) 49 2008 **Fax** (088) 49 2240
Open 7 days 10–5 **Production** 250 000
Winemaker(s) Andrew Tolley
Taylors continues to flourish and expand, with yet further extensions to the vineyard area, a new white wine cellar under construction, and the retention of the services of Geoff Weaver as consultant. The reason is simple: the wines offer consistently good value for money.

Principal Wines Premium range: Chardonnay, Clare Riesling, White Clare, Pinot Noir, Shiraz, Cabernet Sauvignon; lower-priced Clare Valley range: Riesling, Dry White, Sweet White, Shiraz Cabernet.

TAYLORS CABERNET SAUVIGNON
●●●● $12.95
The 120 hectares of cabernet sauvignon attest to the fact that for at least half of its life Taylors was predominantly a red wine producer, indeed initially exclusively so. The wine is 100% cabernet sauvignon, and is matured in predominantly American oak, with increasing amounts of French oak being introduced.
Cellaring 5–7 years. **Best Vintages** '86, '89, '90, '92, '94
Current Vintage '91
Matching Food Mixed grill.
Tasting Note 1991 Medium red-purple; sophisticated spicy oak handling is evident, together with fresh red berry fruits to the bouquet. The palate shows the same sophisticated oak handling in a modern, ever-so-slightly resinous/charry mould, but the sweet berry fruit flavours give life and freshness as well.

TAYLORS CHARDONNAY
●●● ▶ $12.95
Made solely from the low-yielding mendausa clone used throughout the substantial 90 hectares of estate plantings (with further plantings in progress). A portion of the wine was fermented in French oak, which has had a pronounced impact on the overall blend as from 1993. A formerly innocuous wine which is now very much on the improve.
Cellaring 2–3 years. **Best Vintages** '87, '89, '92, '94
Current Vintage '93
Matching Food Guacamole.
Tasting Note 1993 Light to medium green-yellow; quite pronounced, spicy, slightly raw oak is evident on the bouquet, but there is rather more fruit evident on the palate, which has good mouthfeel, and is fleshed out by just a hint of residual sugar to make a clever commercial style.

TAYLORS CLARE RIESLING
●●●● ▶ $11
In the midst of the debate over the use of the word 'Rhine' in connection with Riesling, Taylors throws in a further confusion. Clare Riesling was the name incorrectly given to a second-rate variety called crouchen; this wine is in fact made from riesling, and the incorrect labelling borders on the bizarre. The wine itself is good, particularly the '93 and '94 vintages.
Cellaring 3–4 years. **Best Vintages** '82, '87, '92, '93, '94
Current Vintage '94
Matching Food Avocado.
Tasting Note 1994 Light green-yellow; crisp, clean and fresh with faintly herbaceous notes. The palate is crisp, clean and fresh with lime, citrus and herb flavours and considerable length and grip to the finish.

TAYLORS SHIRAZ
●●●● $11

Previously called Hermitage, but now re-badged Shiraz in conformity
with international standards, which makes Taylors' adherence to
Clare Riesling all the more surprising. Matured for 12 months in
American oak, in more recent years with much success. The '92 is
a very attractive wine.

Cellaring 4–6 years. **Best Vintages** '86, '89, '90, '92, '94
Current Vintage '92
Matching Food Carpaccio of beef.
Tasting Note 1992 Medium to full purple-red; strong liquorice and
spice varietal aromas interwoven with well balanced, albeit quite
pronounced, vanillin American oak. A generous wine in the mouth,
with lots of spicy/liquorice fruit and very well integrated vanillin oak.
Soft tannins.

TEMPLE BRUER WINES

★★★★ 9.95–19.95 R AUSSD
Langhorne Creek **Est.** 1980
Milang Road, Strathalbyn, SA 5255
Ph (085) 37 0203 **Fax** (085) 37 0131
Open Tues–Sun 10–4.30 **Production** 8000
Winemaker(s) David Bruer

Always known for its eclectic range of wines, Temple Bruer (which
also carries on a substantial business as a vine propagation nursery)
has seen a sharp lift in wine quality. Clean, modern, redesigned
labels add to the appeal.

Principal Wines Riesling, Auslese Riesling, Botrytis Riesling,
Cornucopia Grenache, Cabernet Merlot, Shiraz Malbec, Sparkling
Burgundy.

TEMPLE BRUER AUSLESE RIESLING
●●●● $11.95

Made from riesling grapes which were 40% botrytis affected, and
picked at just under 16° baume, with a little over 3° baume residual
sugar, giving the wine Auslese sweetness. Temple Bruer has
occasionally made much sweeter and more intense totally botrytis-
affected Rieslings.

Cellaring Drink now. **Best Vintages** '81, '84, '89, '90
Current Vintage '90
Matching Food Excellent aperitif, fruit-based desserts.
Tasting Note 1990 Glowing yellow-green; clean lime and toast
bottle developed aromas of medium intensity. The palate is nicely
balanced and weighted, with toasty/limey fruit, soft acid, and now
at its peak.

TEMPLE BRUER CORNUCOPIA GRENACHE
●●●● ▶ $9.95

A new venture for Temple Bruer, and made very much in the modern
cafe style. One suspects that there will be many more wines of this
style coming onto the market in the years ahead.

Cellaring Drink now. **Best Vintages** NA **Current Vintage** '93
Matching Food Duck paté.
Tasting Note 1993 Vivid light purple-red; fresh, fruity and lively
with a hint of spicy oak, possibly chips. On the palate the wine is
wonderfully fresh and vibrant, again with a feeling of some chips
use during fermentation followed by early bottling to preserve
freshness. Appropriately low tannins.

TEMPLE BRUER RIESLING

●●●● $9.95
While Temple Bruer has its winery and viticultural base in Langhorne
Creek, it has not hesitated to go to the Eden Valley for the source of
its Rieslings, which both in dry and sweet form have been impressive
in recent years.
Cellaring 3–5 years. **Best Vintages** '87, '89, '91, '93
Current Vintage '92
Matching Food Fish terrine.
Tasting Note 1992 Medium to full yellow-green; a full, soft lime
and honey bouquet leads on to a very pleasant, soft lime-accented,
bottle developed style with plenty of flavour and which finishes
pleasantly dry.

TEMPLE BRUER SHIRAZ MALBEC

●●● ▶ $11.95
A blend of 70% shiraz and 30% malbec from the 1.5 hectares of
shiraz and half a hectare of malbec, both estate plantings. A
traditional Langhorne Creek blend which works very well. It is made
in open fermenters with traditional punch-down techniques and
matured in American oak.
Cellaring 4–5 years. **Best Vintages** '81, '83, '87, '89, '91
Current Vintage '91
Matching Food Mediterranean-style dishes.
Tasting Note 1991 Medium red-purple; a fresh, clean bouquet
which is surprisingly closed and unevolved, but which will surely
open up with age. The palate is elegantly fresh to the point of being
unusually youthful; there are attractive red berry fruit flavours, fine
tannins and crisp acid. A wine which tastes as if it might not have
undergone malolactic fermentation, though it presumably has.

TERRACE VALE WINES

★★☆ 6–18 CD AUS171
Hunter Valley **Est.** 1971
Deasey's Lane, Pokolbin, NSW 2321
Ph (049) 98 7517 **Fax** (049) 98 7814
Open 7 days 9–5 **Production** 6500
Winemaker(s) Alain Le Prince
A long-established but relatively low-profile winery heavily
dependent on its cellar door and local (including Newcastle) trade.
Principal Wines Semillon, Fine Hunter White, Chardonnay
Semillon, Unwooded Chardonnay, Chardonnay, Gewurztraminer,
Shiraz Cabernet Pinot Noir, Fine Hunter Hermitage, Cabernet
Sauvignon, Sparkling.

THALGARA ESTATE

NR 12.50–15 CD AUSSD
Hunter Valley **Est.** 1985
DeBeyers Road, Pokolbin, NSW 2321
Ph (049) 98 7717 **Fax** (049) 98 7717
Open 7 days 10–5
Production 1500
Winemaker(s) Steve Lamb
A low-profile winery not given to answering correspondence, but
produced a lovely Show Reserve Shiraz which won a silver medal at
the 1994 Canberra National Wine Show, showing harmonious fruit
and oak with intriguing nettle/mint characters. Striking and
delicious.
Principal Wines Chardonnay, Semillon Chardonnay, Shiraz,
Shiraz Cabernet.

THE BRIARS

★★★ 15.50 CD AUSSD
Mornington Peninsula **Est.** 1989
Nepean Highway, Mount Martha, Vic 3934
Ph (059) 74 3686 **Fax** (059) 75 7988
Open Wed–Mon 11–5
Production 1000
Winemaker(s) Various
An enterprising venture of the Mornington Shire Council, with grapes
grown at and sold from the historic Briars Homestead, marketed
cellar door, through a few Mornington Peninsula restaurants and
through The Briars Wine Club mailing list. Two of the vines first
planted in the mid 1800s still survive; The Briars Tourist Centre also
offers light lunches and afternoon teas.
Principal Wines Chardonnay, Pinot Noir, Cabernet Sauvignon.

THE COWRA ESTATE

★★☆ 10–18 R AUS111
Cowra **Est.** 1973
PO Box 266, Boorowa Road, Cowra, NSW 2794
Ph (063) 42 1136 **Fax** (063) 42 4286
Open Tue–Sat 11–5, Sun 12–5
Production NFP
Winemaker(s) Simon Gilbert (Contract)
A major producer with a strong export base, the wines of which I
have tasted many times, but which, for a variety of reasons, do not
seem to realise the full potential of the Cowra region for full-bodied
white wines. It is not that they are bad wines, they are not, but they
lack the style of the early Petaluma and the current Rothbury wines
made from similar vintage sources.
Principal Wines Riesling, Gewurztraminer, Chardonnay, Directors
Reserve Chardonnay, Directors Reserve Merlot, Directors Reserve
Pinot Noir, Cabernet Sauvignon.

THE MINYA WINERY

NR 10.50–15.50 CD AUSSD
Geelong **Est.** 1974
Minya Lane, Connewarre, Vic 3227
Ph (052) 64 1397
Open Public hols & by appt **Production** 1330
Winemaker(s) Susan Dans
Geoff Dans first planted vines in 1974 on his family's dairy farm,
followed by further plantings in 1982 and 1988. I have not tasted
any of the wines.
Principal Wines Gewurztraminer, Chardonnay, Grenache,
Cabernet Shiraz, Merlot.

THE PADTHAWAY ESTATE

NR 16.99–19.99 R AUS81–85
Padthaway **Est.** 1980
Keith-Naracoorte Road, Padthaway, SA 5271
Ph (087) 65 5039 **Fax** (087) 65 5097
Open 7 days 10–4.30 **Production** 10 000
Winemaker(s) Nigel Catt
The only functioning winery in Padthaway, set in the superb grounds
of the Estate in a large and gracious old stone woolshed; the
homestead is in the Relais et Chateaux mould, offering luxurious
accommodation and fine food. Surprisingly few wines are presented
to me for tasting, but the last Pinot Brut tasted was truly excellent.
Principal Wines Eliza Pinot Chardonnay Cuvée, Eliza Pinot Noir
Brut, Eliza Chardonnay.

THE RIDGE WINES

★★☆ 9.20–13.50 CD AUSSD
Coonawarra **Est.** 1984
Naracoorte Road, Coonawarra, SA 5263
Ph (087) 36 5071
Open 7 days 9–5 **Production** 2000
Winemaker(s) Sid Kidman
Quite simply, the quality should be better given the area and Sid
Kidman's viticultural expertise, although I must admit, it is some time
since I have tasted the wines.
Principal Wines Riesling, Sauvignon Blanc, Cabernet Sauvignon,
Shiraz.

THE SILOS WINERY

NR 8.50–14 CD AUSSD
South Coast New South Wales **Est.** 1985
Princes Highway, Jaspers Brush, NSW 2535
Ph (044) 48 6082
Open 7 days 10–5 **Production** 1400
Winemaker(s) Alan Bamfield

Aimed purely at the tourist trade; wine quality has left much to be desired, but a delightful, light, pepper-spice 1990 Shiraz redressed the balance.
Principal Wines Chardonnay, Semillon, Sauvignon Blanc, Shiraz, Malbec, Port.

THE WARREN VINEYARD

NR 11–15 CD AUS180
Warren Valley **Est.** 1985
224 Dickinson Street, Pemberton, WA 6260
Ph (097) 76 1115 **Fax** (097) 76 1115
Open 7 days 11–5 **Production** 600
Winemaker(s) Virginia Willcocks
The 1.4 hectare vineyard was established in 1985, and is one of the smallest in the Pemberton region, coming to public notice when its 1991 Cabernet Sauvignon won the award for the Best Red Table Wine from the Pemberton Region at the 1992 SGIO Western Australia Winemakers Exhibition. The wine in question shows very cool growing conditions, being a little leafy and astringent, but with pleasant overall flavour.
Principal Wines Chardonnay, Riesling, Merlot, Cabernet Merlot, Cabernet Sauvignon, Port.

THE WILLOWS VINEYARD

★★★☆ 9–14 R AUS36, 177, UK11
Barossa Valley **Est.** 1989
Light Pass Road, Light Pass, Barossa Valley, SA 5355
Ph (085) 62 1080 **Fax** (085) 62 3447
Open 7 days 10.30–4.30 **Production** 3500
Winemaker(s) Peter Scholz, Michael Scholz
The Scholz family has been grape growers for generations. Current generation winemakers Peter and Michael Scholz could not resist the temptation to make smooth, well-balanced and flavoursome wines under their own label. These are all marketed with some years' bottle age.
Principal Wines Riesling, Semillon, Pinot Noir, Shiraz, Cabernet Sauvignon.

THE WILSON VINEYARD

★★★☆ 11–19.50 CD AUS87, 111, 188
Clare Valley **Est.** 1974
Polish Hill River, Sevenhill via Clare, SA 5453
Ph (088) 43 4310
Open W'ends 10–4.30 **Production** 3700
Winemaker(s) John Wilson
Dr John Wilson is a tireless ambassador for the Clare Valley and for wine (and its beneficial effect on health) in general. His wines are made using techniques and philosophies garnered early in his wine career, and can be idiosyncratic.

Principal Wines Gallery Series Riesling, Cabernet Sauvignon, Hippocrene Sparkling Burgundy, Chardonnay, Zinfandel, Liqueur Gewerztraminer.

THE WILSON VINEYARD CHARDONNAY
●●● ▶ $12.50
As I have written many times, chardonnay is an unusually difficult variety to grow and handle in the Clare Valley. This wine represents a major departure in style for The Wilson Vineyard; after a gap in 1993 when no wine was made, John Wilson has moved from barrel fermentation, malolactic fermentation and lees contact to a much more direct, fruity style which receives only limited exposure to oak and is early bottled without malolactic fermentation.
Cellaring 1–3 years. **Best Vintages** NA **Current Vintage** '94
Matching Food Crab.
Tasting Note 1994 Light green-yellow; firm, crisp and youthful, quite aromatic and with some lift. There are lifted citrus and melon fruit flavours and again a hint of lift. Has length and may develop over the short term.

THE WILSON VINEYARD RIESLING
●●●● ▶ $11
John Wilson has always made powerful Riesling from his Polish Hill River vineyards, almost invariably at the upper end of the Clare Valley hierarchy. 1994 was a low-yielding vintage and the result is a very concentrated, long-lived wine.
Cellaring 4–7 years. **Best Vintages** '85, '90, '91, '92, '94
Current Vintage '94
Matching Food Japanese cuisine.
Tasting Note 1994 Light green-yellow; firm, elegant and intense, with a hint of spice but still developing its full fruit aroma. The palate is crisp with a distinct hint of spice and some ever-so-slightly rough herbal aspects; it has the fruit weight and intensity to smooth out and settle down with time in bottle.

THISTLE HILL VINEYARD
★★★★ 9.95–13.95 CD AUS16
Mudgee **Est.** 1976
McDonalds Road, Mudgee, NSW 2850
Ph (063) 73 3546 **Fax** (063) 73 3540
Open 7 days 9–5 **Production** 3500
Winemaker(s) David Robertson
David and Leslie Robertson produce supremely honest wines, always full of flavour and appropriately reflecting the climate and terroir. Some may be a little short on finesse, but never on character.
Principal Wines Chardonnay, Riesling, Pinot Noir, Cabernet Sauvignon.

THISTLE HILL CABERNET SAUVIGNON
●●●● $13.95
The 5 hectares of cabernet sauvignon amount to half the total estate plantings; this is the most important wine in the Thistle Hill stable,

ageing gracefully into a gently earthy but always-rich regional style.
Cellaring 4–7 years. **Best Vintages** '85, '86, '88, '89, '93
Current Vintage '90
Matching Food English cheddar.
Tasting Note 1990 Medium to full red-purple; ripe,
briary/bramble/chocolate fruit, at once sweet yet not jammy,
dominates the bouquet. The palate is less rich than the bouquet, but
no less attractive, with mouthfilling cedar/cigar box/dark berry
flavours, finishing with soft tannins.

THISTLE HILL CHARDONNAY
●●●● ▶ $12.95
Produced from 3 hectares of low-yielding estate plantings, and
remarkably consistent in style and quality over the years. Generously
flavoured and constructed, it ages into a full-blown traditional
Australian cross of regional and varietal character — what we used
to call White Burgundy.
Cellaring 4–7 years. **Best Vintages** '84, '86, '88, '93, '94
Current Vintage '92
Matching Food Veal cutlets.
Tasting Note 1992 Medium yellow-green; ripe, buttery/honeyed
sweet fruit with subtle oak on the bouquet. The palate has abundant
sweet fruit showing honey and peach, but the finish is not sugary.

THOMAS WINES

NR 4.50–25 CD AUSSD
South-west Coastal Plain **Est.** 1976
23-24 Crowd Road, Gelorup, WA 6230
Ph (097) 95 7925
Open By appt **Production** 600
Winemaker(s) Gill Thomas
I have not tasted the elegant wines of Bunbury pharmacist Gill
Thomas for several years; they are only sold to a local clientele.
Principal Wines Pinot Noir, Cabernet Sauvignon.

THORNHILL/THE BERRY FARM *

NR 6.50–13 CD AUSSD
Margaret River **Est.** 1990
Bessel Road, Rosa Glen, WA 6285
Ph (097) 57 5054 **Fax** (097) 57 5054
Open 7 days 10–4.30 **Production** NFP
Winemaker(s) Eion Lindsay
Although I did not enjoy the Thornhill table wines, the fruit wines
under The Berry Farm label are extraordinarily good. The Sparkling
Strawberry wine has intense strawberry flavour; the Plum Port
likewise, carrying its 16% alcohol with remarkable ease.
Principal Wines Thornhill label: Classic Dry Semillon, Sauvignon
Blanc, Cabernet Sauvignon, Tickled Pink (Sparkling Cabernet
Sauvignon), Still Tickled Pink (Light Cabernet Sauvignon). The Berry
Farm label: a range of fruit-based wines including Sparkling
Strawberry and Plum Port.

TILBA VALLEY WINES

NR 9.50–13.50 CD AUSSD
South Coast New South Wales **Est.** 1978
Glen Eden Vineyard, Corunna Lake via Tilba, NSW 2546
Ph (044) 73 7308
Open Mon–Sat 10–5, Sun 11–5 **Production** 1400
Winemaker(s) Barry Field
A strongly tourist-oriented operation, serving a ploughman's lunch
daily from noon to 2 pm. Draws upon 5 hectares of estate vineyards;
no recent tastings, but 1991 was said to be a very good vintage.
Principal Wines Traminer Riesling, Semillon, Chardonnay,
Cabernet Hermitage.

TIM ADAMS WINES

★★★★ 10.50–17 CD AUS11, 36, 49, 177, UK11
Clare Valley **Est.** 1986
Warenda Road, Clare, SA 5453
Ph (088) 42 2429 **Fax** (088) 42 2429
Open Mon–Fri 10.30–5, W'ends 11–5 **Production** 14 000
Winemaker(s) Tim Adams
Tim and Pam Adams have built a first class business since Tim
Adams left his position as winemaker at Leasingham in 1985. Nine
local growers provide the grapes for the enterprise, which has
consistently produced wines of exceptional depth of flavour.
Principal Wines Riesling, Semillon, Botrytis Semillon, Shiraz,
The Fergus Grenache, Aberfeldy Shiraz, Cabernet.

TIM ADAMS ABERFELDY SHIRAZ
●●●● ▶ $17
The flagship of the Tim Adams range, always generous, rich and
complex, primarily fruit-driven but with some American oak input.
Cellaring 7–10 years. **Best Vintages** '86, '87, '90, '92, '94
Current Vintage '92
Matching Food Spit roast lamb.
Tasting Note 1992 Medium to full red-purple; strong and complex
varietal aromas ranging from chocolate to briar to mint to dark
berries, with an echo of gaminess. The palate is more minty than
the bouquet, with plenty of depth to the fruit, and a touch of
spicy/charry American oak.

TIM ADAMS CABERNET
●●●● $12
As the abbreviated name suggests, in fact a blend of cabernet
sauvignon (80%) and cabernet franc (20%). As with all of the Tim
Adams reds, generously proportioned with fully-ripened fruit.
Cellaring 5–10 years. **Best Vintages** '86, '87, '90, '92, '94
Current Vintage '92
Matching Food Beef casserole.
Tasting Note 1992 Medium to full red-purple; the bouquet has
abundant dark berry and chocolate fruit married with sweet vanillin

oak. The palate is rich and chewy with attractive dark berry and
chocolate fruit, subtle oak, and fine tannins.

TIM ADAMS SEMILLON
●●●● $12
Once the only estate vines, the half-hectare of semillon still provides
the core of the Tim Adams Semillon. It is made to develop early, with
substantial oak input and what appears to be skin contact used prior
to fermentation.
Cellaring 1–2 years. **Best Vintages** '87, '90, '93, '94
Current Vintage '94
Matching Food Rich white meat dishes.
Tasting Note 1994 Medium yellow-green; already very developed
and rich, with good fruit balance and integration to the bouquet. The
palate is complex, rich and full-bodied with sweet, tropical fruits and
spicy oak; a full-blown Australian White Burgundy style.

TIM ADAMS THE FERGUS GRENACHE
●●● ▶ $11
Prior to the 1993 vintage Tim Adams acquired 2 hectares of
40-year-old grenache, which now produces The Fergus. It is made in
a no-holds-barred style; the 1993 vintage achieved 14.5% alcohol.
Whatever else, Grenache has many faces.
Cellaring 3–4 years. **Best Vintages** NA **Current Vintage** '93
Matching Food Braised duck.
Tasting Note 1993 Medium red-purple; pronounced minty aromas
together with some dark cherry and a degree of lift apparent on the
bouquet. On the palate there is lots of bright, essency berry fruit,
with the high alcohol showing itself only on a slightly sweet (alcohol
sweet) finish.

TIM GRAMP WINES *
★★★★ 13–17 R AUS123
Southern Vales **Est.** 1990
PO Box 810, Unley, SA 5061
Ph (08) 379 3658
Open Not **Production** 2500
Winemaker(s) Tim Gramp
Tim Gramp runs an operation very similar to that of Simon Hackett,
owning neither vineyards nor a winery, but simply purchasing
grapes and making the wines in leased facilities.
Principal Wines Shiraz, Grenache.

TIM GRAMP GRENACHE
●●●● $13
Introduced with the 1993 vintage, fermented in new American oak,
and made in the typical full-blooded style which has made the Tim
Gramp label so well known in such a short period of time.
Cellaring 3–4 years. **Best Vintages** NA **Current Vintage** '94
Matching Food Richly-sauced casseroles.
Tasting Note 1994 Medium red-purple; a rich, ripe and perfumed

bouquet with potent plum and berry fruit. On the palate, the 13.7% alcohol is quite evident, giving the wine a chunky feel, but without becoming jammy or porty.

TIM GRAMP SHIRAZ
●●●● ▶ $17
The inaugural 1991 Shiraz won a trophy, six gold and two silver medals, including a gold medal at the 1993 Intervin International Wine Show in New York. The wine is made in a full-throated, full-blooded style, using low-yielding dry-grown grapes and lots of American oak, and works to perfection.
Cellaring 5–10 years. **Best Vintages** '91, '92
Current Vintage '92
Matching Food Barbecued, marinated steak.
Tasting Note 1992 Dense purple-red; a richly-fruited bouquet with abundant dark cherry and plum fruit aromas. The palate is rich and velvety, with delicious cherry, mint and plum flavours running through well integrated and balanced American oak.

TIM KNAPPSTEIN WINES

★★★★☆ 14.60–20 R AUS14, 104, 164, UK41
Clare Valley **Est.** 1976
2 Pioneer Avenue, Clare, SA 5453
Ph (088) 42 2600 **Fax** (088) 42 3831
Open Mon–Fri 9–5, W'ends, Public hols 10–5
Production 36 000
Winemaker(s) Tim Knappstein
While Tim Knappstein has long been regarded as one of Australia's foremost makers of Rhine Riesling and a very good red winemaker, there have been significant changes for the better in the past few years, most notably its acquisition by Petaluma. The Lenswood Vineyard is now entirely separate from Tim Knappstein Wines (see separate entry).
Principal Wines Riesling, Gewurztraminer, Fumé Blanc, Chardonnay, Botrytis Riesling, Cabernet Merlot, Cabernet Sauvignon.

TIM KNAPPSTEIN BOTRYTISED RIESLING (375 ML)
●●●●● $13.20
Only made intermittently when vineyard conditions permit or dictate, five times in the last 15 years. Initially the wine started as an artificially inoculated, rack matured wine, but the cost of this led to its cessation. All of the recent vintages have been outstanding.
Cellaring Up to 5 years, even more. **Best Vintages** '80, '82, '86, '89, '92 **Current Vintage** '92
Matching Food Poached peaches with King Island cream.
Tasting Note 1992 Brilliant green-yellow; intense, piercing lime aromas with just a hint of the tropical/apricot overtones of botrytis. The palate is similar, with unusually pure riesling varietal character preserved notwithstanding the level of botrytis. Outstanding wine.

TIM KNAPPSTEIN CABERNET MERLOT
●●●● $18.50
Made in a distinctive style, and designed to be sold and consumed
virtually immediately on release. The softening is achieved two ways:
firstly by the addition of merlot, and secondly by the use of some
carbonic maceration. It works.
Cellaring Drink now. **Best Vintages** NA **Current Vintage** '92
Matching Food Roast veal.
Tasting Note 1992 Medium to full red, with just a touch of purple;
the bouquet is clean, soft with gentle fruit, of light to medium intensity
and minimal oak influence. The palate is more distinctive, with a
combination of the sappy Merlot and carbonic maceration
characters coming through, finishing with soft tannins.

TIM KNAPPSTEIN CABERNET SAUVIGNON
●●●● $20
Derived from 10 hectares of cabernet sauvignon which is in fact
owned personally by Tim and wife Annie Knappstein, rather than the
company, but is to all intents and purposes estate-grown. The overall
style is very much lighter than most of its Clare Valley counterparts,
and to be perfectly honest, I wish it had a little more concentration.
Cellaring 3–5 years. **Best Vintages** '77, '78, '80, '84, '85, '90,
'93, '94 **Current Vintage** '89
Matching Food Mild cheese.
Tasting Note 1989 Medium purple-red; a gently fruity, plummy
bouquet of medium intensity with subtle oak. The palate shows more
of the '89 vintage character than the bouquet, but still works fairly
well all things considered, even if it does fall away slightly on the
finish.

TIM KNAPPSTEIN FUMÉ BLANC
●●●●● $18.50
A complex blend of Clare Valley and Lenswood sauvignon blanc
and semillon, which has deservedly enjoyed great critical acclaim
and show success since its present formulation in 1993, although the
label goes back much further. 25% barrel fermentation gives that
extra level of complexity, and the Lenswood component has lifted
the quality of the wine out of all recognition.
Cellaring Best young. **Best Vintages** '93, '94
Current Vintage '94
Matching Food Tartare of salmon.
Tasting Note 1994 Light yellow-green; complex aromas running
the gamut through gooseberry, tropical, herbal and smoky. The
palate has length and crispness, with all of the flavours promised
by the bouquet.

TIM KNAPPSTEIN RIESLING
●●●●● $14.60
The reputation of the Rieslings of the Clare Valley are as much due
to Tim Knappstein as to any other winemaker, past or present. Tim
Knappstein himself would be the first to say that the quality and style
of Riesling is in turn strongly dependent upon the terroir and climate,

and that too is true. The combination of man, climate and variety in the outcome produce a classic wine.
Cellaring Up to 20 years. **Best Vintages** '77, '78, '79, '80, '83, '86, '90, '93, '94 **Current Vintage** '94
Matching Food Salads of all kinds.
Tasting Note 1994 The product of an excellent vintage; the bouquet is fine, floral and toasty, with some citrus/herbal notes. The palate has many flavours, predominantly spicy/toasty, but early in its life was not as fruity as the '93.

TIM KNAPPSTEIN THE FRANC
●●●● $14.99
The first release of this wine under the clever name of 'the Franc'. Picked very late (it contains 13.5% alcohol) but nonetheless made as a soft, early-drinking style which is both unusual and engaging.
Cellaring Now–3 years. **Best Vintages** NA
Current Vintage '94
Matching Food Italian.
Tasting Note 1994 Medium to full purple-red; sweet, luscious, ripe raspberry/red berry fruit aromas with little or no oak evident. The palate is similarly luscious and berryish, much sweeter than the relatively rare varietal Cabernet Francs encountered from other makers.

TINGLE-WOOD WINES
★★★★★ 10–12 CD AUSSD
Great Southern **Est.** 1976
Glenrowan Road, Denmark, WA 6333
Ph (098) 40 9218
Open 7 days 9–5 **Production** Nil 1994 (bird damage)
Winemaker(s) John Wade (Contract)
This remote, forest-encircled vineyard has produced some quite lovely wines for owner Bob Wood, with trophy-winning wines from both 1990 and 1991. Sadly, no grapes were picked in 1992 or 1994 owing to seasonal conditions.
Principal Wines Yellow Tingle Riesling, Yellow Tingle Late Harvest Riesling, Red Tingle Cabernet Shiraz.

TINGLE-WOOD RED TINGLE SHIRAZ
●●●● $12
A blend of 50% cabernet sauvignon and 50% shiraz deriving from 0.75 of a hectare of each variety. A very elegant style which ages marvellously well.
Cellaring 7 years. **Best Vintages** '90, '91
Current Vintage '90, '91
Matching Food Roast lamb.
Tasting Note 1990 Medium to full red-purple; clean, distinctly herbaceous style, yet not bitter, with subtle oak. The palate is crisp, lean yet not the least sour or bitter; a clean wine with hints of red berry fruit and considerable length.

TINGLE-WOOD YELLOW TINGLE RIESLING
●●●●● $12

Incredibly, the 1990 and 1991 wines were still available in late
1994 at a mere $12 a bottle. Produced from 1.5 hectares of very
low-yielding vines, and of the highest possible quality.
Cellaring Up to 10 years. **Best Vintages** '90, '91
Current Vintage '90, '91
Matching Food Sashimi, fuller-flavoured fish.
Tasting Note 1990 Light to medium yellow-green; tight lime juice
aromas with just a hint of toast. On the palate, a potent wine with
tremendous length and intensity in classic Riesling style, starting to
show development but still in many respects a baby. The '91 is
every bit as good.

TINLINS WINERY

NR 2.60–4.15 CD AUSSD
Southern Vales **Est.** 1977
Kangarilla Road, McLaren Flat, SA 5171
Ph (08) 323 8649 **Fax** (08) 323 9747
Open 7 days 9–5 **Production** 120 000
Winemaker(s) Warren Randall
A very interesting operation drawing upon 95 hectares of estate
vineyards which specialises in bulk wine sales to the major
Australian wine companies. A small proportion of the production is
sold direct through the cellar door at mouthwateringly low prices.
Principal Wines Generic table, fortified and flavoured wines sold
in bottles, flagons, 6-litre casks and 25-litre kegs for as little as
$1 a litre.

TIPPERARY HILL ESTATE *

NR 9–14.50 CD AUSSD
Bendigo **Est.** 1986
Alma-Bowedale Road, Alma via Maryborough, Vic 3465
Ph (054) 61 3312
Open Sun 10–5 **Production** 1000
Winemaker(s) Paul Flowers
Two hectares of vineyard produce the bulk of the wine for Tipperary
Hill Estate, which is one of the newest arrivals in the Bendigo region.
Principal Wines Shiraz, Pinot Noir, Cabernets.

TISDALL WINES *

★★☆ 6.25–10 R AUS104
Murray River **Est.** 1979
Carmelia Creek Road, Echuca, Vic 3564
Ph (054) 82 1911 **Fax** (054) 82 2516
Open Mon–Fri 9–5, W'ends 10–5 **Production** NFP
Winemaker(s) Toni Stockhausen
After an absence from the market following its acquisition by
Mildara Blass, Tisdall has made a cautious and — it must be said —

unconvincing return with a limited range of wines, of which the '92 Cabernet Merlot is the best.

Principal Wines Chenin Blanc, Chardonnay, Shiraz Cabernet, Cabernet Merlot.

TIZZANA WINES

NR 5.50–16.50 CD AUSSD
Sydney District **Est.** 1887
518 Tizzana Road, Ebenezer, NSW 2756
Ph (045) 79 1150 **Fax** (045) 79 1216
Open W'ends, Hols 12–6 **Production** 200
Winemaker(s) Peter Auld

The only estate wines tasted (several years ago) were not good, but the historic stone winery is most certainly worth a visit, and a wide selection of Tizzana Selection wines from other makers gives a broad choice.

Principal Wines Estate-grown and made Shiraz, Cabernet Sauvignon, Port; cleanskin wines under Tizzana Selection label.

TOLLANA WINES

★★★★☆ 9.95–17 R AUS147, UK83
Barossa Valley **Est.** 1888
Tanunda Road, Nuriootpa, SA 5355
Ph (085) 62 0389 **Fax** (085) 62 2494
Open Mon–Sat 10–5, Sun 12–4 **Production** NFP
Winemaker(s) Neville Falkenburg

As the Southcorp Wine Group moves to establish regional identity for its wines, Tollana is simultaneously gaining the recognition it deserves and emphasising its Eden Valley base.

Principal Wines Riesling, Chardonnay, Sauvignon Blanc, Semillon, Botrytis Riesling, Hermitage, Show Hermitage, Cabernet Sauvignon Bin TR222, all Eden Valley sourced with the exception of the Botrytis Riesling.

TOLLANA BOTRYTIS RIESLING (375 ML)
●●●●● $11

Made from heavily botrytised Coonawarra and Eden Valley riesling harvested at an average of 21° baume, resulting in a massive 148 grams per litre of residual sugar. The '92 vintage has been a prolific trophy and gold medal winner.

Cellaring Drink now. **Best Vintages** NA **Current Vintage** '92
Matching Food Very sweet, rich desserts.

Tasting Note 1992 Medium to full orange; voluminous apricot and cumquat fruit aromas with a necessary touch of volatile acidity. A very complex wine on the palate with great length and strong acid balancing the incredibly rich raisiny apricot palate.

TOLLANA CABERNET SAUVIGNON BIN TR222
●●●● ▶ $15.95

Another Tollana Classic with a proud history. Made entirely from Eden Valley cabernet sauvignon, it is matured in new and one-year-old American and French oak for 15 months. Like the Riesling, it has been a prolific and consistent gold medal winner.

Cellaring 5–7 years. **Best Vintages** '86, '88, '90, '91, '92
Current Vintage '92
Matching Food Braised lamb.
Tasting Note 1992 Medium to full red-purple; concentrated briary/berry fruit aromas with the American, rather than the French, oak dominating the bouquet. A full-flavoured wine on the palate with lots of dark berry fruit with briary undertones; the oak is in restraint, the texture smooth, finishing with soft tannins.

TOLLANA CHARDONNAY
●●●● $11
Another very complex wine with a great deal of sophisticated oak input, costing both time and money. There is some very good fruit lurking underneath the oak, but a lighter touch would surely make an even better wine. A consistent silver medal winner.

Cellaring 2–3 years. **Best Vintages** '88, '90, '92, '93
Current Vintage '93
Matching Food Chicken poached in white wine.
Tasting Note 1993 Medium yellow-green; a very rich and complex bouquet with masses of barrel ferment oak in inimitable Penfolds style. The palate is big, rich and oaky with some citrus and melon fruit lurking in the forest.

TOLLANA RIESLING
●●●● $9.95
For the better part of two decades, the Tollana Riesling has been one of Australia's better kept secrets, particularly under its prior ownerships. It ages superbly well, and has not infrequently collected major trophies at national wine shows as a mature wine.

Cellaring 5–7 years. **Best Vintages** '86, '87, '90, '92, '93
Current Vintage '93
Matching Food Seafood salad.
Tasting Note 1993 Glowing yellow-green; potent fruit aromas ranging from herbaceous through lime and grapefruit. The palate is full, rich and soft, with an amalgam of lime and toast flavours. A quicker developing vintage.

TOLLANA SEMILLON
●●● ▶ $11
A slight slip from the pure Eden Valley region of origin, as it is in fact a blend of 58% Eden Valley and 42% Adelaide Hills material. The wine is 100% barrel fermented and matured in new French oak for six months, which seems a gross case of overkill. The wine would be better still if it were less heavily oaked (and would doubtless cost less to make).

Cellaring 2–3 years. **Best Vintages** '91, '92, '93
Current Vintage '93
Matching Food Pork with apricots.
Tasting Note 1993 Glowing yellow-green; a very rich, full bouquet, dominated by classy French oak. In the mouth, a full-blown

style with lots of honey, butter and toasty oak, but dries out a
fraction on the finish because of all of that oak. Some will love this
style.

TOLLEY WINES

★★★★ 6.95–17.95 R AUS13, 15, 37, 82–85, UK68
Barossa Valley **Est.** 1892
30 Barracks Road, Hope Valley, SA 5090
Ph (08) 264 2255 **Fax** (08) 263 7485
Open Mon–Fri 7.30–5, Sat 9–5 **Production** 150 000
Winemaker(s) Christopher Tolley, Diana Heinrich
A large family-owned and operated winery, known for the sheer
consistency of the quality of its wines; the prices are no less
appealing. The 44 hectares of vineyards established by Tolley in
Padthaway should provide premium wines through the Hope Valley
brand as the vines mature, adding another important string to the
Tolley bow.
Principal Wines There are three ranges. Bottom end: Cellar
Reserve Riesling, Classic Dry White, Traminer Riesling, Late Harvest
Muscat, Chardonnay, Shiraz Cabernet; the principal line of Pedare:
Riesling, Gewurztraminer, Auslese Riesling, Chardonnay, Cabernet
Sauvignon; limited quantity top-of-the-range Hope Valley
Chardonnay and Cabernet Sauvignon, also Port and Sparkling.

TOLLEY PEDARE CABERNET SAUVIGNON
●●●● ▶ $12.50
Yet another surprising performer sourced almost entirely from
12 hectares of Barossa floor estate vineyards. Both the '90 and '91
vintages have been excellent. The wine is usually sold with between
three and four years bottle age, which makes the price even more
attractive.
Cellaring 4–7 years. **Best Vintages** '86, '88, '90, '91, '92
Current Vintage '91
Matching Food Grilled calf's liver.
Tasting Note 1991 Medium red with just a touch of purple; a
clean bouquet with some cedary notes of medium intensity. A well
structured, mature wine on the palate in the secondary phase of its
development with fine tannins and good length to the flavour.

TOLLEY PEDARE GEWURZTRAMINER
●●●● $12.50
Produced from 6 hectares of vines in the thoroughly unlikely
surrounds of the Barossa Valley floor. Somehow or other Tolley has
always managed to produce a special wine, which has won
120 show awards, including three trophies and 20 gold medals
over the years.
Cellaring 1–5 years. **Best Vintages** '87, '91, '92, '93, '94
Current Vintage '94
Matching Food All Asian cuisine.
Tasting Note 1994 Light green-yellow; classic lime, spice and
lychee aromas of medium intensity on the bouquet, and similar lime
and spice flavours on the palate. Finishes dry, as it should.

TOLLEY PEDARE RIESLING
●●●● ▶ $11.50

A far from glamorous wine which has proved its breeding in the show ring in recent years, the '92 vintage winning gold medals in Sydney and Brisbane, the '93 a silver medal at the 1994 Australian National Wine Show in Canberra. A no-frills style, which ages nicely.

Cellaring Up to 5 years. **Best Vintages** '87, '91, '92, '93, '94
Current Vintage '93
Matching Food Salade niçoise.
Tasting Note 1993 Light yellow-green; firm, crisp toasty aromas, neither enzyme nor yeast-driven. The palate is similarly stylish and unforced, with passionfruit and citrus flavours, and excellent balance and length.

TORRESAN ESTATE

NR 6–13 CD AUSSD
Southern Vales **Est.** 1972
Manning Road, Flagstaff Hill, SA 5159
Ph (08) 270 2500 **Fax** (08) 270 3848
Open Mon–Sat 8–5 **Production** 13 000
Winemaker(s) Michael Torresan, John Torresan
A substantial cellar door trade and local clientele account for most sales of mature but uninspiring wines.
Principal Wines Riesling, Semillon, Cabernet Shiraz, Cabernet Sauvignon, Fortifieds.

TREETON ESTATE *

★★★★ 13–15 CD AUSSD
Margaret River **Est.** 1984
North Treeton Road, Cowaramup, WA 6284
Ph (097) 55 5481 **Fax** (097) 55 5051
Open 7 days 10–6 **Production** NFP
Winemaker(s) David McGowan
David McGowan and wife Corinne purchased the 30-hectare property upon which Treeton Estate is established in 1982, beginning to plant the vines two years later. He has done just about everything in his life, and in the early years was working in Perth, which led to various setbacks for the vineyard. Since 1993 the wines have been made at Treeton by David McGowan with some consultancy help, and it is abundantly clear that he has either got great feel for wine or some very good help.
Principal Wines Shiraz, Chardonnay, Semillon, Petit Rouge, Cabernet Sauvignon.

TREETON ESTATE CABERNET SAUVIGNON
●●●● ▶ $15

Like the Shiraz of the same year, spotlessly clean, but seems to have been taken to bottle a little earlier than it should have been, and is

slightly undermade or underworked. For all that, a more than creditable wine.
Cellaring 3–5 years. **Best Vintages** NA **Current Vintage** '93
Matching Food Margaret River brie.
Tasting Note 1993 Medium red-purple; clean, red berry fruit with sweet vanillin oak on the bouquet leads on to a palate with youthful red berry flavours, some caramel/toffee oak, and soft tannins.

TREETON ESTATE SHIRAZ
●●●● ▶ $14
The evocative and elegant label graces an extremely good wine, with razor-sharp varietal definition and technically sound winemaking. A singularly propitious start for on-site winemaking, which was previously carried out at Woody Nook.
Cellaring 3–5 years. **Best Vintages** NA **Current Vintage** '93
Matching Food Lamb Provençale.
Tasting Note 1993 Medium red-purple; a potent, high-toned bouquet with spicy/earthy/berry aromas. The palate, like the bouquet, is essentially fruit- rather than oak-driven, with intense spicy/berry fruit flavours, and a clean finish.

TRENTHAM ESTATE

★★★★ 8–14 R AUS11, 49, 71, 162, 177, UK69
Murray River **Est.** 1988
Sturt Highway, Trentham Cliffs, NSW 2738
Ph (050) 24 8888 **Fax** (050) 24 8800
Open Mon–Fri 9–5, W'ends 10–5 **Production** 22 000
Winemaker(s) Anthony Murphy
Remarkably consistent tasting notes across all wine styles from all vintages since 1989 attest to the expertise of ex-Mildara winemaker Tony Murphy, now making the Trentham wines from his family vineyards. Indeed, Trentham seems to be going from strength to strength with each succeeding vintage. The winery restaurant is also recommended.
Principal Wines Chardonnay, Sauvignon Blanc Fumé, Colombard Chardonnay, Rhine Riesling, Traminer Riesling, Spatlese Lexia, Noble Taminga, Pinot Noir, Merlot, Shiraz, Cabernet Merlot, Trentham, Burke & Wills Tawny Port.

TRENTHAM ESTATE CHARDONNAY
●●●● $10.95
Produced from 6 hectares of estate-grown grapes, which account for 20% of the total plantings of around 30 hectares. Skilfully made, using predominantly French oak. A silver medal winner at the 1994 Australian National Wine Show at Canberra.
Cellaring 2–3 years. **Best Vintages** '90, '92, '93
Current Vintage '93
Matching Food Avocado salad.
Tasting Note 1993 Medium yellow-green; complex aromas with some tropical peach fruit and spicy oak. The palate, too, is complex, with rounded sweet fruit; the oak is just a fraction oily/resinous on the finish.

TRENTHAM ESTATE MERLOT

●●●● $10.95

Tony Murphy has often managed to conjure up something special
with merlot; the Mildura region is not the most likely site for a variety
such as this. The '93, a silver medal winner at the 1994 Royal
Sydney Show, is a particularly good example.

Cellaring 3–4 years. **Best Vintages** '92, '93, '94
Current Vintage '93
Matching Food Marinated rabbit.
Tasting Note 1993 Medium red; a clean bouquet of medium
intensity showing a pleasant amalgam of berry and leaf aromas.
The palate, too, is fresh and clean with juicy red berry fruit flavours,
restrained oak, and a pleasingly soft finish.

TUCK'S RIDGE

★★★★ 11.95–15.95 R AUS113, UK43
Mornington Peninsula **Est.** 1993
37 Red Hill-Shoreham Road, Red Hill South, Vic 3937
Ph (059) 89 8660 **Fax** (059) 89 8579
Open W'ends, Hols 12–5 **Production** 5000
Winemaker(s) Daniel Greene

Tuck's Ridge did not appear on the market until July 1993, and left
no doubt about its intentions of emulating the rapid market
penetration achieved by Scotchmans Hill and Yarra Ridge. A little
under 2 hectares of vines were first planted in 1987; since that time
plantings have been increased to 25 hectares, making it the largest
vineyard on the Mornington Peninsula.

Principal Wines Semillon, Riesling, Chardonnay, Pinot Noir,
Cabernet Sauvignon.

TUCK'S RIDGE RIESLING

●●●● $11.95

Produced in limited quantities (380 cases in 1994) from estate-
grown grapes. There are not many Mornington Peninsula Rieslings;
this is one of the better ones.

Cellaring 2–4 years. **Best Vintages** NA **Current Vintage** '94
Matching Food Char-grilled octopus.
Tasting Note 1994 Light to medium yellow-green; the bouquet is
intense with strong lime juice and passionfruit aromas, leading on to
a well made, high-toned palate with plenty of lime juice flavour. Just
a hint of sweetness from 7 grams per litre of acid.

TUCK'S RIDGE SEMILLON

●●●● ▶ $15.95

Made its debut in 1994, signalling an auspicious first for the
Mornington Peninsula. Only 500 cases were made, but it certainly
points the way for the future.

Cellaring Probably best young. **Best Vintages** NA
Current Vintage '94
Matching Food Grilled goat's cheese salad.
Tasting Note 1994 Light green-yellow; pronounced, pungent

grassy varietal character, a cross between Margaret River and New Zealand in character. There is abundant fruit on the palate, with some spicy notes, and slightly riper, richer, fruit than the bouquet suggests. Long finish.

TUERONG ESTATE

NR 18–22.50 CD AUSSD
Mornington Peninsula **Est.** 1984
Mornington-Flinders Road, Red Hill, Vic 3937
Ph (059) 89 2129
Open W'ends, Public hols 11–5 **Production** 200
Winemaker(s) Peter Cumming
A most unusual operation, which is in reality a family Italian-style restaurant at which the wine is principally sold and served, and which offers something totally different on the Mornington Peninsula.
Principal Wines Chardonnay, Cabernet Sauvignon, Methode Champenoise.

TULLOCH WINES

★★★ 10.95–11.95 R AUS147
Hunter Valley **Est.** 1895
De Beyers Road, Pokolbin, NSW 2321
Ph (049) 98 7580 **Fax** (049) 98 7682
Open Mon–Fri 9–4.30, W'ends 10–4.30 **Production** 20 000
Winemaker(s) Jay Tulloch
A once-great name and reputation which suffered enormously under multiple ownership changes, with a complete loss of identity and direction. In production terms at least, it has found its feet, for it's now the centre of winemaking activities in the Hunter Valley for the Lindeman, Tulloch and Hungerford Hill brands. The wines are dependably boring.
Principal Wines Chablis, Semillon Chardonnay, Verdelho, Limited Release Chardonnay, Hunter River Dry Red, Hector of Glen Elgin Hermitage, Cabernets.

TULLOCH CABERNETS
●●● ▶ $10.95
A first and highly unusual release of a blend of 48% cabernet sauvignon, 30% ruby cabernet and 22% cabernet franc, all grown in the Hunter Valley. Ruby cabernet is mainly found in the Riverlands; it is a vinifera cross which was bred in California by Professor Harold Olmo, and is noted for its good colour. The components come together very satisfactorily in this wine. The wine was matured in one- and two-year-old French and American oak barrels.
Cellaring 2–4 years. **Best Vintages** NA **Current Vintage** '93
Matching Food Calves' liver.
Tasting Note 1994 Bright, full red-purple. A solid bouquet, with plenty of red and blackberry fruits to the fore. The palate, too, is generously flavoured with cassis/redcurrant fruit married with a hint of vanillin oak, and finishing with soft tannins.

TURKEY FLAT VINEYARDS*

★★★★☆ 9.50–15 CD AUSSD, UK11
Barossa Valley **Est.** 1990
Bethany Road, Tanunda, SA 5352
Ph (085) 63 2851 **Fax** (085) 63 3610
Open 7 days 11–5 **Production** 2500
Winemaker(s) Chris Ringland, Roger Harbord
The establishment date of Turkey Flat is given as 1990, but it might
equally well have been 1870 (or thereabouts) when the Schulz
family purchased the Turkey Flat vineyard, or 1847 when the
vineyard was first planted to the very shiraz which still grows today.
In addition there are 6 hectares of very old grenache, and 3
hectares of much younger semillon and cabernet sauvignon. A
significant part of the output is sold to some of the best known
Barossa Valley makers, not the least being Charles Melton, St
Hallett, and Rockford.
Principal Wines Grenache Noir, Semillon, Rosé, Shiraz.

TURKEY FLAT GRENACHE NOIR
●●●● ▶ $11
Peter Schulz, who effectively runs Turkey Flat, is a vigneron, not a
winemaker, and from the word go has had the Turkey Flat wines
made by experts. The Grenache is made by Chris Ringland of
Rockford and right from its first release has been a cult wine. It is
not hard to see why.
Cellaring 3–10 years.
Best Vintages '91, '92, '93
Current Vintage '93
Matching Food Maggie Beer's game pie.
Tasting Note 1993 Medium red-purple; an intensely fragrant and
exotic bouquet with aromas which are at once leafy and spicy yet
sweet. The palate is equally striking, with incredible spice and cherry
flavours which are at once concentrated yet delicate, finishing with
fleshy soft tannins.

TURKEY FLAT SHIRAZ
●●●●● $15
Based upon a precious patch of 145-year-old vines at the heart of
the Turkey Flat Vineyard. It was made at Rockford by Chris Ringland,
and has had the Adelaide wine press in a paroxysm of delight since
it was released. The '91, incidentally, is not in the same class,
suffering from volatility.
Cellaring 10 years.
Best Vintages '90, '92
Current Vintage '92
Matching Food Smoked kangaroo.
Tasting Note 1992 Medium to full red-purple; rich, concentrated
chocolate-accented, dark berry fruit is matched with abundant
vanillin American oak. The palate is packed with flavour in a
dark chocolate/dark cherry spectrum, the oak well balanced and
integrated.

457

TWIN VALLEY ESTATE *

NR 8.90–15 CD AUS96
Barossa Valley **Est.** 1990
Hoffnungsthal Road, Lyndoch, SA 5351
Ph (085) 24 4584 **Fax** (085) 24 4978
Open 7 days 10–5 **Production** 2000
Winemaker(s) Fernando Martin
While Fernando Martin has always had his sights set firmly on the
tourist trade, the Twin Valley Estate wines are more than acceptable.
The spicy, limey Frontignac Spatlese being a particularly good
example of its kind.
Principal Wines Traminer, Frontignac Spatlese, Eden Valley
Rhine, Chardonnay, Cabernet Sauvignon Franc, Classic Burgundy,
Pinot Cabernet, White Port, Martin's Mead.

TYRRELL'S VINEYARDS

★★★★★ 7–28 R AUS171, UK13
Hunter Valley **Est.** 1858
Broke Road, Pokolbin, NSW 2321
Ph (049) 98 7509 **Fax** (049) 98 7723
Open Mon–Sat 8–5 **Production** 550 000
Winemaker(s) Andrew Spinaze
A quite extraordinary family winery which has grown up from an
insignificant base in 1960 to become one of the most influential mid-
sized companies, successfully competing with wines running all the
way from cheap, volume-driven Long Flat White up to the super-
premium Vat 47 Chardonnay, which challenges Roxburgh for the
title of Australia's best. There is a similar range of price and style
with the red wines, but in recent years Tyrrell's has barely faltered
within the parameters of price and style.
Principal Wines At the bottom end the large-volume Long Flat
White and Red; next Old Winery Chardonnay, Semillon,
Chardonnay Semillon, Semillon Sauvignon Blanc, Riesling, Pinot
Noir, Shiraz, Cabernet Merlot; next a range of individual vineyard
wines including Shee-Oak Chardonnay, Stevens Semillon, Lost Block
Semillon, Brookdale Semillon, Forwich Verdelho, Brokenback Shiraz;
at the very top Vat 1 Semillon, Vat 6 Pinot Noir, Vat 9 Shiraz, Vat
47 Chardonnay.

TYRRELL'S BROOKDALE SEMILLON
●●●●● $15
The Brookdale Vineyard was planted by the Drayton family in 1967
on the yellow sandy clay loams of Pokolbin. The individual vineyard
Brookdale label was first introduced in 1994, and will hopefully be
a continuing one. 1000 cases were made of an outstanding wine.
Cellaring A decade or more. **Best Vintages** NA
Current Vintage '94
Matching Food Calamari.
Tasting Note 1994 Light green-yellow; clean, fresh, crisp and
tangy with pristine varietal character. On the palate, one of the best

Semillons from an outstanding vintage, with even greater richness to the fruit than (say) the Brokenwood of the same year.

TYRRELL'S OLD WINERY CABERNET MERLOT
●●●● ▶ $12

Arguably the best of the Old Winery range, although this is to split hairs. 80% cabernet sauvignon and 20% merlot is sourced from the Hunter Valley, Coonawarra and McLaren Vale, and matured in a mix of one- and two-year-old American and French oak barriques. Not only a consistent gold medal winner at national shows, but a trophy winner in recent years.

Cellaring 3–5 years. **Best Vintages** '89, '90, '91, '92, '93
Current Vintage '93
Matching Food Grilled kidneys.
Tasting Note 1993 Medium red-purple; a clean and smooth bouquet with red berry fruits and subtle oak leads on to a balanced and harmonious palate. Gentle red fruit flavours merge with soft tannins and just a hint of oak, without any component dominating.

TYRRELL'S OLD WINERY CHARDONNAY
●●●● ▶ $13

A wine which is as much a testament to the production skills of the Tyrrell's winemaking team as to the vast storehouse of accumulated knowledge in handling this variety. It is deliberately made in a richer, earlier-maturing style than Vat 47, and perhaps for this reason is often very nearly as well treated in wine shows as a young wine, being a prolific medal winner. The message is, drink it, don't cellar it.

Cellaring Drink now. **Best Vintages** NA
Current Vintage '93
Matching Food Ginger pork.
Tasting Note 1993 Glowing yellow-green; a clean, full and rich bouquet with smooth peach and melon fruit, and subtle oak. The palate is very well balanced, with lively, tangy acidity balancing the richness of the fruit, and oak introduced just to the right level.

TYRRELL'S OLD WINERY SHIRAZ
●●●● ▶ $13

Sourced entirely from Hunter Valley shiraz, and made in the traditional fashion in the old, wax-lined concrete vats at Tyrrell's, hand plunged, then matured in large oak casks for 12 months before being given a brief period in one- and two-year-old French oak barriques prior to bottling. Always a complex wine; a regular gold medal winner; and 1991 was, of course, an outstanding vintage.

Cellaring 5–8 years. **Best Vintages** '81, '83, '87, '91, '92
Current Vintage '91
Matching Food Smoked cheese.
Tasting Note 1991 Medium red; attractive, stylish liquorice fruit with a hint of regional earth. A substantial wine on the palate, with masses of dark berry and liquorice fruit flavours, subtle oak and soft tannins on the finish.

TYRRELL'S SHEE-OAK NON WOODED CHARDONNAY
●●●● $14.95
The Shee-Oak Vineyard was purchased by Tyrrell's in 1981 and
planted to chardonnay in 1982. The sandy loam flats are ideal for
white wines, resulting in excellent ripeness. This wine represents a
new departure for Tyrrell's: it is the first non wooded Chardonnay to
come from a winery which pioneered barrel fermentation of
Chardonnay in the mid 1970s.
Cellaring 1–5 years. **Best Vintages** NA
Current Vintage '94
Matching Food Moreton Bay bugs.
Tasting Note 1994 Bright green-yellow; the bouquet is surprisingly
complex and rich, with lots of ripe aromas and characters, and even
a hint of spice. The palate has considerable weight and richness,
again with those spicy characters evident, perhaps deriving from the
13% alcohol.

TYRRELL'S VAT 1 SEMILLON
●●●●● $25
One of the great, classic Hunter Valley Semillons, produced from un-
irrigated vines which, because of their superior soils, do in fact yield
well. Released as a young wine through the Tyrrell's mailing list and
cellar door, but re-released through the retail trade at various
intervals according to the vintage.
Cellaring Up to 15 years. **Best Vintages** '75, '76, '77, '86, '87,
'89, '92, '94 **Current Vintage** '89
Matching Food Pan-fried veal.
Tasting Note 1989 Brilliant green-yellow; a particularly intense
bouquet with tight, herbaceous aromas with a peculiar fruit
character seen in other Hunter Valley Semillons of this year, vaguely
French. The palate is powerful, long and herbaceous, particularly
intense on the mid to back palate. (The last wine to be labelled
Riesling, though in a Burgundy bottle.)

TYRRELL'S VAT 47 PINOT CHARDONNAY
●●●●● $28
First made in the appalling vintage of 1971, sharing with the
Craigmoor wine of the same year the honour of being the first
Chardonnay labelled as such and sold this century. Has since
unequivocally stamped itself as one of the great marques, with recent
vintages going from strength to strength. The '94 vintage won the
Bert Bear Trophy for Best One Year Old White at the 1995 Royal
Sydney Show.
Cellaring 5–15 years. **Best Vintages** '73, '75, '76, '79, '82,
'84, '85, '89, '90, '92, '93 **Current Vintage** '94
Matching Food Fresh, slow-cooked salmon.
Tasting Note 1994 Medium to full yellow-green; intense white
peach/nectarine fruit with obvious but well-integrated oak. A very
rich and full wine in the mouth, showing much more fatness at this
stage of its development than either the '92 or '93 vintages did, and
should develop more quickly in consequence.

TYRRELL'S VAT 9 SHIRAZ
●●●●● $25

First released in 1962, and has been the flagship of the Tyrrell's Shiraz production since that time. Based around the two old blocks of vineyard known as the 'four and eight acre blocks on the righthand side of the winery driveway'. A fruit-driven style, but in recent years the addition of little new French oak has added both to the complexity and appeal of the wine.
Cellaring 10–15 years. **Best Vintages** '81, '83, '85, '87, '89, '90, '91, '92, '93 **Current Vintage** '92
Matching Food Venison.
Tasting Note 1992 Medium to full purple-red; a lifted, lively fragrant bouquet with exemplary spice and liquorice varietal fruit aromas. An absolutely delicious wine in the mouth with similar spice and liquorice varietal fruit, even a touch of cassis. Soft tannins, subtle oak and good acidity.

VASSE FELIX WINES

★★★★ 16–24.95 R AUS138–142, UK38
Margaret River **Est.** 1967
Caves Road, Willyabrup, WA 6280
Ph (097) 55 5242 **Fax** (097) 55 5425
Open 7 days 10–4.30 **Production** 25 000
Winemaker(s) Clive Otto

Long regarded as one of the foremost wineries in the region, founded by Dr Tom Cullity but now owned by Heytesbury Holdings Pty Ltd, the investment company of the Holmes à Courts. Much of its reputation was founded on its elegant Cabernets, but these days the range is much broader. Curiously, the wines seldom cross my horizon.
Principal Wines Classic Dry White, Chardonnay, Classic Dry Red, Cabernet Sauvignon, Sparkling Brut.

VERITAS WINERY

★★★☆ 10–14 CD AUS68, UK52
Barossa Valley **Est.** 1955
94 Langmeil Road, Tanunda, SA 5352
Ph (085) 63 2330
Open Mon–Fri 9–5, W'ends 11–5
Production 7500
Winemaker(s) Rolf Binder

The Hungarian influence is obvious in the naming of some of the wines, but Australian technology is paramount in shaping the generally very good quality. Rolf Binder seeks no publicity for the wines outside South Australia.
Principal Wines Riesling, Semillon Sauvignon Blanc, Tramino, Leanyka, Cabernet Franc Merlot, Cabernet Sauvignon, Shiraz Cabernet, Bikaver Bull's Blood, Heysen Vineyard Shiraz, Fortifieds.

VICARYS WINES

★★★ 6.70–12 CD AUSSD
Sydney District **Est.** 1923
Northern Road, Luddenham, NSW 2745
Ph (047) 73 4161 **Fax** (047) 73 4411
Open Mon–Fri 9–5, W'ends 11.30–5.30
Production NFP
Winemaker(s) Chris Niccol
Vicarys justifiably claims to be the Sydney region's oldest
continuously-operating winery, having been established in a very
attractive, large, stone shearing shed built around 1890. Most of the
wines come from other parts of Australia, but the winery does draw
upon 4 hectares of estate traminer and 2 hectares of chardonnay for
those wines, and has produced some very good wines of all styles
over the years.
Principal Wines Chardonnay, Semillon, Riesling, Fumé Blanc,
Gewurztraminer, Cabernet Sauvignon, Shiraz Cabernet Merlot,
Sparkling, Fortifieds.

VINTINA ESTATE

NR 12–14 CD AUSSD
Mornington Peninsula **Est.** 1985
1282 Nepean Highway, Mt Eliza, Vic 3930
Ph (03) 9787 8166 **Fax** (03) 9775 2035
Open 7 days 9–5 **Production** 400
Winemaker(s) Jim Filippone, Kevin McCarthy (Consultant)
The initial releases of Vintina (the only wines tasted to date), were
mediocre. With competent contract winemaking, improvement can
be expected. However, no recent tastings.
Principal Wines Chardonnay, Semillon, Pinot Gris, Pinot Noir,
Cabernet Sauvignon.

VIRAGE *

★★★ 12–15 R AUSSD
Margaret River **Est.** 1990
Bussel Highway via Cowaramup, WA 6284
Ph (097) 55 5318 **Fax** (097) 55 5318
Open Not **Production** 1000
Winemaker(s) Bernard Abbott
Former Vasse Felix winemaker Bernard Abbott, together with
wife Pascale, acquired (under long-term lease) the former
government research station vineyard at Bramley Estate in 1990.
Bernard Abbott makes the wines at a local Margaret River
winery, and sells them by mailing list and direct to retailer and
restaurants in Perth, Melbourne and Sydney. The wines are
pleasant rather than exciting.
Principal Wines Sauvignon Blanc, Semillon Sauvignon Blanc
Chardonnay, Traminer Riesling, Cabernet Shiraz Zinfandel,
Cabernet Merlot.

VIRAGE CABERNET MERLOT

●●●● $15

One can see Bernard Abbott's years at Vasse Felix come through in this wine, which is elegant, crisp, and has been picked earlier rather than later. Whether one sees it as too green and herbal (or not) is a purely personal decision.

Cellaring 3–6 years. **Best Vintages** NA **Current Vintage** '92
Matching Food Veal shanks.

Tasting Note 1992 Medium red-purple; clean, with leaf/green bean/capsicum/cedar/cigar box aromas and flavours all intermingling. There are some red berry fruits on the palate, too, which finishes with soft, fine tannins.

VIRAGE SAUVIGNON BLANC

●●● ▶ $12

A no-frills direct seafood style made without adornment and best drunk ice-cold on a summer's day.

Cellaring Drink now. **Best Vintages** NA **Current Vintage** '94
Matching Food Cold crustacea.

Tasting Note 1994 Light yellow-green; light, clean and crisp, with strong regional/varietal herbal aromas. The palate is clean, crisp and direct to the point of outright pungency, but not unpleasantly so.

VIRAGE SEMILLON SAUVIGNON BLANC CHARDONNAY

●●● ▶ $14

A cocktail blend of the kind so favoured in the Margaret River, but which seems to work well no matter what the particular ingredients and percentages may be.

Cellaring Drink now. **Best Vintages** NA **Current Vintage** '94
Matching Food Scallop terrine.

Tasting Note 1994 Light to medium yellow-green; the bouquet is firm and crisp, with citrus aromas predominant. The palate is clean and crisp, with citrus and herbal flavours; the finish is long, and adds a touch of class to the wine.

VIRGIN HILLS

★★★★★ 26 R AUS17, 49, 116, 161 UK45 US2
Macedon **Est.** 1968
Salisbury Road, Lauriston West via Kyneton, Vic 3444
Ph (054) 23 9169 **Fax** (054) 23 9324
Open By appt **Production** 2200
Winemaker(s) Mark Sheppard

The Macedon region is not normally a kind host to the cabernet sauvignon family nor shiraz, but in the warmer vintages in particular, Virgin Hills produces one of Australia's great red wines. Very quietly, winemaker Mark Sheppard has moved to sulphur-free red winemaking, adding yet a further dimension of interest to this fascinating winery.

Principal Wines A single Cabernet Sauvignon Shiraz Merlot Blend called Virgin Hills; occasional limited Reserve release.

VIRGIN HILLS
●●●●● $26

An entirely estate-grown blend (in descending order) of cabernet sauvignon, shiraz, merlot, malbec and occasionally a touch of pinot noir. Not only are the grapes organically grown, but since 1988 the wine has been made without the use of added sulphur dioxide. It is a brave move which makes the world's best preservative free red, but there is a tiny seed of doubt about the durability of the wines.
Cellaring I simply don't know. **Best Vintages** '74, '75, '76, '80, '82, '85, '88, '90, '91 **Current Vintage** '92
Matching Food Duck.
Tasting Note 1992 Medium to full red-purple; fine, typically elegant/refined bouquet with cedary fruit and oak. The palate is similarly finely structured and elegant, with cedar and cassis fruit, finishing with fine tannins. The aftertaste, however, does betray the absence of sulphur dioxide.

VOYAGER ESTATE

★★★★ 11–18 R AUS97, 101, 115, 161 UK34
Margaret River **Est.** 1978
Lot 1 Gnarawary Road, Margaret River, WA 6285
Ph (09) 385 3133 **Fax** (09) 383 4029
Open Not **Production** 10 000
Winemaker(s) Stuart Pym
Formerly Freycinet Estate, renamed after its purchase (in May 1991) from Western Australian viticulturist Peter Gherardi. Millions of dollars have been spent by new owner Michael Wright in extending the vineyards and erecting a state-of-the-art winery reminiscent of the more opulent showpieces of the Napa Valley.
Principal Wines Chenin Blanc, Classic Dry White, Semillon, Chardonnay, Cabernet Merlot.

VOYAGER CHARDONNAY
●●●●● $18

In both 1992 and 1993 Voyager Estate has produced a Chardonnay of complexity, style and verve typical of the Margaret River at its very best.
Cellaring 4–7 years. **Best Vintages** '92, '93
Current Vintage '93
Matching Food Braised pork neck.
Tasting Note 1993 Medium yellow-green; concentrated fruit with a slightly French tang and cut, partly deriving from the oak/barrel fermentation treatment. There is tremendous fruit on the palate with concentrated citrus and melon flavours, and a long, lingering finish.

VOYAGER ESTATE CLASSIC DRY WHITE
●●●● $13

Estate-produced from the traditional Margaret River mix of semillon, sauvignon blanc and chenin blanc, but shows the above-average concentration of aroma and flavour one has come to associate with the Voyager Estate label.

Cellaring 1–2 years. **Best Vintages** NA **Current Vintage** '93
Matching Food Coquilles St Jacques.
Tasting Note 1993 Medium yellow-green; the bouquet shows
strong herbal fruit aromas, clean and crisp. A punchy wine on the
palate with concentration and length; herb and lime flavours are
rounded off with crisp acid.

WA DE LOCK VINEYARDS

★★☆ 10–15 CD AUSSD
East Gippsland **Est.** 1987
Stratford Road, Maffra, Vic 3860
Ph (051) 47 3244 **Fax** (051) 43 1421
Open Thur–Tues 10–5 **Production** 1200
Winemaker(s) Graeme Little
The initial plantings of pinot noir, cabernet sauvignon and sauvignon
blanc in 1987 have been progressively expanded, with chardonnay
being added, with 5 hectares now under vine. Grape intake has
been supplemented by purchases of riesling, merlot and cabernet
franc grown at Maffra. Quality (and style) has been erratic, with
resinous oak affecting some of the wines, although there are some
interesting fruit flavours in the Pinot and Cabernet Merlot.
Principal Wines Chameleon, Chardonnay, Sauvignon Blanc,
Pinot Noir, Cabernet Merlot.

WA DE LOCK CHAMELEON
●●● ▶ $13.50
A Rosé style made from pinot noir, and which succeeds admirably.
One assumes the juice has been run-off to make this wine, with the
remaining wine used to make the conventional Pinot from Wa De
Lock.
Cellaring Drink now. **Best Vintages** NA **Current Vintage** '94
Matching Food Salmon.
Tasting Note 1994 Pink-bronze; well made, with a clean
strawberry-accented bouquet. The palate has a similar nice touch of
strawberry with plenty of fruit, finishing crisp and clean. Not sweet,
and an excellent example of the style.

WANDERING BROOK ESTATE *

NR 12–14 CD AUSSD
Warren Valley **Est.** 1989
PO Box 32, Wandering, WA 6308
Ph (098) 84 1064
Open W'ends 9.30–6 **Production** 1000
Winemaker(s) Hotham Valley (Contract)
Laurie and Margaret White have planted 10 hectares of vines on
their 130-year-old family property in a move to diversify. Up to
1994 the wines were made at Goundrey, since 1994 at the nearby
Hotham Valley. A lusciously ripe Cabernet from 1993, albeit slightly
rustic, and a '93 oaked Chardonnay are the best wines prior to

1994. Renamed Wandering Brook Estate late 1994; up till then known as Redhill Estate.
Principal Wines Verdelho, Chardonnay, Unwooded Chardonnay, Dry Red, Cabernet Sauvignon.

WANDIN VALLEY ESTATE

★★★☆ 10–19 CD AUSSD
Hunter Valley **Est.** 1973
Talga Road, Allandale, NSW 2321
Ph (049) 30 7313 **Fax** (049) 30 7814
Open 7 days 10–5 **Production** 4000
Winemaker(s) Geoff Broadfield
The former Millstone vineyard is now owned by the producer of TV series *A Country Practice*; the owner has also acquired the services of Allanmere winemaker Geoff Broadfield. Rapidly developing Chardonnays have been the focal point of Wandin Valley's considerable show success. The estate also boasts a Cope Williams-type village cricket oval and extensive cottage accommodation.
Principal Wines Talga Ridge White, Sauvignon Blanc, Chardonnay, Talga Ridge Red, Shiraz, Pinot Noir, Ruby Cabernet, Cabernet Sauvignon, Muscat.

WANDIN VALLEY ESTATE CHARDONNAY
●●● $13.95
An estate-grown and produced wine made in a full-frontal style. Skin contact and subsequent maturation in American oak barriques maximise the propensity of Hunter Valley Chardonnay to richness, and the oak is at the opulent end of the spectrum.
Cellaring Drink now. **Best Vintages** NA **Current Vintage** '94
Matching Food Scallopini.
Tasting Note 1994 Medium to full yellow-green; the bouquet is big and rich with honeyed fruit and strong, spicy American oak. The palate is almost entirely driven by spicy American oak, with the fruit very much in the background.

WANDIN VALLEY ESTATE RESERVE CHARDONNAY
●●●● ▶ $20
The Reserve Chardonnay was introduced with effect from the 1994 vintage, and was a gold medal winner at the 1994 Australian National Wine Show in Canberra. The '92 and '93 vintages of Chardonnay also did very well in shows in the year of their making, but have developed at an extraordinarily rapid rate since. The moral seems to be to drink the wine the moment it is released. All in all, a wine style which makes Dolly Parton look like Twiggy.
Cellaring Don't. **Best Vintages** '94 **Current Vintage** '94
Matching Food Opulent seafood, white meat dishes.
Tasting Note 1994 Medium to full yellow-green; the bouquet is very complex, but essentially driven by barrel ferment oak. The palate is powerful and intense with peach, melon and grapefruit flavours to accompany the toasty/nutty barrel ferment characters.

WANINGA WINES

★★★★ 7.50–12.50 CD AUSSD
Clare Valley **Est.** 1989
Hughes Park Road, Sevenhill via Clare, SA 5453
Ph (088) 43 4395
Open W'ends, Hols 10–5 **Production** 1200
Winemaker(s) Tim Adams, Jeffrey Grosset
(Contract)
The large vineyards owned by Waninga were established in 1974,
but it was not until 1989 that a portion of the grapes was withheld
from sale and vinified for the owners. Since that time, Waninga has
produced some quite lovely wines, having wisely opted for very
competent contract winemaking.
Principal Wines Riesling (three vintages available), Chenin Blanc,
Chardonnay, Shiraz (two vintages), Cabernet Sauvignon.

WANINGA CABERNET SAUVIGNON
●●●● $12.50
Produced from mature, low-yielding vines which are encouraged to
fully ripen the fruit. Again, shows the philosophy of contract
winemaker Tim Adams.
Cellaring 5 years. **Best Vintages** '89, '91, '92, '93
Current Vintage '93
Matching Food Rump steak.
Tasting Note 1993 Youthful purple-red; complex, ultra-ripe
bouquet of dark berry and mint, with a touch of hay/straw. The
palate is likewise full of ripe berry fruit with minty overtones, all
tasting as if there were an element of berry shrivel before picking.
The strong point of the wine is the finish, which is not too tannic.

WANINGA RIESLING
●●●● ▶ $10
Produced from what are now relatively old estate vineyards, first
planted in 1974. In mainstream Clare style, except that the '93 was
late picked and made fairly sweet, no doubt useful at cellar door.
Made by Jeffrey Grosset.
Cellaring 4–6 years. **Best Vintages** '90, '91, '92, '94
Current Vintage '92, '93, '94
Matching Food Asparagus.
Tasting Note 1994 Light green-yellow; a firm bouquet with classic
toast, herb and lime aromas of medium to full intensity. The palate is
well balanced and constructed with plenty of lime and toast fruit,
and just a hint of residual sugar giving the wine broad appeal.

WANINGA SHIRAZ
●●● ▶ $11.50
Made by Tim Adams, and shows the oak handling which one
expects from this maker. There is abundant fruit, to be sure, but there
is also a generous dollop of American oak to flesh out the style.
Cellaring 4–6 years. **Best Vintages** '89, '91, '92, '93
Current Vintage '91
Matching Food Steak and kidney pie.

Tasting Note 1991 Medium red; clean, with quite complex berry fruit dominated by spicy/coconut/vanillin oak. The palate, too, is in no small measure driven by the American oak, but is not resinous or bitter.

WANTIRNA ESTATE

NR 23 ML AUSSD
Yarra Valley **Est.** 1963
Bushy Park Lane, Wantirna South, Vic 3152
Ph (03) 9801 2367 **Fax** (03) 9887 0225
Open Sat 2–5 May–Feb **Production** 800
Winemaker(s) Reg Egan
Owner/winemaker Reg Egan does not believe in any form of comparative tastings or assessments, and even less in winery or wine ratings.
Principal Wines Chardonnay, Pinot Noir, Cabernet Merlot.

WARDS GATEWAY CELLARS

★★☆ 7.50–9 CD AUSSD
Barossa Valley **Est.** 1979
Barossa Valley Highway, Lyndoch, SA 5351
Ph (085) 24 4138
Open 7 days 9–5.30 **Production** 5000
Winemaker(s) Ray Ward (plus Contract makers)
The very old vines surrounding the winery produce the best wines, which are made without frills or new oak and sold without ostentation.
Principal Wines Riesling, Chablis, Frontignac, Fumé Blanc, Shiraz, Cabernet Sauvignon, Port.

WARRABILLA WINES

NR 14–25 ML AUSSD
North East Victoria **Est.** 1986
Indigo Valley, Rutherglen, Vic 3685 (vineyard only)
Ph (060) 32 9461
Open Not **Production** 800
Winemaker(s) Andrew Sutherland-Smith
Former All Saints winemaker Andrew Sutherland-Smith has leased a small winery at Corowa to make the Warrabilla wines from a vineyard developed by himself and Carol Smith in the Indigo Valley. The opening of the cellar door was postponed to 1995.
Principal Wines Rutherglen Shiraz, Rutherglen Cabernet Merlot, Walla Walla Cabernet Shiraz, Glenrowan Shiraz, Rutherglen Vintage Port, Touriga Vintage Port.

WARRAMATE WINES

★★★★ 13–19 CD AUSSD
Yarra Valley **Est.** 1970
27 Maddens Lane, Gruyere, Vic 3770
Ph (059) 64 9219

Open W'ends 10–6, Mon–Fri by appt **Production** 780
Winemaker(s) Jack Church, David Church
Showed a marked return to form with the 1992 vintage red wines, with the influence of son Dr David Church (possessed of a very good palate) no doubt having much to do with the improvement.
Principal Wines Shiraz, Riesling, Cabernet Sauvignon.

WARRAMATE CABERNET SAUVIGNON
●●● ▸ $19
Produced from 0.8 of a hectare of cabernet sauvignon, with a little merlot included in the plantings. Like the Shiraz, the vines are not irrigated, and are consequently low-yielding.
Cellaring 5 years. **Best Vintages** '88, '92
Current Vintage '92
Matching Food Mature cheddar.
Tasting Note 1992 Medium to full red-purple; a solid, briary bouquet with some leafy characters which run through so many Yarra Valley Cabernets. The palate has lots of concentrated briary fruit, but has leafy notes which are slightly distracting.

WARRAMATE SHIRAZ
●●●● ▸ $15
Produced from just under half a hectare of estate-grown plantings, typically providing around 200 cases of wine. The plantings are not irrigated, and enjoy a prime north-facing slope.
Cellaring 4–8 years. **Best Vintages** '88, '92
Current Vintage '92
Matching Food Spiced lamb.
Tasting Note 1992 Medium to full red-purple; firm and concentrated aromas with mint and dark berry fruits (no spice) and subtle oak. The palate is faultless, with clean, concentrated dark berry fruit, finishing with fine tannins.

WARRENMANG VINEYARD
★★★☆ 11–18.50 CD AUSSD
Pyrenees **Est.** 1974
Mountain Creek Road, Moonambel, Vic 3478
Ph (054) 67 2233 **Fax** (054) 67 2309
Open 7 days 9–5 **Production** 7500
Winemaker(s) Roland Kaval
Warrenmang is now the focus of a superb accommodation and restaurant complex created by former restaurateur Luigi Bazzani and wife Athalie, which is in much demand as a conference centre as well as for weekend tourism. The striking black Bazzani label is gradually overtaking the Warrenmang label in importance, and is responsible for the growth in the volume of production. It is partially sourced from contract growers; the estate wines are, as their name suggests, estate-grown.
Principal Wines Bazzani Chardonnay Chenin Blanc, Chardonnay, Late Harvest Traminer, Bazzani Cabernet Shiraz Dolcetto, Shiraz, Grand Pyrenees, Vintage Port.

WARRENMANG BAZZANI CABERNET SHIRAZ DOLCETTO
●●●● ▶ $12

A deliberately lighter style, predominantly cabernet and shiraz, and with a little dolcetto adding sweet fruit complexity. A direct style, made with minimum oak intrusion, which works very well.
Cellaring 2–3 years. **Best Vintages** NA **Current Vintage** '92
Matching Food Osso bucco.
Tasting Note 1992 Medium red-purple; hints of dark chocolate and vanilla amongst clean red fruit aromas. On the palate the spicy shiraz component comes through a spotlessly clean wine with nice feel and structure; fruit- not oak-driven.

WARRENMANG ESTATE SHIRAZ
●●● ▶ $16

Produced from 3 hectares of very low-yielding estate plantings, vines which have tended to produce wines of awesome power and extract, needing a light touch in the winery. Roland Kaval has started to get things right.
Cellaring 10 years. **Best Vintages** '82, '85, '92, '94
Current Vintage '92
Matching Food Strong cheese or red meat.
Tasting Note 1992 Full red-purple; a concentrated bouquet with briary/spicy/dark berry notes, initially with some earthy astringency which blew off. The palate is rich and concentrated, with liquorice and gamey flavours; the tannins are under control.

WARREN VINEYARD, THE See page 440.

WATER WHEEL VINEYARDS

★★★☆ 9.95–16.50 R AUS137, 182, 188, UK11
Bendigo **Est.** 1972
Bridgewater-on-Loddon, Bridgewater, Vic 3516
Ph (054) 37 3060 **Fax** (054) 37 3082
Open Mon–Sat 9–5, Sun 12–5 **Production** 7500
Winemaker(s) Peter Cumming
Peter Cumming gained great respect as a winemaker during his four-year stint with Hickinbotham winemakers, and his 1989 purchase of Water Wheel was greeted with enthusiasm by followers of his wines. It has to be said that some of the wines have been mildly disappointing.
Principal Wines Chardonnay, Riesling, Sauvignon Blanc, Pinot Noir, Shiraz, Cabernet Sauvignon; grapes from other districts under premium Wing Fields label.

WATER WHEEL CABERNET SAUVIGNON
●●●● $12.95

Produced predominantly from new plantings of cabernet sauvignon established when the Cumming family took over control of Water Wheel. Right from the outset these plantings produced wines with intense fruit flavours, very evident in the '92 vintage wine. A small percentage (15%) of cabernet franc and merlot adds complexity.

Cellaring 3–5 years. **Best Vintages** '90, '91, '92
Current Vintage '92
Matching Food Mild Indian curry.
Tasting Note 1992 Medium to full red-purple; the bouquet is redolent of rich cassis/raspberry fruit together with a touch of slightly resinous, charry oak. There is similar intense cassis, mint and raspberry fruit on the palate, almost recalling the unfermented berries. The oak needed to settle down when the wine was first released.

WATER WHEEL SHIRAZ
●●● ▶ $12.95
Made to be consumed while young, and showing the bright fruit which Peter Cumming always seems to obtain in his wines. The oak makes little or no contribution.
Cellaring Drink now. **Best Vintages** NA **Current Vintage** '93
Matching Food Cold meats.
Tasting Note 1993 Medium red-purple; minty/cherry aromas of light to medium intensity lead on to a lively palate with spice, cherry and fruit flavours all present. The tannins are minimal, and the oak simply not evident.

WATTLEY CREEK WINES

NR 13–20 R AUS34, 48
Southern Tasmania **Est.** 1990
Fleurtys Lane, Flowerpot, Tas 7054
Ph (002) 67 4604 **Fax** (002) 67 4828
Open 7 days at Woodbridge Hotel, Woodbridge 7162
Production 500
Winemaker(s) Leigh Gawith
Leigh Gawith established St Patricks at Pipers Brook in 1983, but sold the vineyard to Pipers Brook Winery in 1990 and has now relocated in the extreme south of Tasmania at Flowerpot. The wines presently being sold are a mixture from his previous location and his new venture. He is also making wines on a contract basis for three other embryonic makers, Roland View, Tunnel Hill and Polley Estate.
Principal Wines Muller Thurgau, Chardonnay, Pinot Noir, Cabernet Blend.

WAYBOURNE WINERY *

NR 7–20 ML AUSSD
Geelong **Est.** 1980
60 Lemins Road, Waurn Ponds, Vic 3221
Ph (052) 41 8477 **Fax** (052) 41 8477
Open By appt **Production** 400
Winemaker(s) Various Consultant/Contract
Owned by Tony and Kay Volpato, who have relied upon external consultants to assist with the winemaking. The first wines were released in January 1992 and have proved to be of extremely variable quality. The best to date has been the '94 Frontignac.
Principal Wines Rhine Riesling, Frontignac, Chenin Blanc, Cabernet Sauvignon, Pinot Gris.

WEIN VALLEY ESTATES

NR 2.55–7.95 CD AUS58, 146
Riverlands **Est.** 1985
Nixon Road, Monash, SA 5342
Ph (085) 83 5255 **Fax** (085) 83 5444
Open Mon–Fri 9–4.30, Sat, Public hols 11–3
Production 777 000
Winemaker(s) Otto König
A major producer of bulk and packaged wine; much is sold to other makers for blending or repackaging. The quality basically reflects the price, although the label design and packaging are quite beautiful.
Principal Wines An array of generic table, fortified and flavoured wines, with premium varietals under the Lone Gum label.

WELLINGTON WINES

★★★★ 15–17.50 ML AUSSD
Huon Valley **Est.** 1990
Cnr Richmond & Denholms Roads, Cambridge, Tas 7170
Ph (002) 48 5844 **Fax** (002) 43 0226
Open By appt **Production** 500
Winemaker(s) Andrew Hood
Consultant winemaker Andrew Hood (ex-Charles Sturt University) and wife Jenny have constructed a brand new, state-of-the-art winery on land leased from the University of Tasmania. The 500-case production of Wellington is dwarfed by the 4500 cases contract made for others.
Principal Wines Chardonnay, Pinot Noir.

WENDOUREE CELLARS

★★★★★ 15–18 CD AUSSD
Clare Valley **Est.** 1895
Wendouree Road, Clare, SA 5453
Ph (088) 42 2896
Open Mon–Sat 10–4.30 **Production** 2400
Winemaker(s) Tony Brady
The iron fist in a velvet glove best describes these extraordinary wines. They are fashioned with passion and yet precision from the very old vineyard with its unique terroir by Tony and Lita Brady, who rightly see themselves as custodians of a priceless treasure.
Principal Wines Shiraz Malbec, Shiraz Mataro, Cabernet Malbec, Cabernet Sauvignon, Muscat of Alexandria.

WENDOUREE CELLARS CABERNET MALBEC
●●●●● $17.50
This is but one of five wines produced in most vintages from the estate. Each one is entitled to be classed as a classic wine, each one a monument to the terroir and to the Bradys' passionate defence of it.

Cellaring 20+ years. **Best Vintages** '83, '86, '89, '90, '91, '92
Current Vintage '92
Matching Food Leave it in the cellar for a decade.
Tasting Note 1992 As one would expect, dense, youthful purple-red colour, with a ripely potent bouquet with briary/berry aromas complexed by an obvious contribution of plummy malbec fruit. Formidably massive in the mouth, with powerful, potent, earth/briary/berry fruit flavours, nowhere near approachable.

WEST END WINES

★★☆ 2.30–8.90 CD AUSSD
Murrumbidgee Irrigation Area **Est.** 1945
12/83 Brayne Road, Griffith, NSW 2680
Ph (069) 64 1506 **Fax** (069) 62 1673
Open Mon–Fri 9–4.30 **Production** 54 200
Winemaker(s) William Calabria
The '82, '84 and '89 Cabernet Sauvignons have each won a gold medal at national wine shows, the '89 at Canberra (in 1990), which is a remarkable achievement in itself for a little-known Riverina winery. Much of the wine is sold in flagons; the market is essentially within the Italian community. A range of current vintage wines tasted at the 1995 Sydney International Winemakers Competitions were, to put it mildly, uninspiring.
Principal Wines Chardonnay, Colombard Chardonnay, Chablis, Traminer Riesling, Hermitage, Cabernet Sauvignon, Liqueur Muscat, Barbera, Fortifieds.

WESTERNPORT ESTATE

NR 10–36 R AUSSD
South Gippsland **Est.** 1981
St Helier Road, The Gurdies, Vic 3984
Ph (059) 97 6208 **Fax** (059) 97 6511
Open 7 days 10–5 **Production** 750
Winemaker(s) Peter Kosik
The only winery in the south west Gippsland region, established on the slopes of The Gurdies hills overlooking Westernport Bay and French Island. Plantings of the 4.5-hectare vineyard commenced in 1981, but no fruit was harvested in 1991 owing to bird attack. A winery has been partially completed, and it is intended to increase the vineyards to 25 hectares and ultimately build a restaurant on site.
Principal Wines Riesling, NV Gurdies Hill Red (Cabernet Shiraz blend), Shiraz, Cabernet Sauvignon, Port.

WESTFIELD WINES

★★★★ 12.95–18 R AUS103
Swan Valley **Est.** 1922
Cnr Memorial Ave & Great Northern Highway, Baskerville, WA 6056
Ph (09) 296 4356

Open 7 days 10–5.30 **Production** 3000
Winemaker(s) John Kosovich
Consistent producer of a surprisingly elegant and complex
Chardonnay; the other wines are more variable, but from time
to time has made attractive Verdelho and excellent Cabernet
Sauvignon. John Kosovich is a perfectionist, and I look forward to
the release of his Pemberton wines from his recently-established
vineyard in that area.
Principal Wines Verdelho, Chardonnay, Chenin Blanc, Semillon,
Riesling, Merlot, Cabernet Sauvignon, Shiraz, Port.

WETHERALL WINES *

★★★☆ 11–14.50 CD AUSSD
Coonawarra **Est.** 1991
Naracoorte Road, Coonawarra, SA 5263
Ph (087) 37 2104 **Fax** (087) 37 2105
Open 7 days 9.30–5 **Production** 1500
Winemaker(s) Michael Wetherall
Wetherall Wines is situated next door to the well known Hermitage
Restaurant in Coonawarra. The wines from 1992, in particular,
are commendable. The business was being offered for sale in
early 1995.
Principal Wines Shiraz, Rhine Riesling, Chardonnay, Cabernet
Sauvignon.

WETHERALL WINES CABERNET SAUVIGNON
●●● ▶ $14.50
As with the Shiraz, but a tiny part of the Wetherall production, and
no doubt utilising some of the best fruit from the now fully-mature
cabernet vines. Traditionally made, with strong American oak input.
Cellaring 4–6 years. **Best Vintages** '90, '92
Current Vintage '92
Matching Food King Island cheddar.
Tasting Note 1992 Medium purple-red; obvious cool-grown fruit
with leafy/tobacco aromas enriched by strong vanillin American
oak. The palate likewise shows a blend of slightly herbaceous
cabernet varietal fruit with sweeter, vanillin American oak, finishing
with soft tannins which provide some flesh to the wine. Significantly
better than either the '91 or '90, mainly through better oak handling.

WETHERALL WINES SHIRAZ
●●●● $13
Wetherall has only recently ventured into winemaking. It has
35 hectares of prime Coonawarra vineyards, and has been growing
grapes for 25 years, supplying many of the major companies. As
one might expect, this represents the pick of the crop.
Cellaring 5–6 years. **Best Vintages** '91, '92
Current Vintage '92
Matching Food Shepherd's pie.
Tasting Note 1992 Medium to full red-purple; a complex bouquet
with cedar, dark chocolate, spice and leaf. The palate shows

cedary/vanillin oak with good peppery/spicy varietal fruit which
became progressively more apparent; finishes with fine tannins.

WICKHAM HILL WINES

★★☆ 4.95 R AUS117
Murrumbidgee Irrigation Area **Est.** 1970
22 Jensen Road, Griffith, NSW 2680
Ph (069) 64 2121 **Fax** (069) 62 7121
Open Not **Production** NFP
Winemaker(s) Orlando
A brand of Orlando with its grape sources and winery based in
the Murrumbidgee Irrigation Area. The wines are basically of cask
quality sold in bottles, but do use the Orlando discipline and
production skills.
Principal Wines Chablis, Riesling, Spatlese Lexia, Capelli
Lambrusco, Nouveau, Dry Red.

WIGNALLS

★★★★☆ 9.80–19.80 CD AUS35, 150, 181, 188, UK99
Great Southern **Est.** 1982
Chester Pass Road (Highway 1), Albany, WA 6330
Ph (098) 41 2848 **Fax** (098) 41 2848
Open 7 days 12–4 **Production** 6000
Winemaker(s) John Wade (Contract)
A noted producer of Pinot Noir which has extended the map for the
variety in Australia. The Pinots have tremendous style and flair, but
do age fairly quickly. The white wines are elegant, and show the
cool climate to good advantage.
Principal Wines Chardonnay, Sauvignon Blanc, Frontignac,
Pinot Noir, Cabernet Sauvignon, Tawny Port, White Port.

WIGNALLS CHARDONNAY
●●●● $19.50
Produced from 2 hectares of estate plantings. It is usually fairly
discrete when first released, but builds flavour and character with
a year or two in the bottle.
Cellaring 3–5 years. **Best Vintages** '85, '88, '91, '92
Current Vintage '93
Matching Food Milk-fed veal.
Tasting Note 1993 Medium to full yellow-green; quite complex,
with some attractive barrel ferment characters and elegant peach
and melon fruit. Quite generous in the mouth with rounded, fleshy
peach and melon fruit, finishing with subtle oak.

WIGNALLS PINOT NOIR
●●●●● $19.80
The rating is given for the better of the vintages, and on the basis
that the wines will be consumed within one or two years of release.
Thereafter they become a little chancy, although they can never be
accused of lack of style. For example, the '92 was wonderful at the

end of 1994. Note also there are tiny quantities of a Reserve Pinot released from time to time.
Cellaring 1–2 years. **Best Vintages** '85, '86, '88, '91, '93
Current Vintage '93
Matching Food Seared Tasmanian salmon.
Tasting Note 1993 Medium red; fragrant, potent stemmy/sappy aromas with light strawberry fruit on the bouquet. The palate is very typical of Wignalls, markedly stemmy, with a long, clean finish and subtle oak. One sometimes wishes for a touch more concentration to the fruit flavour.

WIGNALLS SAUVIGNON BLANC
●●● ▶ $14.80
Made from small estate plantings in limited quantities. The style is crisp and direct, without any particular pretensions.
Cellaring Drink now. **Best Vintages** NA **Current Vintage** '94
Matching Food Scampi.
Tasting Note 1994 Light green-yellow; crisp clean and firm, with gently herbal notes, and a whisker of sulphur dioxide when first released. The palate is firm, clean, crisp and direct, with pleasant intensity and length.

WILD DUCK CREEK ESTATE

NR 12–15.50 CD AUSSD
Bendigo **Est.** 1980
Spring Flat Road, Heathcote, Vic 3523
Ph (054) 33 3133
Open By appt **Production** 500
Winemaker(s) David Anderson
The first release of Wild Duck Creek Estate from the 1991 vintage marks the end of 12 years of effort by David and Diana Anderson, who commenced planting the 4.5-hectare vineyard in 1980, made their first tiny quantities of wine in 1986, the first commercial quantities of wine in 1991, and built their winery and cellar door facility in 1993.
Principal Wines Springflat Shiraz, Alan's Cabernets (65% cabernet sauvignon, 10% merlot, 10% malbec, 10% cabernet franc, 2% petit verdot), Pressings Cabernets (magnums only), Merlot, Reserve Cabernet Sauvignon, Merlot Cabernet Franc.

WILDWOOD VINEYARDS

★★★☆ 15–19 CD AUS56, UK53
Macedon **Est.** 1983
St John's Lane, Wildwood, Bulla, Vic 3428
Ph (03) 9307 1118 **Fax** (03) 9331 1590
Open 7 days 10–6 **Production** 1500
Winemaker(s) Dr Wayne Stott, Peter Dredge
Wildwood is situated at the southernmost part of the Macedon region, just 4 kilometres past Melbourne airport. The vineyard and cellar door are situated at an altitude of 130 metres in the Oaklands

Valley, which provides unexpected views back to Port Phillip Bay
and the Melbourne skyline. Plastic surgeon Wayne Stott has taken
what is very much a part-time activity rather more seriously than most
by undertaking (and completing) the Wine Science Degree at
Charles Sturt University.
Principal Wines Merlot Cabernet Franc, Chardonnay, Cabernets,
Pinot Noir, Shiraz.

WILDWOOD MERLOT CABERNET FRANC
●●●● ▶ $19
The '92 is a thoroughly impressive wine, and the best made yet at
Wildwood. 1992 was an excellent ripening season, important in the
uncompromisingly cool climate of the Macedon region, even at this
low altitude.
Cellaring 5 years. **Best Vintages** '88, '90, '91, '92, '93
Current Vintage '92
Matching Food Cannelloni.
Tasting Note 1992 Medium red-purple; a complex bouquet with
sweet briary/spicy fruit with good oak balance and integration.
There is exceptionally striking sweet juicy fruit on the palate, with
oak in the background, and finishing with soft tannins.

WILLESPIE WINES

★★★☆ 10–19 R AUS34, 184, UK93
Margaret River **Est.** 1976
Harmans Mill Road, Willyabrup via Cowaramup, WA 6284
Ph (097) 55 6248 **Fax** (097) 55 6210
Open 7 days 10.30–5 **Production** 5000
Winemaker(s) Michael Lemmes
Willespie has produced many attractive white wines over the years,
typically in brisk, herbaceous Margaret River style, but its new
plantings of merlot suggest a bright future for this variety once the
wine becomes commercially available.
Principal Wines Sauvignon Blanc, Semillon Sauvignon Blanc,
Verdelho, Riesling, Cabernet Sauvignon, Merlot; Harmans Mill
White, Harmans Mill Autumn White, Harmans Mill Red are cheaper
second label wines.

WILLESPIE SAUVIGNON BLANC
●●●● $15.50
In many ways, the flagbearer for Willespie. The typical Margaret
River herbaceous characters are usually accompanied by a riper
gooseberry spectrum, particularly in outstanding vintages such as
1993.
Cellaring 1–3 years. **Best Vintages** '87, '90, '91, '93
Current Vintage '94
Matching Food Shellfish.
Tasting Note 1994 Light green-yellow; clean, fragrant
gooseberry/herbal fruit of medium intensity on the bouquet. There
is greater intensity and fruit weight on the palate, again with some
gooseberry notes, and a long, slightly smoky finish.

WILLOW BEND WINES

★★★★ 14–15 R AUS36, 99
Barossa Valley **Est.** 1990
Lyndoch Valley Road, Lyndoch, SA 5351; PO Box 107, Lyndoch,
SA 5351
Ph (085) 24 4169 **Fax** (085) 24 4169
Open Not **Production** 750
Winemaker(s) Wayne Dutschke
Wayne Dutschke has had 10 years of winemaking experience with
major wine companies in South Australia, Victoria and New South
Wales, but has returned to South Australia to join his uncle, Ken
Semmler, a leading grape grower in the Barossa Valley and now in
the Adelaide Hills.
Principal Wines Chardonnay, Shiraz Merlot Cabernet Sauvignon
Cabernet Franc.

WILLOW BEND CHARDONNAY

●●●● $15
An extremely rich wine in a full-blown show style which develops
quite quickly. Produced from fully ripened grapes, it spends 10
months in German and French oak on yeast lees.
Cellaring Drink now. **Best Vintages** '93 **Current Vintage** '93
Matching Food Pork chops.
Tasting Note 1993 Medium yellow-green; a stylish bouquet with
good fruit and oak balance and integration, and just a faint hint of
camphor. On the palate, richer and riper than the bouquet suggests
with full butter, honey, peach and butterscotch flavours.

WILLOW BEND SHIRAZ MERLOT CABERNET SAUVIGNON CABERNET FRANC

●●●● $15
A blend of 35% shiraz, 35% merlot, 15% cabernet sauvignon and
15% cabernet franc, all produced on the Semmler Barossa Valley
Vineyard (1991 Vineyard of the Year) which spent 2 years in French
and American oak hogsheads before being bottled mid 1994.
Cellaring 4–6 years. **Best Vintages** '92 **Current Vintage** '92
Matching Food Beef casserole.
Tasting Note 1992 Medium to full red-purple; the bouquet is
clean, full with cedary overtones to complex dark berry fruits. The
palate, as with the Chardonnay, is much bigger than the bouquet
suggests, with more fruit, oak and tannins all present. A dense wine
needing at least three years in bottle.

WILLOW CREEK VINEYARD

NR 12.95–15.95 R AUS188
Mornington Peninsula **Est.** 1989
166 Balnarring Road, Merricks North, Vic 3926
Ph (059) 89 7367
Open Thur–Mon 11–5 **Production** 4000
Winemaker(s) Peter Harris, Katherine Quealy
Yet another significant entrant in the fast-expanding Mornington

Peninsula area, with 15 hectares of vines planted to cabernet
sauvignon, chardonnay and pinot noir. The cellar door sales area
boasts picnic areas, barbecue facilities, trout fishing and bocce;
lunches are served every day, and dinners by appointment.
Principal Wines Chardonnay, Unwooded Chardonnay, Pinot
Noir, Cabernet Sauvignon.

WILLOW CREEK
●●● $17.95
Made in the newly fashionable unwooded style from the pick of
estate-grown grapes; much of the Willow Creek production is sold
to other makers. It is surprisingly light given its 13.5% alcohol, but
these fresh, light styles do have their place in the market.
Cellaring Drink now. **Best Vintages** NA **Current Vintage** '94
Matching Food Sauteed scallops.
Tasting Note 1994 Bright green-yellow; scented citrus and melon
fruit aromas with that ever-so-distinctive Mornington Peninsula
character which is nonetheless difficult to define. The palate is soft,
with pleasant, slightly cosmetic fruit flavours, and without a great
deal of length.

WILLOW CREEK CHARDONNAY
●●● ▶ $15.50
Produced from 4.5 hectares of estate plantings, and technically well
made, any deficiencies coming from fairly light fruit and modest oak.
Cellaring Drink now. **Best Vintages** NA **Current Vintage** '93
Matching Food Ragout of seafood.
Tasting Note 1993 Light straw-yellow; a very light bouquet but
clean fresh and crisp. The palate is likewise light but clean with
minimal oak, sweet fruit and just a hint of sugar on the finish. A
clever commercial wine.

WILLOWS, THE See page 440.

WILSON VINEYARD, THE See page 440.

WILTON ESTATE
★★★☆ 6.95–16.95 CD AUS56, 74, 120, 126, 184
Murrumbidgee Irrigation Area **Est.** 1977
Whitton Stock Route, Yenda, NSW 2681
Ph (069) 68 1303 **Fax** (069) 68 1328
Open Mon–Fri 9–5 **Production** 100 000
Winemaker(s) Adrian Sheridan
The former St Peters distillery has been transformed into a table wine
producer, drawing grapes and wine from various parts of southern
Australia and New South Wales for its dry table wines, but having
outstanding success with its Botrytis Semillon from locally grown fruit.
Principal Wines Semillon Sauvignon Blanc, Chardonnay, Botrytis
Semillon, Marsanne, Cabernet Merlot, Heathcote Shiraz; Hidden
Valley is the second label.

WILTON ESTATE BOTRYTIS SEMILLON (375 ML)

●●●●● $16.95

The 1992 vintage is a magnificent wine which has swept all before it in the wine shows, being rated above the De Bortoli Noble One on many occasions. It has accumulated a De Bortoli-like string of trophies and gold medals, leaving no doubt that Griffith is clearly the best region in Australia for this style of wine.

Cellaring Now–3 years. **Best Vintages** '92
Current Vintage '92
Matching Food Crème brûleé.
Tasting Note 1992 Medium to full yellow; rich, complex and concentrated apricot and peach fruit, subtle oak and just the right amount of volatile lift. A classy wine on the palate with great style, good acid balance and length. Has intensity but not over-blown.

WINCHELSEA ESTATE

★★★☆ 13–19 R AUSSD
Geelong **Est.** 1984
Winchelsea, Vic 3241 (vineyard only)
Open Not **Production** NFP
Winemaker(s) Contract
Owned by Melbourne retailer Nick Chlebnikowski, and the wines are sold only through Nick's chain of stores. Vibrantly peppery Shiraz has been the best of the wines by far.
Principal Wines Riesling, Chardonnay, Shiraz.

WINDOWRIE ESTATE *

NR NA AUSSD
Cowra **Est.** 1988
Windowrie, Canowindra, NSW 2804
Ph (063) 44 3234 **Fax** (063) 44 3234
Open By appt **Production** NFP
Winemaker(s) Rodney Hooper, Simon Gilbert
(Contract)
Windowrie Estate was established in 1988 on a substantial grazing property at Canowindra, 30 kilometres north of Cowra, and in the same viticultural region. 10 hectares of chardonnay, 8 hectares of cabernet sauvignon, and 3 hectares each of sauvignon blanc and pinot noir produced over 230 tonnes in 1994, with further vineyard expansion imminent. Most of the grapes are sold, with small quantities being made for the Windowrie Estate label, the Chardonnays enjoying spectacular show success.
Principal Wines Chardonnay, Sauvignon Blanc, Pinot Noir, Cabernet Merlot.

WINEWOOD WINES

NR 10 CD AUSSD
Granite Bar **Est.** 1984
Sundown Road, Ballandean, Qld 4382
Ph (076) 84 1187 **Fax** (076) 84 1187

Open W'ends, Public hols 9–5 **Production** 700
Winemaker(s) Ian Davis
A weekend and holiday activity for schoolteacher Ian Davis and
town planning wife Jeanette; the tiny winery is a model of neatness
and precision planning. The use of marsanne with chardonnay and
semillon shows an interesting change in direction.
Principal Wines Chardonnay, Chardonnay Marsanne, Marsanne
Semillon, Shiraz, Cabernet Sauvignon Merlot Cabernet Franc.

WINTERS VINEYARD *

NR 8–11 CD AUSSD
Coonawarra **Est.** 1988
Clarke Road, O.B. Flat via Mount Gambier, SA 5290
Ph (087) 26 8255 **Fax** (087) 26 8255
Open Not **Production** 500
Winemaker(s) Bruce Gregory, Jim Brand (Contract)
Former restaurateurs Martin and Merrilee Winter have established
8 hectares of vineyards 6 kilometres south of Mount Gambier and
about 60 kilometres south of Coonawarra proper. The wines are
contract made, with an ultimate production target of 2500 cases.
The light, leafy but pleasant '92 Cabernet Sauvignon shows the cool
climate, but is well made with a nice touch of cedary vanillin oak.
Principal Wines Chardonnay, Cabernet Sauvignon, Dinner House
Flat (Shiraz Pinot).

WIRILDA CREEK WINERY *

★★★☆ 11–13 CD AUS111
Southern Vales **Est.** 1993
32 McMurtrie Road, McLaren Vale, SA 5171
Ph (08) 323 9688 **Fax** (08) 323 9688
Open 7 days 10–5 **Production** 2000
Winemaker(s) Kerry Flanagan
Wirilda Creek may be the newest arrival in McLaren Vale, but it
offers the lot: wine, lunch every day (Pickers Platters reflecting local
produce) and accommodation (four rooms opening onto a private
garden courtyard).
Principal Wines Oak Matured Semillon, Sauvignon Blanc,
Cabernet Malbec Shiraz, Cabernet Merlot, Shiraz, Port.

WIRILDA CREEK SEMILLON
●●● $13
Made from contract-grown grapes, and barrel fermented to produce
a very full-flavoured wine with some unusual flavours, more towards
chardonnay in character.
Cellaring Drink now. **Best Vintages** NA **Current Vintage** '93
Matching Food Veal parmigiana.
Tasting Note 1993 Medium yellow-green; the bouquet is clean
with some peach and passionfruit aromas of medium intensity. The
palate is of medium weight, smooth with more of those peachy
flavours of the bouquet, and oak in restraint; there is a slightly
peppery finish which detracts.

WIRILDA CREEK SHIRAZ
●●● ▶ $13
Wirilda Creek say this is their top red, and I agree. While not a
heavyweight by any means, it shows good varietal character.
Cellaring 3–5 years. **Best Vintages** NA **Current Vintage** '93
Matching Food Italian.
Tasting Note 1993 Medium to full red-purple; good shiraz fruit
with some earthy/gamey overtones allied with American oak. The
palate is solid, with earthy/spicy varietal character finishing with
pleasant acidity and restrained oak.

WIRRA WIRRA

★★★★☆ 12–25 R AUS112, 164, UK17
Southern Vales **Est.** 1969
McMurtie Road, McLaren Vale, SA 5171
Ph (08) 323 8414 **Fax** (08) 323 8596
Open Mon–Sat 10–5, Sun 11–5 **Production** 40 000
Winemaker(s) Benjamin Riggs
Long respected for the consistency of its white wines, Wirra Wirra
has now established an equally formidable reputation for its reds.
Right across the board, the wines are of exemplary character,
quality and style.
Principal Wines The Cousins (Sparkling), Hand Picked Riesling,
Sweet Semillon, Sauvignon Blanc, Chardonnay, Wood Matured
Semillon Sauvignon Blanc, The Angelus Cabernet Sauvignon, Pinot
Noir, Church Block (Cabernet Shiraz Merlot), RWS Shiraz, Original
Blend (Grenache Shiraz), Port.

WIRRA WIRRA CHARDONNAY
●●●● $17.95
Eight hectares of estate vineyards provide the core of what is always
a stylish wine, rising to great heights in years such as 1991. The full
range of modern Chardonnay winemaking techniques are applied,
with as much focus on structure and complexity as on fruit,
producing a wine which ages very well.
Cellaring 2–5 years. **Best Vintages** '82, '89, '91, '92, '94
Current Vintage '93
Matching Food Wiener schnitzel.
Tasting Note 1993 Medium to full yellow-green; reasonably
complex with some malolactic fermentation characters and subtle
oak. A solid wine on the palate with toast and honey characters.
Not one of the best Wirra Wirra Chardonnays.

**WIRRA WIRRA CHURCH BLOCK CABERNET SHIRAZ
MERLOT**
●●●● $14.95
Church Block, typically a blend of around 50% cabernet sauvignon
and 25% each shiraz and merlot, was the first of the Wirra Wirra
red wines to catch the eye, although quality did wander around
somewhat. It has now settled down in a pleasant, straightforward
style designed for relatively early consumption.

Cellaring 2–3 years. **Best Vintages** '90, '91, '94
Current Vintage '93
Matching Food Pasta bolognaise.
Tasting Note 1993 Bright medium red, with just a touch of purple; clean, bright, fresh earthy/berry fruit aromas with just a hint of oak. A bright, fresh relatively simple wine on the palate with soft tannins.

WIRRA WIRRA HAND PICKED RIESLING
●●● ▶ $12
When, well over a decade ago, Wirra Wirra incorporated the words 'Hand Picked' into its Riesling label, it was regarded as another example of owner Greg Trott's notorious sense of humour. In the intervening years it has come to represent a statement of individuality for one of the region's better Rieslings.
Cellaring 2–3 years. **Best Vintages** '82, '89, '91, '92, '94
Current Vintage '94
Matching Food South Australian whiting.
Tasting Note 1994 Light to medium yellow-green; crisp, tingling lemon rind/herbaceous/grassy aromas. The wine is nicely balanced on the palate, with the clever use of just a hint of residual sugar to give the wine some structure, although the fruit is not particularly intense.

WIRRA WIRRA ORIGINAL BLEND GRENACHE SHIRAZ
●●●● $16
Introduced in 1993 in response to the sudden surge of interest in grenache. Wirra Wirra has one hectare of this variety (and 11 hectares of shiraz) which form the core of the wine.
Cellaring Up to 5 years. **Best Vintages** NA
Current Vintage '93
Matching Food Steak and kidney pie (or pie floater).
Tasting Note 1993 Medium red-purple; firm, briary/berry/liquorice fruit with minimal oak on the bouquet. A concentrated wine on the palate, still youthful and with the tannins still to resolve, but has real potential.

WIRRA WIRRA SAUVIGNON BLANC
●●●● $13.50
One of the pioneers of quality Sauvignon Blanc in McLaren Vale. Wine quality is never less than good, in vintages such as 1994 nearing perfection. Draws principally upon 3.5 hectares of estate plantings.
Cellaring Best drunk young. **Best Vintages** '91, '92, '94
Current Vintage '94
Matching Food Blue swimmer crab.
Tasting Note 1994 Bright, light green-yellow; crisp, floral/gooseberry aromas, pure and clean. On the palate there is a perfect balance between grassy and gooseberry flavours, showing perfect fruit ripeness, with a long, dry finish.

WIRRA WIRRA THE ANGELUS CABERNET SAUVIGNON
●●●●● $25
Named after a one-tonne bell which used to ring at St Ignatius

church, Norwood; a Trott whimsy for The Angelus is only made in 'ring the bell' vintages — four in total up to 1992, including the '91 which received national acclaim as the top wine at the 1992 Sydney International Winemakers Competition.

Cellaring Up to 10 years. **Best Vintages** '86, '90, '91, '92
Current Vintage '92
Matching Food Fillet of beef.
Tasting Note 1992 Medium to full red-purple; a spotlessly clean bouquet with faintly austere but perfectly ripened cabernet in a distinctly Bordeaux mould. The same gently astringent/herbaceous classic cabernet fruit with tannins running throughout, drives the palate. The wine is not green or stemmy, and will undoubtedly enchant the classicists.

WISE WINES *

NR 12–16.50 CD AUS181
Margaret River **Est.** 1986
Lot 4 Meelup Road, Dunsborough, WA 6281
Ph (097) 55 3331 **Fax** (097) 55 3979
Open 7 days 10.30–4.30 **Production** 10 000
Winemaker(s) Mark Ravenscroft
Wise Wines is an amalgam of Geographe Estate, Eagle Bay Estate and the Newlands Vineyard at Donnybrook. The head of the syndicate is former medical practitioner and stock market entrepreneur extraordinaire Ron Wise, who has always been a wine connoisseur, and now has the economic means to indulge himself to the full. Wise Wines also offers a spectacular outdoor restaurant overlooking Geographe Bay.
Principal Wines Sauvignon Blanc Semillon, Aquercus Chardonnay (Unwooded), Chardonnay, Late Harvest (Chenin Blanc, Semillon, Muscat), Travigna, Pinot Noir, Classic Soft Red, Merlot, Cabernet Sauvignon.

WOLF BLASS

★★★★ 9.95–25.95 R AUS104
Barossa Valley **Est.** 1966
Bilyara Vineyards, Sturt Highway, Nuriootpa, SA 5355
Ph (085) 236 0888 **Fax** (085) 62 2156
Open 7 days 9–5 **Production** 250 000
Winemaker(s) John Glaetzer (Red), Chris Hatcher (White)
Although merged with Mildara, the brands (as expected) have been left largely intact, and — so far at least — the style of the wines has changed little. The red wines continue to be very oaky, and it may well be that the old adage 'if it ain't broke, don't fix it' is being applied.
Principal Wines White wines under White, Yellow, Green and Gold labels, with emphasis on Riesling and blended Classic Dry White; red wines under Red, Yellow, Brown, Grey and Black labels with emphasis on Cabernet Sauvignon, Shiraz and blends of these. Also sparkling and fortified wines.

WOLF BLASS GOLD LABEL RIESLING
●●●● $10.95

Produced from Wolf Blass's only significant vineyard holdings in the Clare Valley. It is significantly more fruit-driven than enzyme-driven (the latter being the case with the Yellow Label Riesling) and has been a prolific medal and trophy winner in national wine shows over the past four or five years.

Cellaring Now–2 years. **Best Vintages** '90, '92, '94
Current Vintage '94
Matching Food Salad niçoise.
Tasting Note 1994 Light green-yellow; lots of lime juice fruit aromas, with just a hint of spice lurking in the background. The palate is nicely balanced with ample flavour yet not coarse; there is sweet lime juice flavour running throughout, and a long finish.

WOLF BLASS SHOW RESERVE CABERNET SAUVIGNON
●●●● $25.95

For almost two decades Wolf Blass resolutely turned his back on Coonawarra. In the twilight of his involvement with the company, it made a Coonawarra Cabernet Sauvignon which was rewarded with three trophies at the 1991 Adelaide Wine Show. In fruit terms, it is a radical departure from anything made by Wolf Blass.

Cellaring 5–9 years. **Best Vintages** NA
Current Vintage '90
Matching Food Beef satay.
Tasting Note 1990 Medium to full red; potent herbaceous cabernet fruit aromas with tangy lemon and vanilla oak. The palate is a replica of the bouquet, with crisp, herbaceous fruit on the mid palate followed by lemon and vanilla oak on the finish.

WOLF BLASS TRAMINER RIESLING
●●●● ▶ $8.95

Made from a blend of traminer and riesling sourced from the Clare, Barossa and Eden Valleys. Without question the most underrated wine in the Wolf Blass stable, simply because of the relatively unfashionable nature of the blend, and its commercial (and highly successful) targeting of the Asian restaurant market.

Cellaring Drink now. **Best Vintages** NA **Current Vintage** '94
Matching Food Asian.
Tasting Note 1994 Light green-yellow; intense lime, lychee and spice aromas and flavours. The palate is neither phenolic nor sweet, finishing dry, and with great balance. This really is a class wine.

WOODLANDS WINES

★★★☆ 16–20 CD AUS161
Margaret River **Est.** 1973
Cnr Caves & Metricup Roads, Willyabrup via Cowaramup, WA 6284
Ph (09) 274 6155 **Fax** (09) 274 6421
Open W'ends by appt **Production** 850

Winemaker(s) David Watson, Dorham Mann (Consultant)
Burst on the scene with some superlative Cabernet Sauvignons early
on, but did not manage to maintain the momentum; and indeed
made no red wine in 1988, 1989 or 1991. The 1992 red wines
mark a return to form.
Principal Wines Margaret Cabernet Merlot, Chardonnay, Pinot
Noir, Peter Cabernet Malbec.

WOODLANDS MARGARET CABERNET MERLOT
●●● ▶ $16
Produced entirely from estate-grown grapes (there are 5 hectares in
total) showing a hint of the minty characters which so marked the
spectacular releases from the vineyard.
Cellaring 4–6 years. **Best Vintages** '81, '82, '86, '87
Current Vintage '92
Matching Food Beef tartare.
Tasting Note 1992 Medium red-purple; clean, firm, fresh berry
fruits with subtle oak and a hint of mint. Similar fresh, bright red
berry and mint fruit flavours, all suggesting a fairly short sojourn in
oak (and perhaps longer time in tank) before bottling. A nice wine,
nonetheless.

WOODONGA HILL WINES

NR 9–15 CD AUSSD
Hilltops **Est.** 1986
Cowra Road, Young, NSW 2594
Ph (063) 82 2972
Open 7 days 9–5 **Production** 2400
Winemaker(s) Jill Lindsay
Early problems with white wine quality appear to have been
surmounted. The 1993 Rhine Riesling was the top pointed wine
in the (open) Riesling class at the 1993 Cowra Wine Show.
Principal Wines Riesling, Chardonnay, Gewurztraminer,
Shiraz, Cabernet Sauvignon.

WOODSTOCK WINE CELLARS

★★★★☆ 10.95–13.95 R AUS84, UK4
Southern Vales **Est.** 1974
Douglas Gully Road, McLaren Flat, SA 5171
Ph (08) 383 0156 **Fax** (08) 383 0437
Open Mon–Fri 9–5, W'ends, Hols 12–5 **Production** 20 000
Winemaker(s) Scott Collett, John Weeks
One of the stalwarts of McLaren Vale, producing archetypal,
invariably reliable, full-bodied red wines and showing versatility
with spectacular botrytis sweet whites and high quality (14-year-old)
Tawny Port.
Principal Wines Riesling, Semillon, Chardonnay, Sauvignon
Blanc, Botrytis Sweet White, Botrytis Riesling, Cabernet Sauvignon,
Shiraz, Tawny Port. The Stocks Shiraz is a recently-introduced
flagship; the Douglas Gully range is a cheaper, second label.

WOODSTOCK BOTRYTIS SWEET WHITE (375 ML)
●●●● ▶ $8

Made from botrytis-affected chenin blanc and riesling grapes, sometimes with lesser amounts of semillon and/or frontignan. Part of the fermentation is on skins (unusual) and the wine is given brief oak maturation.

Cellaring 2–4 years. **Best Vintages** '90, '91, '92, '93
Current Vintage '93
Matching Food Crème brûlée.
Tasting Note 1993 Deep yellow-green; a veritable cascade of spicy, nutmeg and cumquat fruit aromas on the bouquet, with a similar melange of nutmeg, coconut and fruit on the palate; very luscious, but does not cloy. A bargain at the price.

WOODSTOCK CABERNET SAUVIGNON
●●●● ▶ $14

Produced from a little over 6.5 hectares of estate plantings. The vines are old, and the fruit concentration substantial. Like the Shiraz, has been incredibly consistent over the years, and represents great value.

Cellaring Up to 10 years. **Best Vintages** '82, '84, '91, '92, '94
Current Vintage '92
Matching Food Game pie.
Tasting Note 1992 Medium to full red; a solid briary/chocolatey/earthy bouquet with warm region fruit aromas. A very generous, mouthfilling wine on the palate with lots of dark chocolate and red berry fruit, finishing with solid tannins.

WOODSTOCK SHIRAZ
●●●● $14

Produced from 5.3 hectares of estate plantings, and one of the most reliable — and most typical — examples of McLaren Vale Shiraz. It relies almost entirely on its rich fruit; oak would simply be a distraction.

Cellaring Up to 10 years. **Best Vintages** '82, '84, '91, '92, '94
Current Vintage '92
Matching Food Steak in black bean sauce.
Tasting Note 1992 Medium to full red; solid, clean berry fruit with some earthy varietal notes. The palate is crammed with rich, dark chocolate, berry and earth fruit, finishing with abundant soft tannins.

WOODSTOCK THE STOCKS SHIRAZ
●●●● ▶ $20

First made in the 1991 vintage, and released in late 1994. It is made from century-old (98-year-old, to be precise) vines, and matured in new American oak hogsheads. I remain to be convinced that new American oak improves the wine.

Cellaring 10 years. **Best Vintages** NA **Current Vintage** '91
Matching Food Barbecued steak.
Tasting Note 1991 Medium to full red-purple; dark cherry and liquorice fruit with pronounced vanillin American oak. On the palate there is lots of fruit and lots of oak of full weight, but not extractive.

The flavours run the gamut of rich, sweet berry and chocolate through to vanilla, the latter from the oak.

WOODY NOOK WINES

★★★☆ 9–18CD AUS175
Margaret River **Est.** 1982
Metricup Road, Busselton, WA 6280
Ph (097) 55 7547 **Fax** (097) 55 7565
Open 7 days 10–4.30 **Production** 1120
Winemaker(s) Neil Gallagher
The winery rating represents a compromise between the best and the least wines, for quality, both in red and white wines, does vary somewhat. The best red wines are very good indeed.
Principal Wines Chenin Blanc, Sauvignon Blanc, Late Picked Chenin Blanc, Late Harvest Semillon, Merlot, Cabernet Sauvignon; Gallagher's Choice Cabernet Sauvignon is top of the range.

WOODY NOOK GALLAGHER'S CHOICE CABERNET SAUVIGNON

●●●● ▶ $18
As the name suggests, the pick of the vintage, and winemaker Neil Gallagher certainly got it right in 1993, for this wine is far superior to the standard Cabernet Sauvignon of the same year.
Cellaring 5–7 years. **Best Vintages** NA **Current Vintage** '93
Matching Food Herbed rack of lamb.
Tasting Note 1993 Medium red-purple; fresh, spicy/earthy/berry fruit with subtle oak. A potent wine on the palate with spicy characters vaguely reminiscent of shiraz, rather than cabernet sauvignon, with good weight and concentration.

WRIGHTS WINERY

★★☆ 12–25 CD AUS175, UK74
Margaret River **Est.** 1973
Harmans South Road, Cowaramup, WA 6284
Ph (097) 55 5314 **Fax** (097) 55 5459
Open 7 days 10–4.30 **Production** 2500
Winemaker(s) Henry Wright
The red wines of 1988 were the best for some years, but subsequent vintages slipped back again. There is an omnipresent streak of gravelly astringency which seems to run through all of the red wines, including the '91 Shiraz exhibited at the 1994 Mount Barker Wine Show. Perhaps the style appeals more to others.
Principal Wines Semillon Riesling, White Hermitage, Hermitage Cabernet, Late Picked Shiraz, Vintage and White Port.

WYANGA PARK VINEYARDS

★★☆ 9–17.50 CD AUS16
Gippsland **Est.** 1970
Baades Road, Lakes Entrance, Vic 3909
Ph (051) 55 1508 **Fax** (051) 55 1443

Open 7 days 9–5 **Production** 5000
Winemaker(s) Andrew Smith

Offers a broad range of wines of diverse provenance directed at the tourist trade; the 1992 Warragul Cabernet Sauvignon is the best of the local wines. Winery cruises up the north arm of the Gippsland Lake to Wyanga Park are scheduled four days a week throughout the entire year.

Principal Wines Sauvignon Blanc, Colombard, Riesling, Traminer Riesling, Crouchen, Chardonnay, Pinot Noir, Victorian Cabernet Shiraz, Cabernet Merlot, Warragul Cabernet Sauvignon, Fortifieds.

WYNDHAM ESTATE

★★★ 6.95–13.95 R AUS117 US7
Hunter Valley **Est.** 1828
Dalwood Road, Branxton, NSW 2335
Ph (049) 38 3444 **Fax** (049) 38 1840
Open Mon–Fri 9.30–5, W'ends 10–4 **Production** NFP
Winemaker(s) John Baruzzi

An absolutely reliable producer of keenly-priced mid-range table wines which are smoothly and precisely aimed at those who enjoy wine but don't wish to become over-involved in its mystery and intrigue. Every now and then it comes up with a wine of surprising quality, although there does seem to be some variation between different batch bottlings.

Principal Wines Chablis Superior, Chardonnay Bin 222, Graves Exceptional Bin 777, Hunter Chardonnay, Oak Cask Chardonnay, Traminer Riesling Bin TR2, Show Reserve Verdelho, Cabernet Merlot Bin 888, Cabernet Sauvignon Bin 444, Pinot Noir Bin 333, Selected Hermitage Bin 555.

WYNNS COONAWARRA ESTATE

★★★★★ 8.95–45 R AUS147 UK40, 70, 83 US11
Coonawarra **Est.** 1891
Memorial Drive, Coonawarra, SA 5263
Ph (087) 36 3266 **Fax** (087) 36 3202
Open 7 days 10–4 **Production** 190 000
Winemaker(s) Peter Douglas

The immense production has in no way prevented Wynns from producing excellent wines covering the full price spectrum from the bargain basement Riesling and Hermitage through to the deluxe John Riddoch Cabernet Sauvignon and the newly-introduced Michael Hermitage. In years such as 1990 and 1991 Wynns offers extraordinary value for money.

Principal Wines Riesling, Chardonnay, Hermitage, Cabernet Hermitage Merlot, Black Label Cabernet Sauvignon, Michael Hermitage, John Riddoch Cabernet Sauvignon, Ovens Valley Shiraz.

WYNNS CABERNET HERMITAGE MERLOT

●●●● $11.95

A blend of cabernet and shiraz, with a little merlot added since the end of the 1980s. It is aged in a mixture of new and used American and French barrels for 15 months, and the aim is to produce a more elegant and slightly lighter style of red wine than that offered by the other red wines under the Wynns label.

Cellaring Now–3 years. **Best Vintages** '86, '88, '90, '91, '92
Current Vintage '92
Matching Food Yearling beef.
Tasting Note 1992 Medium red-purple; an elegant bouquet with notes of earth, cedar and briar. The palate is similarly elegant with briary/leafy/minty aspects to the red fruit flavours. Oak has been used in restraint. A multiple gold medal winner.

WYNNS CHARDONNAY
●●●● $11.50

A fast improving style which used to be dominated by phenolic German and American oak, but is now barrel fermented primarily in French wood (with smaller quantities of German and American), a change which culminated in the '93 vintage winning the trophy for Best Commercial Dry White at the 1994 Canberra National Wine Show. The '94 continues the trend, although not on the same high plane.

Cellaring Short term. **Best Vintages** '92, '93, '94
Current Vintage '94
Matching Food Fillet of pork.
Tasting Note 1994 Medium to full yellow-green; voluminous fruit and oak intermingle on both the bouquet and palate in a Baroque style which seems increasingly common in Coonawarra these days. Fleshy, rich and opulent.

WYNNS COONAWARRA ESTATE BLACK LABEL CABERNET SAUVIGNON
●●●●● $17

Given the volume in which this wine is made (said to be over 40,000 cases) it has to be the most important Cabernet in Australia, a powerful testament to the synergy between Coonawarra and cabernet sauvignon. Matured in new and used American and French oak barrels for 16 months; a dyed-in-the-wool classic with a magnificent history.

Cellaring 5–20 years. **Best Vintages** '53, '57, '58, '62, '82, '88, '90, '91 **Current Vintage** '92
Matching Food Roast beef.
Tasting Note 1992 Full red-purple; blackcurrant, mulberry and cedar aromas intermingle on the bouquet, which has exemplary varietal character. In the mouth, the wine shows the same flavours, and has excellent structure, resting on fine but persistent tannins.

WYNNS COONAWARRA ESTATE HERMITAGE
●●●● ▶ $9.95

Estate means what is says; this is 100% estate-grown Coonawarra shiraz, a wine which vies with Penfolds Koonunga Hill dry red for the title of best value red wine in Australia. The wine ages well: witnessed by the top gold in Class 38 (Dry Red Soft Finish) given to the 1989 vintage at the 1994 Australian National Wine Show. A classic.

Cellaring Perfect each way, now or in 10 years. **Best Vintages** '54, '55, '62, '65, '70, '85, '86, '89, '90, '91, '92, '93
Current Vintage '93
Matching Food Spiced lamb.
Tasting Note 1993 Medium to full red-purple; abundant black cherry and varietal spice aromas on the bouquet, fruit- rather than oak-driven. The palate is vibrantly spicy and highly flavoured, again fruit- rather than oak-driven. Outstanding varietal character, particularly in such an inexpensive wine.

WYNNS COONAWARRA ESTATE RIESLING
●●● ▶ $9
If the Black Label Cabernet Sauvignon is Mr Reliable, the Riesling is Mrs Reliable. Year-in, year-out it represents exceptional value for money, and vertical tastings have shown the wine has a surprising capacity to age and develop in bottle.
Cellaring Each way — now or in 5+ years. **Best Vintages** '88, '87, '88, '90, '91, '92, '94 **Current Vintage** '94
Matching Food Grilled whiting.
Tasting Note 1994 Light to medium yellow-green; there are abundant floral/tropical aromas on the bouquet which carry through in precisely the same mode on the palate. Happily, the wine relies on legitimate fruit rather than residual sugar for its impact, and finishes relatively dry.

WYNNS JOHN RIDDOCH CABERNET SAUVIGNON
●●●●● $45
First made in 1982, and only vintaged in the best years, and then from the finest material available. It is matured in new French and American oak hogsheads for 12-15 months, and is a wine of enormous concentration and power. I personally find the power overwhelming, but was one of those who happily awarded a trophy to the 1985 vintage at the 1994 Australian National Wine Show. Just be patient. Incidentally, less than 1% of the annual pick of Wynns Coonawarra Cabernet goes into John Riddoch.
Cellaring 15–25 years. **Best Vintages** '82, '85, '86, '88, '90, '91 **Current Vintage** '92
Matching Food Leave it in the cellar.
Tasting Note 1992 Deep red-purple; chocolate, briar and cassis aromas mingle with strong vanillin oak on the bouquet, in a slightly less forceful mode than either the '90 or '91 vintages. The palate, too, is ever so slightly more accessible at this early stage of its development, no doubt a factor contributing to its three gold medals.

WYNNS MICHAEL HERMITAGE
●●●●● $45
First made in the outstanding Coonawarra vintage of 1990, to stand alongside the John Riddoch Cabernet Sauvignon. It takes its name from the most famous of all of the Wynns wines, the glorious 1955 Michael Hermitage, which still rates as one of the top half-dozen wines made in Australia since the Second World War. A prolific trophy and gold medal winner, every bit as powerful as the Riddoch.
Cellaring 15–25 years. **Best Vintages** '90, '91

Current Vintage '91
Matching Food Leave it in the cellar.
Tasting Note 1991 The bright purple-red colour leads on to a
fragrant, scented bouquet with voluptuous sweet berry fruit and
balanced oak. The palate is very complex and stylish with red
berry/cassis/raspberry fruit flavours with hints of spice in the
background. Will be approachable earlier than the 1990, but still
needs great patience to allow it to show its best.

WYNNS OVENS VALLEY SHIRAZ
●●●● ▶ $9
The early vintages (starting in 1955) were made entirely from shiraz
made by Cliff Booth at Taminick in the Ovens Valley of north-east
Victoria, but within 10 years the north-east Victorian contribution had
fallen to its present level of around 10 per cent. The majority of the
wine now comes from the Barossa Valley and McLaren Vale, albeit
with a small but important contribution from north-east Victoria. The
earliest vintages were great; after a lapse, the wine is once again of
impeccable quality, consistency and style.
Cellaring Up to 20 years. **Best Vintages** '56, '59, '68, '70, '71,
'74, '86, '88, '90, '91, '92 **Current Vintage** '92
Matching Food Beef Provençale.
Tasting Note 1992 Medium to full purple-red; the clean and
smooth bouquet has abundant dark plum and liquorice fruit. The
palate is immaculately balanced, with flavours of plum, and no oak
forcing.

YALUMBA WINERY

★★★★☆ 6.95–21.95 R AUS138–142 UK65 US10
Barossa Valley **Est.** 1849
Eden Valley Road, Angaston, SA 5353
Ph (085) 61 3200 **Fax** (085) 61 3393
Open Mon–Fri 8.30–5, Sat 10–5, Sun 12–5
Production 830 000
Winemaker(s) Brian Walsh
Family-owned and run by Robert Hill-Smith; much of its prosperity in
recent years has turned on the great success of Angas Brut in export
markets, but the company has always had a commitment to quality
and shown great vision in its selection of vineyard sites and brands.
Principal Wines Under the Yalumba label (in ascending order)
Oxford Landing range, Galway Hermitage and Christobels Dry
White, Family Selection range and The Signature Collection.
Separate brand identities for Hill Smith Estate, Pewsey Vale and
Heggies, with strong emphasis on key varietals Riesling,
Chardonnay, Semillon and Cabernet Sauvignon. Angas Brut is a
leader in the sparkling wine market, with Yalumba D at the top end
of the quality tree.

YALUMBA CHRISTOBELS DRY WHITE
●●● ▶ $7.95
An interesting, unwooded varietal blend which, when first
introduced, incorporated viognier, but is now made from semillon,

sauvignon blanc and marsanne. It has also been mirrored by an upmarket version at twice the price — the strikingly labelled Antipodean. The gold medal awarded to '94 Christobels at the 1994 Brisbane Wine Show suggests that Christobels may be the better value.

Cellaring Drink now. **Best Vintages** NA **Current Vintage** '94
Matching Food Seafood salad.

Tasting Note 1994 Light to medium green-yellow; a crisp, clean, fairly lean but bracing bouquet leads on to a similarly fresh and crisp palate with zesty lemony fruit and a quite long finish.

YALUMBA D
●●●● ▶ $21.95

Deliberately and consistently made at the fuller end of the Australian sparkling wine spectrum. Always a complex, rich, mouthfilling style, although the levels of aldehyde in the older vintages were somewhat controversial. The '91 is a blend of 65% pinot noir from Eden Valley, Coonawarra, Adelaide Hills; 31% chardonnay from Coonawarra and Eden Valley; and 4% pinot meuniere from Eden Valley.

Cellaring Buy the late disgorged versions. **Best Vintages** '90, '91, '92 **Current Vintage** '91

Matching Food Richer seafood dishes.

Tasting Note 1994 Full yellow-straw; big, soft and richly complex aromas in a nutty/bready/yeasty/vanilla spectrum. A concentrated but soft palate with buttery/nutty flavours and a hint of anise from the pinot component.

YALUMBA FAMILY RESERVE CHARDONNAY
●●●● ▶ $10.95

Sits underneath the Show Reserve Chardonnay; both are very well priced, but as with the Christobels/Antipodean contrast, one has to say that the Family Reserve offers the best value for money. The wine has often shown rather a lot of oak, but the '93 seems to have got the balance right.

Cellaring 2–4 years. **Best Vintages** '90, '91, '92, '93
Current Vintage '93

Matching Food Calamari.

Tasting Note 1993 Bright, light green-yellow; a markedly fresh and crisp, slightly herbaceous, style with citrussy aromas and subtle oak. The palate is intense, fresh and crisp, with citrus and melon fruit and a long finish.

YALUMBA THE SIGNATURE CABERNET SHIRAZ
●●●●● $17.95

An Australian classic, dating back to 1962, but deriving from Sir Robert Menzies' declaration at a lunch in Adelaide that the '61 Special Vintage Galway Claret was 'the finest Australian wine I have ever tasted'. The 1990 vintage is one of the greatest in a proud line; a blend of 65% cabernet sauvignon and 35% shiraz from Barossa and Coonawarra, it is a multiple gold medal winner.

Cellaring 5–15 years. **Best Vintages** '62, '66, '75, '81, '85, '88, '90, '91 **Current Vintage** '90

Matching Food Rare roast beef.
Tasting Note 1990 An outstanding wine fully reflecting the great vintage. The bouquet shows concentrated briary/berry fruits with good oak integration and balance. The palate, too, is powerful yet balanced, with dark berry, cassis and plum fruit flavours backed by opulent oak.

YANWIRRA *

★★★☆ 15 CD AUSSD
Great Southern **Est.** 1989
Redman Road, Denmark, WA 6333
Ph (09) 386 3577 **Fax** (09) 386 3578
Open Not **Production** NFP
Winemaker(s) John Wade (Contract)
Perth anaesthetist Ian McGlew and wife Liz have a liquorice allsorts 4-hectare vineyard which has produced some quite delicious Sauvignon Blanc; the destruction of the crop by birds in 1994 was a particularly bitter blow given the quality of the '93 wine.
Principal Wines Sauvignon Blanc, Dry White, Cabernet blend.

YANWIRRA SAUVIGNON BLANC
●●●● ▶ $15
Produced from 0.35 of a hectare of lyre trellis-trained sauvignon blanc, with a percentage of estate-grown semillon added. A particularly rich wine for young vines, promising well for the future.
Cellaring Drink now. **Best Vintages** '93 **Current Vintage** '93
Matching Food Pasta with cream sauce.
Tasting Note 1993 Light to medium yellow-green; the bouquet is clean, with good fruit intensity in a gooseberry/tropical spectrum. The palate shows similar flavours, again with good weight, finishing with soft acid. Not the least bit mean, green or herbal.

YARRA BURN VINEYARDS

★★★☆ 14.50–17.95 R AUS138–142
Yarra Valley **Est.** 1976
Settlement Road, Yarra Junction, Vic 3797
Ph (059) 67 1428 **Fax** (059) 67 1146
Open 7 days 10–5 **Production** 8200
Winemaker(s) David Fyffe
Chris and David Fyffe are now firmly in control at Yarra Burn after a prolonged period of financial uncertainty, with national distribution by S Smith & Son. The bluestone restaurant and cellar door sales area are important features in the Yarra Valley, with the restaurant strongly recommended.
Principal Wines Sauvignon Blanc Semillon, Chardonnay, Pinot Noir, Shiraz, Cabernet Sauvignon, Sparkling Pinot.

YARRA BURN SAUVIGNON BLANC SEMILLON
●●●● $14.50
A blend of 60% sauvignon blanc and 40% semillon from various

parts of the Yarra Valley. Made in the modern style, tank fermented without oak, and early bottled.
Cellaring None required. **Best Vintages** NA
Current Vintage '94
Matching Food Bouillabaisse.
Tasting Note 1994 Light green-yellow; light, fresh, crisp lemony/herbal fruit aromas of medium intensity. The palate is fresh and crisp, with clean, direct lemon and herbal fruit flavours, finishing with a barely perceptible hint of sweetness.

YARRA BURN SHIRAZ
●●● ▶ $16.50
Drawn in part from one hectare of estate plantings, and in part from other Yarra Valley growers. A good example of cool-climate shiraz, unforced by oak, and making an attractive early-drinking style.
Cellaring 2–3 years. **Best Vintages** '90, '91, '93
Current Vintage '93
Matching Food Italian.
Tasting Note 1993 Medium to full red; solid, ripish briary liquorice and spice fruit on the bouquet, and with some minty characters which appeared on the palate alongside the spice. A firm but not tannic finish.

YARRA EDGE VINEYARD
★★★★ 17–21 CD AUSSD
Yarra Valley **Est.** 1984
Lot 3 Edward Road, Lilydale, Vic 3140
Ph (03) 9735 3473 **Fax** (03) 9735 4853
Open By appt **Production** 1300
Winemaker(s) Tom Carson, Michael Zitzlaff (Contract)
Up until 1994 the Bingerman family had the wines contract made by Michael Zitzlaff at Oakridge. The 1995 vintage saw split responsibilities, with the red wines made by newly-appointed winemaker Tom Carson at Yarra Edge, but the Chardonnay made at Oakridge. It is planned that all future wines will be made at Yarra Edge.
Principal Wines Chardonnay, Cabernets.

YARRA EDGE CHARDONNAY
●●●● ▶ $16
Made entirely from low-yielding estate-grown grapes, and has typically shown the concentration one would expect from such low yields. The '93 vintage is a little lighter in style than some of the preceding vintages, but is none the worse for that.
Cellaring 3–5 years. **Best Vintages** '90, '91, '92, '93
Current Vintage '93
Matching Food Sweetbreads.
Tasting Note 1993 Medium yellow-green; fine, reserved melon and citrus-tinged fruit, with subtle French oak. An elegant wine on the palate with light melon and fig fruit, and again subtle barrel ferment characters. Will undoubtedly develop richness over the next two to three years.

YARRA RIDGE VINEYARD

★★★★ 14.95–16.95 R AUS104
Yarra Valley **Est.** 1983
Glenview Road, Yarra Glen, Vic 3755
Ph (03) 9730 1022 **Fax** (03) 9730 1131
Open W'ends, Hols 10–5.30 **Production** 50 000
Winemaker(s) Rob Dolan

Production continues to soar under the joint ownership of Mildara Blass and founder Louis Bialkower. The Sauvignon Blanc is no longer Yarra Valley sourced, the status of some of the other wines seemingly indeterminate. Overall, quality has been maintained remarkably well.

Principal Wines Chardonnay, Sauvignon Blanc, Botrytis Semillon, Pinot Noir, Reserve Pinot Noir, Merlot, Cabernet Sauvignon.

YARRA RIDGE CHARDONNAY
●●●● $15.95

A consistent wine which is a testament to the winemaking and wine production skills of winemaker Rob Dolan, particularly given the requirements of batch bottling and the limited size of the winery relative to its total production. A perfect wine for the cafe set.
Cellaring Largely irrelevant. **Best Vintages** '90, '92, '93, '94
Current Vintage '94
Matching Food Scallops, mussels.
Tasting Note 1994 Light yellow-green; a complex bouquet with intense fruit and very cleverly used American oak. The palate is well balanced, with fine citrus/melon fruit and seductive American oak.

YARRA RIDGE PINOT NOIR
●●●● $15.95

Anchored in the Yarra Valley, and with a Reserve Pinot Noir recently added to the range, albeit in small quantities. One of the lesser lights in the Yarra Ridge stable, but always a pleasant wine.
Cellaring Drink now. **Best Vintages** '91, '92, '93
Current Vintage '93
Matching Food Poultry.
Tasting Note 1993 Medium red; a fairly soft bouquet which progressively opens up in the glass revealing plum and spice fruit. The palate is relatively weighty, soft and chewy with some plummy fruit and clever use of oak. A success in a difficult vintage.

YARRA RIDGE SAUVIGNON BLANC
●●● ▶ $13.95

This wine was largely responsible for the initial phenomenal growth of Yarra Ridge. Ironically, the early vintages were from the Yarra Valley; the wine now has an infinitely broader geographic base, and shows it. However, it is certainly adequate for the market it serves.
Cellaring Drink now. **Best Vintages** NA **Current Vintage** '94
Matching Food Fish and chips.
Tasting Note 1994 Light to medium yellow-green; a soft, gently

fruity and only mildly herbaceous bouquet. The palate has soft fruit
and finishes with appreciable residual sugar.

YARRA VALLEY HILLS *

★★★☆ 13–18 CD AUS72
Yarra Valley **Est.** 1989
Old Don Road, Healesville, Vic 3777
Ph (059) 62 4173 **Fax** (059) 62 4173
Open W'ends, Public hols 10–6 **Production** 1465
Winemaker(s) Various Contract
Former schoolteacher Terry Hill has built up a very successful empire
in a short period of time through leasing two substantial vineyards
and principally acting as a grape supplier to others, with a small
proportion of the grapes being contract made by a range of Yarra
Valley winemakers, but henceforth by Yarra Ridge. Wine quality
has been consistently reliable, with conspicuous success for the
'93 Chardonnay.
Principal Wines Riesling, Sauvignon Blanc, Chardonnay, Pinot
Noir, Cabernet Sauvignon.

YARRA VALLEY HILLS CHARDONNAY
●●●● $18
From the Kiah and Yalambie vineyards. Not a heavyweight by any
means, but does show authentic Yarra Valley cool climate fruit
flavours, and should mature quite well.
Cellaring 3–4 years. **Best Vintages** '93, '94
Current Vintage '94
Matching Food Crab, lobster.
Tasting Note 1994 Light to medium yellow-green; crisp, clean
bouquet with melon fruit of light to medium intensity and minimal
oak. The palate is as yet fairly light-bodied, simple and clean with
melon/citrus fruit, yet to build real character.

YARRA VALLEY HILLS PINOT NOIR
●●●● $18
Like the Chardonnay, made primarily from Kiah and Yalambie
vineyards grapes. Light-bodied, but shows authentic varietal
character and regional style.
Cellaring 1–2 years. **Best Vintages** NA **Current Vintage** '94
Matching Food Chicken, quail.
Tasting Note 1994 Medium red-purple; the bouquet is of light to
medium intensity, with light stemmy/cherry fruit and subtle oak.
Scores best on the length of the palate and balance, with
silky/supple cherry and strawberry flavours, and subtle oak.

YARRA VALLEY HILLS SAUVIGNON BLANC
●●● ▶ $15
Produced from grapes grown at the Log Creek vineyard, made in a
direct, unwooded style with threshold residual sugar.
Cellaring Drink now. **Best Vintages** NA **Current Vintage** '94
Matching Food Seafood.

Tasting Note 1994 Light to medium yellow-green; a clean, fresh bouquet with pronounced herbal overtones, of light to medium intensity. The palate has rather more length, with gooseberry tropical flavours to go with the more herbaceous characters, fleshed out at the end with some sweetness.

YARRA YARRA VINEYARD *

★★★★ 16–20 ML AUSSD
Yarra Valley **Est.** 1979
239 Hunts Lane, Steels Creek, Vic 3775
Ph (059) 65 2380 **Fax** (03) 830 4180
Open Not **Production** NFP
Winemaker(s) Ian MacLean

The questionnaire returned by fax to me for the purposes of this work had Domaine de Chevalier at the top as the sender's number. Domaine de Chevalier is, of course, a famous Graves (Bordeaux) Chateau, and it was there that Ian MacLean was doing the 1994 vintage. Other people, it seems, try to do two or more things at the one time. This low profile winery is certainly dedicated to quality, with almost all of the wine sold by mail order and through leading Melbourne restaurants.

Principal Wines Cabernets, Sauvignon Blanc Semillon.

YARRA YARRA CABERNETS

●●●● $20

Produced from 1.5 hectares of cabernet sauvignon, cabernet franc and merlot grown on a north-facing slope, and which are not irrigated. The final wine (a blend of 75% cabernet and 12.5% each of cabernet franc and merlot) reflects the low-yielding vines.
Cellaring 5–10 years. **Best Vintages** '84, '86, '89, '90, '92
Current Vintage '91
Matching Food Osso bucco.
Tasting Note 1991 Medium to full red; a complex briary/cedary bouquet with somewhat subdued fruit, perhaps in transition, leading on to a fresh, leafy/briary palate, with subtle oak and well balanced tannins. Curiously, much less ripe than the '90.

YARRA YERING

★★★★★ 23–100 CD AUS111 UK43 US2
Yarra Valley **Est.** 1969
Briarty Road, Coldstream, Vic 3770
Ph (059) 64 9267 **Fax** (059) 64 9239
Open Sat, Public hols 10–5, Sun 12–5 **Production** 4000
Winemaker(s) Bailey Carrodus, Peter Wilson

Dr Bailey Carrodus makes extremely powerful, occasionally idiosyncratic wines from his 25-year-old, low-yielding un-irrigated vineyards. Both red and white wines have an exceptional depth of flavour and richness, although my preference for what I believe to be the great red wines is well known.

Principal Wines Dry Red No 1 (Sauvignon Blanc Semillon),

Chardonnay, Pinot Noir, Dry Red No 1 (Bordeaux Blend), Dry Red
No 2 (Rhone blend), Merlot (tiny quantities at $100 a bottle),
Underhill Shiraz.

YARRA YERING DRY RED NO 1
●●●●● $24
Predominantly cabernet sauvignon, with small quantities of merlot,
cabernet franc and malbec, and a tiny contribution of petit verdot.
Entirely estate-grown from low-yielding, un-irrigated vines, and
matured in high quality new French oak.
Cellaring 10+ years. **Best Vintages** '80, '81, '86, '89, '90,
'91, '93 **Current Vintage** '93
Matching Food Roast leg of lamb.
Tasting Note 1993 Full purple-red; complex dark berry fruit
aromas with subtle but evident oak. The palate is finely structured
and balanced; a feature is the tannins which run right throughout the
length of the palate, but are fine and soft. Swallows up the 100%
new oak in which it was matured.

YARRA YERING DRY RED NO 2
●●●●● $24
Predominantly shiraz, with a little viognier and a few scraps of other
things from time to time. Entirely estate-grown, of course, and
produced from vines which are now over 25 years old.
Cellaring 10+ years. **Best Vintages** '80, '81, '86, '89, '90,
'91, '93 **Current Vintage** '93
Matching Food Beef bourguignon.
Tasting Note 1993 Full purple-red; the bouquet is more discrete
than the Underhill of the same year, elegant and gently spicy. Those
spice and pepper characters are rather more evident on a long,
elegant palate with cherry and cedar notes also apparent.

YARRA YERING UNDERHILL SHIRAZ
●●●● ▶ $24
Made entirely from the former Prigorje Vineyard, which adjoins that
of Yarra Yering and is now, indeed, part of the Yarra Yering estate
— and has been so for some years. Here, too, the vines are old,
low-yielding and un-irrigated.
Cellaring 5–7 years. **Best Vintages** '91, '92, '93
Current Vintage '93
Matching Food Breast of squab.
Tasting Note 1993 Medium purple-red; a riotous and powerful
bouquet with voluminous pepper, spice and red cherry fruit. The
same splashy, opulent fruit is evident on the palate; great now,
but greater still in 10 years.

YASS VALLEY WINES *

NR 8.50–11 CD AUSSD
Canberra **Est.** 1979
9 Crisps Lane, Murrumbateman, NSW 2582
Ph (06) 227 5592 **Fax** (06) 227 5592
Open W'ends, Public hols 11–5 **Production** 115

Winemaker(s) Michael Withers
Michael Withers and Anne Hillier purchased Yass Valley Wines in
January 1991, and have subsequently rehabilitated the existing run-
down vineyards and extended the plantings. Mick Withers is a
chemist by profession and has almost completed a Wine Science
degree at Charles Sturt University; Anne is a registered psychologist
and has almost completed a Viticulture diploma at Charles Sturt. All
of the wines are now made on the premises, the '94 Riesling being
crisp and toasty, and made very competently.
Principal Wines Riesling, Chardonnay, Shiraz, Cabernet
Sauvignon.

YELLOWGLEN VINEYARDS

★★★★☆ 12.95–28 R AUS104, UK61
Bendigo **Est.** 1975
White's Road, Smythesdale, Vic 3551
Ph (053) 42 8617 **Fax** (053) 33 7102
Open 7 days 9–5 **Production** 220 000
Winemaker(s) Jeffrey Wilkinson
The quality of the top end Yellowglen wines over recent years has
gone from strength to strength. The quality of the commercial, non
vintage wines is, by contrast, no more than adequate for the purpose
and behind that of (say) Seaview, Killawarra or Seppelt.
Principal Wines Brut Cremant, Brut Pinot Chardonnay, Brut Rosé,
Cuvée Victoria, Vintage Pinot Chardonnay, Y.

YELLOWGLEN CUVÉE VICTORIA
●●●● ▶ $28
Sourced from Ballarat, Strathbogie and Yarra Valley fruit; a blend of
pinot noir and chardonnay, with the pinot noir component very much
to the fore in shaping the style of the wine.
Cellaring NA. **Best Vintages** '90, '91, '92
Current Vintage '92
Matching Food Shellfish.
Tasting Note 1992 Light to medium straw-yellow; a relatively firm,
yeasty/bready bouquet leads on to a clean, firm palate which has
quite classic length and intensity. All in all, a quite austere style
driven by pinot noir.

YELLOWGLEN VINTAGE PINOT CHARDONNAY BRUT
●●●● ▶ $18.95
A blend of pinot noir and chardonnay sourced from cool regions
across south eastern Australia, but predominantly Coonawarra, Eden
Valley, Yarra Valley and Ballarat. It first hit the headlines with the
'90 vintage, which was truly delicious, and the '92 is very much in
the same mould.
Cellaring Drink now. **Best Vintages** '88, '90, '92
Current Vintage '92
Matching Food Oysters.
Tasting Note 1992 Bright, light yellow-green; clean, crisp and
stylish aromas with faintly citrussy fruit to the fore. The palate is very

well balanced with citrus notes balanced by more dusty/bready characters. A pleasantly dry finish, and not overtly fruity.

YELLOWGLEN Y
●●●● ▶ $28

First released in 1994 with a package blatantly copied from the Sonoma Valley's Chateau Jordan's J. Equally interesting or controversial is the base wine, an assemblage of 55% chardonnay and 45% pinot noir from the 1990 and 1991 vintages, with part matured in French oak barriques before tiraging and three years lees maturation. The grapes were sourced from Coonawarra, Yarra Valley, Eden Valley and Ballarat.

Cellaring Drink now. **Best Vintages** NA **Current Vintage** NV
Matching Food Aperitif.

Tasting Note NV Bright light green-yellow; clean, fresh, crisp lemony/herbaceous/citrus aromas, with a spotlessly clean and crisp palate on which the chardonnay seems to be the dominant player. There is no sign of the wood maturation, and the wine is nicely balanced.

YERING STATION

★★★☆ 11.50–14.50 CD AUSSD
Yarra Valley **Est.** 1988
Melba Highway, Yering, Vic 3770
Ph (03) 9730 1107 **Fax** (03) 9739 0135
Open Thur–Sun 10–5 **Production** 5600
Winemaker(s) St Huberts (Contract)

The family of leading Sydney merchant banker Jim Dominguez has re-established Yering Station on the site of the first vineyard to be planted in the Yarra Valley in the 1840s. While the wine is presently made at St Huberts under contract, the historic brick winery has been restored as a barrel maturation area and luxurious sales and tasting facility. Well worth a visit.

Principal Wines Chardonnay, Unwooded Chardonnay, Pinot Noir, Cabernet Merlot.

YERING STATION CABERNET MERLOT
●●● ▶ $14.50

A blend of estate-grown cabernet sauvignon (dominant) together with merlot and a little cabernet franc.

Cellaring 2–3 years. **Best Vintages** '90, '91, '92
Current Vintage '92
Matching Food Prosciutto.

Tasting Note 1992 Bright medium red; fresh, albeit somewhat simple, red berry fruit of light to medium intensity. The flavours are direct with some redcurrant/cassis notes, along with a few more herbaceous characters, and the oak held well in restraint.

YERING STATION CHARDONNAY
●●●● $14.50

Caused a minor sensation when it won the trophy at the 1993 Lilydale Wine Show for Best Southern Victorian (including Yarra

Valley) Chardonnay. Has developed nicely, although perhaps not quite as well as some of the other wines it competed with at that show. 100% estate-grown, of course.
Cellaring 2–3 years. **Best Vintages** '93, '94
Current Vintage '93
Matching Food Veal in white sauce.
Tasting Note 1993 Medium yellow-green; the bouquet is clean and smooth with well balanced and integrated oak, showing some vanilla characters. The palate is of medium weight, again showing the sophisticated use of American and French oak; the fruit is of light to medium weight with stony/minerally aspects, and just a hint of melon.

YERINGBERG

★★★★★ 18–22 CD AUS144 UK16 US2
Yarra Valley **Est.** 1862
Maroondah Highway, Coldstream, Vic 3770
Ph (03) 9739 1453 **Fax** (03) 9739 0048
Open By appt **Production** 1000
Winemaker(s) Guill de Pury
Makes wines for the next millennium from the low-yielding vines re-established on the heart of what was one of the most famous (and infinitely larger) vineyards of the nineteenth century. The red wines have a velvety generosity of flavour which is rarely encountered, yet never lose varietal character, while the Yeringberg White takes students of history back to Yeringberg's fame in the nineteenth century.
Principal Wines Chardonnay, Yeringberg White (Marsanne/Roussanne), Pinot Noir, Yeringberg Red (Cabernet blend).

YERINGBERG CHARDONNAY
●●●●● $19
Produced from the half hectare of estate plantings, and made in necessarily very limited quantities. This restricts its opportunity for show entries, but it has been a consistent trophy and gold medal winner at the Lilydale Wine Show, the '94 following in the footsteps of many of its predecessors with a gold medal.
Cellaring 4–7 years. **Best Vintages** '88, '90, '91, '92, '93
Current Vintage '94
Matching Food Sweetbreads.
Tasting Note 1994 Medium to full yellow-green; excellent fruit and oak balance and integration on the bouquet, with lots of melon and peach fruit. A finer wine on the palate, with melon flavours dominant, and excellent length and acidity.

YERINGBERG DRY RED
●●●●● $22
Produced from an estate-grown blend of cabernet sauvignon, merlot, cabernet franc and malbec (with cabernet sauvignon dominant, and the other components in descending order as listed). The vineyard is established on the precise site of the great 19th-century plantings,

albeit but a fraction of the size of those vineyards, enjoying a prime north-facing slope.

Cellaring 20+ years. **Best Vintages** '85, '86, '88, '90, '91
Current Vintage '92
Matching Food Yarra Valley venison.
Tasting Note 1992 Medium purple-red, distinctly lighter than the preceding vintages. The bouquet is fragrant, with faintly gamey edges to the aroma attesting to its cool climate origins. The palate is flavourful and long, with good balance and fine structure, but with less fruit richness than in years such as '91 or '88.

YUNGARRA ESTATE

NR 10.50–12 CD AUSSD
Margaret River **Est.** 1988
Yungarra Drive, Dunsborough, WA 6281
Ph (097) 55 2153 **Fax** (097) 55 2310
Open 7 days 10–4.30 **Production** 1450
Winemaker(s) Erland Happ (Contract)
Yungarra Estate is a combined tourist lodge and cellar door facility set on a 40-hectare property overlooking Geographe Bay. The 8-hectare vineyard was first planted in 1988, producing its first wines in 1992, contract made by Erland Happ. In the meantime, wines purchased from other makers are being sold through cellar door by owners Gerry and Wendy Atherden.
Principal Wines Semillon, Sauvignon Blanc, Quartet (Semillon, Sauvignon Blanc, Chenin Blanc, Verdelho), Chenin Blanc Verdelho, Pink Opal (sweet red table wine made from Cabernet and Merlot), Springtime (sweet Sauvignon Blanc, Verdelho), Cabernet Sauvignon, Cabernet Merlot, Royale.

ZEMA ESTATE

★★★★☆ 9–22 CD AUS111, 123, 183
Coonawarra **Est.** 1982
Main Penola-Naracoorte Road, Coonawarra, SA 5263
Ph (087) 36 3219 **Fax** (087) 36 3280
Open 7 days 9–5 **Production** 6000
Winemaker(s) Matt Zema, Nick Zema
Zema is one of the last outposts of hand pruning and hand picking in Coonawarra, the various members of the Zema family tending a 40-hectare vineyard progressively planted between 1982 and 1994 in the heart of Coonawarra's terra rossa soil. Winemaking practices are straightforward; if ever there was an example of great wines being made in the vineyard, this is it.
Principal Wines Riesling, Shiraz, Cabernet Sauvignon, Family Selection Cabernet Sauvignon.

ZEMA ESTATE CABERNET SAUVIGNON

●●●● ▶ $17
Just as is the case with the Shiraz, produced from dryland, hand-pruned, hand-picked vines. A 100% cabernet sauvignon wine, matured in small French and American wood, but with the fruit —

rather than the oak — driving the wine. Back in form after a
disappointing '91.
Cellaring 5–10 years. **Best Vintages** '84, '86, '88, '92
Current Vintage '92
Matching Food Barbecued lamb.
Tasting Note 1992 Dense red-purple; a ripe and full bouquet
with some chocolate tones to the fruit, and vanillin oak adding
complexity. A solid, ripe, full-flavoured wine with abundant
blackcurrant and chocolate fruit flavours, and nicely controlled
vanillin oak.

ZEMA ESTATE SHIRAZ
●●●● ▶ $14
So far as I know, the only dryland, hand-pruned and hand-picked
vineyard in Coonawarra. This very conservative approach to
viticulture has paid big dividends, with outstanding wines produced
in '84, '86, '88, '92.
Cellaring Up to 10 years. **Best Vintages** '84, '86, '88, '92
Current Vintage '92
Matching Food Bistecca Fiorentina.
Tasting Note 1992 Medium to full red-purple; clean, smooth red
berry fruit of good depth with some varietal spice evident. The palate
is spotlessly clean with lively berry fruit flavours, good acidity, a
fresh finish and subtle oak.

ZUBER ESTATE

★★☆ 6–10 CD AUSSD
Bendigo **Est.** 1971
Northern Highway, Heathcote, Vic 3523
Ph (054) 33 2142
Open 7 days 9–6 **Production** 800
Winemaker(s) A Zuber
A somewhat erratic winery which is capable of producing the style
of Shiraz for which Bendigo is famous, but does not always do so.
Principal Wines Shiraz.

NEW ZEALAND WINERIES AND WINES

AKARANGI

NR 9.90–15 CD NZSD
Hawke's Bay **Est.** 1988
River Road, Havelock North, Hawke's Bay
Ph (06) 877 8228 **Fax** (06) 877 7947
Open W'ends, Public hols 9–5 **Production** 400
Winemaker(s) Morton Osborne
Former contract grape growers now making and selling tiny
quantities cellar door and through one or two local shops. Morton
and Vivien Osborne have 3 hectares of vineyards, and operate the
cellar door sales through a century-old church moved onto the
property.
Principal Wines Sauvignon Blanc, Muller Thurgau, Chenin Blanc,
Chardonnay, Cabernet Sauvignon.

ALLAN SCOTT WINES

★★★★ 11–20 R NZ5 UK44
Marlborough **Est.** 1990
Jacksons Road, RD 3, Blenheim
Ph (03) 572 9054 **Fax** (03) 572 9053
Open 7 days 9.30–4.30 **Production** 15 000
Winemaker(s) Allan Scott
Eight hectares each of sauvignon blanc, riesling and chardonnay
mean all the front-line wines are estate-grown. Highly regarded
wines have emanated since the first release, no surprise given Allan
Scott's career as Corbans' chief viticulturist for many years, not to
mention his involvement in the establishment of Cloudy Bay. A
popular vineyard restaurant also operates seven days a week.
Principal Wines Sauvignon Blanc, Riesling, Autumn Riesling,
Chardonnay, Mount Riley Classic Red.

ALLAN SCOTT AUTUMN RIESLING (375 ML)
●●●● ▸ $11
An elegant demonstration of the capacity of Marlborough to produce Botrytis Rieslings of the highest quality if the conditions are right — as they were in 1993. This is an extremely good wine by any standards.
Cellaring 2–4 years. **Best Vintages** NA **Current Vintage** '93
Matching Food Poached nectarines.
Tasting Note 1993 Brilliant green-yellow; a clean and elegant bouquet showing marked botrytis influence, yet not so marked as to obscure the pure lime varietal character. A similarly stylish and elegant wine on the palate with lime and passionfruit flavours, good length and perfectly balanced acidity.

ALLAN SCOTT RIESLING
●●● ▸ $14
Drawn from around 8 hectares of estate plantings. Both the 1992 and 1993 vintages were outstanding wines, the former winning a gold medal at the Air New Zealand Wine Show, the latter a gold medal at the 1994 Sydney International Winemakers Competition. The '94 comes as a qualified disappointment after the preceding vintages.
Cellaring 2–3 years. **Best Vintages** '92, '93
Current Vintage '94
Matching Food Fresh asparagus.
Tasting Note 1994 Light to medium green-yellow; the bouquet is crisp and spicy, with a hint of herbal astringency which is hard to identify but which also appears fleetingly on the palate. This apart, the wine is firm, crisp and pleasantly dry; may well come together with more bottle age.

ALLAN SCOTT SAUVIGNON BLANC
●●●● ▸ $17
Tasted on three separate occasions in Marlborough, Auckland and Sydney, respectively, at the end of 1994, with exceptionally consistent tasting notes — simply because it is hard to imagine a more disciplined and absolutely correct Marlborough style of Sauvignon Blanc, in which the fruit does all the work.
Cellaring Now–2 years. **Best Vintages** '92, '94
Current Vintage '94
Matching Food Sugar-cured tuna.
Tasting Note 1994 Light green-yellow; clean, fresh and crisp, with hints of herb and capsicum, yet not bitter or leafy. In the mouth, a powerful, direct style with that typical cut to the palate, spotlessly clean, and with a lingering aftertaste suggesting the clever use of subliminal levels of residual sugar.

ASPEN RIDGE ESTATE

NR 7.75–12 CD NZ9, 11
Waikato **Est.** 1968
Waerenga Road, Te Kauwhata
Ph (07) 826 3595 **Fax** (07) 827 3143

Open 7 days 8.30–6 **Production** 4000
Winemaker(s) Alastair McKissock
A specialist in unfermented, non-alcoholic sparkling grape juice,
a strange niche for a former head of the Te Kauwhata Research
Station with a Master's Degree in Oenology from UCLA Davis to
boot. Alastair McKissock is seeking to retire, and was quietly
offering the property for sale in 1994.
Principal Wines Sauvignon Blanc, Rhine Wine (sic), Harvest
White Hock, Harvest Red Claret, Cabernet Merlot, together with a
range of fortified and non-alcoholic sparkling and still grape juices.

ATA RANGI

★★★★★ 20–29 CD NZ5 UK35
Martinborough **Est.** 1980
Puruatanga Road, Martinborough
Ph (06) 306 9570 **Fax** (06) 306 9570
Open 7 days 11–5 Nov–Mar **Production** 2600
Winemaker(s) Clive Paton, Phyll Pattie
Consistently ranks among the best wineries in New Zealand,
let alone Martinborough. Both the Pinot Noir and Celebre are
remarkable for their depth of colour and sweetness of fruit, showing
the impact of full physiological ripeness.
Principal Wines Chardonnay, Pinot Noir, Celebre (Cabernet,
Syrah, Merlot blend).

ATA RANGI PINOT NOIR
●●●●● $29
Made in a very different style from the other consistently great Pinot
Noir from the Wairarapa, that of Martinborough Vineyard. Ata
Rangi is bigger, richer and more fleshy; that of Martinborough
tighter and perhaps more elegant. There should not be a question
of choice between the two styles: both should be in your cellar.
Cellaring 2–4 years. **Best Vintages** '86, '88, '89, '90, '91,
'92, '93 **Current Vintage** '93
Matching Food New Zealand venison.
Tasting Note 1993 Medium to full red-purple; a complex and
solid bouquet with abundant dark plum fruit and well balanced and
integrated spicy oak. A marvellously rich, soft and voluptuous wine
on the palate with briary/plum/berry fruit flavours, finishing with
long but soft tannins.

AWAITI VINEYARDS

NR NA NZSD
Waikato **Est.** 1989
Awaiti Road, RD2, Paeroa
Ph (07) 862 3834
Open Mon–Sat 9–5 **Production** 1500
Winemaker(s) Nick Chan
Cliff and Judith Pett have been producing grapes from their 3-hectare
vineyard since 1978, selling to others, but in 1989 commenced to

508

vinify part of the estate production. It is sold principally through cellar door, with a little through local shops.
Principal Wines Chenin Blanc, Cabernet Sauvignon.

BABICH

★★★★ NA NZSD UK31
Henderson **Est.** 1916
Babich Road, Henderson
Ph (09) 833 7859 **Fax** (09) 833 9929
Open Mon–Sat 9–5.30, Sun 11.30–5 **Production** NFP
Winemaker(s) Joe Babich
Continues to uphold the reputation it gained in the 1960s, but has moved with the times in radically changing its fruit sources and wine styles. Particularly, given the volume of production, quality is admirably consistent.
Principal Wines Irongate Chardonnay, Hawke's Bay Chardonnay, East Coast Chardonnay, Stopbank Chardonnay, Marlborough Sauvignon Blanc, Mara Estate Sauvignon, Hawke's Bay Sauvignon Blanc, Semillon Chardonnay, Fumé Vert.

BABICH MARA ESTATE SAUVIGNON
●●●● $16
A new label from Babich, dropping the words 'blanc' from the varietal name, but doubly identifying itself as of Hawke's Bay origin by the principal brand name of Mara Estate and the subtitle 'Gimblett Road'. A luscious style neatly pinpointing the dramatic difference between Hawke's Bay and Marlborough Sauvignon Blanc.
Cellaring Drink now. **Best Vintages** '93 **Current Vintage** '93
Matching Food Richer seafood, white meats.
Tasting Note 1993 Medium yellow-green; a very smooth and clean bouquet with seductive spicy/peachy aromas, outside the mainstream. A soft, fleshy palate with more of those stone fruit and peach flavours, nicely weighted, and showing no excess acidity.

BABICH MARLBOROUGH SAUVIGNON BLANC
●●● ▸ $13
The wine was first made in 1991, and was an immediate success. Both the wine of that year and the following vintage received gold medals in the New Zealand show system. They are made in a richer, fuller style than many Marlborough Sauvignon Blancs, but without sacrificing varietal character. The '94 follows in very much the same tradition.
Cellaring Drink now. **Best Vintages** '91, '92, '94
Current Vintage '94
Matching Food Marinated calamari.
Tasting Note 1994 Medium yellow-green; the bouquet is full, complex and tending a fraction broad, but with strong fruit and varietal character. A big wine on the palate with lots of flavour and complexity, and a greater than usual number of flavour and structure nuances. Emphatically drink now.

BAZZARD ESTATE

NR NA NZSD
Kumeu **Est.** 1991
Awa Road, RD2, Kumeu
Ph (09) 412 8486
Open By appt **Production** 1500
Winemaker(s) Kim Crawford (Contract)
Charles Bazzard is a former Buckinghamshire solicitor (and transient
waterfront worker) who, together with wife Kay, has developed an
organically-grown hillside vineyard in the Awa Valley, near Huapai.
Only low levels of sulphur dioxide are used, and the wine is matured
in old oak — all designed to produce a European style, not
surprising given that almost all of the production is exported to the
United Kingdom.
Principal Wines Muller Gewurztraminer, Pinot Noir.

BENFIELD & DELAMERE

NR NA NZSD
Martinborough **Est.** 1987
Cambridge Road, Martinborough
Ph (06) 306 9926 **Fax** (06) 306 9926
Open By appt **Production** 350
Winemaker(s) Bill Benfield, Sue Delamere
Wellington architect Bill Benfield and partner librarian Sue Delamere
have single-mindedly set about re-creating Bordeaux, with an ultra
high density, very low trellissed vineyard and utilising 'conservative'
techniques of the kind favoured by the Bordelaise. Recent vintages
have been less than kind, with little or no grapes produced.
Principal Wines 'Martinborough', a single Cabernet Sauvignon
Merlot Cabernet Franc blend.

BLACK RIDGE

★★★☆ NA NZSD
Central Otago **Est.** 1987
Controys Road, Earnscleugh, Alexandra
Ph (03) 449 2059
Open Mon–Sat 9.30–5 **Production** 1000
Winemaker(s) Michael Walter
The formidable, rocky vineyard site at Black Ridge is legendary
even in New Zealand, where toughness is taken for granted. The
8-hectare vineyard will always be low producing, but the wines
produced to date have all had clear and bracing varietal character.
The Pinot Noir is a particularly good example of what the site can
produce.
Principal Wines Riesling, Chardonnay, Gewurztraminer, Pinot
Noir.

BLACK RIDGE PINOT NOIR

★★★★ $NA
Made from the unquestionably inferior bachtebel clone, yet a wine

which has abundant colour, flavour and varietal character. It makes one wonder what might be achieved on this most southerly commercial vineyard in the world if one of the top clones of pinot noir were to be used.
Cellaring 1–2 years. **Best Vintages** NA **Current Vintage** '93
Matching Food Grilled rabbit.
Tasting Note 1993 Medium purple-red; a clean, fresh, though not particularly aromatic bouquet is followed by a nicely balanced, elegant and flavoursome palate with attractive red and black cherry fruit flavours.

BLOOMFIELDS VINEYARDS

NR 14–24 CD NZ7
Martinborough **Est.** 1981
119 Solway Crescent, Masterton
Ph (06) 377 5505 **Fax** (06) 377 5505
Open By appt **Production** 900
Winemaker(s) David Bloomfield
Tiny quantities of the wines sold to date have been eagerly snapped up by the local clientele, but wines are now being distributed (sparingly) through Kitchener Wines. The wines are made by former architectural technician turned winemaker David Bloomfield, drawing upon 2 hectares of estate cabernet sauvignon and a single hectare of pinot noir, sauvignon blanc, merlot and cabernet franc.
Principal Wines Sauvignon Blanc, Pinot Noir, Cabernet Sauvignon Merlot Cabernet Franc under both Solway and Bloomfield labels.

BLUE ROCK VINEYARD

NR NA NZ7
Martinborough **Est.** 1986
Dry River Road, Martinborough
Ph (06) 306 9353
Open 7 days 11–6 **Production** 2500
Winemaker(s) Jenny Clark
Blue Rock is a partnership run by the Clark family in a bid to diversify the activities carried on its 200-hectare sheep and cattle farm. There are now 12 hectares of windswept vineyards servicing a winery which was built in 1992, and a winery tasting room-cum-cafe-style restaurant completed in 1994, overlooking a 4-hectare park complete with lake, wildlife habitat and barbecue facilities.
Principal Wines Chardonnay, Sauvignon Blanc, Riesling, Pinot Noir, Cabernet Sauvignon, Cabernet Franc, Magenta Methode Traditionale.

BLUE ROCK SAUVIGNON BLANC
●●● $NA
A wine which shows the hazards of vintage generalisations in New Zealand (or anywhere else, for that matter). The '93 (from a vintage with a terrible reputation) is a very attractive wine, the '94 not so.
Cellaring Drink now. **Best Vintages** '93

Current Vintage '93, '94
Matching Food Salad Niçoise.
Tasting Note 1993 Medium yellow-green; potent gooseberry fruit aromas showing good varietal character and what appear to be low-yielding grapes. The palate is concentrated and powerful with distinct asparagus flavours, finishing with firm but not untenable acid.

BROOKFIELDS VINEYARDS

★★★☆ NA NZSD
Hawke's Bay **Est.** 1937
Brookfields Road, Meeanee, Napier
Ph (06) 834 4615 **Fax** (06) 834 4622
Open Mon–Sat 9–5, Sun 12–4 **Production** 5000
Winemaker(s) Peter Robertson
Peter Robertson has worked hard since acquiring Brookfields in 1977, producing grassy Sauvignon Blanc, lightly-oaked, understated Chardonnay, blackcurrant-flavoured Reserve Cabernet Sauvignon and, best of all, Cabernet Merlot with distinct overtones of St Emilion.
Principal Wines Chardonnay, Gewurztraminer, Sauvignon Blanc, Fumé Blanc, Pinot Gris, Cabernet, Reserve Cabernet Sauvignon, Cabernet Merlot.

BROTHERS VINEYARDS, THE See page 574.

BROWNLIE BROTHERS

NR NA NZSD
Hawke's Bay **Est.** 1991
6 Franklin Road, Bayview
Ph (06) 836 6250
Open 7 days 9–6 **Production** 650
Winemaker(s) Chris Brownlie
Chris and Jim Brownlie have progressively established 15 hectares of vineyards, selling most of the grapes to other wineries, but recently taking the plunge and vinifying a small part of the production for mail order and cellar door sales.
Principal Wines Chardonnay, Sauvignon Blanc, Gewurztraminer, Pinot Noir.

C J PASK WINERY

★★★★ 10–23.50 CD NZ2 UK58
Hawke's Bay **Est.** 1985
Omahu Road, Hastings
Ph (06) 879 7906 **Fax** (06) 879 6428
Open Mon–Sat 9–5, Sun 11–4 **Production** 17 000
Winemaker(s) Kate Radburnd
Ex-cropduster pilot C J Pask became one of the most highly regarded grape growers in Hawke's Bay; his coup in securing former Vidal winemaker Kate Radburnd (nee Marris) has paid the expected

dividends. Production has increased rapidly, and the wines have had significant and consistent success in New Zealand wine shows.
Principal Wines Sauvignon Blanc, Chardonnay, Reserve Chardonnay, Cabernet Merlot, Cabernet Sauvignon; Roy's Hill White and Red are second label.

CAIRNBRAE WINES *

★★★★☆ 16–19 CD NZSD
Marlborough **Est.** 1981
Jacksons Road, RD3, Blenheim
Ph (03) 572 8048 **Fax** (03) 572 8048
Open 7 days 9–5 **Production** 6000
Winemaker(s) Kim Crawford (Consultant)
The Brown family (Daphne, Murray and Dion) established 18 hectares of vineyard progressively from 1981, selling the grapes to Corbans until 1992, when part of the production was made for them by Kim Crawford, and the label was launched with immediate success. Definitely a label to watch.
Principal Wines Sauvignon Blanc, Chardonnay, Riesling, Semillon.

CAIRNBRAE CHARDONNAY
●●●● ▶ $19
A powerful, fruit-driven style which relies neither on oak nor on prolonged skin contact to give it the depth of flavour it possesses. Like all New Zealand Chardonnays, will develop reasonably quickly, but is no more than pleasantly mature at two years of age.
Cellaring Now–1 year. **Best Vintages** NA
Current Vintage '93
Matching Food Stuffed mussels.
Tasting Note 1993 Glowing yellow-green; a tangy, zesty citrus and melon-driven bouquet of medium to full intensity. The palate follows logically on from the bouquet, with complex grapefruit and melon flavours, and a long finish.

CAIRNBRAE RIESLING
●●●● ▶ $14
Yet another wine to demonstrate just how good riesling can be when grown in the Marlborough region. There may be some bottle variation; encountered several times at the end of 1994, on one occasion showing poor colour, which suggests an oxidised bottle. On the other occasion, quite brilliant. It is on that tasting that the note is given.
Cellaring Now–4 years. **Best Vintages** NA
Current Vintage '94
Matching Food Avocado salad.
Tasting Note 1994 Bright, light green-yellow; a clean, fresh and crisp bouquet with classic lime and toast aromas, together with some faintly herbal tones. The palate is crisp, clean, direct and toasty, with a bracingly long finish. Should develop well in bottle.

CAIRNBRAE SAUVIGNON BLANC
●●●●● $16
Again, tasted on a number of occasions in late 1994, and consistently impressed. Neatly combines elegance with some quite individual aromas and flavours. The '94 is a worthy follow-up to the gold medal winning 1993 Sauvignon Blanc (at the Air New Zealand Wine Show).
Cellaring Drink now. **Best Vintages** '93, '94
Current Vintage '94
Matching Food Grilled flounder.
Tasting Note 1994 Light green-yellow; a lifted bouquet with interesting grassy/green pea fruit aromas, and an almost estery edge. Beautifully balanced and constructed palate which has delicious feel and weight, even if more delicate than some Marlborough wines. The flavours run from herbaceous/green pea through to gooseberry. I really like this wine.

CAIRNBRAE SEMILLON
●●●● ▶ $16
Arguably the most interesting, if not quite the best, of the Cairnbrae wines, simply because it shows less of the extreme herbal/hay/straw characters which so often seem to disfigure Marlborough Semillons. Quite frankly, I have no idea how it will develop, but it does appear to have the structure to age nicely in bottle.
Cellaring 1–4 years. **Best Vintages** NA
Current Vintage '94
Matching Food Angels on horseback.
Tasting Note 1994 Light green-yellow; a fragrant, fresh, gently grassy bouquet, spotlessly clean, with good varietal character and weight. The palate is lively and fresh with pronounced lemony/grassy fruit, and tightly balanced acidity.

CELLIER LE BRUN

★★★★ 18–49.95 CD NZSD UK44
Marlborough **Est.** 1985
Terrace Road, Renwick
Ph (03) 572 8859 **Fax** (03) 572 8814
Open 7 days 9–5 **Production** 15 000
Winemaker(s) Daniel Le Brun
French-born and trained (in Champagne) Daniel Le Brun and wife Adele are now veterans of the Marlborough scene. In 1993 their winery was acquired by Appellation Vineyards Limited, a publicly listed company which also purchased Morton Estate and Allan Scott Wines. Whether the move will prove successful remains to be seen. In the meantime, Daniel Le Brun continues to produce the full-flavoured wines which have always been the mark of the vineyard.
Principal Wines Methode Champenoise specialist, with a large range of both vintage and non-vintage wines, including NV Brut, NV Rosé, Vintage Brut, Vintage Blanc de Blancs and super Cuvées of Blanc de Noirs and Cuvée Adele. Tiny quantities of Chardonnay and Pinot Noir table wine are also made.

CELLIER LE BRUN BLANC DE BLANCS
●●● ▶ $41.95

Made entirely from chardonnay, and given almost three years on yeast lees prior to disgorgement. In the mainstream of the Cellier Le Brun style, rich and full of flavour. Has been particularly successful in New Zealand wine shows.

Cellaring Drink now. **Best Vintages** '89, '90
Current Vintage '90
Matching Food Rich seafood with beurre blanc sauces.
Tasting Note 1990 Deep yellow; a full, deep, complex nutty/buttery bouquet in a particular style, but attractive. The palate shows many flavours, mostly in a similar nutty/buttery spectrum, but with a hint of camphor, and, not unlike some of the other Cellier Le Brun wines, dries out slightly on the finish.

CELLIER LE BRUN BLANC DE NOIRS
●●●● $41.95

Made, obviously enough, from 100% pinot noir, but made from richer material than the Rosé and given even longer on yeast lees before disgorgement. An expensive wine, but, in my view, justifies the price.

Cellaring Drink now. **Best Vintages** '89 **Current Vintage** '89
Matching Food Seared Atlantic salmon.
Tasting Note 1989 Salmon rose in colour; a very complex bouquet with nutty pinot noir varietal aromas of medium to full intensity. Succeeds particularly well in the mouth; a stylish wine with nutty/spicy flavours, with good length, balance and mouthfeel.

CELLIER LE BRUN ROSÉ
●●● ▶ $26.95

Made entirely from hand-picked pinot noir, and described by Daniel Le Brun as a 'red wine drinker's sparkler'. It is held on yeast lees for two years before disgorgement and is typically rich and full bodied.

Cellaring Drink now. **Best Vintages** NA **Current Vintage** NA
Matching Food Fish, veal or chicken dishes.
Tasting Note NV Full salmon pink; the bouquet shows strong bready/yeasty autolysis characters with an equally strong input from the pinot noir, all adding up to complexity. The palate is full flavoured with spicy aspects, and a touch of strawberry, drying off slightly on the finish.

CHARD FARM
★★★★☆ 15–29 R NZSD
Central Otago **Est.** 1987
Gibbston, RD2, Queenstown
Ph (03) 442 6110 **Fax** (03) 442 6110
Open 7 days 11–5 **Production** 6000
Winemaker(s) Rob Hay

Perched precariously between sheer cliffs and the fast-flowing waters of the Kawarau River, Chard Farm is a tribute to the vision and courage of Rob and Gregory Hay. At a latitude of 45°S, viticulture will never be easy, but Chard Farm has made every post a winner to date.

Principal Wines Riesling, Gewurztraminer, Sauvignon Blanc, Judge and Jury Chardonnay, Pinot Noir, Bragato Reserve Pinot Noir.

CHARD FARM BRAGATO RESERVE PINOT NOIR
●●●●● $29

Named in honour of the visionary viticulturist Romeo Bragato who came to New Zealand from Victoria at the end of the 19th century, and momentarily took the New Zealand industry by the scruff of the neck, propelling it in the direction in which it has finally headed 90 years later. He departed, and his vision was lost, but not entirely forgotten. This is a fitting tribute to his memory, even more fittingly packaged in an exotic Italian glass bottle.

Cellaring 3–5 years. **Best Vintages** '91, '93
Current Vintage '93
Matching Food Jugged hare.
Tasting Note 1993 Medium red-purple; smooth, ripe cherry fruit with well handled and balanced high quality charry oak. The palate is lively and multi-flavoured with briary/plummy/berry flavours cut by some more citrussy/stemmy characters. A wine full of flavour, character and style.

CHARD FARM GEWURZTRAMINER
●●● ▶ $15

A wine which reflects Rob Hay's three years study in Germany (after graduating from Otago University with a Bachelor of Science degree). Hay went to Germany to 'study winemaking in a genuinely cool climate' he says. Chard Farm certainly possesses that.

Cellaring Drink now. **Best Vintages** NA **Current Vintage** '94
Matching Food Delicate Asian dishes.
Tasting Note 1994 The colour is so pale as to be almost white; the bouquet is light, crisp and clean with cool climate herbal/spice aromas. On the palate, has as much sauvignon blanc as gewurztraminer character — crisp, bracing and herbal. Happily, not propped up by residual sugar.

CHARD FARM JUDGE AND JURY CHARDONNAY
●●●● ▶ $29

Strikingly packaged in one of the new generation rocket missile-shaped dark green Italian glass bottles, and taking its name from the prominent outcrops of rock across the Kawarau Gorge. Chard Farm clings precariously on the side of the Gorge. There is a great deal more to the wine than innovative (and no doubt expensive) packaging.

Cellaring 2–5 years. **Best Vintages** NA **Current Vintage** '94
Matching Food Breast of chicken, veal.
Tasting Note 1993 Medium to full yellow-green; an extremely complex bouquet with multi-layered aromas of peach, apricot and citrus. The palate shows a similar array of flavours from herbal to honeysuckle to melon and cashew, with a pronounced malolactic fermentation influence.

CHARD FARM PINOT NOIR

●●●● $21

The very unusual climate of southern New Zealand, with its long summer daylight hours, but a relatively short growing season inter-spersed with occasionally very hot days and cold nights, poses a question for any grape variety. It certainly does so for pinot noir, although the majority of winemakers who ply their trade here believe the variety is indeed suited to the climate. This wine supports that view.

Cellaring 2–3 years. **Best Vintages** '91, '93
Current Vintage '93
Matching Food Breast of duck.
Tasting Note 1993 Medium red-purple; the bouquet is full and ripe with plum and raspberry fruit aromas, a hint of spice, and not the least bit vegetal. The palate is high-toned, powerful and rich, with spicy/plummy fruit bordering on jammy, balanced by marked acidity on the finish.

CHARD FARM SAUVIGNON BLANC

●●● ▶ $17.50

Another wine to uncompromisingly reflect the cool climate (and for that matter craggy beauty) of Chard Farm. It takes up where Marlborough Sauvignon Blanc leaves off; piercingly crisp in style.

Cellaring 1–2 years. **Best Vintages** NA **Current Vintage** '94
Matching Food Oysters, mussels.
Tasting Note 1994 The colour is as pale as the Gewurztraminer: water white; the bouquet extreme herbal/tobacco leaf aromas, the palate likewise showing piercing herbal/tobacco fruit flavours with bracing acidity.

CHIFNEY

NR 11–25 CD NZSD
Martinborough **Est.** 1980
Huangarua Road, Martinborough
Ph (06) 306 9495 **Fax** (06) 306 9495
Open 7 days 9–5 **Production** 300
Winemaker(s) Stan Chifney

A retirement hobby which became rather more than that when the 1986 Cabernet Sauvignon won a gold medal at the 1988 Auckland Easter Show; I have tasted that wine, but none more recently and hence do not give a rating.

Principal Wines Chardonnay, Chenin Blanc, Rosé.

CHURCH ROAD WINERY, THE   See page 574.

CLEARVIEW ESTATE

★★★★☆ 10–25 CD NZSD
Hastings **Est.** 1989
Clifton Road, RD2, Te Awanga
Ph (06) 875 0150 **Fax** (06) 875 0974
Open Thur–Mon 10–6 summer; w'ends 10–5 winter

Production 1200
Winemaker(s) Tim Turvey
Clearview Estate is situated on a shingly site first planted by Anthony Vidal in 1916 on the coast of Te Awanga; it has been replanted since 1988 with chardonnay, cabernet sauvignon, cabernet franc and merlot, with grapes also coming from a neighbouring vineyard. All of the wines to date have been of exceptional quality, exemplified by the '93 Fumé Blanc. Alfresco lunches are served throughout the summer months.
Principal Wines Chardonnay, Te Awanga Sauvignon Blanc, Fumé Blanc, Cabernet Franc, Merlot, Chambourcin.

CLEARVIEW ESTATE FUMÉ BLANC
●●●●● $20
The same sophisticated oak handling evident in the Clearview Barrel Fermented Chardonnays appears in the Fumé Blanc. It adds a dimension to the wine without detracting from the fruit, and works wonderfully well.
Cellaring 1–2 years. **Best Vintages** NA **Current Vintage** '93
Matching Food Salmon tartare.
Tasting Note 1993 Medium yellow-green; a rich and complex bouquet, with spicy oak and voluptuously ripe fruit aromas. On the palate, cleverly handled, delicious spicy oak with citrus and peach fruit; almost a fugitive from chardonnay, but none the worse for that.

CLEARVIEW ESTATE TE AWANGA SAUVIGNON BLANC
●●●● ▶ $15
Shares some of the same deliciously ripe fruit characters of the Fumé Blanc although, in this instance, unadorned by oak. This is the type of wine to melt the heart of the most hardened foe of Sauvignon Blanc.
Cellaring Drink now. **Best Vintages** NA **Current Vintage** '94
Matching Food Mussels in white wine sauce.
Tasting Note 1994 Medium to full yellow-green; a ripe, soft vanilla and peach-accented bouquet leads on to a palate with more varietal character apparent; there are abundant gooseberry/tropical fruit flavours in a mouthfilling style.

CLOUDY BAY
★★★★★ 21.75–39.50 R NZ10 AUS65, 66, 167, 169, 181 UK71
Marlborough **Est.** 1985
Jacksons Road, Blenheim
Ph (03) 572 8914 **Fax** (03) 572 8065
Open 7 days 10–4.30 **Production** 50 000
Winemaker(s) Kevin Judd
The other arm of Cape Mentelle, masterminded by David Hohnen and realised by Kevin Judd, his trusted lieutenant from day one. A marketing tour de force, it became a world-recognised brand in only a few years, but the wine quality and style should not be underestimated: quite simply Hohnen and Judd took New Zealand Sauvignon Blanc from curiosity to respectability.

Principal Wines Sauvignon Blanc, Chardonnay, Cabernet Merlot, Pelorus (sparkling).

CLOUDY BAY CHARDONNAY

●●●●● $31.50

The extensive chardonnay plantings of Cloudy Bay (almost 35 hectares in total) are increasingly directed to the production of Pelorus, with the newer plantings dedicated to this purpose. However, Cloudy Bay produces a Chardonnay of real stature and complexity, made using prolonged yeast lees contact, malolactic fermentation and ageing in French oak.

Cellaring 3–5 years. **Best Vintages** '87, '91
Current Vintage '92
Matching Food Sweetbreads.
Tasting Note 1992 Light to medium green-yellow; a wine still coming together when tasted, with some oak influence still to integrate, though far from aggressive; faintly herbal/green citrus aspects to the bouquet. The palate is firm, with fruit sweetness balanced by echoes of the herbal characters of the bouquet. A cool, relatively low-yielding vintage of high quality.

CLOUDY BAY PELORUS

●●●● ▶ $39.50

A blend of pinot noir and chardonnay, made with consultancy advice and direction from Californian-born and trained Harold Osborne. The wine is aged for three years on yeast lees, and is given further bottle age prior to release. One of the most positively flavoured and structured sparkling wines from Australasia.

Cellaring 5–10 years. **Best Vintages** NA **Current Vintage** '90
Matching Food Medium-weight shellfish or fish dishes.
Tasting Note 1990 Full yellow-straw; a very full, bready/yeasty, almost buttery, bouquet, showing strong autolysis characters. The palate has enormous flavour, with buttery/yellow peach flavours together with the nutty/creamy characters deriving from the long period on lees.

CLOUDY BAY SAUVIGNON BLANC

●●●●● $21.75

The most famous New World Sauvignon Blanc, with an international reputation second to none. The creative team of David Hohnen and Kevin Judd are disarmingly modest about the wine; however, correctly, they may point to the perfect marriage between the variety and the climate and soil of Marlborough. There is also the attention to detail, the discipline and the creative intelligence required to make any wine of such distinction with such consistency.

Cellaring Now–5 years. **Best Vintages** '92, '94
Current Vintage '94
Matching Food Virtually any seafood dish.
Tasting Note 1994 Bright, light green-yellow; intense and clean, with beautifully balanced gooseberry/tropical aromas set against more herbal characters, but not the least green or aggressive;

subliminal touch of spice. A wonderful wine on the palate, with very good acid balance and length. Has overt varietal character, yet not at all in the cut-throat razor range. Poor flowering produced a small crop which ripened in perfect conditions.

COLLARDS

★★★★★ 9.35–27 CD NZ1, 6, 11
Henderson **Est.** 1910
303 Lincoln Road, Henderson, Auckland
Ph (09) 838 8341 **Fax** (09) 837 5840
Open Mon–Sat 9–5, Sun 11–5 **Production** 17 000
Winemaker(s) Bruce Collard, Geoff Collard
Fastidious winemaking evidences itself in all of the Collards wines, although it is the white wines which (deservedly) win most praise and show success.
Principal Wines Chardonnay (Rothesay, Gisborne, Hawke's Bay, Marlborough), Chenin Blanc, Sauvignon Blanc (Rothesay, Martinborough), Riesling, White Burgundy, Barrel Fermented Semillon, Late Harvest Semillon, Pinot Noir, Cabernet Sauvignon, Cabernet Merlot, Tawny Port.

COLLARDS ROTHESAY CHARDONNAY

●●●●● $27
Arguably the most distinguished of the Collards wines, proving that the Auckland region — in this case the Waikoukou Valley — can indeed produce high quality Chardonnay and Sauvignon Blanc. Since it was first made in 1986, the wine has won eight gold medals in New Zealand wine shows, but had its ultimate moment of glory at the 1994 Australian National Wine Show in Canberra, where it topped a field of over 100 medal-winning Chardonnays.
Cellaring 2–5 years. **Best Vintages** '86, '87, '89, '93, '94
Current Vintage '93
Matching Food Deep-sea fish.
Tasting Note 1993 Medium yellow-green; firm and clean, with plenty of depth to the fruit, and no hint of the jungle phenolics which so often mark New Zealand Chardonnays. The palate is big, rich and powerful, with ripe white peach fruit flavours and subtle oak.

CONDERS BEND

★★★★☆ 14–19.95 R NZ2
Nelson **Est.** 1991
23 Birdling Close, Richmond
Ph (03) 544 6809 **Fax** (03) 544 6809
Open Not **Production** 3000
Winemaker(s) Craig Gass
Craig Gass, together with wife Jane, has had 20 years experience in the industry, encompassing stints with George Fistonich in the early days of Villa Maria, and overseas, including Coldstream Hills. More recently he has worked with John Belsham's major contract

520

winemaking operation. All of the grapes for Conders Bend are in
fact sourced in Marlborough and made at Belsham's Vinotech
winery.
Principal Wines Sauvignon Blanc, Chardonnay.

CONDERS BEND SAUVIGNON BLANC
●●●●● $15
Produced from 3 hectares of sauvignon blanc now owned by the
Gass family, and stood out as one of the top three wines at a major
regional tasting (under show conditions) held in Marlborough in the
second half of 1994. An absolutely delicious wine which would
please even those who do not much like Sauvignon Blanc.
Cellaring Drink now. **Best Vintages** '92, '94
Current Vintage '94
Matching Food Calamari.
Tasting Note 1994 Bright green-yellow; the bouquet shows
excellent fruit ripeness and weight with hints of gooseberry to go
along with the more conventional green pea/herbaceous characters
of the variety. The palate is superb; there is high-toned, intensely
pure fruit, which is piercing yet not abrasive; some
gooseberry/tropical fruit flavours round the palate off without any
excess residual sugar. A wine to drink, not simply taste.

CONTINENTAL WINES *

NR NA NZSD
Northland **Est.** 1986
Main South Road, Whangarei
Ph (09) 438 7227
Open 7 days 10–4 **Production** 2000
Winemaker(s) Mario Vuletich
Since its establishment, production has shifted away from fortified
wines based on old New Zealand hybrids to conventional premium
varietal wines. These have been well received by wine-writers and
by the judges at local wine shows.
Principal Wines Chardonnay, Gewurztraminer, Pinot Noir,
Merlot, Cabernet Sauvignon, Port.

COOPERS CREEK

★★★★☆ 10–23.50 R NZ5 AUS28, 76, 163 UK33
Huapai **Est.** 1980
State Highway 16, Huapai
Ph (09) 412 8560 **Fax** (09) 412 8375
Open Mon–Fri 9–5.30, w'ends 10.30–5.30
Production 40 000
Winemaker(s) Kim Crawford
A long-term producer of stylish white wines sourced from Gisborne,
Hawke's Bay and Marlborough, respectively. They are full of
character and flavour, but avoid the heavy, coarse phenolics which
were once so much part of the white wine scene in New Zealand.

Principal Wines Hawke's Bay Riesling, Late Harvest Riesling, Hawke's Bay Chardonnay, Chardonnay Swamp Reserve, Marlborough Sauvignon Blanc, Gisborne Fumé Blanc, Gisborne Chardonnay, Hawke's Bay Merlot, Huapai Cabernet Merlot.

COOPERS CREEK GISBORNE CHARDONNAY
●●●● $15
Made in similar style, and with similar winemaking philosophies, as the Hawke's Bay Chardonnay and the deluxe Swamp Reserve Chardonnay. Full-blown, ripe fruit drives a highly commercial style.
Cellaring Drink now. **Best Vintages** '91, '92, '94
Current Vintage '94
Matching Food Veal goulash.
Tasting Note 1994 Glowing yellow-green; a complex bouquet with lots of sweet, honeyed fruit and well integrated and balanced oak. A big, rich wine on the palate with those sweet, yellow peach flavours and what appears to be fairly high alcohol adding to the overall impression of sweetness.

COOPERS CREEK GISBORNE FUMÉ BLANC
●●●● ▶ $15
A blend of 80% sauvignon blanc and 20% semillon, partially barrel fermented. The rich and full flavours which result have caught the attention of show judges and wine-writers alike; the '93 was a gold medal winner at the 1994 New Zealand Royal Easter Show, while the '94 is in much the same class.
Cellaring 1–2 years. **Best Vintages** '93, '94
Current Vintage '94
Matching Food Asian prawn dishes.
Tasting Note 1994 Medium to full yellow-green; the sophisticated use of high quality oak is immediately apparent on the bouquet, with spicy/nutmeg overtones to the fairly rich fruit. The palate, too, is driven primarily by high quality oak, but there is plenty of overall flavour there, and a hint of sweetness on the finish adds to, rather than detracts from, the commercial appeal of the wine.

COOPERS CREEK HAWKE'S BAY CHARDONNAY
●●●● $18.50
Winemaker Kim Crawford believes in ripe grapes, something fairly readily achieved in the Hawke's Bay climate. Barrel fermentation, lees contact and partial malolactic fermentation all add to the impact of a powerful wine style. The '94 won a silver medal at the Australian National Wine Show in classy company.
Cellaring Drink now. **Best Vintages** '86, '89, '91, '92, '94
Current Vintage '94
Matching Food Sweet and sour pork.
Tasting Note 1994 Medium to full yellow-green; a rich, full-blown bouquet with abundant peach and fig fruit together with nicely balanced oak. The palate shows extraordinarily ripe peachy/buttery fruit, almost into canned peach flavours, and will surely develop very quickly in bottle.

CORBANS

★★★★☆ 8.95–35 CD NZSD UK22
Henderson **Est.** 1902
Jacksons Road, Blenheim
Ph (03) 572 8198 **Fax** (03) 572 8199
Open 7 days 10–4.30 **Production** 750 000 plus 3 million casks
Winemaker(s) Alan McCorkindale
New Zealand's second largest wine group, with 37% of the market,
and rapidly closing the gap on Montana. Its almost bewildering
array of labels gives it distinct marketing advantages over Montana,
particularly given the seemingly separate identities that many of
these brands enjoy.

Principal Wines Under the key brands of Corbans, Cooks,
Robard and Butler, Stoneleigh Vineyard and Longridge, Corbans
markets six different cabernet-based reds, seven Chardonnays and
eight Sauvignon Blancs drawn from group-owned vineyards in the
Hawke's Bay and Marlborough regions (heavily supplemented by
purchased fruit) processed through wineries in Gisborne, Hawke's
Bay and Marlborough.

CORBANS COOKS WINEMAKERS RESERVE CHARDONNAY
●●●● ▶ $20
A famous label in New Zealand with a (relatively) long history of
high-class wine production. For many years, indeed, it was the
leading Chardonnay in New Zealand. Released with considerable
bottle age, it shows both concentration and complexity.
Cellaring 3–5 years. **Best Vintages** '83, '86, '89, '91
Current Vintage '91
Matching Food Deep-sea fish.
Tasting Note 1991 Medium to full yellow-green; a smooth and
clean bouquet with peach, melon and a touch of citrus. The palate is
holding together remarkably well and — most impressively — is not
overworked in terms of phenolics. It is a fruit-driven rather than oak-
driven wine of real style.

CORBANS COTTAGE BLOCK MERLOT
●●●● ▶ $35
Winemaker Alan McCorkindale (who presides at the Marlborough
winery) has shown particular flair in handling pinot noir and merlot,
not varieties one immediately associates with Marlborough. This is
a quite delicious wine with pure fruit flavours to the fore.
Cellaring 3–6 years. **Best Vintages** '87, '89, '91, '92, '94
Current Vintage '92
Matching Food New Zealand spring lamb.
Tasting Note 1992 Medium red-purple; fragrant, clean,
juicy/leafy fruit intermingling with more spicy/cedary aromas. On
the palate there are similar intense sweet berry and red cherry fruit
flavours which, in the New Zealand context at least, are fully ripe,
although the cool-grown origins are evident when the wine is tasted
in Australia.

CORBANS COTTAGE BLOCK NOBLE RIESLING (375 ML)
●●●● ▶ $20

The Cottage Block range is a new one for Corbans' Marlborough winery; all of the wines are at the top end, and all are produced in limited quantities. This is a heavily botrytis-infected style which works very well.

Cellaring 3–5 years. **Best Vintages** NA **Current Vintage** '91
Matching Food Fruit tart.

Tasting Note 1991 Medium to full yellow-orange; the aromas are multifaceted, ranging from apricot through to lime, showing some bottle development, but still intense. The palate is as intense as the bouquet promises, with apricot flavours dominant, finishing with excellent acidity on a cleansing finish.

CORBANS COTTAGE BLOCK PINOT NOIR
●●●● ▶ $35

Corbans was the first producer to release a noteworthy Pinot Noir from Marlborough, starring in various Sydney International Winemakers Competitions, most recently in 1995, when the 1992 Pinot Noir won yet another gold medal. Winemaker Alan McCorkindale understands better than most how to get the best out of this temperamental variety.

Cellaring Drink now. **Best Vintages** '91, '92
Current Vintage '92
Matching Food Char-grilled salmon.

Tasting Note 1992 Medium to full red-purple; a fruit-driven bouquet with ripe plummy fruit and a hint of tobacco. A solid wine on the palate with similar briary/plummy fruit flavours, and subtle oak. If there is a fault, it lies in the lack of structural complexity.

CORBANS LONGRIDGE HAWKE'S BAY CHARDONNAY
●●● ▶ $16

The Longridge range is very much the product of the marketing genius of Corbans' general manager Noel Scanlan, and sits alongside the Stoneleigh Marlborough wines in terms of price and market perception. The style is honest and relatively full-bodied, without being especially exciting.

Cellaring 2–3 years. **Best Vintages** '83, '89, '90, '91, '94
Current Vintage '93
Matching Food Pork fillets.

Tasting Note 1993 Medium to full yellow-green; the bouquet is smooth, of medium to full intensity, reasonably complex, with buttery/peachy fruit aromas. The same flavours carry through on the palate, although there are some telltale signs of a fairly difficult vintage on a green-tinged finish.

CORBANS STONELEIGH RIESLING
●●●● $13.95

Draws upon 22 hectares of estate plantings to produce an elegant wine with the highly-perfumed fruit which distinguishes New Zealand Rieslings from those of Australia.

Cellaring 2–5 years. **Best Vintages** '86, '89, '90, '91, '94

Current Vintage '93
Matching Food Fish terrine.
Tasting Note 1993 Bright green-yellow; the bouquet is floral and
perfumed with faintly spicy overtones. In the mouth the wine is dry,
crisp and elegant, with flavours of spice and lime; it has good length
and good balance, and in particular does not suffer from the excess
acidity which dogged the '93 vintage.

COVELL ESTATE *

NR 25 CD NZSD
Waikato **Est.** 1987
Troutbeck Road, Galatea
Ph (07) 366 4827
Open 7 days 10–4 **Production** 1000
Winemaker(s) Bob Covell
Bob Covell began the establishment of his 5-hectare biodynamic
vineyard 13 years ago on the volcanic plateau of the North Island.
The first experimental wines were made in 1987, the first
commercial wine (a Pinot Noir) will be released from the 1991
vintage.
Principal Wines Pinot Noir.

CRAB FARM

NR 10–17 CD NZSD
Hawke's Bay **Est.** 1989
125 Main Road, Bay View, Hawke's Bay
Ph (06) 836 6678
Open 7 days 10–5 **Production** 1800
Winemaker(s) Hamish Jardine
Hamish Jardine has worked at both Chateau Reynella and
Matawhero; the family vineyards were planted in 1980 and are
now mature, so given the equable Hawke's Bay climate there is
no reason why the wines should not succeed.
Principal Wines Gewurztraminer, Sauvignon Blanc, Pinot Noir,
Merlot, Cabernet Sauvignon.

CROSSROADS WINE COMPANY

NR 15 R NZSD
Hawke's Bay **Est.** 1990
SH 50, Korokipo Road, Fernhill, Napier
Ph (06) 835 4538
Open 7 days 9–6 **Production** 6000
Winemaker(s) Malcom Reeves
A partnership between Malcolm Reeves, wine journalist and Massey
University lecturer, and computer entrepreneur Lester O'Brien. Right
from vintage, the wines have received widespread critical acclaim,
and have enjoyed great success in wine shows. Production is
planned to grow to 10 000 cases if all goes well.
Principal Wines Gewurztraminer, Riesling, Chardonnay,
Sauvignon Blanc, Cabernet Sauvignon.

CROSSROADS WINE COMPANY SAUVIGNON BLANC
●●● ▶ $15
A relatively unusual style for Hawke's Bay, which normally produces
white wines which are fleshy and opulent by New Zealand
standards. The winemaker's thumbprint is on the wine.
Cellaring 1–3 years. **Best Vintages** NA **Current Vintage** '94
Matching Food Shellfish.
Tasting Note 1994 Light green-yellow; a crisp, light and fresh
bouquet with flinty/minerally notes which are repeated on the
relatively austere, almost European-style, palate.

DANIEL SCHUSTER (OMIHI HILLS)

★★★☆ 14.95–24.95 R NZ7 UK100
Canterbury **Est.** 1984
Reeces Road, Omihi, North Canterbury (vineyard only)
Ph (03) 337 1763 **Fax** (03) 379 8638
Open By appt **Production** 2000
Winemaker(s) Danny Schuster
Austrian-born, German-trained Danny Schuster is arguably better
known as a viticultural consultant in the Napa Valley than he is as
a winemaker in New Zealand. This despite the fact that he achieved
lasting recognition for the Pinot Noirs he made at St Helena in the
early 1980s, and despite his ongoing interest in Pinot Noir,
and a major (as yet unpublished) book on the subject to his credit. It
is thus the final irony that he has consistently produced better Pinot
Blanc than Pinot Noir since establishing his winery.
Principal Wines Hawke's Bay Chenin Blanc, Hawke's Bay Pinot
Blanc, Hawke's Bay Pinot Noir, Canterbury Pinot Noir, Reserve Pinot
Noir.

DANIEL SCHUSTER HAWKE'S BAY CHENIN BLANC
●●●● ▶ $14.95
The grapes are supplied under an ongoing contract, whole bunch
pressed on site at Hawke's Bay and transported to the Omihi Hills
winery for barrel fermentation and ageing on yeast lees for
11 months in used Vosges and Troncais barriques.
Cellaring 2–4 years. **Best Vintages** NA **Current Vintage** '93
Matching Food Roast turkey.
Tasting Note 1993 Light to medium yellow-green; the bouquet is
stylish, showing excellent barrel ferment characters deriving from
high-quality oak. The palate is likewise driven by excellent oak and
barrel ferment characters; had the base been chardonnay, not
chenin blanc, this would have been a five-star wine.

DANIEL SCHUSTER RESERVE PINOT NOIR
●●● ▶ $24.95
A mere 250 cases produced, sourced from Omihi Hills Vineyard in
Waipara and the 'old vines block' of St Helena, contracted to Daniel
Schuster. The wine is made using Burgundian techniques and aged
for 15 months in a mixture of one- and two-year-old Troncais
barriques.

Cellaring 1–2 years. **Best Vintages** '89, '92, '93
Current Vintage '92
Matching Food Grilled quail.
Tasting Note 1992 Light red; a clean, fault-free bouquet but distinctly stemmy and herbal, needing a touch more sweetness to the fruit. The palate, too, is on the stemmy/herbal side, albeit with some length and style.

DE REDCLIFFE ESTATES

★★★☆ 14–21R NZSD
Waikato **Est.** 1976
Lyons Road, Mangatawhiri Valley, Pokeno, near Auckland
Ph (09) 233 6314 **Fax** (09) 233 6215
Open 7 days 9.30–5 **Production** 15 000
Winemaker(s) Mark Compton
The Waikato's answer to the Napa Valley, with the $7 million Hotel du Vin, luxury restaurant, wine tours, lectures, the lot; briefly listed on the Stock Exchange, but now Japanese-owned. The white wines are by far the best.
Principal Wines Marlborough Riesling, Marlborough Sauvignon Blanc, Mangatawhiri Chardonnay, Hawke's Bay Pinot Noir, Hawke's Bay Cabernet Merlot, Hawke's Bay Cabernet Merlot Franc; Proprietor's Reserve is top end label, along with Mangatawhiri Chardonnay.

DE REDCLIFFE MANGATAWHIRI CHARDONNAY
●●● ▶ $21
Yet another Auckland district Chardonnay to prove its worth, coming from the 6.5-hectare home vineyard of De Redcliffe, which is largely planted to chardonnay. The wine is made in a fairly straightforward style, with the fruit doing the work.
Cellaring Drink now. **Best Vintages** '87, '89, '91, '93
Current Vintage '93
Matching Food Breast of chicken.
Tasting Note 1993 Medium yellow-green; clean, smooth fruit aromas running from lemony through to vanilla and peach. The palate is likewise clean and smooth, with faintly tropical overtones to the peachy/buttery fruit, and soft finish.

DE REDCLIFFE PROPRIETOR'S RESERVE HAWKE'S BAY MERLOT
●●● ▶ $21
A relatively new wine for De Redcliffe, which has hitherto tended to blend merlot with cabernet sauvignon. A pleasant wine of medium weight, showing an interesting array of varietal aromas and flavours.
Cellaring 2–4 years. **Best Vintages** NA **Current Vintage** '92
Matching Food Soft ripened cheese.
Tasting Note 1992 Medium red-purple; the bouquet shows a range of minty/earthy/minerally aromas which are repeated on a palate which, while lacking flesh and richness on the middle, does have length, and finishes well.

DELEGAT'S WINE ESTATE

★★★★ 16.95–24.95 R NZ1 AUS176 UK38
Henderson **Est.** 1947
Hepburn Road, Henderson
Ph (09) 836 0129 **Fax** (09) 836 3282
Open Mon–Fri 9–5, Sat 9–6 **Production** NFP
Winemaker(s) Brent Marris

Delegat's now sources most of its grapes from Hawke's Bay, utilising its own vineyards there and contract growers, but has added the Oyster Bay range from Marlborough to its repertoire. The quality of the wines is seldom less than good, with a number of excellent wines under the Proprietor's Reserve label.

Principal Wines Estate label of Chardonnay, Sauvignon Blanc and Cabernet Merlot; top-of-the-range Proprietor's Reserve label of Chardonnay, Fumé Blanc, Cabernet Sauvignon and Merlot. Also vineyard-designated Chardonnay from Hawke's Bay, Oyster Bay Chardonnay and Sauvignon Blanc, and Sauvignon Blanc from Marlborough.

DELEGAT'S OYSTER BAY CHARDONNAY
●●● ▶ $19.95

Delegat's Oyster Bay vineyards were planted in 1988 on Marlborough's Wairau plains around Spring Creek, Fairhall and Rapaura. Like the Sauvignon Blanc, the Chardonnay has had great success, the '92 vintage winning gold medals at the Air New Zealand National Wine Awards in 1992 and at the International Wine Challenge, London, in 1993. It has to be said that the '93 vintage is not quite up to the same standard.

Cellaring 2–3 years. **Best Vintages** '90, '91, '92, '94
Current Vintage '93
Matching Food Marinated octopus.
Tasting Note 1993 Medium to full yellow-green; a very striking bouquet with plenty of power but some slightly smelly European overtones. The same characters appear on the palate, which is powerful but does not appear to be entirely clean, with some rather vegetal phenolic characters.

DELEGAT'S OYSTER BAY SAUVIGNON BLANC
●●●● $16.95

The first vintage of Delegat's Oyster Bay Sauvignon Blanc, made from two-year-old vines, had extraordinary success in winning the Marquis de Goulaine Trophy for Best Sauvignon Blanc at the International Wine and Spirit Competition in London in July 1991. Not surprisingly, the Oyster Bay label has spearheaded Delegat's export drive since that time. It is made in a classic, no-frills, bracingly direct Marlborough style.

Cellaring Drink now. **Best Vintages** '90, '91, '92, '94
Current Vintage '94
Matching Food Oysters, mussels.
Tasting Note 1994 Light to medium green-yellow; intense, pungent grassy/herbal/minerally aromas lead on to an intense

palate showing pristine grassy/herbal sauvignon blanc varietal character.

DELEGAT'S PROPRIETOR'S RESERVE CHARDONNAY
●●●●● $24.95

One of New Zealand's most distinguished Chardonnays, reaching a peak with the '92. Made from hand-harvested, estate-grown grapes; 50% is barrel fermented in a mixture of new and one-year-old French oak barriques, and a sensibly restrained 10% undergoes malolactic fermentation. A gold medal winner at the Sydney International Wine Competition 1994 and at New Zealand's Royal Easter Show 1994.
Cellaring 2–4 years. **Best Vintages** '86, '89, '91, '92, '94
Current Vintage '92
Matching Food Smoked salmon.
Tasting Note 1992 Full yellow-green; a complex, rich and potent bouquet with good barrel ferment characters and smooth fruit. The palate is stylish and concentrated, with complex melon, fig and peach fruit nicely balanced by oak. Ageing nicely.

DELEGAT'S PROPRIETOR'S RESERVE MERLOT
●●●● ▶ $24.95

A 100% merlot, 100% Hawke's Bay wine. After a warm fermentation, 50% of the wine completed its primary fermentation in new Nevers oak barriques, and all of the wine spent 12 months in wood prior to bottling. A gold medal winner at the New Zealand Royal Easter Show 1994, showing perfectly ripened fruit notwithstanding the relatively cool summer.
Cellaring 4–6 years. **Best Vintages** '86, '89, '91, '92, '94
Current Vintage '92
Matching Food Roast veal.
Tasting Note 1992 Medium red-purple; a clean, relatively intense bouquet with briary/tobacco-accented aromas, but not green or herbal. The palate is clean and long, with dark berry fruit flavours, hints of tobacco, finishing with fine tannins and subtle oak.

DRY RIVER

★★★★★ 17–40 CD NZ5 UK49
Martinborough **Est.** 1979
Puruatanga Road, Martinborough
Ph (06) 306 9388 **Fax** (06) 306 9388
Open Not **Production** 2000
Winemaker(s) Neil McCallum

Winemaker/owner Neil McCallum is a research scientist with a Doctorate from Oxford University, with winemaking very much a part-time occupation. He has justifiably gained an international reputation for the exceptional quality of his wines, which he jealously guards and protects. Each is made in tiny quantities, and sells out immediately on release. Says Dr McCallum, disarmingly, 'We are unable to send wine samples to international critics'. Despite this, one or two Dry River wines do occasionally pass my palate; I only wish more did so.

Principal Wines Dry Riesling, Chardonnay, Gewurztraminer, Sauvignon Blanc, Pinot Gris, Pinot Noir.

ESK VALLEY ESTATE

★★★☆ 10.50–16.40 CD NZSD UK99
Hawke's Bay **Est.** 1933
745 Main Road, Bay View, Napier
Ph (06) 836 6411 **Fax** (06) 836 6413
Open 7 days 10–6 summer, 10–5 winter
Production 25 000
Winemaker(s) Gordon Russell
The little brother in the Villa Maria-Vidal family which has, in typical brash, small boy fashion, on a number of occasions upstaged the others. In more recent years, however, the wines have more accurately reflected their status in the corporate structure.
Principal Wines Chenin Blanc, Sauvignon Blanc, Cabernet Merlot Franc under the Private Bin label; Chardonnay and Cabernet Merlot under the Reserve Bin label; also tiny quantities of Rosé and Botrytised Chenin Blanc.

ESK VALLEY ESTATE PRIVATE BIN CHENIN BLANC
●●● ▶ $10.50
The Esk Valley Chenin Blanc is matured for four months in previously-used French and American oak casks, and is described as wood aged on the label. In fact the oak impact is barely perceptible, but does add to the texture of the wine. It ages well, and in late 1994, no less than four vintages ('90–'93 inclusive) were available at the cellar door — and all at the same price.
Cellaring 3–5 years. **Best Vintages** '87, '89, '91, '92, '94
Current Vintage '93
Matching Food Pork fillet with apricots.
Tasting Note 1993 Medium yellow-green; a complex fruit-driven bouquet with the classic fruit salad aromas of chenin blanc. The palate has plenty of weight and mouthfeel, sweet but not sugary, and a pleasantly long finish.

ESK VALLEY ESTATE PRIVATE BIN SAUVIGNON BLANC
●●● ▶ $14.50
Made from contract-grown grapes sourced throughout the Hawke's Bay region. In 1994, both standard and Reserve bottlings were produced, the standard wine being every bit as attractive in its youth as the Reserve version and, of course, being substantially cheaper.
Cellaring Drink now. **Best Vintages** '87, '89, '92, '94
Current Vintage '94
Matching Food Pan-fried trout.
Tasting Note 1994 Light yellow-green; the bouquet is of light to medium intensity with pleasant passionfruit and peach edges to more conventional but ripe sauvignon blanc aromas. The palate is supple and balanced, again showing nicely ripened fruit, and likewise soft tropical flavours alongside gooseberry/herbal characters.

ESKDALE WINEGROWERS

NR NA NZSD
Hawke's Bay **Est.** 1973
Main Road, Eskdale
Ph (06) 836 6302
Open Mon–Sat 9–5 **Production** Under 1000
Winemaker(s) Kim Salonius
Having gained winemaking experience at McWilliam's, Canadian-
born Kim Salonius and family have established a tiny 2-hectare
estate operation, making wines in very small quantities, sold
cellar door. Their wines have gained a strong reputation for
consistency of quality.
Principal Wines Gewurztraminer, Chardonnay, Cabernet.

FORREST ESTATE

★★★★ 12–20 CD NZSD UK43
Marlborough **Est.** 1989
Blicks Road, Renwick, Marlborough
Ph (03) 572 9084 **Fax** (03) 572 9084
Open Mon–Sun 12–5 Oct–Apr **Production** 5000
Winemaker(s) John Forrest
Former biochemist and genetic engineer John Forrest has had
considerable success since his first vintage in 1990, relying initially
on purchased grapes but with a 4-hectare vineyard now planted.
Wine quality has been remarkably consistent right across the range,
perhaps reflecting John Forrest's strong grounding in chemistry.
Principal Wines Chardonnay, Sauvignon Blanc, Semillon,
Riesling, Cabernet Rosé, Gibsons Creek Cabernet Franc Merlot.

FORREST ESTATE SAUVIGNON BLANC

●●● ▶ $15
An interesting wine which is a blend of 85% sauvignon blanc and
15% semillon; in 1994 a small proportion of botrytis-infected fruit
was deliberately added for extra complexity. As if this were not
enough, the sauvignon blanc was picked on different dates to give
a range of flavours and characters. This is a long way from the
standard Marlborough Sauvignon Blanc.
Cellaring 1–2 years. **Best Vintages** '91, '92, '94
Current Vintage '94
Matching Food Coquilles St Jacques.
Tasting Note 1994 Light to medium yellow-green; a complex
bouquet showing all of the influences of the varied grape input,
including some botrytis-derived phenolics. A big wine on the palate
with lots of flavour and concentration, and a range of flavours from
herbal to far riper characters.

FOXES ISLAND WINES *

★★★★ 26 R NZ10
Marlborough **Est.** 1992
440 Rapaura Road, Blenheim

Ph (03) 572 8393 **Fax** (03) 572 8399
Open 7 days 9–5 at Wairau River Winery **Production** 1400
Winemaker(s) John Belsham
Former Hunter's winemaker John Belsham presides over the vast
contract winemaking business of Vintech, but since 1992 has made
tiny quantities of wine from 4 hectares of vineyards established on
stony barren ground called Foxes Island, from which the name of
the winery is derived.
Principal Wines Chardonnay, Pinot Noir.

FOXES ISLAND CHARDONNAY
●●●● $26
1250 cases of the 1400 output in 1994 was of Chardonnay. John
Belsham deliberately adopts a very low profile for Foxes Island,
emphasising that his main business is the contract-making of wine
for others through Vintech, not Foxes Island. Nor was 1993 a
particularly easy vintage, and the wine is itself on the modest side.
Cellaring 1–2 years. **Best Vintages** '94 **Current Vintage** '93
Matching Food Blanquette of veal.
Tasting Note 1993 Medium yellow-green; a very complex
nutty/buttery/oaky bouquet leads on to a similarly richly textured
palate with fairly broad, nutty, malolactic, ambient fermentation
temperature characters.

FRENCH FARM VINEYARDS

NR NA NZ5 UK43
Canterbury **Est.** 1991
French Farm Valley Road, Akaroa
Ph (03) 304 5784 **Fax** (03) 304 5785
Open 7 days 10–6 **Production** 5000
Winemaker(s) Tony Bish
The name of the enterprise derives from the fact that French
immigrants planted vines at Akaroa (one hour's drive south of
Christchurch) as early as 1840. The luxurious tasting facilities
include a restaurant open every day for lunch, with superb views
back across the bay. Winemaker/owner Tony Bish graduated
with a Wine Science Degree from Charles Sturt University, and is
making wines of consistently good standard.
Principal Wines Fumé Blanc, Riesling, Sauvignon Blanc, Cabernet
Sauvignon, Cabernet Franc, Rosé.

FROMM WINERY *

NR NA NZSD
Marlborough **Est.** 1992
Godfrey Road, Blenheim
Ph (03) 572 9355
Open Mon–Sat 11–5 **Production** 2000
Winemaker(s) Hatsch Kalberer
Former Matawhero winemaker Hatsch Kalberer was planning to
commence wine sales as from December 1994. There are

3 hectares of estate vineyards, with a further 3 hectares to be planted, and an additional 10 hectares under contract from local growers. Production is accordingly planned to substantially increase.
Principal Wines Chardonnay, Pinot Noir.

GATEHOUSE WINES

NR NA NZSD
Canterbury **Est.** 1989
Jowers Road, RD6, Christchurch
Ph (03) 342 9682
Open Mon–Sat 10–5 Nov–Feb, Sat 10–5 Mar–Oct
Production NFP
Winemaker(s) Peter Gatehouse

The Gatehouse family made its first wines in 1989 from estate plantings commenced in the early 1980s. The initial release was under the Makariri label, but the wines will henceforth be released under the Gatehouse label, and it is planned to increase production through the purchase of additional grapes from contract growers.
Principal Wines Chardonnay, Gewurztraminer, Riesling, Pinot Noir, Merlot, Cabernet Sauvignon.

GIBBSTON VALLEY

★★★☆ 14–25 R NZ8 UK43
Central Otago **Est.** 1989
State Highway 1, Gibbston, RD1, Queenstown
Ph (03) 442 6910 **Fax** (03) 442 6909
Open 7 days 10–5.30
Production 7000
Winemaker(s) Grant Taylor

A highly professional and attractive winery, restaurant and cellar door sales facility, which has been an outstanding success since the day it opened. Viticulture poses special problems, and both varietal selection and determining style will inevitably take time. However, a neat, modern production facility and a succession of very competent winemakers have pushed Gibbston Valley firmly down the road to success.
Principal Wines Four wines from Central Otago: Riesling, Sauvignon Blanc, Pinot Gris, Reserve Pinot Noir; from Marlborough: Riesling, Chardonnay, Sauvignon Blanc. The White and Ryecroft Red from Waitiri are cheaper second labels.

GIBBSTON VALLEY RESERVE PINOT NOIR
●●● ▶ $25
Produced in limited quantities from the relatively small estate plantings of the variety. The short growing season carries with it threats at both the start and finish of the season; the yields are low, and the wine is very much subject to vintage conditions.
Cellaring 1–2 years. **Best Vintages** '89, '90, '91, '94

Current Vintage '93
Matching Food Spiced quail.
Tasting Note 1993 Medium red-purple; a complex bouquet with
some sappy/stalky edges to the strawberry fruit, and powerful oak.
The palate shows a similar range of flavours, once again quite oak
dominated, and thins out fractionally on the finish, suggesting
imperfectly ripened fruit assisted by chaptalisation.

GIESEN ESTATE

★★★★☆ 7–30 CD NZ10 AUS112 UK1
Canterbury **Est.** 1981
Burnham School Road, Burnham
Ph (03) 347 6729 **Fax** (03) 347 6729
Open Mon–Sat 10–5 **Production** 30 000
Winemaker(s) Marcel Giesen, Rudi Bauer
Determination, skill and marketing flair have seen Giesen grow
from obscurity to one of the largest family-owned and run wineries
in New Zealand. Given the Giesens' Rhine Valley origins it is
not surprising that they have done so well with aromatic, non-
wooded white wines, but the Reserve Chardonnay extends
the range.
Principal Wines Muller Thurgau, Riesling, Dry Riesling, Extra Dry
Riesling, Late Harvest Riesling, Chardonnay, Reserve Chardonnay,
Ehrenfelser, Dry Gewurztraminer, Port.

GIESEN ESTATE EXTRA DRY RIESLING
●●●● $15
It was the desire to grow riesling — and in particular to make a dry
Riesling — which lured the Giesen family to the very cool Canterbury
district in the first place. The grapes were harvested at the end of
April with a typical German analysis of just under 11 baume,
9.6 grammes per litre of acid and a pH of 3.1. Botrytis was
deliberately excluded.
Cellaring 3 years. **Best Vintages** '89, '90, '91, '94
Current Vintage '91
Matching Food Sashimi.
Tasting Note 1991 Medium to full yellow-green; a very floral
bouquet with lots of lime and fig aromas. On the palate, intense
and high-toned, with powerful citrussy fruit, and cleansing acidity
on the finish.

GIESEN ESTATE LATE HARVEST RIESLING
●●●● ▶ $19
Made from heavily botrytis-infected estate-grown grapes picked in
May at 38° Brix. A stylish wine, although now fully aged.
Cellaring Drink now. **Best Vintages** NA
Current Vintage '90
Matching Food Home-made fruit ice cream.
Tasting Note 1990 Glowing yellow-green; strong botrytis
influence evident throughout a bouquet showing a spectrum of

aromas from lime to apricot to pineapple. The palate is rich, full flavoured with lime and more tropical fruit flavours, and a relatively soft finish.

GIESEN ESTATE RESERVE CHARDONNAY
●●●● $30
Until 1992, the Reserve Chardonnays from Giesen Estate were all produced from Canterbury grapes and released under the Burnham School Road label. In 1992 it was felt the best wine of the vintage had come from grapes purchased from Marlborough, and it is this wine which produced the Reserve. The full gamut of winemaking techniques was used, including malolactic fermentation, lees contact and 50% new French oak.
Cellaring 2–4 years. **Best Vintages** NA **Current Vintage** '92
Matching Food Smoked chicken.
Tasting Note 1992 Deep yellow; a rich, honeyed/buttery bouquet with hints of botrytis in the background. An extremely rich and full-blown wine on the palate, with peach, honey, malt and butter flavours all intermingling. Not a wine to be ignored.

GILLAN WINES *
★★★★ 15.95 R NZ6
Marlborough **Est.** 1992
Rapaura Road, Blenheim, Marlborough
Ph (03) 572 9979 **Fax** (03) 572 9980
Open 7 days 10–5 summer **Production** 3800
Winemaker(s) Sam Weaver
Gillan Wines is a partnership between English-born Toni and Terry Gillan and local vignerons Hamish and Anne Young. The Gillans were involved in the establishment of Grove Mill Wine Company after they moved from London in 1987, but have since gone their own way; Terry Gillan is involved in a number of other tourist ventures in the Marlborough region. The Gillan wines are made at Vintech under the direction of Sam Weaver and Craig Gass.
Principal Wines Eastfields Sauvignon Blanc, Chardonnay, Merlot, Marlborough Cuvée Methode Traditionale.

GILLAN EASTFIELDS SAUVIGNON BLANC
●●●● ▶ $15.95
The only wine released by Gillan to date, with the balance of the range to come in 1995 and thereafter. Produced from the Youngs' Eastfields Vineyard, this wine had instantaneous success, winning a gold medal at the 1994 Air New Zealand Wine Awards, New Zealand's premier wine show.
Cellaring Now–2 years. **Best Vintages** NA
Current Vintage '94
Matching Food Antipasto.
Tasting Note 1994 Light green-yellow; a crisp, clean bouquet with an attractive range of aromas running from herbal through to more tangy/peachy characters. The palate is bright, fresh and pure, with the same range of flavours evident on the bouquet.

GLADSTONE VINEYARD

★★★★ NA NZSD
Martinborough **Est.** 1987
Gladstone Road, Gladstone, Carterton
Ph (06) 379 8563 **Fax** (06) 379 8563
Open 7 days 10–12, 2–5 Sept–May, by appt June–Aug
Production 1500
Winemaker(s) Dennis Roberts
Dennis Roberts has taken early retirement from a professional career
to concentrate on his love of vineyards and wine. A handsome
winery presides over an immaculate vineyard situated roughly
halfway between Martinborough and Masterton on alluvial soils
laid down by the nearby Ruamahanga River. The label design,
incidentally, is a model of elegance and simplicity.
Principal Wines Riesling, Sauvignon Blanc, Chardonnay,
Cabernet Merlot.

GLENMARK WINES

★★★★☆ 9–27 CD NZ11
Canterbury **Est.** 1981
Mackenzies Road, Waipara
Ph (03) 314 6828 **Fax** (03) 314 6828
Open 7 days 11–6 **Production** 1000
Winemaker(s) Kym Raynor
Kym Raynor is a very experienced winemaker, and Glenmark is an
important part of the Canterbury scene, notwithstanding its relatively
small size. Much of the wine is sold cellar door, with the Weka
Plains Wine Garden offering a full restaurant service and wine by
the glass from October through to April. Bookings are essential.
Principal Wines Waipara Riesling, Weka Plains Riesling,
Waipara White, Chardonnay, Gewurztraminer, Pinot Noir.

GLENMARK WAIPARA RIESLING
●●●● ▶ $12
Somewhat surprisingly, this wine could still be purchased at the
winery late in 1994, and fared well at the 1995 Sydney
International Winemakers Competition, narrowly missing out on
selection in the Top 100.
Cellaring Drink now. **Best Vintages** '87, '88, '90, '91
Current Vintage '90
Matching Food Trout mousse.
Tasting Note 1990 Light green-yellow; concentrated lime juice
aromas on the bouquet, with similarly rich and full lime juice flavours
on the palate. If one is to be hypercritical, it is a fraction heavy
towards the finish.

GLENMARK WEKA PLAINS RIESLING
●●●● ▶ $14
Riesling has been one of the most consistent medal winners for
Glenmark, which is part of a much larger mixed farming venture

with crops, Corriedale sheep and one of the foundation herds of Santa Gertrudis cattle. Raynor's Australian background has left its mark on this wine.

Cellaring 4–7 years. **Best Vintages** '88, '90, '91, '94
Current Vintage '94
Matching Food Seafood salad.
Tasting Note 1994 Very light green-yellow; a crisp, toasty, reserved bouquet, strongly reminiscent of the Clare Valley. The palate is likewise very reserved, steely, toasty and bone dry. Should develop superbly.

GLOVER'S VINEYARD

★★★ 11–18 CD NZ6 UK42
Nelson **Est.** 1984
Gardner Valley Road, Upper Moutere
Ph (03) 543 2698
Open 7 days 10–6 **Production** 1200
Winemaker(s) David Glover
David Glover studied winemaking and viticulture at Charles Sturt University in southern New South Wales during a 17-year stay in Australia. He returned with wife Penny to establish their own vineyard in 1984, struggling with birds and other predators before producing their first wines in 1989. The quality of the white wines has been good, although the muscular, brawny Pinot Noir has pleased others more than it has me.
Principal Wines Sauvignon Blanc, Riesling, Late Harvest Riesling, Pinot Noir, Cabernet Sauvignon.

GOLDWATER ESTATE

NR 20–33 CD NZSD UK42
Waiheke Island **Est.** 1978
18 Causeway Road, Putiki Bay, Waiheke Island
Ph (09) 372 7493 **Fax** (09) 372 6827
Open 7 days 11–4 summer, w'ends, hols 11–4 winter
Production 5000
Winemaker(s) Kim Goldwater
Goldwater Estate has established a formidable reputation for the quality of its wines, which sell in impressive volumes given their relatively high prices. Dr Richard Smart has been retained as viticultural consultant for the Waiheke Island red wines.
Principal Wines Marlborough Chardonnay, Delamore Chardonnay, Waiheke Island Cabernet Merlot.

GRAPE REPUBLIC

NR 10–26 R NZSD
Wellington **Est.** 1985
State Highway 1, Te Horo
Ph (06) 364 3284 **Fax** (06) 364 3284
Open 7 days 10–5 **Production** 3000

Winemaker(s) Alastair Pain
A marketing and promotion tour-de-force using direct mail and wine
club techniques, with a vast array of flavoured wines and smaller
quantities of more expensive table wines which are distinctly austere.
Alastair Pain says this is the European style he is aiming for. I am not
so sure, although the 1990 Druid Hill Cabernet Sauvignon is a good
wine. A winery cafe opened for business in 1993.
Principal Wines Chardonnay, Sauvignon Blanc, Riesling, Rosé,
Gewurztraminer, Cabernet Sauvignon; a selection of fruit wines.

GROVE MILL

★★★★ 17.85–29.50 CD NZ5 AUS84 UK47
Marlborough **Est.** 1988
Waihopai Valley Road, Marlborough
Ph (03) 572 8200 **Fax** (03) 572 8211
Open Tues–Sat 11–5 **Production** 12 000
Winemaker(s) David Pearce
Burst onto the scene with a superb '89 Chardonnay, and continued
its success through 1992 and into 1993, when its 1992 Riesling
was judged to be the Top Wine of the Year by *Cuisine Magazine*.
The 1993 Sauvignon Blanc is an attractive wine, but I have
problems with the 1994 vintage of that wine.
Principal Wines From Marlborough: Sauvignon Blanc,
Chardonnay, Riesling, Dry Riesling, Gewurztraminer, Pinot Gris;
Lansdowne Chardonnay.

HERONS FLIGHT

NR 24 CD NZ7
Northland **Est.** 1987
Sharp Road, Matakana
Ph (09) 422 7915
Open 7 days 10–6 **Production** 1500
Winemaker(s) David Hoskins
Herons Flight or Phoenix Flight? Having established a small vineyard
in 1987, David Hoskins and Mary Evans have leased the defunct
Antipodean Winery which was the scene of so much marketing hype
and excitement in the mid 1980s before disappearing in a bitter
family dispute. The first Herons Flight wine (a densely-coloured and
flavoured Cabernet Sauvignon) was produced from the 1991
vintage; production has reached its planned maximum level.
Principal Wines Barrel Fermented Chardonnay, Unoaked
Chardonnay, Cabernet Merlot.

HIGHFIELD ESTATE

★★★★ 9.50–13 CD NZ10
Marlborough **Est.** 1990
Brookby Road, RD2, Blenheim
Ph (03) 572 8592 **Fax** (03) 572 9257
Open 7 days 10–5 **Production** 4000

Winemaker(s) Tony Hooper
Highfield Estate was purchased by an international partnership in
late 1991, the English and Japanese limbs of which are associated
with the French Champagne House Drappier, pointing to the
addition of a Methode Champenoise sparkling wine to the range of
premium varietals. Winemaker Tony Hooper, who spent several
years making wine at Yarra Burn in the Yarra Valley, adds the final
international touch — and skill.
Principal Wines Chardonnay, Riesling, Sauvignon Blanc, Noble
Late Harvest, Merlot.

HIGHFIELD ESTATE CHARDONNAY
●●● ▶ $15
The 4 hectares of estate chardonnay are primarily directed to the
production of sparkling wine (in turn destined for Japan), but small
quantities are made as a table wine under the Highfield Estate label.
It relies on elegance rather than power for its appeal.
Cellaring 2–3 years. **Best Vintages** '91, '94
Current Vintage '93
Matching Food New Zealand crayfish.
Tasting Note 1993 Glowing yellow-green; intense, cool-
grown citrus/melon/herbaceous fruit aromas drive the bouquet.
The palate is elegant, again showing melon and citrus fruit, and
finishing with the fairly hard acid which so marked the 1993
vintage.

HIGHFIELD ESTATE MERLOT
●●●● $15
Produced from 5 hectares of estate-grown grapes and praised by all
and sundry since its debut. It is another convincing demonstration
that the Marlborough region is far more suited to merlot than it is to
cabernet sauvignon — not surprising given the temperature
summation.
Cellaring 2–4 years. **Best Vintages** '90, '91, '94
Current Vintage '93
Matching Food Grilled kidneys.
Tasting Note 1993 Light to medium red; the fruit aromas are ripe,
almost into a slightly confection/jam spectrum. The palate shows
similar very ripe, juicy berry fruit, even a hint of chocolate, and is
quite fleshy and soft.

HIGHFIELD ESTATE SAUVIGNON BLANC
●●●● $13
A classic, piercingly pure, no-frills Marlborough style, very consistent
from one year to the next. Against all the odds, I marginally
preferred the '93 over the '94 in a major tasting held in
Marlborough, but that was more to the credit of the former than the
discredit of the latter.
Cellaring 1–3 years. **Best Vintages** '91, '94
Current Vintage '94
Matching Food Shellfish.

Tasting Note 1994 Light green-yellow; fresh, crisp, powerful varietal aromas running from herbal/capsicum through to melon. The palate is direct, fresh and firm, with unadorned varietal fruit flavour running through to a long, crisply acid finish.

HUNTER'S WINES

★★★★★ 15.95–23.50 R NZSD UK1
Marlborough **Est.** 1980
Rapaura Road, Blenheim
Ph (03) 572 8489 **Fax** (03) 572 8761
Open 7 days 9.30–4.30 **Production** 30 000
Winemaker(s) Gary Duke
Hunter's goes from strength to strength, consistently producing flawless wines with tremendous varietal character. Given the quantity and quality of its production, it is a winery of world standing, and certainly among the top half dozen in Australasia.
Principal Wines Chardonnay, Gewurztraminer, Sauvignon Blanc, Oak Aged Sauvignon Blanc, Riesling, Pinot Noir, Cabernet Merlot, Brut.

HUNTER'S CHARDONNAY

●●●●● $23.05
Just as the Sauvignon Blanc is so often at the head of the field in New Zealand, so is the Chardonnay, although it does seem to me that the '93 vintage invested the wine with some fairly pronounced botrytis characters which have unduly modified the varietal character of this particular wine.
Cellaring 2–5 years. **Best Vintages** '90, '91, '94
Current Vintage '93
Matching Food Honey prawns.
Tasting Note 1993 Pronounced peach and apricot overtones to sweet, honeyed fruit and subtle oak on the bouquet. The palate is similarly very ripe, showing peach and apricot flavours, and with a remarkably soft finish for a '93 vintage.

HUNTER'S OAK AGED SAUVIGNON BLANC

●●●●● $23.50
Having decided to put Sauvignon Blanc in oak, Jane Hunter and her winemaking/consulting team have not done anything by half measures. It is barrel fermented with a substantial percentage of new wood making a pronounced impact on the wine. Whether it is a better wine really depends on one's personal view of oak and, for that matter, of Sauvignon Blanc.
Cellaring 3–5 years. **Best Vintages** '88, '89, '91, '93, '94
Current Vintage '93
Matching Food Grilled spatchcock.
Tasting Note 1993 Medium to full yellow-green; pronounced spicy vanilla oak, well balanced and integrated on both the bouquet and palate. The palate has an array of softly ripe fruit flavours, but, as with the bouquet, it is (pleasantly) dominated by the oak.

HUNTER'S PINOT NOIR

●●●● ▶ $19.95

The '93 was a surprise packet from Hunter's; I have tasted numerous
prior vintages, and been unimpressed. The wine has basically been
sold in the United Kingdom, where it has widespread acceptance. If
there were more vintages like the '93, the wine would no doubt
enjoy international acceptance.

Cellaring 2–4 years. **Best Vintages** '93 **Current Vintage** '93
Matching Food Saddle of hare.

Tasting Note 1993 Medium red; a fragrant bouquet with an array
of stemmy and spicy aromas of light to medium intensity. The palate
shows similar lively, spicy/stemmy flavours with hints of earthy/berry
fruits; the oak handling is good, as is the length to the finish.

HUNTER'S RIESLING

●●●● ▶ $15.95

Not a major item in the Hunter's line-up, but an attractive wine,
showing typical New Zealand (or, rather, Marlborough) elegance.

Cellaring 2–4 years. **Best Vintages** '90, '91, '93, '94
Current Vintage '94
Matching Food Asparagus with hollandaise sauce.

Tasting Note 1994 Light yellow-green; the bouquet is clean, with
a mix of faintly herbaceous/toasty notes running alongside finer lime
characters. The palate is floral and delicate, with a hint of
passionfruit to add further interest.

HUNTER'S SAUVIGNON BLANC

●●●●● $19.95

Made in two versions, this being the major (unoaked) version. Year
in, year out it is one of New Zealand's best. By chance I tasted the
'94 on four different occasions in four different locations towards
the end of 1994, three of them in totally masked or show venues.
On three of the four occasions I unhesitatingly gave it gold medal
points; the fourth simply has to have been a bad bottle, being at the
Cuisine Magazine tasting, when it was consistently judged at a
lower level.

Cellaring 1–2 years. **Best Vintages** '88, '89, '91, '93, '94
Current Vintage '94
Matching Food All seafood.

Tasting Note 1994 Brilliant green-yellow; spotlessly clean,
fragrant and pungent citrus, passionfruit and gooseberry aromas.
The palate mirrors the bouquet, classy and elegant, with gooseberry
fruit tinged with more tropical characters; perfect balance.

HUTHLEE ESTATE *

NR 24–25 R NZSD
Hawke's Bay **Est.** 1991
Montana Road, RD5 Hastings, Hawke's Bay
Ph (06) 879 6234 **Fax** (06) 879 6234
Open Mon–Sat 10–5, Sun 11–4 **Production** 450
Winemaker(s) Devon Lee

Devon and Estelle Lee planted their 6-hectare vineyard in 1984, and established an on-site winery in 1991. The light but clean and well-made wines from the 1992 vintage have been favourably reviewed.
Principal Wines Rosé, Cabernet Franc, Merlot Cabernet, Merlot.

JACKSON ESTATE

★★★★☆ 13.45–30 ML NZ7 UK44
Marlborough **Est.** 1988
Jacksons Road, Blenheim
Ph (04) 569 6547 **Fax** (04) 569 7037
Open Not **Production** 12 000
Winemaker(s) Martin Shaw (Consultant)
Long-term major grape growers John and Warwick Stichbury, with leading viticulurist Richard Bowling in charge, own substantial vineyards in the Marlborough area, and have now established their own winery and brand to vinify part of the production, the balance still being sold to others.
Principal Wines Riesling, Marlborough Dry Riesling, Sauvignon Blanc, Chardonnay, Botrytis Riesling, Pinot Noir.

JACKSON ESTATE RIESLING
●●●● $15.95
As with the Sauvignon Blanc, estate-grown (from 4 hectares of vines) and, again as with the Sauvignon Blanc, showing an unusual degree of ripeness and softness. Perhaps some of these fruit characters derive from the fact that the vines are not irrigated.
Cellaring 1–4 years. **Best Vintages** '92, '94
Current Vintage '94
Matching Food Trout mousse.
Tasting Note 1994 Light to medium yellow-green; the bouquet is clean and soft, of medium intensity, with lime-accented fruit. There is plenty of fruit and flavour on the palate, with the residual sugar seemingly pushing up a little, but making for a thoroughly commercial style.

JACKSON ESTATE SAUVIGNON BLANC
●●●●● $17.95
Produced from 15 hectares of estate plantings established in 1988, and producing the first vintage in 1991. The vines are not irrigated, are hand-pruned and utilise the Scott Henry trellis. The quality of the fruit is beyond dispute, and the winemaking skills of international flying winemaker Martin Shaw add the final touch.
Cellaring 1–3 years. **Best Vintages** '91, '92, '93, '94
Current Vintage '94
Matching Food Calamari.
Tasting Note 1994 Light to medium yellow-green; rich fruit aromas in a ripe spectrum, ranging from gooseberry through to peach. The wine has abundant flavour on the palate, again in a riper spectrum, with gooseberry and stone fruit flavours, finishing with perfectly balanced acidity. A softer but thoroughly satisfying style of Marlborough Sauvignon Blanc.

JOHANNESHOF CELLARS *

NR NA NZSD
Marlborough **Est.** 1993
State Highway 1, Koromiko, RD3, Blenheim
Ph (03) 573 7035 **Fax** (03) 573 7035
Open W'ends 10–5 **Production** 650
Winemaker(s) Edel Everling, Warwick Foley
Marlborough district winemaker Warwick Foley met his wife-to-be
Edel Everling in New Zealand, followed her back to Germany
(where her family has a winemaking history) and spent five years
studying and working, inter alia at Geisenheim. The couple have
returned to New Zealand to make European-style wines in an
underground cellar blasted into a hillside between Blenheim and
Picton. The '92 and '93 Sauvignon Blancs tasted in 1994
showed rather heavy, extractive phenolic characters.
Principal Wines Sauvignon Blanc, Muller Thurgau, Methode
Champenoise.

KEMBLEFIELD ESTATE *

NR 7.95–19.95 CD NZ10
Hastings **Est.** 1993
Aorangi Road, Hastings
Ph (06) 874 9649 **Fax** (06) 874 9457
Open By appt **Production** 11 600
Winemaker(s) John Kemble
With 8.5 hectares of sauvignon blanc, 7.3 hectares of chardonnay,
4.5 hectares of merlot and 2.9 hectares of cabernet sauvignon,
Kemblefield Estate has accelerated out of the blocks since it
graduated from grape growing to winemaking in 1993.
Principal Wines Chardonnay, Reserve Sauvignon Blanc,
Cabernet Merlot, Merlot.

KUMEU RIVER WINES

★★★★ 13–29 CD NZ7 UK17
Kumeu **Est.** 1944
550 Highway 16, Kumeu
Ph (09) 412 8415 **Fax** (09) 412 7627
Open Mon–Fri 9–5.30, Sat 11–5.30 **Production** 18 000
Winemaker(s) Michael Brajkovich
The wines of Michael Brajkovich defy conventional classification,
simply because the highly trained, highly skilled and highly
intelligent Brajkovich does not observe convention in crafting them,
preferring instead to follow his own French-influenced instincts and
preferences. Not altogether surprisingly, the wines have won high
praise overseas.
Principal Wines At the top end, Kumeu River label: Chardonnay,
Sauvignon Semillon, Semillon, Merlot Cabernet; Brajkovich
Auckland Chardonnay; Brajkovich Signature range: Chardonnay,
Sauvignon, Cabernet Merlot, Cabernet Franc.

KUMEU RIVER BRAJKOVICH SIGNATURE SAUVIGNON
●●● ▶ $14

Michael Brajkovich holds firmly to the Auckland region, from whence
all of the grapes for the various Kumeu River wines come. 80% are
estate-grown, but the intake is supplemented for the Brajkovich
Signature range in particular. His faith in the Auckland region is
understandable when it comes to chardonnay and cabernet merlot,
but is rather more debatable with varieties such as sauvignon blanc.
Cellaring 2–3 years. **Best Vintages** '89, '91, '92, '93, '94
Current Vintage '94
Matching Food White-fleshed fish.
Tasting Note 1994 Light to medium yellow-green; the bouquet is
light, clean and smooth, with some nutty/herbal characters. The
palate shows some crisp, herbaceous fruit, but is not particularly
intense, nor yet particularly varietal.

LAKE CHALICE WINES *

NR 11.50–18.50 CD NZ6
Marlborough **Est.** 1989
Vintage Lane, Renwick
Ph (03) 572 9327 **Fax** (03) 572 9327
Open Planned summer 1995 **Production** 1200
Winemaker(s) Chris Gambitsis

Lake Chalice Wines is a partnership of three long-time friends, Chris
Gambitsis, Ron Wichman and Phil Binning. In 1989 they purchased
the 11.5-hectare Falcon Vineyard; the name of the winery comes
from a wilderness lake situated in the Richmond Range which
borders the northern side of Marlborough's Wairau Plain. The first
wine release was in 1993.
Principal Wines Semillon (Barrel Fermented), Sauvignon Blanc,
Chardonnay, Riesling.

LAKE CHALICE SAUVIGNON BLANC
●●● $14.50

The Falcon Vineyard was selected for its potential to produce
outstanding fruit, say the partners. It is, even by Marlborough
standards, extremely stony and free-draining. The '94 vintage does
not show the concentration one might expect, though it is a pleasant
enough wine.
Cellaring Drink now. **Best Vintages** NA **Current Vintage** '94
Matching Food Shellfish.
Tasting Note 1994 Light green-yellow; a crisp, direct bouquet with
slightly dusty/herbal overtones. The palate is light but shows quite
good varietal character in a grassy mould; curiously, the alcohol
seems relatively high.

LANDFALL WINES

★★★ ▶ 23 CD NZSD UK21
Gisborne **Est.** 1987
State Highway 2, Manutuke, Gisborne
Ph (06) 862 8577 **Fax** (06) 867 8508

Open 7 days 10–6 Oct–Easter **Production** 5000
Winemaker(s) John Thorpe
Landfall has managed to change its name and associations with
the regularity of the guards at Buckingham Palace. Revington is no
more, but there is now a separate brand, also owned by the Thorpe
family and which is separately marketed, appearing under the
Longbush entry.
Principal Wines Chardonnay, Pinot Noir.

LARCOMB WINES

★★★☆ 8–16 CD NZSD
Canterbury **Est.** 1985
Larcombs Road, RD5, Christchurch
Ph (03) 347 8909
Open Nov–Feb Tues–Sun 9–5 **Production** 2000
Winemaker(s) John Thom
Highly regarded maker of fine, elegant citrus Rhine Riesling, fleshy,
gently-oaked Pinot Gris, and generous Pinot Noir; the winery
restaurant (open from November to February) is extremely popular
and contributes substantially to sales.
Principal Wines Riesling, Gewurztraminer, Pinot Gris, Pinot Noir.

LAWSONS DRY HILLS *

★★★★★ 15.75–21.50 R NZSD
Marlborough **Est.** 1992
Alabama Road, Blenheim
Ph (03) 578 7674 **Fax** (03) 578 7674
Open 7 days 10–5 **Production** 3300
Winemaker(s) Clair Allan
Lawsons Dry Hills is situated on the Wither Hills, which in turn take
their name from their parched mid-summer look. It is owned by
Barbara and Ross Lawson, who have graduated from being grape
growers to winemakers, with Roseworthy-trained Clair Allan in
charge of winemaking — and doing an absolutely brilliant job.
Principal Wines Gewurztraminer, Sauvignon Blanc, Chardonnay,
Riesling.

LAWSONS DRY HILLS CHARDONNAY

●●●●● $19.50
Just as in the case of the Riesling, the highest-pointed Chardonnay
from 1992 or 1993 in the *Cuisine Magazine* Marlborough regional
tasting at the end of 1994. Sensitive use of high-quality oak is an
outstanding feature of the wine.
Cellaring 2–5 years. **Best Vintages** NA **Current Vintage** '93
Matching Food Ragout of sweetbreads and brains.
Tasting Note 1993 Glowing yellow-green; an exceptionally stylish
bouquet, with sophisticated, spicy/nutmeg oak woven through
powerful fruit. The palate is fresh and lively, almost crisp, with citrus
and melon fruit supported by the same spicy oak evident on the
bouquet. Perfect balance, length and acidity.

LAWSONS DRY HILLS GEWURZTRAMINER
●●●● $17.50
Although it is not absolutely clear, it seems that the Gewurztraminer
is in fact the only estate-grown wine. Even though it is on the delicate
side, it is beautifully made.
Cellaring Drink now. **Best Vintages** NA **Current Vintage** '94
Matching Food Delicate Asian seafood.
Tasting Note 1994 Medium to full yellow-green; a softly fragrant
bouquet with aromas of lychee, lime and pastille. The palate shows
good varietal character with lime and lychee flavours predominant,
and is not too sweet.

LAWSONS DRY HILLS RIESLING
●●●●● $14.50
Of 15 Rieslings from the '93 and '94 vintages which I encountered
during a major regional Marlborough wine tasting in 1994, this
wine was given the highest points. Perfection.
Cellaring 2–5 years. **Best Vintages** NA **Current Vintage** '94
Matching Food Asparagus salad.
Tasting Note 1994 Light green-yellow; a fine, intense bouquet
with classic toast and lime varietal character, recalling the best wines
of the Clare Valley. In the mouth, the wine is fresh, crisp and lively,
with pure varietal fruit, and a long, dry finish.

LAWSONS DRY HILLS SAUVIGNON BLANC
●●●● ▶ $16.50
Another classic Marlborough wine, tasted twice in late 1994, each
time with high points.
Cellaring Now–2 years. **Best Vintages** NA
Current Vintage '94
Matching Food Crayfish.
Tasting Note 1994 Light green-yellow; spotlessly clean,
moderately powerful aromas running from herbal to tropical. A
wonderfully balanced wine on the palate with spotlessly clean,
direct flavours, again running from gooseberry through minerally
to herbaceous. Well-balanced acidity.

LIMEBURNERS BAY
★★★ 7–19.95 CD NZSD
Kumeu **Est.** 1978
112 Hobsonville Road, Hobsonville
Ph (09) 416 8844
Open Mon–Sat 9–6 **Production** 3500
Winemaker(s) Alan Laurenson
Has established a reputation for itself as a producer of high class
Cabernet Sauvignon, doing especially well with its '84, '87 and '89
wines. 50% of the production is exported, with almost all of the
white wines sold in Germany and Denmark; the rest is sold cellar
door.
Principal Wines Muller Thurgau, Semillon Chardonnay,
Sauvignon Blanc, Chardonnay, Cabernet Merlot, Cabernet
Sauvignon.

LINCOLN VINEYARDS

★★☆ 6.95–21.50 CD NZSD
Henderson **Est.** 1937
130 Lincoln Road, Henderson
Ph (09) 838 6944 **Fax** (09) 838 6984
Open Mon–Sat 9–6, Sun 11–5 **Production** 35 000
Winemaker(s) Nick Chan

A substantial family-owned operation drawing its grapes from
Auckland, Gisborne and Hawke's Bay. The labels are avant garde,
but the wines are not: six different Chardonnays entered in the 1995
Sydney International Winemakers Competition showed similar flat
and dull characters, sometimes pointing to overcropping in the
vineyard, and sometimes to handling problems in the winery.
Principal Wines Chardonnay (under a series of labels including
Vintage Selection, Gisborne, Show Reserve and Parklands
Vineyard), Sauvignon Blanc, Chenin Blanc, Rhine Riesling, Muller
Thurgau, Cabernet Sauvignon, Merlot.

LINDEN ESTATE

NR 12.50–22 CD NZSD
Hawke's Bay **Est.** 1991
Napier-Taupo Road, SH5, Eskdale
Ph (06) 836 6806
Open 7 days 10–6 **Production** 450
Winemaker(s) Wim van der Linden, Nick Sage

This is the project of retired civil engineer and long-term grape
grower Wim van der Linden and family, son John being a tutor in
viticulture at the Polytechnic in Hawke's Bay. The estate vineyard
was replanted in 1989 to 12.5 hectares of premium varieties.
Most of the grapes are sold to others.
Principal Wines Sauvignon Blanc, Oak Aged Sauvignon Blanc,
Estate White, Chardonnay, Merlot, Cabernet Sauvignon, Cabernet
Franc Merlot.

LINTZ ESTATE

NR 16–32 CD NZSD UK72
Martinborough **Est.** 1989
Kitchener Street, Martinborough
Ph (06) 306 9174 **Fax** (06) 306 9237
Open By appt while stocks last **Production** 2000
Winemaker(s) Chris Lintz

New Zealand-born Chris Lintz comes from a German winemaking
family, and graduated from Geisenheim. The first stage of the Lintz
winery, drawing grapes from the 9-hectare vineyard, was completed
in 1991, and production is eventually planned to increase to around
13 000 cases. The vineyard is moving towards certification as fully
organic; if it achieves this it will be the first outside Gisborne to do so.
Principal Wines Spicy Traminer, Sauvignon Blanc, Dry White,
Optima Noble Selection Sweet White, Rosé, Pinot Noir, Cabernet
Merlot, Cabernet Sauvignon, Bottle Fermented Riesling Brut.

LINTZ ESTATE OPTIMA NOBLE SELECTION SWEET WHITE 375 ML
●●● ▶ $19.50

Optima is one of the specialised German crossings (bred as recently as 1970) and specifically created for late harvest styles. Lintz Estate has the only commercial plantings in Australasia.
Cellaring 2–4 years. **Best Vintages** NA **Current Vintage** '93
Matching Food Apricot soufflé.
Tasting Note 1993 Full yellow-orange; intense botrytis with voluminous dried peach and dried apricot aromas allied with fairly high volatile acidity. On the palate the volatility intrudes somewhat; although the wine has intense flavour, it sharpens off on the finish.

LINTZ ESTATE SAUVIGNON BLANC
●●●● $18

Labelled 'Barrique Matured' but in fact far more fruit- than oak-driven. In the 1994 *Winewise Magazine* Small Makers Competition it stood out like a beacon in the class because of the intensity of the fruit and the varietal character compared to the Australian entries. (The show was in fact open to both Australian and New Zealand producers.)
Cellaring 3–5 years. **Best Vintages** NA **Current Vintage** '93
Matching Food Spiced Asian.
Tasting Note 1993 Medium yellow-green; a powerful, concentrated bouquet redolent of gooseberry/passionfruit/tropical fruit in a ripe mould. The palate is as rich as the bouquet promises, tending to be slightly phenolic, but with masses of flavour and character.

LOMBARDI WINES

NR 9.95–14.95 CD NZSD
Hawke's Bay **Est.** 1948
298 Te Mata Road, Havelock North
Ph (06) 877 7985
Open 7 days 9–5 **Production** 1000
Winemaker(s) Andrew Coltart
The Australian Riverlands transported to the unlikely environment of Hawke's Bay, with a half-Italian, half-English family concentrating on a kaleidoscopic array of Vermouths and sweet, flavoured fortified wines. New Zealand-born Chris Lintz comes from a German winemaking family, and graduated from Geisenheim.
Principal Wines Riesling Sylvaner, Sauternes, Sherry, Vermouth, Marsala, and flavoured fortifieds.

LONGBUSH WINES *

NR NA NZSD
Gisborne **Est.** 1991
1 Wharf Shed, The Esplanade, Gisborne
Ph (06) 867 5764 **Fax** (06) 867 0963
Open Tues–Sun 10–6 **Production** 4500

Winemaker(s) Landfall (Contract)
Owned by Bill and John Thorpe (of Landfall), with the wines made at
Landfall from purchased grapes and marketed separately through
the Longbush Wharf Cafe and Cellar, which is open for lunches and
light meals.
Principal Wines Muller Thurgau, Rhine Riesling, Sauvignon Blanc,
Chardonnay, Pinot Noir Blush, Pinot Noir.

MARK RATTRAY VINEYARD *

NR NA NZSD
Canterbury **Est.** 1992
SH 1 Waipara
Ph (03) 314 6710 **Fax** (03) 314 6710
Open 7 days 10–5 **Production** 800
Winemaker(s) Mark Rattray
Mark Rattray is a high-profile wine consultant in the Canterbury
district, who has enjoyed much success. Initially involved in Waipara
Springs, he has now gone his own way with wife Michelle under the
Mark Rattray Vineyard label, while continuing to consult to three
other makers in the region.
Principal Wines Chardonnay, Pinot Noir.

MARTINBOROUGH VINEYARD

★★★★★ 15–42.50 CD NZ5 UK44
Martinborough **Est.** 1980
Princess Street, Martinborough
Ph (06) 306 9955 **Fax** (06) 306 9217
Open 7 days 11–5 **Production** 10 000
Winemaker(s) Larry McKenna
Australian-born and trained Larry McKenna has established a firm
reputation as New Zealand's most skilled producer of Pinot Noir,
and with an ability to produce Chardonnay of similarly impressive
ilk. It is on these two wines that the reputation of Martinborough
Vineyard rests, although McKenna also makes classy Sauvignon
Blanc, Gewurztraminer and Riesling.
Principal Wines Riesling, Riesling Late Harvest, Gewurztraminer,
Sauvignon Blanc, Chardonnay, Chardonnay Late Harvest, Pinot
Noir, Pinot Noir Reserve.

MARTINBOROUGH VINEYARD CHARDONNAY
●●●●● $27.50
Larry McKenna works very hard with all his wines, focusing as much
on structure and mouthfeel as on varietal or primary fruit flavours.
These are complex, sophisticated wines, as far removed from the
jungle-juice, phenolic, skin contacted Chardonnays of bygone years
or lesser producers as one could imagine.
Cellaring 3–6 years. **Best Vintages** '88, '89, '91, '93, '94
Current Vintage '93
Matching Food Pan-fried veal.
Tasting Note 1993 Medium to full yellow-green; an exceptionally
complex bouquet with tangy barrel ferment and malolactic

fermentation characters, which, taken together, give the wine a
distinctly French cast. The palate continues in the same style;
complex, with obvious malolactic influence, and a long,
mealy/minerally finish.

MARTINBOROUGH VINEYARD PINOT NOIR
●●●●● $35
The Martinborough Vineyard Pinot Noirs are made in much the
same style as the Chardonnays, with as much focus on structure
and complexity as on fruit. Larry McKenna has never been afraid to
experiment, and deliberately walks the razor's edge in the quest for
ultimate quality. The '93 was a gold medal winner at the 1995
Sydney International Winemakers Competition.
Cellaring 3–6 years. **Best Vintages** '86, '88, '91, '94
Current Vintage '93
Matching Food Breast of duck.
Tasting Note 1993 Light red; a complex bouquet with
minerally/earthy/sappy notes together with hints of plum and
strawberry. The wine really comes alive on the palate, with style and
length in that slippery/sappy/stemmy mode which one finds in better
Burgundies. For all that, does not look as if it will be long-lived.

MATAWHERO WINES

★★☆ 11–24.50 CD NZ5
Gisborne **Est.** 1975
Riverpoint Road, Matawhero
Ph (06) 868 8366 **Fax** (06) 867 9856
Open Mon–Sat 9–5 **Production** 10 000
Winemaker(s) Denis Irwin
The wines have always been cast in the mould of Matawhero's
unpredictable founder and owner Denis Irwin: at their best, in the
guise of the Gewurztraminer from a good vintage, they are quite
superb, racy and powerful; at their worst, they are poor and exhibit
marked fermentation problems. The four wines entered in the 1995
Sydney International Winemakers Competition fell into the latter
category.
Principal Wines Gewurztraminer, Chardonnay, Sauvignon Blanc,
Chenin Blanc, Pinot Noir, Cabernet Merlot.

MATUA VALLEY

★★★★☆ 10.90–27.50 CD NZ1, 6, 11 AUS142 UK57
Waimauku **Est.** 1974
Waikoukou Road, Waimauku
Ph (09) 411 8301 **Fax** (09) 411 7982
Open Mon–Sat 8.30–5, Sun 11–4.30 **Production** 110 000
Winemaker(s) Ross Spence, Mark Robertson
One of the undoubted high-fliers of the New Zealand wine industry,
producing a wide range of wines of quite remarkable consistency of
quality. The Shingle Peak label has been particularly successful,
while the presentation of the Ararimu Chardonnay and Cabernet
Sauvignon sets new standards of excellence for New Zealand.

Principal Wines A very large range, from generic and varietal white and red table wines at the bottom end of the price scale, to the Shingle Peak Marlborough range of Sauvignon Blanc, Riesling, Chardonnay, Cabernet Sauvignon, and then to the premium white and red table wines under the Reserve, Ararimu or Judd Estate labels.

MATUA VALLEY ARARIMU CHARDONNAY
●●●● ▶ $27.50
First introduced in 1991, the Ararimu label has become the flagship of the large Matua Valley range. It was based on the best grapes produced on the Judd Estate in Gisborne, as is the '94 vintage, although there was a release from 1993 which came from Auckland fruit, subtitled 'Waimauku' (and which was a useful wine).
Cellaring Drink now. **Best Vintages** '91, '94
Current Vintage '94
Matching Food Veal Italian style.
Tasting Note 1994 Medium yellow-green; spicy oak is immediately evident on the bouquet, but there is good clean fruit to accompany that oak. On the palate, there is abundant ripe peach fruit, and even more abundant spicy oak. Has all the hallmarks of a quick maturing style.

MATUA VALLEY JUDD ESTATE CHARDONNAY
●●● ▶ $17.90
Judd Estate is not a Matua Valley-owned vineyard, but is in fact owned by Morris Judd. It has long produced what Ross Spence regards as 'special fruit' and — even though less fashionable than Hawke's Bay — provided Matua Valley with its flagship wine for many years. It has now been effectively relegated by Ararimu, but remains a better than average wine.
Cellaring 1–2 years. **Best Vintages** '91, '94
Current Vintage '93
Matching Food Pasta with creamy sauce.
Tasting Note 1993 Medium to full yellow; a complex bouquet with those distinctive New Zealand phenolic characters which lead on to a potent, high-toned palate with abundant, multi-faceted fruit. One has the feeling that the wine needs to be drunk young.

MATUA VALLEY SHINGLE PEAK SAUVIGNON BLANC
●●● ▶ $10.90
The Shingle Peak label, based on contract-grown grapes purchased from Marlborough, was developed for the export market. While a relatively recent addition to the Matua Valley product portfolio, it has had great success, no doubt due to its competitive pricing.
Cellaring Drink now. **Best Vintages** NA **Current Vintage** '94
Matching Food New Zealand whitebait.
Tasting Note 1994 Light green-yellow; a clean, crisp and bracing bouquet in the mainstream of Marlborough style. The palate is clean, fresh, crisp and well made; it lacks final intensity, but no doubt comes from a high-cropping vineyard given the price at which it sells.

MAZURAN'S VINEYARD

NR NA NZSD
Henderson **Est.** 1938
255 Lincoln Road, Henderson
Ph (09) 838 6945
Open Mon–Sat 9–6 **Production** 1000
Winemaker(s) Rado Hladilo
A Sherry and Port specialist, still surviving on the reputation built for
its wines by George Mazuran, who died in 1980.
Principal Wines Sherries and Ports.

MERLEN WINES

★★★ 12.50–17.50 CD NZSD
Marlborough **Est.** 1987
Rapaura Road, Renwick
Ph (03) 572 9151 **Fax** (03) 572 9151
Open 7 days 9–5 **Production** 6000
Winemaker(s) Almuth Lorenz
If wines resembled their makers (as owners do their dogs)
Geisenheim-trained Almuth Lorenz would make striking, full-bodied
reds. Since she doesn't like red wines, she instead makes striking
white wines which reflect her sunny disposition and outgoing
personality. All can be tasted at the winery restaurant, which
operates seven days a week, with a selection of six 50 ml glasses
of wine available for only $5.
Principal Wines Riesling, Sauvignon Blanc, Chardonnay,
Semillon, Gewurztraminer.

MERLEN CHARDONNAY

●●● $17.50
Not surprisingly, Almuth Lorenz makes her Chardonnays using
what might loosely be called European techniques, including barrel
fermentation of partially clarified juice, lees contact and malolactic
fermentation. 1992 was not the easiest vintage in Marlborough,
and this particular wine shows the influence of some botrytis.
Cellaring Drink now. **Best Vintages** '87, '88, '89, '91, '94
Current Vintage '92
Matching Food Kassler.
Tasting Note 1992 Medium straw-yellow; there is a range of
tropical aromas over and above the normal chardonnay varietal
fruit, showing some influence of botrytis. Both the bouquet and
palate show substantial vanillin oak influence, and the wine is
overall quite sweet, though not necessarily from residual sugar.

MERLEN SEMILLON

●●● $15.50
While semillon is grown extensively in Marlborough, it is seldom
produced as a straight varietal. Most is blended (in proportions of
10%–20%) with Marlborough sauvignon blanc, this blend being one
of Cloudy Bay's so-called secrets. This wine is a very typical example
of the variety grown in the cool Marlborough climate.

Cellaring 2–4 years. **Best Vintages** '87, '88, '89, '91, '94
Current Vintage '92
Matching Food Tandoori chicken.
Tasting Note 1992 Medium to full yellow-green; an extremely potent bouquet with strong aromas of dry grass and straw. A powerful wine on the palate, showing the influence of the cool climate in no uncertain fashion, again with those hay/straw flavours, finishing with pronounced acidity.

MILLS REEF WINERY

★★☆ 11.95–29.95 CD NZSD
Bay of Plenty **Est.** 1989
143 Moffat Road, Bethlehem, Tauranga
Ph (07) 543 0926 **Fax** (07) 543 0728
Open 7 days 8–5 **Production** 20 000
Winemaker(s) Paddy Preston
At the end of 1994 Mills Reef had begun the construction of a lavish new winery, situated on an 8-hectare site within five minutes of Tauranga, incorporating wine tasting and display rooms, a restaurant and a conference/meeting room, together with usual winemaking facilities. The initial releases from Mills Reef were impressive, but subsequent wines (including three submitted to the 1995 Sydney International Winemakers Competition) have been, to say the least, disappointing.
Principal Wines Mills Reef Mere Road Selection label: Riesling, Sauvignon Blanc, Chardonnay, Pinot Blush; Mills Reef Hawke's Bay range: Chardonnay, Dry Riesling, Traminer Riesling, Cabernet Merlot, Cabernet Sauvignon; Elspeth Chardonnay, Elspeth Sauvignon Blanc; also Methode Champenoise.

MILLTON VINEYARD, THE See page 575.

MISSION VINEYARDS

★★★ 8–14 CD NZSD
Hawke's Bay **Est.** 1851
Church Road, Taradale
Ph (06) 844 2259 **Fax** (06) 844 6023
Open Mon–Sat 8–5, Sun 1–4 **Production** 55 000
Winemaker(s) Paul Mooney
New Zealand's oldest winemaker, owned by the Society of Mary, making honest, basically unpretentious wines at suitably modest prices. Two Sauvignon Blancs from '94, one with a touch of sugar, were acceptable, particularly at the price; that with a touch of residual sugar worked best.
Principal Wines Predominantly varietal designated wines; Sauvignon Blanc, Fumé Blanc, Semillon Sauvignon Blanc, Semillon, Pinot Gris, Chardonnay, Cabernet Merlot, Cabernet Sauvignon. Also proprietary brands including Sugar Loaf Semillon, White Heritage, St Marys Riesling Sylvaner and Estella Sauternes.

MONTANA WINES

★★★★ 10.95–19.95 CD NZSD AUS46
Auckland, Gisborne & Marlborough **Est.** 1977
171 Pilkington Road, Glen Innes, Auckland
Ph (09) 570 5549 **Fax** (09) 527 1113
Open 7 days 9.30–5.30 **Production** 26 000 tonnes (equivalent
to 1.65 million cases)
Winemaker(s) John Simes
Has a far more dominant position than does Southcorp through
Seppelts-Penfolds-Lindemans in Australia, as it produces 50% of New
Zealand's wine. Having parted company with Seagrams many years
ago, it is now seeking equity partners, and has formed joint ventures
with Deutz for sparkling winemaking and Cordier with its Church
Road winery offshoot. As one might expect, the wines are invariably
well crafted right across the range, even if most attention falls on its
Marlborough Sauvignon Blanc.
Principal Wines A vast range, headed by Marlborough
Sauvignon Blanc, Rhine Riesling, Chardonnay and Cabernet
Sauvignon; Renwick Estate Chardonnay, Brancott Estate Sauvignon
Blanc and Fairhall Estate Cabernet Sauvignon (also all from
Marlborough); Ormond Estate Chardonnay (Gisborne); important
sparkling wines, headed by Deutz Marlborough Cuvée (Brut and
Blanc de Blancs) and Lindauer (Special Reserve Brut de Brut, Brut,
Sec and Rosé); large volume Wohnsiedler Muller Thurgau,
Blenheimer and Chablisse; then a range of export-oriented brand-
name products; also wines under the Penfolds label.

MONTANA BRANCOTT ESTATE SAUVIGNON BLANC
●●●● ▶ $12
Montana's Brancott Estate must be one of the most photographed
vineyards in the world; it can also boast being the birthplace of New
Zealand Sauvignon Blanc. What is more, the aged-vintage releases
of Brancott Estate Sauvignon Blanc (along with the principal
Montana label and Cloudy Bay) demonstrate that given the
appropriate vintage conditions, the wines can age very well.
Cellaring 2–7 years. **Best Vintages** '80, '82, '83, '87, '89, '91
Current Vintage '91
Matching Food Bluff oysters.
Tasting Note 1991 Medium yellow-green; a clean bouquet of
medium to full intensity with lemon grass and asparagus aromas, in
some ways veering towards aged riesling. The palate shows similar
flavours, of medium weight, avoiding phenolics, and with a
pleasantly dry finish.

MONTANA FAIRHALL ESTATE CABERNET SAUVIGNON
●●●● $15
The Fairhall Estate of Montana is primarily planted to red grapes,
and a small section provides by far the best Marlborough red wine
to be released by Montana. It retains unmistakable cool climate
characteristics, but has more flesh and ripeness than the standard
Marlborough Cabernet Sauvignon of Montana.

Cellaring 3–5 years. **Best Vintages** '83, '87, '89, '91
Current Vintage '91
Matching Food Leg of lamb.
Tasting Note 1991 Youthful medium to full purple-red; a stylish bouquet with cedary/tobacco aromas, and by no means overtly green. A well made wine on the palate with cedary/herbaceous fruit, a touch of redcurrant; soft tannins on a long finish.

MONTANA LINDAUER BRUT

●●● ▶ $10
First made in 1981, and for a long time the leading sparkling wine to come from New Zealand, although now overtaken by Deutz. It is made from pinot noir and chardonnay grown in Gisborne and Marlborough, and matured on yeast lees for 18 months.
Cellaring Not required. **Best Vintages** NA
Current Vintage NV
Matching Food Aperitif, shellfish.
Tasting Note NV Light straw, even with a hint of partridge-eye from the pinot. A gently fruity, clean and quite stylish bouquet leads on to a fresh, fruity and lively palate, highly commercial in terms of its mouthfeel, balance and flavour.

MONTANA MARLBOROUGH CHARDONNAY

●●●● ▶ $14
Not a wine which normally comes to the fore in any discussion of the Montana portfolio, but this particular vintage ('93) excelled at the major Marlborough District Tasting in 1994. As one would expect from a Montana wine, it is primarily fruit-driven, although there is surprising complexity on the palate.
Cellaring 3–5 years. **Best Vintages** '83, '87, '89, '91, '93
Current Vintage '93
Matching Food Fresh salmon.
Tasting Note 1993 Bright green-yellow; an intense fruit-driven bouquet with tangy melon and grapefruit aromas. The palate shows a similar array of fruit flavours, made more complex by a hint of spice and vanilla oak. Has intensity and length.

MORTON ESTATE

★★★☆ 9.50–21.60 CD NZSD UK15
Waikato **Est.** 1982
State Highway 2, RD2 Kati Kati
Ph (07) 552 0795 **Fax** (07) 552 0651
Open 7 days 10.30–5 **Production** 48 000
Winemaker(s) John Hancock, Steve Bird
Various ownership changes have not led to any changes in the very well established and equally consistent style of the Morton Estate wines. They are all at the baroque end of the New Zealand style, and — try as I may — I really cannot come to terms with them, either in blind or open tastings. However, they clearly have broad appeal, for Morton Estate is a highly regarded producer.
Principal Wines The White Label Range consists of Chardonnay, Sauvignon Blanc, Fumé Blanc and Pinot Noir (all from Hawke's

Bay). Marlborough Riesling and Blush (a blend of Hawke's Bay and
Marlborough Pinot Noir); the top-end Black Label range is Hawke's
Bay Chardonnay and Hawke's Bay Fumé Blanc; the sparkling wines
are Methode Champenoise Vintage Brut and NV Morton Brut.

MOTEO WINES

NR NA NZSD
Hawke's Bay **Est.** 1991
RD3 Moteo, Pa Road, Purketapu, Napier
Ph (06) 844 9911
Open Not **Production** 10 000
Winemaker(s) Peter Gough
Peter Gough is a graduate of Roseworthy College, and worked in
the Hunter Valley and Coonawarra before returning to Hawke's Bay.
He is also manager and partner of a vineyard partnership which
supplies Moteo Wines with its grapes. His experience showed in the
1992 Sauvignon Blanc, a wine with strong oak and rich fruit.
Principal Wines Chardonnay, Sauvignon Blanc, Cabernet
Merlot Franc.

MOUNT LINTON WINE COMPANY *

NR 16.50 R NZ12
Marlborough **Est.** 1992
Hammerichs Road, Rapaura, Blenheim
Ph (03) 572 9911 **Fax** (03) 572 9486
Open Not **Production** 800
Winemaker(s) Tim MacFarlane
An embryonic wine business with only one wine produced to date,
made from contract-grown grapes.
Principal Wines Sauvignon Blanc.

MUIRLEA RISE

NR NA NZSD
Martinborough **Est.** 1991
50 Princess Street, Martinborough
Ph (06) 306 9332
Open Not **Production** 800
Winemaker(s) Willy Brown
Former Auckland wine distributor Willy Brown has established a
1.9-hectare vineyard. The first wine released, a 1991 Pinot Noir,
was a consistent show award winner, and is another affirmation of
the suitability of the Martinborough region for pinot noir. It has to be
said that the 1992 Pinot Noir was not in the same class.
Principal Wines Pinot Noir, Shiraz, Cabernet Sauvignon, Port.

NAUTILUS WINES

★★★★☆ 15.95–18.95 CD NZ10 AUS142 UK38
Auckland **Est.** 1986
Bucks Road, Renwick, Marlborough

Ph (09) 366 1356 **Fax** (09) 366 1357
Open 7 days 10.30–4.30 **Production** 10 000
Winemaker(s) Alan Hoey

Nautilus is ultimately owned by Yalumba of Australia; the wines are made by Yalumba winemaker Alan Hoey at Matua Valley from Hawke's Bay sauvignon blanc and Marlborough chardonnay. The wines, in particular the Sauvignon Blanc, have been consistently good.

Principal Wines Chardonnay, Sauvignon Blanc, Cabernet Sauvignon Merlot Franc, Cuvée Marlborough Brut.

NAUTILUS WINES SAUVIGNON BLANC
●●●●● $15

Sauvignon Blanc was the first wine to be released under the striking and beautiful Nautilus label, and remains the most important wine in terms of quantity. Invariably clearly defined, but the '94 is the best yet. The wine was tasted on three occasions in late 1994, doing particularly well on two of the three occasions.

Cellaring Now–3 years. **Best Vintages** '89, '90, '91, '94
Current Vintage '94
Matching Food Crayfish.
Tasting Note 1994 Light to medium green-yellow; a pungent, powerful bouquet with complex layered fruit in mainstream Marlborough style. Comes alive on the palate with rich, round, mouthfilling flavours, and far more richness and depth than the bouquet would suggest.

NEUDORF VINEYARDS
★★★★★ 16–30 CD NZ5 UK43
Nelson **Est.** 1978
Neudorf Road, Upper Moutere, Nelson
Ph (03) 543 2643 **Fax** (03) 543 2955
Open 7 days 10–5 Nov–Easter **Production** 4000
Winemaker(s) Tim Finn

Tim Finn has produced some of Australasia's most stunningly complex and rich Chardonnays, with the 1989 and 1991 wines outstanding in any class. But his skills do not stop there; they span all varieties. He produces wines which are consistently of show medal standard.

Principal Wines Chardonnay, Sauvignon Blanc, Semillon, Riesling, Pinot Noir, Cabernet Sauvignon.

NEUDORF VINEYARDS CHARDONNAY
●●●●● $30

Tim Finn has mastered the temperamental Nelson climate, producing consistently rich and opulent Chardonnays of quite exceptional complexity. Part of the answer lies in the non-irrigated vineyard, which is planted on Moutere clays, interspersed with layers of gravel. Part lies in the barrel fermentation (50% new oak), malolactic fermentation and extended lees contact.

Cellaring 2–5 years. **Best Vintages** '87, '89, '91, '92, '94

Current Vintage '93
Matching Food Veal, pasta.
Tasting Note 1993 Light to medium yellow-green; a complex, multifaceted bouquet with both barrel ferment and malolactic ferment characters interwoven with ripe, peachy fruit. A powerful and interesting wine on the palate, with strong nutty malolactic characters, finishing slightly sweet, almost certainly from the fairly high alcohol.

NEUDORF VINEYARDS PINOT NOIR
●●●● ▶ $26
If chardonnay presents a challenge in the Nelson climate, pinot noir presents an even greater one — the relatively high summer rainfall often poses particular difficulties. The contrast between the '91, '92 and '93 vintages shows how big an impact vintage plays, for these are all quite different wines in style: the '91 muscular, the '92 fragrant and cherry-accented, the '93 spicy.
Cellaring 1–3 years. **Best Vintages** '83, '90, '91, '92, '94
Current Vintage '93
Matching Food New Zealand venison.
Tasting Note 1993 Medium red-purple; a potent bouquet, with strong peppery/spicy aromas to the plummy fruit. On the palate the wine is spicy and peppery to the point of looking more like cool climate shiraz than pinot noir, and hardens off fractionally on the finish.

NGA WAKA VINEYARD *

NR 20 ML NZSD
Martinborough **Est.** 1988
Kitchener Street, Martinborough
Ph (04) 471 0550 **Fax** (04) 471 0550
Open Not **Production** 500
Winemaker(s) Roger Parkinson
Roseworthy-trained Roger Parkinson produces the Nga Waka wines from 4 hectares of estate plantings in the heart of the Martinborough Terraces. The vines are still coming into full bearing, but the early vintages are showing the intensity of flavour which Parkinson believes Martinborough can and should produce.
Principal Wines Riesling, Sauvignon Blanc, Chardonnay.

NGA WAKA SAUVIGNON BLANC
★★★★ $20
A most interesting wine with a strong regional identity, recalling the Sauvignon Blancs of Palliser Estate and Martinborough Vineyards. Sensibly, made without the use or intervention of oak.
Cellaring 1–3 years. **Best Vintages** NA **Current Vintage** '94
Matching Food Seafood pasta.
Tasting Note 1994 Light to medium yellow-green; an intense bouquet with potent herbal and tropical fruit characters both evident, and appearing again on the ultra-concentrated palate. Some sweaty fermentation characters early in the wine's life need to settle down; if they do, the wine could be sensational.

NGATARAWA WINES

★★★★ 10–25 CD NZ6 AUS1 UK96
Hawke's Bay **Est.** 1981
Ngatarawa Road, Bridge Pa, RD5 Hastings
Ph (06) 879 7603 **Fax** (06) 879 6675
Open 7 days 11–5 **Production** 14 000
Winemaker(s) Alwyn Corban
Alwyn Corban is a highly qualified and highly intelligent winemaker
from a famous New Zealand wine family, who has elected to grow
vines organically and make wines which sometimes (but certainly not
always) fall outside the mainstream. Challenging and interesting,
and not to be taken lightly.
Principal Wines Alwyn Chardonnay is the flagship; the lesser-
priced Stables range comprises Chardonnay, Sauvignon Blanc,
Classic White, Late Harvest Riesling and Cabernet Merlot.

NOBILO WINES

★★★ 8–34 CD NZ5 AUS63 UK13
Auckland **Est.** 1943
Station Road, Huapai
Ph (09) 412 9148 **Fax** (09) 412 7124
Open Mon–Fri 9–5, Sat 10–5, Sun 11–4
Production 200 000
Winemaker(s) Greg Foster
One of the more energetic and effective wine marketers, with
production heavily focused on white wines sourced from Gisborne,
Hawke's Bay and Marlborough. The Marlborough Sauvignon Blanc
and Reserve Chardonnays are the best wines in a substantial and
diverse portfolio.
Principal Wines Marlborough Sauvignon Blanc, Chardonnay and
Cabernet Sauvignon; Poverty Bay Chardonnay, Reserve Dixon
Chardonnay and Reserve Tietjen Chardonnay; Muller Thurgau,
White Cloud, Huapai Pinotage and Hawke's Bay Cabernet.

NOBILO MARLBOROUGH SAUVIGNON BLANC
●●●● ▶ $15
Made in conventional, unwooded style from contract-grown grapes
and — as one might expect — shows the impact of varying vintage
conditions, the style ranging from overtly grassy in the cooler years
to more rich and tropical in the warmer years. The excellent 1994
vintage falls very much in the latter category.
Cellaring Now–2 years.
Best Vintages '86, '89, '91, '92, '94
Current Vintage '94
Matching Food Steamed crab with black bean sauce.
Tasting Note 1994 Light to medium yellow-green; an unusually
ripe and luscious aroma almost into peach, the palate luscious, ripe
and soft, again showing peachy flavours more akin to chardonnay.
While non-varietal, a delicious mouthful.

OHINEMURI ESTATE

NR NA NZSD
Waikato **Est.** 1989
Moresby Street, Karangahake
Ph (07) 862 8874
Open 7 days 10–6 **Production** NFP
Winemaker(s) Horst Hillerich
German-born, trained and qualified winemaker Horst Hillerich
came to New Zealand in 1987, first working at Totara before
establishing Ohinemuri Estate. A restaurant was duly opened
at the newly-constructed winery in the Karangahake Gorge in
1993; Hillerich has produced some highly regarded Sauvignon
Blanc.
Principal Wines Chardonnay, Chenin Blanc, Gewurztraminer,
Riesling, Sauvignon Blanc, Pinotage, Cabernet Sauvignon.

OKAHU ESTATE

NR 12.95–22.95 CD NZSD
Northland **Est.** 1984
Okahu Road, Kaitaia
Ph (09) 408 0888 **Fax** (09) 408 0890
Open 7 days 10–6 summer; w'ends 10–6 winter
Production 1000
Winemaker(s) Monty Knight
The 90 Mile wines (respectively blends of chardonnay, semillon
and arnsburger, and cabernet merlot, pinotage and pinot noir)
signal the location of Okahu Estate at the bottom end of the
90 Mile Beach. The other wines are made from grapes purchased
from other regions.
Principal Wines 90 Mile White and Red; Clifton Chardonnay,
Montgomery Chardonnay, Rhine Riesling, Te Hana Pinot Noir, Old
Brother John's Tawny Port.

PACIFIC VINEYARDS

★★★ 10.50–11.95 CD NZSD
Henderson **Est.** 1936
90 McLeod Road, Henderson
Ph (09) 838 9578
Open Mon–Sat 9–6
Production 12 000
Winemaker(s) Steve Tubic
One of the more interesting New Zealand wineries, notwithstanding
its low profile, which has at various times produced very large
quantities of wine (sold in cask and bulk) but is now refocusing on its
bottled wine production in more limited quantities and, on the other
side of the fence, a venture into beer brewing.
Principal Wines Phoenix Gewurztraminer, Phoenix Chardonnay,
Phoenix Cabernet Sauvignon, Quail Farm Cabernet Rosé.

PALLISER ESTATE

★★★★☆ 16–24 CD NZ10 UK74
Martinborough **Est.** 1989
Kitchener Street, Martinborough
Ph (06) 306 9109 **Fax** (06) 306 9946
Open 7 days 10–6 **Production** 10 000
Winemaker(s) Allan Johnson
Palliser Estate has produced a series of highly regarded and highly-awarded wines from its state-of-the-art winery right from its first vintage in 1989. My tasting notes indicate consistently high scores across the full range of the wines produced.
Principal Wines Chardonnay, Sauvignon Blanc, Riesling, Pinot Noir.

PALLISER ESTATE CHARDONNAY
●●●● $24
As with the Riesling, produced almost entirely from the large estate plantings. Highly protective winemaking and cool fermentation are obvious in the wine, which has ageing potential.
Cellaring 3–5 years. **Best Vintages** '91, '92, '93, '94
Current Vintage '93
Matching Food Abalone.
Tasting Note 1993 Light green-yellow; a fragrant, lively, zesty bouquet, still seemingly showing some fermentation characters. An intensely-flavoured palate, with similar zesty/lemony characters, needing another year or so in bottle to soften and open up.

PALLISER ESTATE RIESLING
●●●●● $18
Produced both as a dry Riesling (as in this case) and, occasionally, in delectable late harvest, botrytised versions. The '93 was the top gold medal in its class at the 1994 National Wine Show of Australia in Canberra, outscoring all of the leading Australian Rieslings (and numerous New Zealand contenders).
Cellaring 2–4 years. **Best Vintages** '91, '92, '93, '94
Current Vintage '93
Matching Food Seafood salad.
Tasting Note 1993 Bright green-yellow; intense lime aromas with some slightly herbaceous edges which add to, rather than detract from, the appeal of the bouquet. A highly-flavoured wine on the palate, with intense lime and herb flavours on a long, lingering finish.

PARKER METHODE CHAMPENOISE

NR NA NZSD
Gisborne **Est.** 1987
91 Banks Street, Gisborne
Ph (06) 867 6967 **Fax** (06) 867 6967
Open 7 days 9.30–6 **Production** 1000
Winemaker(s) Phil Parker

A new and highly-rated Methode Champenoise specialist which has caused much interest and comment. Has not entered the show ring and I have not tasted the wines. The winery also has a restaurant open for lunch and dinner every day of the week.
Principal Wines Dry Flint, Classical Brut, Rosé Brut, Light Red.

PEGASUS BAY *

NR 14–23 CD NZ5
Canterbury **Est.** 1992
Stopgrove Road, Waipara
Ph (03) 314 6869 **Fax** (03) 355 5937
Open 7 days 10–5 **Production** 6500
Winemaker(s) Matthew Donaldson
Leading wine-writer and wine judge Professor Ivan Donaldson (a neurologist) has, together with his wife and family, established a very large operation in Canterbury, with 20 hectares of vineyards coming into bearing and a large and striking cathedral-like winery commissioned in time for the 1992 vintage. Son Matthew is a Roseworthy graduate, and in every respect this is a serious operation. A winery restaurant adds to the attraction.
Principal Wines Chardonnay, Sauvignon Blanc Semillon, Riesling, Cabernet Caress (Rosé), Pinot Noir, Cabernet Merlot.

PEGASUS BAY PINOT NOIR
●●●● ▶ $23
Pegasus Bay has produced astonishing rich, deeply-coloured and full-bodied Pinot Noirs over the past few vintages. Indeed, the only question mark about the wines has been whether or not they are too much of a good thing. Intriguingly, Professor Donaldson likes to pop the bottle into a microwave for half a minute or so to slightly warm the wine before service.
Cellaring 3–6 years. **Best Vintages** '93 **Current Vintage** '93
Matching Food Venison.
Tasting Note 1993 Dark red-purple; voluminous, rich, ripe plum and cherry fruit aromas lead on to substantial wine on the palate, very rich and full flavoured, so luscious it is almost heavy. The oak is well handled.

PELORUS

NR 8–18.50 CD NZSD
Nelson **Est.** 1983
Patons Road, Richmond, Nelson
Ph (03) 542 3868 **Fax** (03) 542 3868
Open Mon–Sat 10–5 Dec–Mar **Production** 600
Winemaker(s) Andrew Greenhough
Previously called Ranzau, but new owners Andrew Greenhough and Jennifer Wheeler now have four vintages under their belt, drawing their grapes from a 3-hectare vineyard predominantly planted to chardonnay and pinot noir. The winery is in no way connected with Pelorus Methode Champenoise of Cloudy Bay.

Principal Wines Riesling, Gewurztraminer, Waimea Plains
Sauvignon Blanc, Chardonnay, Muller Thurgau, Dry White, Pinot
Noir, Cabernet Sauvignon.

PELORUS WAIMEA PLAINS SAUVIGNON BLANC
●●● $16
This is an interesting wine, with real echoes of the Loire Valley,
paradoxically held back by a touch of bitterness, which is the very
thing which recalls the Loire.
Cellaring Now–2 years. **Best Vintages** NA
Current Vintage '94
Matching Food Marinated mussels.
Tasting Note 1994 Light green-yellow; a range of aromas from
nectarine through gooseberry to cut grass lead on to a palate with
quite intense fruit, good structure, but then a strange bitter character
on the finish, which may soften with time.

PENINSULA ESTATE

NR 21–25 CD NZ10
Waiheke Island **Est.** 1986
52A Korora Road, Oneroa, Waiheke Island
Ph (09) 72 7866 **Fax** (09) 72 7866
Open W'ends 11–4 **Production** 1400
Winemaker(s) Doug Hamilton
The single wine comes from a 2-hectare estate vineyard situated on
a peninsula overlooking Oneroa Bay. The '89 was an inspired start,
redolent of high-toned cassis berry fruit and sweet oak, followed by
a firmer and less exotic '90, well balanced and with a cellaring
future. The '91 was awarded four stars in the September 1994 issue
of *Cuisine Magazine*.
Principal Wines A single wine labelled Peninsula Estate Cabernet
Merlot in 1991, and Oneroa Bay Cabernet Merlot in 1992, but also
in fact including a small percentage of cabernet franc and malbec.

PIERRE ESTATE

NR 13.95–19 ML NZSD
Waikanae **Est.** 1969
Elizabeth Street, Waikanae
Ph (04) 293 4604
Open Not **Production** NFP
Winemaker(s) Peter Heginbotham
Waikanae is situated on the coast north of Wellington; the wines are
estate-grown, made and produced in the 'Chateau' and
underground cellars completed in 1991. I have not tasted the wines.
Principal Wines Blanc du Noir (Pinot Noir), Cabernet Sauvignon.

PLEASANT VALLEY WINES

NR 5.95–14.95 CD NZ3
Henderson **Est.** 1902
322 Henderson Valley Road, Waitakere

Ph (09) 838 8857 **Fax** (09) 838 8456
Open Mon–Sat 9–6, Sun 11–6 **Production** 5000
Winemaker(s) Rebecca Salmond
A former moribund fortified winemaker, revitalised since 1984 and
now complementing its stocks of old fortified wines with well-made
table wines sourced from Hawke's Bay, Gisborne and Marlborough.
Principal Wines Gewurztraminer, Sauvignon Blanc, Chenin
Chardonnay, Chardonnay, Riesling, Pinotage, plus a range of
fortified wines; chiefly Sherries, but also Port.

PONDER ESTATE *

NR 17.50 CD NZSD
Marlborough **Est.** 1987
New Renwick Road, Blenheim
Ph (03) 572 8642 **Fax** (03) 572 9034
Open By appt **Production** 11 000
Winemaker(s) Mike Ponder
With 8.5 hectares of sauvignon blanc, 7 hectares of chardonnay
and 2.5 hectares of riesling established in 1987 and coming into
bearing, Ponder Estate expects to more than double its production
to well over 20 000 in 1995. The 1994 Sauvignon Blanc was its
first wine, and already is distributed in the United Kingdom.
Principal Wines Marlborough Sauvignon Blanc, Chardonnay.

PONDER ESTATE SAUVIGNON BLANC
●●● ▶ $17.50
Produced from 8.5 hectares of estate planting. While well made,
it is relatively light, perhaps reflecting young vines. One judge at a
Cuisine Magazine Tasting in 1994 was particularly taken with the
wine, which does have attractive flavour.
Cellaring Drink now. **Best Vintages** NA **Current Vintage** '94
Matching Food Shellfish.
Tasting Note 1994 Light green-yellow, with considerable carbon
dioxide evident. A clean, direct, relatively light bouquet leads on to
a clean and crisp palate with hints of passionfruit and stone fruit.
Pleasant, easy drinking style.

RIPPON VINEYARD

★★★★☆ 12–45 CD NZSD UK35
Central Otago **Est.** 1975
Mount Aspiring Road, Lake Wanaka
Ph (03) 443 8084 **Fax** (03) 443 8084
Open 7 days 2–5 Aug–May **Production** 2500
Winemaker(s) Clotilde Chauvel
Claimed, with some justification, to be the most beautifully sited
vineyard in the world, situated on the edge of Lake Wanaka (which
is responsible for the remarkable site climate), with the snow-clad
New Zealand Alps painting a striking backdrop. Right across the
range, Rippon has produced some outstanding wines, none more
so than the Pinot Noir.

Principal Wines Gewurztraminer, Riesling, Osteiner, Hotere White, Chardonnay, Gamay Rosé, Pinot Noir, Pinot Noir Selection.

RIPPON VINEYARD PINOT NOIR SELECTION
●●●●● $45

Produced in minuscule quantities, and these days packaged in the same tall Italian bottle favoured by Chard Farm. Packaging to one side, this is an extraordinarily opulent and rich wine, with consistent character showing through from one year to the next.
Cellaring 2–3 years. **Best Vintages** '89, '90, '91, '92, '93
Current Vintage '93
Matching Food Marinated venison.
Tasting Note 1993 Full red-purple; an opulent and striking bouquet with masses of ripe plummy fruit together with cinnamon spice aromas. The palate is rich and full blown, with abundant plummy fruit and richness.

RIVERSIDE WINES

NR 10–18 CD NZSD
Hawke's Bay **Est.** 1989
Dartmoor Road, Puketapu, Napier
Ph (06) 844 4942
Open Summer, Thur–Sun 10.30–5 **Production** 1650
Winemaker(s) Rachel Cadwallader, Nick Sage (Consultant)
Ian and Rachel Cadwallader have established 14 hectares of vines on their farm, and they are coming progressively into production. The wine is made on site in the small winery above the Dartmoor Valley.
Principal Wines Chardonnay, Cabernet Rosé, Cabernet Merlot.

RONGOPAI WINES

★★★★ 13.80–45 CD NZ6
Waikato **Est.** 1985
Te Kauwhata Road, Te Kauwhata
Ph (08) 826 3981 **Fax** (08) 826 3462
Open Mon–Fri 9–5, Sat 10–5, Sun 11–5
Production 8500
Winemaker(s) Tom van Dam
Now owned solely by Tom van Dam and wife Faith, but going from strength to strength, it would seem. The reputation of Rongopai rests fairly and squarely upon its spectacular botrytised wines, the 1993 Botrytised Reserve being a gold medal winner at the 1994 Royal Easter Show, and the 1993 Botrytised Chardonnay described by Tom van Dam as 'awesome and the best Rongopai sweet wine ever made', with 5.5% alcohol, 273 grammes per litre of residual sugar and 12.8 grammes per litre of acid.
Principal Wines Sauvignon Blanc, Winemakers Selection Sauvignon Blanc, Chardonnay, TK Reserve Chardonnay, Reserve Botrytis Chardonnay, Botrytised Reserve, Waerenga (Cabernet blend), TK Reserve Merlot.

RONGOPAI SAUVIGNON BLANC
●●● ▶ $16
Very much an expression of the Te Kauwhata region climate, with
ripe, tropical, slightly botrytis-influenced flavours. It is a wine which
will appeal to those who do not like the more
steely Marlborough style.
Cellaring Drink now. **Best Vintages** NA **Current Vintage** '94
Matching Food Sweet and sour pork.
Tasting Note 1994 Medium to full yellow; a big, fairly broad
bouquet showing some botrytis influence and, like the palate, with
some faintly oily characters. The palate is rich with full-bodied,
somewhat modified fruit, and a heavy finish.

ROSEBANK ESTATE *

NR 12–20 R NZSD
Canterbury **Est.** 1993
Cnr Johns and Groynes Drive, Belfast, Christchurch
Ph (03) 323 7353 **Fax** (03) 323 8538
Open 7 days 10–5 **Production** 2000
Winemaker(s) Mark Rattray (Consultant)
Situated only minutes from the city centre and six minutes from
Christchurch airport, this is as much an entertainment centre as it is a
winery, with a beautiful garden setting containing hundreds of roses,
rhododendrons and camellias, and lunch served in the restaurant
each day, and à la carte dinner Wednesday to Sunday from 6 pm.
The Waipara vineyard will ultimately provide 50% of the
production; in the meantime all of the grapes are being sourced from
Marlborough.
Principal Wines Riesling, Chardonnay, Muller Thurgau, Pinot
Noir, Cabernet Sauvignon.

ROSEBANK ESTATE MARLBOROUGH RIESLING
●●●● $15
Made in Canterbury from Marlborough-grown grapes by consultant
winemaker Mark Rattray, and a quality wine in all respects.
Cellaring 2–3 years. **Best Vintages** NA **Current Vintage** '93
Matching Food Antipasto.
Tasting Note 1993 Light green-yellow; a highly aromatic bouquet
with herbaceous/garden mint aromas. The palate, too, is highly
flavoured, with potent mint and herb alongside citrus.

RUBY BAY WINES

NR 10.50–15.80 CD NZ5
Nelson **Est.** 1976
Korepo Road, RD1, Upper Moutere, Nelson
Ph (03) 540 2825
Open 7 days 10–6 **Production** 650
Winemaker(s) David Moore
The beautifully sited former Korepo winery, purchased by the Moore
family in 1989, is well known for its restaurant. Wine quality has

been variable, but the 1991 Cabernet Sauvignon won a gold medal and trophy at the Air New Zealand Wine Awards, an outstanding achievement.

Principal Wines Chardonnay, Sauvignon Blanc, Riesling, Gewurztraminer, Pinot Noir, Cabernet Sauvignon, Pinot Rosé.

SACRED HILL

NR 15–20 CD NZSD
Hawke's Bay **Est.** 1986
Dartmoor Road, RD6, Napier
Ph (06) 844 2576
Open By appt **Production** 5000
Winemaker(s) Mark Mason

Sacred Hill has had its ups and downs, both financially and in terms of wine quality, since it was founded in 1986. The barrel fermented Sacred Hill Fumé Blanc is its best known wine, but the '92 and '93 vintages are not impressive.

Principal Wines Top-of-the-range wines are Sacred Hill Fumé Blanc, Chardonnay and Cabernets; then come Whitecliff Sauvignon Blanc, Gewurztraminer, Chardonnay and Chenin Blanc; then Dartmoor Pinot Noir, Merlot and Cabernet Sauvignon.

SACRED HILL WHITECLIFF SAUVIGNON BLANC

●●● ▶ $15

Produced from the 6-hectare Whitecliff Vineyard, established on a site overlooking white limestone cliffs carved by the Tutaekuri River. Made in a very different style from the Sacred Hill Fumé Blanc, and there does appear to be a faint hint of oak in the background of the wine.

Cellaring Drink now. **Best Vintages** NA **Current Vintage** '94
Matching Food Asian cuisine.
Tasting Note 1994 Very light straw-yellow; a slightly strange, multifaceted bouquet showing stony/minerally/spicy characters, rather than fruity. The palate is no less a chameleon, crisp and acidic, but then also with spicy aspects.

SEIBEL WINES

★★★ 12–20 CD NZSD
Henderson **Est.** 1988
113 Sturges Road, Henderson
Ph (09) 836 6113 **Fax** (09) 836 6113
Open Wed–Mon 11–6 **Production** 5500
Winemaker(s) Norbert Seibel

Significantly increasing production shows that Norbert Seibel is doing well, but I have to confess to having difficulties with the white wines I have tasted, including the yet to be released 1993 Nelson Chardonnay.

Principal Wines Limited Edition Hawke's Bay Chardonnay, Hawke's Bay Sauvignon Blanc and Select Noble Late Harvest Chardonnay lead the roster; then come Scheurebe, Barrel Fermented

White Riesling, Late Harvest White Riesling, Barrel Fermented
Chenin Blanc, Semi-Dry Gewuztraminer, Medium Dry Riesling,
Cabernet Franc Merlot, Cabernet Sauvignon.

SEIFRIED ESTATE

★★★★☆ 9.40–19.60 R NZSD
Nelson **Est.** 1973
Main Road, Upper Moutere, Nelson
Ph (03) 543 2795 **Fax** (03) 543 2809
Open 7 days 11–5 **Production** 33 000
Winemaker(s) Jane Cooper
With 40 hectares of vineyards established progressively between
1973 and 1988, and a production in excess of 250,000 litres,
Seifried Estate is by far the largest of the Nelson wineries. The
production is heavily biased towards white wines, which are of
wholly admirable consistency of style and quality.
Principal Wines A white specialist with Riesling, Dry Riesling,
Oak Aged Rhine Riesling, Chardonnay, Sauvignon Blanc, Chablis,
Gewurztraminer, Muller Thurgau, Old Coach Road Classic Dry
White, Old Coach Road Chardonnay, Late Harvest Riesling, Ice
Wine; the two principal red wines are Pinot and Cabernet
Sauvignon.

SEIFRIED ESTATE CHARDONNAY

●●●● $19
Not in the class of Neudorf's Chardonnay, but nonetheless complex
and in full-blown, robust New Zealand style. Not surprisingly, the
Nelson summers sometimes introduce a note of botrytis, as in the
case of the '93.
Cellaring Drink now. **Best Vintages** '83, '85, '86, '93, '94
Current Vintage '93
Matching Food Sweet and sour pork.
Tasting Note 1993 Deep yellow; a soft, rich bouquet with
mandarin and apricot overtones, presumably botrytis-induced. On
the palate there is soft, peachy/malty/mead-like fruit, with a tweak
of acidity on the finish.

SEIFRIED ESTATE ICE WINE (375 ML)

●●●● $19.20
A blend of highly-botrytised rhine riesling and gewurztraminer,
although neither the Germans nor Hermann Seifried's native
Austrians would approve of the use of the term 'Ice Wine', even
if freeze concentration has been used in its making.
Cellaring 2–3 years. **Best Vintages** NA
Current Vintage '93
Matching Food Fruit tart.
Tasting Note 1993 Full yellow, with a suspicion of orange-brown
starting to appear. The bouquet is complex, with spice and vanilla
aromas, leading on to a sweet, spicy multi-flavoured palate, finishing
with bracing acidity.

SEIFRIED ESTATE SAUVIGNON BLANC
••••• $17

Made without the use of oak, from estate-grown grapes. Good in 1991, 1992 and 1993, and outstanding in 1994, when it received five stars in the annual *Cuisine Magazine* Sauvignon Blanc Tasting.
Cellaring Now–2 years. **Best Vintages** '91, '92, '93, '94
Current Vintage '94
Matching Food Sugar-cured tuna.
Tasting Note 1994 Light green-yellow; a highly aromatic bouquet with aromas ranging from gooseberry/grassy through to passionfruit. An exceptionally elegant wine on the palate, with length and persistence to the flavour, running from nectarine to peach to citrus, finishing with typical regional acidity.

SELAKS WINES

★★★★☆ 7.30–20.80 CD NZSD AUS62 UK84
Kumeu **Est.** 1934
15 Old North Road, Kumeu
Ph (09) 412 8609 **Fax** (09) 412 7524
Open Mon–Fri 9–5, Sat 10–5.30, Sun 11–4.30
Production 45 000
Winemaker(s) Darryl Woolley

With Montana, Selaks first brought Sauvignon Blanc to the attention of overseas markets, especially Australia. Its Sauvignon Blanc and Sauvignon Semillon blends continue to be its forte, always good, frequently outstanding — as they were in 1994.
Principal Wines Marlborough Sauvignon Blanc, Drylands Estate Sauvignon Blanc, Marlborough Chardonnay, Marlborough Sauvignon Blanc Semillon, White Burgundy, Gisborne Fumé, Marlborough Rhine Riesling, Muller Thurgau, Ice Wine, Private Bin Claret, Cabernet Sauvignon, Methode Champenoise.

SELAKS DRYLANDS ESTATE SAUVIGNON BLANC
••••• $NA

A new label for Selaks which made its debut at the 1995 Sydney International Winemakers Competition, being very highly pointed in the Top 100 and duly receiving a gold medal.
Cellaring 2–3 years. **Best Vintages** NA **Current Vintage** '94
Matching Food Slow-cooked Tasmanian salmon.
Tasting Note 1994 Light green-yellow; pristine gooseberry aromas from perfectly ripened, intense fruit. A wonderful wine on the palate, with all the varietal intensity one could wish for, yet is not aggressive or acidic, and went wonderfully well with food.

SELAKS MARLBOROUGH SAUVIGNON BLANC
•••• ▶ $11.95

Produced from the Matador Estate at Blenheim in Marlborough, stainless steel fermented and given no wood. In the mainstream of Marlborough Sauvignon Blanc, except, perhaps, for the faint trace of residual sugar, just at threshold level, but doing no more than balancing the other flavours.
Cellaring Now–2 years. **Best Vintages** '85, '89, '91, '92, '94

Current Vintage '94
Matching Food Shellfish.
Tasting Note 1994 Light green-yellow; a clean bouquet showing good fruit ripeness, with tropical/gooseberry overtones. The palate is very well flavoured and balanced, with nicely ripened fruit and that flick of residual sugar set against pleasant acidity.

SELAKS MARLBOROUGH SAUVIGNON BLANC SEMILLON
●●●● ▶ $14.65
Typically a blend of 60% sauvignon blanc and 40% semillon, partly tank fermented and partly barrel fermented, then matured in oak. The '94 vintage, which was selected in the Top 100 at the 1995 Sydney International Winemakers Competition, showed little evidence of oak, but a great deal of attractive fruit.
Cellaring 2–3 years. **Best Vintages** '85, '89, '91, '92, '94
Current Vintage '94
Matching Food King prawns.
Tasting Note 1994 Light green-yellow; an array of aromas running from herbal through to riper gooseberry but intense and potent. The palate has plenty of depth, is essentially fruit-driven, with clean, positive flavours and nicely balanced acidity.

SHERWOOD ESTATE

NR 10.50–26.50 CD NZSD
Canterbury **Est.** 1987
Weedons Ross Road, Christchurch
Ph (03) 347 9060 **Fax** (03) 347 8225
Open 7 days 11–5 **Production** 5000
Winemaker(s) Dayne Sherwood
Sherwood Estate produced its first wines in 1990; situated close to Christchurch (15 minutes drive) it also offers a garden setting tasting room with snacks and lunches available in the Vineyard Bar throughout summer. Production has soared since the early days, making Sherwood Estate an important part of the Christchurch landscape. Made a five-star 1993 Reserve Pinot Noir, rated in the Top Ten Wines of the Year by *Cuisine Magazine*.
Principal Wines Riesling, Muller Thurgau, Chardonnay, Reserve Chardonnay, Pinot Noir, Reserve Pinot Noir, Cabernet Franc.

SILVERSTREAM VINEYARD

NR 18–24 CD NZ3
Canterbury **Est.** 1990
65 Giles Road, Clarkville, Kaiapoi
Ph (03) 327 5678 **Fax** (03) 327 5678
Open By appt **Production** 500
Winemaker(s) Peter Todd
One of the newest of the Canterbury wineries, situated on the Waimakari Plains north of Christchurch. Owned by Peter and wife Zeke Todd (of Anglo-Italian and Dutch ancestry, respectively), with 4 hectares of estate plantings.
Principal Wines Chardonnay, Pinot Noir.

SILVERSTREAM VINEYARD PINOT NOIR
●●●● $24

Two vintages have so far been released, from the 1992 and 1993 vintages, respectively. The rating is given on the basis of the '92 vintage, which is significantly better than the '93, the former with lots of ripe, dark plum fruit and considerable intensity.

Cellaring 2–3 years. **Best Vintages** '92 **Current Vintage** '93 **Matching Food** Quail.

Tasting Note 1993 Slightly blackish aspects to the hue suggest high pH; there are pronounced sappy/vegetal edges to the aroma, once again suggesting elevated pH; the palate does, however, have some sappy/tangy pinot style; there can be no doubting the potential of the vineyard.

SOLJANS WINES

★★★ 7.40–18.50 CD NZSD
Henderson **Est.** 1937
263 Lincoln Road, Henderson
Ph (09) 838 8365 **Fax** (09) 838 8366
Open Mon–Sat 9–6, Sun 11–5 **Production** 8000
Winemaker(s) Tony Soljan
Well-made wines sold at very modest prices which deserve a wider audience.
Principal Wines Muller Thurgau, Chardonnay, Gewurztraminer, Sauvignon Blanc, Cabernet Sauvignon, Pinotage, many fortifieds.

ST GEORGE ESTATE

NR 8.50–17.50 CD NZSD UK54
Hawke's Bay **Est.** 1985
St Georges Road South, Hastings
Ph (06) 877 5356 **Fax** (06) 877 5356
Open 7 days 9–4 **Production** 2500
Winemaker(s) Michael Bennett
Former Te Mata Estate winemaker (1980–84) Michael Bennett produces a range of well regarded wines which I, for some obscure reason, have not tasted. They may be purchased by the glass at the winery's well patronised restaurant. The range includes such esoteric wines as a mischievously labelled Cheval Blanc, a white blend, and New Zealand's only Petite Syrah.
Principal Wines Chardonnay, Sauvignon Blanc, Riesling, Gewurztraminer, Cheval Blanc, Rosé, Cabernet Merlot, Petite Syrah, Muscat.

ST HELENA ESTATE

NR 7.50–17 CD NZSD UK44
Canterbury **Est.** 1978
Coutts Island Road, Christchurch
Ph (03) 323 8202 **Fax** (03) 323 8202
Open Mon–Sat 10–4.30, Sun 12–5 **Production** 8000

Winemaker(s) Peter Evans
Whether in its moments of success or otherwise, controversy has never been far from St Helena's door. After a spectacular debut for its Pinot Noir in 1982, there has been a roller-coaster ride since, with more downs than ups.
Principal Wines Riesling, Muller Thurgau, Southern Alps Dry White, Chardonnay, Pinot Gris, Pinot Blanc, Pinot Noir, Port Hills Dry Red.

ST JEROME WINES

★★★★ 7.50–35 CD NZSD UK43
Henderson **Est.** 1968
219 Metcalfe Road, Henderson
Ph (09) 833 6205 **Fax** (09) 833 6205
Open Mon–Sat 9–6, Sun 12–5 **Production** 5000
Winemaker(s) Davorin Ozich, Miro Ozich
The Cabernet Merlots made by Davorin Ozich between 1987 and 1991 reflect his Master of Science Degree and practical training at Chateau Margaux and Chateau Cos d'Estournel in Bordeaux. They are hugely powerful wines, the 1991 in particular. It was rated number two in New Zealand's Top Ten Reds of the Year in the September 1994 edition of *Cuisine Magazine*, but did not impress the judges at the 1995 Sydney International Winemakers Competition, being described as 'harsh and overextractive'. Herein lies the rub: these are wines which demand cellaring and a certain degree of understanding.
Principal Wines Riesling, Sauvignon Blanc, Chardonnay, Chablis, Gewurztraminer, Cabernet Merlot, Port.

ST NESBIT

★★★★★ 20–30 R NZ4 UK35
South Auckland **Est.** 1980
Hingaia Road, RD1, Papakura
Ph (09) 379 0808 **Fax** (09) 376 6956
Open Not **Production** 700
Winemaker(s) Dr Tony Molloy QC
Tony Molloy is a leading tax lawyer with a weekend passion; his Bordeaux-blend is revered in New Zealand and very well regarded elsewhere. His Cabernet Merlot is produced in minuscule quantities, much of it exported, leaving a mere 250 cases for the New Zealand market.
Principal Wines A single Cabernet Merlot (Cabernet Sauvignon, Cabernet Franc, Merlot, Malbec, Petit Verdot) Bordeaux blend has been supplemented more recently by a Rosé.

ST NESBIT CABERNET MERLOT
●●●●● $30
Produced from 4 hectares of low-yielding grapes, especially low-yielding in 1989 when birds destroyed much of the cabernet, forcing the release of a Merlot Cabernet, rather than a Cabernet

Merlot, for that year. The wines are given extended bottle age before release, and benefit marvellously from it, as a mini vertical tasting of the '89 to '91 vintages showed in late 1994.

Cellaring 7–15 years. **Best Vintages** '84, '87, '89, '90, '91
Current Vintage '89
Matching Food Loin of lamb.
Tasting Note 1989 Medium to full red; a wonderfully complex bouquet with cedar and cigar box intermingling with hints of earth and forest floor. On the palate, the richest, fullest and ripest of the wines, with briary/chocolatey fruit and again some most attractive earthy undertones. Has developed superbly since first tasted in 1990. The 1990 will be a worthy successor.

STONECROFT VINEYARD

NR NA NZ5
Hawke's Bay **Est.** 1987
Mere Road, RD5, Hastings
Ph (06) 879 9610
Open W'ends, Public hols 11–5 **Production** 700
Winemaker(s) Dr Alan Limmer
Analytical chemist Dr Alan Limmer produces very full-bodied, rich and ripe wines from his 3-hectare vineyard situated on free-draining, gravelly soils which promote early ripening.
Principal Wines Chardonnay, Sauvignon Blanc, Gewurztraminer, Cabernet Sauvignon.

STONYRIDGE VINEYARD

★★★★★ 55 R NZ2 UK35
Waiheke Island **Est.** 1982
80 Onetangi Road, Waiheke Island
Ph (09) 372 8822 **Fax** (09) 372 8822
Open Fri–Sun 1.30–5 **Production** 800
Winemaker(s) Stephen White
The winery which justifies the hype about Waiheke Island; the '87 was a quite lovely wine, balanced, fine and cedary, the '89 even better, with tremendous concentration of rich, sweet fruit, good tannins and again some of those hallmark cedary/briary aromas. Respected New Zealand critic Bob Campbell regards the 1991 as even better, classing it as 'Waiheke's most impressive red made to date'. Larose Cabernet Blend is produced from 3.5 hectares of cabernet sauvignon, merlot, cabernet franc, malbec and petit verdot.
Principal Wines Larose Cabernet Blend.

TE KAIRANGA WINES

★★★★ 13.50–22 CD NZ2
Martinborough **Est.** 1984
Martins Road, Martinborough
Ph (06) 306 9122 **Fax** (06) 306 9322
Open 7 days 10–5 **Production** 8000
Winemaker(s) Chris Buring

Te Kairanga is now fulfilling the potential it always had to produce high quality wines fully representative of the Martinborough region. What is more, it is doing so consistently across the style range.
Principal Wines Castle Point Dry White, Chardonnay, Sauvignon Blanc, Dry Rosé, Castle Point Red, Pinot Noir.

TE KAIRANGA CHARDONNAY
●●●● ▶ $21
Produced entirely from Martinborough grapes; 33% was barrel fermented in new French oak, and 30% taken through malolactic fermentation. Aged for five months on lees in barrel before bottling.
Cellaring 2–4 years. **Best Vintages** '91, '94
Current Vintage '93
Matching Food Richer fish dishes.
Tasting Note 1993 Light green-yellow; a clean, crisp and fresh bouquet with melon/herbal aromas and no phenolic characters whatsoever. The palate is crisp and clean, with citrus and melon fruit balanced by subtle oak.

TE KAIRANGA PINOT NOIR
●●●● ▶ $22
Like the Chardonnay, made entirely from estate-grown Martinborough grapes, and matured for 10 months in French oak. Four different pickings at different levels of ripeness were utilised. A gold medal winner and Top 100 finalist in the 1995 Sydney International Winemakers Competition.
Cellaring Drink now. **Best Vintages** '91, '94
Current Vintage '93
Matching Food Squab.
Tasting Note 1993 Medium red, with just a touch of purple. The bouquet is clean and spicy, with subtle oak. The palate has attractive cherry fruit, together with pronounced spicy characters; perhaps a fraction light overall.

TE KAIRANGA SAUVIGNON BLANC
●●●● ▶ $17
In fact produced from a blend of 60% Martinborough and 40% Gisborne fruit. Each component was clearly allowed to reach full ripeness, producing a voluptuous style.
Cellaring Drink now. **Best Vintages** '94 **Current Vintage** '94
Matching Food Scallops in cream sauce.
Tasting Note 1994 Light green-yellow; a crisp, fresh and clean bouquet with aromas running through nectarine to apple. The palate is fleshy and full, with most attractive nectarine flavours, and a well-balanced, long finish.

TE MATA ESTATE
★★★★★ 11.20–25.65 CD NZ5
Hawke's Bay **Est.** 1896
Te Mata Road, Havelock North
Ph (06) 877 4399 **Fax** (06) 877 4397
Open Mon–Sat 9–5, Sun 11–4 **Production** 15 000

Winemaker(s) Peter Cowley

In the eyes of many, New Zealand's foremost producer of Cabernet Merlot, notwithstanding a consistency of the show success of the Vidal/Villa Maria group. The wines of Te Mata are made in a different style, restrained and elegant but always packed with fine fruit. Nor should the consistently stylish and varietally correct white wines be ignored; these too are of the highest quality.

Principal Wines Elston Chardonnay, Castle Hill Sauvignon Blanc, Cape Crest Sauvignon Blanc, Rosé, Cabernet Merlot, Awatea Cabernet Merlot (premium).

TE WHARE RA

★★★ 11–17 CD NZSD

Marlborough **Est.** 1979

Anglesea Street, Renwick, Marlborough

Ph (03) 572 8581

Open 7 days 9–5 **Production** 2500

Winemaker(s) Allen Hogan

Best known for intermittent superb releases of botrytised wines, made variously from riesling, muller thurgau, traminer and sauvignon blanc. A low-profile winery which shuns publicity, selling most of its wine from cellar door and by mailing list.

Principal Wines Chardonnay, Fumé Blanc, Gewurztraminer, Riesling, Botrytis, Cabernet Merlot.

THE BROTHERS VINEYARDS *

NR 14.50–20 R NZSD AUS34 UK45

Marlborough **Est.** 1991

Brancott Road, Blenheim RD2

Ph (04) 386 3873 **Fax** (04) 386 3853

Open By appt **Production** 3000

Winemaker(s) Douglas Holmes

A new arrival drawing upon 25 hectares of vineyards, with much of the grape production sold to other makers. It has wasted no time in establishing export markets in the United Kingdom, Canada and Australia.

Principal Wines Chardonnay, Sauvignon Blanc Semillon, Semillon.

THE CHURCH ROAD WINERY *

NR NA NZSD

Hawke's Bay **Est.** 1897

200 Church Road, Taradale

Ph (06) 844 2053 **Fax** (06) 844 3378

Open Mon–Sat 9–5 **Production** NFP

Winemaker(s) Tony Prichard

Montana's acquisition of the historic McDonald winery in 1989 and its investment of $2 million on refurbishment followed by the announcement of the Cordier joint venture, together with the acquisition of premium Hawke's Bay vineyards, signalled Montana's

determination to enter the top end of the market with high quality
Chardonnay and Cabernet Sauvignon. Legal squabbles have forced
the adoption of The Church Road name for both winery and labels.
Principal Wines Chardonnay, Cabernet Sauvignon.

THE MILLTON VINEYARD

★★★★ 15.50–31.50 CD NZ6 UK92
Gisborne **Est.** 1984
Papatu Road, Manutuke, Gisborne
Ph (06) 862 8680 **Fax** (06) 862 8869
Open By appt **Production** 15 000
Winemaker(s) James Millton
The only registered organic vineyards in New Zealand, using bio-
dynamic methods and banning insecticides and herbicides;
winemaking methods are conventional, but seek to limit the use of
chemical additives wherever possible. The white wines, particularly
botrytised, can be of the highest quality; the germanic, lime-
flavoured Riesling Opou Vineyard is almost always outstanding.
Principal Wines Chardonnay, Clos de Ste Anne Chardonnay,
Chenin Blanc, Te Arai River Sauvignon Blanc, Riesling Opou
Vineyards, Clos de Ste Anne Pinot Noir, Te Arai River Cabernet
Merlot.

TORLESSE *

NR 8.45–19.90 R NZSD
Canterbury **Est.** 1990
Waipara Village, Waipara, Canterbury
Ph (03) 377 1595 **Fax** (03) 377 1595
Open Not **Production** NFP
Winemaker(s) Kym Raynor
Torlesse was effectively reborn in 1990 when its existing
shareholders purchased the business from a receiver. They include
Dr David Jackson, author of several books on viticulture, and
winemaker Kym Raynor; all have vineyards in the Canterbury
region which supply Torlesse with grapes, supplemented by grapes
purchased from Marlborough.
Principal Wines Muller Thurgau, Riesling (Dry and Medium),
Southern Blush, Beidecker Dry, Gewurztraminer, Marlborough
Sauvignon Blanc, Marlborough Chardonnay, Marlborough
Cabernet Franc.

TOTARA VINEYARDS

★★★☆ 10–16 R NZSD
Waikato **Est.** 1950
Main Road, Thames
Ph (07) 868 6798 **Fax** (07) 868 8729
Open Mon–Sat 9–5.30 **Production** 10 000
Winemaker(s) Gilbert Chan
A substantial operation which, however, has had its share of
problems, leading to a decision to remove all its vineyards in 1986

under the Vine-Pull scheme; it now relies on local growers to provide the grapes for its wines. Had its moment of glory in the 1992 Air New Zealand Wine Show when the '90 Reserve Chardonnay won the Chardonnay Trophy.

Principal Wines Muller Thurgau, Chardonnay, Reserve Chardonnay, Sauvignon Blanc, Chenin Blanc, Cabernet Sauvignon.

TUI VALE *

NR NA NZSD
Hawke's Bay **Est.** 1990
Omahu Road, Hastings
Ph (09) 521 2503 **Fax** (09) 528 9688
Open Not **Production** NFP
Winemaker(s) Keith Crone

Owner and winemaker Keith Crone is one of the most experienced viticulturists in New Zealand, having studied oenology and viticulture at the UCLA Davis, and later becoming chief viticulturist first at McWilliam's, and later at Cooks. The first wines under the Tui Vale label were made by Keith Crone at the C J Pask winery, but he has now developed his own winery at Omahu Road, Hastings.

Principal Wines Sauvignon Blanc, Chardonnay, Pinot Noir, Cabernet Sauvignon.

VAVASOUR WINES

★★★★☆ 12–27.45 CD NZ7 UK1
Marlborough **Est.** 1986
Redwood Pass Road, Awatere Valley, Marlborough
Ph (03) 575 7481 **Fax** (03) 575 7240
Open Mon–Fri 9–5, Sat 10–4 **Production** 10 000
Winemaker(s) Glenn Thomas

A high-profile newcomer which has quickly fulfilled the expectations held for it. The drier, slightly warmer climate of the Awatere Valley and the unique river terrace stony soils on which the 12.5-hectare vineyard is established are producing grapes of great intensity of flavour, which are then being skilfully handled in the winery.

Principal Wines At the top end come Vavasour Reserve Chardonnay, Reserve Cabernet Sauvignon; then Dashwood Chardonnay, Sauvignon Blanc and Pinot Noir; and Stafford Brook Chardonnay and Cabernet.

VAVASOUR DASHWOOD SAUVIGNON BLANC

●●●● $16

In contrast to the Vavasour Reserve, 60% of which is barrel fermented and which is drawn solely from the Awatere Valley vineyard, the Dashwood Sauvignon Blanc is fermented in steel and comes from a mix of Awatere and Wairau Valley grapes.

Cellaring Now–2 years. **Best Vintages** '89, '90, '91, '93
Current Vintage '94
Matching Food Pickled octopus.
Tasting Note 1994 Light green-yellow; a firm, powerful herbaceous/green pea bouquet at the tarter end of the spectrum.

The palate shows ultra classic, powerful herbaceous/green pea flavours in what I describe as the jugular or razor blade style.

VAVASOUR RESERVE CABERNET SAUVIGNON
●●●● ▶ $23.25

A blend of cabernet sauvignon and cabernet franc which is matured for 18 months in French oak barriques, and drawn entirely from the Awatere Valley. It has been Vavasour's contention since the outset that the Awatere Valley — and, in particular, the rocky alluvial vineyard site — is capable of producing red wines every bit as good as the whites. So far that remains to be proven, although not so much through the fault of the reds as because of the sheer quality of the top-end whites.

Cellaring 3–5 years. **Best Vintages** '89, '90, '91
Current Vintage '91
Matching Food Moroccan lamb.
Tasting Note 1991 Medium to full purple-red; the bouquet is ripe, with a spectrum of aromas running from briary to blackcurrant to a hint of cinnamon stick. The palate is full and relatively rich, with solid tannins; shows ripe fruit throughout, with hints of mint in the background. Still needs time to soften.

VICTORY WINES

NR 6–8 CD NZSD
Nelson **Est.** 1968
774 Main Road South, Stoke **Ph** (03) 547 6391
Open 7 days 9–5 **Production** 500
Winemaker(s) Rod Neill

A part-time occupation for orchardist Rod Neill. The vineyard is Nelson's oldest; the vines were planted in 1968 and the first wine produced in 1973.

Principal Wines Chasselas, Seibel, Cabernet Sauvignon, Gamay Beaujolais.

VIDAL ESTATE

★★★★☆ 10.50–39.95 CD NZSD UK35
Hawke's Bay **Est.** 1905
913 St Aubyns Street East, Hastings
Ph (06) 876 8105 **Fax** (03) 876 5312
Open Mon–Sat 1–6, Sun 10.30–5 **Production** 34 500
Winemaker(s) Elise Montgomery

Together with Te Mata, Villa Maria and Esk Valley, consistently produces New Zealand's finest red wines; they have ripeness, richness and balance, a far cry from the reds of bygone years. Elise Montgomery seems to have put the white wines on a similar path, much improved from earlier years.

Principal Wines Under the Private Bin range: Sauvignon Blanc, Chardonnay, Fumé Blanc, Gewurztraminer, Merlot Rosé, Cabernet Merlot; under the Reserve label: Gewurztraminer, Fumé Blanc, Chardonnay, Gimblett Road Chardonnay, Cabernet Merlot, Cabernet Sauvignon.

VIDAL ESTATE PRIVATE BIN FUMÉ BLANC
●●●● $10.50

Partially barrel fermented, and made entirely from Hawke's Bay sauvignon blanc. The '94 was a gold medallist and in the Top 100 of the 1995 Sydney International Winemakers Competition.

Cellaring 1–2 years. **Best Vintages** '86, '89, '90, '91, '94
Current Vintage '94
Matching Food Seafood terrine.
Tasting Note 1994 Light green-yellow; a quite complex bouquet with gooseberry/herbal fruit and oak still coming together. The palate is similar, with the flavours and textures still marrying, but with abundant gooseberry/herbal fruit flavours and length to the finish. Should mature well.

VIDAL ESTATE PRIVATE BIN GEWURZTRAMINER
●●●● $10.50

The principal difference between the Private Bin and the Reserve Gewurztraminer lies in the amount of residual sugar: the Private Bin has 7.5 grammes per litre (still technically dry under Australian wine show rules), the Reserve Bin is below the taste threshold at 3.85 grammes per litre. No doubt, too, slightly lower-yielding or better-quality fruit is used in the Reserve Bin range. For all that, I think the Private Bin works better.

Cellaring Drink now. **Best Vintages** NA
Current Vintage '93
Matching Food Japanese.
Tasting Note 1993 Light green-yellow; there are gentle lychee aromas, tinged with spice on the bouquet. The palate is delicate to the point of lightness, but does have length and avoids phenolics and tannins. The sugar is well balanced.

VIDAL ESTATE RESERVE CABERNET MERLOT
●●●● ▸ $28

Consistently one of New Zealand's top red wines; the currently available '92 vintage was rated number five in *Cuisine Magazine*'s Top Ten New Zealand Reds for 1994, and was a finalist in the 1995 Sydney International Winemakers Competition.

Cellaring 3–5 years. **Best Vintages** '87, '89, '90, '91
Current Vintage '92
Matching Food Grilled calf's liver.
Tasting Note 1992 Medium red; a clean bouquet with leafy/cedary aromas of light to medium intensity, with some vanillin oak. The palate is elegant, again with cedar, vanilla and berry fruit flavours, finishing with soft tannins.

VILAGRAD WINES

NR NA NZSD
Waikato **Est.** 1922
Rukuhia Road, RD2, Ohaupo
Ph (07) 825 2893
Open Tues–Sat 10–6 **Production** 2000
Winemaker(s) Peter Nooyen

A low-profile operation making wines of modest but consistently acceptable quality that age surprisingly well.
Principal Wines Chardonnay, Sauvignon Blanc, Muller Thurgau, Riesling, Pinot Noir, Cabernet Sauvignon.

VILLA MARIA

★★★★★ 8.50–36 CD NZ1, 11
Auckland **Est.** 1961
5 Kirkbridge Road, Mangere, Auckland
Ph (09) 275 6119 **Fax** (09) 275 6618
Open 7 days 10–6 **Production** 120 000
Winemaker(s) Grant Edmonds
Whether viewed on the basis of its performance at the 1995 Sydney International Winemakers Competition, or on any other show result over the last few years, Villa Maria has to be rated New Zealand's best large winery. The quality of the wines, both white and red, is exemplary, the flavours magically full without going over the top.
Principal Wines A large range of wines under the Private Bin label, basically varietally identified, stands at the bottom end of the portfolio; next comes the Cellar Selection range of Chardonnay, Sauvignon Blanc, Cabernet Merlot; at the top end the Reserve Bin range of Barrique Fermented Chardonnay, Marlborough Chardonnay, Sauvignon Blanc, Gewurztraminer, Noble Riesling, Cabernet Merlot and Cabernet Sauvignon.

VILLA MARIA CELLAR SELECTION CHARDONNAY
●●●●● $16.50
Earlier vintages of Marlborough Chardonnay have been released under the Reserve label; this gold medalist and Top 100 winner at the 1995 Sydney International Winemakers Competition appears to be due for release under the Cellar Selection label at a mouthwatering price.
Cellaring Now–3 years. **Best Vintages** '90, '91, '94
Current Vintage '93
Matching Food Pan-fried trout.
Tasting Note 1993 Bright yellow-green; a wonderfully complex and intense bouquet with peach, melon and grapefruit interwoven with high-quality oak. On the palate, an intense, high-flavoured, fruit-driven wine with melon and fig flavours to the fore, and only the barest hint of oak evident.

VILLA MARIA PRIVATE BIN RHINE RIESLING
●●●●● $10.90
A totally delicious wine which was one of Villa Maria's four gold medal winners and Top 100 successes in the 1995 Sydney International Winemakers Competition. An outstanding wine in its price category.
Cellaring Now–3 years. **Best Vintages** '86, '89, '90, '91, '94
Current Vintage '94
Matching Food Asparagus with prosciutto.
Tasting Note 1994 Light green-yellow; a delicate, elegant

bouquet with floral/lime aromas. The palate is fine, intense and lingering, with tight lime juice fruit, perfectly balanced acidity and subliminal residual sugar.

VILLA MARIA PRIVATE BIN SAUVIGNON BLANC
●●●●● $12.50
Another totally delicious wine from Villa Maria which was one of the top-rated (five-star) Sauvignon Blancs in the 1994 *Cuisine Magazine* annual tasting.
Cellaring Drink now. **Best Vintages** '90, '91, '94
Current Vintage '94
Matching Food Salmon roulade.
Tasting Note 1994 Light green-yellow; a clean and crisp bouquet with aromas ranging from gently grassy through to sweet gooseberry. Perfection on the palate, with beautifully ripened fruit and texture, and flavours in the tropical/passionfruit/gooseberry spectrum. A touch of sweetness only helps the wine.

VILLA MARIA RESERVE BARRIQUE FERMENTED CHARDONNAY
●●●●● $27
One can legitimately argue about the level of oak in this wine; whether one really likes it or not is a question of personal style preference, but there is no doubting the complexity and power of the wine. A gold medallist and Top 100 finalist in both the 1994 and 1995 Sydney International Winemakers Competitions, and a medal winner at the 1994 Australian National Wine Show in Canberra.
Cellaring Now–2 years. **Best Vintages** '90, '91, '94
Current Vintage '93
Matching Food Stir-fried chicken.
Tasting Note 1993 Medium yellow-green; a stylish, complex and intense bouquet with strong barrel ferment oak influence. The palate is initially dominated by the positive use of high-quality, barrel ferment oak, but does have the melon and fig fruit to sustain it.

VILLA MARIA RESERVE MERLOT CABERNET
●●●●● $30
To my palate, not only the best New Zealand red wine in the 1995 Sydney International Winemakers Competition, but one of the outstanding red wines of the entire show. Whereas the Vidal Reserve seems to me to be distinctly New Zealand in character, and a bit on the leafy/herbal side, this wine has outstanding generosity and richness. For good measure, I also preferred it markedly to the highly-rated 1992 Esk Valley Reserve Red.
Cellaring 3–7 years. **Best Vintages** '85, '87, '90, '91, '94
Current Vintage '92
Matching Food Fillet of beef.
Tasting Note 1992 Strong purple-red; while showing herbaceous, cool-grown fruit, has generosity, and is neither leafy nor mean. An outstanding wine on the palate, with great structure, flavour, balance and length; luscious red berry fruit flavours on the mid palate are followed by fruit and oak tannins to sustain the wine for a long life.

VOSS ESTATE

NR 16.50–22 CD NZSD
Martinborough **Est.** 1988
Puruatanga Road, Martinborough
Ph (06) 306 9668
Open 7 days 10–6 summer **Production** 800
Winemaker(s) Gary Voss

Voss Estate has been established by Annette Atkins, Gary Voss and
Murray Voss, with 3 hectares of vineyards (one hectare each of
chardonnay, pinot noir and cabernet sauvignon/merlot) still coming
into bearing after a disastrous frost in 1992. In the meantime,
grapes are purchased from other regions.
Principal Wines Hawke's Bay Chardonnay, Reserve Chardonnay,
Sauvignon Blanc, Pinot Noir, Cabernet Merlot Franc.

VOSS ESTATE SAUVIGNON BLANC

●●● ▶ $16.50
Unlike the early Voss Estate wines, made from Martinborough fruit,
and although perhaps showing some young vine characters, has
been very cleverly made.
Cellaring Drink now. **Best Vintages** NA **Current Vintage** '94
Matching Food Whitebait.
Tasting Note 1994 Light green-yellow; the bouquet is of light to
medium intensity but with an interesting spectrum of aromas running
from cut apple to grass to peach. The palate is fresh, crisp and fairly
grassy; the grassiness is balanced by the use of residual sugar.

WAIMARAMA ESTATE

NR 18.50–24.50 ML NZ5 UK16
Hawke's Bay **Est.** 1988
31 Waimarama Road, Havelock North
Ph (06) 877 6794 **Fax** (06) 877 6789
Open Not **Production** 2600
Winemaker(s) Nick Sage

An exciting newcomer which had already gathered much critical
attention and praise before its two entries in the 1992 Air New
Zealand Wine Show received a top gold medal (1991 Cabernet
Merlot) and strong silver medal (1991 Cabernet Sauvignon),
respectively. It would seem that this vineyard, situated on a north-
facing slope at the foot of Te Mata peak, may well be one of the
stars of the Hawke's Bay region in years to come.
Principal Wines Cabernet Sauvignon, Undercliffe Cabernet
Merlot, Dessert Cabernet.

WAIPARA SPRINGS WINES

NR 13–21 CD NZSD UK97
Canterbury **Est.** 1990
Waipara Springs Vineyard, RD 3, Amberley
Ph (03) 314 6777
Open 7 days 11–5 summer **Production** 3500

Winemaker(s) Kim Raynor

Owned by Bruce and Jill Moore, who commenced planting the vineyard way back in 1982, establishing 4 hectares of chardonnay, the grapes of which were sold to Corbans. The Waipara Springs label was established in 1990 and much of the wine is exported.

Principal Wines Sauvignon Blanc, Chardonnay, Riesling, Pinot Noir.

WAIRAU RIVER WINES

★★★★ 11.90–21.50 CD NZSD AUS166 UK78
Marlborough **Est.** 1978
Cnr Rapaura Road and State Highway 6, Blenheim
Ph (03) 572 8584 **Fax** (03) 572 8584
Open 7 days 9–5 **Production** 11 500
Winemaker(s) John Belsham (Contract)

Phil and Chris Rose have been long-term grape growers in the Marlborough region, having established a 60-hectare vineyard progressively since 1978. The first wines were made under the Wairau River label in 1991 by contract winemaker John Belsham, and all of the vintages to date have been of exemplary quality ('91 to '93), particularly the tropical-accented Sauvignon Blanc.

Principal Wines Sauvignon Blanc, Chardonnay.

WAIRAU RIVER SAUVIGNON BLANC

●●●● ▶ $16

The Sauvignon Blanc accounts for 8000 cases of the total Wairau River production, and is exported to both the United Kingdom and Australia with great success. The consistency of the wine over the '91 to '93 vintages shows why.

Cellaring 1–3 years. **Best Vintages** '91, '92, '93, '94
Current Vintage '93
Matching Food Deep-fried calamari.
Tasting Note 1993 Light green-yellow; a complex bouquet with a range of herbal to riper fruit aromas present. On the palate, one of the best Sauvignon Blancs from the '93 vintage, with greater complexity and more softness. A particularly good outcome from a difficult year for this variety.

WAITAKERE ROAD VINEYARD

★★★★ 16–30 CD NZSD
Kumeu **Est.** 1986
748 Waitakere Road, RD1, Kumeu
Ph (09) 412 7256 **Fax** (09) 412 7256
Open Sat 12–6 **Production** 3000
Winemaker(s) Tim Harris

The project of Auckland lawyer and wine-writer Tim Harris, who purchased half of the vineyard in 1986, and the balance (with 15-year-old cabernet sauvignon planted) in 1988. Bloomers and Bigney Coigne have to be two of the most unusual proprietary names I have encountered in the English-speaking world. Bigney Coigne is a synonym for Merlot and an old English word for corner,

thus literally 'Merlot Corner'. Quaint names to one side, wine quality
has been exemplary.

Principal Wines Uppercase Red, Bloomers (Merlot, Seibel,
Cabernet Franc), Harrier Rise (Cabernet Sauvignon), Bigney Coigne
(Reserve Merlot).

WEST BROOK WINERY

★★★☆ 7–15.50 CD NZSD
Henderson **Est.** 1937
34 Awaroa Road, Henderson
Ph (09) 838 8746 **Fax** (09) 838 8746
Open Mon–Sat 9–6, Sun 12–5 **Production** 7000
Winemaker(s) Anthony Ivicevich
Unpretentious producer of wines of reliable quality, seldom aspiring
to greatness but capable of a very pleasant surprise from time to
time. The 1993 Blue Ridge Sauvignon Blanc (warm, tropical
gooseberry fruit) and 1993 Henderson Merlot (Italianate/spicy/
dusty/cedary) both impressed at the 1995 Sydney International
Winemakers Competition although not making the Top 100.
Principal Wines Blue Ridge Sauvignon Blanc, Sauvignon Blanc
Semillon, Semillon, Chardonnay, Chenin Blanc, Traminer Riesling,
Cabernet Sauvignon, Cabernet Merlot, Henderson Merlot.

WILLIAM HILL WINERY

NR NA NZSD
Central Otago **Est.** 1982
Dunstan Road, RD1, Alexandra **Ph** (03) 448 8436
Open By appt **Production** 300
Winemaker(s) Black Ridge (Contract)
Notwithstanding that the William Hill vineyards extend to 3 hectares,
production has remained at minuscule levels, and almost all of the
wines are sold by mail order and through selected local outlets.
Principal Wines Gewurztraminer, Chardonnay, Sauvignon Blanc,
Pinot Noir, Cabernet Sauvignon.

WINSLOW WINES *

NR NA NZSD
Martinborough **Est.** 1987
Princess Street, Martinborough
Ph (06) 306 9710 **Fax** (06) 306 9710
Open Mon–Sat 9–5 **Production** 500
Winemaker(s) Ross Turner
The estate plantings of 2.2 acres are devoted to cabernet sauvignon
(75%), cabernet franc (15%) and merlot (10%); the rhine riesling and
chardonnay are contract-grown. The 1991 Winslow Cabernet
Sauvignon Franc Merlot won silver medals at local wine competitions.
Principal Wines Winslow is the top label, Louis the second; wines
produced include Rhine Riesling, Chardonnay and Cabernet
Sauvignon Franc Merlot.

DISTRIBUTORS

AUSTRALIAN DISTRIBUTORS

1. Alexander & Paterson
   600 Dawson St, Brunswick Vic 3056
   Tel: (03) 9380 6199

2. Allied Vintners
   PO Box 96, Erindale ACT 2903
   Tel: (06) 291 7361

3. Andrew Waterman Wholesales
   3 Clark St, Wayville SA 5034
   Tel: (08) 271 4858

4. Angoves Pty (NSW)
   Cnr Queen & Marion Sts, Auburn NSW 2144
   Tel: (02) 649 6044

5. Angoves Pty (Qld)
   30 Bellrick St, Acacia Ridge Qld 4110
   Tel: (07) 3345 2344

6. Angoves Pty (SA)
   1320 North East Rd, Tea Tree Gully SA 5091
   Tel: (08) 264 2366

7. Angoves Pty (Tas)
   14 Bingley St, Howrah Tas 7018
   Tel: (002) 47 1196

8. Angoves Pty (Vic)
   PO Box 547, Mulgrave Vic 3170
   Tel: (03) 9561 6111

9. Angoves Pty (WA)
   325 Treasure Rd, Welshpool WA 6106
   Tel: (09) 353 1900

10. Appellation Wines & Spirits
    9 Woodvale Close, St Ives NSW 2075
    Tel: (02) 449 7677

11. Aria Wine Co
    PO Box 536, Randwick NSW 2031
    Tel: (02) 314 5730

12. Arrowfield Wines P/L
    3/19–21 Bourke Rd, Alexandria NSW 2015
    Tel: (02) 698 8033

13. Australian Liquor Marketers
    Lot 3241 College Rd, Berrimah NT 0828
    Tel: (089) 84 4622

14. Australian Liquor Marketers
    GPO Box 910, Hobart Tas 7000
    Tel: (002) 73 2760

15. Australian Liquor Marketers
    PO Box 3519, Alice Springs NT 0871
    Tel: (089) 0266

16. Australian Prestige Wines
    PO Box 325, Northcote Vic 3070
    Tel: (03) 600 0133

17. Barrique Fine Wines
    PO Box 34, Stones Corner Qld 4120
    Tel: (07) 395 3355

18. Bio Dynamic Marketing
    Main Rd, Powelltown Vic 3797
    Tel: (03) 689 5241

19. Brian Downie & Associates
    7A Daveys Bay Rd, Mt Eliza Vic 3930
    Tel: (03) 9787 7260

20. BRL Hardy Wine Co (NSW)
    104 Bay St, East Botany NSW 2019
    Tel: (02) 665 5855

21. BRL Hardy Wine Co (Qld)
    43 Murray St, Bowen Hills Qld 4006
    Tel: (07) 3252 7933

22. BRL Hardy Wine Co (SA)
    Reynalla Rd, Reynella SA 5161
    Tel: (08) 381 2266

23. BRL Hardy Wine Co (Vic)
    61–63 Nantilla Rd, Clayton Vic 3168
    Tel: (03) 9561 2455

24. BRL Hardy Wine Co (WA)
    Dale Rd, Middle Swan WA 6056
    Tel: (09) 274 5100

25. Broadway Liquor Distributors P/L
    96 Glebe Point Rd, Glebe NSW 2037
    Tel: (02) 660 3908

26. Busby Wine Co
    PO Box 433, Wahroonga NSW 2076
    Tel: (02) 989 8280

27. Caon Tucker Classic Wines
    11 Kings Court, Adelaide SA 5000
    Tel: (08) 211 7599

28. Capital Fine Wines
    PO Box 7, Barker Centre ACT 2603
    Tel: (06) 239 6968

29. Carlton Special Beverages Co (NSW)
    26 Broadway, Sydney NSW 2000
    Tel: (02) 217 1405

30. Carlton Special Beverages Co (Qld)
    20 Ivory St, Fortitude Valley Qld 4006
    Tel: (07) 3212 0115

31. Carlton Special Beverages Co (SA)
    34–36 Rosberg Rd, Wingfield SA 5013
    Tel: (08) 262 2844

32. Carlton Special Beverages Co (Vic)
    PO Box 318, Mt Waverly Vic 3149
    Tel: (03) 9565 7177

33. Carlton Special Beverages Co (WA)
    39 McDowell St, Welshpool WA 6106
    Tel: (09) 451 7577

34. Carol-Ann Martin Classic Wines
    Box 1065, Potts Point NSW 2011
    Tel: (02) 356 2007

35. CC Taffs & Co
    5/28 Boyland Ave, Coopers Plains Qld 4108
    Tel: (07) 3875 1980

36. Chace Agencies
    Box 227, Hindmarsh SA 5007
    Tel: (08) 346 9555

37. Chancellors Wines & Spirits
    GPO Box 88A, Hobart Tas 7001
    Tel: (002) 23 6377

38. Chateau Yaldara P/L (NSW)
    PO Box 383, Homebush Bay NSW 2140
    Tel: (02) 748 1258

39. Chateau Yaldara P/L (Vic)
    PO Box 188, Black Rock Vic 3193
    Tel: (03) 9589 5900

40. Chateau Yaldara P/L (WA)
    6 Elmton Court, Duncraig WA 6023
    Tel: (09) 447 7388

41. Classical Wines of Australia
    313A Homer St, Earlwood NSW 2206
    Tel: (02) 558 8588

42. Combined Wines & Spirit Merchants
    Lot 5 Sheridan Close, Milperra NSW 2214
    Tel: (02) 792 3033

43. Concorde Liquor (NSW)
    5 Bennelong Rd, Homebush NSW 2140
    Tel: (02) 647 2877

44. Concorde Liquor (Qld)
    836 Boundary Rd, Coopers Plains Qld 4108
    Tel: (07) 3277 8500

45. Concorde Liquor (SA)
    87 Holbrooks Rd, Underdale SA 5032
    Tel: (08) 43 7011

46. Concorde Liquor (Vic)
    4 Trade Place, Vermont Vic 3133
    Tel: (03) 9873 5399

47. Country Wine Agencies
    Suite 1/106 George St, Port Melbourne Vic 3207
    Tel: (03) 9416 2355

48. David Johnson & Assoc
    67 Montpelier Retreat, Battery Point Tas 7004
    Tel: (002) 24 0653

49. David Mullen Wine Agencies
    23 Fircroft Way, Hammersley WA 6022
    Tel: (09) 447 5426

50. David Ridge
    205 Grote St, Adelaide SA 5000
    Tel: (08) 231 3450

51. De Bono Wine Merchants
    43 Buffalo Rd, Gladesville 2111
    Tel: (02) 809 7522

52. De Bortoli Wines Pty Ltd (NSW)
    De Bortoli Rd, Bilbul NSW 2680
    Tel: (069) 64 9444

53. De Bortoli Wines Pty Ltd (Qld)
    23 Collinsvale St, Rocklea Qld 4106
    Tel: (07) 3274 2923

54. De Bortoli Wines Pty Ltd (Vic)
    874 Mountain Hwy, Bayswater Vic 3153
    Tel: (03) 9720 3153

55. Dilaterre
    PO Box 60, Essenden Vic 3040
    Tel: (03) 9462 2763

56. Domaine Wine Shippers
    Box 69, Doncaster East Vic 3109
    Tel: (03) 9894 3888

57. Draper Agencies
    PO Box 293, Gosford NSW 2256
    Tel: 018 22 0000

58. Estate Wines
    314–316 Marrickville Rd, Alexandria NSW 2204
    Tel: (02) 550 0300

59. Evans & Tate
    Swan St, Henley Brook WA 6055
    Tel: (09) 296 4666

60. Evans & Tate (NSW)
    Level 23 Tower 1 Bondi Junction Plaza,
    Bondi Junction NSW 2029
    Tel: (02) 369 3766

61. F M Liquor Pty
    1/136 Railway St, Cottesloe WA 6011
    Tel: (09) 385 3885

62. Farmer Bros
    42 Mort St, Canberra ACT 2601
    Tel: (06) 247 2344

63. Fesq Dorado (NSW)
    Level 1, 9 Underwood Ave, Botany NSW 2019
    Tel: (02) 316 7400

64. Fesq Dorado (Qld)
    PO Box 53, Mt Gravatt Qld 4122
    Tel: (07) 3892 7222

65. Fesq Dorado (Tas)
    7A Pillinger St, Dynnyrne Hobart Tas 7005
    Tel: (002) 23 3823

66. Fesq Dorado (Vic)
    584 Nicholson St, Fitzroy North Vic 3068
    Tel: (03) 9482 4244

67. Fesq Dorado (WA)
    9 Bowman St, South Perth WA 6151
    Tel: (002) 23 3823

68. Festival Wines & Spirits
    984 Port Rd, Albert Park SA 5014
    Tel: (08) 268 8066

69. Fin Vin Agencies P/L
    PO Box 367, Strawberry Hills NSW 2012
    Tel: (02) 310 2077

70. Fine Wine Wholesalers
    1 Sleeman Rd, O'Connor WA 6163
    Tel: (09) 314 7133

71. Fleurieu Wine Merchants,
    O'Connell St, North Adelaide SA 5006
    Tel: (08) 239 1980

72. Flinders Wholesale Wines & Spirits
    3 Wandarri Crt, Cheltenham Vic 3192
    Tel: (03) 584 5233

73. Halloran Manton P/L
    3 Welder Ave, Seven Hills NSW 2147
    Tel: (02) 624 7244

74. Harry Williams Ltd
    24 Essington St, Mitchell ACT 2911
    Tel: (06) 241 7591

75. Haviland Wine Co
    12 Hopetoun Ave, Chatswood NSW 2067
    Tel: (02) 419 3877

76. Hill International Wines (NSW)
    Unit 4A 6 Boundary Rd, Northmead NSW 2152
    Tel: (02) 630 5429

77. Hill International Wines (Qld)
    PO Box 66, Coopers Plains Qld 4108
    Tel: 018 603 677

78. Hill International Wines (SA)
    PO Box 501, McLaren Vale SA 5171
    Tel: (08) 383 0054

79. Hill International Wines (Vic)
    PO Box 47, Glen Waverly Vic 3150
    (03) 9550 1838

80. Hollick Wines P/L
    184 Grandview Rd, Rosanna Vic 3084
    Tel: (03) 9459 9856

81. Inchcape Liquor Marketing (SA)
    70–72 Pym St, Dudley Park SA 5008
    Tel: (08) 344 3577

82. Inchcape Liquor Marketing (NSW)
    208–426 Victoria Rd, Gladesville NSW 2111
    Tel: (02) 879 6766

83. Inchcape Liquor Marketing (Qld)
    10 Success St, Acacia Ridge Qld 4110
    Tel: (07) 3227 7600

84. Inchcape Liquor Marketing (Vic)
    1834 Princes Hwy, Clayton Vic 3168
    Tel: (03) 9543 2333

85. Inchcape Liquor Marketing (WA)
    16 Aitken Way, Kewdale WA 6015
    Tel: (09) 353 3737

86. Inglewood Wines P/L
    18–20 Cleg St, Artarmon NSW 2064
    Tel: (02) 436 3022

87. J Harvey Long Wine Co
    7 Ramsey St, Burwood East Vic 3151
    Tel: (03) 9808 6004

88. Jayberry Wines
    8 Wesley Place, Cherry Brook NSW 2126
    Tel: (02) 9980 7400

89. John Burke Wine Portfolio
    63 Tuart Rd, Greenwood WA 6024
    Tel: (09) 246 2092

90. John Collar
    173 Mt Pleasant Rd, Eltham Vic 3095
    Tel: (03) 9439 1071

91. John Parker
    45 Piccadilly Rd, Salisbury East SA 5109
    Tel: (08) 258 2906

92. Jumbuck Marketing
    PO Box 190, Edwardstown SA 5039
    Tel: (08) 371 1237

93. Karen Hunter
    101 Grosvenor Rd, Lindfield NSW 2070
    Tel: (03) 9482 6985

94. Kenneth Graham Brokerage
    PO Box 479, Woodend Vic 3442
    Tel: (054) 27 1739

95. La Forgia Wine Agency
4/348 Richmond Rd, Netley SA 5037
Tel: (08) 352 1588

96. Leading Wines of Australia
89-109 Gray St, Adelaide SA 5000
Tel: (08) 211 8966

97. Lionel Samson & Son
PO Box 80, Fremantle WA 6160
(09) 335 7444

98. Lofton Agencies
PO Box 286, Newtown NSW 2042
Tel: (02) 557 4782

99. McLaren Vale Cellars
Townsville St, Fyshwick ACT 2609
Tel: (06) 280 6329

100. McWilliams Wines Pty
68 Anzac St, Chullora NSW 2190
Tel: (02) 707 1266

101. Melbourne Wine Distributors
PO Box 280, Mount Hawthorn WA 6016
Tel: (03) 9482 6985

102. Metro Wine Distributors
PO Box 280, Mount Hawthorn WA 6016
Tel: (09) 273 6252

103. MGM Wine Distributors
Carbon Crt, Osborne Park WA 6017
Tel: (09) 244 3299

104. Mildara Blass Ltd
101 Dundas Place, Albert Park Vic 3206
Tel: (03) 9690 9966

105. Miranda Wines Pty
PO Box 405, Griffith NSW 2680
Tel: (069) 62 4033

106. MLM Pty
5/43 Kirwan St, Floreat WA 6014
Tel: (09) 387 5877

107. National Liquor Co (Qld)
Unit 6A 2958 Logan Rd, Underwood Qld 4119
Tel: (07) 3841 0077

108. National Liquor Co (Vic)
5 Weald Crt, Frankston, Vic 3199
Tel: 018 34 9502

109. National Liquor Co (WA)
210 Bannister Rd, Canning Vale WA 6155
Tel: (09) 455 2477

110. National Wine Brokers
121 Adair St, Scullin ACT 2614
Tel: (06) 254 8203

111. National Wine Merchants
     185 Sturt St, Adelaide SA 5000
     Tel: (08) 231 1066

112. Negociants
     205 Grote St, Adelaide SA 5000
     Tel: (08) 231 3963

113. Nelson Wine Company
     584 Nicholson St, North Fitzroy Vic 3102
     Tel: (03) 9482 3866

114. Norman Zerbe
     Box 4843, Cairns Qld 4870
     Tel: (070) 351 5544

115. Oak Barrel Wines
     24 Barrier St, Fyshwick ACT 2609
     Tel: (06) 280 6371

116. Options Fine Wines
     218 Carrington St, Adelaide SA 5000
     Tel: (08) 223 7554

117. Orlando Wyndham
     33 Exeter Terrace, Devon Park SA 5008
     Tel: (08) 208 2444

118. Parker Evans
     45 Piccadilly Rd, Salisbury East SA 5109
     Tel: (08) 363 3060

119. Pat Dilling
     7/57 Raleigh St, Carlisle WA 6101
     Tel: 018 94 9188

120. PAT Foods Ltd
     100 O'Riordan St, Alexandria NSW 2015
     Tel: (02) 693 2477

121. Peter Bourne Wine Emporium
     127 Bayswater Rd, Rushcutters Bay NSW 2011
     Tel: (02) 361 4885

122. Pinnacle Wine Merchants
     PO Box 332, Brighton Le Sands NSW 2216
     Tel: (02) 567 5443

123. Porter & Co
     PO Box 351, Kingswood SA 5062
     Tel: (08) 373 3010

124. Premier Vineyards
     PO Box 367, Strawberry Hills NSW 2012
     Tel: (02) 363 9855

125. Queensland Fine Wines
     PO Box 535, Mt Gravatt Qld 4122
     Tel: (07) 3849 6896

126. Regional Liquor Merchants
     PO Box 121, St Agnes SA 5097
     Tel: (08) 363 0733

127. Regional Wines Pty Ltd
PO Box 4, Darlinghurst NSW 2010
Tel: (02) 331 2961

128. Remy Australie P/L
484 Victoria Rd, Gladesville NSW 2111
Tel: (02) 816 5000

129. RHL Wine Consultants
11 Bridge St, Port Melbourne Vic 3207
Tel: (03) 9419 1006

130. Richard Mackie Fine Wines
155 Stephen Terrace, Walkerville SA 5081
Tel: (08) 269 1162

131. Roger Brown Wine Agencies
20 Raglan St, Turramurra NSW 2074
Tel: (02) 9988 3400

132. Rosemount Estates Pty (NSW)
18 Herbert St, Artarmon NSW 2064
Tel: (02) 9906 2613

133. Rosemount Estates Pty (Qld)
14 Campbells St, Bowen Hills Qld 4006
Tel: (07) 3252 2795

134. Rosemount Estates Pty (SA)
14 Ingoldby Rd, McLaren Vale SA 5171
Tel: (08) 383 0001

135. Rosemount Estates Pty (Vic)
2 River St, South Yarra Vic 3141
Tel: (03) 9826 1327

136. Rosemount Estates Pty (WA)
252 Cambridge St, Wembley WA 6014
Tel: (09) 388 3154

137. Rutherglen Wine Co
241 Normanby Rd, South Melbourne Vic 3205
Tel: (03) 9646 6666

138. S Smith & Son Pty Ltd (NSW)
30-32 Skarrat St, North Auburn NSW 2144
Tel: (02) 648 4511

139. S Smith & Son Pty Ltd (Qld)
13 Shoebury St, Rocklea Qld 4106
Tel: (07) 3892 5022

140. S Smith & Son Pty Ltd (Vic)
109 Hyde St, Footscray Vic 3011
Tel: (03) 9689 1-122

141. S Smith & Son Pty Ltd (WA)
114 Radium St, Welshpool WA 6106
Tel: (09) 451 9822

142. S. Smith & Son Pty Ltd (SA)
PO Box 10, Angaston SA 5353
Tel: (085) 61 3200

143. S & V Wine Merchants
     11/47 OG Road, Klemzig SA 5087
     Tel: (08) 364 4242

144. Select Vineyards
     56 Clarke St, South Melbourne Vic 3205
     Tel (03) 9696 0200

145. Selwyn Wines
     26–28 Coolgardie St, West Perth WA 6005
     Tel: (09) 481 2355

146. South Australia Liquor Co
     75 Hardys Rd, Underdale SA 5032
     Tel: (08) 352 5611

147. Southcorp Wines
     PO Box 38, Millers Point NSW 2000
     Tel: (02) 321 0222

148. Sullivan Wine Agencies
     12 Walnut Rd, North Balwyn Vic 3104
     Tel: (03) 9857 9298

149. Suntory (Aust) P/L (NSW)
     PO Box 171, Rosebery NSW 2018
     Tel:(02) 698 9200

150. Sutherland Fine Wines
     31 Victoria Pde, Collingwood Vic 3066
     Tel: (03) 9417 3066

151. Swift & Moore (NSW)
     8 Egerton St, Silverwater NSW 2141
     Tel: (02) 647 1599

152. Swift & Moore (Qld)
     57 Assembly St, Salisbury Qld 4107
     Tel: (07) 3875 1921

153. Swift & Moore (SA)
     10 Rosberg Rd, Wingfield SA 5013
     Tel: (08) 349 6233

154. Swift & Moore (Vic)
     424 Princes Hwy, Noble Park Vic 3174
     Ph (03) 9795 5633

155. Swift & Moore (WA)
     10 Tipping Rd, Kewdale WA 6105
     Tel: (09) 353 3578

156. Tasmanian Fine Wine Distributors
     124 Davey St, Hobart Tas 7000
     Tel: (002) 34 5211

157. Taylors Wines (NSW) Pty Ltd
     1–3 Charles St, Petersham NSW 2049
     Tel: (02) 560 2122

158. Taylors Wines (Qld) Pty Ltd
     67 Bellrick St, Acacia Ridge Qld 4110
     Tel: (07) 3344 3022

159. Taylors Wines (Vic) Pty Ltd
     1 Yarra Pl, South Melbourne Vic 3205
     Tel: (03) 9696 2066

160. Taylors Wines (WA) Pty Ltd
     9 Collingwood St, Osborne Park WA 6017
     Tel: (09) 445 1920

161. The Fine Wine Specialist
     Level 1, 9 Underwood Ave, Botany NSW 2019
     Tel: (02) 363 4845

162. The Territory Wine Co
     GPO Box 3620, Darwin NT 0801
     Tel: (089) 454 999

163. The Wine Company
     4/56 Smith St, Springvale Vic 3171
     Tel: (03) 9562 3900

164. Tim Seats Pty
     PO Box 39613, Winellie NT 0821
     Tel: (089) 81 2418

165. Tootells Wine & Spirits
     45 Plantation Ave, Brighton East Vic 3187
     Tel: (03) 9592 4853

166. Trimex Pty
     213 Botany Rd, Waterloo NSW 2017
     Tel: (02) 698 5155

167. Tucker Seabrook (NSW)
     11 Rosebery Ave, Rosebery NSW 2018
     Tel: (02) 662 2725

168. Tucker Seabrook (WA)
     87 Knutsford Ave, Rivervale WA 6103
     Tel: (09) 277 1100

169. Tucker Seabrook (Qld)
     Unit 4/19 Murdoch Crt, Acacia Ridge Qld 4110
     Tel: (07) 3272 1711

170. Tucker Seabrook (Vic)
     6 Syme St, Brunswick Vic 3056
     Tel: (03) 9388 0400

171. Tyrrell's Vineyards P/L
     Broke Rd, Pokolbin NSW 2320
     Tel: (008) 04 5501

172. Victorian Wine Consultants
     34 Millton St, West Melbourne Vic 3003
     Tel: (03) 9328 3033

173. Victuals Pty Ltd
     467 Hawthorn Rd, Caulfield South Vic 3162
     Tel: (03) 9530 0666

174. Vinco
     90 Prince Alfred Rd, Newport NSW 2106
     Tel: (02) 979 8709

175. Vinimpex
Box 414, Bassendean WA 6054
Tel: (09) 377 4699

176. Vintage Estates of Australia
10 Jasmine St, Botany NSW 2019
Tel: (02) 316 7129

177. Vintners Pty Ltd
176 Rathmines Rd, Hawthorn East Vic 3123
Tel: (03) 9882 1879

178. WAZA Wines
86 Alexander St, Wembley WA 6014
Tel: (09) 383 9113

179. Webster Wine & Spirits
9 Patrick St, Hobart Tas 7000
Tel: (002) 38 0200

180. West Australian Fine Wines
19 Arulen St, Kingsford NSW 2032
Tel: (02) 349 1259

181. West Coast Wine Cellars
94 Thompsons Rd, North Fremantle WA 6159
Tel: (09) 430 5430

182. Western Wine Agency
4 Judd St, South Perth WA 6151
Tel: (09) 368 1888

183. Westwood Wine Agencies
6 Wharton St, Surrey Hills Vic 3127
Tel: (03) 9836 7341

184. Wine 2000
11 Eurella St, Kenmore Qld 4069
Tel: (07) 3878 4586

185. Wine Partners
94 Moray St, New Farm Qld 4005
Tel: (07) 3254 0685

186. Wine Profile Pty
PO Box 256, Sandy Bay Tas 7006
Tel: 018 125 623

187. Winestock
241 Normanby Rd, South Melbourne Vic 3205
Tel: (03) 9645 2111

188. Young & Rashleigh Wine Merchants
Unit 3, 19–21 Bourke Rd, Alexandria NSW 2015
Tel: (02) 310 3233

NEW ZEALAND DISTRIBUTORS

1. Allied Liquor Merchants
   Private Bag 94–303, Pakuranga, Auckland
   Tel: (09) 274 4279

2. Burleigh Trading
   PO Box 36–251, Northcote, Auckland
   Tel: (09) 480 0789

3. Charles Henry Ltd
   75 Blenheim Rd, Christchurch

4. Delmaine Trading Ltd
   PO Box 58–453, Greenmount, Auckland
   Tel: (09) 274 8797

5. Eurowine
   188 Thorndon Quay, Thorndon, Wellington
   Tel: (04) 499 1734

6. Glengarry–Hancocks Ltd
   PO Box 47–191, Ponsonby, Auckland
   Tel: (09) 379 3740

7. Kitchener Wines
   6 Heather St, Parnell, Auckland
   Tel: (09) 377 3264

8. Lace Fine Wine Merchants
   220 Blockhouse Bay Rd, Avondale, Auckland 7
   Tel: (09) 820 2256

9. Lakeland Liquor
   40 Sumner St, Rotorua

10. Negociants
    130-138 St Georges Bay Rd, Parnell, Auckland
    Tel: (09) 366 1356

11. NZ Wines & Spirits
    PO Box 58741, Greenmount, Auckland
    Tel: (09) 274 2500

12. Tim McFarlane
    643 Old Renwick Rd, RD2 Blenheim
    Tel: (03) 572 9911

UNITED KINGDOM DISTRIBUTORS

1. A.H. Wines
   Back St, West Camel, Nr Yeovill
   Somerset BA22 7QB
   Tel: (0935) 850 1167

2. A L Vose & Co
   Town House, Main St
   Grange-over-Sands LA11 6DY
   Tel: (05395) 33328

3. Adam Bancroft Associates Ltd
   The Mansion House,
   57 Lambeth Rd
   London SW8 1RJ

4. Adnams
   High St, Southwold
   Suffolk IP18 6JW

5. Alex Finlater & Co
   77 Abbey Rd
   London NW8 OAE
   Tel: (071) 624 7311

6. Alliance Wine Co
   Bridge of Weir
   Scotland
   Tel: (505) 506060

7. Amadio Import
   18 Somers Cres
   London W2 2PN
   Tel: (071) 724 3480

8. Andrew Garret Wines (UK)
   Stonehouse Farm, Ashby Rd
   Woodville, Swadlincote
   Derbyshire DE9 7BP

9. Anthony Byrne Fine Wines Ltd
   88 High St, Ramsey
   Cambridgeshire PE17 1BS
   Tel: 0487 814555

10. Australian Estates
    31 Hitchin St, Baldcock
    Herts AL5 1RH

11. Australian Wine Centre
    50 The Strand
    London WC2N 5LW
    Tel: (0781) 92 50751

12. Australian Wineries (UK) Ltd
    20 Craddocks Pde, Ashstead
    Surrey KT21 1QJ
    Tel: 037 22 74065

13. Avery's of Bristol Ltd
    7 Park St Bristol BS1 5NG
    Tel: 0272 214141

14. Barwell & Jones
    24 Fore St, Ispwich
    Suffolk IP4 UU
    Tel: (0473) 23 2322

15. BerkmannWine Cellars
    12 Brewery Rd
    London N7 9NH
    Tel: (071) 609 0018

16. Bibendum Wine Limited
    113 Regents Park Road
    London NW1 8UR
    Tel: (071) 722 5577

17. Boxford Wine Co
    Spring Cottage, Butchers Lane
    Colchester, Essex CO10 5EA
    Tel: (0787) 210187

18. BRL Hardy (Europe)
    Hardy House,
    4 Dorking Rd
    Epsom, Surrey

19. Broke Estate (UK) Pty Ltd
    5 Great College St
    Westminster SW1P 3SJ

20. Brown Brothers Wines (Europe)
    29A Swan St, Sudbury
    Suffolk CO1 05NZ

21. Bywater & Broderick
    7 Main St, Nether Poppleton
    York YO2 6H5

22. Caxton Tower Wines
    4 Harlequin Ave, Brentford
    Middlesex TW8 9EW
    Tel: (081) 758 5400

23. Charles Taylor Wines Ltd
    64 Alexandra Rd, Epsom
    Surrey KT17 4B2
    Tel: (0372) 728 330

24. Chennell & Armstrong Ltd
    Manor Lane, Shipton Rd
    York YO3 6TX
    Tel: (0904) 647001

25. Chittering Estate (UK)
    7 Rickett St, London SW
    26. Cockburn & Campbell
    20-30 Buckhold Rd
    London SW18 4AP

26. Cockburn & Campbell
    20–30 Buckhold Rd
    London SW18 4AP

27. Corney & Barrow Ltd
    12 Helmet Row
    London EC1V 3QJ
    Tel: (0638) 662068

28. Crescent Wines
    c/- Christopher & Co
    80 Cranmore Rd
    Chislehurst Kent BR7 6ET

29. Crestview Wines Ltd
    205B Old Dover Rd
    Canterbury, Kent

30. D & D Wines Ltd
    Adams Court, Knutsford
    Cheshire WA16 6BA
    Tel: (0565) 65092

31. Deinhard & Co
    95 Southwark St
    London SE1 OJF
    Tel: (071) 262 1111

32. Domaines Direct
    29 Wilmington Sq
    London WC1X OEG
    Tel: (071) 837 1142

33. Ehrmanns Wine Shippers
    29 Corsica St
    London N51 JT

34. Fields Wine Merchants
    55 Sloane Ave, Chelsea
    London SW3 3DH
    Tel: (071) 589 5753

35. Fine Wines of New Zealand
    Box 467, London NW5 2NZ
    Tel: (071) 482 0093

36. Forth Wines
    Crawford Pl, Milnathort
    Kinrosshire KY13 7XF

37. Francis Stickney Fine Wines
    1 The Village, North End Way
    London
    Tel: (081) 201 9096

38. Geoffrey Roberts Agencies
    430 High Street
    London MW10 2HA
    Tel: (081) 451 8880

39. Granby Wines
    28 Granby Ave, Harpenden
    Herts AL5 5QR

40. Grants of St James
    56A Packhorse Rd
    Bucks SL9 3EF

41. Griersons
    430 High Rd London NW10 2HA
    Tel: (081) 459 8011

42. Hallgarten Wines
    Dallow Rd, Luton
    Beds LU1 1UR
    Tel: (0582) 22538

43. Haughton Fine Wines
Sole Bay Brewery, Southwold
Suffolk IP18 6JW
Tel: (0502) 72 4488

44. Hedley Wright & Co
10–11 Twyford Centre, London Rd
Bishops Stortford Herts
Tel: (0279) 506512

45. Heyman Bros Ltd
130 Ebury St, London SW1
Tel: (071) 730 0324

46. Jackson Nugent Vintners
60 High St, Wimbledon Village
London

47. John E Fells & Sons
Fells House, Birbreck Grove
London W3 7QD
Tel: (081) 749 7775

48. Just-In-Case
1 High St, Bishops Waltham
Hants SO32 1AB

49. Justerni & Brooks
61 St James St
London SW1
Tel: (071) 258 5000

50. Laurence Hayward & Partners
The Old Stables, Foxhole Oasthouse
Wadhurst, East Sussex TBE 6NB

51. Lawlers
88/92 South St
Dorking Surrey RH4 2EZ
Tel: (0306) 884412

52. Lay & Wheeler
John Lay House, 95 Gosbecks Rd
Colchester Essex CO1 1JA
Tel: (0206) 764 446

53. Malcolm Desborough
21 George St, St Albans
Herts AL3 4ES
Tel: (0727) 61101

54. Marchant Wine Cellars
Marchant Rise, Northian
Rye, East Sussex

55. Mayor Sworder & Co Ltd
21 Duke St Hill, London SE1 2SW
Tel: (071) 407 5111

56. McKinley Vintners
50 Lanercost Rd, London SW2 3DN
Tel: (081) 671 7219

57. Mentzendorff & Co
31 Greater Peter St
London SW1P 3LS

58. Merchant Vintners
Red Duster House, York St
Hull HU2 0QX
Tel: (0482) 29443

59. Michael Druitt Agency
136-142 New Kent Rd
London SE1 6TU
Tel: (071) 493 5412

60. Michael Morgan Ltd
Swan Crt, 3rd Floor, 9 Tanner St
London SE1 3LE

61. Mildara Blass (UK) Ltd
10 Smith's Yard, Summerly St, Earlsfield
London SW18 4HR

62. Milton Sandford
PO Box 3, Twyford, Reading
Berks RG10 8QS
Tel: (0734) 345251

63. Moet et Chandon Ltd
13 Grosevnor Cres, London SW1X 7EE
Tel: (071) 235 9411

64. Mount Helen Wines (UK)
April Cottage, Anvil Rd
Pimperne Blandford Forum
Dorset DT11 8UQ

65. Negociants UK
64A High St, Harpenden
Herts AL5 25P

66. Oddbins Ltd
31 Weir Rd, Wimbledon
London
Tel: (081) 944 4400

67. Olsen Wine Shippers
The White House, Roxby Pl
London SW6 IRS

68. OW Loeb & Co Ltd
64 Southwark Bridge Rd
London SE1 0AS
Tel: (071) 928 7750

69. Oxbury Wine Co
Knoll Farm, Damerham
Fordingbridge, Hants SP6 3JL

70. Pacific Coasters Enterprises
Highfield Ave, Fareham
Hants PO14 1HY

71. Paragon Vintners Ltd
    91 Park St, London W1Y 4AX
    Tel: (071) 491 0623

72. Parfitz Wine Ltd
    30 Main Rd, Dowsby
    Bourne, Lincs PE10 OTL
    Tel: (0778) 440 594

73. Percy Fox & Co
    Templefields House, Riverway
    Harlow, Essex CM20 2EA

74. Peter Diplock Limited
    William Blake House, Warshire St
    London W1
    Tel: (071) 734 2099

75. Peter Lehmann (UK) Ltd
    Godmersham Park, Godmersham
    Nr Canterbury, Kent CT4 7DT
    Tel: (0227) 731 1353

76. Peter Watts Wines
    Wisdoms Barn, Colne Rd
    Coggeshall, Essex CO6 1TD
    Tel: (0376) 561130

77. Pol Roger Ltd
    Lanark House, New St
    Ledbury, Herts HR8 2DX
    Tel: (0531) 6111

78. Reid Wines
    The Mill, Marsh Lane
    Hallatrow nr Bristol BS18 5EB
    Tel: (0761) 452645

79. Remy & Associates (UK)
    The Malthouse, 45 New Street
    Henley on Thames, Oxon RG9 2BP
    Tel: (0491) 410777

80. Renvic Wines Ltd
    2 School Cottages, North Royston
    Herts SG8 0S4
    Tel: 76 385 2470

81. Richards Walford
    Manor House, Pickworth
    Stamford, Lincs PE9 4DJ
    Tel: (0780) 410 242

82. Rosemount Estates Pty Ltd
    Hatchlands, East Clandon
    Guildford, Surrey GU4 790
    Tel: (0483) 211466

83. Southcorp (Europe)
    12 King St, Richmond
    Surrey TW9 1ND
    Tel: (081) 332 6600

84. Stevens Garnier Ltd
3/4 Hythe Bridge St
Oxford OX1 2EW

85. Stones of Belgravia
6 Pont St, London SW1X 9EL

86. Stratford Wine Merchants
High St, Cookham-on-Thames
Berks SL6 9SQ
Tel: (0628) 810606

87. Taltarni (UK)
PO Box 2040, Boxford
Sudbury, Suffolk CO10 5DY
Tel: (0787) 211411

88. Tanners Wines
26 Wyle Cop, Shrewsbury
Shropshire SY1 1XD
Tel: (0743) 232400

89. The Wine Treasury
143 Edbury St
London SW1W 9QN
Tel: (071) 730 6774

90. Thos Peatling Ltd
Westgate House, Bury St Edmunds
Suffolk IP33 1QP

91. Vickery Wines
5 Maldon Crt, Carlton Rd
Harpenden, Herts

92. Vinceremos Wines
65 Raglan Rd
Leeds LS2 9DZ
Tel: (0532) 431691

93. Viniceros – Cornwall Wine Merchants
Chapel Rd, Tuckingmill
Camborne, Cornwall TR14 8QY
Tel: (0209) 7157765

94. Vintage Estates of Australia
Marlborough House, 68 High St
Weybridge, Surrey

95. Vintage Roots
Shepherds Farm, Wargrave Rd
Berks RG10 8DT
Tel: (0734) 401222

96. Walter S Seigal Ltd
50 Battersea Park Rd
London SW11 4JP

97. Waterloo Wine Co
6 Vineyard Borough
London SE1 1QI
Tel: (071) 403 7967

98. Waverly Vintners Ltd
 PO Box 22, Creiff Rd
 Perth PH1 25L Scotland
 Tel: (0738) 29621

99. Whittaker Wines
 35 Chatsworth Rd, High Lane
 Stockport, Cheshire SK6 8DA
 Tel: (0663) 64497

100. Windrush Wines Ltd
 The Barracks Cecily Hill
 Cirencester, Glouc GL7 2EF
 Tel: (0285) 650466

101. Wine Cellars
 153-155 Wandsworth High St
 London SW18 4JB

102. Wine Importer
 Unit 7 Beaverhall House
 27 Beaverhall Rd
 Edinburgh EH7 4JE

UNITED STATES DISTRIBUTORS

The following are some of the major Australian wine importers in the USA.

1. Arrowfield Wines (Arrowfield)
 424 Wood Hollow Drive, Novato CA 94945
 Tel: (415) 898 9123 Fax: (415) 898 8082

2. Old Bridge Cellars
 1232 Market St, Suite 101, San Francisco CA 94102
 Tel: (415) 863 9463 Fax: (415) 863 9487

3. Parliament Import Co.
 3303 Atlantic Ave, Atlantic City NJ 08401
 Tel: (609) 348 1100 Fax: (609) 3690

4. Pasternak Wine Imports
 777 West Putnam Ave, Greenwhich CT 06830
 Tel: (203) 531 3740 Fax: (203) 531 3429

5. Duggans Distillers Products Corp.
 523 Route 303 Suite 22, Orangeburg NY 10962
 Tel: (914) 359 1107 Fax: (914) 359 0753

6. Cabo Distributing Co.
 9657 East Rush St, South El Monte CA 91733
 Tel: (818) 575 8080 Fax: (818) 350 3880

7. Austin Nichols & Co., Inc.
 156 East 46th St, New York NY 10017
 Tel: (212) 455 9495 Fax: (212) 455 9431

8. BRL Hardy
 4515 Daly Drive, Suite H, Chantilly VA 22021
 Tel: (703) 968 0067 Fax: (703) 968 0070

9. Kooka Wines, Inc.
   8038- 17th Ave N.E., Seattle WA 98115
   Tel: (206) 523 7379 Fax: (206) 523 7380

10. Negociants (USA), Inc.
    3664 Dayspring Drive, Hilliard OH 43026
    Tel: (614) 876 0056 Fax: (614) 876 9156

11. PWG Vintners (USA), Inc.
    60 Garden Ct Suite #220, Monterey CA 93940
    Tel: (408) 655 4848 Fax: (408) 655 0904

12. Rosemount Estates, Inc.
    583 First Street West, Sonoma CA 95476
    Tel: (707) 996 4504 Fax: (707) 996 5063

CANADIAN DISTRIBUTORS

Please note that these Canadian distributors of Australian wines
are general contacts; no corresponding code numbers are given
throughout the *Wine Companion*.

Academy Brands Int.
 700 Dorval Dr, Ste. 300
 Oakville ON L6K 3V3
 Tel: (905) 844 5040

Allegro Wine
 142 Browning Avenue
 Toronto ON M4K 1W5
 Tel: (416) 466 2720

Australian Trade Commission
 175 Bloor Street East, Ste. 316
 Toronto ON M4W 3R8
 Tel: (416) 323 3909

Carriage Trade W & S
 R.R #3
 Schomberg ON L0G 1T0
 Tel: (905) 939 8330

Charton Hobbs Inc. W & S
 5080 Timberlea Blvd, Ste. 40
 Mississauga ON L4W 4M2
 Tel: (905) 238 3222

Cipelli Wines & Spirits
 109 Woodbine Downs Ave, #6
 Etobicoke ON M9W 6Y1
 Tel: (416) 798 9463

Clos Des Vignes
 716 Taschereau
 Sainte-Therese Quebec J7E 4E1
 Tel: (514) 434 3339

Depot des Bieres et Vins Inc.
 1967 Baile
 Montreal Quebec H3H 1P6
 Tel: (514) 933 1961

Dumont Vins & Spiritueux Inc.
175 Marieville
Rougemont Quebec J0L 1M0
Tel: (514) 891 2404

Esprit Agencies
56 Claymore Drive
Toronto ON M8Z 2S2
Tel: (416) 762 4133

Eurovintage Int. Inc.
27 Allengrove Crescent
Agincourt ON M1W 1S4
Tel: (416) 494 2881

Featherstone & Co. Ltd
5230 Harvester Road
Burlington ON L7L 4X4
Tel: (416) 601 7308

Gilbey Canada Inc.
401 The West Mall, Ste. 700
Toronto ON M9C 5J4
Tel: (416) 626 2000

Gladstone & Company Wine Imports
1224 Hamilton Street, Ste. 302
Vancouver BC V6B 2S8
Tel: (604) 689 5333

Grady Wine Marketing
3134 East 20th Avenue
Vancouver BC V5M 2V5
Tel: (604) 254 4608

Groupe Paul Masson Inc.
50 de la Barre #110
Longueuil Quebec J4K 5G2
Tel: (514) 878 3050

BRL Hardy Wine Co.
1532 King Street W
Toronto ON M6K 1J6
Tel: (416) 536 5113

HHD Imports Inc.
Box 2364, Station B
Kitchener ON N2H 6M2
Tel: (519) 884 7600

Inniskillin Wines
142 Davenport Road
Toronto ON M5R 1J2
Tel: (416) 413 9463

John F. Kelly & Assoc.
3057 West 44th Avenue
Vancouver BC V6N 3K5
Tel: (604) 266 9211

Lacey International
171 Midland Avenue
Scarborough ON M1N 4A4
Tel: (416) 264 3491

L.C.C. Vins & Spiritueux Inc.
716 Taschereau
Sainte-Therese Quebec J7E 4E1
Tel: (514) 434 7404

Lifford Agencies Inc.
45 St. Clair Avenue W, Ste 602
Toronto ON M4V 1K9
Tel: (416) 963 9631

Lorac Wine Inc.
204 Old Forest Hill Road
Toronto ON M6C 2G9
Tel: (416) 783 2516

Maison Remy & Associes
999 de Maisonneuve Ouest, #560
Montreal Quebec H3A 3L4
Tel: (514) 285 8910

Marchand de Vin, Inc.
4920 de Maisonneuve Ouest, #207
Westmount Quebec H3Z 1N1
Tel: (514) 481 2046

Mark Anthony Group
2600 Skymark Avenue, Bldg. 11, Ste. 202
Mississauga ON L4W 5B2
Tel: (905) 238 6731

Noble Estates W & S
3875 Keele Street, Ste. 201
North York ON M3J 1N6
Tel: (416) 398 0031

Pacific Wine & Spirits (Ontario) Ltd
208 Evans Avenue
Toronto ON M8Z 1J7
Tel: (416) 259 8588

Reserve & Selection Inc.
3464 de Lorimier
Montreal Quebec H2K 3X6
Tel: (514) 524 3993

Sainsbury & Company
2345 Yonge St, Ste. 703
Toronto ON M4P 2E5
Tel: (416) 485 3000

Select Wine Merchants
2850 Lakeshore Blvd W, Box 80010
Etobicoke ON M8V 3B2
Tel: (416) 251 1066

Societe Comm. Clement Int. Inc.
  1225, rue Volta
  Boucherville Quebec J4B 7M7
  Tel: (514) 526 9209

Termes Agencies
  3721 Delbrook Avenue, Ste. 120
  North Vancouver BC V7N 3Z4
  Tel: (604) 983 9444

The Delf Group
  13020 Delf Place
  Richmond BC V6V 2A2
  Tel: (604) 278 4600

The Merchant Vintner Ltd
  13 Fairmount Crescent
  Toronto ON M4L 2H1
  Tel: (416) 463 9496

Torion Trading Ltd
  Box 844 Bradford ON L3Z 2B3
  Tel: (905) 775 7578

Totally Awesome Wine Company
  104–5562 Balsam Street
  Vancouver BC V6M 4B7
  Tel: (604) 263 4401